MOORESTOWN LIBRARY
3 2030 00125 7210

CRITICAL SURVEY OF DRAMA

CRITICAL SURVEY OF DRAMA

REVISED EDITION

Sha-Zin

6

Edited by
FRANK N. MAGILL

SALEM PRESS
Pasadena, California Englewood Cliffs, New Jersey

∞ The paper used in these volumes conforms to the American National Standard for Permanence of Paper for Printed Library Materials, Z39.48-1984.

Library of Congress Cataloging-in-Publication Data

Critical survey of drama. English language series/ edited by Frank N. Magill.—Rev. ed.

p. cm.

Includes bibliographical references and index.

1. English drama—Dictionaries. 2. American drama—Dictionaries. 3. English drama—Bio-bibliography. 4. American drama—Bio-bibliography. 5. Commonwealth drama (English)—Dictionaries. 6. Dramatists, English—Biography—Dictionaries. 7. Dramatists, American—Biography—Dictionaries. 8. Commonwealth drama (English)—Bio-bibliography.

I. Magill, Frank Northen, 1907- .
PR623.C75 1994
822.009'03—dc20 93-41618
ISBN 0-89356-851-1 (set) CIP
ISBN 0-89356-857-0 (volume 6)

PRINTED IN THE UNITED STATES OF AMERICA

LIST OF AUTHORS IN VOLUME 6

CRITICAL SURVEY OF DRAMA

WALLACE SHAWN

Born: New York, New York; November 12, 1943

Principal drama

The Hotel Play, wr. 1970, pr. 1981; *Play in Seven Scenes*, pr. 1974; *Our Late Night*, pr. 1974, pb. 1984; *In the Dark*, pr. 1976 (libretto); *Three Short Plays: Summer Evening, The Youth Hostel, Mr. Frivolous*, pr. 1976; *The Mandrake*, pr. 1977 (adaptation of Niccolò Machiavelli's play *La mandragola*); *Marie and Bruce*, pr. 1979, pb. 1980; *My Dinner with André*, pr. 1980, pb. 1981 (with André Gregory); *The Music Teacher*, pr. 1982 (libretto); *Aunt Dan and Lemon*, pr., pb. 1985; *The Fever*, pr. 1990, pb. 1991.

Other literary forms

In addition to his stage plays, Wallace Shawn has also written two opera librettos (*In the Dark* and *The Music Teacher*) and a screenplay (*My Dinner with André*, 1981, adapted from his stage play).

Achievements

After a slow start, Shawn has established himself as a leading writer in the Off-Broadway theater. His first play to receive a major production, *Our Late Night*, as staged by André Gregory's Manhattan Project at the Public Theatre, received an Obie Award in 1975. His play *Aunt Dan and Lemon* shared that same award with several other plays in 1985. Shawn's work, though often taking as its subject extremely violent thoughts or antisocial behavior, has been praised for its accuracy in representing the emotional qualities of contemporary American life. His plays make unusual demands upon audiences, who must respond to his characters with comic insight and intellectual energy. Shawn's distinctive voice is one of insidiously timid argumentation, an impression that is reinforced by his frequent appearances as a humorously innocuous character in contemporary films, yet he is also capable of writing shrill, viscerally affecting drama. Shawn's major works are distinctively unconventional, and he is among the most provocative writers in the American theater today.

Biography

Wallace Shawn's upbringing was without question a privileged one. His father, William Shawn, was the editor of *The New Yorker* for several decades, and so Shawn grew up in the atmosphere of Manhattan literary society. His education has been extensive, including the best schools in the English-speaking world. From the Dalton School (1948-1957) and Putney School (1958-1961), Shawn went on to take a B.A. in history from Harvard (1965).

He then took additional degrees at Magdalen College, Oxford: a B.A. in philosophy, politics, and economics (1968) and an M.A. in Latin under G. J. Warnock (1968). The time between universities was spent teaching English on a Fulbright Scholarship at Indore Christian College, India.

Shawn's dramatic talents were encouraged by his parents, who provided him with creative tools such as a toy theater and a motion-picture camera. His childhood theatrics included the composition and performance of lurid murder mysteries with his younger brother Allen. Shawn recalls that an important turning point in his perception of drama came when his father took part in a different kind of play, about a botanist in Japan. From this point, Shawn developed the conviction that a play could be almost anything, and other performances included a four-hour version of John Milton's *Paradise Lost* (1667), a play featuring Ludwig Wittgenstein, and a Chinese dynastic drama. Many of these performances featured music by Allen Shawn, with whom Wallace continued to collaborate.

The young Shawn attended frequent professional productions in New York, including acclaimed productions of work as varied as Eugene O'Neill's *The Iceman Cometh* (1946) and the early classics of the absurdist drama. This exposure reinforced Shawn's conviction that the potential topics for dramatization are infinite.

Shawn's career after Oxford started with two years of teaching Latin at the Church of the Heavenly Rest Day School in Manhattan. During that time, Shawn began to write regularly, drafting plays such as *Four Meals in May* and *The Old Man*. Shawn then took a succession of odd jobs, including work as a shipping clerk in the garment district and as a copy-machine operator, while drafting a number of short plays and one full-length script, *The Hotel Play*. During this time, Shawn also studied acting with Katherine Sergava at the H.B. studio.

Shawn has maintained a long-term relationship with writer Deborah Eisenberg. His play *Marie and Bruce* is dedicated to her, and she is mentioned several times in *My Dinner with André*. Her book of short stories, *Transactions in a Foreign Currency* (1986), carries a dedication to Shawn, and her long story "A Cautionary Tale" (published in *The New Yorker*) features characters resembling them both. Eisenberg has also authored one play, *Pastorale* (1982), which features the same sorts of casually cryptic dialogue and frustrated young characters that appear in Shawn's dramatic output.

Shawn's first break came through André Gregory's Manhattan Project. The hour-long production of *Our Late Night*, Shawn's first professional production, was awarded an Obie for Best Play Off-Broadway. Shawn was then engaged by the Public Theater to prepare the adaptation of Niccolò Machiavelli's *La mandragola*. The production was staged by Wilford Leach, and Shawn was featured as an actor in the prologue. Leach later directed *Marie and Bruce*, with Louise Lasser and Bob Balaban, in a widely reviewed Public

Theater production in 1980 that led to Shawn's publishing contract with Grove Press.

Shawn's plays have also received several productions in London, including an early stage version of *My Dinner with André* in 1980. The first British production of his work was a *succès de scandale*, a staging of the trilogy *Three Short Plays* by Max Stafford-Clark for the Joint Stock Company in 1977. One part of the trilogy, an orgiastically sexual play called *The Youth Hostel*, aroused a public outcry over alleged obscenity. The author fortunately escaped prosecution, but concern over the representation of sex precluded any impression that might have been created by the play's artistic qualities. Later productions of *Marie and Bruce* and *Aunt Dan and Lemon* were received more responsibly.

The development of Shawn's acting career since 1977 has allowed him the comfort of a regular income and the time to pursue his writing projects. Shawn has had large character roles in a number of films, such as an obsessed psychiatrist in Marshall Brickman's *Lovesick* (1983), a depraved priest in the schoolboy drama *Heaven Help Us* (1985), and the diminutive innkeeper Freud in *The Hotel New Hampshire* (1984), but he is still perhaps best known for a brief appearance as Diane Keaton's former lover in Woody Allen's *Manhattan* (1979), as well as his role as himself in the film version of *My Dinner with André*. Shawn has also appeared frequently in his own plays, including the 1981 La Mama E.T.C. production of *The Hotel Play*, the stage and screen versions of *My Dinner with André*, and the London and New York productions of *Aunt Dan and Lemon.* He has also appeared as the sole performer in *The Fever.*

By his own admission, writing does not come particularly easily to Shawn. Nevertheless, he has consistently pursued the images and themes that capture his imagination, always with the assumption that a personal concern with the material will arouse some similar response in the audience. Shawn has not developed any formulaic approach, though his work has distinctive stylistic traits and persistent themes. His plays have shown a steady improvement, and his following has continued to grow as his works enter the repertoire of major regional playhouses such as the Magic Theater and the Mark Taper Forum.

Analysis

Wallace Shawn's major plays exhibit a concern with vivid images of violence, whether political or sexual, as they are manifested in the imaginations and behavior of his contemporary characters. These images connect Shawn's work with the traditional themes of surrealism, yet the apparently harmless characters and situations in the plays' narrative structures cause a kind of contradictory tension between the force of obsessive imagination and the ordinary experience of daily life. Shawn has consistently improved his ability to express this juxtaposition of qualities, while emphasizing the immediate importance of his major themes. No detailed line of development can be established in Shawn's career because so much of his work has not yet been published or professionally produced, but the later major plays show a definite connection to the material of his early writings.

Shawn's first play to receive a major production, *Our Late Night*, raised the eyebrows of critics with its simultaneously scatological and intelligent style. The situation involves a young couple and their party guests and proceeds anecdotally from the final preparations of the couple, through the recitations of their guests' unusual feelings and experiences, to the empty moments after the party ends. The play's action—or what there is of action in the play—concerns the lusts of the partygoers for one another in combination with their visceral reactions to what gets said (and eaten). The longest, most memorable monologue is an impassioned shaggy-dog story about one single-minded male guest's sexual exploits in the tropics.

The language of the play reveals one of Shawn's characteristic devices: the polite utterance of unconscionably rude sentiments. Obscenity begins to flow so freely that it becomes the normal discourse of the play, along with the frequent use of proper names, salutations, and other conventionally respectful phrases. The language becomes the stylistic equivalent of the characters themselves: well-dressed and pleasant-seeming, but sexually obsessed at the core. The final effect of the play, in the right sort of sophisticated performance situation, is not obscene but satirical, exposing the thin veneer of manners that strains to hold back the force of human desire.

Shawn's second professional production raised more than eyebrows. The London production of *Three Short Plays* provoked antiobscenity complaints that resulted in a government investigation of the theater and an initiative to rewrite British obscenity laws. Of the three plays which constituted the production, the objectionable material was contained in *The Youth Hostel*. The play is unique for Shawn because the actors do not merely talk about their fantasies, they enact the fulfillment of their sexual desires onstage. Yet stylistically, the play has passages very similar to the successful satire of *Our Late Night*. Characters copulate, masturbate, and have violent fistfights, but they continue to express themselves in the polite, matter-of-fact idiom of contemporary young Americans.

The other two plays in the trilogy are less likely to offend audiences than *The Youth Hostel*, but they address the same themes. In *Summer Evening*, a young couple in a foreign hotel pass the time between meals by trying on clothes, discussing the mundane details of their vacation, and snacking. Yet lurking under the surface of the action, which Shawn suggests should have an extremely quick, unrealistic pace, are the desires of the man to possess the woman to the point of death, and the woman's fears of the injury that could come with her submission. The language, dotted with interruptions to encourage the tempo, remains oddly formal and polite, even while the intimacy of the characters' revelations gradually leads them to make love at the play's end. The last play of the set, a monologue titled *Mr. Frivolous*, features the eponymous character at breakfast, fantasizing about companionship and sexual pleasure. The title suggests the principal theme: Despite the intimacy and even the quaintness of his recitation, the young man is vacuous to the point of complete superfluity.

In *Marie and Bruce*, Shawn combines his stylistic habits with his psychological thematic concerns to create an elegantly crafted, if sometimes painful, portrait of a woman's life. Marie narrates the action, a typical day that includes abusing her husband at breakfast, going about her housework, taking a walk, going to a party with her husband, and then abusing him again over dinner. The shrillness of Marie's scatalogical vilifications of Bruce is countered by a patient, quizzical humility on his part, which carries the relationship through a final, horrible denunciation by Marie and back into a pattern of everyday life. The language of the play contains descriptive passages of unusual beauty that are deeply felt by the characters and are strangely moving. Both of the main characters also have an extended narrative solo, in which they describe their adventures when they leave the familiar surroundings of home and office. The images in these monologues are almost lush—erotically charged with the power of each character's frustrated sexuality.

As in *Our Late Night*, Shawn uses the device of a party scene. The supporting characters' scenes are short, with quick crosscutting between snatches of dialogue and actors doubling the many characters in such a way that the overall impression is like an overheard pastiche of party conversation. Some of the scenes, as they are juxtaposed to Marie's narration and short scenes with Bruce, are very funny. Later, at a restaurant, the couple is forced to overhear another conversation, this time a disgusting description of an intestinal ailment. This encounter triggers a blast from Marie that causes the amusing frustration and sexual flirtation of the earlier scenes to be seen from the tragic perspective of human mortality. Her enormous anger and disappointment expressed, Marie settles down at home with Bruce for the quiet end of her Sisyphean day. The dehumanizing experiences of the party scene, of urban confinement, and of powerlessness are reinforced in even the smallest details of the play, such as Bruce's search for the typewriter that Marie has destroyed, a machine made to express human feelings.

The Hotel Play is much less accomplished than *Marie and Bruce* and much more diffuse and vague. Its tropical setting suggests that the play has some connection to the sexual narration of the guest in *Our Late Night*. In fact, the central character of this episodic nightmare play is a diminutive but mysterious hotel clerk. The action shifts between various settings in the hotel, with a human menagerie passing through the more public scenes, while sex and gunfire punctuate the play's more private encounters. Shawn notes in a foreword that the play's atmosphere is intentionally dreamlike, and the most prominent themes are, like those of dreams, full of sexual fascination, eating, laughter, and the fear of death. The random ordering of the work creates the impression of a dream logic as well, which finally culminates in the death of one of the clerk's several paramours. Like the young people in *The Youth Hostel*, the impulsive characters of *The Hotel Play* have a detached, casually polite attitude toward the extreme situations that confront them.

My Dinner with André shows a considerable shift away from this relaxed attitude, mostly because André Gregory's part of the extended conversation that constitutes the play is so fraught with concern over the state of humanity and the nature and potential of the human condition. The play's tight form, even as it pretends to be a rambling dialogue in a restaurant, has an important antecedent in the balance and meticulousness of composition in *Marie and Bruce*. Shawn provides a narrative frame for the action, which consists almost entirely of Gregory's extended description of his search for an absolute human meaning in places such as Jerzy Grotowski's retreat in the Polish forest, in Findhorn, in Tibet, and in the Sahara. Once Gregory has almost concluded his fascinating litany of hope and despair, Shawn begins to answer from his domestic perspective, which he views as potentially infinite in its extension. *My Dinner with André*, while not a play in the conventional sense, is a carefully edited, scripted, and objectified conversation with a range of dynamic effects and a wealth of themes that recapitulate those of Shawn's other work: the emptiness of sex, the automatizing influence of routine, the frustrations of desire, and even the horror of the Nazi cruelties. This last point is much more clearly amplified, however, in Shawn's most ambitious play, *Aunt Dan and Lemon*.

The narrative frame for *Aunt Dan and Lemon* is provided by Leonora, nicknamed Lemon, as she shares her thoughts and memories with an audience that she welcomes into the theater. The play's progress begins along autobiographical lines, as the audience becomes familiar with Lemon's parents and their friends. Then the action begins to focus on one of the friends, an articulate and conservative Oxford intellectual called Aunt Dan, who forms a peculiar, destructive attachment to Lemon. Once Aunt Dan is introduced, much of the play consists of her storytelling, as she describes sordid acquaintances and political situations to Lemon from her confused, eccentric perspective. The squalid events from Aunt Dan's stories, her conservative background and political instruction, and the impression made on Lemon by her friend's eventual illness and death are gradually coalesced into a fascination on the girl's part for the Nazi war crimes. The primary theme of the play, then, seems to be Shawn's demonstration of how an intelligent, sensitive, privileged individual can be persuaded, through the influence of a few frustrated teachers and poor examples, to take a political position sympathetic to radical Fascism.

Interestingly, Shawn includes very little material in the play's dialogue that confronts or questions the despicable beliefs of the main characters. Their voices and attitudes, through conventional habits of expression such as those used in the earlier plays, disarm the audience, leading spectators to suppose that the characters are normal, pleasant people. Yet once the stage material begins to include political content, Shawn depends upon the audience to carry on a perceptive dialogue of its own, a kind of internal running commentary in the mind of each viewer that confronts and ridicules the beliefs of the characters. Shawn's only manipulation of the audience comes in his choices for the humorous juxtaposition of images and the improbable choice of characters: Aunt Dan's explanation of the Vietnam bombing uses stuffed animals to demonstrate her points, and her story about a seedy group of London friends involves the seduction and murder of an exaggerated Latin Lothario. In the right kind of performance situation, where an educated audience is likely to have strong views that they can oppose to those of the characters, the play is instructive, terrifying, and often quite amusing. Yet the ideological aspect of this play is much like its affective side, almost completely dependent upon the competence and the insight of the audience response. For this reason, Shawn was accused of irresponsible playwriting in some of the New York reviews, an accusation that prompted him to write a special afterword on the context of the play.

In *The Fever*, Shawn brings to the forefront many of the themes and devices of his earlier work in a theatrically severe but verbally complex conversation between an unnamed, Shawn-like narrator and an audience of intimates—a group of ten or twelve people in a private home. Shawn himself considers the work to be a "fable or fairy tale," yet the personal role he took in its performance and the close relation of the material to earlier monologues in his work (such as Lemon's, or the party guest's in *Our Late Night*) caused some critical confusion over Shawn's distance from the character and the fictional experiences narrated in the play. The text concerns the struggle of liberal conscience faced by a genteel American character who must confront and then try to come to terms with the everyday poverty and political torture suffered by ordinary people in a Central American country. The play has no clear narrative, mixing travel episodes about the discovery of another way of life with political ideas, personal moral reflections, descriptions of real or imagined illness, imprisonment, and domestic life. The crucial consideration of the play is one of social justice; why, Shawn's narrator asks, does he lead a life of moneyed privilege, while poor people lead lives of humiliation and terror? The search for answers runs the gamut from commodity fetishism to capitalist defense, but the asking of the play's questions never really implies coherent answers, and no such pat conclusions are forthcoming. Consequently *The Fever* continues, in even more concentrated form, Shawn's call for the audience to consider ambiguous political problems for themselves. Listeners are provoked to ponder, as the feverish character does, the "thin book of life" that comprises their birth, social position, accomplishments, values, and reasons for being in the world. The tale ends not in righteous condemnation but with a plea for forgiveness.

Despite problems with its critical reception and its potential for misunderstanding, *Aunt Dan and Lemon* is probably Shawn's most challenging and absorbing play. Shawn's most important works, such as *My Dinner with André* and *Marie and Bruce*, tend to proceed from a narrative framework into a carefully constructed series of dialogues and monologues, arriving finally at a kind of stillness in resolution. Shawn's strengths as a playwright include an unusual flair for formal innovation, in plays as different as *The Hotel Play*, with its innumerable sets and characters, and *The Fever*, almost minimalist in its simple theatricality. He also writes dialogue of enormous sophistication, allowing him to represent the language of intellectuals by credibly imitating rather than satirizing their discourse. Yet his most remarkable quality as a writer comes in his persistent posing of difficult, even painful, questions about contemporary life. Given the temptations of the commercial marketplace, Shawn could easily use his comic skills to write successful teleplays or screenplays. Yet he has sustained his commitment to the theatrical exploration of obsessive, subconscious desire and the way it shapes human experience, not only in daily life but also in the broader perspectives of the appreciation of history and the value of human culture.

Other major work

SCREENPLAY: *My Dinner with André*, 1981.

Bibliography

Billington, Michael. "A Play of Ideas Stirs Political Passions." *The New York Times*, October 27, 1985, p. B1. Billington discusses with Shawn the controversy over the political implications of *Aunt Dan and Lemon*. Shawn explains his dialogic theory of audience communication.

Posnock, Ross. "New York Phantasmagoria." *Raritan* 11 (Fall, 1991): 142-159. Shawn's concerns in *The Fever* are cleverly juxtaposed with those of New York intellectual Richard Sennett. Both writers are concerned with the contemporary crisis of human values in urban culture.

Savran, David. "Wally Shawn." In *In Their Own Words: Contemporary American Playwrights*. New York: Theatre Communications Group, 1988. This long interview covers Shawn's career up to 1986. Shawn talks specifically about his processes of composition and revision for production.

Shawn, Wallace. "Why Write for the Theater? A Roundtable Report." *The New York Times*, February 9, 1986, p. B1. Shawn discusses his creative process and commitment to theater with Arthur Miller, Athol Fugard, and David Mamet. The most concise statement of his philosophy of composition.

Shawn, Wallace, and William Shawn. "Interview with William and Wally Shawn." Interview by Lucinda Franks. *The New York Times*, August 3, 1980, p. B1. Shawn and his father discuss their memories of Wallace's childhood and their common interests. Shawn recalls his earliest dramatic efforts, which sometimes included his brother and father.

Shewey, Don. "The Secret Life of Wally Shawn." *Esquire* 100 (October, 1983): 90-94. This personal portrait, undertaken in conjunction with the release of *My Dinner with André*, outlines several of the playwright's basic beliefs.

Wetzsteon, Ross. "The Holy Fool of the American Theater." *The Village Voice*, April 2, 1991, pp. 35-37. Wetzsteon explains the critical reception of *The Fever*, and Shawn responds to criticisms of his politics and his use of alternative dramatic forms with some explanations of his intentions.

Michael L. Quinn

PERCY BYSSHE SHELLEY

Born: Field Place, Sussex, England; August 4, 1792
Died: Off Viareggio, Italy; July 8, 1822

Principal drama

The Cenci, pb. 1819, pr. 1886; *Prometheus Unbound: A Lyrical Drama in Four Acts*, pb. 1820; *Oedipus Tyrannus: Or, Swellfoot the Tyrant*, pb. 1820; *Hellas: A Lyrical Drama*, pb. 1822; *Charles the First*, pb. 1824 (fragment); *The Cyclops*, pb. 1824 (translation of Euripides' play).

Other literary forms

In addition to his dramas, Percy Bysshe Shelley wrote essays of considerable power and has long been recognized as one of England's greatest poets. His first published work, however, was the thoroughly undistinguished Gothic novel *Zastrozzi: A Romance* (1810), which was followed later in the same year by the equally unimpressive *St. Irvyne: Or, The Rosicrucian* (mistakenly dated 1811 on the title page). Also appearing in 1810 were *Original Poetry by Victor and Cazire*, a collaboration with his sister Elizabeth which, despite its title, included plagiarized material, and *Posthumous Fragments of Margaret Nicholson*, a collection of six poems purportedly by the madwoman who had attempted, in 1786, to assassinate George III.

Of considerably greater significance was the appearance in 1811 of *The Necessity of Atheism*, a pamphlet written by Shelley and his Oxford friend, Thomas Jefferson Hogg, and which caused both to be expelled from the university. Having painfully established his credentials as a freethinker, Shelley then published two pamphlets, *An Address to the Irish People* (1812) and *Proposals for an Association of . . . Philanthropists* (1812), and an anonymous broadside, *Declaration of Rights* (1812), which further manifested his extreme liberalism. Another production of 1812, *A Letter to Lord Ellenborough*, expressed Shelley's support for freedom of the press with such passionate eloquence that it was quickly suppressed.

Queen Mab: A Philosophical Poem, whose 2,305 lines were accompanied by 118 pages of notes, was printed in 1813 but was too radical in content for the printer to risk public sale. Instead, copies were circulated privately, and this private dissemination was eventually supplemented by the appearance of pirated editions. In addition, a revision of a part of the poem appeared as *The Daemon of the World* in the 1816 volume *Alastor: Or, The Spirit of Solitude, and Other Poems*. At about this time, Shelley also planned to publish a number of his shorter poems, but his plans misfired, and the collection, referred to as *The Esdaile Notebook*, remained unpublished until 1964.

The previously mentioned *Alastor* appeared in February of 1816 and was

Shelley's first significant attempt to gain public recognition as a poet. The volume's title poem concerns the destruction of an artistic young man who succumbs to the lure of an unattainable ideal, a temptation to which Shelley himself was highly susceptible. Intricately symbolic in content and abstract in theme, *Alastor* is stylistically consistent with much of the poetry of Shelley's great maturity. The year 1816 also witnessed the writing of the "Hymn to Intellectual Beauty" and "Mont Blanc," two of his finest lyrics.

In 1817, with *A Proposal for Putting Reform to the Vote Throughout the Kingdom* and *An Address to the People on the Death of the Princess Charlotte* (only the former of which is known with certainty to have been published during his lifetime), Shelley brought to a close his career as a political pamphleteer. Political themes continued to be of great importance in his poetry, however, as the title of his next major poem, *The Revolt of Islam* (1818), suggests. A narrative of the struggles of Laon and Cythna, *The Revolt of Islam* is a vision of selfless revolution, revolution shorn of the vengefulness which produced the Reign of Terror, but revolution ultimately, if gloriously, defeated. Its stirring "Dedication" includes one of Shelley's most eloquent statements of the altruistic nature of the true reformer:

> . . . I will be wise,
> And just, and free, and mild, if in me lies
> Such power, for I grow weary to behold
> The selfish and the strong still tyrannise
> Without reproach or check. . . .

Rosalind and Helen: A Modern Eclogue, with Other Poems was published in 1819, and though *Rosalind and Helen* itself is not among Shelley's more notable works, the volume also included the considerably more successful "Ozymandias" and "Lines Written Among the Euganean Hills." Two other poems of approximately this same period, *Prince Athanase*, a reworking of the *Alastor* theme, and the slightly later *Julian and Maddalo: A Conversation*, an attempt by Shelley to distill the philosophical differences between himself and his famous friend, Lord Byron, appeared first in *Posthumous Poems of Percy Bysshe Shelley* (1824).

Two poems of 1819 which were also published posthumously are *The Masque of Anarchy* (1832), inspired by the Peterloo Massacre, and *Peter Bell the Third* (1839), a parody of William Wordsworth's *Peter Bell* (1819). In addition, the years 1819-1820 produced "Ode to the West Wind," "To a Skylark," "The Sensitive Plant," and "The Cloud," all of which were included in *Prometheus Unbound: A Lyrical Drama in Four Acts, with Other Poems* (1820). "The Indian Serenade," of 1819; the "Letter to Maria Gisborne" and *The Witch of Atlas*, both of 1820; and "When the Lamp Is Shattered" and *The Triumph of Life*, both of 1822, were contained in the posthumous 1824 volume, only the 1819 poem having appeared during Shelley's lifetime. *The Witch of Atlas* and *The Triumph of Life*, the latter of which Shelley was working on during the days preceding his death, are presented in the intricate symbolic mode characteristic of Shelley's most distinctive poetry.

Two of Shelley's poetic masterworks, *Epipsychidion* (1821) and *Adonais: An Elegy on the Death of John Keats* (1821), remain to be mentioned. The former, inspired by Shelley's acquaintance with Teresa Viviani, whose father had confined her to a convent school during the months preceding her marriage, is an attempt to define man's spiritual essence, his *epipsyche*. The latter, written after the death of John Keats, is one of the most beautiful elegies in the English language.

Finally, a great many of Shelley's letters and a number of his more important essays have been published since his death. Among the latter are "A Defence of Poetry," included in *Essays, Letters from Abroad, Translations and Fragments* (1840), "An Essay on Christianity," contained in *Shelley Memorials* (1859), and the separately printed *A Philosophical View of Reform* (1920).

Achievements

Shelley was long a lover of drama but not always a lover of the theater. Under the influence of Thomas Love Peacock and Leigh Hunt, however, he appears to have overcome much of his natural distaste for theatrical extravagance, and after a number of enjoyable experiences in London, he continued his attendance at plays and operas during his years in Italy. Still, unlike Lord Byron, who acted on more than one occasion in amateur stage productions and served for a time on the Drury Lane Committee of Management, Shelley knew drama from the point of view of the avid reader and occasional spectator, not from the perspective of the practical man of the theater. The strengths and weaknesses of most of his dramatic works, effective—even magnificent—in the study but inappropriate for the stage, are consistent with this indirect knowledge of stagecraft, but the undeniable dramatic power of one particular play, *The Cenci*, suggests that, if he had lived longer, Shelley might have become the dramatic genius which England during the Romantic era so sadly lacked.

Very early in his literary career, Shelley is said to have attempted dramatic collaborations with his sister Elizabeth and with a friend, Andrew Amos, but what appear to be the first surviving dramatic fragments are a handful of lines written in Italy in 1818 for a play to have been entitled "Tasso." According to Mary Shelley, her husband, at about this same time, was also thinking of composing a biblical drama based on the Book of Job, no farfetched project when one considers that Byron was about to undertake *Cain: A Mystery* (pb. 1821). If Thomas Medwin, Shelley's cousin and biographer, is to be believed, the plan for *Charles the First* was a product of 1818 as well, though the writing of this promising fragment was deferred to 1819 and thereafter. The only dramatic project of 1818 which Shelley ultimately completed, however, was *Prometheus Unbound.*

As Mary Shelley relates in her notes to the play, *Prometheus Unbound* was begun during a period in which Shelley was thoroughly inbued with the spirit of the Greek tragedies, especially with "the sublime majesty of Aeschylus," which "filled him with wonder and delight." He was also aware, as later critics have pointed out, of the uses of the Promethean myth by his poetic contemporaries, such as Johann Wolfgang von Goethe and Byron. He was familiar, too, with recent experiments, including Goethe's *Faust* (pb. 1808, 1833) and Byron's *Manfred* (pb. 1817), in a highly symbolic mental drama with which his own great talents were wonderfully compatible. The result of this amalgam of influences was Shelley's composition, during 1818 and 1819, of one of literature's great lyric dramas, an exultant statement of Shelley's faith in the ultimate triumph of justice and love over hatred and oppression.

Despite its poetic beauty, however, *Prometheus Unbound* is not a practical stage play. Shelley had long considered himself unsuited for composing such a play, but while he was at work on *Prometheus Unbound*, he was introduced to a subject on which he based one of the few nineteenth century tragedies in English worthy of continued theatrical attention, *The Cenci*. He had been shown a rare manuscript in which the brutal history of the Cenci family was recorded, and he had been drawn to this tale of incest and murder because it so perfectly illustrated themes that had long obsessed him. As they occur in the play, the savagery of Count Francesco Cenci exemplifies the corrupting influence of absolute, oppressive power, and the vengefulness of his victimized daughter, Beatrice, with its terrible spiritual consequences, illustrates the destructive results of surrendering to hatred. In a sense, the joyous conclusion of *Prometheus Unbound* and the tragic conclusion of *The Cenci* are obverse images of the same truth, that fortitude and forgiveness, rather than violent retaliation, are the proper responses to injustice.

Oedipus Tyrannus is a slighter accomplishment. Inspired at least in part by the squealing of pigs near Shelley's rooms in the vicinity of Pisa, Italy, the play is a raucous burlesque of events surrounding George IV's attempt to divorce his estranged wife, Caroline. Its virulent mockery of commoners, cabinet ministers, and members of the royal family alike brought about its quick suppression.

Oedipus Tyrannus was begun on August 24, 1820, a year after Shelley had finished *The Cenci* and soon after he had completed *Prometheus Unbound*. The year before, he had translated Euripides' *The Cyclops* and had begun the fragment *Charles the First*. Both appeared in *Posthumous Poems of Percy Bysshe Shelley*, as did his translations of scenes from Pedro

Calderón de la Barca's *El mágico prodigioso* (1637) and Goethe's *Faust*. An additional fragment, an untitled work centering on an Indian enchantress, was also included in the 1824 volume. Among the above, Shelley had the highest hopes for *Charles the First*, a tragedy which was to trace the complexities of the Cromwell uprising. Unfortunately, the subject presented so many problems that he gave it up by June, 1822.

The last of Shelley's dramatic works to be published during his lifetime, *Hellas*, was written in support of the Greek revolutionaries under the leadership of Prince Alexander Mavrocordato, to whom the play is dedicated. Like *Prometheus Unbound*, *Hellas* has affinities to Aeschylean tragedy. Aeschylus' *Prometheus Bound* (fifth century B.C.) provided much of the inspiration for the earlier work, while his *Persians* (472 B.C.) gave impetus to the writing of *Hellas*. The play's most familiar lines, from the concluding choral song, are an eloquent cry of hope for the regeneration of the world:

> The world's great age begins anew,
>   The golden years return,
> The earth doth like a snake renew
>   Her winter weeds outworn:
> Heaven smiles, and faiths and empires gleam,
> Like wrecks of a dissolving dream.

The Cenci is the only play by Shelley with a substantial stage history, the others having received no more than rare experimental treatment. Even *The Cenci*, in fact, was long neglected, having been performed for the first time in London on May 7, 1886, under the sponsorship of the Shelley Society. During the next forty years, productions occurred in Paris (1891), Coburg (1919), Moscow (1919-1920), Prague (1922), London (1922 and 1926), Leeds (1923), Frankfurt am Main (1924), and New York (1926). The London production of 1922, with Dame Sybil Thorndike as Beatrice, was the most instrumental in establishing *The Cenci*'s fitness for the stage.

Biography

Percy Bysshe Shelley, born on August 4, 1792, at Field Place in Sussex, England, near the town of Horsham, was the eldest of seven children. His father was Timothy Shelley, a longtime Member of Parliament and eventual baronet, and his mother, the former Elizabeth Pilfold. The young Shelley lived in privileged comfort, a circumstance which later offended his reformist sensibilities, and was the object of considerable family affection. His education was begun near Field Place by the Reverend Evan Edwards and was continued at Syon House Academy (from 1802 to 1804) and Eton (from 1804 to 1810). His experiences at Syon House and Eton, where he underwent considerable bullying, helped inspire his passionate hatred of oppressive power. These were also the years in which he developed his fascinations with science and literature. The former brought about his successful attempt to burn down a willow tree with a magnifying glass and his unsuccessful attempt to summon the Devil; the latter led to the publication of his first book, a Gothic novel, before his eighteenth birthday.

Shelley entered University College, Oxford, in October of 1810, and was expelled on March 25, 1811, for his distribution of *The Necessity of Atheism*, a collaboration with Hogg. His expulsion aggravated the difficulties that already existed between him and his father, and finding himself unwelcome at home, Shelley took up residence in London, where he became reacquainted with Harriet Westbrook, a classmate of his sister. Westbrook soon replaced Harriet Grove in Shelley's affections, Grove having rejected the young poet earlier in the year, and after the sixteen-year-old Westbrook had made herself irresistible by claiming to be a sufferer of persecution, the two ran off to Edinburgh, where they were married on August 29, 1811. Although the marriage appears to have been reasonably happy at first, it eventually became one of the great disasters of Shelley's life.

Hogg lived with the Shelleys in Edinburgh and later in York, but Hogg's unsuccessful attempt to seduce Harriet during a short trip by Shelley to Sussex resulted in the couple's quick departure for Keswick, this time accompanied by Harriet's meddlesome sister, Eliza. At Keswick, Shelley became acquainted with Robert Southey, who saw in Shelley's radical ways a reflection of what he had once been, and began corresponding with his future father-in-law, William Godwin, celebrated among liberals as the writer of *An Inquiry Concerning the Principles of Political Justice, and Its Influence on General Virtue and Happiness* (1793). Godwin's ideas were among the most powerful influences on Shelley's own early political ethos.

In February of 1812, Shelley traveled to Dublin, Ireland, where he issued pamphlets and delivered speeches in favor of increased Irish autonomy. He then took himself and his household to Wales and later to Lynmouth, Devon, where *A Letter to Lord Ellenborough* was refused publication, most of the copies being burned by the printer, and where his servant was arrested for handing out sheets of his *Declaration of Rights*. Having come under government surveillance, he then retired to Tremadoc, Wales, after which he departed for London, arriving on October 4, 1812.

During the six weeks he spent in London, Shelley met Godwin, Thomas Hookham, and Peacock, all of whom were to figure prominently in his later career. Shelley's explicit purpose in going to London, however, was to raise money for an engineering project near Tremadoc which was being supported by one of his liberal friends and to deal with some of his own financial difficulties. Having done what he could, he returned to Tremadoc for the winter but left for Ireland after someone purportedly tried to shoot him on February 26, 1813.

Shelley was back in London by April, where *Queen Mab* was published in May (by Hookham) and where Shelley's daughter, Eliza Ianthe, was born in June. During the next several months, the Shelleys' wanderings continued, but most of their time was spent in or near London, thus giving them continuing access to the Godwin household and allowing the growth of their friendship with the amiable Peacock. This seems to be the period, too, when Harriet and Shelley began drifting apart. Their differences in temperament were becoming less easy to ignore, and the annoying presence of the irascible Westbrook was driving her brother-in-law to distraction. The inevitable crisis occurred after Shelley, to Godwin's horror, expressed his love for Godwin's teenage daughter Mary on June 27, 1814. Harriet was not amenable to Shelley's suggestion that Mary become part of the family, and after a period of melodramatic chaos, Shelley and Mary, with Mary's half sister Claire Clairmont, fled to France on July 27, 1814. After an impromptu Continental tour, the errant lovers returned to England on September 13. During the next six months, both Harriet and Mary gave birth to children by Shelley, but only Charles Bysshe Shelley, Harriet's son, survived infancy.

Shelley and Mary found that they were not welcome among most of their old friends, though Peacock remained loyal, and Shelley spent a great deal of his time dodging creditors. His financial troubles were somewhat eased when his father, in June, 1815, began providing him with a generous annual allowance, but his social problems continued. In August of that year, he and Mary rented a cottage outside Bishopsgate, where they lived for a time in somber seclusion. Following a journey up the Thames with Peacock and Charles Clairmont, however, Shelley recovered his equanimity and began work on the poetry of the *Alastor* volume. *Alastor* was published in February, 1816, shortly after the birth of William Shelley, the poet's second son.

Shelley, with Mary, their son, and Claire Clairmont, embarked on a second Continental tour in May. Claire, who had secretly carried on an affair with Lord Byron and was carrying his child, urged the group on to Lake Geneva, where they soon encountered the celebrated author of *Childe Harold's Pilgrimage* (1812-1818, 1819). Byron and Shelley, though vastly different in personality, quickly became friends, and their many conversations proved fruitful to the poetry of both. The friendship was also beneficial to Mary, who began work on *Frankenstein* (1818) during an evening at Byron's quarters in the Villa Diodati. The encounter was less fortunate for Claire, who discovered that Byron felt no love for her, though he expressed a willingness to rear their child so long as its mother kept discreetly at a distance.

Shelley was generous in his attempts to assist Claire, who accompanied the Shelley household to Bath after their return from the Continent in late summer. Even without the complication of Claire's pregnancy, the next few months were among the most tumultuous of Shelley's life. The first shock occurred in October, when Mary's half sister Fanny Imlay took her own life. This was soon followed by the disappearance of Harriet Shelley, whose body was found on December 10, 1816, floating in the Serpentine, where she, too, had become a suicide. Shelley and Mary were married three weeks later, after which a custody fight for Ianthe and Charles ended in failure on March 27, 1817. Shelley was judged an unfit father because of his "immoral and vicious" principles.

In the midst of these troubles, Shelley found himself winning recognition as a poet, most notably through Leigh Hunt's "Young Poets" article in *The Examiner* in December, 1816. Shelley quickly took advantage of the opportunity offered by the article, which grouped him with John Hamilton Reynolds and Keats, to introduce himself to Hunt, through whom he met Keats, Horace Smith, and other members of the London literary scene. With the birth of Clara Allegra Byron at Bath on January 12, 1817, and with his own involvement in the child custody case, Shelley found it not only possible but also necessary to spend considerable time in the capital, a circumstance that augmented his chances for literary friendships.

A few weeks before the handing down of the Chancery decision, Shelley moved his entourage to Albion House in Great Marlow, where he had easy access to London and where he could accommodate his many literary visitors. The Marlow period, despite its occasional traumas, was a time of comparative stability, during which Shelley did the last of his political pamphleteering and published the longest of his poems, *The Revolt of Islam*. He also began *Rosalind and Helen* and became a father for the fifth time. His daughter Clara was born on September 2, 1817. Unfortunately, because of new financial worries brought on largely by loans to his improvident father-in-law and because of concern that the courts might take custody of William and Clara, Shelley and Mary left Marlow in February, 1818. On March 11, they sailed from England, intending to reach Italy. After that date, Shelley never saw England again.

The Shelley party crossed France and passed through the Alps to Turin and Milan. While in Milan, Shelley exchanged letters with Byron concerning Allegra, and it was finally decided that Byron's daughter would be sent to his apartments in Venice under the protection of a nurse. The Shelleys then traveled to Pisa and Leghorn, where they lingered for several weeks. They next occupied the Casa Bertini at the Baths of Lucca, where Shelley completed *Rosalind and Helen*, which was published during the spring of 1819.

Because of disturbing letters from Allegra's nurse, Shelley and Claire departed for Venice on August 17, 1818, arriving five days later. Byron and Shelley resumed their friendship, a circumstance that inspired Shelley's *Julian and Maddalo*, and Claire was pleased to find Allegra in good health, though the chaos of Byron's bizarre household had necessitated her being placed, for a time, with another family. More significant, as a result of Shelley's misleading statements to Byron concerning the whereabouts of Mary and the annoying Claire, Shelley was forced to ask Mary to make a quick journey from Lucca to Este, where Byron had offered him the use of a house. During the trip, Clara became infected with dysentery; she died in Venice on September 24, 1818.

Clara's death brought Shelley and Mary grief and a cooling of their love, but the months at Este were, nevertheless, productive. In addition to his work on *Julian and Maddalo*, Shelley composed "Lines Written Among the Euganean Hills" and began *Prometheus Unbound*. Their journey to Rome during November showed less production, but their three-month stay in Naples saw the completion of *Prometheus Unbound*, act 1. Following their return to Rome in March, 1819, Shelley wrote the play's second and third acts and became interested in the history of the Cenci family. During June, however, in the midst of the poet's fruitful literary activities, William became ill. The crisis came quickly, and after a sixty-hour struggle, the child died on June 7, 1819.

Soon thereafter, the grieving parents moved to Leghorn, where Shelley immersed himself in further literary endeavors, primarily the writing of *The Cenci*, though *The Masque of Anarchy* was also written there. In October, the Shelleys were again on the move, this time to Florence, where Shelley's last child, Percy Florence, was born on November 12, and where the literary deluge continued. While living at the Palazzo Marino, Shelley wrote *Peter Bell the Third*, "Ode to the West Wind," portions of *A Philosophical View of Reform*, and act 4 of *Prometheus Unbound*. Shelley himself considered *Prometheus Unbound*, published in August of 1820, to be his greatest work, a view which many, if not most, critics have since shared.

In late January, 1820, the Shelleys took inexpensive lodgings in Pisa, in and around which they were to reside during most of the remainder of Shelley's life. With the birth of Percy Florence, Mary's spirits had improved considerably, and much of what had made life bitter for the couple during the previous months appears to have faded from prominence. There were disasters still to come, but there were moments, too, of idyllic tranquillity, as well as further periods of creative accomplishment. Shelley divided 1820 among Pisa itself and nearby Leghorn and San Giuliano. In addition, he traveled with Claire to Florence, where she was to live in the household of a prominent physician. During the year, he seems to have done further work on *A Philosophical View of Reform* and also wrote "The Sensitive Plant," "To a Skylark," the "Letter to Maria Gisborne," *The Witch of Atlas*, and *Oedipus Tyrannus*.

During the first months of 1821, after making the acquaintance of the charming Teresa Viviani, Shelley wrote *Epipsychidion*, a poem inspired by Teresa's virtual imprisonment in the St. Anna convent school. In February and March, after reading a somewhat cynical essay by Peacock, he composed his brilliantly idealistic response, *A Defence of Poetry*, published in 1840. *Adonais* was written on April 11, after he received the shocking news of the death of Keats, whom he had tried to persuade to join him in Pisa for the sake of Keats's health, and the stirring *Hellas* was completed in October.

This was the period, too, when the celebrated Pisan Circle began to form. Thomas Medwin had arrived in late 1819, and Shelley met Edward and Jane Williams in January of 1820. In August of 1820, Shelley traveled to Ravenna to lure Byron to Pisa. Experiencing considerable difficulties because of his own political activities and those of his mistress' family, Byron joined the group late in 1820, along with Teresa Gamba Guiccioli and members of her family. With the addition on January 14, 1822, of Edward Trelawny, a friend of Edward Williams, the Pisan Circle was complete.

With the arrival of Trelawny, 1822 began well, but subsequent months would bring a double catastrophe to Shelley and his friends. The first tragedy occurred in April, when Allegra Byron died in a convent at Ravenna. Claire had been terribly concerned about Allegra from the moment she was told that Byron had left the child behind during his retreat from governmental authorities. He had left Allegra in good hands, but the convent, as Claire had feared, was vulnerable to epidemics, and on April 20, Allegra had succumbed to typhus.

The second tragedy involved Shelley himself. Shelley had continued his literary endeavors in 1822, working primarily on his poems *Charles the First* and *The Triumph of Life*, but with every encouragement from Williams and Trelawny, he also developed an interest in sailing, despite not knowing how to swim. So interested was he, in fact, that he ordered a small boat to be built, delivery of which he accepted on May 12. On July 1, he and Williams sailed the boat, the *Don Juan*, to Leghorn to meet Hunt, whom Shelley had invited to Italy to found a literary journal. On July 8, Williams and Shelley began the return voyage in threatening weather. Their bodies were washed ashore several days later, and under Trelawny's supervision, they were cremated on the beach. In a typically Romantic gesture, Trelawny snatched Shelley's heart from the ashes, and it was eventually given to Mary.

Analysis

For all practical purposes, the narrative of Percy Bysshe Shelley's importance to theatrical history is the tale of *The Cenci*, and the bulk of the following comments will center on that play. Because *Prometheus Unbound* was the first of his substantial literary undertakings to be cast in dramatic form, however, and because this earliest effort is thematically related to *The Cenci*, a few preliminary remarks about *Prometheus Unbound* are appropriate.

Prometheus Unbound considers on the ideal level what *The Cenci* examines on the level of gritty reality, the relationship between good and evil, between benevolent innocence and that which would corrupt it. Shelley's Prometheus is the traditional fire-giver redefined, as his preface tells us. The primary change which Shelley makes in his subject is a reworking of the events leading to Prometheus' release. In the lost Aeschylean play from which Shelley borrowed his title, there occurred a "reconciliation of Jupiter with his victim" at "the price of the disclosure of the danger threatened to his empire by the consummation of his marriage with Thetis." In Shelley's version, Prometheus earns his freedom more nobly, by overcoming himself, by forswearing hatred and the desire for revenge, embracing love, and achieving, through extraordinary fortitude, a merciful selflessness.

In a sense, Prometheus combines a Christ-like forbearance with the traits which the Romantics often admired in Satan. Shelley makes this modified Satanism explicit when he writes:

> The only imaginary being resembling in any degree Prometheus, is Satan, because, in addition to courage, and majesty, and firm and patient opposition to omnipotent force, he is susceptible of being described as exempt from the taints of ambition, envy, revenge, and a desire for personal aggrandisement, which, in the Hero of *Paradise Lost*, interfere with the interest.

By contrast with Satan,

> Prometheus is . . . the type of the highest perfection of moral and intellectual nature, impelled by the purest and the truest motives to the best and noblest ends.

This perfection is absent as the play begins, but when, in act 1, Prometheus relents in his hatred and says, "I wish no living thing to suffer pain," his ultimate triumph and Jupiter's defeat are inevitable. Evil can succeed only if it is allowed access to one's innermost being, only if one allows it to re-create oneself in its own vile image. With "Gentleness, Virtue, Wisdom, and Endurance," a person can win out, though the success of goodness requires a great deal of him as is shown in the play's final lines:

> To suffer woe which Hope thinks infinite;
> To forgive wrongs darker than death or night;
> To defy Power, which seems omnipotent;
> To love, and bear; to hope till Hope creates
> From its own wreck the thing it contemplates;
> Neither to change, nor falter, nor repent;
> This, like thy glory, Titan, is to be
> Good, great and joyous, beautiful and free;
> This is alone Life, Joy, Empire, and Victory.

In *The Cenci*, Beatrice exhibits the necessary defiance of evil, but she lacks the fortitude to resist hatred. She confuses physical violation, which any person with sufficient opportunity can inflict on any other, with spiritual violation, which requires willful complicity. By hating, she comes partially to resemble the thing she hates.

The object of Beatrice's hatred is her father, Count Francesco Cenci, the embodiment of everything the Romantics distrusted in those possessed of power. In characterizing the count, Shelley had a rich gallery of Gothic and melodramatic villains upon which to draw, and among them all, few can match the count for wickedness. The count is a plunderer, a murderer, and an incestuous rapist. He takes delight in destroying the lives of those around him, and he especially enjoys inflicting spiritual torture. He will only "rarely kill the body," because it "preserves, like a strong prison, the soul within my power,/ Wherein I feed it with the breath of fear/ For hourly pain."

Like many a villain of the period, the count commits his vilest crimes against the holy ties of sentiment. His egomania destroys his capacity for fellow-feeling, and out of the horror of his isolating selfhood, he performs deeds of unnatural viciousness against those who most deserve his love. He abuses Lucretia, his wife, and Bernardo, his innocent young son. He prays for the deaths of two other sons, Rocco and Cristofano, and invites guests to a banquet of thanksgiving when their deaths occur. He refuses to repay the loan of his daughter-in-law's dowry, which he had borrowed from the desperately poor Giacomo, his fourth son, and after taking Giacomo's job away and giving it to another man, he alienates this son from his wife and children by claiming that Giacomo used the lost dowry for licentious carousing. He reserves his greatest cruelty, however, for Beatrice. Beatrice possesses the courage to denounce him and to seek redress for the injustices inflicted upon herself and her family. She goes so far as to petition the pope for aid in her struggle. In order to break her rebellious spirit, to crush her will to resist him, the count rapes his daughter and threatens to do so again.

The count's unnatural cruelty inspires unnatural hatred in Lucretia, Giacomo, and Beatrice. As Giacomo tells us, "He has cast Nature off, which was his shield,/ And Nature casts him off, who is her shame;/ And I spurn both." The son, "reversing Nature's law," wishes to take the life of the man who "gave life to me." He wishes to kill the man who denied him "happy years" and "memories/ Of tranquil childhood," who deprived him of "home-sheltered love." Beatrice and Lucretia share this wish to destroy the perverter of love. When Count Cenci proves impervious to their pleas that he relent, and when every external authority refuses to intervene, the family members take action against this most unnatural of men.

Because Beatrice is strongest and most sinned against, she becomes the prime mover of her father's murder. Giacomo refers to her victimization as "a higher reason for the act/ Than mine" and speaks of her, in lines ironically recalling the biblical injunction *against* vengeance, as "a holier judge than me,/ A more unblamed avenger." In becoming the avenger, though, Beatrice must steel herself against those qualities of innocence and compassion that have rendered her superior to her persecutor. She thinks, in fact, that exactly those qualities that militate against the murder can be twisted around to give the strength needed to commit it. She advises Giacomo to

> . . . Let piety to God,
> Brotherly love, justice and clemency,
> And all things that make tender hardest hearts
> Make thine hard, brother.

When assassins have been recruited to do the deed, Giacomo utters a momentary hope that the assassins may fail. When the first attempt does fail, Lucretia takes the opportunity to urge Francesco to confess his sins so that, if a second attempt succeeds, at least she will have done nothing to condemn his soul to eternal torment. Beatrice, by contrast, is as relentless in pursuing revenge as her father had been in pursuing evil pleasures. At a key moment, when even the assassins quail at taking the life of "an old and sleeping man," Beatrice takes up the knife and shames them into performing the murder by threatening to do it herself.

Beatrice is like her father, too, in claiming that God is on her side. Francesco had seen the hand of God in the deaths of his disobedient sons; the ultimate Father had upheld parental authority by killing the rebellious Rocco and Cristofano. Similarly, as Beatrice plots her father's death, she feels confident of having God's approval for her actions; as His instrument, she is permitted, even obligated, to wreak vengeance on this most terrible of sinners. Neither character is right. Both are appealing to the silent symbol of all external authority to justify the unjustifiable, to second the internal voice that has turned them toward evil.

The dangers of religion are further embodied in the machinations of Orsino and the unconscionable actions of the pope and his representatives. Orsino is God's priest, but his priestly garb merely wraps his lustfulness in the hypocritical guise of sanctity. In order to eliminate Count Cenci, the greatest obstacle to his possession of Beatrice, Orsino urges the conspirators on at every turn. When the conspiracy is discovered, he is the only participant in the count's murder to slink safely away. The pope's role in the play's events is even more reprehensible. For years, he has allowed the count's depredations at the price of an occasional rich bribe. He refuses to intervene to end the count's crimes because it is in his self-interest to allow them to continue. When he finally does take action, apparently because he can now achieve more by eliminating the count than by keeping him alive, the pope is too late; the count is already dead. He then turns on those who have accomplished, outside the law, what he would have done with the full authority of the papal office. As the earthly representative of ultimate power, he orders the deaths of those who have become a threat to all power; the conspirators are to be executed. The irony of this situation is that the prop to the papal authority is the same false notion that lured his victims to act as they did, the assumption that everything, even the shedding of human blood, is allowed to those who have God on their side.

In a world as corrupt as the one in which Beatrice Cenci finds herself, her fall is all the more terrible because it is so easy to sympathize with. The most perceptive comments concerning the nature of Beatrice as a tragic heroine and the appropriateness of her life as a tragic subject are Shelley's own:

> Undoubtedly, no person can be truly dishonoured by the act of another; and the fit return to make to the most enormous injuries is kindness and forbearance, and a resolution to convert the injurer from his dark passions by peace and love. Revenge, retaliation, atonement, are pernicious mistakes. If Beatrice had thought in this manner, she would have been wiser and better; but she would never have been a tragic character. . . . It is in the restless and anatomizing casuistry with which men seek the justification of Beatrice, yet feel that she has done what needs justification; it is in the superstitious horror with which they contemplate alike her wrongs and their revenge, that the dramatic character of what she did and suffered, consists.

In her capacity to endure evil and to forgive the evildoer, Beatrice is no Prometheus, but in her very understandable human frailty, she is a far superior subject for dramatic representation.

Other major works

NOVELS: *Zastrozzi: A Romance*, 1810; *St. Irvyne: Or, The Rosicrucian*, 1810.

POETRY: *Original Poetry by Victor and Cazire*, 1810 (with Elizabeth Shelley); *Posthumous Fragments of Margaret Nicholson*, 1810; *Queen Mab: A Philosophical Poem*, 1813 (revised as *The Daemon of the World*); *Alastor: Or, The Spirit of Solitude, and Other Poems*, 1816 (includes *The Daemon of the World*); *Mont Blanc*, 1817; *The Revolt of Islam*, 1818; *Rosalind and Helen: A Modern Eclogue, with Other Poems*, 1819; *Prometheus Unbound: A Lyrical Drama in Four Acts, with Other Poems*, 1820; *Epipsychidion*, 1821; *Adonais: An Elegy on the Death of John Keats*, 1821; *Posthumous Poems of Percy Bysshe Shelley*, 1824 (includes *Prince Athanase, Julian and Maddalo: A Conversation, The Witch of Atlas, The Triumph of Life, The Cyclops, Charles the First*); *The Masque of Anarchy*, 1832; *Peter Bell the Third*, 1839; *The Poetical Works of Percy Bysshe Shelley*, 1839; *The Wandering Jew*, 1887; *The Complete Poetical Works of Shelley*, 1904 (Thomas Hutchinson, editor); *The Esdaile Notebook: A Volume of Early Poems*, 1964.

NONFICTION: *The Necessity of Atheism*, 1811 (with Thomas Jefferson Hogg); *An Address to the Irish People*, 1812; *Declaration of Rights*, 1812; *A*

Letter to Lord Ellenborough, 1812; *Proposals for an Association of . . . Philanthropists*, 1812; *A Refutation of Deism, in a Dialogue*, 1814; *History of a Six Weeks' Tour Through a Part of France, Switzerland, Germany and Holland*, 1817 (with Mary Shelley); *A Proposal for Putting Reform to the Vote Throughout the Kingdom*, 1817; *An Address to the People on the Death of the Princess Charlotte*, 1817(?); *Essays, Letters from Abroad, Translations and Fragments*, 1840; *A Defence of Poetry*, 1840; *Shelley Memorials*, 1859; *Shelley's Prose in the Bodleian Manuscripts*, 1910; *Note Books of Shelley*, 1911; *A Philosophical View of Reform*, 1920; *The Letters of Percy Bysshe Shelley*, 1964 (2 volumes; Frederick L. Jones, editor).

TRANSLATIONS: *The Cyclops*, 1824 (of Euripides' play); *Ion*, 1840 (of Plato's dialogue); "The Banquet Translated from Plato," 1931 (of Plato's dialogue *Symposium*).

MISCELLANEOUS: *The Complete Works of Percy Bysshe Shelley*, 1926-1930 (10 volumes; Roger Ingpen and Walter E. Peck, editors); *Shelley's Poetry and Prose: Authoritative Texts and Criticism*, 1977 (Donald H. Reiman and Sharon B. Powers, editors).

Bibliography

Chernaik, Judith. *The Lyrics of Shelley.* Cleveland, Ohio: Press of Western Reserve University, 1972. Although Chernaik studies the lyrics, she describes a context for *The Cenci*, *Prometheus Unbound*, and *Hellas.* She identifies Shelley's style and thought in his most personal poems and reveals a political and psychological basis for his dramatic poems. Includes manuscript illustrations, newly edited texts of the lyrics discussed, appendices of textual puzzles, a bibliography, and an index.

Cronin, Richard. *Shelley's Poetic Thoughts.* New York: St. Martin's Press, 1981. An incisive study of Shelley's thought within his poems and his manner of handling language. Cronin scrutinizes poetic forms as they manage realism and fantasy, elegy and dream. The central chapter analyzes *Prometheus Unbound* as a dramatization of the history of civilization. Contains notes and an index.

Curran, Stuart. *Shelley's "Annus Mirabilis": The Maturing of an Epic Vision.* San Marino, Calif.: Huntington Library, 1975. Drawing on three Huntington Library notebooks, Curran focuses on 1819 as a miraculous year for Shelley's developing genius. The key is Shelley's exile to a paradisiacal Italy, where he identified with Dante and John Milton. Includes illustrations, extensive notes, and an index.

____________. *Shelley's "Cenci": Scorpions Ringed with Fire.* Princeton, N.J.: Princeton University Press, 1970. A detailed study of Shelley's *The Cenci*, focusing on the play's meaning and influence. Curran recognizes the lack of critical attention to this work and encourages other studies to add to the understanding of this major piece. The play is first studied as a poem, then it is examined as theater for the stage. Includes illustrations, footnotes, and an index.

Holmes, Richard. *Shelley: The Pursuit.* New York: E. P. Dutton, 1975. This major biography presents Shelley as a sinister and sometimes cruel artist of immense talent. Holmes claims new answers to questions about Shelley's Welsh experiences and about his paternity of a child born in Naples. Critical readings of Shelley's writings are less valuable than their biographical context. Contains illustrations, bibliography, notes, and an index.

Keach, William. *Shelley's Style.* New York: Methuen, 1984. Admitting difficulties in Shelley's style, Keach focuses on the figurative transformations that illustrate the poet's special workmanship as a consequence of his divided views of language. Mirror and veil images are examined in *A Defence of Poetry* as preliminary to understanding Shelley's dependence on reflexive images in his poetry. Includes notes and index.

McNiece, Gerald. *Shelley and the Revolutionary Idea.* Cambridge, Mass.: Harvard University Press, 1969. A study of Shelley's calls for rebellion on behalf of energetic virtues that made the poet a spokesperson for good during a period of many evils. Focuses on origins and development of Shelley's idea of revolution and on his concept of heroism, particularly in *Prometheus Unbound* and *Hellas.* Bibliography, notes, index.

Robert H. O'Connor
(Updated by *Richard D. McGhee*)

SAM SHEPARD
Samuel Shepard Rogers

Born: Fort Sheridan, Illinois; November 5, 1943

Principal drama

Cowboys, pr. 1964 (one act); *The Rock Garden*, pr. 1964, pb. 1971 (one act); *Chicago*, pr. 1965, pb. 1967; *Icarus's Mother*, pr. 1965, pb. 1967; *4-H Club*, pr. 1965, pb. 1972; *Fourteen Hundred Thousand*, pr. 1966, pb. 1967; *Melodrama Play*, pr. 1966, pb. 1967; *Red Cross*, pr. 1966, pb. 1967; *La Turista*, pr. 1966, pb. 1968; *Cowboys #2*, pr. 1967, pb. 1968; *Forensic and the Navigators*, pr. 1967, pb. 1969; *The Unseen Hand*, pr., pb. 1969; *Operation Sidewinder*, pb. 1969, pr. 1970; *Shaved Splits*, pr. 1969, pb. 1972; *The Holy Ghostly*, pr. 1970, pb. 1972; *Cowboy Mouth*, pr., pb. 1971 (with Patti Smith); *The Mad Dog Blues*, pr. 1971, pb. 1972; *The Tooth of Crime*, pr. 1972, pb. 1974; *Geography of a Horse Dreamer*, pr., pb. 1974; *Action*, pr. 1974, pb. 1975; *Angel City*, pr., pb. 1976; *Curse of the Starving Class*, pb. 1976, pr. 1977; *Suicide in B Flat*, pr. 1976, pb. 1979; *Buried Child*, pr. 1978, pb. 1979; *Seduced*, pr. 1978, pb. 1979; *True West*, pr. 1980, pb. 1981; *Fool for Love*, pr., pb. 1983; *A Lie of the Mind*, pr. 1985, pb 1986; *States of Shock*, pr. 1991, pb. 1992.

Other literary forms

Sam Shepard has written a number of screenplays, including the ill-fated *Zabriskie Point* (1969) for Michelangelo Antonioni, the award-winning *Paris, Texas* (1984), and *Far North* (1988), which Shepard also directed. Shepard has also written poetry and short fiction, in *Hawk Moon* (1973) and *Motel Chronicles* (1982), and recorded the major events of Bob Dylan's Rolling Thunder Revue tour in a collection of essays titled *Rolling Thunder Logbook* (1977).

Achievements

Shepard is one of the United States' most prolific, most celebrated, and most honored playwrights. Writing exclusively for the Off-Broadway and Off-Off-Broadway theater, Shepard has nevertheless won eleven Obie Awards (for *Red Cross*, *Chicago*, *Icarus's Mother*, *Forensic and the Navigators*, *La Turista*, *Melodrama Play*, *Cowboys #2*, *The Tooth of Crime*, *Curse of the Starving Class*, *Buried Child*, and *Fool for Love*). In 1979, he received a Pulitzer Prize for *Buried Child.* His screenplay for Wim Wenders' film *Paris, Texas* won the Palme d'Or at the Cannes Film Festival, and Shepard himself received an Oscar nomination for his portrayal of Colonel Chuck Yeager in *The Right Stuff* (1983). *A Lie of the Mind* was named the outtstanding new play of the 1985-1986 season by the Drama Desk.

Biography

Born Samuel Shepard Rogers, Jr., on an army base in Fort Sheridan, Illinois on November 5, 1943, Sam Shepard's early years were marked by repeated moves from one place to another: South Dakota, Utah, Florida, Guam, and eventually Southern California. Shepard's father was severely wounded during World War II, became an alcoholic, and progressively withdrew from the family until he became a desert-dwelling, storytelling recluse; Samuel Rogers VI, the playwright's father, died after being struck by a car in 1983. Shepard recalls that his mother, Jane Schook Rogers, would fire her army-issued Luger pistol at the Japanese soldiers sneaking out of the jungle on Guam in the years following World War II. After Shepard's father retired from the army, the family moved to an avocado ranch in the San Bernardino valley, in Southern California, where Shepard spent his adolescent years. In 1962, Shepard joined a barnstorming acting company with a religiously based repertory, the Bishop's Repertory Company. When the company reached New York, Shepard, nineteen years old, dropped out of the company and into the Lower East Side bohemian lifestyle, busing tables at the Village Gate, dabbling with acting, doing drugs, and running the streets with Charles Mingus, Jr., an old California friend.

In 1964, the twin bill of Shepard's first two plays, the original *Cowboys* and *The Rock Garden*, premiered at one of Off-Off-Broadway's most important theaters, Theater Genesis, and Shepard's career was launched. Shepard wrote prolifically for the Off-Off-Broadway theater during the last half of the 1960's, gaining recognition and critical acclaim with each play, many of which contained made-to-order parts for his girlfriend, Joyce Aaron. By 1967, Shepard had gathered three Obie Awards, produced his first full-length play, and could boast of plays being produced on the West Coast, in New York, and in London. In 1969, Shepard married O-Lan Johnson (they had one son, Jesse Mojo), the actress who played the eponymous Oolan in *Forensic and the Navigators*. The following year, however, brought many difficulties for Shepard: *Operation Sidewinder* was produced at the Vivian Beaumont Theater at New York's Lincoln Center, but the frustrations posed by an expensive Broadway production and the generally unfavorable reaction to the play prompted Shepard to return to Off-Off-Broadway. Further, Shepard's romance with the emerging rock star Patti Smith severely taxed his nascent domestic life. Finally, losing patience with the New York theater scene, Shepard and his family moved to London in 1972. Upon his return to the United States in 1976, Shepard joined Bob Dylan on his Rolling Thunder Tour and then moved to San Francisco, where he began working with Joseph Chaikin and the Magic Theatre. The move to California also marks the beginning of Shepard's career as a film star; his portrayal of Colonel Chuck Yeager in *The Right Stuff* earned for him an Oscar nomination. While on the set of *Frances* (1982), Shepard met Jessica Lange; they later bought a ranch together in New Mexico and subsequently moved to Virginia.

Analysis

Nearly all Sam Shepard's plays examine the functions (and dysfunctions) of the relationships between individuals that constitute either family structures or social structures that approximate family structures—close friendships or tight-knit business alliances. The conflict between the two halves of what can be considered a single unit (brother and brother, father and son, husband and wife, boyfriend and girlfriend) as they struggle either for supremacy or for survival amid surrounding pressures can be found at the core of most of Shepard's plays. Further, his principal characters tend not only to be alienated from their immediate circumstances but also to be victimized by their drive toward a destructive self-isolation. The wake of devastation left by figures who are incapable of bridging the abysses they have created shapes the central conflict in many of Shepard's plays.

The pulsating rhythms of those conflicts can be tracked through Shepard's unique use of dramatic language. Instead of the series of natural exchanges between characters found in plays constructed on the principle of mimetic realism, the language in Shepard's plays reflects his extensive musical background. His dialogue ranges from realistic banter to highly metaphoric and figurative speech, to the beat and patter of rock and roll, to free-form, yet highly complex, jazzlike improvisational riffs. Characters frequently disrupt the flow of the dialogue with abrupt shifts in voice (such as Hoss's switch from the street talk of a rock and roll star to the argot of an old Delta blues singer in *The Tooth of Crime*), sudden shifts in character (such as Chet's and Stu's metamorphosis from modern urban cowboys to old-time prospectors in *Cowboys #2*), or unexpected irruptions into convoluted soliloquies that arrest the flow of the action (such as Wesley's recollection of his drunken father's return in *Curse of the Starving Class*). Even when it is primarily realistic, the plays' language is highly figurative, establishing a layer of metaphoric significance that points toward the plays' thematic center.

The setting of Shepard's plays also contributes figurative significance to their dominant theme. The action often unfolds against a backdrop composed of commonplace materials such as bathtubs, old wrecked cars, kitchen tables, refrigerators, living-room sofas, hotel beds, children's bedrooms, or hospital rooms, but these articles suggest an environment that is primarily metaphoric, not realistic. Shepard uses the icons of American pop culture to represent the mythic landscape of the American psyche, thereby demonstrating how personal identity is so often assembled out of the bits and pieces of the social iconography that dominates American culture. His figurative settings also underscore the predominant tensions dramatized, as in *Curse of the Starving Class*, where the lack of food in the refrigerator represents the lack of love and nurture in the family. Because Shepard is primarily interested in depicting figurative conflicts and actions, he is free to draw on a wide variety of materials in the physical setting as well as the dialogue in order to create his mythic landscapes. Hence, Shepard's plays are filled with borrowings from, and allusions to, what he sees as the core of the United States' mythology: rock and roll and country-western music, Hollywood and films of all kinds (Westerns in particular), the trappings of middle-class suburbia, the physical geography of the West (the desert in particular), science fiction, and the conflict between generations that shredded American society and culture during the Vietnam era.

Shepard's earliest extant play, *The Rock Garden*, sketches many of the themes that resonate throughout his work. In the first of the play's three scenes, Shepard defines the estrangement between generations: A Boy and a Girl sit in silence, sipping milk, while a Man, absorbed in his magazine, ignores them. In the second scene, the Boy signals his alienation from the mother figure (the Woman) by donning more and more clothing, which metaphorically suggests the barriers erected between the family members. The third scene repeats this figurative action, with the mother replaced by the father figure, the Man, who bores his son almost to death. Finally, the Boy shatters the superficial complacency of the relationships with a graphic and intensely personal recounting of his sexual preferences and prowess. Thus, the rock garden metaphorically defines this typical Shepardian family: sterile, arid, and empty.

Most of the one-act plays that Shepard wrote for the Off-Off-Broadway theater during the 1960's explore themes that emerged in *The Rock Garden*. *Chicago* examines the dynamics of isolation. The alienation of Stu—who reposes in a bathtub naked from the waist up but wearing jeans and tennis shoes—from the other cast members cannot be overcome by the figurative barriers that Stu creates through his active imagination. In *4-H Club*, three men, Joe, John, and Bob, take turns imposing improvised antics on the other two; in *Red Cross*, Jim, a tourist infested with crab lice, imposes imaginative scenarios on two women: Carol (Jim's girlfriend) and a hotel maid. All three plays present characters who are markedly alienated from their selves and their surroundings; moreover, Shepard suggests that the imposition of personal desires on others leads typically to irreversible alienation. *Cowboys #2* is perhaps Shepard's best depiction of the ability of the imagination to assert a separate reality as Chet and Stu, two urban cowboys, take turns imposing imaginative vistas on each other. For example, Chet assumes the voice and posture of an Old West prospector and addresses Stu as Mel, who plays along. The two urban cowboys and old-time prospectors rollick through a number of fanciful incidents: calisthenics, a rainstorm, an Indian attack, a descant on the decay of the modern West, and a trek across the desert. The play suggests that the imaginative world is just as "real" as the actual world.

In a series of plays from the late 1960's to the early 1970's, Shepard explores isolation and alienation by employing metaphoric sets, characterizations, and actions. *Icarus's Mother* depicts a conflict between five metaphorically "grounded" characters and a jet pilot—a transcendent Icarus figure. When the two females (Jill and Pat) respond to the pilot sexually, the pilot reacts sexually, looping, rolling, climbing, and finally plunging to an explosive climax in the ocean. The play suggests that sexual desire is both irresistible and destructive, that permanent transcendence is not possible, and that males and females cannot communicate successfully. *Forensic and the Navigators* examines the antiwar movement of the 1960's. Two would-be revolutionaries, Forensic (whose name suggests talk but no action) and Emmet, ineptly attempt to chart out a revolutionary action. When the radicals' hideout is suddenly invaded by California Highway Patrol-like exterminators, the fundamental distinctions between the revolutionaries and the forces of oppression progressively disintegrate, since neither side is capable of significant action.

Shepard's first full-length play, *La Turista*, examines the inexorable decay of American society. Set in a Mexican hotel room for the first act, *La Turista* depicts the inability of two middle-class Americans, Kent and Salem, to overcome their cultural and spiritual sickness, symbolized by the dysentery they have contracted. Kent and Salem's internal malaise contrasts sharply with the vitality of the Mexican Boy, who symbolizes both the Third World peoples exploited by American materialism and the son caught in an Oedipal conflict with his father. Moreover, Kent's symbolic role as the epitome of American cultural dominance is undercut by Kent's ironic attack on the obsessions that have made the United States irrecoverably weak. After Kent faints upon seeing the Boy in bed with Salem, the remainder of the first act consists of an attempt to revive Kent (who is described as dead), which involves a Witch Doctor, his son, and sacrificial chickens. The second act of *La Turista* duplicates the first in action, although it employs a separate metaphorical structure. Set in a drab American hotel room, Kent's revival continues. The Witch Doctor and the Boy from the first act enter, dressed now like country doctors from the Civil War era. Kent's disease is the result of a psychological and emotional starvation endemically linked to the structure of the typical American family. Kent and the Doctor become enmeshed in a mutually imposed *Frankenstein* scenario that recalls the father/son conflicts of the first act with Kent in the role of monster/son and the Doctor as the creator/father. As the imaginative play reaches its peak, Kent transforms into the monster and escapes his repressive society by crashing through the upstage wall, leaving a cutout of his body. *La Turista* compellingly suggests that the barren American family and its disposable society are incurably diseased structures that produce generation after generation of monsters.

The Unseen Hand and *Operation Sidewinder* also explore unresolvable conflicts. *The Unseen Hand*, a cross between a science-fiction adventure and a television Western, pits Willie the Space Freak and the Morphan brothers (a trio of Old West outlaws) against the High Commission of Nogoland with its powerful Unseen Hand, a force that squeezes the mind. The conflict unfolds on a stage cluttered with the detritus of the American consumer society (symbolized by the play's setting: Azusa, everything from A to Z in the United States). Nogoland and Azusa are but two different names for the tyrannizing force of established culture that opposes those who seek true freedom. Willie's ability to escape the Unseen Hand's power seems to be a qualified endorsement of revolutionary action. *Operation Sidewinder*, Shepard's big-budget Broadway production, develops the structure sketched in *The Unseen Hand.* The plot brings together a group of revolutionaries consisting of Mickey Free (an Indian), a hippie known as the Young Man (who symbolizes all the impatience, violence, and frustrations of American youths during the 1960's and 1970's), and Blood (a Black Panther type), all of whom struggle against the forces of political oppression led by a Central Intelligence Agency goon (Captain Bovine), a mad scientist (Dr. Vector), and Dr. Vector's gigantic and deadly missile/computer shaped like a sidewinder rattlesnake. When Mickey Free liberates Honey, the play's only significant female, by cutting off the Sidewinder's head, the action suggests that violent political confrontation can lead to true liberation, but the remainder of the play does not fulfill that promise. Shepard uses satiric language and irony to undercut the pretentiousness of both the antiestablishment and the establishment. Only Mickey Free's desire to use the Sidewinder's head as a source of spiritual renewal provides a viable alternative to the sterile and debilitating social mythologies embraced by both the revolutionaries and the establishment. The play ends with a pyrotechnic encounter between a group of Desert Tactical troops who futilely discharge their machine guns into Mickey Free, the Young Man, Honey, and a group of Hopi Indians who are caught up in the spirituality of the snake dance and have thereby achieved a higher level of existence. Although the play preaches too much, *Operation Sidewinder* is perhaps Shepard's most hopeful offering, suggesting that the futility of political and generational conflict can at last be transcended.

Although *Geography of a Horse Dreamer* is on the surface a play about a group of gamblers who are trying to squeeze information from Cody, an artistically minded young man with the ability to dream the winners of horse or dog races, it is really an extended metaphor that reproaches the tendency of a culture to treat its most gifted artists like disposable goods, demanding that they produce more and more until the artists themselves are consumed. Cody's abilities steadily wither since he cannot meet the demands of the Mafia-like gangsters until he is liberated from them by his shotgun-wielding brothers from the West in a violent scene at the play's end.

Angel City also examines the role of the artist in society. Rabbit, a film-script fixer, is hired by a motion-picture studio to repair the script of the company's latest big-budget disaster film. The line between films and the "real," however, is a tenuous distinction in *Angel City.* Miss Scoons, the type of the vacuous American female, desires beyond all else to become the people she sees on the silver screen since she believes their lives to be more "real" than hers. Further, the great disaster that Rabbit is supposed to script becomes the cataclysm that destroys both the world without and the world within the play; *Angel City*'s apocalyptic ending suggests that the American film industry, and the mythology it creates, is a primary source of the United States' cultural and spiritual corruption.

The Tooth of Crime is best described as a rock-and-roll gunfight between a top-of-the-charts but aging rocker, Hoss, and his up-and-coming rival, Crow. Set in a stylized future where rockers mark out territory through acts of violence much like members of rival gangs stake out their turf, *The Tooth of Crime* examines the dynamics by which males relate to one another when establishing their fundamental identities. As Hoss and Crow square off in the musical battle that dominates the play's second act, it becomes clear that Hoss and Crow, like so many of Shepard's other male characters, are locked into the battle of identity that pits father against son. Hoss quickly recognizes that "father" and "son" are locked into a generational cycle in which the younger will inevitably usurp the place of the elder, and the play's conclusion, in which Crow takes possession of Hoss's entourage, goods, and status, suggests that father and son are locked in an endless cycle in which the younger generation is doomed to repeat patterns of its forebears.

That cyclical pattern etched into the relationship between the generations provides the dominant structure for what have been called Shepard's "family" plays: *Curse of the Starving Class*, *Buried Child*, *True West*, *Fool for Love*, and *Lie of the Mind.* The "curse" in *Curse of the Starving Class* is quite clearly the curse of generational repetition: Children inevitably duplicate the actions of their parents. The natures of the parents are planted within the psyches of the children and emerge in actions that emphasize the familial curse passed down from generation to generation. Weston, the father, recalls the poison of his father's alcoholism; Wesley, the son, provides a chilling account of Weston's drunken attack on the home's locked front door; and in the third act, Wesley dons Weston's discarded clothes and admits that his father's essence is beginning to control him. Ella, the mother, passes on to her daughter Emma the curse of menstruation as well as the mother's desire to escape her family. The curse of starvation is overtly symbolized by the perpetually empty refrigerator, which underscores the family's physical, emotional, psychological, and spiritual starvation. Further, the curse of denial pervades all the play's relationships and colors almost every action. Clearly beset from within, this typical Shepardian family is also beset from without by those forces that Shepard believes threaten the mythic (and therefore true) West: the march of progress that wants to destroy the natural world and replace it with shopping malls, freeways, and tract housing developments. There is, obviously, no salvation for this family. Weston runs off to Mexico with the money he has received from the sale of the farm; Emma is blown up in Weston's car by thugs who are looking to extort money from Weston; Ella refuses to acknowledge what happens right in front of her and repeatedly addresses Wesley as Weston; Wesley completes the transformation into his father by adopting his father's attitudes and behaviors. The anecdote that Ella and Wesley jointly tell to close the play becomes the play's second great symbol: An eagle and a tomcat, tearing at each other in a midair struggle, crash to earth. Like that pair of animals, there is no salvation or escape that awaits the family in *Curse of the Starving Class*, only inevitable destruction.

Shepard's vision of the family in *Buried Child* is even darker; long and deeply buried familial secrets constitute the hereditary curse in Shepard's Pulitzer Prize winner. The family patriarch, Dodge, spends all of his time wrapped in an old blanket on the sofa, staring at the television. His wife, Halie, speaks at her husband (not to him) of trivial matters when she is not busy soliciting the local clergyman, Father Dewis. Their eldest son, Tilden, is a burned out and mentally defective semimute who brings armload after armload of corn onto the stage. The second son, Bradley, had one leg cut off by a chain saw and now spends most of his time wrestling with Dodge for control of the blanket and television set or threatening to cut Dodge's hair. In a series of statements that recalls the pattern of denial that occurs in *Curse of the Starving Class*, Dodge refuses to acknowledge that Bradley is his own son, claiming that his flesh and blood are buried in the backyard. To complicate matters, Halie frequently mentions yet another son, Ansel, who (according to Halie and Halie alone) was a hero and basketball star. Into the midst of this dysfunctional home comes Vince, Tilden's son, who wants to reestablish his family ties, and Shelly, Vince's girlfriend. Tilden, however, refuses to recognize Vince, claiming that the son he once had is now dead and buried. The denial of family connections suggests both the physical and the emotional rejection that pervades the home in *Buried Child*. On a physical level, the dead child refers to Halie and Tilden's incestuously conceived child who was killed by

Dodge and buried in the field behind the house. Metaphorically, the dead child represents all the children in the family, all of whom are dead to their father and mother and to one another. Unable to gain recognition from any of his progenitors, Vince stomps out one evening and goes on an alcoholic binge, leaving Shelly at the mercy of Bradley, who menaces her sexually. When Vince returns the next morning, thoroughly drunk, his open violence provides Halie and Dodge with the clue to Vince's identity, once again suggesting that behavior is mechanically passed from generation to generation. When Dodge dies, Vince proclaims himself the family's new patriarch just as Tilden enters carrying the exhumed body of the buried child. The play's highly equivocal ending juxtaposes the hope symbolized by the rebirth of a new generation against despairing images of denial, disease, and death.

True West explores the conflict between two brothers: Lee, a reclusive and violent thief who has been living in the Mojave desert, and Austin, a suburban Yuppie and screenwriter. Austin is trying to close a motion-picture deal with a Hollywood movie mogul, Saul Kimmer, but when Kimmer hears Lee's impromptu outline for a motion picture about two cowboys chasing each other across the plains of Texas, Kimmer decides to drop Austin's project and develop Lee's. *True West*, in addition to analyzing the fate of the artist in a manner that recalls *Angel City* and *Geography of a Horse Dreamer*, questions which version of the West is indeed true. Lee claims that the desert, with its brutally harsh environment that forces its denizens to live by their wits and strength, is the true West, while Austin claims that suburban California, with its shopping malls, highways, and tract housing, constitutes the real West. Further, the numerous references to famous Western films suggest that the only true West is Hollywood's West. The pressure of Kimmer's decision to pursue Lee's screenplay causes the brothers to switch roles: Austin, responding to Lee's taunts, steals a variety of toasters from the neighbors; Lee slaves over the typewriter roughing out the dialogue. The reversal of roles indicates the fundamental similarities that bind the brothers. Upon their Mother's abrupt return from Alaska (who, showing rare good sense for a Shepardian mother, claims to recognize nothing and immediately leaves), Lee and Austin square off in a physically violent but unresolved confrontation. *True West* not only questions the mythology that defines the American West but also probes the violence spawned by the fundamental psychological and behavioral equivalence of family members.

Shepard also examines the equivalency of siblings in *Fool for Love*, replacing the brother-brother conflict of *True West* with a love/hate relationship between half-brother and half-sister, Eddie and May. Reared in different towns by different mothers, Eddie and May meet, fall in love, and begin their incestuous relationship before discovering that they share the same father, the Old Man. Although the friction dramatized in Eddie and May's emotional and sexual relationship points toward Shepard's signature characterization of men and women as two opposite animals who cannot coexist, *Fool for Love* also examines how the same event is often shaped and reshaped by different individuals to create widely divergent memories and understandings of what happened. Eddie and May do not share the same recollection of their meeting and cannot come to terms with the implications of their relationship; moreover, none of their stories agrees with versions of the same incidents told by the Old Man, who at times seems to be Eddie's and May's mental projection but who at other times seems to be an independent character. Despite her attempt to establish a different life-style with Martin, the new man in her life, May is as inextricably bound to Eddie as he is to her. Even though Eddie leaves at the end of the play and May believes that he is not coming back, the play suggests that the audience has witnessed but one episode in a continually repeating cycle in which Eddie and May are victimized by their repetitive actions just as surely as Wesley and Weston were by theirs in *Curse of the Starving Class*.

A Lie of the Mind explores the dysfunctional structure of the American family as well as the delusions that individuals impose on others and themselves. Beaten nearly to death by her husband Jake, Beth creates lies of the mind—fictions that permit her to survive. The play suggests that each character assembles a personal reality in his or her mind. For example, Jake's mother, Lorraine, blocks out the pain of being abandoned by her husband by pretending indifference; Beth's father, Baylor, hides from his family by erecting a façade of the crusty frontier hunter; Jake represses all of his memories of the race in Mexico that led to his father's death. Further, *A Lie of the Mind* suggests that the "two opposite animals," the male and the female, even when yoked together by an irresistible and consuming love, are torn apart by the violence of their fundamental incompatibility. Both Beth and Jake are trapped by their love—neither can be complete without the other—and their obsessive need to be reunited thrusts Beth into delusions of marriage and propels Jake to Montana to find Beth. Their drive for reunification, however, at last proves futile. After kissing Beth, Jake exits into the darkness, and Beth compulsively turns to Jake's wounded brother, Frankie. *A Lie of the Mind* suggests that the American family, like Beth, is fundamentally crippled.

States of Shock is a heavily symbolic exercise in antiwar sentiment that pits a demented, saber-waving colonel against Stubbs, a wheelchair-bound armed-services veteran (who still has a conspicuously large and bloody hole in his chest) in a battle over the symbols and myths that permeate and define large-scale war. Set in a thoroughly American family restaurant, *States of Shock* exposes all the glorious contradictions that surround the concept of war in post-Vietnam America without offering any more than the violence of the inevitable collisions.

Although Shepard has spoken of his personal aversion for the 1960's and early 1970's, the pulsing beat of his scintillating dramatic language, the resonant depth of the mythic images that permeate his plays, and the unwavering intensity of the conflicts that give his plays an unmatched toughness all have their ultimate source in the turmoil both caused and embraced by the sex, drugs, and rock-and-roll generation. The center of Shepard's work moves steadily and inexorably toward a distinctly American version of the domestic drama defined by his predecessors Henrik Ibsen, Anton Chekhov, and Eugene O'Neill, but the conflicts between siblings, husbands and wives, or parents and children are consistently played out against the backdrop of the icons that created the American national identity during the Vietnam era: cowboys, rock and roll music, Hollywood films, middle-class suburbia, science fiction, and the West. It is Shepard's consistent ability, however, to use the particular to suggest the universal that indicates his greatness. In a play written by Shepard, the foreground and shading of a conflict between father and son will inevitably be couched in terms of rock music, cars, gunfights, and liquor, but the outline of that conflict is as old and as evocative as Sophocles' *Oedipus the King* (c. 429 B.C.).

Other major works

NONFICTION: *Rolling Thunder Logbook*, 1977.

SCREENPLAYS: *Me and My Brother*, 1967 (with Robert Frank); *Zabriskie Point*, 1969; *Ringaleevio*, 1971; *Paris, Texas*, 1984 (with L. M. Kit Carson); *Far North*, 1988.

MISCELLANEOUS: *Hawk Moon: A Book of Short Stories, Poems, and Monologues*, 1973; *Motel Chronicles*, 1982.

Bibliography

Auerbach, Doris. *Shepard, Kopit, and the Off Broadway Theater.* Boston: Twayne, 1982. One of the first important academic analyses of Shepard's plays, Auerbach's book provides a valuable analysis of Shepard's work as Off-Broadway drama. Auerbach also provides extensive information on the directors, actors, and theatrical spaces that made up the Off-Broadway theater during the 1960's and 1970's.

Hart, Lynda. *Sam Shepard's Metaphorical Stages.* Westport, Conn.: Greenwood Press, 1987. Hart argues that Shepard's plays from *Cowboys #2* to *A Lie of the Mind* are influenced by techniques developed by the Theater of the Absurd, particularly by the work of Samuel Beckett, Antonin Artaud, and Eugène Ionesco. The book contains a brief chapter on Shepard's work for the television and film industries as well as a pithy biography and an extensive bibliography.

King, Kimball, ed. *Sam Shepard: A Casebook.* New York: Garland, 1988.

This collection of essays written mostly by academics approaches Shepard's work from many angles and demonstrates the range of response the plays evoke. The casebook includes a solid annotated bibliography and a piece by Patrick Fennel that identifies and discusses Shepard's unperformed and unpublished works.

Marranca, Bonnie, ed. *American Dreams: The Imagination of Sam Shepard.* New York: Performing Arts Journal Publications, 1981. A compendium of essays written by academics, directors, and actors, this volume is a good introduction to Shepard's early work for the Off-Broadway theater. A number of short pieces by Shepard himself round out the volume, including Shepard's influential short essay, "Language, Visualization, and the Inner Library."

Mottram, Ron. *Inner Landscapes: The Theater of Sam Shepard.* Columbia: University of Missouri Press, 1984. Perhaps the best sustained examination of Shepard's plays, Mottram's biographical analysis offers many insightful readings of Shepard's work by comparing incidents in the plays to parallel episodes from Shepard's life or to stories from *Hawk Moon* or *Motel Chronicles* with similar characters or incidents. Mottram also includes a brief chronology of Shepard's work to 1985.

Oumano, Ellen. *Sam Shepard: The Life and Work of an American Dreamer.* New York: St. Martin's Press, 1986. Although something of a "pop" biography, as the title indicates, Oumano's book is eminently readable and contains most of the important details about Shepard's professional and personal life. Contains a number of pictures chronicling Shepard's life as an actor as well as a complete and accurate performance record of the plays.

Gregory W. Lanier

RICHARD BRINSLEY SHERIDAN

Born: Dublin, Ireland; October 30, 1751
Died: London, England; July 7, 1816

Principal drama

The Rivals, pr., pb. 1775; *St. Patrick's Day: Or, The Scheming Lieutenant*, pr. 1775, pb. 1788; *The Duenna: Or, The Double Elopement*, pr. 1775, pb. 1776 (libretto; music by Thomas Linley the elder and Thomas Linley the younger, and others); *A Trip to Scarborough*, pr. 1777, pb. 1781 (adaptation of Sir John Vanbrugh's *The Relapse*); *The School for Scandal*, pr. 1777, pb. 1780; *The Critic: Or, A Tragedy Rehearsed*, pr. 1779, pb. 1781; *Pizarro: A Tragedy in Five Acts*, pr., pb. 1799 (adaptation of August von Kotzebue's *Die Spanier in Peru*); *Complete Plays*, pb. 1930; *Plays*, pb. 1956 (L. Gibbs, editor).

Other literary forms

Richard Brinsley Sheridan's other literary efforts, all minor, include the early poems "Clio's Protest" and "The Ridotto of Bath," published in *The Bath Chronicle* (1771); a youthful translation, *Love Epistles of Aristaenetus* (1771), in collaboration with Nathaniel Brassey Halhed; and later occasional verses in connection with the theater—such as prologues and epilogues to other writers' plays—the most important being "Verses to the Memory of Garrick, Spoken as a Monody" (1779). Of far greater significance, especially to biographers and historians, are Sheridan's speeches in Parliament, collected in five volumes (1816), and his letters, which are collected in three volumes, entitled *The Letters of Richard Brinsley Sheridan* (1966). Unfortunately, his speeches are preserved only in summary or imperfect transcript.

Achievements

Sheridan was the best playwright of eighteenth century England, a time of great actors rather than great playwrights. Judged on theatrical rather than strictly literary merit, Sheridan also ranks with the best English writers of comedy: William Shakespeare, Ben Jonson, William Congreve, Oscar Wilde, George Bernard Shaw. Until the era of Wilde and Shaw, only Shakespeare's plays had held the stage better than Sheridan's.

Of Sheridan's plays, *The School for Scandal*, a comedy of manners, is universally acclaimed as his masterpiece. Also applauded are *The Rivals*, another comedy of manners; *The Duenna*, a comic opera; and *The Critic*, a burlesque. The two comedies of manners have fared better over time than have the two more specialized works, perhaps because their attractions are apparent even in printed form, perhaps because changes of taste have gone against the specialized works. The topical allusions in *The Critic* are mostly lost on modern audiences, and *The Duenna* affronts modern sensibilities with episodes of anti-Catholicism and anti-Semitism. In Sheridan's own opinion, his best piece of work was act 1 of *The Critic*.

In recent times, Sheridan's reputation has waned: His "artificial" comedies lack the high seriousness that the modern age demands. Yet the basis of his appeal remains: effective theater embodied in smooth traditional plots, stock characters fleshed out by Sheridan's observations of his time, and some of the wittiest dialogue ever written. Sheridan has never been known for the originality of his plots and characters, some of which can be traced through Shakespeare and Jonson all the way back to Roman comedy, but—like Shakespeare and Jonson—he had the assimilative genius to transform the old into something lively and new. Revolving around a trickery motif, chronicling the age-old battles of the sexes or the generations, culminating in a marriage or marriages, his plots still entertain with their well-paced intrigues and discoveries. Onto the old stocks he grafted such memorable characters as Mrs. Malaprop, Joseph Surface, Lady Teazle, and Sir Fretful Plagiary. One reason why Sheridan does not seem dated is his language, a distinctly modern prose idiom, supple, utilitarian, informal, expressing the hopeful coherence of the early modern era.

Sheridan's achievement is even more impressive when one considers that he wrote all of his plays (except for the adaptation of *Pizarro*) during a period of five years when he was in his mid-twenties and during a period of severe restrictions on the theater. The upper- and upper-middle-class establishment controlled the theater with an iron grip through limitations on the number of theaters, official censorship, and the unofficial censorship of its tastes. No play could be presented that did not satisfy the political and social assumptions of the ruling classes. It is remarkable that, under these restrictions, Sheridan could get away with saying as much as he did.

Biography

In eighteenth century Great Britain, Richard Brinsley Sheridan's lot was pretty much cast when he was born into a genteelly poor Irish theatrical family. All of these social disadvantages, however, worked to his advantage in the theater. Being Irish has given numerous British writers of comedy special insight into the vices and follies of their fellow Britons, as well as the rhetorical skills to air their observations. Being in a theatrical family was obviously an advantage for the aspiring playwright. Finally, being genteelly poor sparked his ambitions with both positive and negative charges. Combined, these factors made Sheridan acutely aware of the disparity between his personal worth and his actual place in society—always a great aid to developing a sense of comic incongruity.

Although lacking wealth and social position, Sheridan's family was both well educated and talented. Both his father and mother were children of scholarly clergymen. Upon being graduated from Trinity College, Dublin, Sheridan's father, Thomas, already a playwright, entered the theater as an actor and soon advanced to manager. Sheridan's mother, the former Frances Chamberlaine, wrote novels and plays. After initial prosperity, the family of six (Richard was the third son) ran into hard times when a minor political indiscretion—reminiscent of an indiscreet sermon which ruined his own father—forced Thomas out of his position: He suppressed some antigovernment lines in a play, thus antagonizing the Irish public. After two years of acting in London, Thomas tried to reestablish himself in Dublin, but without success. Taking his family with him, he returned to England, where, moving from place to place, he pursued an impecunious existence as actor, author, editor, lecturer on elocution, and projector of ambitious undertakings.

After attending Sam Whyte's Seminary for the Instruction of Youth in Dublin, Richard was entered into Harrow School, despite the family's precarious financial situation. How precarious that situation was became evident when, to escape creditors, the rest of the family fled to France, where they lived for several years and where Frances Sheridan died. Left behind at Harrow, Sheridan, lonely and destitute, suffered the abuse heaped upon him by his well-bred schoolmates and masters. The unhappy scholar later maintained that he learned little at Harrow.

When his family returned to London, Sheridan, by then a young man, rejoined them. There his education continued informally, and it was completed when, in the fall of 1770, the family moved to Bath, where the father presented entertainments and tried to establish an academy of oratory. The favorite spa of eighteenth century England, Bath gave young Sheridan a close-up study of *le beau monde*, the fashionable world later depicted in his comedies of manners. He managed to join this scene on the basis of few credentials except a ready wit and charm. In Bath, he also met young Elizabeth Ann Linley, a great beauty and singing member of the musical Linley family, which sometimes collaborated with the Sheridans on entertainments. Elizabeth's public performances brought her the unwanted attentions of numerous suitors, most notably one Thomas Mathews. The boorish Mathews importuned her so closely that, to escape him, Elizabeth (already the subject of a racy play, Samuel Foote's *The Maid of Bath*, 1771) ran away to France—accompanied by Richard Brinsley Sheridan as her protector. After a few weeks, the couple returned, Sheridan fought two duels with Mathews, and, on April 13, 1773, Sheridan and Elizabeth were married.

With this background, Sheridan wrote his plays. He and Elizabeth settled in London, where the need to make a living turned him, like his father, toward the theater. In 1775, he took London by storm, presenting three plays, the first (*The Rivals*) reflecting his recent romantic past. By 1780, however, his playwriting career was over. Although he owned a managing interest in Drury Lane Theatre, he was beginning a distinguished career in Parliament, which consumed much of his efforts.

Sheridan's long service in Parliament has no bearing on his playwriting (aside from the considerable fact that it stopped) but much on his reputation. A liberal Whig, Sheridan sympathized with the American and French revolutions and supported such programs as Catholic emancipation. A principled politician, he could not be bribed despite his constant need for money to pay for elections and entertaining. An independent thinker, he sometimes bucked his own party. Such a man was obviously dangerous, especially when he was also such a powerful speaker. Thus, the leaders of his party used his powers but never allowed him to become a leader. Sheridan even became an adviser and a friend to the Prince of Wales, later George IV, but it was the snobbish prince who led the establishment's strategy against the upstart Sheridan. That strategy was to depict Sheridan as an unreliable lightweight—a strategy dictated at first by Sheridan's background and later by his drinking and debts.

When Drury Lane Theatre burned in 1809, Sheridan's debts drained his resources so that he lacked sufficient funds to win an election in 1812, and his political and princely associates swiftly fell away. Although he died in poverty, he was honored with a lavish funeral in Westminster Abbey, attended by scores of solemn dignitaries and peers of the realm. He is buried in the Poets' Corner of Westminster Abbey.

Analysis

"Poor Sherry," said the Prince of Wales, a line echoed by other noble contemporaries of Richard Brinsley Sheridan and even by Sheridan's admirer Lord Byron. Unhappily, the verdict of the Prince of Wales and his crowd still represents the official response to Sheridan, coloring understanding of his plays with an *argumentum ad hominem*. This official line runs something as follows: "Poor Sherry was motivated by overwhelming vanity and self-interest. That is why he entered the theater and why he left the theater to enter politics. A poor Irish actor's son, he always wanted to hobnob with the rich and powerful, to be part of *le beau monde*, whose attitudes he reflects in his plays. There was something calculating, something insincere and insubstantial, about the fellow. Same thing about his plays." This is the establishment Sheridan safely tucked away in the Poets' Corner.

There is also, however, an antiestablishment Sheridan—the penniless child suffering at Harrow, the spirited young man dueling for his girl, the member of Parliament sympathizing with the American and French revolutions, whose servants in his plays are smarter than their masters. True, Sheridan's leading characters are usually gentry or better. True, Sheridan usually exhibits the doings of *le beau monde*. True, he does not issue a clarion call for revolution and the institution of a republic. He was working within the restrictions of accepted traditions, theatrical tastes, and official censorship. Within those restrictions, however, he exhibited *le beau monde* as vain, money-grabbing, and scandalmongering. As a playwright, Sheridan enjoyed the satisfaction of seeing the fashionable world pay and applaud to see itself pilloried.

Sheridan lived in the midst of what one of his characters calls "a luxurious and dissipated age," but the people enjoying the luxuries and dissipations were standing on the heads of a mass of poor people. He could not attack the upper classes directly, even though they offered big targets for satire. In particular, their illusions about themselves, their pretensions of nobility and gentility, made them vulnerable. Sheridan knew a whoring society when he saw one, and he satirized its illusions and pretensions relentlessly.

Sheridan's satire is milder in tone, however, than that of cynical Restoration comedy or the savage attacks Alexander Pope and Jonathan Swift could deliver. The tone of Restoration comedy harks back to the dark, stinging satire of Ben Jonson, who presented the world as little better than a zoo. Such satire incorporates the conservative vision of the Great Chain of Being, wherein human nature is permanently flawed, half angel, half animal. The animal side must be cynically accepted or flogged into good behavior by Church, State, and satirists. Sheridan's satire is more optimistic, softened by the influence of the sentimental mode which grew up in the eighteenth century as the main competitor of the satiric mode, especially in the novel and drama.

Originating in Nonconformist religious thought and maturing in Romanticism, sentimentalism rested on the revolutionary doctrine that human nature is essentially good. Stressing empathy and the humane emotions, sentimentalism was susceptible to hypocrisy. It also had a devastating effect on drama: Tragedy turned into melodrama, and comedy turned to provoking sympathetic tears. The two most notorious examples of sentimental literature, Henry Mackenzie's novel *The Man of Feeling* and Richard Cumberland's play *The West Indian* both came out in 1771, just before Sheridan began writing. Like his fellow countryman Oliver Goldsmith, Sheridan accepted the underlying doctrine of sentimentalism but reacted against its excesses. Not unnaturally, Goldsmith and Sheridan thought comedy ought to provoke laughter.

To produce "laughing comedy," Sheridan returned to the witty, satiric comedy of manners of the Restoration, but without the Restoration cynicism and sexual license. Whereas the Restoration offered refinement and style as a substitute for goodness, Sheridan still believed in its possibilities. The result is a warmly human balance similar to that in Henry Fielding's novels. As William Hazlitt said of *The School for Scandal*, "it professes a faith in the natural goodness, as well as habitual depravity, of human nature." Human frailties are laughed at and, if acknowledged, usually forgiven. Among prominent failings is hypocrisy, and anyone too good is suspect. Most of all, empathy has become a sense of participation—the author's and the audience's—in the vices and follies of humankind. This laugh of recognition is perhaps Richard Brinsley Sheridan's greatest gift to "high seriousness."

Sheridan's first play, *The Rivals*, reflects his own experiences—his life in Bath, his elopement with Elizabeth Linley, his duels—but it is not strictly autobiographical. Nor was it only a *succès de scandale*, although being the talk of the town probably helped Sheridan at the time. Rather than seeing parallels to Sheridan's life in *The Rivals*, modern audiences are more likely to notice parallels to Shakespeare's plays, for Sheridan drew unashamedly not only on his own experiences but also on his predecessors' work. These two seams in the play reveal Sheridan's apprentice patchings, but what is amazing is that he sewed them all up so well. When the play failed in its first performance, Sheridan revised it within a few days and turned *The Rivals* into one of the great English comedies of manners.

Set in the fashionable resort town of Bath, *The Rivals* concerns the efforts of Captain Jack Absolute, "son and heir to Sir Anthony Absolute, a baronet of three thousand a year," to win the hand of Miss Lydia Languish, an heiress who "could pay the national debt." Miss Languish, however, entertains romantic notions of marrying only for love: She is determined to wed a penniless suitor who will elope and live with her in blissful poverty. To humor her fantasies, Captain Absolute pretends to be Beverley, "a half-pay ensign." His wooing is further complicated by the opposition of Mrs. Malaprop, Lydia's battle-ax guardian aunt; and by two rivals, bumbling country squire Bob Acres and duelist Sir Lucius O'Trigger (whose love letters are actually being delivered to Mrs. Malaprop by the maid, Lucy). The final complication is the appearance of Sir Anthony with news of an arranged marriage for Jack. After a heated confrontation between father and son, this complication proves to be the resolution of the plot: The young lady intended for Jack Absolute is Miss Lydia Languish. The discovery of Beverley's true identity alienates Lydia, but she is brought around when Jack's life is threatened by a duel with the rivals. Averted at the last moment, the threatening duel also convinces Julia Melville to forgive Mr. Faulkland, Jack's friend, for doubting her love.

Drawn out too long, Mr. Faulkland's almost psychotic behavior mars the tone of the play, but his fantasies of doubt correspond to Lydia's fantasies of romance, perhaps pointing up the theme that a good marriage must be rooted in reality: true love and a solid bank account. The other characters provide a display of diverse human nature. Reminiscent of Shakespeare's

Sir Andrew Aguecheek, the cowardly suitor Acres contrasts with the equally ridiculous O'Trigger, whose name describes his ready disposition. Lydia's whims and Sir Anthony's commands typify the ludicrous demands that sweethearts and fathers can make, and Mrs. Malaprop's comical misuse of words ("a nice derangement of epitaphs") epitomizes the cavalier misunderstanding of reality which the characters exhibit.

The play is full of notable examples of human illusion—O'Trigger's "honor," Sir Anthony's parental authority, Bob Acres' "polishing" (that is, new clothes, hairdo, dancing lessons, and swearing), Mrs. Malaprop's vanity, Faulkland's doubts, and Lydia's romance. Their illusions make them easy marks for one another and for the streetwise servants. To manipulate them, one simply plays up to their fantasies. For example, Jack is "Beverley" to Lydia, a dutiful son to Sir Anthony, and a flatterer to Mrs. Malaprop. All the characters with illusions are worthy of study, but perhaps the most important are Mrs. Malaprop, Faulkland, and Lydia.

On the periphery of the action, Mrs. Malaprop is symbolically at the play's center. She provides a simplified example of how illusion works. Her funny misuse of words, symbols of reality, epitomizes the break with reality. She thinks her big words make her, as O'Trigger says, "a great mistress of the language," "the queen of the dictionary," or, as Jack says, a leader in "intellectual accomplishments, elegant manners, and unaffected learning." The reality is summed up in Jack's intercepted letter: ". . . I am told that the same ridiculous vanity, which makes her dress up her coarse features, and deck her dull chat with hard words which she don't understand, does also lay her open to the grossest deceptions from flattery and pretended admiration. . . ." To Sir Lucius O'Trigger, she is "Delia," a female counterpart of romantic Beverley. When Sir Lucius sees the real thing, however, he turns her down—as do Jack and Acres. Clinging to her illusions, Mrs. Malaprop stomps off the stage, huffing that "men are all barbarians."

The illusions of Faulkland and Lydia are essentially overreactions of the young to the sterile social order represented by Mrs. Malaprop and the older generation: Their illusions are examples of sentimentalism, the gross exaggeration of feeling that Goldsmith and Sheridan deplored. Faulkland is a man of sensibility, but unfortunately, as he notes, love "urges sensibility to madness." His "too exquisite nicety" leads him constantly to question and torture Julia, a "mild and affectionate spirit" any man would be lucky to find. The least suggestion can send him into paroxysms of doubt: Jack and even the "looby" Acres are able to play on his sensibility at will. He is, as he finally admits, a "fool." Lydia's overreaction contrasts with that of Faulkland, but she would agree with him that "when *Love* receives such countenance from *Prudence*, nice minds will be suspicious of its birth." Fed by sentimental novels, her overheated mind throws prudence to the wind. Jack easily deceives her by playing her romantic games and speaking the language of the novels she has read. Thinking to outwit and shock her relatives, she is shocked to discover herself "the only dupe at last." The young lady who had hoped for a "sentimental" elopement with all the trimmings must settle for being "a mere Smithfield bargain." Actually, she gets more than she bargained for: When confronted by the reality of a truly romantic situation—men dueling to the death over her—she comes to her senses.

The illusions of all these characters in *The Rivals* say something about the society in which they live. First, being born in the upper strata apparently encourages illusions about oneself: Only wealth and privilege could create a Mrs. Malaprop. Second, to sustain those illusions apparently requires a lot of lying and deceiving. Third, with all the lying and deceiving, it becomes difficult to find anything genuine—hence the hard search of Faulkland and Lydia for true love. That Sheridan himself sought the genuine is suggested by his repeated use throughout the play of the word "sincerity," apparently a quality he found in short supply in eighteenth century England.

Musically untalented, Sheridan wrote the comic opera *The Duenna* in collaboration with his father-in-law and brother-in-law (both named Thomas Linley) and probably with the help of his wife. Despite this piecemeal method of composition, the completed opera was an immense success. In particular, the opera is a testimony to Sheridan's patchwork skill and to the talented Linleys, whose tunes were hummed about London streets. Typically, however, the words of the songs are bland, and so are the opera's stock characters, some of whom are almost indistinguishable from one another. Of all Sheridan's works, *The Duenna* most requires performance, since it depends so much on acting, spectacle, and music (twenty-seven songs in all).

Set in Seville, *The Duenna* features not one but two pairs of lovers thwarted by tyrannical parents. Donna Louisa's father has arranged an unsuitable match for her, notwithstanding her love for Don Antonio, and Donna Clara's father and stepmother are forcing her into a convent, even though she is loved by Don Ferdinand. Both young ladies run off and, assisted by bribed nuns and priests (the latter also drunk), marry their lovers in a convent. Louisa tricks her father, Don Jerome, with the help of her governess, old Margaret the Duenna. When Don Jerome vows "never to see or speak to" Louisa until she marries his choice, Louisa and the Duenna trade places, and the penniless old Duenna marries Louisa's intended, Isaac Mendoza, a rich Jew who has never seen Louisa and who thinks he is adding to his coffers.

Like most of Sheridan's works, *The Duenna* offers sparkling intrigue and dialogue. Here again, a female servant masterminds the plotting, but to a great extent the fathers and the villain outsmart themselves. The scheming Mendoza, recently converted to Christianity and hence standing "like the blank leaves between the Old and New Testament," is well known for being "the dupe of his own art." Of the characters, only the ugly Duenna, the obnoxious Mendoza, and the drunken priest Father Paul stand forth with any distinction, and they are stereotypes.

The broad strokes of the stock characters and action do provide simplified versions of some of Sheridan's themes. For example, the hypocritical nuns and priests show, as Louisa notes, that "in religion, as in friendship, they who profess most are ever the least sincere"—a forewarning of Joseph Surface in *The School for Scandal.* Louisa herself seems of two minds on the relationship of love and wealth. Early in the opera, she sings that she loves Don Antonio "for himself alone," since he has no wealth. Later in the play, faced with the prospect of being disinherited, she changes her tune: ". . . there is a chilling air around poverty that often kills affection that was not nursed in it. If we would make love our household god we had best secure him a comfortable roof." At least her aims are different from her father's, who sets forth his marriage as a proper example: "I married her for her fortune, and she took me in obedience to her father, and a very happy couple we were. We never expected any love from one another, and so we were never disappointed." Such cold-blooded reasoning is a reminder of how often, in Sheridan's plays, the older and younger generations are at odds on the subject of marriage. The two views presuppose radically different ideas not only of marriage but also of personality and society: The vital difference is between valuing someone "for her fortune" and "for himself alone." Thus, in Sheridan's plays, the struggle within the family is a microcosm of the larger struggle between the old and new order in society. There is no doubt about which side Sheridan took, since his own father opposed his marriage to Elizabeth Ann Linley (old Thomas had the absurd notion that the Sheridans were too good for "musicians").

Another theme in *The Duenna* revolves around the idea of "seeing." There are a number of observations on how subjective states, especially love, affect one's seeing, especially of the beloved. The merging of subject and object here, encouraged perhaps by eighteenth century empathy, foreshadows Romantic "seeing," wherein what is observed takes its coloring from the imagination. *The Duenna* also contains a number of warnings about such "seeing": Don Jerome gets so angry that he does not recognize his daughter posing as the veiled Duenna, and Don Ferdinand gets so jealous he does not recognize his beloved dressed as a nun. In the opera's most philosophical song, however, Don Jerome gets the final word on "seeing":

> Truth, they say, lies in a well,
> Why, I vow I ne'er could see;
> Let the water-drinkers tell,
> There it always lay for me;

For when sparkling wine went round,
  Never saw I falsehood's mask;
But still honest truth I found
  In the bottom of each flask.

He seems to say that people need their illusions, or at least their opiates.

Possibly Don Jerome was speaking for Sheridan, since the opium of entertainment is precisely what Sheridan provided in *The Duenna*. The first English comic opera to use specially composed music, *The Duenna* was a forerunner of the operettas by W. S. Gilbert and Sir Arthur Sullivan and the Broadway musical, which by now have institutionalized sentimental "seeing."

If *The Rivals* shows the fashionable world on vacation, *The School for Scandal* shows it back home in London, working hard to "murder characters" and "kill time." If the duelist O'Trigger is deadly, he is nothing to this school of piranhas, which renders "a character dead at every word." The difference between vacation and work is precisely the difference in tone, theme, and achievement between *The Rivals* and *The School for Scandal*. No seams or weaknesses obtrude in *The School for Scandal*, the title of which sums up the play's prevailing imagery and unity.

The play begins with a marvelous expository device: The "scandalous college" is in session, headed by its "president," Lady Sneerwell. As the pupils gather—Snake, Joseph Surface, Mrs. Candour, Crabtree, Sir Benjamin Backbite—the audience hears juicy bits of scandal about the president and each pupil. The key information is that Sir Peter Teazle has a pack of trouble. The Surface brothers, to whom Sir Peter is "a kind of guardian," are competing for Maria, Sir Peter's rich ward. Joseph, the older brother, is a scheming knave who, with "the assistance of his sentiment and hypocrisy," passes for a paragon of virtue, while Charles is "the most dissipated and extravagant young fellow in the kingdom." Joseph enjoys the favor of Sir Peter, Charles, of Maria. During a recess, Sir Peter is also shown having fits with his young wife. Country-bred Lady Teazle has blossomed into a London woman of fashion, even joining Lady Sneerwell's group and carrying on a flirtation with Joseph. The scandalmongers, however, have linked her to Charles.

The Surfaces are unmasked when Sir Oliver Surface, a rich uncle, returns from many years in the East Indies and puts the brothers to the test. Posing as a moneylender, Sir Oliver observes Charles's dissipation, even purchases the family portraits from him—but forgives the young man when Charles will not part with the portrait of dear Uncle Oliver. Charles also sends some of the money to old Stanley, a poor relation in distress, but when Sir Oliver, posing as Stanley, applies to Joseph, he is given the brushoff. In a famous scene, Joseph is also discovered hiding Lady Teazle behind a screen and Sir Peter Teazle in a closet, where each has heard an earful. The screen symbolizes Joseph's character and the nature of the society in which he flourishes, and the closet suggests where Sir Peter has been hiding. The truth comes out, however—confirmed by the confessions of Snake—and the people have to live with it. Now the centerpiece of a raging scandal, stodgy Sir Peter mellows; Lady Teazle and Charles will reform; Joseph's punishment is being "known to the world"; and Snake hopes his good deeds will not spoil his professional reputation. Meanwhile, the audience, schooled by a master, has been treated to a delightful exposition of illusion and reality in society.

Sheridan exposes a shallow society where appearances rule: It is not what you are but what you appear to be that counts; reputation is all. The main proponent of this philosophy—still not entirely discredited even in modern society—is the well-spoken Joseph Surface, whose hypocrisy illustrates another danger inherent in sentimentalism. Actually, the talented Joseph represents both types prominent in his society: the hypocrite, who manipulates appearances to enhance his own reputation, and the scandalmonger, who manipulates appearances to tear down the reputations of others (as Joseph shows, the two callings go together). Behind façades of gentility, both types feel free to indulge their basest instincts. For example, the motives acknowledged by scandalmongers include bitterness over being slandered oneself, personal spite, impersonal malice, fun, and following the fashion, though the dullness of their lives is also a factor: They have nothing better to do than sit around and gossip about other people's lives, with perhaps a touch of envy. As Lady Teazle makes clear, these "are all people of rank and fortune." They represent a society rotten at the core.

Luckily, this decadent society includes a saving remnant that is not fooled by appearances. There is the faithful old servant Rowley, who believes in the goodness of a reprobate's heart. There is crusty Sir Oliver, who is sickened by scraps of morality and who believes that a man is not sincere if he has not made any enemies. There is Lady Teazle, whose personal development through the play marks the course of the plot. At first she is drawn to the world of appearances, of high fashion and rich furnishings, of the circle of scandalmongers and Joseph. Her turning point comes when Joseph suggests that she go to bed with him, literally and figuratively. She returns to her country wisdom and rejects him. When the screen is pulled down and she is caught in Joseph's quarters, she refuses to second his story and dubs him "Good Mr. Hypocrite." Thereafter, she withdraws from the "scandalous college" and turns over a new leaf.

Finally, there is Charles, the reprobate himself. His regeneration is harder to believe than Lady Teazle's, but Sheridan shrewdly keeps him offstage until halfway through the play, by which time he contrasts favorably with Joseph and the scandalmongers. Although dissolute and bankrupt, Charles has two important qualities that Joseph lacks: benevolence and honesty. Unlike the hypocritical Joseph Surface, Charles Surface is exactly what he appears to be. His loss of reputation has, in fact, freed him to be himself, and his experience has prepared him to see himself and others clearly. He is given the two main symbolic gestures in the play: pulling down the screen and selling off the family portraits. Symbolically, he attacks both the pretensions of his society and their hereditary basis. Charles's auction of the family portraits now seems merely funny, but the mockery involved in "knocking down" one's ancestors "with their own pedigree" was probably a shock to the eighteenth century system, even though Sheridan softened the revolutionary gesture by keeping it in the family.

In the tradition of *The Rehearsal* (pr. 1671) by George Villiers, Duke of Buckingham, and Henry Fielding's *Tom Thumb: A Tragedy* (pr. 1730), Sheridan's *The Critic* is a burlesque, a type of comedy especially popular in eighteenth century England. *The Critic* provides an engaging and informative survey of the theatrical world in Sheridan's time. Despite its many topical references, the play also has potential for revival in the contemporary age of self-conscious art, in which burlesque is a staple of television comedy. The topical references, in fact, would reverberate with a certain irony, since it appears from *The Critic* that things have not changed all that much in the theater.

Act 1 opens on a breakfast scene, where the critic Mr. Dangle holds court, entertaining all sorts of solicitations. This day there appear Mr. Sneer, another critic; Sir Fretful Plagiary, a vain playwright (based on Richard Cumberland); Mr. Puff, an advertising writer who has authored a play; and Signor Pasticcio Ritornello and a chorus of Italian girls come for audition (the scene probably gives some insight into the Sheridan household). Repartee, malice, and dissimulation fly around the table, in the manner of theatrical shoptalk, with Mrs. Dangle occasionally clearing the air in straightforward language.

In the other two acts, Dangle and Sneer attend a rehearsal of Puff's play, a wretched tragedy entitled *The Spanish Armada*. Again there is much opportunity for satire. Puff has given the actors permission "to cut out or omit whatever they found heavy or unnecessary to the plot"; thus, the play is very brief. Brief as it is, it is a smashing parody of the kind of tragedy written in Sheridan's time, full of clumsy exposition, bombastic verse, stilted characters, and improbable, sensational events, ending with a triumphant sea battle and a procession of all the English rivers accompanied by George Frederick Handel's water music and a chorus.

The faked feelings of the actors in the play-within-the-play are reminders that theater is the essence of illusion, and the framing action of *The Critic* is a reminder of how theater people are often caught up in the illusion. To Mr. Dangle, the theater is more important than the real world: When he reads "the news," it is the theatrical news rather than the news of the impending French invasion. He is such a stargazer because he considers himself a moving force in the theatrical world, as he tells Mrs. Dangle: ". . . you will not easily persuade me that there is no credit or importance in being at the head of a band of critics, who take upon them to decide for the whole town, whose opinion and patronage all writers solicit, and whose recommendation no manager dares refuse!" Representing a commonsense point of view, Mrs. Dangle is a counterweight to the vanity which is such an occupational hazard for theatrical (and literary) people. At regular intervals, she tells Mr. Dangle that he is ridiculous: "Why should you affect the character of a critic?" and "Both managers and authors of the least merit laugh at your pretensions. The Public is their Critic. . . ."

The real critic in the play is the play itself, as the double meaning in the title indicates. Taking a hard look at the eighteenth century theater, *The Critic* first notes the ideal: ". . . the stage is 'the mirror of Nature'. . . ." The statement is a reminder of how theatrical illusion, and art in general, can paradoxically arrive at the truth. The theater (and art), however, can also go astray, as it did in Sheridan's time. First there is comedy, which strayed into two sorts: "sentimental" comedy, which contains "nothing ridiculous in it from the beginning to the end," and "moral" comedy, which treats "the greater vices and blacker crimes of humanity." To her discredit, Mrs. Dangle prefers the former sort, and Mr. Sneer defends the latter: ". . . the theatre, in proper hands, might certainly be made the school of morality; but now, I am sorry to say it, people seem to go there principally for their entertainment." As for what was happening to tragedy, Mr. Puff's *The Spanish Armada* is sufficient example. Choosing Mr. Puff to be the featured author was an inspired symbolic stroke: as a master of "puffing" (advertising) who commands the language of "panegyrical superlatives," the ability to exaggerate or even invent reality ("to insinuate obsequious rivulets into visionary groves"), he truly represents the spirit of the age in the theater.

Sheridan's remaining plays little enhance his literary reputation, but they do reveal a great deal about his political and social attitudes. The plays are *St. Patrick's Day*, a two-act comedy; *A Trip to Scarborough*, an adaptation of Sir John Vanbrugh's comedy *The Relapse* (pr., pb. 1696); and *Pizarro*, an adaptation of August von Kotzebue's tragedy *Die Spanier in Peru* (1794).

Pizarro is an embarrassing reminder of the kind of tragedy which Sheridan parodied in *The Critic*. Treating the depredations of European invaders against the noble Incas, the play gives evidence of Sheridan's antipathy to colonial oppression (it echoes his speeches in Parliament against British rule in India) and his ability to satisfy the growing popular taste for romantic melodrama. In its day, *Pizarro* was a tremendous box-office success.

Like *Pizarro*, *St. Patrick's Day* was probably a vehicle for specific actors.

The short farce also satisfied the requirements of an afterpiece, a slighter work presented after the main play. Full of scheming and disguising, it dramatizes Lieutenant O'Connor's winning of Miss Lauretta Credulous over the opposition of her father, Justice Credulous, who hates Irishmen and soldiers. Aside from its lighthearted action, *St. Patrick's Day* is notable for its Irish sentiments and its sympathy for the lot of poor soldiers (in Sheridan's time, often Irishmen).

A Trip to Scarborough, a much more substantial work, was adapted from *The Relapse*, a favorite Restoration comedy. In his adaptation, Sheridan trimmed the plot and cleaned up the sexual innuendo of the original. The adaptation has many features similar to those of Sheridan's other comedies of manners—in particular, an intrigue centering on assumed identity and rivalry between two brothers for a rich heiress. In the course of the intrigue, the penniless Tom Fashion triumphs over his older brother, Lord Foppington, "an ungrateful narrow-minded coxcomb." Furthermore, Lord Foppington is roughly handled by the father-in-law, Sir Tunbelly Clumsy, a jovial Yorkshireman whose personality and household (Muddymoat Hall) are in a tradition stretching to Emily Brontë's *Wuthering Heights* (1847) and Charles Dickens' *Nicholas Nickleby* (1838-1839).

The humbling of a lord in *A Trip to Scarborough* is another example of the antiestablishment Sheridan, a side that the official pronouncements have preferred not to mention. Yet it is as much a part of Sheridan as his inspired ability to write entertaining comedy. A subversive element in eighteenth century Britain, Sheridan was constantly chipping away at the illusions and pretensions of the old order and interjecting stirrings of the egalitarianism that was sweeping away the old order elsewhere. His attack on primogeniture, at the heart of the old system, is typical:

> LORD FOPPINGTON: . . . Nature has made some difference 'twixt me and you.
> TOM FASHION: Yes—she made you older.

Something of a transitional figure in British drama, Sheridan looked back to Restoration comedy for his inspiration, but his social attitudes looked forward to George Bernard Shaw. During the long barren stretch of two hundred years between Restoration comedy and Shaw, Sheridan preserved the comic spirit in British drama largely through the force of his talent.

Other major works

POETRY: "Clio's Protest," 1771; "The Ridotto of Bath," 1771; *A Familiar Epistle to the Author of the Heroic Epistle to Sir William Chambers*, 1774; "Epilogue to *The Rivals*," 1775; "Epilogue to *Semiramis*," 1776; "Verses to the Memory of Garrick, Spoken as a Monody," 1779; "Epilogue to *The Fatal Falsehood*," 1779; "Prologue to *Pizarro*," 1799; "Lines by a Lady of Fashion," 1825.

NONFICTION: *Speeches of the Late Right Honourable Richard Brinsley Sheridan (Several Corrected by Himself)*, 1816 (5 volumes); *The Letters of Richard Brinsley Sheridan*, 1966 (3 volumes; C. J. L. Price, editor).

MISCELLANEOUS: *The Plays and Poems of Richard Brinsley Sheridan*, 1928, 1962 (3 volumes; R. Compton Rhodes, editor).

Bibliography

Ayling, Stanley. *A Portrait of Sheridan*. London: Constable, 1985. More than two hundred pages on Sheridan's life and work. Ayling offers glimpses of Sheridan's true nature, including the unflattering views on the theater expressed in his letters. Provides good treatment of Sheridan's political hopes, the Warren Hastings affair, and the regency crisis involving the Prince of Wales. The treatment of the early plays is rather brief. Includes some comments on the management of the Drury Lane in later chapters.

Davison, Peter, ed. *Sheridan: Comedies*. Basingstoke, England: Macmillan, 1986. A casebook for the two best-known plays, plus discussions of *The Critic* and *A Trip to Scarborough*. Contains an introductory section on Sheridan's family, his orations, his life and letters; general commentary on Restoration comedy and Sheridan's plays; and final sections on each of the four plays with commentaries by William Hazlitt, Max Beerbohm, George Bernard Shaw, Sir Laurence Olivier, and numerous others. Bibliography surprisingly slight. Index.

Durant, Jack D. *Richard Brinsley Sheridan*. Boston: Twayne, 1975. Investigates Sheridan's career as a writer, manager of the Drury Lane Theatre, and member of Parliament, and discusses Sheridan as a poet and literary theorist. Contains separate chapters on *The Rivals*, *The Duenna*, *The School for Scandal*, and *The Critic*, and a final chapter on the unfinished plays, collaborations, adaptations, and other miscellanea. The organization is basically chronological and topical. Includes an index, a select bibliography, and a portrait of Sheridan by Sir Joshua Reynolds.

Hare, Arnold. *Richard Brinsley Sheridan*. Windsor, England: Profile Books, 1981. This thin volume sketches the major details about Sheridan's life and family: his theatrical father, the sojourn in Bath, his flight to Paris with Elizabeth Ann Linley, their subsequent marriage, and his theater career. Pays brief attention to the theatrical milieu, but analyzes the plays, including some relatively minor ones. Complemented by a select bibliography and a portrait from a pastel by John Russell.

Loftis, John. *Sheridan and the Drama of Georgian England*. Cambridge, Mass.: Harvard University Press, 1977. This authoritative volume examines, in the opening chapter, Sheridan's relationships with his dramatic predecessors, then analyzes extensively Sheridan's plays. Loftis considers *The Rivals* and *The Duenna* for their burlesque elements; examines *A*

Trip to Scarborough and *The School for Scandal* for their neoclassical characteristics; judges *The Critic* as greatly reflective of Sheridan's recent experiences in the theatrical world, including his ill-fated venture with the King's Theatre; and analyzes *Pizarro* for its association with Sheridan's literary and theatrical careers. The bibliography is divided into editions, biographies, critical studies, and background studies. Lengthy index.

Norwood, James. *The Life and Works of Richard Brinsley Sheridan.* Edinburgh: Scottish Academic Press, 1985. Norwood believes that Sheridan's career as a writer and theatrical manager is inseparable from his private and political life. He attempts a lengthy biographical study in which extensive discussion of the writing career appears. Makes a fresh effort to evaluate Sheridan's political career and to create a balanced assessment of his thirty-two years as manager of the Drury Lane. Several illustrations, bibliography, index.

Smith, Dane F., and M. L. Lawhon. *Plays About the Theatre in England, 1737-1800.* Lewisburg, Pa.: Bucknell University Press, 1979. Interprets *The Critic* as an attack on the sentimentalism of the contemporary comedy and of the writers and critics who supported it. Also sees parts of *The School for Scandal* and *The Rivals* as attacks on sentimentalism. Some comparisons are made with Oliver Goldsmith's comedies.

Harold Branam
(Updated by *Howard L. Ford*)

R. C. SHERRIFF

Born: Kingston-on-Thames, England; June 6, 1896
Died: London, England; November 13, 1975

Principal drama

Journey's End, pr. 1928, pb. 1929; *Badger's Green*, pr., pb. 1930; *St. Helena*, pb. 1934, pr. 1936 (with Jeanne de Casalis); *Miss Mabel*, pr. 1948, pb. 1949; *Home at Seven*, pr., pb. 1950; *The White Carnation*, pr., pb. 1953; *The Long Sunset*, pr., pb. 1955; *The Telescope*, pr., pb. 1957; *A Shred of Evidence*, pr. 1960, pb. 1961.

Other literary forms

In addition to his nine professionally produced stage plays, R. C. Sherriff wrote five novels. He is, however, remembered chiefly for his first stage play, *Journey's End*, as well as for a number of screenplays that have come to be regarded as classics.

Achievements

Journey's End, a drama about World War I, is a legend and landmark in the modern British theater. It is notable as the first grimly realistic war play. In it, there is none of the romanticism about war that led the naïve young poet Rupert Brooke to write in his poem "1914," "Now God be thanked who has matched us with His hour" and to sentimentalize the dead soldiers as dreaming happy dreams of "laughter, learnt of friends; and gentleness,/ In hearts at peace, under an English heaven." Both Brooke and the young Thomas Mann saw war as a cleansing, liberating, and purifying process, and Mann called peace "an element of civil corruption." Such views were soon annihilated by the horrors of trench warfare. Sherriff, a wounded veteran of that war, knew better, and his play shows the stress, boredom, suffering, and slaughter that war produces. When the play was first staged, critic Hannen Swaffer called it "the greatest of all war plays," and in 1962, G. Wilson Knight still judged it "the greatest war play of the century."

Sherriff's other plays—an ecological drama, a play about Napoleon in exile, several comedy-mysteries, a ghost story, and a drama about Romans in Britain—are literate, civilized, thoughtful, and forgettable, as are his novels. The success of *Journey's End*, however, led its director to hire Sherriff to write screenplays, and as a screenwriter, Sherriff did some of his most notable work, including the production of such classics as *The Invisible Man* (1933), *Goodbye, Mr. Chips* (1939), *The Four Feathers* (1939), *That Hamilton Woman* (1941), *Odd Man Out* (1947), *Quartet* (1949), and *Trio* (1950).

Biography

Robert Cedric Sherriff was born on June 6, 1896, at Kingston-on-Thames, near London. His father, Herbert Hankin Sherriff, worked for the Sun Insurance Company; his mother was Constance Winder Sherriff. Robert grew up in Kingston-on-Thames, where he attended the local grammar school. He was graduated at seventeen, after which he followed his father into the insurance business, but his career was interrupted after nine months by the outbreak of World War I. Sherriff volunteered, became a second lieutenant in the Ninth East Surrey Regiment, was wounded so severely at Ypres (where four-fifths of the original British Expeditionary Force died) that he was hospitalized for six months, returned to active duty, and was mustered out at the war's end as a captain.

Back in civilian life, Sherriff returned to the Sun Insurance Company, where he worked for the next ten years as a claims adjuster. For recreation, he joined the Kingston rowing club, and to raise funds for the organization, he and some fellow members wrote and produced plays. Sherriff took to playwriting with zeal and studied William Archer's *Play-Making* (1912) so thoroughly that he claimed to have memorized it. In addition, he began to read modern plays systematically and commuted to London to see the latest productions. Returning home on the train, he sometimes developed dialogue for a play he had in mind for the rowing club.

After writing plays for six years for amateur productions, Sherriff turned to a more serious project—a drama based upon his firsthand knowledge of trench warfare. His parents had saved the letters he had written to them from the trenches, and these helped him revive the immediacy of the experience, its realistic details, and his friendships and feelings at the time. Throughout 1928, he worked alone on the play. Gradually, the play, at first called "Suspense" and then "Waiting," took final shape as *Journey's End*.

Realizing that this drama was not the stuff of amateur theatricals, Sherriff sent it to the Curtis Brown theatrical agency. Impressed but unable to see the play's commercial possibilities, Brown sent it on to Geoffrey Dearmer at the Incorporated Stage Society. Dearmer advised Sherriff to send a copy to George Bernard Shaw, who sent it back with the comment that it was "a document, not a drama," and that as a slice of "horribly abnormal life" it should be "performed by all means, even at the disadvantage of being the newspaper of the day before yesterday." Even so, all the London theatrical managements rejected *Journey's End*; they were strongly opposed to war plays, and this one lacked all the standard ingredients for a popular success. It had no leading lady, no romance, no conventional heroics, and all the action took place offstage. Though this was the author's seventh play, the first six were all amateur productions, and the insurance agent earning six pounds a week was utterly obscure.

Nevertheless, Dearmer arranged for a production by the noncommercial

Incorporated Stage Society. To direct, he picked a minor actor named James Whale. Whale, in turn, looked for a leading actor to play Captain Stanhope. All of the eminent London actors had declined the role, but twenty-one-year-old Laurence Olivier, who was hoping to win the lead in a stage version of *Beau Geste* (pr. 1929?) that director Basil Dean was then casting, saw the role of Stanhope as a chance to prove that he could play a soldier and thus handle the lead in the Foreign Legion drama. Ronald Colman had had a smash hit in the film version of *Beau Geste* (1926), and Olivier, an admirer of Colman, hoped to repeat the success. As for *Journey's End*, Olivier recalled in his *Confessions of an Actor* (1982) that "Although I could recognize the possibilities of the part of Stanhope, I told James Whale, the director, I didn't think all that highly of the play. 'There's nothing but meals in it,' I complained. He replied: 'That's about all there was to think about in Flanders during the War.'" Though he was performing in a romantic comedy each evening at the Royalty Theatre, with two weekly matinees, and though *Journey's End* was to have only two performances at the Apollo Theatre, Olivier undertook the role as an audition for *Beau Geste*. There were only two weeks for rehearsal, but Olivier dug into the character of the burned-out Stanhope and later called the part his "favorite stage role," though later yet he reserved this designation for Archie Rice in *The Entertainer*.

Cast as young Raleigh was Maurice Evans, then an unknown, who was also hoping to get the lead in *Beau Geste*. George Zucco, later a memorable villain in Hollywood films, was cast as "Uncle" Osborne, the gentle, middle-aged schoolmaster who quotes from Lewis Carroll's *Alice in Wonderland* before going on a virtual suicide mission. Cast as Trotter, the fat officer concerned chiefly about provisions, was Melville Cooper, who later played Mr. Collins in the film version of Jane Austen's *Pride and Prejudice* (1940), in which he again appeared with Olivier. In 1928, no member of the cast was well-known.

The first performance, on the evening of Sunday, December 9, 1928, went off flawlessly but received only moderate applause, though Barry Jackson commended the play's honest realism. The critics did not appear *en masse* until the second and final performance at the Monday matinee. The play and production so overwhelmed them that Hannen Swaffer, London's most scathing critic, hailed *Journey's End* as "the greatest of all war plays." James Agate devoted his entire weekly radio talk show to praising it, concluding, "But you will never see this play. I have spoken with several managers, urging them to give you the opportunity of judging it for yourselves, but they are adamant in their belief that war plays have no audience in the theatre."

When six weeks passed with no sign that the play might be revived by a commercial producer, Olivier accepted the lead in *Beau Geste*. Now that the leading man was gone, chances for a revival of *Journey's End* seemed even more unlikely. Sherriff noted that "all the rest of the cast stood by the play. They refused other parts in the hope of remaining in it, and they believed in it so much that they tried in vain to form a combine and raise the cash among themselves. But it seemed hopeless."

Then a fan named Maurice Browne persuaded a millionaire friend to put up the money. There was a search for a new leading man, and a relatively unknown actor named Colin Clive got the part and joined the rest of the cast from the Apollo Theatre. The new production opened on January 21, 1929, at the Savoy Theatre. The first performance received nineteen curtain calls, and the success of *Journey's End* became a theatrical legend. It went on to play 594 performances in London. A second production, also directed by James Whale, with Colin Keith-Johnston in the lead, opened at the Henry Miller Theatre in New York on March 22, 1929, and ran for 485 performances. Translated into twenty-seven languages, *Journey's End* played around the world. *Beau Geste*, a flop, closed after a month, and Olivier went on to act in seven more flops during the nearly two years in which Colin Clive starred as Stanhope.

Journey's End made the reputation and fortune of three men. It raised Sherriff from obscurity to fame and fortune; it established James Whale as an important director; and it made Colin Clive a star. D. W. Griffith wanted to direct the film version, but James Whale was retained as director. Colin Clive again played Stanhope, but the rest of the cast was new, with David Manners replacing Maurice Evans as Raleigh.

As for Sherriff, his friends urged him to write another play. At the moment, he had no ideas for one and instead, collaborating with Vernon Bartlett, turned *Journey's End* into a novel (1930). It did not have the overwhelming success of the play and film versions, and Sherriff turned back to playwriting with his next venture, a problem comedy called *Badger's Green*, about the conflict between developers trying to exploit the imaginary village of the title and the conservationists opposing them. Perhaps the problem, now a vital one, was ahead of its time, for the 1930 production fared poorly.

Discouraged, Sherriff feared that he might not be able to continue supporting himself by his pen, and being unwilling to return to the insurance business, he entered New College at Oxford University to earn a degree in history and become a schoolmaster. While a student, he wrote another novel, *The Fortnight in September* (1931), about a middle-class family's annual vacation at a seaside resort. Favorably reviewed, it sold well in England and abroad. Still at Oxford, Sherriff joined an undergraduate rowing crew, though he was then thirty-five years old, but before he could participate in the annual races or earn his degree, he received an invitation from James Whale to collaborate with Philip Wylie on a screenplay of

H. G. Wells's *The Invisible Man* (1897). The scenarios for Whale's *Frankenstein* films had departed drastically from the novel, but the script for *The Invisible Man* followed Wells with reasonable fidelity. To play the lead, who is heard throughout but whose features are seen only in the final shot, Whale wanted an actor with a distinctive voice, and Claude Rains made an impressive film debut in the role. Released in 1933, *The Invisible Man* was one of the year's most memorable films, and its literate script, which constituted the best of all horror and science fiction screenplays until the 1950's, helped make it one of the most successful film adaptations of a Wells novel.

The Invisible Man was important in Sherriff's career, introducing him to screenwriting, a genre in which he was to do some of his most memorable work. Immediately after it, however, he first returned to the stage, collaborating with actress Jeanne de Casalis (the wife of Colin Clive) on *St. Helena*, a play about the exiled and imprisoned Napoleon. Written and published in 1934, it was not produced until 1936, when it had a faltering start until Winston Churchill wrote to *The Times* (London) in its defense, calling it "a work of art of a very high order." Churchill added, "I was among the very first to acclaim the quality of *Journey's End*. Here is the end of the most astonishing journey ever made by mortal man." The letter boosted ticket sales from fewer than one hundred for a performance to overflow houses; when the demand held for almost two months, the management moved the production to a larger theater in the West End. Possibly the house was wrong for the show, but for whatever reasons, the move was a disaster, and attendance plunged precipitously.

Fortunately for Sherriff, James Whale once more invited him to write a screenplay for him, this time an adaptation of Erich Maria Remarque's novel *The Road Back* (1931). Though the 1937 film was only moderately successful, it was important in Sherriff's career in that it returned him to screenwriting; during the next eighteen years, he wrote the scripts for an impressive number of outstanding films, among them *Goodbye, Mr. Chips*, *The Four Feathers*, *That Hamilton Woman*, *This Above All* (1942), *Odd Man Out*, *Quartet*, and *Trio*.

Sherriff did not return to playwriting until 1948, with *Miss Mabel*, a popular comedy-mystery. From 1950 to 1960, he wrote five more plays: *Home at Seven*, *The White Carnation*, *The Long Sunset*, *The Telescope*, and *A Shred of Evidence*. The last two were not successful, and after 1960, Sherriff went into semiretirement; his last publication, in 1968, was an autobiography, *No Leading Lady*, the title of which refers to complaints about *Journey's End* before its unexpected triumph. It is valuable as a lively account not only of Sherriff's life and career but also of forty years in the history of British theater and cinema. In those forty years, Sherriff played a prominent part.

Analysis

R. C. Sherriff's major achievement as a playwright, and his only enduring play, is *Journey's End*, the first grimly realistic drama about modern war. Trench warfare was quite different from anything in previous wars; instead of dashing cavalry charges and "the pomp and circumstance of glorious war," the men were holed up interminably, suffering from boredom, trenchfoot, vermin, perpetual bombardment, and shell shock. The entire action of *Journey's End* takes place in a dugout in the British trenches before St. Quentin between Monday evening, March 18, 1918, and the following Thursday, toward dawn. As the play opens, Captain Hardy is handing over the command to Captain Stanhope; before Stanhope arrives, Hardy explains the setup to Stanhope's second-in-command, Lieutenant Osborne (and thus to the audience as well). The audience learns that, after a tremendous bombardment, the Germans are planning a major attack. The audience also learns about conditions in the dugout—the rats, vermin, cockroach races, and supplies. Finally, the audience learns that Stanhope, the best company commander in the area, has been drinking so heavily that he is considered a freak. Defending him, Osborne explains that Stanhope, who is only twenty-one years old, has been at the front for three years and has not had a furlough for twelve months. He drinks because his nerves are shattered.

A replacement officer arrives, Second Lieutenant Raleigh, eighteen years old and just out of school. For years, Raleigh has worshiped Stanhope (who was ahead of him in school and who is engaged to his sister) as a hero. Unaware of the change in Stanhope, Raleigh has used the influence of his uncle, General Raleigh, to get a posting under his idol. He tells Osborne about Stanhope in their school days together, and Osborne instructs him about the trenches. The Germans are only a hundred yards away, the length of a football field, and between them is no-man's-land. In the English dugout the remaining staff include only Second Lieutenant Trotter, short and fat, whose chief concern seems to be food, and Second Lieutenant Hibbert. The minimal plot develops tensions among these men and between the men and the stresses of trench warfare and the impending attack. Hibbert is a coward, and in one dramatic moment, Stanhope threatens to shoot him and then rallies the man's courage temporarily. Raleigh tries to conceal his dismay at Stanhope's nervous drinking. When Raleigh writes a letter to his sister, Stanhope shocks them all by demanding to censor it; he fears that Raleigh will have revealed his deterioration but finds that the younger man has written only praise of him. The colonel assigns Raleigh and Osborne to make a raid to capture a German prisoner; though the Germans are ready and waiting, Raleigh succeeds, but Osborne is killed. Before going over the top, Osborne lays his pipe down with the line, "I do hate leaving a pipe when it's got a nice glow on the top like that"—a finely understated exit. When the attack comes, Raleigh is shot through the spine and dies with only Stanhope present. Stanhope then goes up to join in the fighting as shelling hits the dugout and caves it in. The play ends in darkness with the rattle of machine-gun fire.

In this war, there is no magnificence—only mud, monotony, and mortality. Unlike Ernest Hemingway's *A Farewell to Arms* (1929), an adaptation of which was staged the same year, *Journey's End* offers no romance, except for references to the never-seen sister of Raleigh. The cast is exclusively masculine; women are available only on furlough, which the men seem never to get. Interestingly, the stage version of *A Farewell to Arms*, like *Beau Geste*, died a quick death; apparently it was impossible to mount a believable staging of an Arab attack on Fort Zinderneuf or the retreat from Caporetto, the escape into a raging torrent, the escape across an Alpine lake, or the rest of Hemingway's broad panorama. By confining *Journey's End* to the dugout, Sherriff not only avoided the necessity of trying to stage battle scenes but also conveyed beautifully the claustrophobia of trench warfare, which imprisons the soldiers within their own defenses.

Journey's End is sometimes thought of as an antiwar play, but this is not necessarily the case. Certainly it portrays war as horrible, but it never investigates the causes of war or questions the war's justification. The closest it comes to doing so is a brief scene in which Raleigh says, "The Germans are really quite decent, aren't they? I mean, outside the newspapers?" and Osborne tells how the Germans refrained from shooting a patrol that came out to drag a wounded soldier to safety, and how, instead, a German officer shouted "Carry him!" and fired some flares to help the rescue mission. "The next day," Osborne comments dryly, "we blew each other's trenches to blazes." He and Raleigh agree that "it all seems rather—*silly*. . . ." Otherwise, the play takes warfare for granted. Like Stephen Crane's *The Red Badge of Courage* (1895), which never even mentions the Civil War or the battle at hand, *Journey's End* is concerned with the conduct of men under the stress of warfare. Certainly, it is not an antimilitary play in the way that such films as *All Quiet on the Western Front* (1930), *Paths of Glory* (1957), *Catch-22* (1961), *Gallipoli* (1981), or the novel *Slaughterhouse-Five* (1969) attack the corruption, cruelty, or absurdity of the military mind. Instead, its protagonists do their best to adhere to the British "stiff upper lip" tradition; when they crack momentarily, they show exactly how much they have been holding themselves in under intense pressure.

St. Helena, the play about Napoleon that Sherriff wrote with Jeanne de Casalis, tries to humanize the exiled emperor but never asks about the justice or injustice of his role in keeping all Europe at war for twenty years. In this respect, it resembles *Journey's End*; both plays show the immediate human factor but decline to challenge the morality or necessity of war.

For theatergoers who did not share Churchill's admiration of Napoleon, *St. Helena* lacked impact. A drama of the deposed emperor's frustration and stagnation, it does not build up dramatic intensity but rather winds down in a series of anticlimaxes. The play's structure indicates this, for instead of the traditional three acts, it has twelve scenes spanning six years. Napoleon spends his time dictating his memoirs, frustrating the British authorities, arbitrating petty disputes among members of his staff, complaining about living conditions on the island, reliving his past moments of glory, and wondering whether he should not have died at one of them. The individual roles in *St. Helena* are well written; a good cast could have fun with them, but the overall drama is as tedious as life on the island must have been.

After World War II, Sherriff took time out from screenwriting to write several plays. *Miss Mabel* is a comedy-mystery about elderly twin sisters, one a miserly, rich widow, the other, Miss Mabel, a poor, humanitarian spinster. The play begins with the widow dead; to everyone's surprise, her will leaves her sizable fortune to a physician to use in building a hospital, to a vicar to establish a home for children, to the widow's gardener to have his own nursery, and to a nephew to marry and to study architecture. Miss Mabel receives nothing but wants nothing. It turns out that she has poisoned her sister and forged the will. When the heirs discover this crime, they are torn between staying silent and fulfilling their dreams or clearing their consciences by disclosing the crime. They choose to inform the police, but the play implies that the law will be lenient to the murdering philanthropist, who seems a bit like a refugee from *Arsenic and Old Lace*. The play was quite popular and played to full houses for more than six months.

Sherriff's next play appeared in 1950. *Home at Seven* concerns David Preston, a mild-mannered bank teller who comes home one night at seven o'clock to find his wife distraught because he has been missing for more than a day. Preston has no recollection of the lost time, but during his amnesia, five hundred pounds have been stolen from the club of which he is treasurer, and the club steward, whom Preston disliked, has been murdered. Circumstantial evidence seems to point to Preston's guilt, but he is finally proved innocent. Sir Ralph Richardson starred in a successful London run of nearly a year and proceeded to direct as well as star in a film version, retitled *Murder on Monday* (1952).

Sherriff's next play, *The White Carnation*, is a comedy about a ghost. It opens outside the house of John Greenwood, a wealthy stockbroker, who is entertaining his guests at an annual Christmas Eve party. It is close to midnight, supposedly in 1951, in a small town outside London. As the guests depart, "a strange, eerie gust of wind" slams the front door shut, leaving Greenwood locked out in the cold. Unable to rouse anyone, he breaks a window and lets himself in, only to discover a deserted, unfurnished, partly bombed-out interior. A policeman, attracted by Greenwood's shouting, tries to evict him as a trespasser, but Greenwood refuses to leave his own house. When a sergeant who knows him arrives to establish his identity, the man cries out in horror. A doctor finds Greenwood "healthy" but with no pulse, heartbeat, circulation, or temperature; the doctor informs Greenwood that he has been dead for seven years. According to the sergeant, Greenwood and all of his guests were killed in 1944 when a German fly-bomb fell on the house. The sergeant even attended Greenwood's funeral and saw the corpse dressed, as Greenwood is now, in his dinner clothes, with a white carnation in his buttonhole.

Instead of staying in the twilight zone, the play develops into a droll comedy. As portrayed by Sir Ralph Richardson, Greenwood is not at all an ectoplasmic spook; instead, he is a sturdy, phlegmatic, seemingly flesh-and-blood Englishman. Playing against the expectations of the supernatural, Sherriff derives considerable comedy from satirizing bureaucracy as it comes into conflict with the not-so-spectral Greenwood. The house has been sold and is to be torn down to make room for a housing development, but Greenwood refuses to leave. He does not know how to dematerialize, is utterly ignorant of spectral ways, and wants his furniture and radio back. The question of whether ghosts can own property is debated. What are the legal rights of ghosts? What government bureau has jurisdiction over them? Greenwood's case is passed from the Ministry of Health, which decides that its responsibility ends with death and burial, to the Ministry of Works, which maintains Ancient Monuments but decides that Greenwood's house does not qualify and will not accept him without the house, to the chancellor of the Duchy of Lancaster, who passes the matter on to the Home Office, which deals with passports and which determines that, upon his death, Greenwood ceased to be a citizen and that therefore his ghost entered the country illegally and can be deported. No one knows how to deport him, however, and he still refuses to leave.

Meanwhile, Greenwood intends to enjoy himself, reading the greatest literature and listening to the greatest music—pursuits for which he never found time when he was alive. Despite his lofty plans, however, he discovers that he cannot enjoy reading anything but the *Financial Times*; he also learns that he had been insensitive to his wife, thoughtlessly neglecting her and wounding her feelings.

Unable to prevail against Greenwood in any other way, the authorities undermine the house and plan to collapse it at midnight on Christmas Eve, 1952. As they make the final preparations, Greenwood disappears, and we are back at the Christmas Eve party in 1944. In the "interval," however, Greenwood has learned to be more humane, and he is loving and considerate to his wife as once again the bomb falls, together with the final curtain. *The White Carnation* is a *jeu d'esprit*, worlds away from the grim dugout of *Journey's End*, but it shows Sherriff's skill at civilized comedy.

Though Sherriff never took his degree in history, he remained an enthusiast of the subject; besides writing *St. Helena* and screenplays for two historical films—*The Four Feathers* and *That Hamilton Woman*—he became an amateur archaeologist and dug among the Roman ruins in southern England. In his play *The Long Sunset*, he tried to reconstruct the life of the Romans in Britain as the empire was dying and the legions were being withdrawn. Sherriff noted in his preface to the play that little is known about the way in which the Romans faced the end. The play deals with Julian, a Roman farmer, and his family. To save their land when the legions leave, they recruit the aid of Arthur and Gawain, who, in Sherriff's play, are much more primitive figures than the romanticized heroes of Camelot. Sherriff's Arthur is closer to the misty figures recorded in the early chronicles by Gildas and Nennius than to the chivalric monarch of Sir Thomas Malory. The play was not a success, but it is noteworthy in that it foreshadowed a whole genre of neo-Arthurian novels that sometimes tried to recapture a sense of the primitive background of the Matter of Britain.

In 1960, Sherriff's last play appeared, a comedy-mystery entitled *A Shred of Evidence*. In it, Richard Medway learns that while he was out drunk the night before, a cyclist had been killed by a hit-and-run driver on the road Medway had taken. Medway can recall nothing, and the evidence seems to point to him, but his innocence is established. Though the details differ, the play is, in some ways, merely a reprise of *Home at Seven*, and though its plot-twists are entertaining, it is Sherriff's weakest work.

Of Sherriff's novels and plays, only *Journey's End* is a masterpiece; the rest are well-crafted, entertaining, but justly forgotten works. Aside from *Journey's End*, it may well be that Sherriff's best work was in films; his screenwriting was always craftsmanlike, and *Journey's End*, *The Invisible Man*, *Goodbye, Mr. Chips*, *The Four Feathers*, *That Hamilton Woman*, *Odd Man Out*, *Quartet*, and *Trio* are film classics.

Other major works

NOVELS: *Journey's End*, 1930 (with Vernon Bartlett; adaptation of Sherriff's play); *The Fortnight in September*, 1931; *Greengates*, 1936; *The Hopkins Manuscript*, 1939; *King John's Treasure*, 1954.

NONFICTION: *No Leading Lady: An Autobiography*, 1968; *The Siege of Swayne Castle*, 1973.

SCREENPLAYS: *The Invisible Man*, 1933 (with Philip Wylie; adaptation of H. G. Wells's novel); *The Road Back*, 1937 (with Charles Kenyon; adaptation of Erich Maria Remarque's novel); *Goodbye, Mr. Chips*, 1939 (with Claudine West and Erich Maschwitz; adaptation of James Hilton's novel); *The Four Feathers*, 1939 (adaptation of A. E. W. Mason's novel); *That Hamilton Woman*, 1941 (with Walter Reisch); *This Above All*, 1942 (adaptation of Eric Knight's novel); *Forever and a Day*, 1943 (with others); *Odd Man Out*, 1947 (with F. L. Green; adaptation of Green's novel); *Quartet*, 1949 (adaptation of W. Somerset Maugham's stories); *Trio*, 1950 (adaptation of Maugham's stories); *No Highway in the Sky*, 1951 (with Oscar Millard and Alec Coppel; adaptation of Nevil Shute's novel); *The Dam Busters*, 1954; *The Night My Number Came Up*, 1955 (based on an article by Air Marshal Sir Victor Goddard).

Bibliography

Cottrell, John. *Laurence Olivier.* Englewood Cliffs, N.J.: Prentice-Hall, 1975. Olivier, in 1928, was the star of the first production of *Journey's End*, which was staged by the Incorporated Stage Society before it reopened in London. Cottrell gives an elaborately detailed account of the play's first two stagings.

Darlington, William A. "'Keying Down': The Secret of *Journey's End.*" *Theatre Arts Monthly* 13 (July, 1929): 493-497. A critic who has seen all the performances of *Journey's End* compares the play's first two productions and the New York production.

Hill, Eldon C. "R. C. Sherriff." In *Dictionary of Literary Biography*, edited by Stanley Weintraub. Vol. 10, part 2, M-Z, *Modern British Dramatists, 1900-1945.* Detroit, Mich.: Gale Research, 1982. Hill goes into considerable detail in his discussion of *Journey's End,* quoting G. Wilson Knight's 1962 statement that it is "the greatest war play of the century" and comparing it to Stephen Crane's *The Red Badge of Courage* (1895) and George Bernard Shaw's *Arms and the Man* (pr. 1894, pb. 1898). He gives a briefer account of the other plays and novels and says little about the screenplays. Hill claims that Sherriff has "outlived his reputation as a dramatist" and is one of "fame's disinherited." Includes two photographs of the author, a reproduction of the program, and a photograph of the 1929 production of *Journey's End.*

Kunitz, Stanley J., and Howard Haycraft, eds. *Twentieth-Century Authors: A Biographical Dictionary of Modern Literature.* New York: Wilson, 1942. Contains a photograph of Sherriff with a brief biographical sketch of his childhood, war experience, work as an insurance claims adjuster, and beginnings as a playwright and screenwriter. Tells of his unmarried domestic life in a small town in Surrey, where he rowed and played cricket. The sketch is updated to 1955 in the first supplement.

Robert E. Morsberger

ROBERT E. SHERWOOD

Born: New Rochelle, New York; April 4, 1896
Died: New York, New York; November 14, 1955

Principal drama

The Road to Rome, pr., pb. 1927; *The Love Nest*, pr. 1927 (adaptation of Ring Lardner's story); *The Queen's Husband*, pr., pb. 1928; *Waterloo Bridge*, pr., pb. 1930; *This Is New York*, pr. 1930, pb. 1931; *Reunion in Vienna*, pr. 1931, pb. 1932; *Acropolis*, pr. 1933; *The Petrified Forest*, pr., pb. 1935; *Idiot's Delight*, pr., pb. 1936; *Tovarich*, pr., pb. 1936 (adaptation of Jacques Deval's comedy); *Abe Lincoln in Illinois*, pr. 1938, pb. 1939; *There Shall Be No Night*, pr., pb. 1940; *The Rugged Path*, pr. 1945; *Miss Liberty*, pr. 1949 (libretto; music by Irving Berlin); *Small War on Murray Hill*, pr., pb. 1957.

Other literary forms

Robert E. Sherwood made his reputation as a dramatist, although he received considerable recognition and a Pulitzer Prize for *Roosevelt and Hopkins* (1948), a detailed historical study of the relationship between Franklin D. Roosevelt and Harry Hopkins during the war years; the British edition, entitled *The White House Papers of Harry Hopkins*, followed in 1949. Sherwood also wrote *The Virtuous Knight* (1931), a badly received novel. Both of these works demonstrate Sherwood's interest in history. *The Virtuous Knight* is set in the time of the Crusades and was a product of the period during which some of Sherwood's plays, most notably *The Road to Rome* and *Acropolis*, were based on historical events.

Achievements

Robert E. Sherwood was not a dramatic innovator. He produced fifteen full-length plays, two of which—*The Love Nest* and *Tovarich*—were adaptations, the former based on a Ring Lardner short story, the latter based on a comedy by Jacques Deval. *Miss Liberty* was a musical for which Irving Berlin wrote the music. Sherwood also wrote the ending for Philip Barry's *Second Threshold* (pr. 1951) after Barry's death. Nine of his plays ran for more than one hundred performances on Broadway, making them commercial successes. *Abe Lincoln in Illinois* had the longest run, 472 performances.

Sherwood received Pulitzer Prizes in drama for *Idiot's Delight*, *Abe Lincoln in Illinois*, and *There Shall Be No Night*. *Roosevelt and Hopkins* won for Sherwood a fourth Pulitzer Prize. His film script *The Best Years of Our Lives* took an Academy Award for Best Screenplay of 1946, one of nine Academy Awards garnered by the film. Sherwood also received the Gold

Medal for Drama of the National Institute of Arts and Letters in 1941, the Gutenberg Award in 1949, and the Bancroft Prize for Distinguished Writing in American History in 1949. He was awarded honorary doctorates by Dartmouth College (1940), Yale University (1941), Harvard University (1949), and Bishop's University (1950). Such is a bare outline of Sherwood's achievements.

To flesh out this listing, one must recognize that Sherwood was also an activist in his profession and in national affairs. In 1935, he became secretary of the Dramatists' Guild and rose to the presidency of that organization in 1937, the year in which he combined forces with Maxwell Anderson, S. N. Behrman, Sidney Howard, and Elmer Rice to form the Playwrights' Company, which was incorporated in 1938 for the purpose of permitting playwrights to stage their own plays, either directing the plays themselves or appointing directors of their own choosing. Sherwood was elected president of the American National Theatre and Academy in 1939.

Although Sherwood had been a strident pacifist, Adolf Hitler's ascendancy in Germany forced him to rethink his stand. A political idealist, Sherwood was finally forced to recognize the impossibility of allowing a dictator to run roughshod over Europe. *There Shall Be No Night* calls for action against aggressors of Hitler's ilk and represents an important turning point in Sherwood's thinking. In his presidential address to the Dramatists' Guild in 1939, Sherwood called upon writers to turn their talents to writing in support of freedom. *There Shall Be No Night* is in line with this imperative.

Long a friend and political supporter of Franklin D. Roosevelt, Sherwood was asked by the Roosevelt Administration to write war propaganda. He did so willingly, and in time became not only a confidant of the president, visiting him often at the White House, but also one of his chief speech writers. In 1940, Sherwood was appointed as a special assistant to the secretary of war, and in 1942, he was appointed director of the overseas branch of the office of war information. In 1945, he served as a special assistant to the secretary of the navy.

Sherwood was also active as a screenwriter. As early as 1932, he had collaborated with Charles Lederer on *Cock of the Air* for United Artists, followed in 1935 by *The Scarlet Pimpernel*, a collaboration with Arthur Wimperis. In 1936, he was involved in writing the screenplay for *Rembrandt*, although he was not the sole author. His screenplay for *The Ghost Goes West* was produced in 1936 by Alexander Korda. The following year, with Aben Kandel, he wrote the screenplay for *Thunder in the City* and also did considerable rewriting on a Metro-Goldwyn-Mayer script, *Conquest*. In 1938, he was coauthor with Lajos Biro of the screenplay for *The Divorce of Lady X* and also wrote *The Adventures of Marco Polo*, the latter of which was cited by Francis Marion in *How to Write and Sell Fiction*

Stories as a splendid example of scenario writing. Sherwood adapted *Idiot's Delight* for the screen in 1939, the year in which *Abe Lincoln in Illinois* was also filmed. *Rebecca* followed in 1940. His finest Hollywood effort was *The Best Years of Our Lives*, in 1946. It was followed in 1947 by *The Bishop's Wife*, on which he collaborated with Leonardo Bercovici, and in 1953 by his last screenplay, *Man on a Tightrope*.

Biography

Robert Emmet Sherwood was the product of an affluent and artistic family. His mother, the former Rosina Emmet, was sufficiently well-known as an artist to be listed in *Who's Who*. His father, Arthur Murray Sherwood, was a prominent investment broker and held a seat on the New York Stock Exchange. Arthur Sherwood was a frustrated actor and had been an active member of the Hasty Pudding Club during his student days at Harvard, where he was also the first president of the Harvard *Lampoon*. Robert Sherwood followed in his father's footsteps at Harvard, both as a member of the Hasty Pudding Club and as editor of the *Lampoon*.

Sherwood was named for the Irish patriot Robert Emmet, brother of his mother's great-grandfather, who led an attack on Dublin Castle and was hanged in 1803. Sherwood was proud of his renegade namesake. Mary Elizabeth Wilson Sherwood, mother of Sherwood's father, had been honored both by the French government and by Queen Victoria of Britain. She was active in literary and artistic circles and in her lifetime wrote more than twenty books and hundreds of articles.

Thus, Robert Sherwood, the next to the youngest of five Sherwood children, was born into an artistically active family of considerable means. Shortly after his birth, the family moved to a house on Lexington Avenue in New York City. The family also maintained a forty-room Georgian mansion, Skene Wood, set on three hundred acres bordering Lake Champlain. It was there that Sherwood spent most of his childhood summers.

During the summers at Skene Wood, Sherwood and his siblings put on amateur dramatic productions, and Sherwood produced a handwritten newspaper, *Children's Life*. At eight, he wrote an ending for Charles Dickens' unfinished novel *The Mystery of Edwin Drood* (1870), and two years later he wrote his first play, *Tom Ruggles' Surprise*, soon to be followed by *How the King Was Saved* and *The Curse of Bacchus*.

When he was nine years old, Sherwood was sent to the Fay School in Southborough, Massachusetts, and at thirteen, he was sent to the Milton Academy near Boston to begin his preparatory studies for Harvard. Both in preparatory school and later at Harvard, Sherwood's energies were to be directed more toward literary matters than toward academic ones. He was managing editor of Milton's monthly magazine, *Orange and Blue*, for much of his final year at Milton; he was deeply in trouble with his studies, however, and in April, the school forced his withdrawal from this post. Ultimately, his grades were so low that Milton Academy refused him a diploma, giving him instead a certificate of attendance. Despite this, Sherwood was elected valedictorian by his classmates, and he gave the valedictory address.

Sherwood's academic career at Harvard was no more distinguished than his career at Milton Academy had been, although his contributions to Harvard's dramatic and literary clubs were substantial. On the brink of expulsion three times during his freshman year alone, Sherwood did not make it through to graduation. In July of 1917, having been rejected on account of his great height by the various branches of the United States armed forces in which he attempted to enlist, Sherwood became a member of the Canadian Expeditionary Force, serving in the Forty-second Battalion of the Fifth Royal Highlanders and achieving the distinction of being very probably the tallest serviceman in World War I to wear kilts. At six feet seven inches, he towered over his fellow combatants. He served six months in France, where he was gassed on Vimy Ridge. In 1918, Harvard awarded him a bachelor's degree in absentia although he had not met the academic standards for this degree.

On his return from the war, Sherwood was offered a position at *Vanity Fair*, a magazine that the *Lampoon* under Sherwood's editorship had burlesqued so effectively that its editor wanted Sherwood on his staff. At *Vanity Fair*, Sherwood shared an office with Robert Benchley and Dorothy Parker; the three were fired in 1920 for rebelling against *Vanity Fair*'s editorial staff, but soon they were all hired by *Life* magazine, to whose editorship Sherwood rose in 1924. During this period, Sherwood was a regular participant in the Round Table which met at the Algonquin Hotel.

Sherwood married Mary Brandon in 1922. Their turbulent marriage lasted until 1934, when they were divorced. The following year, Sherwood married Marc Connelly's former wife, actress Madeline Hurlock Connelly. Sherwood's extravagant life-style during the early years of his marriage to Mary Brandon caused him to sink deeply into debt, from which he extricated himself in 1926 by writing *The Road to Rome* in three weeks' time. When the play opened on Broadway the following year, it was an immediate success and ran for 392 performances. Throughout his career, Sherwood frequently relied on his gift for rapid composition to free himself from debts.

The activism that had led Sherwood to serve in the armed forces during the war and to speak his mind at *Vanity Fair* shifted its focus to the problems of actors and writers. It led Sherwood to assume prominent roles in the Dramatists' Guild and in the American National Theatre Association and to be instrumental in forming the Playwrights' Producing Company.

It was natural that, with the spread of Fascism in Europe, Sherwood's basically activist personality should lead him to encourage his fellow writers to strike out against aggression of the sort that Hitler was practicing and should lead him to write a play, *There Shall Be No Night*, which departed drastically from his romantic liberalism and pacifism of the 1920's and 1930's. It is also significant that Sherwood at this time tried to rewrite his pacifist play *Acropolis*, for which he could never arrange a production in New York and which ran for only twelve performances when it played in London in 1933. Sherwood was unable to rewrite it satisfactorily, probably because he no longer believed in the kind of pacifism that the play promulgated.

Always a man of the world, Sherwood's insights were deepened by his direct contact with high levels of government during the war. His work with the Hopkins papers was meticulously researched, although some scholars think that Sidney Hyman deserves more credit than he was given for the high level of research apparent in *Roosevelt and Hopkins*.

Sherwood became a propagandist in the years following Hitler's invasion of Poland in 1939. The quality and effectiveness of his dramatic writing declined after the war. He died in 1955 at age fifty-nine.

Analysis

Although Robert E. Sherwood's writing was seldom profound, it was often effective and moving. He had an excellent sense of timing and was able to balance his characters and play them off against one another in such a way as to achieve and maintain dramatic tension. His major characters are largely romantics, dreamers of one sort or another, who envision a more perfect world, a more felicitous state of affairs.

Sherwood's plays are urbane, idealistic, and often quite witty. They may seem somewhat dated to modern readers; both the situations on which they are focused and Sherwood's suggested solutions to the problems posed are out of keeping with the pragmatic temper of the 1970's and 1980's.

The most consistent element found in the plays is pacifism. Sherwood was convinced of the futility of war. *There Shall Be No Night*, although it is a war play, wrestles with the question of pacifism quite substantially. In this play, Sherwood was led to abandon his idealism to the extent of calling for action against the sort of aggression that leads to genocide. In nearly all of his other plays, Sherwood examines the options available to humankind to avoid war.

Even Sherwood's earliest play dealt with the question of pacifism and of human conflict in the face of war. *The Road to Rome* would be flippant if it were less urbane. In this historical comedy, Sherwood risks using modern slang and contemporary situations in an ancient Roman setting and gets away with it. The subject of the play had always interested Sherwood: Why had Hannibal and his army come to the very gates of Rome, only to turn away and retreat from a sure victory?

Taking a number of liberties with historical fact, Sherwood suggests an answer: Amytis, the wife of Rome's dictator, Fabius Maximus, allows herself to be captured by the enemy and is about to be stabbed to death by Hannibal when she seduces him. Amytis returns to Rome and to her unexciting husband. Hannibal retreats.

Essentially, *The Road to Rome* is a satire which compares the Rome of Fabius with American society after World War I. Fabius and his mother, Fabia, represent conventional social values. They are much concerned with appearance and with what people think, and they take themselves quite seriously. Amytis, on the other hand, has an Athenian mother; she is an iconoclast in this dreary, somewhat backward Roman society. When she hears that Hannibal is about to invade Rome, Amytis flees to Ostia, admonishing Fabius not to eat too much starch while she is away. She leaves in the company of two slaves, Meta and Varius, around whom a useful subplot is constructed.

Before the end of act 1, it is obvious that Amytis, bored with her life and unsympathetic to her husband and her monotonous mother-in-law, is thrilled by the thought of the aggressor outside the city gates. She claims that Hannibal "sounds like a thoroughly commendable person" and goes on to ask, "Is it wrong for me to admire good, old-fashioned virility in men?"

Thus, the stage is set: When Amytis and her slaves are captured, it is clear that she will entrap Hannibal. More important, through Amytis, Sherwood suggests that Hannibal comes to realize that there is no glory in sacking Rome. Rationality prevails in the tradition of true liberal romanticism found in much of Sherwood's writing before *There Shall Be No Night*.

If Sherwood was attempting to convey the message that reason can prevail over might, he fell somewhat short of his mark. Hannibal can be brought to the point of uttering that "there is a thing called the human equation," but he arrives at this point not through reason so much as because he has yielded to his lust for Amytis. Nevertheless, if the decision not to sack Rome is Hannibal's, it is clear that the focus of the play is on Amytis, whose reason prevails.

The Meta-Varius subplot portrays the true and lasting love the two slaves have for each other. Because they are slaves, they are unable to marry. Their love stands in sharp contrast to the barren relationship that exists between Amytis and Fabius. Amytis persuades Hannibal to free these two lovers so that they can return to their native Sicily and marry.

The last two acts of *The Road to Rome* are weakened by heavy-handed pacifist diatribes, but the play's general wittiness and the excellence of Sherwood's characterizations are sufficient to overcome such shortcomings. It is ironic that Amytis' relationship with her husband is based upon her frivolousness, while her relationship with Hannibal succeeds because of her wit and intellect. The play attacks conformity and examines closely the difference between public and private morality. In Amytis, one can see shadows of the bright young Sherwood whose nonconformity led him to disaster on more than one occasion. Amytis is drawn delightfully and convincingly and is ever the recipient of the audience's warm compassion.

As the play ends, Rome has been spared, Hannibal is in retreat, and Amytis returns to Fabius, who will undoubtedly receive the credit for saving Rome. The audience is also left with the strong impression that Amytis has been made pregnant by Hannibal, and it can savor the delicious irony that Hannibal's child will be reared as Fabius' and may himself eventually come to rule Rome. In the final scene of the play, Hannibal says to Fabius, "I wish happiness and prosperity to you, your wife, and your sons." When Fabius responds that he has no sons, Hannibal replies, "You may."

Sherwood's next play, *The Love Nest*, was based on a splendid Ring Lardner short story, but the adaptation failed utterly, both artistically and commercially, playing only twenty-three performances. Perhaps Sherwood was drawn to the story by his own domestic complications at the time. A secondary theme of the play is censorship, a subject in which Sherwood was becoming quite interested and on which he debated in 1927 with John Sumner, president of the Society for the Prevention of Vice.

The play revolves around Celia Gregg, the actress wife of a much disliked motion-picture director, Lou Gregg. Celia has risen to her present position not through her own talent but because she married a director whose reputation is shady, partly because of nudity in his film, *Hell's Paradise*, and partly because of rumors about his own private life. Celia and the butler, Forbes, an unemployed actor, love each other, and before the play is over, they decide to leave and have a life together, though there is little to suggest that they have any real future. *The Love Nest* has some witty lines, and Celia's dramatic drunk scene in act 2 is splendid, but the play fails because its psychological motivation is unconvincing and underdeveloped, and the dramatic tension is uneven.

Newspaper accounts of the official visit of Queen Marie of Romania to the United States in 1926 gave Sherwood the substance for his next play, *The Queen's Husband*, a thin yet diverting comedy that ran for 125 performances on Broadway, making it moderately successful commercially. During Queen Marie's visit, her consort was very much in the background. Sherwood's play focuses on the consort, Ferdinand, who in the play becomes Eric VIII, consort of Queen Martha. The principality over which Eric and Martha rule is much in the hands of the military, led by General Northrup, who seeks to annihilate the opposition by executing them. Queen Martha goes along with this. The king, however, must sign the orders for the executions, and he subverts the plan simply by losing the orders. When his private secretary, Freddy Granton, finds the death warrants, Eric tells him to "take them out and lose them again."

Eric is first presented as a doddering nonentity, but it soon becomes apparent that he knows what he is doing and that he ultimately gets his way. In a romantic subplot, Princess Anne is in love with Freddy Granton, but there are impediments to her marrying a commoner; indeed, a royal marriage is being arranged for her. On the day of the wedding, however, the king finally asserts himself, sees to it that Princess Anne marries the man she loves, sends them off on a trip to Panama, and clears the way for free elections by dissolving the Parliament. The play is filled with fairy-tale elements, and its resolution is improbable at best. It was received with some public enthusiasm as a diverting, witty entertainment, well-staged and competently acted, but it is not a play that contributes to Sherwood's artistic stature in any way.

Waterloo Bridge has little more to recommend it than does *The Queen's Husband*, and its run of only sixty-four performances clearly indicated a lack of public acceptance. The play succeeded better as a film, for which S. N. Behrman wrote the major portion of a screenplay that fleshed out the plot and essentially discarded Sherwood's original script. Universal Studios produced the film in 1931, and Metro-Goldwyn-Mayer released other film versions of the play in 1940 and 1956.

Sherwood wrote the play from the memory of an experience in London in 1918 when he was recovering from war injuries. During the festivities celebrating the Armistice, Sherwood had met an American chorus girl who had been stranded in London, where she was in the cast of *The Pink Lady*. She invited Sherwood to come to her flat, but he lost the address so was unable to accept her invitation.

In the play, a remarkably innocent American soldier, Roy Cronin, meets Myra Deauville on Waterloo Bridge and is too inexperienced to realize that she is a prostitute out plying her trade. He goes to her apartment and, mistaking her for a symbol of purity, proposes marriage to her. She accepts, but then she has a change of heart, leaves Roy a note, and fades from the scene. They meet again by accident on Waterloo Bridge, where she confesses to being a whore, but Roy urges her to forget her past. He loves her and shows that he does by signing over his life insurance to her and arranging for her to receive part of his pay each month. As the second act of this two-act play ends, enemy bombers are flying overhead and Roy must return to his unit. Myra lights a match and holds it up for the German bombardiers to see. The play ends with a pacifist diatribe that Sherwood puts rather unconvincingly into Roy's mouth. *Waterloo Bridge* was less successful than *The Queen's Husband* because it lacked the wit of its predecessor and because it often wallowed in sentimentality.

Not to be daunted by the failure of *Waterloo Bridge*, Sherwood wrote

This Is New York, which also failed, running for only fifty-nine performances on Broadway. He produced the play quickly after he had put aside a play about the Crusades entitled "Marching as to War." This historical play was never completed, but much of the material Sherwood used in it found its way into his only novel, *The Virtuous Knight*.

This Is New York shows Sherwood as a loyal and patriotic New Yorker, but not as a consummate playwright. Irked by the provincial attitudes which had helped to defeat Al Smith in the 1928 presidential election, Sherwood set out to write a play about the hypocrisy of the provinces. He partially succeeded by lining up Senator Harvey L. Krull, of Iowa, and his self-righteous wife against a group of New Yorkers, including racketeers, bootleggers, blackmailers, and other such marginal figures. In the end, the Krulls are shown up as the hypocrites Sherwood set out to create, while the socially marginal characters show a warmth and humanity that ingratiate them to audiences. The key figure in the play is the Krulls' daughter Emma, who wants to marry a New Yorker, Joe Gresham. Emma is an appealing character, believably depicted and necessary to the development of the play's theme. After a somewhat tedious and talky first act, the play moves to a dramatically tight second act with a strong climax. The play is significant only as a step in Sherwood's development toward being able to create and control a believable microcosm, an ability that was to serve him well in plays such as *The Petrified Forest* and *Idiot's Delight*.

Sherwood visited Vienna in 1929 to attend a performance of *The Road to Rome*, called *Hannibal ante portes* in the Austrian production. While in Vienna, he met Frau Sacher of the Hotel Sacher, who became the model for Frau Lucher in *Reunion in Vienna*, a sophisticated comedy that came to Broadway in 1931 for a highly successful run. Alfred Lunt and Lynn Fontanne played in the starring roles, with Helen Westley as Frau Lucher. Sherwood called the play an escape from reality. This witty play contained in its printed version a preface as pessimistic as anything Sherwood was ever to write. He warned, "Man may not have time to complete the process of his own doing before the unknown forces have combined to burst the bubble of his universe."

Set in the Vienna of 1930, *Reunion in Vienna* shows a city from which the Habsburgs have been exiled and in which the bourgeoisie has taken command. Frau Lucher—like her prototype, Frau Sacher—works to keep the concept of the nobility alive. She has given clandestine parties for exiled leaders who have returned for visits, and she is now planning a party to celebrate the one hundredth birthday of Franz Josef. Much to everyone's surprise, the Archduke Rudolf Maximilian von Habsburg, now a taxicab driver in Nice, returns for the occasion. Rudolf's former mistress, Elena, is married to one of the bourgeoisie who has risen in power, Anton Krug, a surgeon until the Habsburgs, whom he had opposed, had him sent from his medical post in their army to do hard labor in a rock quarry, where he destroyed his hands. When he finally gained his release, Anton no longer had the manual sensitivity to perform surgery, so he entered the practice of psychiatry.

Anton, who has every reason to hate the Habsburgs, is a rational man. Not only is he able to put past bitterness behind him, but also he is sure enough of his relationship with Elena to encourage her, when they learn that Rudolf is back in Vienna, to see her former lover and to attend Frau Lucher's reunion. She does so and finds that Rudolf is still dashing and romantic. Anton leaves the two of them alone, and the inevitable occurs, much as it did between Amytis and Hannibal, to whom Elena and Rudolf can legitimately be compared.

Rudolf's entry in act 2 is one of the best-prepared entries in any contemporary play. The deposed archduke is still every inch a Habsburg. The audience has been tantalized through act 1, wondering how Rudolf will appear after a decade away. Two minor characters give hints, but his entry is a breathtaking moment of pure theater. In act 3, the civilized interchange between Rudolf and Anton is well handled. Anton is the voice of reason and control, Rudolf that of emotion and soul. The night that Elena and Rudolf have together does not destroy the Krugs' union but rather strengthens it. If their marriage is dull, it is at least secure; it provides each party with the dependable reference point that husbands and wives need.

Reunion in Vienna helped to reestablish Sherwood's reputation after three plays that had been either outright failures or very limited successes. The play represented a turning point for Sherwood, who, after its production, was a much surer writer, even though he was to produce one more failure, *Acropolis*. *Reunion in Vienna*, dashed off in three weeks, was produced at a time when Sherwood's marriage was foundering and when there was little reason for cheer on the world scene. Hitler and Benito Mussolini were on the rise in Europe, and the world was in the grips of the Depression. Broadway needed a drawing-room drama such as *Reunion in Vienna* to divert its attention from the social and political realitites that caused Sherwood to write such a gloomy preface to the play.

Acropolis was an important play for Sherwood. It deals with ideas concerning human freedom and dignity that Sherwood considered fundamental—ideas present in many of his works but frequently diminished in impact by his witty manner. Sherwood wrote *Acropolis* in 1932 while he was traveling in France with his wife and the Connellys. He had long been mulling over the ideas that were the substance of the play. He gave the script to the Theatre Guild, which turned it down because it was not sufficiently theatrical and because it had too much talk in it. The play was finally produced in London in the fall of 1933, financed largely by Paul Hyde Bonner, Sherwood's neighbor at Grand Enton, Surrey. The play ran for only twelve performances, making it Sherwood's worst commercial disaster.

Unlike Sherwood's other plays, *Acropolis* went through many revisions. Indeed, the author was revising it up to the time he wrote *There Shall Be No Night* in 1940. The play, however, never seemed to coalesce into a dramatic whole, and with Sherwood's shift away from his romantic liberalism of the early 1930's, *Acropolis* in its various forms came to represent his thinking less and less each year. The play remained unpublished, although a number of manuscript versions of it exist.

When he went to Reno for six weeks in 1935 to obtain his divorce from Mary Brandon, Sherwood rented an office and began to write. His attention turned to an Arizona tourist attraction, the Petrified Forest, which in his play by that name provides an almost eternal backdrop before which ephemeral men and women play out their small roles. The microcosm of *The Petrified Forest* is the Black Mesa Filling Station. The cast of characters includes Gramp Maple, an old pioneer, now senescent; his son Jason, a bit of a dolt; and his granddaughter, Jason's daughter Gabrielle, nicknamed Gabby.

Gabby's French mother married Jason when he was an American soldier fighting in World War I, and she returned to Arizona with him but could not tolerate the isolation. She returned to France, abandoning both husband and daughter. Boze Hertlinger is a former college football player who pursues Gabby. Into this scene enters Alan Squier, the ideological center of the play in many respects, who has recently come from France and is hitchhiking across the country. Although he is sophisticated, cultivated, and intelligent, Alan is almost bankrupt, and his future is bleak. The cast is rounded out by the Chisholms, a banker and his wife, and their chauffeur, who are all in the filling station when Duke Mantee, a desperado recently escaped from an Oklahoma prison, arrives and holds all of them hostage.

Gabby's dream in life is to visit France, from which her mother came. Gabby, who has the vocabulary of a stevedore, quotes lines from François Villon, and paints watercolors, which she will show only to Alan, who predictably begins to be attracted to her. He decides to help her realize her dream by signing over to her his five-thousand-dollar life insurance policy and then getting Duke Mantee to shoot him.

The focus of the play is badly distorted. Alan represents what is good in the world, yet he enters into a suicide pact to help Gabby. One can only conclude that Sherwood is implying that the dark forces will prevail over the bright forces in society, for with Alan's death, which ultimately occurs onstage, the world—or at least Sherwood's microcosm—is left to the Boze Hertlingers and the Jason Maples, people who have ceased to have a discernible purpose in society.

One important theme in *The Petrified Forest* is that the pioneer, who led to the development of the United States, is fading from the scene. Gramp was a pioneer, but now he is too old to qualify as one. If Alan has the potential to be a sort of ideological pioneer, his death precludes that possibility. Duke Mantee comes across as the man of action, suggestive of Harry Glassman, the racketeer in *This Is New York*; Mantee is, despite his criminal record, infinitely more decent and promising than the senator and his wife.

Although *The Petrified Forest* is flawed structurally and thematically, as John Howard Lawson has demonstrated quite brilliantly in his *Theory and Technique of Playwriting* (1936), it was theatrical in the highest sense, and Broadway received it well. It played for nearly two hundred performances. Adapted for the screen in 1936, *The Petrified Forest* featured Leslie Howard as Alan Squier, Bette Davis as Gabby, and Humphrey Bogart as Duke Mantee. It is in its film version that the work is best remembered.

In *Idiot's Delight*, Sherwood again employed the device of placing a diverse group of people in a confined microcosm and putting them under considerable tension. *Idiot's Delight* could not have been more appropriate for its time: Its New York opening followed Mussolini's invasion of Ethiopia by two days; its London opening came a week after Hitler had invaded Austria. The world was tense, and Sherwood's play captured and exploited this tension.

As the play opens, the audience is presented with a cast that includes a weapons manufacturer and his mistress; a French Marxist labor leader who is executed before the play is over; two British honeymooners; a German scientist who is about to develop a cure for cancer but must now rush home to the *Vaterland* to work on developing poison gases; and Harry Van, a "hoofer" who is the guardian of a group of traveling showgirls. This mismatched group is stranded at the Hotel Monte Gabriele, just over the Italian border from Austria and Switzerland. All of them are being held by the Italian government because of the international tensions which have developed. They are essentially unable to control their own destinies, much as the people being held by Duke Mantee in *The Petrified Forest* were unable to control their own destinies, save for Alan Squier, who willed his own execution.

Lynn Fontanne, who played the role of Irene, the munitions manufacturer's mistress, urged upon Sherwood the revision from which the title is drawn. Sherwood expanded Fontanne's part and wrote into it the speech about God as a "poor, lonely old soul. Sitting up there in heaven, with nothing to do but play solitaire. Poor, dear God. Playing Idiot's Delight."

The play, although it is a delightful comedy, reflects the same sort of futility that was evidenced in *The Petrified Forest*. In it, Sherwood clearly expresses the conviction that intelligent people do not run things but rather are pawns in a system controlled by those of evil intent. In Sherwood's own eyes, the play missed its mark as a seriously intended comedy. Although it ran for more than three hundred performances and won for its author his first Pulitzer Prize for Drama, Sherwood was forced to admit that "the trouble with me is that I start off with a big message and end with nothing but good entertainment." The play is best understood if it is viewed essentially as a moral rather than a political statement.

Sherwood also wrote the film scenario for *Idiot's Delight*, for which he was paid $135,000 by Metro-Goldwyn-Mayer. The play represented an important step in Sherwood's development and in his public recognition.

It was two years before Sherwood was to have another opening on Broadway. During this time, he was much occupied with setting up the Playwrights' Producing Company, whose first production was to be *Abe Lincoln in Illinois*. Six feet, seven inches tall himself, Sherwood knew something of the isolation of being very tall, and in significant ways, he identified personally with Lincoln. The play, in three acts, is divided into twelve scenes and covers a thirty-year time span. It begins in New Salem, where the young Lincoln was postmaster, moving in the second act to Springfield, where Lincoln practices law and meets Mary Todd, whom he marries after once refusing to marry her on their appointed wedding day. In the last act, Lincoln is seen debating Douglas, becoming a presidential candidate, and winning the election. The play ends just as Lincoln is to leave for Washington to assume the presidency.

The character of Lincoln is psychologically well drawn, particularly in regard to his early association with and ultimate marriage to Mary Todd. She represents what the young Lincoln most fears—duty. Had he not married her, one must wonder whether he would ever have become president. Certainly, he is brought to the brink of leaving Illinois and going out to Nebraska with Seth Gale, in which case he could never have become president. Mary is persistent, however, and Lincoln marries her, thus beginning on the course which she has carefully plotted.

The themes of *Abe Lincoln in Illinois* were timely for the late 1930's. The problems that Lincoln faced, the moral dilemmas with which he wrestled, were not unlike those that perplexed the pacifist Sherwood, who was being forced to question his moral stand as Hitler threatened the whole of Europe.

Parts of the play are sketchy. The first-act curtain falls on a young Lincoln, immature and uncertain, only to rise years later on a Lincoln who has matured between the acts. Sherwood does not demonstrate the maturing process but rather presents it for the audience to accept, which it can easily do because the Lincoln story is so well-known. Similarly, the play ends before the crucial events of Lincoln's term of office, but this is quite immaterial to audiences who are fully aware of the tragic story of the Lincoln presidency. The play, an initial Broadway success that ran longer than any other Sherwood production, has probably been performed more often and been seen by more people that any other Sherwood play, and it is the play with which he is most readily identified today.

Sherwood's pacifism had been severely put to the test as the 1930's drew to a close. On the last Christmas Day of the decade, Sherwood heard William Lindsay White's broadcast from Finland called "Christmas in the Mannerheim Line," and it convinced him more than had anything else previously that the United States could not isolate itself from the rest of the world but must intervene to stop the spread of totalitarianism. His patriotism reached new heights, but this was no narrow patriotism. Rather, it had to do with the survival of the highest ideals that Sherwood held. Within six months, he was to make his stand clear, first by writing *There Shall Be No Night*, which he began on January 15, 1940, and which he delivered to the Lunts three weeks later, and then, in May, 1940, by spending $24,000 of his own money to run a full-page advertisement in more than one hundred American newspapers, calling upon his compatriots, and particularly upon writers, to stop Hitler. It was this advertisement that attracted President Roosevelt's attention and drew Sherwood into government service.

There Shall Be No Night was based on the Russian invasion of Finland in 1939; before the play ran in London, however, by which time Finland had fallen, Sherwood rewrote it, changing the locale from Finland to Greece and making the aggressors German rather than Russian. The play revolves around the Valkonen family and their trials as their country moves into a state of war. Valkonen is an eminent neurologist, a winner of the Nobel Prize. He, his wife Miranda, and his son Erik, are gentle people who live lives of great civility in Helsinki, until the war comes and their lives crumble. Before the play is over, they are all dead or about to die except for Erik's fiancée, Kaatri, pregnant with Erik's child; she escapes to the safety of America, where her delivery will give the Valkonens "one little link with the future." "It gives us the illusion of survival," says Miranda as the play ends, "and perhaps it isn't just an illusion." The play is filled with ironies, the chief one being that the most worthwhile people are defeated and destroyed. Dr. Ziemssen, the German Consul in Helsinki, is by training an anthropologist, yet he is supporting a plan of genocide, clearly stating that the plan outlined in Hitler's *Mein Kampf* is now operative.

An immensely moving play, *There Shall Be No Night* probably did more to mold the consciences of American audiences of its day than any play on the New York stage. It offers no strong ray of hope; rather, Sherwood brings audiences right into the vortex of a cosmic problem and leaves them there to struggle against the forces into which he has plunged them. *There Shall Be No Night*, Sherwood's first full-fledged tragedy, was unrelenting in its pessimistic realism and in its call to action.

Sherwood was never again to write a notably successful play, although he continued to score successes in his screenplays, and his *Roosevelt and Hopkins* was one of the great books to come out of the war period. Of his final plays, *Miss Liberty* was a popular light musical which ran for 308 performances, while *The Rugged Path* and *Small War on Murray Hill* were both artistic and commercial failures. Morey Vinion, the protagonist in *The Rugged Path*, speaks toward the end of the play for Sherwood and helps to explain his inability to write with the verve and wit that he achieved so easily in the 1930's: "I am no longer impressed by the power of the pen. For years I wrote about what was coming. I tried to tell what I had seen and heard and felt. I wrote my heart out. But it did no good." By the time the United States had entered and fought in a world conflict, Sherwood was too dispirited to be able to write with the conviction which earlier drove him.

Other major works

NOVEL: *The Virtuous Knight*, 1931.

NONFICTION: *The Best Moving Pictures of 1922-1923*, 1923 (editor). *Roosevelt and Hopkins*, 1948 (also as *The White House Papers of Harry Hopkins*, 1949).

SCREENPLAYS: *Cock of the Air*, 1932 (with Charles Lederer); *The Scarlet Pimpernel*, 1935 (with Arthur Wimperis; adaptation of Baroness Orczy's novel); *The Ghost Goes West*, 1936; *Thunder in the City*, 1937 (with Aben Kandel); *The Adventures of Marco Polo*, 1938; *The Divorce of Lady X*, 1938 (with Lajos Biro; adaptation of Biro's play *Counsel's Opinion*); *Abe Lincoln in Illinois*, 1939 (adaptation of his play); *Idiot's Delight*, 1939 (adaptation of his play); *Rebecca*, 1940; *The Best Years of Our Lives*, 1946; *The Bishop's Wife*, 1947 (with Leonardo Bercovici); *Man on a Tightrope*, 1953.

Bibliography

Brown, John Mason. *The Ordeal of a Playwright: Robert E. Sherwood and the Challenge of War.* Edited by Norman Cousins. New York: Harper & Row, 1970. Brown's uncompleted second biography (the first is listed below) furnishes a fragmentary but telling portrait of Sherwood as being wrenched away from devout pacifism to become aroused by world affairs. As a presidential speech writer, he wrote, on the eve of World War II, a pro-interventionist play, *There Shall Be No Night*, portraying a brave Finnish family resisting Finland's invasion. Complemented by an index and a complete text of *There Shall Be No Night.*

__________. *The Worlds of Robert E. Sherwood: Mirror to His Times, 1897-1939.* New York: Harper & Row, 1965. This thoroughly documented and admiring biography extends from Sherwood's early childhood and up through his career as a critic and playwright to include the writing of *Abe Lincoln in Illinois*. The volume contains a list of Sherwood's work and an index, in addition to twenty-eight illustrations of Sherwood, his family and friends, and several productions.

Gould, Jean. *Modern American Playwrights*. New York: Dodd, Mead, 1966. In a discussion of twentieth century American "realistic" playwrights, Gould devotes a lucidly compressed, eighteen-page chapter to Sherwood's life and works. Readable and informal, Gould's essay is particularly suited to the understanding and research needs of high school students. The book contains a select bibliography, an index, and a 1953 photograph of Sherwood along with those of his playwright contemporaries.

Meserve, Walter J. *Robert E. Sherwood: Reluctant Moralist*. New York: Pegasus, 1970. In addition to examining Sherwood as a dramatist, Meserve considers the playwright's role as an adviser and speech writer for Franklin D. Roosevelt, as a prominent member of the Author's League, and as a founding partner in the Playwright's Company. The book offers a valuable, objective, detailed analysis of all Sherwood's plays, determining him to be more of a superior maker of plays than a dramatist of searching ideas. Supplemented by an informative, select bibliography and an index.

Shuman, R. Baird. *Robert E. Sherwood*. New York: Twayne, 1964. An accessible and comprehensive biographical and critical treatment of the playwright and his work. It contains a chronology, a detailed examination of Sherwood's plays within the context of his life and career, and an annotated listing of secondary sources.

Sievers, Wieder David. *Freud on Broadway*. New York: Hermitage House, 1955. In investigating Freudian influence on American dramatists' work, Sievers devotes a six-page essay to Sherwood's plays from *The Road to Rome* to *The Rugged Path*. He identifies Sherwood as a playwright whose psychoanalytical thinking was always distinctly original and distilled out of his own political and social ideas.

R. Baird Shuman
(Updated by *Christian H. Moe*)

JAMES SHIRLEY

Born: London, England; September 7, 1596 (baptized)
Died: London, England; October 29, 1666

Principal drama

The School of Compliment, pr. 1625, pb. 1631 (also known as *Love Tricks: Or, The School of Compliments*); *The Brothers*, pr. 1626, pb. 1652; *The Maid's Revenge*, pr. 1626, pb. 1639; *The Wedding*, pr. 1626(?), pb. 1629; *The Witty Fair One*, pr. 1628, pb. 1633; *The Grateful Servant*, pr. 1629, pb. 1630 (also known as *The Faithful Servant*); *The Traitor*, pr. 1631, pb. 1635; *Love's Cruelty*, pr. 1631, pb. 1640; *The Duke*, pr. 1631; *The Changes: Or, Love in a Maze*, pr. 1631, pb. 1632; *Hyde Park*, pr. 1632, pb. 1637; *The Ball*, pr. 1632, pb. 1639 (with George Chapman); *The Bird in a Cage*, pr. 1632, pb. 1633 (also known as *The Beauties*); *The Young Admiral*, pr. 1633, pb. 1637; *The Gamester*, pr. 1633, pb. 1637; *The Triumph of Peace*, pr., pb. 1634 (masque); *The Coronation*, pr. 1635, pb. 1640; *The Lady of Pleasure*, pr. 1635, pb. 1637; *Chabot, Admiral of France*, pr. 1635, pb. 1639 (with George Chapman); *The Duke's Mistress*, pr. 1636, pb. 1638; *The Constant Maid*, pr. 1636-1640(?), pb. 1640; *The Royal Master*, pr. 1637, pb. 1638; *The Doubtful Heir*, pr. c. 1638, pb. 1652 (also known as *Rosania: Or, Love's Victory*); *The Politician*, pr. 1639(?), pb. 1655; *The Gentleman of Venice*, pr. 1639, pb. 1655; *Patrick for Ireland*, pr. 1639(?), pb. 1640; *The Humorous Courtier*, pr., pb. 1640 (revision of *The Duke*); *The Imposture*, pr. 1640, pb. 1652; *The Cardinal*, pr. 1641, pb. 1652; *The Sisters*, pr. 1642, pb. 1652; *The Court Secret*, wr. 1642, pb. 1653, pr. after 1660; *The Contention of Ajax and Ulysses for the Armour of Achilles*, pr. c. 1645, pb. 1658 (masque); *Dramatic Works and Poems*, pb. 1833 (6 volumes).

Other literary forms

Both before and after his career as a dramatist, James Shirley was a schoolmaster; among the fruits of that vocation are several grammar texts. Of greater significance are his accomplishments as a Cavalier poet, one of the Sons of Ben who sometimes wrote witty verse—"a sort of [Thomas] Carew without Carew's genius," according to Douglas Bush—and whose 1646 collection of poems is in the tradition of the Ovidian poetry of the Elizabethans. In that volume is *Narcissus: Or, The Self-Lover*, which is patterned after William Shakespeare's *Venus and Adonis* (1593). Shirley's best-known poetic work and a frequent anthology piece is a later product: the "noble dirge" from the masque *The Contention of Ajax and Ulysses for the Armour of Achilles.* "The glories of our blood and state/ Are shadows not substantial things. . . ." Though the source of the masque probably is Ovid's *Metamorphoses* (c. A.D. 8), the dirge that Calchas speaks over the body of Ajax strikes an Augustan note. The poetry in Shirley's plays has been praised for its "lightness," "spontaneity of movement," and "richness of decoration," and its similarity to that of John Fletcher has been noted, but since Shirley is a transitional figure between the Elizabethan poetic playwrights and the more prosaic Restoration dramatists, there is little noteworthy verse in his plays, except for the tragicomedies.

Achievements

For the seventeen years between 1625 and 1642, Shirley, a prolific playwright in a variety of modes, dominated the Caroline stage. His more than thirty extant plays (several more are lost or of uncertain attribution) demonstrate his facility at creating comedies, tragedies, tragicomedies, and masques for the aristocratic and upper-class audiences of the private theaters. Flourishing as he did in the last years of the golden age of Renaissance drama, he wrote in the traditions of his predecessors: the revenge tragedy of Thomas Kyd and John Webster, the city comedy of Thomas Dekker and Philip Massinger, the humors comedy of Ben Jonson, and the tragicomedy of Francis Beaumont and John Fletcher. Whereas Shirley's tragedies are largely derivative and suggest the decadence common to the serious drama of the decade preceding Oliver Cromwell, the comedies not only recall the past but also look forward to the Restoration comedies of manners written by such men as Sir George Etherege, William Wycherley, and William Congreve, though Shirley is more moral. Among his tragedies, *The Cardinal* does not pale in comparison with Webster's *The Duchess of Malfi* (pr. 1613-1614) or *The White Devil* (pr. 1609-1612), and the comedies *Hyde Park* and *The Lady of Pleasure* still sparkle.

Shirley cannot be credited with any landmark innovations or lasting influence on the stage, but he produced a steady stream of popular plays in which he exploited the themes, devices, and character-types of others while creating dramas uniquely his own, and he was in large measure responsible for the continued vitality of the Renaissance drama into the 1640's. When Massinger died in 1640, Shirley became the principal playwright for the King's Men; only the closing of the theaters two years later ended his career as a dramatist. He had the satisfaction of seeing many of his works (tragedies as well as comedies) revived successfully in the 1660's (though sometimes adapted and presented as if by new playwrights), a distinction that few of his Renaissance predecessors or contemporaries shared. John Dryden's mocking scorn in *Mac Flecknoe* (1682) is undeserved.

Biography

James Shirley was born in London, probably on September 3, 1596, and baptized on September 7 in St. Mary Woolchurch. On October 4, 1608, he entered the Merchant Taylors' School, which offered the standard classical curriculum, and studied there until 1612. His activities in the next three years are uncertain, though he may have gone to St. John's College, Oxford, while also being apprenticed to a scrivener, Thomas Frith, in London.He was matriculated at St. Catherine's College, Cambridge, in 1615, received the bachelor of arts degree in 1617, and was ordained. Between 1617 and 1625, he worked for his master of arts at Cambridge; married Elizabeth Gilmet; accepted a curacy in Lincolnshire; published his first work, a narrative poem, *Eccho: Or, The Infortunate Lovers* (1618), which is believed to be the same poem as *Narcissus: Or, the Self-Lover*; had two daughters and a son; vacated his living to become headmaster of a St. Albans grammar school; and may have converted to Catholicism.

In 1624, Shirley went to London to become a playwright, and his play *The School of Compliment* was "The first fruits of a muse that before this/ Never saluted audience. . . ." A satiric comedy with a pastoral element that recalls Shakespeare's *As You Like It* (pr. c. 1599-1600), it was revived in the Restoration to Samuel Pepys's delight. During the next decade, Shirley averaged two plays per year, mainly produced for the Phoenix, and became a favorite of Queen Henrietta Maria. When the theaters were closed in 1636 because of the plague, Shirley went to Dublin, where he stayed until 1640, writing plays for John Ogilby's company at the Warburgh Street Theatre. This sojourn in Ireland may have cost him the post of poet laureate, which fell vacant upon Jonson's death in 1637 and was awarded the next year to William Davenant. Shirley returned to London in April, 1640, to succeed Philip Massinger as chief dramatist for the King's Men at Blackfriars, but when the Puritans closed the theaters in September, 1642, only three of his plays for the company had been produced; a fourth, *The Court Secret*, was not performed until the Restoration.

Shirley's career as a playwright ended with the Puritan rebellion, at the start of which he reportedly fled London with his patron William Cavendish, later Duke of Newcastle, "to join him in the wars." He came back to the city about 1645 and returned to teaching, mainly in the Whitefriars section of London, where he lived. Over the next twenty years he published poetry, masques, a collection of plays, and grammar texts. During the Great Fire of London in October, 1666, Shirley and his second wife, Frances, fled to St. Giles in the Fields, Middlesex, where they died on the same day, October 29, 1666.

Analysis

The pervasive anti-licentiousness present in his plays is a trait that links James Shirley to his Elizabethan predecessors more closely than to his Restoration successors. Whatever the genre—tragicomedy, comedy, or tragedy—virtue is either rewarded or, at least, honored; while sexual wrongdoing is not condoned, reformation is accepted. The plays are not, however, homiletic; they are entertainments in the mainstream of earlier Elizabethan practice. As such, careful development of plots and rapid pacing are primary, sometimes to the detriment of characterization. Compare, for example, the Duchess in *The Cardinal* with her counterpart in *The Duchess of Malfi*; the former is shallow, the latter more fully realized. Perhaps because character development is not a central concern in his plays, there are more stereotypes than individuals. This does not detract from the realism of the comedies, however, because the characters are recognizable types, and the action takes place in a realistically portrayed world, a London that Shirley's aristocratic audience would recognize. Not the London of Dekker or Jonson (city merchants and their apprentices are rarely seen in Shirley's comedies), it is closer to the Restoration London of Etherege, Wycherley, and Congreve.

In most of Shirley's plays there are echoes of earlier dramas; like his contemporaries and predecessors, he borrowed situations and devices with impunity. Nevertheless, Shirley was more original than most of his fellow playwrights, for though there are frequent similarities or parallels between his and earlier plays, one rarely can point to a direct source. Thus, while *The Cardinal* is in the same revenge-tragedy tradition of *The Duchess of Malfi* and certainly must have been written with Webster's play in mind, the earlier work is not its source; there is not even close borrowing. Similarly, although the Enoch Arden motif in *Hyde Park* has an analogue in Dekker's *The Shoemaker's Holiday: Or, The Gentle Craft* (pr. 1600), Dekker's play is not at all a source and, according to Norman Rabkin, "There are no known sources" for *Hyde Park*.

In almost all of his many and varied plays, Shirley utilizes the old conventions, but he infuses them with a new life. *The Cardinal* may reflect the decadence common to tragedies of the previous decades, but it offers interesting variations on a hackneyed theme. That Shirley's comedies have a distinctive artfulness is confirmed by the critical consensus that they herald the next age as much as they recall the past.

Shirley's most noteworthy plays are the comedies *Hyde Park* and *The Lady of Pleasure* and the tragedy *The Cardinal*; a fourth, *The Wedding*, is an early work that is of interest as a Fletcherian tragicomedy. *The Wedding* was a popular play, both on the Caroline stage and in the Restoration. Probably first done at the Phoenix on May 31, 1626, it was printed several times (the first in 1629 with a commendatory poem by John Ford) and was considered a valuable enough property to be included in a 1639 repertory list as a "protected" play. Though Shirley calls it a comedy, it fits Fletcher's description of tragicomedy: "In respect it wants deaths, which is enough to make it no tragedy, yet brings some near it, which is enough to make it no comedy. . . ." There are two plots, one serious and one comic, and as in so many early seventeenth century plays, the comic underplot functions fairly independently of the serious business.

The main plot involves the planned marriage of Gratiana, daughter of Sir John Belfare, to Beauford, her "passionate lover." Marwood, Beauford's friend, claims to have seduced Gratiana, which leads to a duel in which Marwood apparently is fatally injured. Beauford then confronts Gratiana, and though she proclaims her chastity and labels Marwood's charge false, Beauford renounces her, and they decide to end their lives. Meanwhile, Marwood, believing he is dying, affirms the truth of his charge, claiming that Cardona, a gentlewoman, had served as bawd. Beauford, having arrayed his quarters as for a funeral, receives news of Marwood's death ("His last breath did forgive you") and a warning that he "must expect/ No safety from the law." Cardona then is brought to Beauford and confesses that while Marwood did "viciously affect" Gratiana, "I knew her virtue was not/ To be corrupted in a thought." Therefore, she reveals, "I did, in hope to make myself a fortune/ And get a husband for my child . . . woo my daughter to/ Supply Gratiana's bed. . . ." Gratiana is brought to Beauford in a coffin, still very much alive, though she has "solicited" her death with prayers, and they renew their vows to each other. Belfare recovers from his temporary madness (brought on by his daughter's disappearance on the eve of her wedding), and Marwood reappears, alive after all and fully recovered. When Cardona tells him of the switch she engineered, he asks forgiveness ("I never had a conscience/ till now.") and agrees to marry Milliscent, the girl he unwittingly had seduced.

The subplot deals with the pursuit of Jane, Justice Lanby's daughter, by three suitors: Rawbone, "a thin citizen," and Lodam, "a fat gentlemen," both Jonsonian humor characters; and Haver, a poor young gentleman who disguises himself as Rawbone's servant in order to have freer access to Jane. The first of the men is a penurious usurer, but Lanby tests his daughter by pretending that he wants her to marry Rawbone. To Lodam—who brings no wealth to a bride, only his own ample self and an imperfect knowledge of foreign languages—Lanby says: "I must refer you, sir, unto my daughter. If you can win her fair opinion, my consent may happily follow." Jane, however, is in love with Haver, who provokes a duel between Lodam and Rawbone and then takes Rawbone's place (in disguise) in the combat. When the men meet at Finsbury to duel, the result is a broadly comic scene. In its aftermath, the benevolent Lanby pretends to force an immediate marriage between Jane and Rawbone, knowing full well that the apparent Rawbone is Haver in disguise. Jane goes along with the gambit, though believing that her father is cozening her. Lodam's consolation for his lost quest is a dinner; Rawbone gets to deliver the epilogue of the play.

In that epilogue, Rawbone asks the audience "to wake a fool dormant amongst ye. I ha' been kicked, and kicked to that purpose. Maybe they knocked at the wrong door—my brains are asleep in the garret . . . you must clap me . . . I shall hardly come to myself else." Shirley thus draws the attention of the audience to a prevailing theme of the play: people coming to their senses, realizing the truth about themselves, and perhaps even reforming. Hence, the moral ambivalence that is present through most of the play (a trait common to tragicomedy) is confronted in the resolution, when Shirley has his characters face the consequences of their actions. Exclaims Marwood: "Into how many sins hath lust engag'd me!/ Is there a hope you can forgive, and you,/ And she whom I have most dishonour'd?/ I never had a conscience till now. . . ."

The Wedding concludes with a typical assembly and reconciliation scene. The plots are linked not only by this scene but also by their common focus upon marriage and the subplot's function as a comic contrast to the serious (and potentially tragic) love story of the main plot; the presence of duels in both plots highlights this difference. The device of rival suitors recalls earlier plays, such as Shakespeare's *The Taming of the Shrew* (pr. c. 1593-1594), which also features disguise, while the slapstick duel recalls Shakespeare's *Twelfth Night* (pr. c. 1600-1602) and anticipates Richard Brinsley Sheridan's *The Rivals* (pr. 1775). Belfare's madness harks back to the revenge tragedy of Thomas Kyd, and the bed trick was used earlier in Shakespeare's *Measure for Measure* (pr. 1604), Thomas Middleton and William Rowley's *The Changeling* (pr. 1622), and other Elizabethan plays. In sum, the play is highly derivative, with Shirley utilizing familiar devices, situations, and character-types; the combination, however, does work, and the play apparently evoked from audiences the contradictory mix of responses typical of tragicomedy. Because of its genre, it lacks the realistic sophistication of Shirley's later comedy of manners, but considered for what it is—an early work in the Fletcher mode—*The Wedding* certainly succeeds.

A better play, *Hyde Park* was licensed on April 20, 1632, and probably was first performed at the Phoenix Theatre on or about that date, to coincide with the seasonal opening of Hyde Park, which King James I had made into a public facility under Sir Henry Rich, Earl of Holland. It is an urbane comedy of manners that develops a realistic portrait of Cavalier London at the height of the Caroline period. Popular when it premiered, *Hyde Park* was revived in the Restoration, on which occasion actual horses were brought onstage for the racing scenes.

The action of the play, which occurs on a single day, consists of three plots, each of which, a critic has noted, is "constructed about a love triangle involving a woman and two male rivals." Further, "each plot turns on a surprising change in the woman's position within the triangle," and each is developed as a different kind of comedy: "high comedy appealing to the intellect, sentimental comedy appealing to ethical sensibilities, and simple situation comedy."

On the seventh anniversary of the disappearance at sea of Bonavent, a merchant, his widow finally is ready to remarry, and Lacy is an anxious suitor. Advising against the marriage is the widow's kinswoman, Mistress Carol ("We maids are thought the worse on, for your easiness"), "a malicious piece," according to Lacy, who also says," 'tis pity any place/ But a cold nunnery should be troubled with her." Carol is herself involved in a battle of the sexes with Fairfield, whom she persuades not to make any amorous overtures ("I had rather hear the tedious tales/ Of Holinshed than any thing that trenches/ On love"), and he goes home to "think a satire." She does, however, trifle with two of her servants, she says, "when I have nothing else to do for sport." The supposedly dead Bonavent returns in disguise at the start of the second act, learns of his wife's remarriage that day, and meets Lacy, who invites him to join the wedding celebrations. The third story line concerns Fairfield's sister Julietta; Trier, who is her suitor; and Lord Bonvile, who intrudes upon Trier's turf.

The third and fourth acts are set in Hyde Park and afford an opportunity for Shirley to depict the leisure class at play. Lord Bonvile advances his pursuit of Julietta as Trier hovers, Fairfield bids what he thinks is his final farewell to Carol, and the impending races (among men and horses) become a metaphor for all the competing lovers in the play. As the action progresses, Carol loses a second round to Fairfield, tricked by him and her servant into revealing her true feelings ("O love, I am thy captive . . ."), though still attempting to maintain some distance while Fairfield has the upper hand. The fourth act ends with Bonavent making his first move toward discarding his disguise and revealing himself to his wife.

At the start of the last act, Carol tells Julietta of her fears for Fairfield's well-being as a result of a letter from him. When the presumably distraught suitor is found, Carol proposes to him—not for love, she avers, but because she is merciful and desires to save his life. He denies authorship of the plaintive piece (which was written by one of Carol's servants) and tells her: "To save thy life, I'll not be troubled with thee." She pleads, "I know you love me still; do not refuse me," and he relents: "Each other's now by conquest, come let's to 'em." In the concluding assembly scene, Julietta rejects Trier and accepts Lord Bonvile, and Bonavent removes his disguise and reclaims his wife. In each of the pairings, therefore, a dark horse eventually triumphs, and the losers good-naturedly accept their unexpected misfortune.

Hyde Park is a successful play whose portrait of London life reminds one commentator of "the genre-painting of Dekker . . . as in *The Shoemaker's Holiday* and [Middleton and Dekker's] *The Roaring Girl*, the portrayal of London as subject to itself as audience is much of the play's *raison d'être*." The play is also Elizabethan in other respects, too: clever servants, letters that advance the plots, disguise, and multiple plots. The romance between Carol and Fairfield recalls Beatrice and Benedick of Shakespeare's *Much*

Ado About Nothing (pr. c. 1598-1599), and Carol is a descendant of Beaumont and Fletcher's scornful lady character. Shirley also anticipates his Restoration successors, for *Hyde Park* is a comedy of manners—though one in which pre-Restoration standards of sexual propriety are observed—and Carol and Fairfield also look ahead to Millamant and Mirabell of Congreve's *The Way of the World* (pr. 1700); their verbal sparring parallels the proviso scene and marital conditions agreement that are central to that play and other Restoration comedies.

Hyde Park, then, is a typical Shirley city comedy, as lively and as realistic as those of Middleton or Dekker, but concerned with a very different London, that of the upper classes and their pastimes. What problems they have revolve about romantic entanglements and intrigues of the love chase and little else, but all of this Shirley handles with dexterity and in conformity with his moral precepts. The thematic core of the play is Lord Bonvile's attempted seduction of Julietta, to which she reacts with a lengthy and eloquent paean to chastity (". . . unless you prove/ A friend to virtue, were your honor centupled,/ Could you pile titles till you reach the clouds,/ Were every petty manor you possess/ A kingdom, and the blood of many princes/ United in your veins . . ./ Yet I . . . am/ As much above you in my innocence."); he is moved to immediate repentance ("If this be true, what a wretched thing should I/ Appear now, if I were anything but a lord?/ I do not like myself.—") and asks for her hand: ". . . since there's no remedy,/ Be honest!" Lord Bonvile's conversion from libertinism not only distinguishes him from the ubiquitous rake of the Restoration but also highlights the primary difference between this play and its successors in the next age.

The Lady of Pleasure also is a comedy of manners, and in it Shirley develops variations on the theme of honor; it may even be a commentary upon a Platonic love cult in the Caroline court. Licensed in 1635 and performed at the Phoenix Theatre, the satiric play was not as popular in the seventeenth century as other Shirley works, but later playwrights did adapt characters, plot elements, and bits of dialogue from it for their use. Most notable, perhaps, is Sheridan's indebtedness in *The School for Scandal* (pr. 1777); Sheridan's Sir Peter and Lady Teazle are obvious descendants of Shirley's Sir Thomas Bornwell and his wife Aretina, and the conceit of the scandal school also owes something to Shirley.

The play begins with Sir Thomas, a country gentleman, and his wife newly arrived in London so that she can enjoy the city's pleasures, including gambling and partying and wasting their wealth on paintings, furniture, and clothing. The profligate Aretina quickly develops a salon, which includes a bawd named Madam Decoy, and a pair of gallants, Alexander Kickshaw and John Littleworth. The men are interested in Celestina, Lady Bellamour, a young widow whose year of mourning has passed. Aretina sees Celestina as a potential rival, and Bornwell comments: "Now my

Lady/ Is troubled, as she feared to be eclipsed/ This news will cost me somewhat." He decides, therefore, to pretend to renounce thrift and embrace her life-style, hoping that when she sees an image of herself, she will be frightened into reformation. Meanwhile, Celestina's steward cautions her about living beyond her means, but she resolves "to pay some delight; my estate will bear it." The parallel patterns of the two plots are obvious from the start of the play: Celestina, too, has a gentleman caller and looks forward to lady visitors, whom she will instruct in the social graces.

When Aretine's nephew Frederick arrives from the university in his scholar's black satin uniform, she is appalled: "What luck [misfortune] I did not send him into France!" She commends him to Kickshaw's breeding, Littleworth offers to teach Frederick "postures and rudiments," and Aretina's steward opens the wine cellar to him. The second act ends with Bornwell visiting the young widow Celestina to become acquainted and to invite her to his home; the third act begins at the home of a nobleman who is distantly related to Aretina. Mourning for fair Bella Maria, he rejects Madam Decoy's services as bawd to effect a liaison with Aretina; rather, he warns Aretina of the designs that Decoy has upon her honor. When she receives his warning, Aretina decides to use the bawd's services to enter instead into a secret liaison with Kickshaw. She also employs Kickshaw and Littleworth to embarrass Celestina, but the younger woman holds her own against the onslaught, and Bornwell comes to her aid when he realizes that she is being victimized. The act ends with Kickshaw receiving a summons to a tryst with a secret admirer.

In the farcical first scene of the fourth act, Decoy—disguised as a hag—entices Kickshaw to her bedroom, where Aretina awaits him under cover of darkness. The largely satiric second scene focuses initially upon young Frederick's transformation into a fop; then, when Aretina and Bornwell are alone, Bornwell attempts to make his wife jealous by confessing his love for Celestina: "I must/ Acknowledge twas thy cure to disenchant me/ From a dull husband to an active lover." Instead of being offended, Aretina replies: "I must acknowledge Celestina/ Most excellently fair, fair above all/ The beauties I ha' seen. . . ." Further, "she is a piece so angelically moving, I should think/ Frailty excused to dote upon her form,/ And almost virtue to be wicked with her." Bornwell is confused. In the final scene of the act, a seriocomic one, Aretina's distant kinsman visits Celestina, who tests him ("I am man enough, but knew not where,/ Until this meeting, beauty dwelt"), but when he is tempted to make advances, she reminds the nobleman of his honorable reputation and his devotion to the late Bella Maria. Virtue will be rewarded.

The fifth act, though a single scene, also falls into three sections, the first of which has Aretina becoming aware of her husband's large gaming losses and learning that he has "summed up" his estate "and find we may have/ A month good yet." As for their prospects beyond the month, he proposes to become a soldier and suggests that she could "find a trade to live by." As Aretina starts to assess her uncertain future, Decoy, Kickshaw, and Frederick arrive. The boastful talkativeness of Kickshaw and her drunken nephew's romantic overtures ("My blood is rampant too, I must court some body,/ As good my Aunt as any other body") shock her, and she is ready for conversion. Momentarily left alone, she looks in a mirror: " 'Tis a false glass; sure I am more deformed./ What have I done? My soul is miserable." The lord who earlier warned his kinswoman Aretina about Decoy comes in, followed by Bornwell and Celestina. While Bornwell consoles his repentant wife, the lord and young widow form "an honorable alliance." The Bornwells will return to the country with "wealth enough,/ If yet we use it nobly," Frederick will return to college, and Kickshaw is implored to "purge . . . foul blood by repentance."

While *The Lady of Pleasure* foreshadows Restoration comedy of manners in subject matter, plot, character-types, and witty dialogue, its focus upon honor and the movement from folly and libertinism to repentance and reformation distinguish it from the later plays, for ultimately it celebrates moderation, honor, and innocence. In addition, Shirley makes it clear, as a critic has noted, that "the highest classes share with the lowest responsibility for conducting themselves in a manner that becomes their station in life."

Notable, too, as a pre-Restoration quality is the unemotional tone of the play, for superficial flirtation rather than romantic involvement is what Shirley largely portrays, and Celestina, wise beyond her sixteen years, delivers the keynote, assuring Mariana and Isabella that "men shall never/ Make my heart lean with sighing, nor with tears/ Draw on my eyes the infamy of spectacles," and then advising them: " 'Tis the chief principle to keep your heart/ Under your own obedience; jest, but love not." Finally, there is a shallowness to the upper-class life-style depicted in *The Lady of Pleasure*, still another trait that it shares with the post-1660 comedies of manners.

Licensed in 1641, *The Cardinal* is one of four extant tragedies by Shirley and his first tragedy for the King's Men at Blackfriars. Both in his dedication (in which he calls it "the best of my flock") and in his prologue ("this play/ Might rival with his best"), Shirley indicates his own high regard for the play. Many critics agree with him, rating it among the best tragedies of the period, but some point to Shirley's indebtedness to Kyd, Webster, and other predecessors in the revenge tragedy tradition, and one labels the play a "shallow imitation." Derivative though it may be, *The Cardinal* is powerful theater and was a popular stage vehicle both before the closing of the theaters and during the Restoration period; coming as it does at the end of a half century of revenge tragedy that began with Kyd's *The Spanish Trag-*

edy (pr. c. 1585-1589), one is surprised at how much originality and vitality it possesses.

The Duchess Rosaura of Navarre, widowed before her youthful marriage was consummated, is betrothed to Don Columbo, a grim-faced and rough-hewn soldier who is nephew to the cardinal, the power behind the throne; her true love is Count d'Alvarez, a young man who is said to be perfectly suited to her (says a lord: "Hymen cannot tie/ A knot of two more equal hearts and blood"), but she has wisely deferred to the king's wishes and "given this treasure up." When war with Aragon begins, the arranged marriage is postponed because Columbo is chosen to lead Navarre's forces. Learning of the unexpected turn of events, the duchess is joyous ("I have not skill to contain myself"), but in the presence of the king, the cardinal, and Columbo himself, she dissembles and maintains the proper façade. When Alvarez comes in, however, she prods him to respect their "mutual vows," but he is unwilling to risk the others' displeasure unless Columbo is killed in battle or renounces his claim.

The action of the second act begins on the battlefield; Columbo is impatient to storm the enemy, but Hernando advises restraint. The disagreement leads Hernando to resign his commission, and he returns to Navarre with a letter giving Columbo's decision to attack. Complementing this action is the arrival of a letter for Columbo from the duchess in which she asks him to resign his "interest to her person, promise, or love." He decides that she is testing him ("'Tis a device to hasten my return;/ Love has a thousand arts") and sends the desired release. The duchess gives Columbo's reply to the king and obtains his permission to wed Alvarez. The cardinal is angry at the unexpected turn of events. He calls Alvarez effeminate and counsels the duchess to leave him, but she is defiant, and the act closes with the cardinal vowing that "action and revenge/ Must calm her fury."

Preparations for the marriage are under way when news arrives of Columbo's triumph and imminent return. The cardinal's passion rises: "He has not won so much upon the Aragon/ As he has lost at home; and his neglect/ Of what my studies had contrived to add/ More lustre to our family by the access/ Of the great duchess' fortune, cools his triumph,/ And makes me wild." Masquers who have prepared a wedding entertainment are asked to delay their presentation so "a company of cavaliers in gallant equipage, newly alighted" can present their revels. At the start, they beckon to the bridegroom, and Alvarez accompanies them. A moment later they return with his body, and Columbo removes his disguise and admits to having committed the murder. The duchess calls for justice, but the king wavers and seeks a way out, for Columbo is a military hero and the Cardinal's nephew. Ultimately, though, he decides that not the murder but a breach of decorum deserves punishment: "This contempt/ Of majesty transcends my power to pardon,/ And you shall feel my anger, sir."

Columbo soon is freed, and while not formally pardoned, he is "graced now more than ever" and "courted as preserver of his country." His rehabilitation is attributed to the cardinal's influence, and there is speculation that a match between him and the duchess again may be in prospect. When Columbo visits her, he warns her not to remarry: "I'll kill the next at th' altar and quench all/ The smiling tapers with his blood. . . ." Hernando then comes to her, expresses his devotion to her and Alvarez, and promises to exact vengeance upon Columbo and the cardinal. The cardinal then approaches the duchess in a conciliatory manner, but she sees through the deceitful ploys of "this cozening statesman" and remains determined that "this Cardinal must not be long-lived." Toward this end, she will feign madness. The act concludes with a duel between Hernando and Columbo in which the latter is killed.

The death grieves the king and cardinal, and Hernando's disappearance causes suspicion to fall on him. Hernando returns in disguise, renews his pledge to the duchess, and hides in her room when the cardinal (who has been made guardian of the apparently mad duchess) comes for dinner. Though the cleric is troubled that "her loss of brain" means she "is now beneath [his] great revenge" and "is not capable to feel [his] anger," he nevertheless intends to rape and poison her and make it seem as if she committed suicide. Once he embraces and kisses her, however, he feels "a strong enchantment from her lips" and he fears that he "shall forgive Columbo's death" if she yields to him. In the event, she denies his overtures, he forces her, and Hernando rushes from behind the arras, stabs the cardinal, and kills himself. To the king and others, the cardinal (who believes his wounds are fatal) says he has poisoned the duchess, but as proof of his repentance he offers an antidote "to preserve her innocent life." Both drink it, after which he reveals that it really was a deadly poison, and both he and the duchess die. The cardinal, however, has been caught in his "own engine," for the surgeon tells him before his death, "Your wounds, sir, were not desperate."

The Spanish Tragedy, *Hamlet*, *The Duchess of Malfi*, John Ford's *The Broken Heart* (pr. c. 1627-1631), and Cyril Tourneur's *The Atheist's Tragedy* (pr. c. 1607) are the most obvious antecedents of *The Cardinal*, and the links between it and its predecessors are immediately apparent: murder of a rival by a jealous lover; support for the murderer by a Machiavellian villain anxious for advancement or wealth; madness (real or feigned) as a result of grief; a play-within-a-play; revenge as an obsessive motive.

Though Fredson Bowers' judgment that *The Cardinal* is "clear-cut, coherent Kydian revenge tragedy" is valid, Shirley departs significantly from past practice in his mystifying prologue. In these lighthearted, even flippant, twenty-six lines of heroic couplets, the playwright teases his audience, refusing to reveal whether *The Cardinal* is a comedy or a tragedy and even suggesting by his style and tone that it is the former: "Whether the comic Muse, or ladies' love,/ Romance, or direful tragedy it prove,/ The bill determines not; and would you be/ Persuaded, I would have 't a Comedy." Self-mockery and a satiric reference to classical dramatic theory increase the mysteriousness of the prologue, and their presence may reflect Shirley's sensitivity at offering an old-fashioned revenge tragedy to his new Blackfriars constituency.

Variations on the color red and frequent allusions to blood pervade *The Cardinal* and create an imagistic texture that complements the horror of the events. The nobility of the duchess, Alvarez, and Hernando contrasts sharply with the depravity of the cardinal and Columbo, and the equivocal morality of the king and Celinda (a court lady) completes the social picture. Shirley falters a bit, however, in his delineation of the character of his heroine, for the duchess makes a fundamental error when she misjudges the true nature of Columbo, and her unnecessary avowal to Hernando further diminishes her. Finally, she mistakenly considers the cardinal responsible for the murder of Alvarez. In other words, Duchess Rosaura, memorable though she is, is no Duchess of Malfi, nor has Shirley given her dramatics moments that match Webster's mad scenes.

It is ironic that at the close of his career as a playwright, James Shirley's most memorable work should be one that recalls past stage practice, since so many of his earlier plays anticipate those of the next age. The success of *The Cardinal* notwithstanding, Shirley was at his best as a comic playwright, and within the parameters that he set for himself, he wrote creditable comedies of manners that struck a responsive chord not only among his Caroline audience but also on the Restoration stage in the 1660's.

Other major works

POETRY: *Poems &c. by James Shirley*, 1646 (includes *Narcissus: Or, The Self-Lover*).

NONFICTION: *Via ad Latinam Linguam Complanata: The Way Made Plain to the Latin Tongues*, 1649 (also as *Grammatica anglo-latina*, 1651); *The Rudiments of Grammar*, 1656 (enlarged as *Manductio*, 1660); *An Essay Towards an Universal and Rational Grammar*, 1726 (compiled and edited by Jenkin Thomas Philipps from Shirley's writings on grammar).

Bibliography

Bowers, Fredson. *Elizabethan Revenge Tragedy, 1587-1642.* Princeton, N.J.: Princeton University Press, 1940. Still an important source on the subject, Bowers' study traces the dramatic currents and the literary and ethical influences that affected dramatists who wrote revenge tragedies. Shirley's tragedies are examined in chapter 7, "The Decadence of Revenge." Bowers considers Shirley the best of the last of the Elizabethans writing revenge plays.

Forsythe, Robert Stanley. *The Relations of Shirley's Plays to the Elizabethan Drama.* 1914. Reprint. New York: Benjamin Blom, 1965. An early, but important, historical approach to Renaissance drama, Forsythe's work is a thorough study of the influences of conventional elements in Elizabethan dramatic literature on Shirley's plays. Includes a lengthy but outdated bibliography containing biographical, critical, and nondramatic illustrative material.

Lucow, Ben. *James Shirley.* New York: Twayne, 1981. Opening chapters on the dramatist's biography, masques, and nondramatic verse are followed by a chronological discussion of the plays. An excellent introduction to Shirley's drama combines plot summaries with pertinent background material and critical analyses. Contains a chronology of the author's life and a select bibliography of primary and secondary sources.

Nason, Arthur Huntington. *James Shirley Dramatist: A Biographical and Critical Study.* 1915. Reprint. New York: Benjamin Blom, 1967. Nason's book, the first thorough biographical, critical study of Shirley, establishes a chronology of the playwright's life, plots the course of his development as a dramatist, and assesses the distinctive characteristics of his dramatic works. Nason concludes with a list of Shirley's works and an annotated bibliography of critical sources.

Wertheim, Albert. "James Shirley." In *The Later Jacobean and Caroline Dramatists: A Survey and Bibliography of Recent Studies in English Renaissance Drama*, edited by Terence P. Logan and Denzell S. Smith. Lincoln: University of Nebraska Press, 1978. This bibliographical essay identifies essential biographical and critical studies of Shirley. Wertheim expresses surprise that so little has been written about the dramatist: "Shirley wrote more plays in more different genres than any other single playwright of his time. The large number of plays means that there is an excellent opportunity for studying Shirley in considerable detail—and not only Shirley, but also the nature of the Caroline stage and the tastes of its audience. As yet none of these possibilities has been explored."

Zimmer, Ruth K. *James Shirley: A Reference Guide.* Boston: G. K. Hall, 1980. Zimmer annotates works by and about Shirley published through 1978. The secondary sources include bibliographies, books and articles, commentaries on Shirley within larger works, theses and dissertations, and poems in praise of the dramatist. Also includes a brief sketch of Shirley's life, a chronology of his extant works, and an overview of his dramatic career.

Gerald H. Strauss
(Updated by *Ayne Cantrell*)

NEIL SIMON

Born: Bronx, New York; July 4, 1927

Principal drama

Come Blow Your Horn, pr. 1960, pb. 1961; *Little Me*, pr. 1962, pr. 1982 (revised version), pb. 1981 (music by Cy Coleman, lyrics by Carol Leigh; based on the novel by Patrick Dennis); *Barefoot in the Park*, pr. 1963, pb. 1964; *The Odd Couple*, pr. 1965, pb. 1966; *Sweet Charity*, pr., pb. 1966 (music and lyrics by Coleman and Dorothy Fields; based on Federico Fellini's film *Nights of Cabiria*); *The Star-Spangled Girl*, pr. 1966, pb. 1967; *Plaza Suite*, pr. 1968, pb. 1969; *Promises, Promises*, pr. 1968, pb. 1969 (music and lyrics by Hal David and Burt Bacharach; based on the film *The Apartment* by Billy Wilder and I. A. L. Diamond); *Last of the Red Hot Lovers*, pr. 1969, pb. 1970; *The Gingerbread Lady*, pr. 1970, pb. 1971; *The Comedy of Neil Simon*, pb. 1971 (volume 1 in *The Collected Plays of Neil Simon*); *The Prisoner of Second Avenue*, pr., pb. 1971; *The Sunshine Boys*, pr. 1972, pb. 1973; *The Good Doctor*, pr. 1973, pb. 1974 (adapted from stories by Anton Chekhov); *God's Favorite*, pr. 1974, pb. 1975 (based on the story of Job); *California Suite*, pr. 1976, pb. 1977; *Chapter Two*, pr. 1977, pb. 1979; *They're Playing Our Song*, pr. 1978, pb. 1980 (music by Marvin Hamlisch, lyrics by Carole Bayer Sager; based on Patrick Dennis' novel); *The Collected Plays of Neil Simon*, pb. 1979 (volume 2); *I Ought to Be in Pictures*, pr. 1980, pb. 1981; *Fools*, pr., pb. 1981; *Brighton Beach Memoirs*, pr. 1982, pb. 1984; *Biloxi Blues*, pr. 1984, pb. 1986; *Broadway Bound*, pr. 1986, pb. 1987; *The Odd Couple*, pr., pb. 1986 (female version); *Rumors*, pr. 1988, pb. 1990; *Jake's Women*, pr. 1990, pb. 1991; *Lost in Yonkers*, pr., pb. 1991; *The Collected Plays of Neil Simon*, pb. 1991 (volume 3).

Other literary forms

In addition to his plays, Neil Simon has written numerous scripts for motion pictures. Among these are *After the Fox* (1966, with Cesare Zavattini), *The Out-of-Towners* (1970), *The Heartbreak Kid* (1972), *Murder by Death* (1976), *The Goodbye Girl* (1977), *The Cheap Detective* (1978), *Seems Like Old Times* (1980), *Max Dugan Returns* (1983), *The Lonely Guy* (1984), and *The Slugger's Wife* (1985). He has also adapted dozens of his plays to the screen, from *Barefoot in the Park* (1967) to *I Ought to Be in Pictures* (1982) and *Biloxi Blues* (1988). Along with his brother, Simon wrote during the 1940's and 1950's for a variety of television shows, including the *Phil Silvers Show* (1948), the *Tallulah Bankhead Show* (1951), the *Sid Caesar Show* (1956-1957), and the *Garry Moore Show* (1959-1960). His teleplay *Broadway Bound* was produced in 1992.

Achievements

Simon has established himself as a leading American playwright of the late twentieth century. As a master of domestic comedy and one-line humor, his popular appeal was established early in his career. Though considered by some to be lighter or less serious because of his comedic talents, as his career progressed, Simon infused his comedy with greater amounts of social relevance, autobiographical inspiration, and dramatic depth. Many of his plays explore the thin line that separates comedy from pathos, provoking audiences to laugh through their tears. His plays focus on character and personal relationships in primarily middle-class, urban settings in the United States. Nevertheless, the stories he dramatizes are about basic human problems and aspirations, and his plays have proven to have universal appeal.

Simon has been the recipient of numerous awards and honors. They include two Emmy Awards for his work in television in 1957 and 1959; a Tony Award for Best Author for *The Odd Couple* in 1965, and another for *Biloxi Blues* in 1985; a New York Drama Critics Circle Award in 1983 for *Brighton Beach Memoirs*; A New York State Governor's Award in 1986; and a Pulitzer Prize in Drama and a Tony Award for Best Play for *Lost in Yonkers*, both in 1991.

Biography

Marvin Neil Simon was born in the Bronx, New York, on July 4, 1927. His father, Irving, was a salesman in Manhattan's garment district; his mother, Mamie, worked at Gimbel's department store. The family moved to Washington Heights in northern Manhattan when Simon was young. The family's life was not always tranquil. Irving was an errant husband who occasionally abandoned the family altogether, leaving Mamie, a frustrated and bitter woman, alone to deal with Neil and his older brother Danny. Eventually, the parents were divorced, and Neil went to live with relatives in Queens. From an early age, he exhibited a quick wit and an active imagination. He earned the nickname "Doc"—which stayed with him into adult life—because of his penchant for imitating the family doctor. He loved films and sometimes was asked to leave the theater for laughing too loud. In high school, Simon was sometimes ostracized as a Jew, an experience that would later inform his work. That changed, however, when he joined the baseball team and became a star center fielder. Meanwhile, he and his brother began collaborating on comedy material that they sold to stand-up comics and radio announcers. Simon was graduated from DeWitt Clinton High School in 1944 at the age of sixteen.

He entered New York University under the U.S. Army Air Force Reserve program and was sent to basic training in Biloxi, Mississippi, and then to Lowry Field, Colorado. Throughout his military career, he continued to hone his writing skills, reading favorite authors such as Mark Twain and Robert Benchley and writing for military newspapers. Discharged in 1946, Simon took a job in the mail room at Warner Brothers in New York, where Danny worked in the publicity department. The brothers were soon hired to write for Goodman Ace of the Columbia Broadcasting System (CBS), and over the next decade they provided material for such television comedians as Tallulah Bankhead, Jackie Gleason, Carl Reiner, and Red Skelton. During the summers of 1952 and 1953, they wrote sketches for the professional acting company at Camp Tamiment in Pennsylvania, some of which were featured on Broadway several years later. At Camp Tamiment, Simon fell in love with a young actress named Joan Baim, and the couple was married on September 30, 1953. Five years later, Joan gave birth to a daughter, Ellen; a second daughter, Nancy, was born in 1963.

In 1956, Danny Simon moved to California to be a television director. Neil stayed in New York and wrote for Phil Silvers' *Sergeant Bilko*, Sid Caesar's *Your Show of Shows*, and the *Garry Moore Show*. He also adapted Broadway plays for television, including Lorenz Hart's and Richard Rodgers' musical *Dearest Enemy* (pr. 1925). By the later 1950's, however, he wanted more independence than television writing could offer. He began writing a play of his own. For three years, he wrote and revised, as many as fifty times, his first full play. *Come Blow Your Horn* was optioned by twenty-five producers before it was finally staged in 1960 at the Bucks County Playhouse in New Hope, Pennsylvania. A greatly improved version opened on Broadway the following February. The play received positive notice, and, in 1962, Simon's book for the musical *Little Me* reinforced his growing reputation. It was his third full script, however, *Barefoot in the Park*, that firmly established him on the American stage. It ran for four years, with a total of 1,532 performances. In 1965, Simon had a second smash hit with *The Odd Couple*, which ran for two years and earned for him his first Tony Award.

Over the next decade, Simon's work was characteristically prodigious, with a new play appearing every year or two. While the plays were not all unqualified successes, Simon's popularity continued to rise. At the same time, he accrued a list of screenplay credits. Many were adaptations of his own plays; others were original screenplays or adaptations of other people's works. These films helped spread his notoriety beyond primarily urban, middle-class theater audiences to a wider range of viewers. Despite his popular success, however, Simon was still regarded by serious critics as a lightweight scenarist writing for laughs.

In 1972, Simon faced a harrowing personal tragedy. His wife, Joan, was diagnosed with cancer. Simon nursed her through fifteen agonizing months until she succumbed to the disease in 1973. After twenty years of happy marriage, the loss affected him deeply. Later that year, Simon met an actress named Marsha Mason. The two had a whirlwind romance and within weeks were husband and wife. While never rediscovering the deep passion he had known with Joan, Simon enjoyed a good marriage with Mason that lasted nine years.

In 1974, Simon received a special Tony Award for his contributions to the American theater. His plays continued to appear regularly, and on the screen he scored with such films as *The Goodbye Girl* and *The Cheap Detective.* In 1983, he received a singular honor: The Nederlander Organization renamed a Broadway theater after him.

In the mid-1980's, the trilogy composed of *Brighton Beach Memoirs*, *Biloxi Blues*, and *Broadway Bound* showed a more serious, mature, and openly autobiographical Simon. The three plays garnered many awards, including a Tony Award for *Biloxi Blues* as Best Play of 1985. More important, critics began to take Simon seriously as a respectable dramatist.

His third marriage came in 1987, to Diane Lander, a former actress and model. Though divorced in 1988, the couple remarried in 1990, and Simon adopted Lander's daughter Bryn.

By the 1990's, through four decades of diligent writing, Simon had developed great skill and technique. He divided his time between homes in Manhattan and Bel Air, California, and wrote methodically for seven hours every day. Behind each play that reached fruition, Simon had another ten beginnings that had been put aside, and many more ideas not yet even committed to paper. Nevertheless, with the prodigious output already behind him, he has claimed his position in the history of American theater.

Analysis

Neil Simon's plays have so set the standard for American domestic comedy that they almost form a subgenre in themselves. His work is certainly marked by a distinct style and mastery of certain principles of comic writing. Though the mood, subject matter, and focus of his writing has developed over the years, the Neil Simon signature can still be read throughout.

His plays tend to be domestic comedies focusing on family life and relationships. Almost all are set in New York City and, explicitly or not, depict the concerns and values of middle-class, Jewish family life, writers and show-business people, and Americans in touch with the liberal movements of the 1960's and 1970's. As a keen observer of contemporary life, Simon fills his plays with recognizable topical references and details. Dealing with such themes as marriage, divorce, sexual liberation, and intergenerational conflict, his work effectively chronicles late twentieth century American life-styles and values.

Coming as Simon did from a training ground in stand-up comedy and television writing, he is technically expert at coining and structuring one-line jokes. One-liners are not restricted to token "comic" characters;

rather, they are distributed among all the characters in his plays. Furthermore, Simon is skilled at connecting the jokes and embedding them in the texture of the conflict in a way that reinforces the integrity of a scene. The jokes serve rather than divert the flow of action; they inform characterization rather than reduce characters to mere mouthpieces for the author's wit. Simon supports his quick humor with characters who are clearly delineated, defined not only by their backgrounds, tastes, idiosyncrasies, and language but also by their larger objectives and outlooks on life. They are drawn with eccentricity and excess, but with sympathy and warmth as well. The tendency toward stereotypes and caricatures that Simon sometimes indulged early in his career gradually disappeared as he honed his craft.

Creating rich characters, Simon serves them well by carefully structuring his plays to maximize the potential for both conflict and humor. Knowing that the line between tragedy and comedy is a thin one, he heightens the stakes of his characters' desires. Indeed, many a Simon play, drained of its wit, could easily be transformed into serious high drama, with situations worthy of Henrik Ibsen or August Strindberg. The people of Simon's plays are frustrated, sometimes nearly neurotic; they take their problems head-on and search earnestly for solutions. Like William Shakespeare, Simon lets the meaning of his plays inhabit the surface, so there is rarely a deep subtext to unearth. As his characters are generally intelligent and perceptive, they police one another against emotional subterfuge. Unlike Shakespeare, however, Simon does not utilize subplots but rather provides a single, clear conflict to propel the action.

This technique is certainly true of his first two major successes, *Barefoot in the Park* and *The Odd Couple*. Both plays are simply constructed, consisting of four scenes in three acts, taking place in a single locale within a span of several weeks, and built upon the conflict between two distinctly defined characters.

Barefoot in the Park is about newlyweds Paul and Corie Bratter. The young lawyer and his wife are moving into their first New York apartment, a living space too small, cold, dilapidated, expensive, and high up to induce peaceful living. In the first scene, they take inventory of their new home, amid visits from Corie's well-intentioned mother from New Jersey and a flamboyant older gentleman from the upstairs apartment. Corie hatches a plan to make a match between Mother and the exotic Mr. Velasco.

The second scene is the dinner gathering, pitting Mother's tender stomach against Velasco's gourmet hors d'oeuvres, Corie's enthusiasm against Paul's reluctance, and the foursome against a cold apartment and a catastrophic kitchen. In the third scene, the group returns from a dinner out, Mother leaves with Velasco, and Corie and Paul become embroiled in a fight that ends in a decision to divorce. In facing the challenges of the apartment and the evening, the newlyweds have come to believe that they have nothing in common. Paul considers his wife irrational and irresponsible; she thinks that he is a stuffed shirt incapable of enjoying life.

In the final scene, Mother is unaccounted for, divorce plans proceed apace, and Corie and Paul are miserable. Ultimately, Mother appears, no worse for wear from a night at Velasco's, and Paul and Corie discover the importance of surrender and compromise. She recognizes her need for order, he relaxes enough to take a walk—"barefoot in the park"—and they both realize the depth of their love.

From the start, Simon creates a situation rife with possibilities. The setting offers opportunities for visual jokes and offstage action: For example, there are ongoing references to the six-flight ascent to the apartment. As newlyweds adapting to a new home, job, and life-style, Corie and Paul are portrayed in the midst of major upheaval. The stolid Mother and the splendiferous Velasco are great foils for each other and for the younger couple as well. Furthermore, in Corie and Paul, Simon creates protagonists whose personalities, often in harmony, easily become diametrically opposed through their responses to difficult circumstances.

Even more than in *Barefoot in the Park*, the conflict in Simon's next play, *The Odd Couple*, is built squarely on the collision of opposites. Oscar Madison is a divorced sportswriter living alone, who hosts five friends for a weekly poker game, including his good friend Felix Ungar. (During his childhood, Simon's mother used to run poker games in the family home for extra income.) In the first scene, Felix, usually quite punctual, arrives hours late in emotional distress, with the horrific news that his wife kicked him out. Oscar invites Felix to become his roommate, and the "odd couple" is formed.

Simon established Felix's sensitive and fastidious nature in the opening scene, so it is no surprise when, in the second scene, two weeks later, Felix is driving the slovenly Oscar crazy with his devotion to detail and cleanliness. Their relationship is implicitly a send-up of marriage in an age of rising divorce rates and precarious gender roles. The bachelor life is clearly threatened by Felix's uxoriousness. To break the tension and salve their solitude, Oscar suggests a double date with their upstairs neighbors, the Pigeon sisters. Felix reluctantly agrees.

In the third scene, Cecily and Gwendolyn Pigeon come downstairs for dinner, straight out of an Oscar Wilde drawing room. As in *Barefoot in the Park*, however, the menu is sabotaged by circumstance, and, instead of succumbing to the double seduction that Oscar envisions, the Pigeons both take sisterly pity on the heartbroken Felix. The failed date precipitates a climactic conflagration between the two men, and, as in *Barefoot in the Park*, the only solution seems to be separation.

In the final scene, amid a cold war of silence and anger, Oscar and Felix vent their rage and passion, coming to understand that their conflict reflects an unhappy combination of personality types and the larger tragedies of failed marriages and solitary middle age. These themes reappear time and again in Simon's work—the distance between people, the effects of time on relationships, and the different ways that men and women deal with emotion. In the end, Oscar and Felix reach a mutually respectful peace, forged of patience, humility, and a willingness to laugh.

The formula established by these early comedies provides the basis for many of the plays that followed. In 1966, Simon wrote the book for *Sweet Charity*, a Bob Fosse musical based on the Federico Fellini film *Nights of Cabiria* (1957). In *The Star-Spangled Girl*, he pitted liberal journalists against an old-fashioned Southern belle. Both of these pieces met mixed response. Years later, Simon called *The Star-Spangled Girl* "simply a failure," a play "where I did not have a clear visual image of the characters in my mind as I sat down at the typewriter." Nevertheless, with the opening of *The Star-Spangled Girl*, Simon could claim the singular distinction of having four plays running simultaneously on Broadway.

In 1968, Simon tried something new: a series of three one-act plays set in the same hotel room. The result, *Plaza Suite*, is vintage Simon with an added bittersweetness. The first piece focuses on a stale marriage and a revelation of infidelity; the second, on high school flames reuniting in midlife; and the third, on a bride's wedding day jitters and what they bring out in her parents' marriage. That same year, Simon wrote the book for *Promises, Promises*, a Burt Bacharach-Hal David musical version of the 1960 film *The Apartment*.

His next play, *Last of the Red Hot Lovers*, focuses on the romantic woes of a middle-aged man. Then came *The Gingerbread Lady*, dealing with the subject of alcoholism; *The Prisoner of Second Avenue*, about the nervous breakdown of a man caught in the vertigo of urban life; and *The Sunshine Boys*, depicting the deteriorating relationship of a pair of old comedians. These plays signaled an attempt by Simon to move into issue-oriented material with a more serious tone. While still striking with characteristic wit and receiving popular acclaim, he sometimes overindulges in sentiment and high seriousness. Some critics lambasted the attempt and urged him to stay on familiar, lighter terrain.

In 1972 and 1973, during the period of his wife's illness and death, Simon's writing reflected his personal tragedy. *The Good Doctor* was his adaptation of the tragicomic stories of Russian dramatist Anton Chekhov. More penetrating was *God's Favorite*, a modern reworking of the biblical story of Job, in which a man challenges God and the universe to help him understand the extremity of his sufferings. It was Simon's attempt to find solace and peace through his writing.

California Suite, a Pacific Coast retake of the *Plaza Suite* concept, appeared in 1976. Like its predecessor, and much of the intervening work, it takes a more sophisticated approach to relationships and social situations. It consists of four short plays set in a two-room suite at the Beverly Hills Hotel. The first and third have definite pathos beneath their comic gloss; the second and fourth are lighter and broader.

The second of the four pieces is about Marvin and Millie, a husband and wife from Philadelphia who have come to Los Angeles for a nephew's Bar Mitzvah. Marvin arrived a night early and returned to the suite to find a gift from his brother waiting for him: a prostitute. It is the next morning, and Millie arrives; the other woman, however, is still drunk and asleep in the bed, and for most of the play, Marvin scrambles to conceal her inert form. Eventually, he confesses his sin to Millie, and they face the crisis with equal guilt and stoicism. The play runs on frantic energy, physical comedy, and the audience's discrepant awareness of the other woman's presence.

The fourth play is also built on physical comedy emerging from a situation that is out of control. Mort and Beth and Stu and Gert are two couples from Chicago who have taken a three-week vacation together. Best friends at the start, their rapport has steadily eroded. At last, an accidental injury on the tennis court unleashes torrents of accumulated hostility; the feuding then triggers a series of freak accidents, a veritable comedy of mishaps. The barroom brawl-like mayhem ends in unresolved pandemonium. Simon here displays his ability to bring together one-liners, character conflict, and physical comedy into an orchestrated whole.

Set against these two lighter plays are the first and third pieces. In the first, a divorced couple negotiate where their daughter will live for her last year of high school. Billy and Hannah are both brashly intelligent and piercingly sarcastic. What begins as a brittle, venomous battle of words and wits subtly evolves into a deep struggle for pride and control. Knowing each other all too well, they ultimately bring their hopes, fears, and even some of their long-abandoned love into the open. While the characters use humor as a weapon throughout, their true feelings are always evident, and Simon allows and validates their enduring anger. Ultimately, a deal is struck, but the tone and outcome make it clear that there are no winners in this struggle.

The same is true of the third piece, in which a British actress and her husband have come to Hollywood for the Academy Awards. Dividing the action into two scenes, Simon contrasts their hopeful harmony before the ceremony with their bitter and drunken divisiveness after it. Diana has not won the coveted Oscar but instead has made a fool of herself at the ensuing parties. At the heart of her recklessness is a deep dissatisfaction with her marriage. Her husband, Sidney, an unassuming antiques dealer, is a "bisexual homosexual," and his flirtation with a young actor over dinner has brought dangerous issues to the surface. In the end, Sidney will hold, soothe, and probably make love to Diana, but it is evident that the connection is only temporary. That they can come together at all is a sign of hope, but Simon allows no illusions about the sacrifices they are making and the evanescence of their union.

This mix of pieces and tones, all still focused on relationships, marriages, sex, and love, bespeaks an unapologetic honesty that cannot be found in Simon's earlier work. Indeed, in 1979, Simon said that he believed the third play of *California Suite* was his best and most honest writing.

While parts of his earlier plays are drawn loosely from personal experience, by the late 1970's Simon was ready to take on autobiographical material more directly. *Chapter Two* was the first play in this direction. It tells the story of a recently widowed man who meets and falls in love with a woman, a story the playwright had known firsthand several years before. During this period, he also wrote a second version of *The Odd Couple*, this time with two women in the leading roles; the book for a Marvin Hamlisch-Carole Bayer Sager musical called *They're Playing Our Song*; a play called *I Ought to Be in Pictures*, about a screenwriter and his daughter; and *Fools*, a comic fable based on a Ukrainian folktale. This last was Simon's only unequivocal flop.

The real breakthrough came with *Brighton Beach Memoirs*, which, with *Biloxi Blues* and *Broadway Bound*, forms Simon's acclaimed autobiographical trilogy. In these plays, the playwright's own past is clear and unmistakable. The plays center on Eugene Morris Jerome, a teenage writer and baseball enthusiast growing up in Brighton Beach, New York, in the 1940's. Eugene has an older brother, unhappily married parents, and great aspirations. These aspirations lead him to chronicle his family's trials and tribulations, and his writings become a vehicle for narrating and commenting on the action directly to the audience. As Eugene is representative of the young Simon, his direct address offers an intimacy between playwright and audience that Simon had never before attempted or allowed.

In the trilogy, Simon also effectively explores dramatic structure. "I really made a quantum leap in *Brighton Beach* as a playwright," Simon said in 1985, "because it was the first full-bodied play I had ever written, in terms of dealing with a group of people as individuals and telling all their stories." Before, he would focus on a central character or conflict; now, though Eugene was the connecting thread, Simon was portraying a more integrated and balanced world. In *Brighton Beach Memoirs*, Eugene's adolescent fascination with his cousin Nora, his aunt Blanche's quandary over reestablishing her independence, his older brother Stanley's moral crisis at work, Nora's dreams of a show business career, her sister Laurie's fragile health, and Jack and Kate Jerome's precarious marriage and difficult economic straits are all woven together into a delicate tapestry of events and emotions. The play, suffused with characteristic wit but a deeper sense of poignancy, won the New York Drama Critics Circle Award, the first truly critical recognition of Simon's work.

The New York Times critic Frank Rich wrote that he would love to see a "chapter two" to *Brighton Beach Memoirs*, so Simon decided to continue Eugene's story. *Biloxi Blues* takes place at an army training camp in Biloxi, Mississippi, no doubt the camp that Simon had attended four decades earlier. It is one of his few plays set outside New York City, and one of the few that feature a group of strangers. Like its predecessor, it balances the stories of several characters. Simon introduces Arnold Epstein, a tender Jewish youth with a will of steel; Sergeant Toomey, a career military man facing his mortality and determined to make soldiers of the last group assigned to him; Wykowski and Selridge, the company bullies; and Carney and Hennesey, who bring other colors of adolescence to the complete picture. Outside the barracks, there are Rowena, the weekend prostitute who takes Eugene's virginity, and Daisy, the lovely schoolgirl who wins his heart.

The play gains steady momentum through a variety of means: the rigors of training, the competitive banter of the barracks, the young men's unrelenting fears and hormones, the often blatant bigotry and anti-Semitism, the lurking suspicions of homosexuality, and the implicit challenges to pride and manhood. In the climactic scene, Simon distills all the play's themes into a tense confrontation between the old soldier Toomey and the unwilling hero Epstein, in a way that seals the play's uncanny, but human, logic.

In *Biloxi Blues*, Eugene again takes the audience into his confidence, sharing his process of maturing as both man and writer. The one-liners are ever-present, but the world of the play is darkened by the shadow of World War II, establishing a type of meaningful historical context that is unseen in Simon's work before the trilogy. The fourteen scenes, spanning months and moving through a variety of settings, are also unusual for Simon. *Biloxi Blues* is a rite-of-passage play, and Simon treats the inherent issues—adolescence, manhood, fear, sexuality, separation—with deep warmth, sensitivity, and subtlety.

Broadway Bound completed the trilogy in 1986. Eugene is back in Brighton Beach, and the tapestry interweaves his fledgling career, writing comedy with his brother Stanley, with the quickly unraveling threads of his parents' marriage. Past and family are inescapable even as the future looks bright, and, when their homegrown skit actually comes across the radio waves, Eugene and Stanley learn an important lesson about the dangers of mixing humor and autobiography. It is no doubt an issue that had crossed the playwright's mind as well.

In *Broadway Bound*, Eugene still narrates and comments, and audiences who followed him through the first two plays can appreciate his ripening maturity. The most powerful scene of the play is remarkably simple: Eugene dances with his mother Kate, amid the disarray of the kitchen and her crumbling marriage, to her lyrical reminiscences of a girlhood infatuation with a dashing celebrity and a magical night when she danced with him. The intimacy of the story embarrasses even Eugene, a fact that he candidly confesses to the audience. The Oedipal implications of the scene magnify both the young man's coming-of-age and his mother's life of pain and frustration. By using details taken directly from his own youth, Simon frankly investigates his filial memories and feelings, and the result is powerful. The writing shows a level of dramatic achievement of which the author of *Come Blow Your Horn* could only have dreamed.

The trilogy was followed by *Rumors*, Simon's first attempt at all-out farce, and *Jake's Women*, a whimsical play about a writer and the women who populate his mind. *Jake's Women* endured many rewrites and an aborted out-of-town trial before finally coming to Broadway, a process that testified to Simon's power and diligence as a playwright. In 1991, continuing in the spirit of the trilogy, *Lost in Yonkers* appeared on Broadway. Portraying the sojourn of two boys with their brusque grandmother and eccentric aunt and uncle, it earned Simon critical praise, his second Tony Award for Best Play, and a prestigious Pulitzer Prize in drama.

Through more than two dozen plays and nearly as many film scripts, Simon has become the wealthiest dramatist in history and the most produced playwright on the contemporary American stage behind Shakespeare. More important, in addition to his supremacy over the popular American theater, his devotion to craft, hard work, simplicity, and honesty have secured him a primary position in its literary annals.

Other major works

SCREENPLAYS: *After the Fox*, 1966 (with Cesare Zavattini); *Barefoot in the Park*, 1967; *The Odd Couple*, 1968; *The Out-of-Towners*, 1970; *Plaza Suite*, 1971; *The Last of the Red Hot Lovers*, 1972; *The Heartbreak Kid*, 1972; *The Prisoner of Second Avenue*, 1975; *The Sunshine Boys*, 1975; *Murder by Death*, 1976; *The Goodbye Girl*, 1977; *California Suite*, 1978; *The Cheap Detective*, 1978; *Chapter Two*, 1979; *Seems Like Old Times*, 1980; *Only When I Laugh*, 1981; *I Ought to Be in Pictures*, 1982; *Max Dugan Returns*, 1983; *The Lonely Guy*, 1984; *The Slugger's Wife*, 1985; *Brighton Beach Memoirs*, 1987; *Biloxi Blues*, 1988.

TELEPLAY: *Broadway Bound*, 1992.

Bibliography

Henry, William A., III. "Reliving a Poignant Past." *Time*, December 15, 1986, 72-78. Henry describes the success of the play *Broadway Bound* and its biographical sources, and includes in-depth material about Simon's marriages, life-style, writing habits, and older brother Danny. Compares Simon's life with its fictional parallels, especially in *Broadway Bound.*

Johnson, Robert K. *Neil Simon.* Boston: G. K. Hall, 1983. In this thoughtful and penetrating study, Johnson examines Simon's career and output through 1982, providing thorough synopses, analysis, and criticism of both plays and screenplays. Includes a chronology, a select bibliography, notes, and an index.

McGovern, Edythe. *Not-So-Simple Neil Simon: A Critical Study.* Van Nuys, Calif.: Perivale Press, 1978. McGovern examines twelve of Simon's earliest plays with an even, theoretical, scholarly tone, occasionally tending toward unqualified praise. The slim volume includes a preface by the playwright, a list of characters from the plays, twenty-two production photographs, and seven illustrations by renowned Broadway caricaturist Al Hirschfeld.

Richard, David. "The Last of the Red Hot Playwrights." Review of *Lost in Yonkers. The New York Times Magazine*, February 17, 1991, 30. Celebrating Simon's success with *Lost in Yonkers*, this reviewer describes the play and production and profiles the playwright. The article brings together personal and professional material, using quotes from Simon, his family members, and actors associated with his plays. Personal and in-depth, with nine photographs.

Simon, Neil. "The Art of Theater X." Interview by James Lipton. *The Paris Review* 34 (Winter, 1992): 166-213. A chatty, revealing interview. The first half of the interview is largely given to discussion of how Simon became a playwright and the strong autobiographical elements in his work: "I think my greatest weakness is that I can't write outside my own experience." Other topics include the "almost invisible line" between comedy and tragedy and the gradually darkening vision of Simon's plays, which he sees as a movement toward greater truthfulness. Simon's ongoing enthusiasm for theater is clear; he concludes, "Every time I write a play it's the beginning of a new life for me."

__________. "Simon Says." Interview by David Kaufman. *Horizon* 28 (June, 1985): 55-60. In this smooth, candid interview with the playwright, Simon talks openly about the autobiographical impulses in his plays, the critical response, and his popular and critical success. Through his own words, Simon's humility, directness, and commitment to craft are evident.

Barry Mann

BERNARD SLADE
Bernard Slade Newbound

Born: St. Catharines, Ontario, Canada; May 2, 1930

Principal drama

Simon Says Get Married, pr. 1960; *A Very Close Family*, pr. 1962; *Fling!*, wr. 1970, pr. 1977, pb. 1979; *Same Time, Next Year*, pr., pb. 1975; *Tribute*, pr., pb. 1978; *Romantic Comedy*, pr., pb. 1979; *Special Occasions*, pr., pb. 1982; *Fatal Attraction*, pr. 1984, pb. 1986; *Return Engagements*, pr. 1986, pb. 1989; *Sweet William*, pr. 1986; *An Act of the Imagination*, pr. 1987; *Every Time I See You*, pr. 1991.

Other literary forms

Prior to his first (and highly successful) efforts on Broadway with *Same Time, Next Year*, Bernard Slade spent seventeen years as a writer for television, first as a playwright and later as a series creator and writer. Slade's work in television drama goes back to the days of live broadcasts in the 1950's and 1960's, including a number of hour-long plays first produced by the Canadian Broadcasting Corporation between 1957 and 1963. Several of these plays were also produced on American television for the *U.S. Steel Hour* series. Between 1964 and 1974, Slade wrote a number of pilot films for American television that eventually became successful television series. His major achievements in this genre include *Love on a Rooftop*, *The Flying Nun*, *The Partridge Family*, *Bridget Loves Bernie*, *The Girl with Something Extra*, *The Bobby Sherman Show*, and *Mr. Deeds Goes to Town*, all comedies. Slade's television credits also include authorship of approximately one hundred episodes for these and other series, including *Bewitched* and *My Living Doll*. Slade has said of his experiences as a writer for television that "the controls built into network television, which is basically an advertising medium, don't exactly encourage creativity. Still, TV was my choice. It gave me the financial freedom to sit down and write a play." In 1974, Slade left television to devote full time to writing plays for the theater.

The successful Broadway run of *Same Time, Next Year* made possible Slade's continued work in still another entertainment medium: major motion pictures. Slade has written screenplays for *Stand Up and Be Counted* (1971), *Same Time, Next Year* (1978), *Tribute* (1980), and *Romantic Comedy* (1983). The film versions of Slade's plays will no doubt continue to entertain audiences for years to come through the medium that gave their author his start.

Achievements

Throughout Slade's career, his major works have attracted the prompt and generally enthusiastic attention of the major New York newspapers, including *The New York Times*, the *New York Post*, and the *New York Daily News*. Magazines such as *Time* and *Newsweek* have also carried half-page articles on Slade's works, and scenes from his plays have appeared alongside reviews of all three major television networks. In 1975, *Same Time, Next Year*, long on the list of the top ten longest-running shows, received nominations from all the major awards institutions. The stage version received a Tony nomination, the American Academy of Humor Award, and the prestigious Drama Desk Award, while the screen version received the Academy Award and Writers Guild nominations for Best Screenplay.

Slade's works have also resulted in awards and nominations for actress Ellen Burstyn and actor Jack Lemmon. Burstyn received the Tony Award for Best Actress in 1975 for her portrayal of Doris in *Same Time, Next Year*, and Lemmon earned Tony and Academy Award nominations for his stage and film work as Scottie Templeton in *Tribute*.

Slade is recognized as a major talent both on Broadway and in Hollywood, and his international following continues to increase with each new production. All of his major plays have done well in foreign countries, especially England and France, and *Same Time, Next Year* has been produced in some thirty-five countries around the world. Foreign productions of Slade's plays have traditionally retained the plays' American settings. Slade himself was the first to break with tradition when he Anglicized *Special Occasions* for his directorial debut in London in 1983.

Biography

Bernard Slade Newbound was born in St. Catharines, Ontario, Canada, on May 2, 1930. His parents, Fred and Bessie (née Walbourne) Newbound, were originally from England. When he was four, Slade moved to England with his family and settled in London near the Croydon airport, where his father worked as a mechanic. With the threat of war, Slade, like many children, was evacuated from London, spending the year 1939 in a foster home. Shortly after his return to London at the age of ten, the Battle of Britain broke out in full force: The first daylight bombing of London destroyed the Croydon airport, four blocks from Slade's home, and Slade's father was one of the few workers there to survive the attack.

Life in England took on a restless quality during the war years. The family moved often, and Slade attended some thirteen schools around the country between the late 1930's and 1948. Despite the war, Slade found time to attend the theater and to act in several amateur productions, among them Noël Coward's *I'll Leave It to You* (pr. 1919). In 1948, the family left

England to return to Canada, Slade taking with him his love for the theater and a few pages of notes for plays of his own.

In Canada, Slade worked briefly at a customs office but soon quit his job to resume acting, first in summer stock and later for year-round theaters, where he often did a different play each week. He acted in more than three hundred plays in all, including virtually every romantic comedy written in the 1930's and 1940's. Although Slade disliked the indignity of looking for work as an actor, the experience of being in front of an audience every night eventually paid off as he absorbed a sense of how and when a play works.

In 1957, after nine years of acting in winter and summer stock theater, Slade sat down during a break in the play in which he was performing and wrote a television play designed to provide himself with a good part. Both the Canadian Broadcasting Corporation and, in the United States, the National Broadcasting Company bought the play but found different actors to take Slade's part. *The Prizewinner*, Slade's first television play, was very much in the tradition of live broadcast drama popularized by the *U.S. Steel Hour* and the *Goodyear TV Playhouse* in New York, particularly the work of such writers as Paddy Chayefsky and Tad Mosel; he went on to write many more teleplays, a number of which were produced in the United States as well as in Canada in the late 1950's and early 1960's.

In 1963, having realized that Hollywood was quickly establishing itself as the center for North American television production, Slade moved to California with his wife, Jill Foster Hancock, and their two children and began writing scripts for a new television series entitled *Bewitched*. Soon afterward, he signed a contract (later to become a succession of three-year contracts) with Screen Gems to write pilot films, rarely staying with a show once it became a series. In all, Slade wrote seven pilots, each of which became a successful series, and more than one hundred episode scripts. In 1974, Slade, financially secure, left television and turned his sights on the theater.

Begun on an airplane en route to Hawaii, *Same Time, Next Year* surpassed all Slade's expectations at its opening at Boston's Colonial Theatre in February, 1975. The play quickly moved to New York's Brooks Atkinson Theatre, where it opened on March 13 to standing room only and the unanimous acclamation of New York's best-known theater critics. Soon afterward, Slade wrote the screenplay, and in 1978 Universal Studios released *Same Time, Next Year*, starring Alan Alda and Ellen Burstyn. Earlier, in 1977, Slade had returned to the stage with his wife to star in a Canadian production of *Same Time, Next Year*.

Same Time, Next Year was followed by *Tribute* and, one year later, *Romantic Comedy*, the former originally designed for and offered to Jack Lemmon, who opened the play at Boston's Colonial Theatre on April 6, and in New York on June 1, 1978. Reviews focused primarily on Lemmon's outstanding performance as Scottie Templeton, and criticism of the play was for the most part favorable. Slade then wrote the screenplay for *Tribute*, and, in December, 1980, Twentieth Century-Fox released the film version, starring, once again, Lemmon. Like its predecessors, *Romantic Comedy* opened in Boston and moved to New York, where it played for a year and earned high praise from the critics (Clive Barnes called it Slade's best) before being adapted for the screen. More than any of Slade's other plays, *Romantic Comedy* reflects the enormous influence of the romantic comedies of the 1930's and 1940's on its author.

By all critical accounts, *Special Occasions* was Slade's first failure: The play closed after only one night at the Music Box in New York. Critics pointed their collective finger at the staging primarily and at the story secondarily and found little to like about either. In 1983, Slade took a slightly different version of *Special Occasions* to England, where the play was received with more sympathy by critics and public alike. Slade thus continues to be a major figure in world theater, although the economic rigors of Broadway have prevented his later works from enjoying the same box-office success as his early plays. The 1987 broadcast of his television play *Moving Day* marked his return to the genre in which he enjoyed his first success.

When asked by *Who's Who in America* to describe his work and career, Slade responded, "I am a prisoner of a childhood dream: to write for the theatre. The fulfillment of that dream has lived up to all my expectations. I believe the theatre should be a celebration of the human condition and that the artist's job is to remind us of all that is good about ourselves. I feel privileged to be given a platform for my particular vision of life, and, whether my plays succeed or fail, I am always grateful for the use of the hall."

Analysis

One might best approach Bernard Slade's major works—*Same Time, Next Year*, *Tribute*, *Romantic Comedy*, and *Special Occasions*—by first surveying their common ground. All Slade's plays are comedies for the most part, although *Tribute* and *Special Occasions* contain more frequent departures into the pathetic than do *Same Time, Next Year* and *Romantic Comedy*. (*Tribute* is, at its simplest level, a story about a man who knows when and how he is going to die, while the "special occasions" in the play of that title include divorce, disfiguring automobile accidents, and alcoholic blackouts.) The time frame of a typical Slade play is usually quite broad: *Special Occasions* covers one night of Amy and Michael Ruskin's marriage and ten years of their divorce; *Romantic Comedy* spans thirteen years of an on-again, off-again professional writing relationship; and *Same Time, Next Year* begins in 1951 and ends in 1975, with every indication that its adulterous affair will continue into a fourth decade.

Time is always significant in Slade's works. All four major productions plot the maturation of one or two principal characters over a period of years or months. Quite often the chief protagonist is a male, between thirty and fifty years of age, who makes his living as a writer of one sort or another (Michael Ruskin in *Special Occasions* and Jason Carmichael in *Romantic Comedy* are playwrights). The liberal time frame allows for a wide variety of situations that culminate in self-recognition on the part of the protagonists and a happy ending for the audience. Slade's characters typically experience an illicit affair (not always at center stage), a divorce, a career crisis, and problems with their children and their own maturation. The crowd onstage is always sparse. Two plays—*Special Occasions* and *Same Time, Next Year*—have only two characters each; *Romantic Comedy* and *Tribute* have six and seven characters, respectively. Children rarely appear onstage (*Tribute* is again the exception), yet despite their absence they are often crucial to the plot. Amy and Michael Ruskin's children in *Special Occasions* never appear in the spotlight, but all three younger Ruskins have highly individual personalities, and all are so carefully drawn that the audience is convinced of their existence in spite of their incorporeity. Stephen is at a stage that everyone is hoping he will grow out of, Jennifer is a musical genius (her piano playing is audible), and Kelly is dull. One might assess other characters' personalities with similar ease, even though they are never seen. Indeed, whole scenes in *Same Time, Next Year* are devoted to the unsuspecting husband and the more astute wife (both absent) of the lovers, and most of *Special Occasions* concerns people who are not formally in the play. Thus, just as the extended time frame convinces the audience members that they are not simply spectators at a play but observers of continuous human history, so do Slade's offstage personalities convince them that the principal characters are real people with lives beyond the spotlights.

If there is an all-encompassing thesis that one might extract from Slade's major productions, it is this: Life does not distill itself into isolated instances of time but is instead an evolving process that touches other people who may or may not be present in the flesh but whose influence is felt from moment to moment. The isolated moment can say much (as is the case in *Special Occasions*), but every moment has its context in things outside. While Slade's focus is always on center stage, one senses from the very beginning the presence of a background—historical and densely populated—that gradually comes to life and establishes itself as the source of what one sees and hears onstage. Like his earlier plays for television, Slade's Broadway productions offer little slices of life, complete with triumphs and tragedies, while the whole from which the slice is taken remains conspicuously and deliberately close at hand. Finally, though they sometimes place a strain on credulity, the triumphs win out over the tragedies with remarkable consistency. When Slade's world becomes dark—and it does so almost rhythmically—the darkness lasts only for its appointed duration. There is always a character ready with a joke, however nervously he may tell it, or a stagehand ready with a curtain, to bring one back to the realization that everything will be all right—in time.

In no other play does Slade use time more conspicuously than in *Same Time, Next Year*, his most successful Broadway production. The plot is simple enough: George and Doris leave their spouses at home with the children and meet at the same country inn near San Francisco for one weekend every year from 1951 to 1975. They make love 113 times (George, an accountant, uses his calculator to arrive at the figure), taking a brief but unexpected respite in 1961 because of Doris' pregnancy (and early labor) and George's impotence. (The timing is not always so perfect: In 1965, Doris refuses to have sex with him because he voted for Barry Goldwater.) Yet despite the play's dependence on the affair for its plot, *Same Time, Next Year* is only superficially about adultery. Its real focus is on growing up and on the 364 or so days a year that make George and Doris appear different each time the audience sees them.

The play opens on the morning following the pair's initial encounter. There are awkward moments at first, and George has grave misgivings about the whole situation. He tells lies, he calls Doris by a wrong name, and he is sure that his wife knows all about his infidelity. Doris, despite her Roman Catholic upbringing, is much more relaxed. She even eats George's breakfast for him. George's appetite, when it returns, is for sex: "The Russians have the bomb!" he exclaims, using world events and the threat of annihilation to justify sexual license. Having become familiar with each other sexually, the two decide to tell stories about the good and the bad sides of their spouses as a means of getting to know each other better. George already has his stories prepared, so he begins what later will become part of the ritual celebrated every February in the small country inn that never changes.

Despite the static quality of the setting and the fact that each of the five-year intervals follows closely the formula established in the first encounter, *Same Time, Next Year* is a story about the profound change in the lives of the principal characters and in the larger world outside. The year 1961, for example, matches George's impotence against Doris' pregnancy (both conditions say a good deal about what 1960 must have been like for them). In 1965, Doris is liberated both in her dress and in her philosophical and sociological outlook, while George is on Librium, and by 1970, Doris has bought into the new "chic" establishment and opened an exclusive and highly successful French catering business, while George has exchanged his conservative life-style for denim and sandals. His conversation summarizes up the age of analysis with accuracy and charm: "When you first walked into the room I picked up your high tension level. Then after we made love I sensed a certain anxiety reduction but now I'm getting a definite negative feedback."

The source of the high tension level lies in the people and events in the world and outside the inn. George's impotence is only aggravated by his mother calling long distance to discuss possible cures, and his flirtation with Librium dependency is a direct result of his son's death in Vietnam. Although his psychoananalytic jargon is amusing, there are, nevertheless, serious reasons behind his decision to seek psychiatric help. The decision comes not a moment too soon, for, in 1975, George, now a widower, tells his last story about his wife with a degree of equanimity that comes only after years of dealing with life-altering experiences. The years have been kinder to Doris, whose only crisis comes in 1970 when her husband, Harry, leaves her. Significantly, it is George, in the guise of a Father Michael O'Herlihy, who brings about the couple's reconciliation. Once again, analysis has its real-life rewards.

In spite of its occasional crossovers into the realm of domestic tragedy, *Same Time, Next Year* is first and foremost a comedy in the tradition of the 1970's vintage Broadway. With a few notable exceptions, every situation has its comic moments, and the humor always has something to say about character growth. Doris' discussion of what it is like to have grown from a high school dropout to a wealthy businesswoman is a typical example. Fulfillment, she tells George, is going into Gucci's and buying five suede suits at seven hundred dollars each for her bowling team—simply to spite the unpleasant salesgirl. George, too, has come a long way in twenty years. The same man whose guilt sends him into paroxysms of despair in the 1950's and 1960's is able to confront Doris' husband with amazing composure in 1970. Confessing that honesty is everything, George shamelessly tells Harry about the very intimate relationship he has had with Doris for twenty years. That his first and only conversation with Harry takes place over the telephone makes things a little easier for George and provides one of the play's most humorous moments: "My name? My name is Father Michael O'Herlihy. No, she's out saying a novena right now—Yes, my son, I'll tell her to call you."

One might easily point out any number of similar instances in the play, but the two above will serve to illustrate one final point about the humor in *Same Time, Next Year*. Doris is, from 1956 on, a woman motivated by one outstanding quality—spontaneity. She welcomes every moment as it comes, and she perfectly fits George's definition of life (saying "yes"). So accustomed is the audience to her love of the moment that the episode in the Gucci store comes as no surprise; her reaction represents in every way the classic Doris. George's long-distance triumph is equally revealing. His composure represents an achievement of great proportions, and he revels in it. He knows he is being clever, and so he stretches the moment for as long as he can make it last. Rarely is his self-perception at such a high point; his comic lines come at his own expense for three-quarters of the play. By 1970, a little of Doris has rubbed off on him, and the change is welcome. "I grew up with you," he tells her in 1975, and his words have an unmistakable ring of truth to them. There is only one kind of ending for a play that has so much to celebrate, and that is the kind Doris loves best. "I love—happy—endings!" she says at the end. One feels that she and George have earned one all their own.

Same Time, Next Year is one of Slade's most celebrated works. His next play, *Tribute*, is a celebration, for the audience as well as for the characters. The occasion is Scottie Templeton's fifty-first birthday and his first appearance in public since his near-fatal bout with leukemia. His twenty-year-old son, Jud, and his boss, Lou Daniels, have rented a theater in New York and gathered Scottie's friends to pay tribute to the man who has left a legacy of love and laughter to all who know him. Lou opens the evening with a welcome (he knows many of us, he says) and an anecdote about Scottie and a crowded elevator. Dr. Gladys Petrelli, Scottie's physician, appears next and relates a little story about how Scottie's insomnia is contagious.

So much for the play's first beginning. *Tribute* begins a second time in Scottie's New York town house as Scottie entertains Sally Haines, a young model he met during an earlier stay in the hospital. The time is three months prior to the tribute to Scottie. As Sally leaves, Scottie's ex-wife, Maggie Stratton, enters with Jud, whom Scottie has not seen for two years. Still hurting from his parents' divorce and still feeling neglected, Jud is rather cold toward his father and informs him that he will be staying for only a week—he knows it will make little difference one way or the other to Scottie. Jud thus releases his first arrow, but he has brought a full quiver along with the rest of his baggage.

Scottie's stubborn refusal to receive any medical treatment and Jud's aloofness provide the raw materials for a series of confrontations over the next three months. Dr. Petrelli tells Scottie, who remains an incurable jester from start to finish, that using jokes to shut out reality is no longer going to work. She tries to enlist Jud's help, but Jud's "why me?" attitude has only hardened with age. He tells Sally, with whom he is now romantically involved, that his father is little more than a "court jester and a glorified pimp" (in fact, Scottie is a successful public relations man with a few false career starts in his past). Jud's assessment of his father's character only worsens when he accidentally walks in on his parents' lovemaking. The situation looks hopeless until Lou talks to Jud. Scottie's real talent, he tells Jud, is in making friends and in convincing them that life is better than it really is. He is worth saving, says Lou, and there are hundreds of people who feel the same way. Something clicks. Scottie and Jud have one more confrontation—this one about going to the hospital. Lou interrupts things in mid-crisis only long enough for Jud to pack Scottie's suitcase. They are going to the hospital.

Thus, with a little help, Scottie creates one more friendship where before there was only indifference, and his new friend saves his life and then arranges its celebration. Back onstage for the tribute with which the play began, a handful of Scottie's many friends have been telling stories in between the scenes from Scottie's life, as Jud's slides of his father illuminate the stage. Dr. Petrelli tells of the late hours she has kept because of Scottie's simultaneous attacks of hypochondria and insomnia; Hilary, a retired prostitute, recounts the testimonial dinner that Scottie arranged for her ($250 a plate and a gold watch); Maggie tells a story about a special birthday dinner with Scottie; and Sally sums up what Scottie's new friends in the audience must be saying to themselves by now: "Hi! Whenever I think of Scottie—I smile."

Tribute thus celebrates the little man and dares to call him a hero in spite of his littleness. Life is Scottie Templeton's battleground, and humor, love, and forgiveness are his weapons. He uses them wherever he finds tragedy and indifference—in elevators, on city buses, or in his own town house. Hundreds of people have applauded the funny man in the corduroy cap, and it is Slade's intention that hundreds more will follow suit. *Tribute* offers no real clear-cut alternative once Jud's conversion is complete, and Maggie's enduring love for her ex-husband only confirms the rhetorical message of the play. *Tribute* has the effect of transforming the spectator (or reader) into a friend. By the end, the fact that *Tribute* is a play occurs to one only as an afterthought. Slade intends that one's first thoughts should be about one's new friends, and they are.

Clive Barnes, in a 1978 *New York Post* article, has called *Tribute* an "honest truism" in a "serious funny" vein. A less serious play with less serious truths is *Romantic Comedy*. Slade has called the play a Valentine to the romantic playwrights of the 1930's and 1940's, and the phrase is especially apt. *Romantic Comedy* has all the seriousness of the genre it imitates (which is to say, very little) and all the day-to-day reality of a Valentine card. It achieves, therefore, precisely what it sets out to do: to close the doors on reality and engage in two hours of old-fashioned fun.

Jason Carmichael, a self-centered and highly successful playwright, is about to marry Allison St. James, a young society woman whose father is the ambassador to New Zealand. Anxiously awaiting his prenuptial rubdown at the hands of Boris, Jason walks naked into his study only to find that Phoebe Craddock, a young Vermont schoolteacher and an aspiring playwright, has arrived for a brief interview. She stays for the next ten years and coauthors one Broadway hit after another with the now clothed Jason.

Marriage and partnership go smoothly until Jason decides to use his body where his mind has failed to remedy a bad working relationship with one of his leading ladies. Wife and partner both exit, leaving Jason on his own for the first time in years. He writes nothing of any worth for two years, while Phoebe, now living in Europe with her journalist husband, Leo, writes a best-selling novel called *Romantic Comedy*. She returns to New York to write a stage play based on her novel and to enlist Jason's help. The story is the one that the audience has been viewing onstage, with one supposed difference: Phoebe has "fantasized the relationship to make it interesting."

Romantic Comedy—the play—is already a fantasy, however, and all the crises are resolved: Jason realizes that he loves Phoebe only after a mild heart attack brought on by her return causes him to reevaluate his life; Allison, with qualifications known only to herself, runs for Congress; Leo literally gives Phoebe to Jason and then runs off to Spain to write a novel; and Phoebe outdoes them all by staying with Jason to consummate their unspoken love and to finish the play. There is certainly ample room in *Romantic Comedy* for a little sadness to creep in, but the treatment always says otherwise. *Romantic Comedy* has something of the comedy of manners about it, and, like its eighteenth century forebears, it never opts for realism when a humorous approach presents itself. Still, as Jason remarks in defense of his own plays, it takes a considerable amount of thought to write a play about entertaining an audience for an evening and to make the whole thing look easy.

Romantic Comedy has a whole tradition behind its less than serious view of life. *Special Occasions* is an altogether more innovative work that portrays life in all its bittersweet reality. Like *Same Time, Next Year*, *Special Occasions* follows the lives of two characters over a period of years (in this case, ten), charting their ups and downs and their gradual metamorphosis from strangers into friends. The structure is once again episodic, if less neatly so than before. Circumstances and other occasions bring Amy and Michael Ruskin together for brief moments every now and then, often when they least expect an encounter.

The play opens as Amy and Michael celebrate their fifteenth wedding anniversary and discuss their upcoming divorce. Amy's drinking problem quickly suggests itself as one of the reasons behind their separation, and subsequent occasions soon confirm the suggestion as fact. The rest of the play studies the personal growth not only of Amy and Michael but also of their children—Stephen, Kelly, and Jennifer. Michael's decision to undergo analysis marks his first step toward self-understanding, even if he does rehearse what he is going to say to his analyst. The audience next sees him at his mother's funeral, where he plays the flute in compliance with the last request of the deceased. Amy turns up for the viewing but misses the service, attending instead the eulogy for an eighty-five-year-old Japanese woman. Alcohol is responsible for her mistake.

The funeral home incident leads Amy to her next special occasion: her first Alcoholics Anonymous meeting, the rough equivalent of Michael's analysis. The occasion represents her first step toward personal well-being. Unlike Michael, she never deviates from the course she establishes for herself, although the years that follow unfold incident after incident to threaten her serenity. More often than not, it is Michael who suffers from what life offers over the years and Amy who pulls him through. The remaining special occasions follow in quick succession and include the unsuccessful production of Michael's first play, Stephen's high school graduation, Christmas Eve (an especially *un*festive one), Amy's marriage to Michael's lawyer, the christening of Kelly's son, Stephen's car accident, and Michael's fiftieth birthday. *Special Occasions* has more than enough material for a lifetime—indeed, for several lifetimes—but throughout, the emphasis is on how Amy and Michael come to terms with each occasion and, finally, with each other.

Two questions surface time and time again as Amy and Michael discuss their relationship and the circumstances that bring them together. The first, "Why didn't you tell me?" eventually gives way to the second, "Why did you tell me?" Amy's answer to the second question sums up the theme of the play: Friends, she tells Michael, can tell friends anything. By the end of the play, Amy and Michael, still divorced, have established a firm friendship based on individual growth and shared experience. Like father and son in *Tribute*, they have reframed their relationship out of materials close at hand and can now look forward to filling in the details together. Michael proposes remarriage, but Amy, ever the more sensible of the two, suggests that they pause and enjoy the friendship that has taken ten years and some very special occasions to create.

The critical response to *Special Occasions* was generally unfavorable, but at least part of the negative reaction can be traced to the critics' confusion over what to call the play. *Special Occasions* has been called a comedy, a situation comedy, a soap opera, a television drama, and a failure at each for allowing the others to enter unannounced, yet none of the labels captures the complexity of the play's attitude toward life or the uniqueness of its design. Perhaps it would be more accurate to say that *Special Occasions* is a record of life, complete with its high and its low moments, that seeks to be objective and cumulative. Clearly the play mixes comedy with pathos, but so does life, according to the playwright. The structure is equally mimetic: When one looks back, Slade seems to be saying, one remembers the special occasions. In *Special Occasions*, as in all Slade's plays, looking back turns out to be a pleasurable experience.

Slade has said that no one has yet convinced him that life is not a comedy, and his plays clearly exist to give dramatic expression to his conviction that it is. Slade writes the way he does because he enjoys the sound of laughter and because life regularly affords laughable moments. All Slade's plays are, in the final analysis, profiles in friendship. Doris and George, Scottie and Jud, Jason and Phoebe, Michael and Amy—all affirm Slade's belief that time and a sense of humor can shape experience and bond friend to friend. Since *Special Occasions*, Slade has begun to experiment with (for him) new dramatic forms. *Fatal Attraction* represents his first attempt at writing a thriller. Still, Slade's view of life and the way he presents that view on the stage seem to persist. Some things have not changed with time.

Other major works

SCREENPLAYS: *Stand Up and Be Counted*, 1971; *Same Time, Next Year*, 1978; *Tribute*, 1980; *Romantic Comedy*, 1983.

TELEPLAYS: *The Prizewinner*, 1957; *Moving Day*, 1987.

Bibliography

Beaufort, John. "A Twenty-four-Year Love Story." Review of *Same Time, Next Year. The Christian Science Monitor*, March 21, 1975. Takes a mildly remonstrative tone, with such phrases as "non-married couple" involved in "illicit, once-a-year trysts" representing "changing mores." Good description of voice-over and set transitions, which "give the new comedy an underlying tone of reminiscent recognition." The play is "slight and facile" but is "graced with humanity."

Kerr, Walter. "Stage: Slade's *Romantic Comedy.*" Review of *Romantic Comedy. The New York Times*, November 9, 1979, p. 63. Anthony Perkins and Mia Farrow star in this Broadway hit, which Kerr faults for some of the comic business and improbable laughs. He cites Perkins for his "smartness, high style, the lofty and chilly bon mot" and finds Farrow's character, "eternally childlike, eternally composed," to be well acted.

Watt, Douglas. "Even in Skilled Hands, Being Glib Isn't Easy." Review of *Romantic Comedy. New York Daily News*, November 9, 1979. This review is slightly different in viewpoint and tone from those in other New York newspapers. Watt credits Slade's artistry, mentions the earlier success with *Same Time, Next Year*, and cites Anthony Perkins' and Mia Farrow's personalities, which bring the characters to light in a way that the genre needs.

Wilson, Edwin. "Laughter on Broadway." *The Wall Street Journal*, November 9, 1979. Wilson examines Slade's handling of the writing craft and discusses how the play intentionally works against the form: "Mr.

Slade . . . capitulates" to the form in the end, in a noble effort, but "has not solved his [dramatic] problem" entirely.

____________. "The Redeeming Qualities of an Affair." Review of *Same Time, Next Year. The Wall Street Journal*, March 17, 1975. A long review and analysis of why the play *Same Time, Next Year* works, putting the play in a generic perspective: "More than the saga of two individuals, or even their life together; more than anything it is a love story." Wilson discusses Slade's Broadway debut with this play, and its "ingenious framework." Gives some credit to Gene Saks's direction.

William A. Davis
(Updated by *Thomas J. Taylor*)

WOLE SOYINKA

Born: Abeokuta, Nigeria; July 13, 1934

Principal drama

The Swamp Dwellers, pr. 1958, pb. 1963; *The Lion and the Jewel*, pr. 1959, pb. 1963; *The Invention*, pr. 1959 (one act); *The Trials of Brother Jero*, pr. 1960, pb. 1963; *A Dance of the Forests*, pr. 1960, pb. 1963; *Camwood on the Leaves*, pr. 1960, pb. 1973 (radio play); *The Strong Breed*, pb. 1963, pr. 1964; *Three Plays*, pb. 1963; *Five Plays*, pb. 1964; *Kongi's Harvest*, pr. 1964, pb. 1967; *The Road*, pr., pb. 1965; *Madmen and Specialists*, pr. 1970 (revised version pr., pb. 1971); *Jero's Metamorphosis*, pb. 1973; *The Bacchae*, pr., pb. 1973 (adaption of Euripides' play); *Collected Plays*, pb. 1973, 1974 (2 volumes); *Death and the King's Horseman*, pb. 1975, pr. 1976; *Opera Wonyosi*, pr. 1977, pb. 1980 (adaptation of Bertolt Brecht's play *The Three-Penny Opera*); *A Play of Giants*, pr., pb. 1984; *Six Plays*, pb. 1984; *Requiem for a Futurologist*, pb. 1985.

Other literary forms

Wole Soyinka is not only a dramatist but also a poet, novelist, and critic. His poetry has appeared in several collections, including *Idanre and Other Poems* (1967), *Poems from Prison* (1969), *A Shuttle in the Crypt* (1972), and *Mandela's Earth and Other Poems* (1988). The long poem *Ogun Abibiman*, connecting Yoruba mythology with African liberation, was first published in 1976. Soyinka has also written a few short stories as well as *The Interpreters* (1965) and *Season of Anomy* (1973), two accomplished novels. He has also translated the Yoruba novel of D. O. Fagunwa, *Forest of a Thousand Daemons: A Hunter's Saga* (1968). His most famous piece of criticism is *Myth, Literature, and the African World* (1976). In addition, Soyinka has produced two autobiographical works—*The Man Died* (1972), a memoir of his prison experiences, and *Aké: The Years of Childhood* (1981), a dramatic and imaginative re-creation of his early life—and a memoir to his father, *Ìsarà: A Voyage Around "Essay,"* 1989.

Achievements

In spite of frequent criticism of his obscure and difficult style, Soyinka is generally regarded as a major literary figure in the contemporary world; by some he is considered to be the most sophisticated writer to emerge in Anglophone Africa. He has achieved success in the three major forms—poetry, fiction, and drama—and in the drama, for which he is best known, his range extends from broad farce and satire to tragedy. If he often seems obscure, it is usually because of the density of the text: the constant reliance on imagistic and rhythmic expression and on the ever-present mythic and metaphysical dimension. An ambitious and experimental writer, he invites close textual analysis, as do many other twentieth century figures. His success as a dramatist extends to the practical arts of acting and directing as well. He has been the prime mover in the establishment of theater companies and the encouragement of the theatrical arts in Nigeria.

Behind all of this literary activity lies Soyinka's loyalty to traditional Yoruba culture. He has had the intellectual capacity to understand and adapt it to his own needs and to the needs of his country. This has, perhaps inevitably, led him into the political arena, since his primary concern for human freedom is based largely on the identity of Ogun, the dynamic god of Yoruba mythology. Soyinka is one of those rare writers of genius whose productions appeal both to the professional critic and to the general public. Soyinka's social consciousness has given his works a moral force that has made him a leader among political activists in Africa. His plays are translated into French and have been produced in Africa's Francophone countries; his influence on African theater has been tremendous, and the fear of Soyinka's revolutionary themes has led at least one African country to ban his plays.

Soyinka received first prize at the Dakar Negro Arts Festival in 1960, the John Whiting Drama Prize in 1966, the Jock Campbell Award for Fiction in 1968, and the Nobel Prize in Literature in 1986.

Biography

Akinwande Oluwole Soyinka was born July 13, 1934, at Abeokuta, in Western Nigeria, his mother, a strong-willed businesswoman, his father, a school supervisor. The dominant culture in Western Nigeria is Yoruba. Soyinka has remained Yoruba all his life. He has studied its mythology and theology as a scholar, has developed a theory of tragedy from it, and has used it as the basis and inspiration of his fiction, poetry, and drama. His works are filled with its gods and spirits, its rituals and festivals. The traditional leader, the Oba, retains his spiritual and moral authority. The Yoruba language influences Soyinka's rhythmic and imagistic English style. Soyinka's formal education, however, has been basically Christian and European. Biblical and literary echoes pervade his work. Still, he considers himself African, writing for an African audience. He defends his eclecticism as the right of any artist and insists that even his representation of Yoruba culture is necessarily and justifiably personal.

Soyinka's primary and secondary education was in Nigeria. He attended St. Peter's School in Aké, Abeokuta (1938-1943), Abeokuta Grammar School (1944-1945), and Government College in Ibadan (1946-1950). His undergraduate preparation began at University College, Ibadan (later the University of Ibadan), where he studied from 1952 to 1954 with such future notables as Chinua Achebe and Christopher Okigbo. He then went on to the University of Leeds, where he received his bachelor of arts degree with honors in English in 1957. He was later to receive an honorary degree from Leeds in 1973. His academic career began four years after graduation. He received a Rockefeller Research Fellowship to the University of Ibadan (1961-1962) and became Lecturer at the University of Ife (1962-1964). In 1969, he became drama director, and soon established a drama department and an acting company at the University of Ibadan. He has held various university academic posts, including a visiting professorship at Yale University in 1981, and has also delivered papers at academic meetings and published critical reviews and articles.

As early as his high school days, Soyinka was writing sketches for presentation and, soon after, clever comedies for the radio. At Leeds, he concentrated on the dramatic component in his course work. His career as a dramatist actually began when he became a play reader at the Royal Court Theatre in London, where some of his own early work was performed. Believing that special skills were necessary for the performance of his Nigerian plays, he determined upon his return to Lagos in 1960 to organize theater companies: The 1960 Masks Company in Lagos and The Orisun Theatre group in Ibadan (1964). Since then, he has argued that the best place for such companies, to ensure that they remain nonpolitical, is the university campus. This insistence on political nonalignment points to a final aspect of Soyinka's life—his social commitment. He has continually spoken out on public issues and, as a result, has risked the constant displeasure of existing authorities and institutions; he was detained in prison during the Biafran War, from August, 1967, to October, 1969. Even his early work contains political themes, but the Biafran War and his prison experiences have made his subsequent work more explicitly committed to social justice. He lived in exile from Nigeria for five years (1970-1975). His plays of those years and afterward, produced both abroad and at home, exhibit a political pessimism and employ varying degrees of political rhetoric, from subtle, intricate, metaphysical exploration to overt, satirical attack in public forums and over the radio. The dominant theme in his drama, as well as in his poetry and fiction, is individual human freedom, with its capacity for creation and destruction. Soyinka's own life is an example of that exertion of will, the responsibility of the individual to understand, reinterpret, and act upon his cultural surroundings.

Analysis

For Wole Soyinka, art and morality are blood brothers. This does not mean simply that sensitivity to beauty is a good indicator of moral awareness, though that is strongly suggested in *A Dance of the Forests*. What is more to the point is that the primary obligation of art is to tell the truth:

That obligation implies exposure and denunciation of falsehood. Even in Soyinka's broad farces—for example, the two plays that feature the prophet Jero—the object is not entertainment for its own sake but satire against any religious, social, or political leader who makes a mockery of human freedom. Soyinka also insists—with an eye on the romantic notion of negritude—that human beings have a dual nature whether they be African or Western; that is, they have destructive as well as creative urges. Part of his purpose as an artist is to expose the self-serving idealization of primitive African virtue; the problems in contemporary Africa may exist in a context of Western colonial oppression, but moral responsibility lies within the individual person as much as in the cultural milieu.

What is special about the moral content of Soyinka's drama is its metaphysical dimension, based upon his own personal rendering of Yoruba myth. It assumes a continuum between the worlds of the dead, the living, and the unborn. That continuum is made possible by a fourth realm which, in *Myth, Literature, and the African World*, Soyinka calls "the fourth stage," a realm which links the living with their ancestors and with the future. The myth of Ogun, the god who risked the dangers of the abyss and created a road from the spiritual to the human world, is the key to an understanding of all Soyinka's work, including his drama. The worship of Ogun is a ritual repetition of the god's feat. Yoruba drama, in a comparison which Soyinka himself makes, thus resembles Greek drama in its ritual essence and its origin. Ogun is the Yoruba counterpart of Dionysus. To emphasize its ritual nature, Soyinka incorporates in his drama elements of dance, music, mime, and masquerade. Characters are not merely actors playing a role—which in itself has ritual suggestions—but, in moments of high tension, are symbolically possessed by a god. The central actions are variations of rites of passage, with transformation or death-rebirth being the central archetypal pattern. Soyinka's most frequently used term for the terrifying experience of the numinous fourth stage is "transition." In some plays, the transition experience is artificial or incomplete, or it is parodied (the Jero plays); in others, it is the most pervasive theme.

Soyinka has a remarkable ability to combine the dramatic and theatrical device of peripeteia with the metaphysical experience of transition. The climactic event of the play—that is, the key reversal—is at the same time the moment of divine possession. Generally, the plays move from ordinary realism to ritual enactment, with the nonverbal elements of dance, song, and masquerade receiving increasing prominence as the climax approaches. Thus, for Soyinka, drama is a serious matter. He may say in a facetious moment that it must be primarily entertainment, but in fact he treats it not only as a social and moral force but also as an act of human freedom and a ritual reenactment of human beings' relationship to divinity.

Among Soyinka's early plays, *A Dance of the Forests* is the most ambitious; it is also the most complex treatment of the chthonic realm of transition. Even in what seems to be Soyinka's earliest major play, *The Swamp Dwellers*, the sensitive protagonist, Igwezu, appears as an outcast from ordinary society, as one who has returned from a confrontation with the gods and is not yet able to deal with the compromising and capricious worlds of society and nature. His climactic decisions are those of a man dazed by his revolutionary experiences. The wise old Beggar (an incarnation of the god?) cannot persuade him to turn his knowledge to account. *The Lion and the Jewel*, a comic rendition of society, presents the archetype of transition in at least two ways: through a parody of transformation as the ridiculous country schoolteacher, Lakunle, imagines his passage from bachelor to husband, and through the real rite of passage experienced by the heroine, Sidi, from maiden to wife. *A Dance of the Forests*, as the title itself suggests, is in another world entirely. All of the action is set in the forest, a universal symbol of the unknown, of the mysterious secrets of nature. It relies heavily on ritual, with its accompanying music, mime, dance, and masquerade. In the forest are representatives of the three other realms—the ancestors from the past, the living, and spiritual projections of posterity—as well as the gods and spirits who participate in and organize an extraordinary ritual to bridge the abyss between them.

A Dance of the Forests was written for the Nigerian independence celebrations in 1960, represented in the play as the Gathering of the Tribes. The principal human figures, Adenebi, Rola, and Demoke, have left the public festivities and sought the solitude of the forest. They are all guilty of some crime, hence uneasy in public, though the degree of their awareness varies considerably. Adenebi remains a lost soul because he cannot admit his guilt, even to himself. Rola, a prostitute, and Demoke, an artist who has just murdered his rival, at first, like Adenebi, try to hide their shame, but eventually they face the truth about themselves as human beings and achieve redemption. This is the essential plot of the play; it requires that these three characters—especially Demoke, as the central figure upon whom the climax turns—pass from the ordinary world of the living to the world of the dead and the gods—that is, that they enter the "fourth stage." The first people they meet are Dead Man and Dead Woman, who have come in answer to the summons of the tribes. These ancestors turn out to be not the glorious heroes of Africa's imaginary past but fallen human beings who led unsatisfactory lives. They are accusers rather than celebrators of humankind. Part 1 ends with some of the townspeople trying, through divination, ritual proverbs, dance and song, and a smoking, air-polluting lorry, to chase them away. Early in part 1, the three human protagonists also meet the Supreme Deity, called in the play Forest Head but temporarily disguised as an ordinary man named Obaneji. He guides them to the appointed place for the ritual Welcome of the Dead, which he has decided to hold in the forest because human society has refused to acknowledge the two dead guests as true ancestors out of their past.

Part 2 depicts a conflict between the forces of chance, retribution, and destruction, represented by the god Eshuoro, and the creative forces, represented by the god Ogun and his human agent, Demoke. It is a spiritual conflict that takes place in the realm of transition, symbolically rendered by the swamplike setting deep in the forest. The actual conflict between Eshuoro and Demoke is preceded by an elaborate Welcome of the Dead. Forest Head in Prospero-like fashion stages a drama that re-creates the crucial event in the lives of Dead Man and Dead Woman. Dead Man, a warrior in the court of Mata Kharibu three centuries earlier, had defied the order of his ruler and refused to fight a senseless war. His punishment was emasculation and slavery, which he had to endure in two subsequent incarnations. What he wants now is rest. Forest Head is sympathetic, but Eshuoro is not. Dead Woman was Dead Man's pregnant wife, who, overcome by grief, committed suicide and hence doomed her unborn child to the fate of an *abiku*, an infant that dies repeatedly in childbirth. This scene, designed to arouse fear and pity for the suffering in human life, especially of those whose motives are pure, becomes in the hands of Eshuoro, an uninvited guest who appears in disguise as the Questioner of the Dead, further evidence of the weakness and sinfulness of human nature. The scene also includes two other figures, previous incarnations of Rola and Demoke as Madame Tortoise, the archetypal prostitute, and the Court Poet, who along with the Warrior, resists her charms. What the scene also suggests, therefore, is the ever-recurring cycle of human history, and what follows is a dramatic and symbolic investigation of the question: Do human beings have the freedom and the will to change the pattern? Again it is Eshuoro who attempts to control the inquisition.

Up to this point, the three human protagonists have remained in the background (partly through dramatic necessity, since Rola and Demoke are actors in the flashback), but now the magic of Forest Head concentrates on their redemption. He insists that he cannot change anything himself; he can only provoke self-awareness. Thus, he designs a spiritual projection of the future but remains a passive observer. Significantly, the three humans are masked and become possessed by the spirits who speak through them. Having lost their identities, they enter totally the abyss of transition. The spirit voices from the intangible void are purposely obscure in their dire warnings. Scattered among them are the cries of Half-Child, whom Forest Head has meanwhile taken from the womb of Dead Woman. Its voice, too, is a voice of the future; it wants a full existence with a living mother.

With Eshuoro directing the action, the future of man appears desolate, but Eshuoro's power is not absolute. The play's climactic events, couched as they are in symbolic mime and dance, have elicited numerous interpretations. Eshuoro appears bent upon separating Half-Child from its mother, as though a reunion would mean salvation. Demoke becomes a principal actor (once Forest Head has restored his consciousness), as he attempts to protect the child. With Ogun's help, he succeeds in returning the child to the mother, but Eshuoro emits a shout of victory even at this, suggesting perhaps that Demoke's act may save the child but place his own life in jeopardy, for he is taking upon himself the responsibility of changing the pattern of history. A ritual scene follows in which Eshuoro forces Demoke, a "sacrificial basket" on his head, to climb the totem that Demoke had carved for the tribal festivities. Eshuoro then sets fire to the totem in order to kill both the artist and his creation, but his vengeance is foiled by Ogun, who catches the falling Demoke.

These scenes, depicting the saving of the child and of Demoke himself, are symbolically taking place within the unconscious and are a resolution to Demoke's particular problem and to the central issue raised by the play. As the tribe's carver, Demoke occupies a vital position. Without his art, ritual contact with the gods is impossible, yet in the act of carving the totem he had through jealousy flung his assistant and rival to his death. The incident reflects Soyinka's insistence on the creative and destructive tendencies in man. How can Demoke atone for his crime? The play dramatizes his inner acceptance of his human nature, his admission of guilt, and his redemption through the saving of Half-Child. Soyinka seems to suggest that all salvation is essentially personal and must follow the path of self-awareness, confession, and risk—a rite of passage across the abyss that separates human beings and the gods. The public celebration at the Gathering of the Tribes is pointless and meaningless, even hypocritical, since it denies the realities of the past and the destructive, darker side of human nature. The play thus offers both a tragic vision of life and hope for the future through the courageous acts of individual men. It also identifies the artist as the key provoker of self-awareness. Like Demoke, he is closest to the abyss; he possesses "fingers of the dead."

Between *A Dance of the Forests* in 1960 and *The Road* in 1965, Soyinka devoted his energies to the writing of his first novel, *The Interpreters*, but he did complete two plays during this period, *The Strong Breed* and *Kongi's Harvest*, both of which present a young man taking the responsibilities of the community on his own shoulders. In *The Strong Breed*, Eman first tries to deny the very fact of ritual atonement, especially his own inherited role as the "carrier" of tribal guilt; eventually, however, he plays out this role in another tribe with such obsession that he pays for his rebellion with his life. Daodu, in *Kongi's Harvest*, assumes the Hamlet-like role of avenger as he challenges the authority of the usurping President Kongi, forcing him in the climactic scene to face the horrors of death, of the abyss, which in his egotism he had ignored. In both plays, the myth of transition clearly remains the key to self-awareness.

These two plays were followed by *The Road*, Soyinka's first drama centered on the danger to human sanity posed by contact with the chthonic realm. The setting of *The Road* differs significantly from that of *A Dance of the Forests*. The latter takes place entirely within the realm of passage—symbolically the forest—and hence is essentially an inner experience; in contrast, *The Road* takes place in society—although a very specialized and symbolic segment of it—and is mainly concerned with the effects of death on social behavior. The vision of *A Dance of the Forests* is, broadly speaking, tragic, but with a comic ending: Demoke receives both atonement and a sobering projection of the future. *The Road*, on the other hand, maintains a comic atmosphere through most of its scenes but ends on a tragic note; it actually contains every conceivable dramatic mode, from satire and realism to symbolism and the absurd. Like *A Dance of the Forests*, it is a complex, multifaceted, and ambiguous play.

Structurally, *The Road* proceeds in a manner similar to *A Dance of the Forests*, from the ordinary to the ritualistic. Throughout, Soyinka maintains a tension between the practical world of survival and the spiritual world of essences, between the self and the other. Samson is a realist. He always retains contact with the ordinary world and fulfills the role of mirror or "narrator" even though he never steps out of his role as character. He is the reference point by which one measures the psychological states and obsessions of the other characters. In part 1, he remains onstage and controls the action until the final scene, when Professor, the epitome of obsession with death and the other major figure in the play, takes over the action. The same pattern emerges in part 2, in which Samson and Professor are usually onstage together and in which the balance gradually shifts in the direction of ritual. The setting for the play is a kind of run-down truck stop. Samson is a "tout" for the truck driver Kotonu, who has recently given up his job for psychological reasons that the play gradually makes clear. Professor, a former lay reader in the adjacent church, now runs the truckers' rest stop, which doubles as a spare-parts shop and headquarters of his Quest for the meaning of Death. He holds his own communion every evening for his followers and hangers-on. Murano, his assistant and palm-wine tapster, symbol of the transition stage and Professor's best hope for enlightenment, leaves every morning and returns in the evening with wine for the ritual service.

The play deals with one day in the lives of these characters, a day made decisive by two recent occurrences that bring Professor's Quest to its crisis. In part 1, the occurrences are merely suggested; part 2 contains their reenactment as past merges with present. Kotonu and Samson narrowly missed being killed in an accident on the road; a truck passed them and then fell through a rotted portion of a bridge. Though Samson viewed the near-miss stoically, Kotonu was so disturbed by the thought of death that he has given up driving, much to the displeasure of Samson, whose main preoccupation throughout the play is to restore Kotonu to his common sense. To this end, Samson solicits the aid of Professor, who has hired Kotonu to manage the spare-parts store. Samson insists that Kotonu's genius is in driving, not in scavenging parts off wrecked vehicles and selling them. Professor, however, is sympathetic with Kotonu's sudden concern with death. The second incident is even more significant. Kotonu and Samson were involved in a hit-and-run accident in which they "killed" a man masquerading as Ogun (the "guardian of the road") in a ritual ceremony; he was in the *agemo* phase, in transition from the human to the divine essence. They hid the body in the back of the truck and carried it to the truck stop, where Professor found it. This victim is the Murano of the play, in dumb suspension between life and death and hence supposedly in possession of secrets that Professor is after. The incident intensified Kotonu's withdrawal, especially since he was required to don Murano's bloody mask to escape capture by the other celebrants. Thus, Kotonu himself symbolically became the god Ogun in the rite of passage. The reenactment of these scenes, together with several others in which Samson mimicks Professor or recalls past incidents, dramatizes the impact of death on the living and structurally prepares for the final ritual act.

One other significant event has also recently occurred. Usually Professor leaves every morning for his tour of the road and, like Murano, does not return until evening. On this particular day, he has broken that pattern after coming upon a wreck and finding a road sign with the word "Bend" on it, which he takes to be symbolic. He returns to his headquarters more absentminded than usual and then departs in a daze. Part 1 ends with a funeral service at noon for the victims of the accident at the bridge, and with the return of Murano, confused by the organ music which usually calls him back in the evening. The day is clearly ominous. Murano is almost "killed" as a thief by one of the hangers-on. The communion service at the end of part 2 is the culmination of the various "performances" during the play that have become progressively more intense. The policeman, Particulars Joe, is at the truck stop in search of the hit-and-run victim, whom no one has as yet identified as Murano. The identification soon becomes clear as Murano discovers the Mask he had worn, puts it on, and begins the dance that is to continue until Professor's closing speech. Everyone at the communion, already intoxicated by the wine, senses the power of the moment, the traditional reenactment of the rite of passage from human to divine. Murano is becoming possessed by the god Ogun. Professor hopes to use the moment to gain secret knowledge of death without dying himself. Salubi, to retain his sanity, wants to leave. Say Tokyo Kid, apparently the Eshuoro figure, symbolic of retribution and destruction, skeptical of such ritual behavior, challenges Murano and, during the struggle, stabs Professor with a knife passed to him by Salubi. Murano, completely possessed by the god, hurls Say Tokyo Kid to his death. Professor ends the play with a sermon to his followers, enjoining them to imitate the Road by lying in wait and treacherously destroying the unsuspecting traveler.

The key figure in this play is Professor, but he is such a strange composite that the play remains an ambiguous statement. He is an archetypal character, or rather a composite of archetypes. He is Faust, Falstaff, Jesus, and Don Quixote mixed up in a bundle of conflicting motives. Like Falstaff, he insists on the survival instincts in human nature. Like Faust, he challenges the gods to achieve knowledge denied to the descendents of Adam. He has messianic fantasies, but he is maddened by his preoccupation with death as surely as Don Quixote's romance with literature blinds him to ordinary reality. It is as though the mind of Professor has become a chaotic image of the chthonic realm he so desperately searches out but which he as a human being cannot understand. He never learns that the road of his daily wanderings on which his drivers make their living is not a real substitute for the Road that Ogun traveled to make contact with the human. Whereas Demoke in *A Dance of the Forests* undergoes the transition experience but retains his human perspective, Professor becomes obsessed with the realm itself and intellectualizes himself out of human society. To a large extent, of course, he is a comic figure—the proverbial absentminded professor—but the ambivalent messianic-Machiavellian Quest gives him a certain magnificent dimension and elevates his flaw to the hubris of classical tragedy.

The chaotic misdirection of *The Road*—and, indeed, of much of Soyinka's work in the 1960's, with its motifs of political chicanery, moral inertia, and death in modern Nigeria—anticipated the horrors of the Biafran War at the end of the decade. The war and Soyinka's two-year detention in prison did not, in fact, drastically change his philosophical approach to his craft, but they did intensify his concerns. *The Trials of Brother Jero*, for example, written before the war, is political and social satire, but Jero as the trickster is essentially a comic figure mixing farce and wit. The political caricature who undergoes a mock transformation in the final scene is more ridiculous than dangerous. In a companion piece, however, *Jero's Metamorphosis*, written after the war, the ritual transformation of the beach prophets into an Apostolic Salvation Army is a thinly veiled attack on a military regime that has, as the play reiterates, made public execution a national spectacle. Jero, dressed in his general's uniform, sitting underneath his own portrait as the curtain falls, is a sinister threat to moral sanity. The very subject of *Madmen and Specialists*, written soon after Soyinka's release, is the war's devastating effect on every phase of human life. Its central character, Bero, is hubris itself in his absolute denial of the essence of Yoruba culture: the continuity of life, the gods, the ancestors, and humankind's responsibility toward the future. He renders meaningless the realm that links human beings with the gods, and he violates the primary law of existence—return to nature as much as or more than is taken from it—and reduces people to organisms.

Soyinka's willingness to undertake an adaptation of Euripides' *The Bacchae* thus comes as no surprise: It, too, deals with a madman in defiance of the gods and of the basic rhythms of human society and human nature. Dionysian possession and retribution are the closest thing in Western culture to the worship of Ogun among the Yoruba: *The Bacchae*, like *Madmen and Specialists*, constitutes a warning to militaristic oppression. In all three of these postwar plays, the motif of death, the numinous realm of passage, has retained its central place within the philosophical and dramatic structure; it has simply taken on added significance and urgency because of the realities through which Soyinka has had to live. It has become part of a greater political commitment and a deeper pessimism.

The new commitment and tone are nowhere more evident than in *Death and the King's Horseman*, a play which addresses the failure of the older generation to preserve intact the traditional Yoruba culture and which pessimistically depicts the attempt of their children to undertake the responsibility. According to Yoruba custom, when a king dies, his horseman must, at the end of the thirty days of mourning, commit suicide and join him in the passage to the underworld; otherwise, the king remains in the passage, subject to evil forces. Soyinka builds his play around the king's horseman, Elesin Oba, whose weakness of will breaks the age-old formula and places the entire society in danger of extinction. As with the other plays, much of the action is ritual, and, as is common in Soyinka, the climactic scenes combine dramatic peripeteia with divine possession and entrance into the transition phase. The structure also reflects another aspect of the play, the clash of African and Western cultures, a theme common in African literature but rather rare in Soyinka; the scenes alternate between Nigerian and British settings. Soyinka insists in a prefatory note that the British presence is only accidental: Elesin's failure is not imposed from without but is self-inflicted.

Soyinka organizes the play with his usual economy. All the action takes place within the span of a few hours. Act 1 presents Elesin's procession through the market just at closing time, on the way to his own death: He and his Praise Singer chant his fate. His love of the market as a symbol of earthly activity and life, however, suggests his ambivalence toward his role, and when he sees a beautiful young girl and arranges with Iyaloja, her future mother-in-law and leader of the market women, to marry and enjoy this maiden as his last earthly act, his eventual failure to carry out his appointed role is almost certain. Both Iyaloja and the audience, however, yield temporarily to Elesin's sophistic arguments. He insists that this is not mere sexual indulgence but a mingling of the "seeds of passage" with the life of the unborn; he deceives himself and his audience with poetic fancies and beautiful language. Iyaloja grants him the gift of the girl but warns him of his responsibility: His poetic fancy will not become a reality unless he dies.

In act 2, the scene changes to the home of the British District Officer, Simon Pilkings, and his wife, Jane; the accompanying music changes from sacred chant and rhythm to the tango. The *egungun* mask, used in Ogun worship to represent divine possession, has been turned into a costume for the masquerade later that evening. Here, Soyinka presents ritual suicide through the eyes of the supercilious Pilkings, who rejects Yoruba culture as barbaric; Jane is more sympathetic but still uncomprehending. Simon arranges for Amusa, a Nigerian sergeant in his employ, to arrest Elesin and prevent the completion of the ritual.

Act 3 begins with a comic scene in which the market women and their daughters turn Sergeant Amusa's duty into a mockery and send him packing back to his white superior. This moment of hilarious triumph gives way to what appears to be the climactic scene of the play, Elesin's emergence from his wedding chamber and his hypnotic dance of possession as he symbolically enters the abyss of transition.

This sacred event is replaced again by the artificiality of British custom, as act 4 begins with a mime at the masquerade ball, with the Prince of Wales (having come to Nigeria as a gesture of courage and solidarity during World War II) and his entourage dressed in seventeenth century costume, dancing to a Viennese waltz and admiring Pilkings' demonstration of the *egungun* dance movements and vocal accompaniments. When he learns that Amusa has failed in his mission, Pilkings departs for the market to halt the suicide. Meanwhile, Jane has a long discussion with Elesin's son, Olunde, who has just returned from studying medicine in England to oversee his father's ritual burial. Jane is shocked that Olunde still clings to barbaric customs in spite of his Western education; in turn, Olunde suggests the greater barbarism of world wars, and there is no meeting of minds. The act closes with the unexpected return of Pilkings with Elesin. Olunde, who had assumed with absolute confidence that his father had completed the ritual obligation, senses immediately the cosmic reversal of roles, represented onstage by the father on his knees begging forgiveness from his son and the son judging the father.

Act 5 sees Elesin in chains imprisoned at the Residency. Iyaloja and the other market women bear the body of Olunde to his cell. She condemns Elesin for forcing his son to die in his place, thus reversing the cycle of nature. At the sight of his son, Elesin strangles himself with his chain and enters the abyss, though perhaps too late to satisfy the demands of the gods. What is especially significant about this scene is Elesin's second attempt to conceal the truth from himself. In act 2, he had refused to face his excessive love of life, his inability to leave the world of pleasure to the young. Now, in his conversation with Iyaloja before his recognition of his son, he is denying responsibility for his failure of will. He blames the tempting touch of young flesh and mentions Iyaloja's own complicity in the temptation; he blames especially Pilkings for his abrupt intervention. His most significant statement, however, is his self-serving appeal to the cultural situation. The power and influence of British culture, he says, caused him to question the loyalty of his own gods, and he came to doubt the validity of the ritual itself. The play ends with a dirge over the deaths of Olunde and Elesin, but also, perhaps, over the death of a culture. Iyaloja and Olunde have completed the ritual as best they could, but she is not sure whether the son's death will satisfy the gods. The question remains, whether the younger generation of Nigerians will be able to save the civilization that their parents, in self-indulgence, doubt, and cowardice, have abandoned.

Two satirical plays of the 1980's, *A Play of Giants* and *Requiem for a Futurologist*, insist that neither the political leaders nor the people have emerged from the chaos. In the first, set in New York City, Field-Marshal Kamini (a thinly disguised Idi Amin of Uganda) is a con artist who leads three other heads of state in a hostage-taking, blackmailing, terrorist challenge against the United Nations. It is an all-out, farcical attack on the worship of power by those who wield it and those who submit to it. In the second play, the con artist is an opportunistic servant, Alaba, who uses various disguises to "overthrow" his master, Dr. Godspeak, a well-known prophet or "futurologist," by convincing the public and the doctor himself that he is dead. At Godspeak's "death," Alaba becomes the futurologist, a reincarnation of the famous French astrologer Nostradamus, who can use his supposed powers to exploit a gullible population. In Kamini and Alaba, Soyinka thus metamorphoses once again the Jero of the 1960 play. Nigeria—and the world—still plays the grotesque, exhausting, and futile game of the quack and the dupe.

Other major works

NOVELS: *The Interpreters*, 1965; *Season of Anomy*, 1973.

POETRY: *Idanre and Other Poems*, 1967; *Poems from Prison*, 1969; *A Shuttle in the Crypt*, 1972; *Ogun Abibiman*, 1976; *Mandela's Earth and Other Poems*, 1988.

NONFICTION: *The Man Died*, 1972 (autobiography); *Myth, Literature, and the African World*, 1976; *Aké: The Years of Childhood*, 1981 (autobiography); *Art, Dialogue, and Outrage*, 1988; *Ìsarà: A Voyage Around "Essay,"* 1989; *The Credo of Being and Nothingness, 1991.*

TRANSLATION: *Forest of a Thousand Daemons: A Hunter's Saga*, 1968 (of D. O. Fagunwa's novel *Ogboju Ode Ninu Igbo Irunmale*).

Bibliography

Gibbs, James, ed. *Critical Perspectives on Wole Soyinka.* Washington, D.C.: Three Continents Press, 1980. Contains two introductory essays by Bernth Lindfors and Abiola Irele; fifteen essays on a few individual plays (including *A Dance of the Forests*, the Jero plays, *The Road*, and *Death and the King's Horseman*) and on such subjects as popular theater, tragedy, Third World drama, and dramatic theory; and other essays on Soyinka's poetry and prose. A helpful introduction includes chronological charts on Soyinka as academic, dramatist, and political activist. The select bibliography of primary and secondary sources is thorough.

__________. *Wole Soyinka.* New York: Grove Press, 1986. This general, introductory study of Soyinka as a dramatist, a volume in the *Grove Press Modern Dramatists* series, provides a sketch of the author's life, a chapter entitled "Sources and Influences," and a seven-chapter, chronological survey of the plays, from the beginning through *A Play of the Giants*, with summaries, historical background, and commentary. It treats both dramatic and theatrical concerns and includes photographs from several productions, a bibliography, and an index.

Jones, Eldred Durosimi. *The Writing of Wole Soyinka.* 3d ed. Portsmouth, N.H.: Heinemann, 1988. This introductory survey of Soyinka's works opens with a background essay on the author. Subsequent essays deal with individual texts under the general chapter headings, "Autobiography," "Plays," "Poetry," and "Fiction." Essays on thirteen plays follow a summary-commentary format, approaching them as individual, literary texts, but with some cross-referencing, a few production and theatrical notes, and occasional attention to stylistic development. Includes a biographical outline and a brief bibliography.

Maduakor, Obi. *Wole Soyinka: An Introduction to His Writing.* New York: Garland, 1986. A helpful, critical study designed to clarify difficult aspects of Soyinka's more difficult works. Its four parts include "The Poems," "Fictional and Autobiographical Prose," "Five Metaphysical Plays," and "The Literary Essays." The drama section, around one hundred pages, contains individual chapters on the more abstract and "elliptical" plays (*A Dance of the Forests*, *The Road*, *Madmen and Specialists*, *The Bacchae*, and *Death and the King's Horseman*), under the general topics of "dramatic technique, dramatic structure, theme, characterization, and language."

Moore, Gerald. *Twelve African Writers.* Bloomington: Indiana University Press, 1980. The chapter on Soyinka, "Across the Primeval Gulf," examines the works that appeared after the civil war, including several plays, as manifestations of the Ogun myth, the god's creative act of will bridging the gulf between gods and humans, and his later act of mad genocide. The plays exhibit comparable human tendencies toward creation and destruction and the need for "social renewal" that the god symbolizes.

———. *Wole Soyinka.* 2d ed. London: Evans Brothers, 1978. This expanded, second edition of Moore's chronological study devotes more than half of its 165 pages to the plays. It begins with a biographical introduction that helps explain "the foundations of Soyinka's dramatic career." "Early Work in the Theatre," "A Dance in the Forests," and "The Tragedies" treat the plays before Soyinka's imprisonment, and later chapters look at postwar plays through *Death and the King's Horseman.* Moore's analysis connects the drama with Soyinka's "total activity in the theatre and in society." Production illustrations and select bibliography.

Thomas Banks

SIR RICHARD STEELE

Born: Dublin, Ireland; March, 1672
Died: Carmarthen, Wales; September 1, 1729

Principal drama

The Funeral: Or, Grief à-la-mode, pr. 1701, pb. 1702; *The Lying Lover: Or, The Ladies' Friendship*, pr. 1703, pb. 1704 (based on Pierre Corneille's play *Le Menteur*); *The Tender Husband: Or, The Accomplished Fools*, pr., pb. 1705 (based on Molière's play *Le Sicilien*); *The Conscious Lovers*, pr. 1722, pb. 1723 (based on Terence's play *Andria*); *The Plays of Richard Steele*, 1971 (Shirley Strum Kenny, editor).

Other literary forms

Sir Richard Steele's periodical essays, even more than his four plays, had a major impact upon early eighteenth century sensibility. Beginning his journalistic career as the anonymous author of the Whig government's *The London Gazette*, Steele later joined with Joseph Addison to produce *The Tatler* (1709-1711; 188 by Steele) and *The Spectator* (1711-1712, 1714; 236 by Steele), the most influential vehicles of opinion and taste of their day, comprising short, fictional essays illustrating an idea, theme, or moral. Steele later wrote, also with Addison, *The Guardian* (1713), also a vehicle for periodical essays. *The Englishman* (1713-1714, first series; 1715, second series; periodical essays), *The Theatre* (1720, later edited by John Loftis and published as *Richard Steele's "The Theatre,"* 1920, 1962), and lesser periodicals also came from Steele's pen. Taken together, these more than seven hundred essays constitute Steele's major literary achievement. Steele was also an occasional poet, a writer of political tracts such as *The Importance of Dunkirk Considered* (1713), and a moral philosopher, author of *The Christian Hero* (1701).

Achievements

Although not a dramatist of the first rank, Steele had some notable successes and is important in theater history. He came to write for the theater when, in his words, successful comedies were "built upon the ruin of virtue and innocence." An advocate of reform, Steele hoped to demonstrate that a play could provide effective entertainment without pandering to the worst tastes of the town; he believed that high spirits and a healthy didacticism could coexist. In practice, his demonstrations were mixed successes. Steele stressed domestic virtues and worked hard to make them seem attractive. He appealed to emotion in ways not customary in comedy, helping to usher in a hybrid form known as sentimental comedy, a forerunner of melodrama. These features, as well as Steele's characters and themes, caused him to be among the first to reflect the consciousness of the new middle class.

Steele was a competent manager of dramatic structure, a fashioner of believable characters who speak intelligibly and who, when they are not whining excessively, can gain one's sympathy. Often robust in movement, Steele's comedies sometimes suffer from being too studied, too obviously written as prescriptions and thus lacking in natural ease. Steele's plays, along with his drama criticism, had considerable influence in England and in France. Unfortunately, it was an influence in a direction that has not found much esteem—though the enormous audience for the twentieth century soap opera may owe him a debt of gratitude.

Biography

Sir Richard Steele was born into a family of the English governing class in Ireland. His paternal grandfather was a successful merchant adventurer and courtier who enjoyed the favor of both James I and Charles I. Steele's father (both forebears were also named Richard) led a less colorful life, but he had begun a promising career as a lawyer when young Richard was born in 1672. Steele's mother, born Elinor Sheyles (a Celtic name), was the widow of Thomas Symes of Dublin. She became Mrs. Steele in 1670. Because Steele's father died at a young age without establishing a sure footing for his children, it fell to Richard's aunt, Katherine Steele Mildmay, to provide for the family. Her second marriage, to Henry Gascoigne in 1675, placed her in a position to help her nephew, and it was through Gascoigne's influence (he was private secretary to the Duke of Ormonde) that Steele entered Charterhouse, a prestigious "public" school, in the fall of 1684. At Charterhouse, Steele met his famous friend and collaborator, Joseph Addison, though the two men attended different colleges at Oxford. In 1695, Steele became an ensign in Lord Cutt's regiment, and, partly as a result of his earliest literary efforts, he soon gained a commission and later a captaincy.

Steele made his mark in literary circles with his essay *The Christian Hero* and then with a series of comedies—*The Funeral*, *The Lying Lover*, and *The Tender Husband*—all produced between 1701 and 1705. His success made him an early member of the Kit-Kat Club, founded by leading Whigs, where he enjoyed the company of London's literary intelligentsia and made important Whig connections. By 1707, Steele was "the Gazetteer," the writer of the official government newspaper. After this political hackwork, he joined forces with Addison to create two successful and influential papers, *The Tatler* and *The Spectator*. These periodicals, of which Steele wrote more than four hundred between 1709 and 1712, established for him a second and more permanent reputation. First befriended and then attacked by Jonathan Swift, Steele found himself increasingly a political creature and gave less attention to his other periodical ventures during the last years of the Tory ministry under Queen Anne. An active Whig scribe, Steele found himself in and out of the House of Commons and ready to share the spoils of the coming Whig triumph of 1714.

Early in 1715, Steele was made governor of Drury Lane Theatre, regained a seat in Parliament, and (in April) was knighted by George I. He held the Drury Lane post, at least nominally, until his death. Reform of the stage was Steele's mission, as it had been in his early plays and in his many essays about the theater, but only during the first five years was he active in his duties, and even then he had only limited success in administering the reforms he advocated. His last play, *The Conscious Lovers*, is the best testimony to the sincerity of his goals. Ill health plagued Steele's later years, which he divided between Hereford and Carmarthen, Wales, where he died in 1729.

Steele's domestic life was a study in contrasts. He had an illegitimate daughter by Elizabeth Tonson, the sister of his then future publisher. His first marriage, in the spring of 1705 to Margaret Ford Stretch, a widow of considerable property, ended with her death late the following year. Steele managed to encumber her estate with debts. In 1707, he married Mary Scurlock of Carmarthen. Their marriage of eleven years was marked by Steele's utmost tenderness and devotion, as his constant letters to her attest. She died in childbirth. Neither of Steele's two legitimate daughters lived to have children of her own, though his illegitimate daughter did. His two sons did not survive childhood.

Analysis

Of Sir Richard Steele's four plays, *The Funeral* and *The Tender Husband* are at once the most humorous and the least sentimental. *The Funeral*, Steele's most original play, was written in part to relieve him of the reputation he had made as a pious drone through his essay *The Christian Hero*. Even these sprightly pieces, however, reveal Steele's concern with curing the corruption of the London stage. He shunned the licentiousness that had been rampant but gave each piece enough wit, zest, and characterization to make it popular for many years to come. It is as the author of *The Lying Lover* and *The Conscious Lovers* that Steele's reputation as a founder of the sentimental comedy rests. The earlier play was not a stage success, and it is clearly the weakest of Steele's dramatic efforts. *The Conscious Lovers* was both a success and a major influence. An analysis of *The Tender Husband* and *The Conscious Lovers* allows representation of what M. E. Hare called Steele's "purely amusing and his didactic veins."

The Tender Husband presents Biddy Tipkin, a young girl whose guardian uncle has arranged her marriage to a country cousin, one Humphry Gubbin. Biddy, whose head is filled with the excesses of the airy romances she reads so voraciously, has let herself imagine something far more exotic and impassioned than this dry arrangement. For his part, Humphry does not want to be forced into anything. When the two meet, they pledge to be friendly enemies; they will not have each other, but they will cooperate toward each other's freedom.

Before the audience is introduced to this pair, it learns that Captain Jack Clerimont is seeking his financial ease through a careful marriage. His older brother, Clerimont Senior, has heard of Biddy and helps set a plot in motion that will give Jack a chance at that prize. Everything Jack hears about Biddy's wealth is translated into a positive personal attribute in his playful formulations. Apprised of her fortune of ten thousand pounds, Jack responds: "Such a stature, such a blooming countenance, so easy a shape!" The play's humor, and part of its meaning, derives from interchanges of this sort. By making Jack a good-natured rogue, Steele softens the cynicism in this conventional equation of love and money.

With the wily lawyer Samuel Pounce as helpful (and bribed) intermediary, Jack is given the opportunity to meet and to woo Biddy. He imitates the manner and language of romance literature, quickly winning her heart. He has already convinced himself that he is rescuing her from the hard fate her uncle has in mind. Biddy, because she wants to be, is an easy conquest. Pounce, by distracting Biddy's stern Aunt Barsheba with talk of the stock-market (her true passion), makes Jack's path as smooth as can be.

In a later scene, Jack, disguised as the artist hired by Barsheba to paint her niece's portrait, completes his courtship of Biddy while warning her of how her romantic notions will have to be adjusted to reality. By this time, Steele has modulated Jack's intentions so that his cynical first motive has changed into something far more acceptable; he has discovered a genuine affection for the girl. No longer simply deceiving her for her money, he has been transformed from Restoration rake into earnest suitor.

Wrapped around the Humphry-Biddy-Jack plot is another, more sinister one. Clerimont Senior has been using his soon-to-be-cast-off mistress, Lucy Fainlove, in a most despicable manner. He has had her disguise herself as a man, not only to pass unsuspected before Mrs. Clerimont but also to put that lady in a compromising position so that her husband can "discover" the infidelity that he assumes to be the consequence of the fashionable liberty she desires and he seems to grant. Although his scheme works, he gains little by it. Because he is softened by his wife's tears and somewhat sorry for his deceit, Clerimont Senior becomes Steele's way of suggesting that even a man of generous heart can be temporarily led astray by social fashions that magnify vice by encouraging human frailties. His wife, too, has allowed herself to be victimized. Her love of appearances and affectations provided her, for a while at least, with more pain than pleasure.

Everyone ends up reconciled and happy with the final state of affairs.

Jack gets Biddy, the older Clerimonts passionately patch things up, and Lucy Fainlove captures Humphry, who is quite pleased with himself. Lucy turns out to be the sister of lawyer Pounce, a neat twist that allows Steele to link the two plots together.

If *The Tender Husband* (an ironic title) says anything, it says that people will behave as these people do. It also suggests that those most concerned with forms and appearances are most easily deceived. Steele, like William Congreve in *The Way of the World* (pr. 1700), advocates marriages based on love rather than on parental arrangements, but he (again like Congreve) recognizes the importance of financial security. Jack begins by seeking a fortune; Biddy begins by longing for a romantic dream. Each ends up at a humane, caring, yet practical middle ground.

In many ways, *The Tender Husband* is like much of the Restoration comedy that predates it. Clerimont Senior is the familiar libertine type, though his reformation precludes either a significant victory or any kind of punishment. The far more appealing Jack is still not a paragon of virtue, as the true sentimental hero must be. The tone of the play, however, is far less cynical and the satire is far more gentle than that to which audiences had been accustomed. It is easy to feel sympathy for Jack, for Biddy, and even for Humphry, who is a very special version of the stock country bumpkin and a clear model for Oliver Goldsmith's famous Tony Lumpkin in *She Stoops to Conquer* (pr. 1773). Biddy's aunt, her Uncle Hezekiah, and Humphry's father are all recognizable types, but Steele gives them life. The many songs in the play add their own charm. Colloquially convincing, witty, unburdened by preachiness, *The Tender Husband* is to many critics Steele's best play. It "reforms" the excesses of Restoration comedy without losing touch with what made them work. It remains, first and last, an entertainment.

The same cannot be said for *The Conscious Lovers*. In his preface to the first edition, Steele asserted that "the chief design of this was to be an innocent performance." The prologue asked the audience to value "wit that scorns the aids of vice" and to help "moralize the stage" by giving the work a kind reception. Clearly, then, *The Conscious Lovers* was designed as a model for a new type of drama. As governor of Drury Lane, Steele had made but the slightest advances in his campaign for reform. With his own play he hoped to make his intentions clear while pleasing a discriminating audience.

The play's plot concerns Bevil Junior's desire to please his heart without displeasing his father. Bevil is a model son: loving, respectful, and particularly unwilling to bring his father any pain. Sir John, though a bit formal, is a caring father who has his son's interests at heart. In standard comic tradition, he has arranged a marriage between his son and Lucinda Sealand. It would be a sensible match, except that the two are not in love.

Because Bevil does not wish to go against his father, he has not given any hint of his dismay. He acts exactly as his father wishes as the marriage day approaches. The audience learns that he is counting on being rebuffed, as he knows that Lucinda has her heart set elsewhere. This is a very risky charade, however, especially since Mr. Sealand has favored the match with Bevil.

Recently, though, Mr. Sealand has begun to have doubts about Bevil, and he is about to break off the engagement. Bevil was seen paying suspicious attentions to a mysterious young lady at a masked ball. Questioned by Sir John, Bevil insists that everything is honorable, that he is still worthy of his father's trust, and that the planned marriage should take place.

The mysterious beauty is Indiana, an unfortunate girl who has lost first her parents and then her guardians in a series of calamities. She had been threatened by pirates and sent to prison; then fortune sent Bevil into her life. Her rescuer has set her up in respectable London lodgings with her Aunt Isabella and is "keeping" the young lady without making any demands. Believing himself tied to Lucinda, Bevil has not spoken to Indiana of his love for her, but she hopes that she has read signs of love in his deeds and in his eyes. Isabella expects base motives and keeps her niece worried. Poor Indiana is desperately in love with her benefactor and is tortured by doubt.

There are two genuine suitors for Lucinda's hand. One is Bevil's friend Mr. Myrtle, whose sincere love is returned by Lucinda. The other is Cimberton, a formal, distant, wealthy oaf who is Mrs. Sealand's choice. These complications introduce a battle of wills between Lucinda's parents concerning who will control the girl's future. A conflict, thus, springs up between Bevil, whose behavior is confusing to those around him, and Myrtle, whose jealousy leads him to suspect Bevil of treachery.

The play is a framework for Bevil's moral dilemmas. Should he disobey his father? Can he do so without hurting him? When Myrtle challenges him to a duel, should he partake of this honorable custom—or should he prove to Myrtle that his jealousy is groundless by revealing an exchange of letters between Lucinda and himself against Lucinda's wishes? The audience is intended to feel the struggle within the sensitive and scrupulous young man, and, to some extent, Steele's strategy does succeed. Because Steele detested the dueling custom, he has Bevil argue his way out of the challenge, though Bevil finally must break the confidence that Lucinda has placed in him. Myrtle, once enlightened, is properly thankful, almost tearful, as he recognizes the difficulty of Bevil's stance and the purity of his motives. In true sentimental-comedy form, the two can now work together toward the end of matching Myrtle with Lucinda.

While Mr. Sealand is planning to seek out the mysterious Indiana to discover the truth about Bevil's behavior, Mrs. Sealand is busy concluding arrangements for Lucinda's marriage to Cimberton. She calls in lawyers to determine if Cimberton can bestow an estate on Lucinda without his uncle's consent. Seeing an opportunity for information and delay, Myrtle and Bevil's man Tom disguise themselves as the lawyers. Their expert exchange of opinion naturally ends in confusion. Sir Geoffry Cimberton is then expected. Now Myrtle disguises himself as the uncle, buying time for himself, slightly discouraging the match, then revealing himself and his bold, passionate nature to Lucinda. Mrs. Sealand, not sure what to do next, decides to take everyone and follow her husband as he inquires into the Indiana matter.

A tearful discovery scene ensues as Indiana first reveals the delicacy of her situation and then, by reviewing her history, leads Mr. Sealand to understand that he is face-to-face with his daughter (by a first wife) who was lost in infancy. Through this happy accident, a Bevil-Sealand match is made possible after all. Sir John, when he learns all, is properly proud of his son's behavior and is happy to welcome Indiana in Lucinda's place. He has learned his lesson about arranged marriages. Cimberton, upon hearing that Lucinda's fortune has now diminished by one half (that becomes her sister's), leaves the field, and Myrtle is quick to take advantage of the opening. The play concludes with assurances that "Whate'er the generous mind itself denies/ The secret care of Providence supplies."

Though Steele has made virtue attractive in terms of the plot, the stock discovery scene cheapens the resolution somewhat. One cannot depend on providence being this fantastic. The question is whether Steele has made virtue attractive in terms of the virtuous characters themselves. The moral scruples of Bevil Senior and Junior create a strained situation in which they cannot deal frankly with each other, and Bevil's constant rationalizing of his behavior is not especially attractive. One is made to believe that, in the end, Bevil would not have gone through with the marriage to Lucinda. Thus, saving a miracle, a rupture between father and son would be inevitable. Would it not be better for Bevil to make an early declaration of his feelings for Indiana? Certainly Indiana would have been spared much anguish. While it is clear that the hero never acts out of malice, his caution and sensibility lead him into behavior that is deceitful and hurtful.

Isabella's constant questioning of Bevil's motives creates the trial of Indiana's fortitude that is an emotional center of the play; more important, this persistent doubt reveals the pervasive cynicism of the play's social world. To others, if not to the audience, Bevil's behavior is unbelievable if understood as altruistic. Isabella is sure there is a trap somewhere: Bevil must expect something for paying Indiana's bills. Thus, Steele creates a sort of Platonic mistress while keeping vice offstage. Because Bevil, however, perceives Indiana's warm feelings for him, is it fair—is it manly—for him to withhold his own?

The Bevils, father and son, remain compromised and tedious figures, whatever Steele's intentions. Real wisdom lies in Sir John's servant, Humphrey, and to a lesser extent in the truly comic characters, Tom and Phillis. The romance between Tom and Lucinda's maid is high-spirited and reasonably straightforward. Their bantering and jests at the upper classes are a source of genuine humor, as are the disguise scenes of Tom and Myrtle and the stuffy indifference of Cimberton. It is as if Steele has two plays going on at once: a solemn, didactic tearjerker and an old-fashioned farce. The sentimental part is not comic, and the comic part is not sentimental.

If he had continued to write for the theater, Steele might have improved on the formula—he had the tools and the inspiration. In itself, *The Conscious Lovers* only points in a direction it cannot reach.

Other major works

SHORT FICTION: *The Tatler*, 1709-1711 (with Joseph Addison; periodical essays); *The Spectator*, 1711-1712, 1714 (with Addison; periodical essays); *The Englishman*, 1713-1714, 1715 (periodical essays); *The Guardian*, 1713 (with Addison; periodical essays); *The Lover*, 1714 (periodical essays).

POETRY: *The Procession*, 1695; *Prologue to the University of Oxford*, 1706; *Epilogue to the Town*, 1721; *The Occasional Verse of Richard Steele*, 1952 (Rae Blanchard, editor).

NONFICTION: *The Christian Hero*, 1701; *The Importance of Dunkirk Considered*, 1713; *The Theatre*, 1720 (later published as *Richard Steele's "The Theatre,"* 1920, 1962; John Loftis, editor); *Tracts and Pamphlets by Richard Steele*, 1944 (Blanchard, editor); *The Correspondence of Richard Steele*, 1968 (Blanchard, editor).

Bibliography

Boas, F. S. *An Introduction to Eighteenth-Century Drama, 1700-1780.* Oxford, England: Clarendon Press, 1953. An informative chapter on Steele discusses the military situation that led him into the theater to regain his reputation as a good fellow. Boas judges *The Funeral* unconvincing in its plot but finds that it has good characters, good dialogue, and a firm moral position. Believes that the sentimentality appearing in *The Lying Lover* and *The Tender Husband* mars both works. Compares *The Conscious Lovers* with its source.

Hare, M. E. *Steele and the Sentimental Comedy.* Oxford, England: Clarendon Press, 1909. Hare gives credit to Steele for creating a new comedy that exhibited the private virtues instead of exposing the vices, and that created dramatic interest through the anxieties, rather than the faults, of humankind. Believes, however, that a serious decline of English comedy resulted from these endeavors.

Kenny, Shirley S. *The Plays of Richard Steele.* Oxford, England: Clarendon

Press, 1971. Contains a substantial introduction to each Steele play, providing information on the sources, the manner of composition, the stage history, and the fame and influence of the play, with notes on the text. Readers are greatly aided by valuable sections of commentary.

Schneider, Ben Ross, Jr. *The Ethos of Restoration Comedy.* Urbana: University of Illinois Press, 1971. Schneider discusses Steele passim but provides a commentary related to major elements in late seventeenth century comedy: satire, the plain-dealing versus the double-dealing characters, criticism of characters who show self-love, and others. He finds that Steele, unlike other dramatists, did not deride characters involved in trade and concludes that Steele finally understood Restoration comedy, then helped kill it, with *The Conscious Lovers* delivering the death blow to the earlier type of comedy.

Winton, Calhoun. *Sir Richard Steele, M.P.: The Later Career.* Baltimore: The Johns Hopkins University Press, 1970. Provides an extensive treatment (more than two hundred pages) of Steele from 1714 to 1729. The critical discussion of the plays, however, is highly limited. This basically chronological study includes several appendices (one including papers on the revocation of the license for the Drury Lane Theatre) and a useful index. A continuation of Winton's earlier volume.

Philip K. Jason
(Updated by *Howard L. Ford*)

TOM STOPPARD
Tomas Straussler

Born: Zlin, Czechoslovakia; July 3, 1937

Principal drama

A Walk on the Water, pr. 1964 (televised; revised and televised as *The Preservation of George Riley*, 1964; revised and staged as *Enter a Free Man*, pr., pb. 1968); *The Gamblers*, pr. 1965; *Rosencrantz and Guildenstern Are Dead*, pr. 1966, pb. 1967; *Tango*, pr. 1966, pb. 1968 (adapted from the play by Sławomir Mrożek); *Albert's Bridge*, pr. 1967 (radio play), pr. 1969 (staged), pb. 1969; *The Real Inspector Hound*, pr., pb. 1968 (one act); *After Magritte*, pr. 1970, pb. 1971 (one act); *Dogg's Our Pet*, pr. 1971, pb. 1976 (one act); *Jumpers*, pr., pb. 1972; *Travesties*, pr. 1974, pb. 1975; *Dirty Linen and New-Found-Land*, pr., pb. 1976; *The Fifteen-Minute Hamlet*, pb. 1976, pr. 1992; *Every Good Boy Deserves Favour*, pr. 1977, pb. 1978 (music by André Previn); *Night and Day*, pr., pb. 1978; *Dogg's Hamlet, Cahoot's Macbeth*, pr. 1979, pb. 1980; *Undiscovered Country*, pr. 1979, pb. 1980 (adapted from Arthur Schnitzler's play *Das weite Land*); *On the Razzle*, pr., pb. 1981 (adaptation of Johann Nestroy's play *Einen Jux will er sich machen*); *The Real Thing*, pr., pb. 1982; *The Dog It Was That Died, and Other Plays*, pb. 1983; *The Love for Three Oranges*, pr. 1983 (adaptation of Sergei Prokofiev's opera); *Rough Crossing*, pr. 1984, pb. 1985 (adaptation of Ferenc Molnár's play *Play at the Castle*); *Dalliance*, pr., pb. 1986 (adapted from Arthur Schnitzler's play *Liebelei*); *Hapgood*, pr., pb. 1988; *Arcadia*, pr. 1993.

Other literary forms

In addition to composing plays and occasionally adapting the dramas of others, Tom Stoppard has written several short stories, radio plays, television plays, screenplays, and the novel *Lord Malquist and Mr. Moon* (1966). He prides himself on his versatility, eschewing the notion of the dedicated author plowing a lonely furrow and sacrificing almost all other concerns on the altar of high art. Instead, as he told an interviewer in 1976:

> I've got a weakness . . . for rather shallow people who knock off a telly play and write a rather good novel and . . . interview Castro and write a good poem and a bad poem and . . . every five years do a really good piece of work as well. That sort of eclectic, trivial person who's very gifted.

Stoppard's novel *Lord Malquist and Mr. Moon* is "rather good." It is an exuberant farce that uses a collage of literary styles and allusions ranging from those of Joseph Conrad to Oscar Wilde, and from James Joyce to T. S. Eliot. Lord Malquist is a modern-day earl who seeks to sustain the dandyish refinements of his eighteenth century ancestors. His hired diarist, Mr. Moon, is a pathetically ineffectual man obsessively nursing a home-made bomb. Where the imperious and selfish Malquist anticipates such later dramatic characters as Sir Archibald Jumper of *Jumpers*, the confused, Prufrockian Moon models for the rebuffs experienced by the same text's George Moore. Malquist sums up what seems to be the novel's thesis when he declares, "since we cannot hope for order, let us withdraw with style from the chaos."

Achievements

Stoppard's dramaturgy has a uniquely wide appeal in the contemporary theater, since he often manages to combine comedy with social concern, farce with moral philosophy, and sometimes absurdism with naturalism. He and Harold Pinter, beginning in the 1960's, came to be considered the English-speaking world's leading playwrights. Both owe a large debt to Samuel Beckett and exhibit a willingness to experiment with theatrical forms. Pinter's sparse language, pauses, and silences, however, contrast sharply with Stoppard's free-flowing fountains of verbal play and display. Moreover, Pinter's carefully guarded characters and often baffling, static plots could not differ more from Stoppard's accessible people and vividly detailed, fast-paced action sequences.

Stoppard's work is postmodernist in its self-conscious artfulness and intricate game playing. He loves to confound his audience with abrupt shifts of time and convention, unreliable narrations, and surprising twists of plot. His eclectic borrowings fuse high and low culture, invading the texts of William Shakespeare, Wilde, George Bernard Shaw, Joyce, Eliot, and many more to combine them with "whodunit" thrillers, journalistic techniques, music-hall comedies, and popular love songs.

The leading debate among Stoppard's critics is whether his works are too frivolous and waggish to be taken seriously, whether, despite his eye for striking situations and ear for witty talk, he is no more than an ingenious but juvenile sprinter, too short-winded to complete the potential of his promising situations. His supporters, who seem to command a clear majority, insist that Stoppard is able to fuse his fertile comic sense with intellectual substance. They find his vision of life mature and profound as he dramatizes such concerns as free will versus fate (*Rosencrantz and Guildenstern Are Dead*), moral philosophy (*Jumpers*), art versus politics (*Travesties*), totalitarianism (*Every Good Boy Deserves Favour*), the press's freedoms and responsibilities (*Night and Day*), and married love (*The Real Thing*). They assert that Stoppard's career has shown an increasing commitment to ethical humanism and freedom of conscience while his dramatic craft has forged a rare compact between high comedy and the drama of ideas.

Biography

Tomas Straussler was born on July 3, 1937, in the town of Zlin, Czechoslovakia, since renamed Gottwaldov. He was the youngest of two sons of a physician, Eugene Straussler, and his wife, Martha. Since either the father or mother had at least one parent of Jewish descent (Stoppard is reticent about discussing his childhood), the family moved to Singapore in early 1939, on the eve of the German invasion of their homeland. In 1942, all but the father moved again, to India, just before the Japanese invasion, in which Dr. Straussler was killed. In 1946, Martha Straussler married Kenneth Stoppard, a major in the British army who was stationed in India. Both children took their stepfather's name when the family moved to England later that year. Demobilized, Kenneth Stoppard prospered as a salesman of machine tools.

Despite this globe-trotting background—in one interview he called himself "a bounced Czech"—Stoppard has spoken and written in English since the age of five. His first school in Darjeeling, India, was an English-language, American-run institution. He attended preparatory schools in Nottingham and Yorkshire, leaving at the age of seventeen after having completed his "A" levels. In 1954, he began working as a local journalist in Bristol, rejoicing in the life of a newspaper reporter for the next six years. He did not consider becoming a playwright until the late 1950's, when a new breed of English dramatists, led by John Osborne and Arnold Wesker, asserted themselves on the London stage. Simultaneously, a new breed of actors emerged, prominent among them Peter O'Toole, whose blazing performances for the Bristol Old Vic repertory company definitively turned Stoppard to the theater.

In July, 1960, Stoppard wrote *The Gamblers*—a one-act clumsily derived from Beckett's *En attendant Godot* (pb. 1952, pr. 1953; *Waiting for Godot*, pb. 1954, pr. 1955)—which was unsuccessfully staged in Bristol in 1965. Later in 1960, he composed his first full-length play, *A Walk on the Water.* Considerably rewritten and retitled *Enter a Free Man*, it was staged in London in 1968 after *Rosencrantz and Guildenstern Are Dead* had established Stoppard as a major playwright. In 1962, Stoppard moved to a London suburb and became the drama critic of a new magazine, *Scene*, which folded after eight months. Fortunately, he had begun by then a steady career as a writer of radio plays for the British Broadcasting Corporation (BBC).

With the aid of a Ford Foundation grant, he wrote, in 1964, a first, one-act version of *Rosencrantz and Guildenstern Are Dead*, which he rewrote and expanded for the Royal Shakespeare Company in 1965, then for the

Oxford Theatre Group in 1966, which performed it at that year's Edinburgh Festival. An enthusiastic review in *The Observer* caused Laurence Olivier to buy the play for his National Theatre, which staged it in 1967. Critical acclaim showered on this production, which continued in the National Theatre's repertoire for an unprecedented three and a half years.

In 1965, Stoppard married Jose Ingle; they became the parents of two sons, Oliver and Barnaby. They were divorced in 1972, however, whereupon Stoppard married, the same year, Dr. Miriam Moore-Robinson, a physician and television personality, with whom he had additional sons, William and Edmond.

Since the worldwide success of *Rosencrantz and Guildenstern Are Dead*, Stoppard not only has produced a number of one-act and full-length dramas but also has adapted the plays of several European writers. He has written film scripts as well as radio and television plays. He has directed several stage plays, usually but not always his own, and has supervised the filming of *Rosencrantz and Guildenstern Are Dead*. In 1983, he adapted Sergei Prokofiev's *The Love for Three Oranges* for the Glyndebourne Opera.

Analysis

Tom Stoppard's dramaturgy reveals a cyclical pattern of activity. He tends to explore certain subjects or techniques in several minor works, then creates a major play that integrates the fruits of his earlier trial runs. Thus *Rosencrantz and Guildenstern Are Dead* explores the dialectic of individual freedom opposed to entrapment, which such earlier plays as *A Walk on the Water* had rehearsed.

In *Rosencrantz and Guildenstern Are Dead*, Stoppard assumes the audience's close knowledge of Shakespeare's *Hamlet, Prince of Denmark* (pr. c. 1600-1601, pb. 1603). In the Elizabethan tragedy, Rosencrantz and Guildenstern are two former schoolmates of Hamlet who have been summoned to Elsinore by King Claudius to probe the puzzling behavior of the prince. Hamlet soon intuits that they have become Claudius' spies. When Claudius has them accompany Hamlet on the ship to England, Hamlet discovers the King's letter ordering his execution. He coolly substitutes his escorts' names for his in the letter and shrugs off their consequent deaths as resulting from their dangerous trade of espionage.

From a total of nine scenes in *Hamlet, Prince of Denmark* involving Rosencrantz and Guildenstern, Stoppard incorporates six, omits two, and distributes the other in scenes wholly devised by him. Stoppard's Ros and Guil know that they have been summoned to Elsinore but can remember nothing more of their past. They are two bewildered young men playing pointless games (such as coin flipping) in a theatrical void, while the real action unfolds offstage. They are adrift in a predetermined plot, bumbling Shakespeare's lines on the occasions when the palace intrigue sweeps their way.

Just as Beckett's Vladimir and Estragon engage in mock-philosophizing disputations and vain recollections as they await Godot, so Ros and Guil pursue frequent speculations about their past, their identity, and the baffling world around them.

Stoppard has here constructed an absurdist drama that owes its largest debts to Franz Kafka and Beckett. His Ros and Guil are unaccountably summoned to a mysterious castle where, between long periods of waiting, they receive cryptic instructions that eventually lead to their deaths. They remain uncertain whether they are the victims of chance or fate, mystified by events that are within the boundaries of their awareness but outside the circumference of their understanding.

Like Beckett's Vladimir, Ros is the one who worries and protects; like Beckett's Estragon, Guil is the one who feels and follows. Beckett's world is, however, considerably bleaker than Stoppard's. He offers no comforting irony behind his characters' somber metaphysical flights, while Stoppard's buffoonery is humane. He presents his coprotagonists as likable though confused and frightened strangers in a world somebody else seems to have organized.

Stoppard's literary borrowings include a generous slice of Eliot's poetry, as Ros and Guil imitate Prufock in their roles as attendants and easy tools, playing insignificant parts in a ferociously patterned plot featuring mightier powers. This sympathy for the ineffectual underdog is a constant in Stoppard's dramatic world, as he demonstrates, over and over, his compassionate concern for decent people shouldered aside and manipulated by more brutal peers. Is *Rosencrantz and Guildenstern Are Dead* an immensely entertaining but ultimately shallow exercise, or is it a brilliant transposition of Shakespeare's universe to Beckett's absurdist world? Most critics and large audiences have cast their votes in favor of this erudite, witty, crackling clever drama.

A second group of Stoppard's plays dramatizes the conflict between a protagonist's wish to know and the many difficulties that frustrate this desire, such as the limitations of human perceptions, the frequent deceptiveness of one's senses, and the complexity of ethical choices in a world where guidance is either uncertain or unavailable. Plays belonging to this category include such one-acts as *After Magritte* and the radio play *Artist Descending a Staircase* (1972), as well as Stoppard's two most ambitious, full-length dramas, *Jumpers* and *Travesties*.

Jumpers is a kaleidoscopic work, part bedroom farce, part murder mystery, part political satire, part metaphysical inquiry, and part cosmic tragedy, creating new configurations of ideas and themes from each angle of vision. Stoppard's hero is George Moore, a work-obsessed, seedy, middle-aged professor of moral philosophy, whose name is identical with that of the great English thinker who wrote *Principia Ethica* (1903). George's career has ground to a halt because his adherence to absolute values—beauty, goodness, God—makes him odd man out in a university dominated by logical positivists who hold that value judgments cannot be empirically verified and are therefore relative and meaningless.

George's main adversary is Sir Archibald Jumper, vice-chancellor of the university, who is authoritative in a staggering number of roles: He holds degrees in medicine, philosophy, literature, and law, and diplomas in psychiatry and gymnastics. He is organizer of the Jumpers—a combination of philosophical gymnasts and gymnastic philosophers—all members of the Radical Liberal Party that Archie also heads. The Radical Liberals embody Stoppard's satiric vision of Socialism in action. Having just won an election—which they may have rigged—they have taken over the broadcasting services, arrested all newspaper owners, and appointed a veterinary surgeon Archbishop of Canterbury.

The female principle in the George-Archie struggle is represented by George's beautiful but aptly named wife, Dotty. She is a neurotic musical-comedy star, many years younger than her husband, who retired from the stage after having suffered a nervous breakdown because she believed that the landing of a human being on the Moon had eliminated that planet as a source of romance and thousands of songs. In an ironic reversal of the selflessly heroic British Antarctic Expedition of 1912, Dotty sees, on her bedroom television set, a fight for survival between the damaged space capsule's commander, Captain Scott, and his subordinate officer, Oates. To reduce the weight load, Scott kicks Oates off the capsule's ladder, thereby condemning him to death. Pragmatism has sacrificed moral values—an indictment of logical positivism's slippery ethics. George and Archie are not only philosophic but also erotic rivals. While Dotty has barred her husband from her body—and he makes little effort to overcome her resistance—she is available at all hours to Archie, who visits her in the mornings in her bedroom and is her doctor and psychiatrist and presumably her lover, leaving her room "looking more than a little complacent."

In the first scene, as the Jumpers tumble in the Moores' apartment to celebrate the Rad-Lib victory, a bullet suddenly kills one of them. He turns out to be Duncan McFee, a logical positivist who was scheduled to debate with George at a symposium the next day. Dotty is left whimpering with the corpse, while George, concentrating on composing his lecture, knows nothing of the killing, so that he and his wife talk at cross-purposes while the body hangs behind her bedroom door, always unseen by him. Stoppard parodies the whodunit formula by having Inspector Bones bumble the murder investigation. The resourceful Archie persuades Bones to drop the case by having Dotty trap him in an apparently compromising position. At the close of act 2, McFee is revealed as probably the victim of George's vengeful secretary, who had been McFee's mistress and had learned that he was married and that he planned to enter a monastery.

Holding together the frequently delirious action is the shabby but lovable person of George, shuffling distractedly between his study and Dotty's bedroom, preparing his case against Archie's cynical materialism, which insists that observability has to be a predicate of all genuine knowledge. He does his best—and clearly advocates Stoppard's position—to defend a God in whom he cannot wholly bring himself to believe, so as to support his adherence to moral and aesthetic standards, which he considers a necessary basis for civilization.

The condescending Archie dismisses George as no more than the local eccentric: "[He] is our tame believer, pointed out to visitors in much the same spirit as we point out the magnificent stained glass in what is now the gymnasium." George is less mocked by Stoppard as bumbler and clown than he is admired as a fragmented culture's last humanist, clinging with mad gallantry to lasting values.

In *Jumpers*, Stoppard has written his best play. It is not only a swiftly paced farce and mystery but also a brilliantly humane comedy about the only animal in the cosmos trapped in the toils of an overdeveloped consciousness: the human being. The ultimate mystery, *Jumpers* suggests, is the meaning of life. The work constitutes Stoppard's richest and most brilliant exploration of ethical concerns.

In *Artist Descending a Staircase*, a radio play, Stoppard undertook what he has called "a dry run" of *Travesties. Artist Descending a Staircase* uses a continuous loop of recording tape to involve the audience with three artists engaged in an inquiry into the meaning of art. A more striking bond, between *Jumpers* and *Travesties*, has been summarized by Stoppard in an interview:

> *Jumpers* and *Travesties* are very similar plays. . . . You start with a prologue which is slightly strange. Then you have an interminable monologue which is rather funny. Then you have scenes. Then you end up with another monologue. And you have unexpected bits of music and dance, and at the same time people are playing ping-pong with various intellectual arguments.

Travesties is aptly named. In one of those travesties of probability, the writer James Joyce, the Romanian poet Tristan Tzara, and the Russian revolutionary Vladimir Ilich Ulyanov (who assumed the name of Lenin) were all living in Zurich in 1917: the Irishman working on *Ulysses*, the Romanian helping to set off the Dadaist explosion, and the Russian planning the Armageddon of the Bolshevik Revolution. Stoppard uses his literary license to have the trio interact, and adds, as his protagonist, a British consular official, Henry Carr, historically a minor clerk but promoted by the author to head the British consulate, while the name of the real consul in Zurich—Bennett—is assigned to Carr's butler. The work's structure consists of the sometimes fantastic recollections of old Carr, who, like Beckett's Krapp, replays the spool that contains his past.

The play's plot is both a pastiche and a travesty of Oscar Wilde's great comedy *The Importance of Being Earnest* (pr. 1895, pb. 1899). Stoppard discovered that Joyce had been the business manager of an amateur theatrical company that had staged Wilde's work in Zurich in 1918 and had cast Carr in one of the leading roles as Algernon Moncrieff. This prompted Stoppard not only to have his Carr also echo Algernon but also to double Tzara as Wilde's Jack Worthing, Bennett as Wilde's manservant Lane, and to name his romantic interests Gwendolen and Cecily to mirror, of course, Wilde's Gwendolen and Cecily. Rather surprisingly, Joyce intermittently becomes Lady Bracknell; after all, his middle name, Augusta, corresponds to Bracknell's first.

Travesties is a tour de force of spirited language and convoluted situations that fuses Wilde's high comedy of manners with Shavian dialectic, Joycean fiction, Epic theater, Dadaist spontaneity, music-hall sketches, and limerick word-games. Underneath the bouncy mattress of witty farce is a hard board: Stoppard's lust for ideas. He takes a piercingly cross-eyed look at those movers and shakers of everything that is not nailed down: artists and revolutionaries. The drama revolves four views on art through its ironic prism: Tzara represents Dadaist antiart; Joyce advocates the formalist tradition of art that emphasizes its long-meditated artifice; Lenin subordinates art to an instrument of state policy; and Carr holds a Philistine suspicion of the artist as an ungrateful drone.

In an interview, Stoppard declared himself particularly pleased with a scene, late in act 1, in which Tzara and Joyce confront each other on several levels: Joyce quizzes Tzara along the lines of the catechism chapter involving Bloom and Dedalus in *Ulysses*; Lady Bracknell quizzes Jack about his eligibility for her niece's hand; Tzara informs the audience about the nature of Dadaism; and Joyce affirms the mission of art to shape the ephemeral fragmentation of life into quasi-eternal objects.

Tzara may be the play's most attractive personality. He is not only a Romanian eccentric but also a sardonic social critic and an irreverent deconstructionist of platitudinous slogans. Stoppard has Tzara demand the right both to create a poem out of words jumbled in his hat and to urinate in different colors. Stoppard's Joyce is eloquent in his devout allegiance to the religion of art but less convincing as a shamrock-jacketed spouter of limericks and scrounger of money.

The characterization of Lenin, encountered in the public library but never in Carr's drawing room, proves most problematic. While the artists and bourgeoisie play, he acts, preparing to depart for Russia. His admirer, the librarian Cecily, opens the second act with an earnest lecture on Marxism, interrupted only by Carr's wooing of her. Lenin does not participate in any parallel pairing with Wilde's play—his political weight negates travesty except, perhaps, that his role as Cecily's instructor faintly resembles Miss Prism's. Theatrically, Stoppard's shift from the high-spirited merriment of act 1 to the solemn opening of act 2 is audacious and controversial; some critics have demurred at the drastic undercutting of comic momentum, since it upsets the audience's assumption that the play is made up of the blurred and unreliable recollections of a senile Henry Carr.

Carr is shocked by Tzara's and Lenin's demands that society should be transformed. He tells Tzara, who has expressed sympathy for Lenin's ideas, "You're an amiable bourgeois . . . and if the revolution came you wouldn't know what hit you. . . . Multicoloured micturition is no trick to these boys, they'll have you pissing blood." Yet Carr, while inveighing against artists as self-centered and hostile, also insists that an individual artist's freedom is the most reliable test of a society's freedom.

In the play's coda, old Carr concludes that he learned these lessons from his Zurich experiences: One should be a revolutionary; if not, one should be an artist; and then there is a third lesson—which he cannot recall. Carr may well be a travesty of the sentiments of the public at large, trying to make sense of the meaning of history and the nature of art—and usually failing to do so.

In *Travesties*, Stoppard has composed a witty test whose laughs may outweigh the moral force of its ideas. "In the future," he told Ronald Hayman in June, 1974, "I must stop compromising my plays with this whiff of social application. . . . I should have the courage of my lack of convictions." Yet most of Stoppard's plays after *Travesties* show a marked increase in his political concerns and the deepening of his social conscience.

In *Dirty Linen and New-Found-Land*, Stoppard for the first time takes an unequivocal political stance, opposing any absolute right of the press to wash any and all linen in the glare of trash journalism's exposures. Even politicians, the play contends, are entitled to their confidential lives, as long as their private conduct does not handicap their public performance.

Starting in 1975 with his participation in a protest march against the mistreatment of Soviet dissidents, Stoppard has consistently voiced, both on and off the stage, his outrage at totalitarian violations of human rights. He has particularly befriended and championed the Czech playwright and later statesman Václav Havel, who is in significant ways his mirror image: Havel was born nine months before Stoppard, shares Stoppard's perspectives of absurdism and penchant for wordplay as well as Czech nativity, but he has consistently committed his work as well as his person to social causes, while Stoppard's recognition of social responsibilities has been intermittent. Both playwrights value as their highest goods freedom of expression and individualism.

In *Every Good Boy Deserves Favour*, Stoppard created what he termed "a piece for actors and orchestra." With music by André Previn and a setting in a psychiatric prison in the Soviet Union, the work uses for its title a mnemonic phrase familiar to students of music, since the initial letters, EGBDF, represent in ascending order the notes signified by the black lines of the treble clef. This play-oratorio is a sharply ironic, point-blank attack on the ways in which Soviet law is perverted to stifle dissent. The work is unfortunately flawed by Stoppard's and Previn's self-contradictory uses of the orchestra: On the one hand, it evokes a totalitarian society based on a rigid notion of harmonious order in which improvisation and nonconformity are forbidden; on the other hand, the orchestra seeks to offer a lyrical and humane commentary on the action. The text fails to resolve these opposing purposes.

A far more accomplished attack on the suppression of individual freedom is Stoppard's teleplay *Professional Foul* (1977), dedicated to Havel. The text explores the same ethical problems posed in *Jumpers* and is one of Stoppard's most impressive works. While *Every Good Boy Deserves Favour* and *Professional Foul* represent ambitious advances in Stoppard's dramaturgy, *Night and Day* is a disappointing sidestep into a naturalism that none of Stoppard's previous plays has embraced. He does continue his new role as a didact, opposing any force that might inhibit the untrammeled passage of information, whether it be a union-closed shop or venal media tycoons or a totalitarian state. The drama takes place in a convulsed African country, possibly Uganda, which is agitated by a rebellion against a despotic government led by equally despotic officers. The play's serious concerns, however, are often obscured by stylish posturing and excessive verbal sparks that subvert the serious circumstances of the action. As a result, the text toys with difficult subjects, trivializing them in a manner reminiscent of Noël Coward's flip cleverness.

In *The Real Thing*, Stoppard again harks back to Coward (as well as Wilde) for an exercise in love among the leisured classes, in which aristocrats of style spend their time polishing epigrams and tiptoeing into one another's penthouse souls. This play, however, also has a heart, throbbing with the domestic passion to which even an intellectual playwright, the protagonist Henry, can succumb. Henry has an affair with his good friend's wife, Annie; they fall in love, divorce their spouses, and marry. They are happy for two years, but Annie takes Henry's complaisance for complacence and has trysts with other men. Henry discovers howling-wolf pain in his cuckoldry before he and Annie realize that their marriage is, for better and worse, the real thing.

As so often in his dramatic practice, Stoppard mines his play with parallel phrases and repeated allusions. Yet this time his characters do more than skate on brittle surfaces. They suffer recognizable pain in the throes of romance, sharp darts of regret and ardor, frustration and anguish as they find themselves betrayed and rejected by those they love. This time, Stoppard has created recognizable people as well as flashed the laser beams of his intellect.

More than five years after *The Real Thing*, and after a series of adaptations, Stoppard wrote *Hapgood*, first performed in London in 1988 and subsequently revised for its American tour. Stoppard was inspired by quantum mechanics and the discovery that light consists of particles and waves. He took his fascination with physics' duality and applied it to *Hapgood*, in the form of dual human nature, that is, double agents and double dealings—or, more specifically, espionage. The principal character, Hapgood (also code-named Mother), is a female spy who has been ordered by the Central Intelligence Agency to get rid of a double agent who has been serving the Soviet government. The kind but at the same time merciless Hapgood carries out her mission amid thrilling scenes of kidnappings that are not exactly what they seem to be, double agents who may actually be triple or even quadruple agents, and sexual delusions, in a cerebral drama unequivocally demonstrating its author's love of paradox.

Between screenplays, adaptations, and original dramas, Stoppard wrote perhaps one of his best works, the 1991 radio play *In the Native State*. Like other writers fascinated with British imperialism and India, such as E. M. Forster, Stoppard deals here with the ambiguous theme of India's gaining of independence, or, as it can also be seen, India's losing its status as a territory of the British Empire. *In the Native State* is also about the Anglo-Indian taboo of sexual relations between British women and Indian men.

While on a visit to India, the young poet Flora Crewe has her portrait painted by Nirad Das, an Indian artist. Das, however, has painted two portraits of Crewe: a "proper" one and a nude, the latter remaining in the possession of his son. The nude represents the "more Indian" side of Nirad Das, which is exactly how Crewe wants him to be, for if he anglicized himself she would despise him, since he would be attempting to bring the bloodlines closer together and eventually erase the distinction between ruler and ruled.

Although after *The Real Thing* Stoppard began devoting most of his time to screenplays and to adapting other writers' dramas, his 1993 play *Arcadia*, which was produced after a break of five years, has been greeted with enthusiasm among theater critics, who saw the play returning Stoppard to the stage world.

In *Arcadia*, Stoppard again manages to throw his audience into confusion with sudden shifts from one time period to another; he also continues his experiment of borrowing authentic literary figures, such as Lord Byron, whom spectators find here involved in a murder mystery, one requiring a certain level of intellectual gymnastics on their part.

Arcadia is set in 1809 in the garden room of a beautiful country house in Derbyshire, England. The play's two principal characters, Thomasina Coverly, a thirteen-year-old pupil of Lord Byron's contemporary Septimus Hodge, and Bernard Nightingale, a detective/academic, are separated in time by 180 years. Nightingale, who visits the Coverly house in the 1990's, has as a motive a desire to expose a scandal that occurred in the country house and that involved Lord Byron. The fictional poet Ezra Chater, whom Byron criticized in *English Bards and Scotch Reviewers*, is shot following an erotic meeting in the country house. The shooting of Chater, her fictitiousness (as viewers discover that she is Nightingale's invention), and the insinuated quarrel between her and Lord Byron are only some of the mysteries that engage spectators into becoming detectives.

While his creativity has passed through an extended period of minor productions, Stoppard has already earned an honored place in the ranks of England's playwrights. Like Wilde, his ferocious wit and intellectual acuity dazzle audiences; like Shaw, he stylishly explores intellectual and emotional dilemmas; and like Beckett, his comedy is sometimes bathed in pain and sadness. Altogether, Stoppard is an immensely talented, uniquely unclassifiable writer who invites his public to discover the humaneness of plays and the glory of the English language's density and richness.

Other major works

NOVEL: *Lord Malquist and Mr. Moon*, 1966.

SCREENPLAYS: *The Engagement*, 1970; *The Romantic Englishwoman*, 1975 (with Thomas Wiseman); *Despair*, 1978 (adaptation of Vladimir Nabokov's novel); *The Human Factor*, 1979 (adaptation of Graham Greene's novel); *Brazil*, 1986; *Empire of the Sun*, 1987; *The Russia House*, 1990; *Rosencrantz and Guildenstern Are Dead*, 1990; *Billy Bathgate*, 1991; *Medicine Man*, 1992.

TELEPLAYS: *A Separate Peace*, 1966; *Teeth*, 1967; *Another Moon Called Earth*, 1967; *Neutral Ground*, 1968; *The Engagement*, 1970; *One Pair of Eyes*, 1972 (documentary); *Boundaries*, 1975 (with Clive Exton); *Three Men in a Boat*, 1975 (adaptation of Jerome K. Jerome's novel); *Professional Foul*, 1977; *Squaring the Circle*, 1984.

RADIO PLAYS: *The Dissolution of Dominic Boot*, 1964; *M Is for Moon Among Other Things*, 1964; *If You're Glad I'll Be Frank*, 1965; *Where Are They Now?*, 1970; *Artist Descending a Staircase*, 1972; *In the Native State*, 1991.

TRANSLATION: *Largo Desolato*, 1986 (from the play by Václav Havel).

Bibliography

Billington, Michael. *Stoppard the Playwright.* London: Methuen, 1987. Long the drama critic of *The Guardian*, Billington, who writes from a leftist perspective, admires Stoppard's eloquence but mistrusts his conservative ideas. Still, Billington praises *The Real Thing* and expresses his hopes that Stoppard will increase his passion for both people and causes.

Brassell, Tim. *Tom Stoppard: An Assessment.* New York: St. Martin's Press, 1985. Brassell's study is detailed, elegantly written, and learned. He applies a considerable knowledge of modern drama as well as philosophy.

Hayman, Ronald. *Tom Stoppard.* London: Heinemann, 1977. Hayman's compact text is chiefly valuable for two highly revealing interviews conducted in 1974 and 1976.

Rusinko, Susan. *Tom Stoppard.* Boston: Twayne, 1986. Mainly summarizes the views of other critics and reviewers. Its chief service is an extended bibliography of secondary as well as primary sources.

Whitaker, Thomas. *Tom Stoppard.* New York: Grove Press, 1983. Whitaker's text is succinct, perceptive, and smoothly worded. He stresses the performance aspects of Stoppard's plays, often commenting on particular productions that he has seen.

Gerhard Brand

DAVID STOREY

Born: Wakefield, England; July 13, 1933

Principal drama

The Restoration of Arnold Middleton, wr. 1959, pr. 1966, pb. 1967; *In Celebration*, pr., pb. 1969; *The Contractor*, pr. 1969, pb. 1979; *Home*, pr., pb. 1970; *The Changing Room*, pr. 1971, pb. 1972; *Cromwell*, pr., pb. 1973; *The Farm*, pr., pb. 1973; *Life Class*, pr. 1974, pb. 1975; *Mother's Day*, pr. 1976, pb. 1977; *Sisters*, pr. 1978, pb. 1980; *Early Days*, pr., pb. 1980; *Phoenix*, pr. 1984; *The March on Russia*, pb. 1989; *Stages*, pr. 1992.

Other literary forms

This Sporting Life, David Storey's first—and still most widely read—novel, appeared in 1960; it won the Macmillan Fiction Award and was later made into a successful film with a screenplay by Storey (1963). *Flight into Camden*, which received both the John Llewelyn Rhys Memorial Prize and the Somerset Maugham Award, also reached print in 1960. Among Storey's many other novels are *Pasmore*, published in 1972 and winner of the Faber Memorial Prize, and the autobiographical *Saville* (1976), awarded the prestigious Booker Prize. Storey has also written *Edward* (1973), a book for children.

Achievements

Although Storey considers himself primarily a novelist whose plays are offshoots of his fiction, it now appears certain, at least on the American side of the Atlantic, that he will be known and remembered more as a dramatist. If his novels are in the vein of D. H. Lawrence—with their attention to human beings' physical and spiritual disharmony and their criticism of modern humankind's separation from the elemental processes of nature—his plays qualify him as the principal disciple of Anton Chekhov in postwar British theater. Like the Russian master before him, Storey writes dramas in the mode of symbolic naturalism which, while they are firmly rooted in a specific social milieu, touch on the most universal of themes at the same time that they become swan songs for a dying civilization. Storey admits to finishing his plays very quickly, sometimes within a few days during periods when he is blocked in his novel writing, claiming that they "compose themselves" after a first sentence flashes into his mind. Several of the plays, in fact, reveal a close connection to one or another of the novels; *The Changing Room*, for example, takes a situation from *This Sporting Life* and expands upon it, as *The Contractor* does from *Radcliffe* (1963) and *Life Class* from *A Temporary Life* (1973). Storey finds the writing of drama therapeutic, since work in the theater removes him from the solitary, inner process of creating a novel and transplants him into the outer, communal world of theatrical production.

Not that such a split is at all an unusual experience for this man of letters who was simultaneously both rugby player and art student. Such dichotomies are the wellspring of his creativity, and if they converge fortuitously with the central disharmonies of twentieth century life, so much the better. If the twentieth century is the century of the disintegration of society, of the dissociation of sensibility, and of schizophrenic man, fragmented and alienated, then Storey perfectly captures this widespread sense of vulnerability and mortality within both his fiction and his drama. Several of his works (especially *This Sporting Life* and *The Changing Room*) focus on the split between flesh and spirit, body and soul, the physical and the mental; others (such as *Life Class*), on the pull between life and art, reality and illusion, form and feeling; still others (including *This Sporting Life*, *Radcliffe*, and *The Farm*), on the conflict between the masculine and feminine sensibilities, discipline and intuition, activity and passivity. Further polarities that Storey explores include those between past fact and present memory (*Home* and *Early Days*), between nature and progress (*The Contractor*), between the word and the sword as well as between existence and essence (*Cromwell*), and between commitment and betrayal and dreams and practicality (*Sisters*). Furthermore, throughout Storey's plays there is a wealth of imagery of the sterile wasteland, of what one of his characters terms the "computerized, mechanized, de-humanized, antiseptic society" that is modern industrial culture. As his characters search for meaning and order and some means to achieve integration, they look to the values of work, of communal spirit and support, and of an art whose essence is faithfully to record life so that human beings can see not only the literary reality but also the way in which moments in that reality, especially daily rituals, can achieve a transcendent, sacramental effect that allow people to reclaim some purpose and value—at least temporarily.

Biography

Although a character in one of David Storey's plays remarks that "sport and art don't mix," those two apparent opposites did indeed mix at a crucial period in Storey's own development. The son of a coal miner, Storey was born on July 13, 1933, in Wakefield, Yorkshire—located in northeastern England. In 1953, after attending local schools, Storey began his studies at the Slade School of Fine Art in London, receiving his diploma in 1956. During that time, he commuted on weekends back up to the north, where he played professional football for the Leeds Rugby League Club from 1952 to 1956. After his marriage in 1956, he worked at a number of odd jobs—among them teacher, farm worker, and erector of circus tents, all of which would be reflected in his plays—before he turned to writing. In 1959, when his earliest attempts at fiction proved to be unmarketable, he tried drama, but his first work in the medium, *The Restoration of Arnold Middleton*, did not finally reach the stage until it was produced in Edinburgh, Scotland, in 1966. (After its London production in 1967, Storey received the London *Evening Standard* Award, which he won a second time in 1970.) Following the phenomenal success of *This Sporting Life* in 1960 and the publication of two more novels within three years, Storey turned his energies once again to the theater and, in a tremendous burst of creative inspiration, wrote four of his most important plays: *In Celebration* and *The Contractor*, both written in 1969; *Home*, written in 1970; and *The Changing Room*, written in 1971. With the production of *In Celebration*, Storey began his long and fruitful association with George Devine's English Stage Company at the Royal Court Theatre in London's Sloane Square (where John Osborne's *Look Back in Anger* had premiered in 1956) and director Lindsay Anderson; Anderson would later direct the movie version of *In Celebration* (1975) for the American Film Theater's second season. *Home*, which gained for its author the Variety Club of Great Britain Award, also won for Storey the New York Drama Critics Circle Award in 1971, which Storey received again in 1973 for the New York production of *The Changing Room* by the Long Wharf Theatre of New Haven. Both *The Changing Room* and *The Contractor*—which the same Long Wharf group had presented two years earlier—demand the kind of ensemble acting that, in America, a regional theater seems best able to provide. Storey's theatrical activity continued unabated during the 1970's with more plays, including *The Farm* and *Cromwell*, *Life Class*, *Mother's Day*, *Sisters*, and *Early Days*. Of these, only *Life Class* and *Early Days* appear likely to have much continued life in the theater.

By the early 1980's, Storey hinted that his career as a dramatist was winding down, declaring that "the plays are a dead duck now." In fact, only one play, *Phoenix*—about the artistic director of a theater that loses its government subsidy and is finally demolished—would be produced later in the decade, and that only in the provinces rather than in London. Another play, *Stages*, was produced in 1992.

Analysis

In nearly all of his plays, David Storey practices an almost documentary realism, an absolute fidelity to the facts, even to the minutiae, of daily existence; yet in his best dramas he transcends this level of realism so that the events become, as they do for Chekhov, symbolic of much larger concerns, even allegories of human beings in the modern age. In 1973, Storey himself distinguished between the three types of plays which he writes: the decidedly literary plays, those written in the mode of poetic naturalism, and the overtly stylized works. Among the first group, he included *The*

Restoration of Arnold Middleton, which focuses on one man's use of elaborate pretense to escape confronting reality; *In Celebration*, which is set, like Storey's own early life, in a coal-mining town in the North Country; and *The Farm*, which, while revolving like Arnold Wesker's *Roots* (1959) around an engagement that does not come to pass, explores a mother's attachment to the poet-son and a father's anger over his daughters' failures to regenerate life. To these must be added *Mother's Day*, an unsuccessful farce in the manner of Joe Orton, and *Sisters*, which, like Tennessee Williams' *A Streetcar Named Desire* (1947), sees a woman's arrival threaten the arrangement between her sister and brother-in-law, until the woman's retreat into insanity saves them all. These works, all of which are family problem plays, are literary in that their dialogue and handling of character are novelistic, their plots linear and generally well made, their settings basically representational and not overtly symbolic.

The second group, those works that Storey designates as poetic naturalism, are closest to Chekhov in that their plots are minimal, with the external action that does exist unfolding on a highly symbolic plane. In the two plays that Storey included in this category, *The Contractor* and *The Changing Room*, the event that would appear to be central actually happens offstage (as is also true of *In Celebration*). One can add to this group *Life Class*, in which Storey hints at his philosophy of the artist as a singer of life, recording life in order that others may see it; if human beings partake of existence simply by "being" in the fullest sense of that word, then for Storey the work of art primarily "should not mean but be." Storey's opening direction for *Life Class*, as for *Cromwell*, specifies simply "A Stage," providing an aesthetic comment about the empty space that needs to be filled, in the same way that the dramatist's mind (like a blank page) is peopled through the imaginative act.

Among his third group of overtly stylized works for the stage, Storey had completed only *Home* and *Cromwell*—a history play for an unlocalized Shakespearean stage filled with imagery of light and dark—by 1973, but also belonging to this group is *Early Days*, as Pinteresque in its language of lyric threnody as is *Home*. Most characteristic of the plays in this category is the manner in which stage activity is stripped down to a minimum, in which the rhythmic dialogue becomes sparser and more poetic, sometimes elegiac, and almost at times a liturgical sequence of antiphons with responses. No matter, however, which of the three groups they fall into, almost all of Storey's plays are characterized by a use of the visual and verbal rituals of everyday life, the communal celebrations through which his men and women attempt to redeem the fallen world and to discover a validation for their own existence and some shared values in a diminished and precarious world akin to a modern wasteland.

In its surface details, *In Celebration* is Storey's most Lawrentian and openly autobiographical play. Set in a coal-mining town in the North Country, it focuses on the conflict between the mother and the son-artist. In its structure, *In Celebration* is a traditional family problem play: Three sons return home to honor their parents' fortieth wedding anniversary, and, while there, they dredge up a hurt from the past that continues to influence the present. The play's observance of the unities of time and place, the emphasis on the parents' guilt and its effects upon the children, and the complex mix of love and hate that binds the family together, all make the work reminiscent of Eugene O'Neill's *Long Day's Journey into Night* (pb. 1956). Furthermore, the strategy of a slow disclosure of a secret from the past puts the audience in mind of the realistic, well-made plays of Henrik Ibsen's middle period, such as *Ghosts* (pb. 1881). Mr. Shaw, proud head of the family, refuses to retire even after forty-nine years in the mines, despite seemingly tenuous health, since hard work serves as a means of making retribution for his "sins." Shaw idolizes his wife, whom he got pregnant before they married. The daughter of a pig breeder, better educated than her husband (ironically, she holds a diploma in domestic hygiene), and significantly more religious, she must have felt it a "let-down" to marry him. Their first child, Jamey, who could "draw like an angel," was only seven when he died; Shaw had prayed, to no avail, that the son be spared and his own life taken instead, and Mrs. Shaw, six months pregnant at the time with their youngest child, Steven, had attempted to commit suicide. Shaw refused to have his three surviving sons follow him into the mines, seeing instead that they all went to college. Consequently, they have been forced from the working class into the lower middle class, with all the problems in social dislocation that this change traditionally causes for a Britisher.

The youngest son, Steven, a father of four, teacher, and sometime writer, is a brooding, sensitive, mostly silent man disturbed by what he terms a "feeling of disfigurement." Although he would have died in the womb had his mother's attempted suicide succeeded, he now appears to be her favorite. As a young man, he was disdainful of the establishment and for several years worked on a novel highly critical of the moral flabbiness of modern industrial society. Recently, however, he has reached an accommodation with life and given up his writing; he views this not as a compromise, but rather as an acceptance of things as they are. What deeply disturbs him now is more personal: nightmares and crying spells about the dead brother. The middle son, Colin, a card-carrying Communist during his school days, is now an industrial arbitrator of disputes between workers and management. Colin insists that the family not measure one another by their failures and, solely to raise his mother's spirits at a troubled time and ease her mind about the future, fabricates the news that he will finally marry. The eldest living son, Andrew, has left a career in law to become an artist, a painter of—as he describes them—abstracts with "no sign of life." As a thirteen-year-old boy, he announced to his family that he had no belief in anything, and he continues to be an angry young man, reviling the factory automation that turns workers into robots and continually goading Steven into reasserting his lost venom. Most of all, Andrew's present intention is revenge against his parents, particularly against his mother, who, after Jamey's death, had sent him off for six weeks to stay at a neighbor's and repeatedly had been deaf to his desperate cries to be let back into the house. He resents the way in which his father has always enshrined his mother as a goddess out of some mishandled sense of guilt for having violated her, and he accuses the parents of needing to fashion Jamey into some impossible ideal of perfection to atone for their sins and of having too strictly controlled his life and that of his brothers as well. The home, to him, was a fetid atmosphere, and the parents' guilt was responsible for their sons' problems. Now, as his anniversary memento, he wants to bring all this out into the open, which to some extent he does—although Mrs. Shaw seems oblivious to much of it, perhaps deliberately refusing to face these truths. Steven, however, forbids Andrew to harm or damage their mother and father, and so a full confrontation is narrowly averted. Andrew dances with his mother—tellingly, with no music playing—and, like Arnold in Storey's first play, somewhat unaccountably senses redemption, "salvation in his bones." What undercuts the resolution, however, and marks the ending with uneasiness, is the way that the family's final meal together—a breakfast of cold tea and dry toast—is left uneaten. No real communion has been established as the sons go off, leaving Mrs. Shaw with only Mr. Shaw to support her, a stage image much like that which concludes Storey's next and finest play.

The Contractor retains elements of the conventional family problem play that Storey mined in *In Celebration*, but overlaying this probing of a family's deterioration through three generations are new directions in Storey's dramatic artistry that might even warrant the adjective "Storeyean": the minimization of plot, the fascination with exact reproduction of minute details of daily activity (here the onstage erecting of a huge canvas marquee for a wedding reception), and the investing of concrete image and event with a multilayered network of symbolic meaning.

To describe the external action of *The Contractor* is to discover, from one perspective, how much meaning Storey can evoke from so little. Five workmen erect a tent on the lawn of the company owner's house in the first two acts, then dismantle the tent in act 3, so that the stage image of three tent poles at the end of the play exactly replicates that at the beginning. The tent, like everything else that exists—family relationships, social institutions and structures, value systems—is transitory and ephemeral: All things under the sun pass away, and Storey examines the bedrock, if any, that remains. The workmen are carefully individuated (especially Kay, the foreman, who has been in prison for embezzlement and is sensitive to the emotional distress of others, and Glendenning, the sweets-loving, stuttering half-wit), but it is the group activity, the common goal of erecting the tent, that matters. Ewbank, the tent company owner and father of the bride, is set apart from his workmen by his economic and social status, and yet he insists on pitching in and helping. Not jaded by his station in life, he feels more comfortable with the laborers; he disparages money as more trouble than it is worth, and responds with compassion to Glenny, whom the others torment, and with heartbreak at the senseless damage done to the tent during the party. If Ewbank as overseer of the sewing of the beautifully stitched tent is a craftsman, Old Ewbank, his father, who is a rope maker, is an artisan. Throughout the play, Old Ewbank walks on and off, carrying a piece of rope that he is weaving (but that he eventually misplaces), contrasting it with today's machine-made rope that lacks resilience, and commenting that the laborers, too, have lost their stamina, dependent on pills and drink. His handmade rope is a precious bit of the past, which loses out to the machine-made product of the present.

In contemporary life, there exists a dissociation between art and work, a devaluing of the artifact as impractical. Nevertheless, the possibility that work and art might once again merge, at least fleetingly, is hinted at in the setting up of the marquee. The third generation of the family is represented by Ewbank's indolent son Paul, university-educated yet lacking any marketable skill. He admits to having no incentive to work purposefully and is content to loaf around the world (unsure of his destination) after the wedding. Alienated, rootless, not knowing his place in modern society, Paul does, however, have a flair for arranging the pots of flowers that decorate the tent; his grandmother recognizes this talent as the lingering touch of the artist in him, as the remnant of his grandfather's artistry, yet his father can only disparage such a nonutilitarian skill.

The tent as symbol is amenable to richly various interpretations. Storey himself has spoken of it, first, in terms of "a metaphor for artistic creation": the imaginative act of beginning with very little (three tent poles) and spinning around it a marvelous and ingenious structure, but then wondering, or having others wonder, what it is all worth. Second, Storey has connected the tent with "the decline of capitalistic society." It is being erected on the grounds below the Ewbank home, itself beautiful yet tainted because it was built from the sweat of the laborers, and on a rise above the town; once the valley boasted only farms and mills, yet now it is covered by a cloud of smoke from the industrialized city, where a television aerial adorns every roof. If human beings have become separated from nature and lost the connection between themselves and the earth, they have also lost any fixed point of reference for themselves as social beings. The long-overdue breakdown of the oppressive class system has arrived, and yet people, particularly those of the middle class, find it difficult to know where they belong in the new society, while many in the lower class still look back wistfully on the old stratification.

If the tent symbolizes art and empire, it also suggests the transitoriness of relationships between parent and child, and husband and wife, and the brevity of life itself. The action of *The Contractor*, which occurs in very late summer, exudes an autumnal air: Ewbank remarks that he wishes he had time to do everything over again but that he is too old to start anew. "Come today. Gone tomorrow" might well serve as the play's epigraph. The only things that might endure in the face of constant change and diminishment are close personal relationships—though even those may no longer be lasting—and the value of work. The picture at play's end of Ewbank and his wife, alone now that their children have left, standing arm-in-arm and mouthing stoically "We'll manage" in the face of loss, is somewhat consoling, even if a shadow is cast over the new marriage of daughter Claire to a doctor when she must plead with him to stay sober at their reception. With everything else breaking down and dying out, what provides cohesion and meaning is work, in which individuals lose their egotism and exert their energies to create something together outside themselves. If the ritual dance of the family members, which in traditional romantic drama would signify generativity, is here undercut since it is performed without music, the shared meal retains all its religious force as a secular sacrament. After the tent is dismantled, Ewbank comes out from the house carrying a tray with a bottle of whiskey and the leftover wedding cake. The men partake in a ritual of eating and drinking that symbolizes the communion, however temporary, between them—with Ewbank even hiding away a little extra cake for Glenny.

The Contractor remains Storey's most Chekhovian play—and perhaps the most Chekhovian in all of modern British drama—as well as his most impressive work for the theater. It even verbally echoes *Uncle Vanya* (1899) when Mrs. Ewbank announces near the end, "They've gone, then." The departure is yet another among the many symbols in the play of things passing away with nothing new to take their place.

Storey received his inspiration for *Home* from an image at the end of *The Contractor* of an ornamental metal table and two chairs, which become virtually the only elements in the setting of the later play. If plot in drama is understood as a causally connected series of events that rises to some resolution of a conflict, then *Home* is nearly plotless. Storey here eschews action in favor of a more lyric structure, related to musical composition in its reverberation of motifs: It is a tone poem for voices. The play opens with two early-middle-aged men in a garden: Harry, who in his youth played amateur football, acted bit parts in the theater, and dreamed of becoming either a dancer or a flutist, and Jack, more dandyish in his dress, formerly in the Royal Air Force, who in his youth thought of becoming a priest. They talk and, in scene 2, walk on and off the stage as they are joined by two women of a lower social class. It is here, when Kathleen reveals that her shoelaces have been taken away and that she has painted on the walls, that the audience first realizes that the characters live in an asylum. The gentlemen, each of whom breaks into tears at three points in the play, escort the ladies to lunch; when they return for act 2, the furniture has been disarranged by Alfred, the play's only other—and totally silent—character, whose ritualized movements of lifting and carrying off the metalwork chairs and table suggest that this apparently purposeless activity is all that remains of their lives.

On its literal level, the simple action creates the impression of lost souls, each locked into the home of his or her own psyche, only able to break out sporadically by means of communication with another person. Marjorie is Kathleen's helpmeet, someone the other woman can physically lean on; the basis of their camaraderie is gossiping and tattling on others and sharing slightly bawdy ripostes. Harry and Jack, less well adjusted because clearly more sensitive, have developed a private language of their own, answering each other's incomplete sentences almost intuitively. They are aware of time passing, very slowly, and of eventual mortality. Although they must wait—a favorite image in the contemporary theater—for their next meal to interrupt the monotony of the day and have devised other private means for filling up time, they do not, unlike the tramps in Samuel Beckett's *Waiting for Godot* (pb. 1952), wait in hopeless expectation for anything astounding and meaningful to happen to them. Rather, the mood is again elegiac: Everything notable and noble has already happened in the past, and is not likely to occur again.

If, in this play, with its multivalent symbolism, the home of the title is the psychic retreat of these four souls, it is also England itself, just as Chekhov's orchard was Russia. At one time, a lord and lady occupied the house now turned into the asylum; at one time, England's unique geography as an island led to the creation of a civilized culture and democracy. In a reverent litany of the poets and discoverers and inventions that once made England great, Harry and Jack name Charles Darwin, Sir Isaac Newton, John Milton, and Sir Walter Raleigh; radar, the steam engine, and penicillin. Perhaps Storey even wishes his audience to recall John of Gaunt's famous set piece from William Shakespeare's *Richard II* (pr. c. 1595-1596) apostrophizing England as "this sceptred isle" and "other Eden, demi-paradise," for one of the characters inhabiting what little garden remains at the asylum recalls the local tale that Adam and Eve actually lived in the Vale of Evesham. As the characters remark, however, the "sun has set" on the Empire, and its like will not be seen again. Where once great minds and great ideas flourished, now there is only uniformity and boredom; where once there was camaraderie in battle, responsibility for family members in need, and respect for the "gentler sex," now there is aimlessness, appalling manners, and lack of moral fiber; where once there was sun, now there is little beauty in an industrialized, soot-covered wasteland. Everything, now, has become little, and just as the patients have no hope of release from their home, there is little hope of a future for the larger home that is England. Kathleen yearns for death, lest she go mad—not realizing that she already has; Harry recognizes that there no longer exist any great roles for the actors on the great stage of the world, but only tiny parts on a little platform. Jack muses over metaphysical concerns, the why for God's actions, the mystery at the center of existence, finding no answers. To make life bearable, one can only hold out a hand to another person once in a while and be tolerant of the lapses of others, of the little falls from grace in the midst of the larger fall that has overtaken Western civilization. This swan song for a dying world that apparently is not waiting for anything to be born ends with an image of Harry and Jack desolate and in tears over their awareness of loss.

Just as the central action of the wedding reception that the audience expects to see in *The Contractor* happens between the acts, so, too, the action of the rugby match occurs offstage in *The Changing Room*. What the audience does see is the preparation for the football game (the stripping, bandaging, greasing of bodies, and suiting up), the treatment of the wounded gladiator during the match, and the aftermath of victory (the ritual of bathing, locker-room badinage, singing, and dressing in street clothes before returning to the world). Much of this activity, observed with Storey's usual eye for concrete detail, is choreographed almost like a ballet in performance. Storey manages, despite the large ensemble cast of twenty-two, to give some individuality to members of the team, among them the narcissistic Patsy, who lovingly stands in front of mirrors combing and recombing his hair; the studious-looking schoolmaster Trevor, who wears a club blazer and has an economist for a wife; the fastidious team captain Owens, evidently in his next to last season in the rugged sport, who takes full advantage of the special privileges due him; Walsh, quick with bawdy jokes and gestures as a cover for his sexual insecurity; and most of all the childlike Kendal, who treasures the electric tool kit he has bought to build bookshelves for his wife and who is brought in bloodied from a broken nose. If the location of Storey's play is literally a changing room where men discard their everyday clothes and don their rugby shirts and shorts, it is also a setting employed symbolically, for these men undergo not only a change in clothing; they change from individuals into a group, as the lining up and passing of the ball from one to another before the match indicates, imbued with a sense of team spirit and commitment. The team breaks down social distinctions, equalizing workers and professionals, who can use the game as a means of improving, on one level, their economic condition; even the team's owner, Sir Frederick Thornton, though he sees the players as robots, likes to feel himself one of the men, as Ewbank does in *The Contractor*. More important, playing rugby is a way of escaping the dulling routine of a machine-dominated existence through a physical ritual that takes on religious overtones of purification and renewal, since it enables these men to get in touch with the energies of their bodies (playing football is "life at the extreme," claims Storey, who knows from his own experience); the bodily exertion becomes a means of enlivening the spirit and, even though the fusion is only temporary, an organic harmony replaces fragmentation and dissociation. Like man alone, however, even men together are still subject to vulnerability and mortality. Storey even turns the nudity, occurring naturally here and with greater aesthetic justification than in almost any other contemporary drama, into a visual symbol of man's shared humanity: Bodies may be fine-tuned, yet they can become broken, and they do age; even pain, however, can be a measure of a man. If it is fashionable for contemporary writers to use sport as a metaphor for war or for the struggle for existence, or to portray it as a sublimation for sex or a substitution for power, Storey eschews such negative connotations to focus instead on the way in which sport, like art, can be a transcendence of the moment in time and of the purely self-centered tendency in man.

If there is a central character in *The Changing Room*, it is, ironically, the only one onstage who neither participates in nor watches the game, the menial workman Harry, who hoses out the bath, stokes the fire, lays out the clothes and towels, and sweeps up after the men. The broken-down, hymn-singing Harry, mentally deficient as the result of an accident years ago, is, for the players, a nearly anonymous presence, taken for granted and noticed only when he fails to supply their needs. Harry is obsessively paranoid over the threat of Russia and what he sees as its vast plot to destroy the West. Russia is even responsible for the cold weather that has turned the playing field into a frozen waste; the Communists, he claims, have planted listening devices in the changing room and are using a poison gas to slow the thinking processes and thus brainwash mankind. What Harry says about England is more pointed and closer to the truth: Convinced that his own job has value, that he knows precisely who he works for, he decries—as Old Ewbank had—the detrimental effects of machinery on man's energy and the blurring of class distinctions which mean that men no longer know their place. Like old Fiers in Chekhov's *The Cherry Orchard* (pr. 1904), who longed to maintain the days of serfdom when he felt secure in a lowly station in life, Harry questions progress, feeling that the present cannot measure up to the past, that it is "too late" for any redemption. The final image of Harry sweeping the empty room symbolizes the way that the present continually displaces the past and all that it stands for.

The certainty of old values has broken down, and man appears unable to discover ways to reinvigorate and renew his existence. Even the game can serve only as a temporary ritual that gives the pain of existence during the rest of the week a meaning. Storey's final attitude, then, is deliberately ambiguous and as double-edged as Chekhov's: There is mostly loss, but there is also some possibility for gain. The only certainty for man, however, is the fact of change, which is always unsettling.

The Changing Room, like other plays by Storey, such as *The Contractor* and *Home*, might seem, on the surface, to be apolitical, to be an exercise in documentary realism raised to the level of art. The surface reality is so precisely observed and re-created that the symbolic levels and allegorical equivalencies never seem to be imposed from without but always appear to be discovered by Storey as emanating from within that very reality and then subtly articulated. It could, however, be argued that Storey is the quintessential nonproselytizer among the contemporary British social and political dramatists. His plays are about England. He differs from most other—and usually younger—British social dramatists of the present day in the breadth of his vision. Working by symbol and indirection, he reveals the ills of the time but espouses no narrow platform for curing them. His political attitude, as he suggested in a remark in *Cromwell*, might sound like a self-serving excuse, but perhaps it is simply the realistic if somewhat cynical conclusion of a sensitive man thrown up against an insensitive system: No matter what side a person takes politically, and no matter what political decision that person makes, the decision ends by defeating the very values that the person originally tried to uphold. Storey proposes no answer, for probably none exists. He recurrently dramatizes diminution, decay, and mortality, with every once in a while a moment of compassion and shared humanity, through a daily ritual such as a bath or a meal, to help his often-times desolate people along the way.

Other major works

NOVELS: *This Sporting Life*, 1960; *Flight into Camden*, 1960; *Radcliffe*, 1963; *Pasmore*, 1972; *A Temporary Life*, 1973; *Saville*, 1976; *A Prodigal Child*, 1982; *Present Times*, 1984.

SCREENPLAY: *This Sporting Life*, 1963 (adaptation of Storey's novel).

CHILDREN'S LITERATURE: *Edward*, 1973.

Bibliography

Hutchings, William. *The Plays of David Storey: A Thematic Study.* Carbondale: Southern Illinois University Press, 1988. The first full-length study devoted solely to Storey's work for the theater, Hutchings' valuable book provides detailed critical analyses of each drama. Hutchings sees Storey as stressing the importance of physical work and daily rituals to help the individual achieve a sense of community in a modern society that has been radically desacralized by industrialism and technology. Contains an extensive bibliography.

Kerensky, Oleg. *The New British Drama: Fourteen Playwrights Since Osborne and Pinter.* New York: Taplinger, 1977. Kerensky focuses on the conflict between working-class parents and well-educated middle-class sons in Storey's plays, wherein fidelity to naturalistic detail often takes precedence over plot. He devotes his lengthiest comments to *Mother's Day*, Storey's negatively reviewed farce about English domestic life.

Quigley, Austin E. "The Emblematic Structure and Setting of David Storey's Plays." *Modern Drama* 22, no. 3 (1979): 279-276. In response to conflicting assessments over whether Storey should be regarded as a traditional or an experimental playwright, Quigley probes the basis for Storey's originality as a dramatist. He proposes that it rests in his uncanny ability to reconceive conventional theatrical devices as "structuring images" that contain the plays' themes.

Randall, Phyllis R. "Division and Unity in David Storey." In *Essays on Contemporary British Drama*, edited by Hedwig Bock and Albert Wertheim. Munich: Max Hueber Verlag, 1981. Randall sees as major themes in Storey's writing the disintegration of both the individual and the family or social unit, and "the struggle to make life work on both the external and internal levels." The dramas, she argues, accept the impossibility of full integration, often ironically undercutting the spiritual values. Concludes with a useful chart indicating the interrelationships between Storey's novels and plays.

Taylor, John Russell. *David Storey.* London: Longman, 1974. This pamphlet, written by one of the principal authorities on contemporary British drama as part of the British council's Writers and Their Work series, charts the connections between Storey's novels and plays up through 1973. Taylor emphasizes the tension between the physical and the spiritual in the fiction and the blending of realistic with symbolic or allegorical levels in the dramas. Includes a photograph of Storey as a frontispiece.

Worth, Katharine J. *Revolutions in Modern English Drama.* London: G. Bell & Sons, 1972. In brief yet sensitive remarks, Worth explores Storey's use of physical objects as a focal point and his expert handling of space (stage space in *The Contractor* and screen space in the television adaptation of *Home*). Worth believes that audiences relish the process through which space is transformed, and the characters too, as they participate in fleeting moments of communion.

Thomas P. Adler

ALGERNON CHARLES SWINBURNE

Born: London, England; April 5, 1837
Died: Putney, England; April 10, 1909

Principal drama

The Queen-Mother, pb. 1860; *Rosamond*, pb. 1860; *Atalanta in Calydon*, pb. 1865; *Chastelard*, pb. 1865; *Bothwell*, pb. 1874; *Erechtheus*, pb. 1876; *Mary Stuart*, pb. 1881; *Marino Faliero*, pb. 1885; *Locrine*, pb. 1887; *The Sisters*, pb. 1892; *Rosamund, Queen of the Lombards*, pb. 1899; *The Duke of Gandia*, pb. 1908.

Other literary forms

Algernon Charles Swinburne is best known as a poet, though he also wrote literary criticism and fiction. His drama must be considered a part of his poetic output, since it is written exclusively in verse, the bulk of it in blank verse (unrhymed iambic pentameter). It should also be added that his poetic drama is among his least distinguished work and shares many of the shortcomings of his nondramatic poetry: overdecoration, excessive use of alliteration, and an uneasy tension between vulgarity and pomposity. Conversely, the best passages in his plays reveal the brilliancies that ensure him a place among the best of the late Victorian poets: a remarkable verbal facility and an equally remarkable capacity for metric innovation.

Swinburne is generally classified among the Pre-Raphaelite poets and painters of the latter third of the nineteenth century. Along with his friends and associates Dante Gabriel Rossetti, William Morris, and Sir Edward Burne-Jones, Swinburne was committed to a theory of art that rebelled against the smugness and prudishness of Victorian England by insisting that art must be considered on its own terms, quite apart from any moral value it might possess. Swinburne was a latecomer to the so-called Pre-Raphaelite Brotherhood, a group of writers and painters whose founding members included the painters Holman Hunt and Sir John Everett Millais; those mentioned above came later. The Pre-Raphaelites took their name from an aesthetic theory propounded by the essayist John Ruskin. Simply stated, the idea is this: Art must seek to reproduce nature to the smallest detail, using only nature as a model. For Ruskin, his contemporaries erred in studying Raphael, for in doing so they imitated and reproduced Raphael's mistakes. Artists should instead do what Raphael did: study nature only—hence the term "Pre-Raphaelite."

This original doctrine was eventually abandoned by Rossetti and his disciples—among them Swinburne—who replaced it with a philosophy closely resembling the French critic Théophile Gautier's *l'art pour l'art* (art for art's sake). It is perhaps to this later school, subsequently known as the Aesthetes, that Swinburne properly belongs. Though some of his poems, notably those contained in *A Song of Italy* (1867), do have some sort of moral or political purpose behind them, his best work is truly concerned with art for its own sake and with the role of the artist. He was perhaps one of the last of the Romantic poets, his best work showing many more affinities with Lord Byron, Percy Bysshe Shelley, and John Keats than with his contemporaries, Alfred, Lord Tennyson, Robert Browning, and Matthew Arnold.

Swinburne's novels *Lesbia Brandon* (1952) and *Love's Cross-Currents* (1901) deserve more attention than they have yet received. The latter, a satire on Victorian morality, is one of Swinburne's most consistently interesting works. His literary criticism, much of it published in periodicals, is unhappily short on objectivity; it is too personal, too full of unrestrained praise and harsh invective to be of much value except as Victoriana.

Achievements

Any discussion of Swinburne must take into account that his career was divided into two pronounced stages: that up to 1879 and that after 1879. From 1879 until his death in 1909, Swinburne lived a reclusive life under the guardianship of his agent and friend, Walter Theodore Watts-Dunton, removed from the literary mainstream, and while he continued to write prolifically, there was a certain falling off in quality and imagination in the works he produced during this later period. The works of the 1860's and 1870's are the portions of Swinburne's canon that remain of interest today, and similarly it is the drama of the early period that is most noteworthy.

Like such varied Romantic poets as Byron, Shelley, Keats, and William Wordsworth, Swinburne wrote "closet dramas," plays never intended to be performed, but rather to be read as works of literature. His plays have seldom if ever been produced on the stage, and for good reason: Swinburne knew next to nothing about stagecraft, and his poetic dramas betray his ignorance of the practical demands of the theater. They are, almost without exception, too long; the dialogue is often unnaturally poetic, even for verse drama; and the character motivation is too often obscure, with too much background being assumed of the audience.

The bulk of Swinburne's plays deal with history or myth, a choice of subject matter that was both a blessing and a curse to his career as a playwright. While he was widely read in British and continental history, his scholarliness often gets the best of his artistry in his plays: Artistic license is far too seldom exercised. In the Mary, Queen of Scots trilogy, for example—*Chastelard*, *Bothwell*, and *Mary Stuart*—Swinburne is far too steeped in the history of the era to exploit fully the dramatic possibilities of Mary Stuart, the woman and the myth.

This tension between history and art does not exist in his myth plays—to this group belong *Atalanta in Calydon* and *Erechtheus*—and yet in these last-named works the modern reader finds an overly heavy dependence on Greek tragedy. Although it could be argued that *Atalanta in Calydon* (Swinburne's only acclaimed play) substantially subverts Greek conventions, adapting the methods of Sophocles to serve Swinburne's nineteenth century intentions, still one finds the speeches too long, the meter too forced, the chorus too vocal. *Erechtheus* is even more derivative than *Atalanta in Calydon*, more often than not a virtuosic imitation of Sophoclean tragedy. Similarly, Swinburne's plays in the Elizabethan mode are much too obviously derivative of Thomas Kyd, Francis Beaumont, John Fletcher, and their contemporaries. Replete with bloodshed, vendettas, and murders, such early pieces as *Rosamond* and *The Queen-Mother* are heavily influenced by the revenge tragedies of the minor Renaissance dramatists, but they, too, often lack the dramaturgical mastery of their precursors.

Swinburne must therefore be considered an imitative rather than an original playwright. His most interesting plays—*Atalanta in Calydon*, *Chastelard*, and (for very different reasons) *The Sisters*—succeed not because of their dramatic merit but because of the poetic ingenuity of many of their parts. Like his early nineteenth century precursors, Swinburne was an innovative poet who felt compelled to try his hand at the drama. Too often the results are such that one wishes he had devoted his time to the lyric poetry of which he was an undisputed master. Nevertheless, like the closet dramas of his great Romantic predecessors, Swinburne's plays retain historical interest.

Biography

Algernon Charles Swinburne was born into two of England's proudest old aristocratic families, the Swinburnes and the Ashburnhams. His father was Captain (later Admiral) Charles Henry Swinburne; his mother, the former Lady Jane Henrietta Hamilton, the daughter of the third Earl of Ashburnham. He enjoyed a privileged childhood, dividing his time between the estate of his parents, East Dene on the Isle of Wight, and Capheaton Hall, the Swinburne family seat in Northumberland near the Scottish border. For the rest of his life, he would be fascinated by Scottish history and myth, using it as subject matter for works of such diverse merit as the early poem "The Queen's Tragedy" (1854) and his dramatic trilogy centering on Mary Stuart. He was never close to his father—a conventional man who was away much of the time—but he was pampered by his mother, to whom he remained close until her death in 1896. His paternal grandfather, Sir John Swinburne, was a surrogate father to the boy, treating him with an affection and respect that the poet never forgot.

Although he was the eldest of six children, young "Hadji" Swinburne was a lonely child, made, from early childhood, to feel like an outcast. He was at best unusual in appearance, with bright red hair, a too-slight build, and a perpetual nervous twitch. In the midst of a notably red-blooded extended family, Swinburne appeared effeminate, reared as he was in the company of his mother and four sisters. As a hedge against solitude, he turned to books. Taught to read by his mother, Swinburne at a young age mastered the Bible, Sir Walter Scott's novels, and the plays of William Shakespeare.

In 1849, Swinburne was enrolled at Eton, a move that ultimately proved disastrous. The sensitive boy did not fare well in the restrictive and patriarchal public-school atmosphere, where conformity and team spirit reigned. Always a rebel, young Swinburne was at once terrified and enraged by the oppressive discipline that characterized the place. Though a brilliant student—he was able to profit at least from Eton's heavily classical curriculum, which emphasized Latin and Greek—he was a social failure and a constant source of embarrassment to the school's administration. In the summer of 1853, Swinburne left Eton for good, at least two years earlier than expected.

Swinburne had begun writing even while at Eton, turning out heavily Elizabethan tragedies and even a mock eighteenth century poetic tribute to Queen Victoria entitled "The Triumph of Gloriana." Upon entering Oxford in 1856, he continued his literary career, falling naturally and almost instantly into membership in Old Mortality, a literary group that later published the short-lived literary magazine *Undergraduate Papers*. A more important and farther-reaching influence came in 1857, when Swinburne met Dante Gabriel Rossetti, who, along with his disciples Sir Edward Burne-Jones and William Morris, was down from London decorating the Oxford Union Society building with murals. Swinburne, already seriously questioning religious and political orthodoxy and the hypocrisies of official Victorian morality, was immediately drawn to Rossetti's Svengali-like personality and to the doctrine of art for art's sake. In Swinburne, Rossetti had found his newest disciple.

Rossetti's influence on Swinburne cannot be overstated, and it is generally considered an unhealthy one. Rossetti seems to have cultivated an apostlelike devotion from the young men who constantly surrounded him, often then publicly ridiculing them or dropping them altogether. In addition, Swinburne found Rossetti's Bohemian life-style much too enticing; Rossetti practiced to a remarkable degree the decadent doctrine that he preached. His life was riddled with alcoholic bouts and heterosexual affairs, and under this master's influence, Swinburne learned to give free rein to the sadomasochistic sexual urges that had been festering in him since his Eton days. Swinburne's love of bondage and flagellation figures prominently in some of his best poetry; indeed, such poems as "Dolores" and "Laus Veneris" are anomalies of English literature: They are poetic works of the highest order that until recently could not be candidly or openly discussed by the literary establishment.

Whatever else Rossetti's aesthetic doctrines accomplished, they at least succeeded in prompting Swinburne to take up writing more seriously than ever before. While at Oxford, Swinburne produced a number of poems, plays, and essays, among them the "Ode to Mazzini," a tribute to the leader of the fight for Italian democracy (later to become a friend and admirer of Swinburne); the long poem "Queen Iseult," a treatment of the Tristram and Isolde legend; and the two tragedies mentioned earlier, *The Queen-Mother* and *Rosamond*. As a result of Swinburne's intense literary activity, his academic standing suffered. In 1860, he left Oxford as he had left Eton—for reasons never made public.

The story of Swinburne's subsequent life in London is one of personal dissipation, literary acclaim (and notoriety), and sexual liberation to the point of excess and beyond. Through the offices of Rossetti and his friends—the politician and biographer Richard Monckton Milnes, the explorer Richard Burton, the painter Simeon Solomon—Swinburne led a life of unrestrained bohemianism, as if to make up for years of repression and conformity at Eton and Oxford. He discovered the poetry of Charles-Pierre Baudelaire and the sexually explicit writing of the Marquis de Sade; both of these writers he championed through editorials and reviews in the British popular press in a deliberate attempt to shock the staid literary establishment. The publication of *Atalanta in Calydon* in 1865 met with official approval, but in the same year *Chastelard*, the first of the Mary Stuart plays, brought condemnation, scandalizing, among countless others, the poet laureate Tennyson. *Poems and Ballads* (1866), which includes such "abnormal" poems as "Anactoria" and "Sapphics," gave Swinburne the reputation that he had long craved. He would forever be known as the British Baudelaire, the deviant rebel of English letters.

Swinburne's physical frailty was never quite able to withstand his excesses, and from time to time his father would quietly come to London and fetch Swinburne home to recuperate. One such rescue occurred in 1871 during a long and bitter public battle in which the minor poet Robert Buchanan attacked Rossetti and Swinburne as members of the amoral "Fleshly School of Poetry." Naturally, Swinburne mounted a counterattack. The peevish and juvenile mudslinging continued for five years, culminating in a libel suit in 1876—a suit that Buchanan won. In 1877, Swinburne's father died, and the poet returned to London, hell-bent on spending his inheritance on liquor and sexual pleasure. In June, 1879, his friend Walter Theodore Watts (later Watts-Dunton) did what Admiral Swinburne had so often done: He rescued the poet from a collision course with death and installed him at The Pines, Watts's home in suburban Putney.

Swinburne never left The Pines, and little is known of the last thirty years of his life. He continued to write and to publish, with Watts-Dunton acting as a shrewd literary agent. The poet who everyone thought would die young died at the age of seventy-two on April 10, 1909.

Analysis

Algernon Charles Swinburne very likely got the idea for his most renowned drama, *Atalanta in Calydon*, from Ovid's *Metamorphoses* (c. A.D. 8). The myth concerns Meleager, son of King Oeneus and Queen Althaea of Calydon, at whose birth the three Fates decree a glorious life and an early death: Meleager will die, say the Fates, when the brand then in the fire is consumed. To circumvent their prophecy, Althaea takes the brand from the fire and conceals it. Years later, Artemis, goddess of chastity and of the hunt, demonstrates her anger at Oeneus, who has neglected to pay her sufficient homage, by sending a wild boar to Calydon to devastate the fields and vineyards. The world's greatest hunters are convened to try to slay the boar, among them Meleager, recently returned from Jason's voyage in quest of the Golden Fleece, and Atalanta, skilled huntress and priestess of Artemis, a native of Arcadia.

Meleager falls in love with Atalanta almost immediately, despite his parents' misgivings. When he succeeds in killing the boar, he presents the head and skin to Atalanta. His mother's brothers Plexippus and Toxeus, however, who are angry that a woman should be allowed to join the hunt in the first place, take exception to Meleager's action and threaten to take the trophies for themselves. Meleager, provoked by their challenge to his manhood and by their treatment of Atalanta, kills both of his uncles in a fit of rage. When Althaea hears the news of her brothers' murders, she resurrects and destroys the forgotten brand, in effect killing her son. Meleager dies, but not before forgiving his mother and restating his love for Atalanta.

Too much has been made of the play's classicism. While it is in many ways a skillful imitation of the plays of the Greek masters Sophocles and Euripides—a Greek chorus, for example, intermittently intones the tragic themes, and the Aristotelian unities of time, place, and action are for the most part observed—the most compelling aspects of *Atalanta in Calydon* are decidedly nineteenth century. The theme of the play is the unavoidable control of fate over human life. More specifically, the play questions the benevolence of gods (and, by implication, the Christian God) who allow human tragedies to occur. Some of the most beautiful passages are those in which the chorus takes the gods to task, and the modern reader cannot but detect in these passages a direct affront by Swinburne to Victorian religious piety.

The play is also fundamentally modern in its treatment of love. Althaea repeatedly warns her son against the snares of love, and the chorus frequently takes up Althaea's sentiment, solemnly chanting about the dangers of romantic involvement and the attractions of celibacy. Oeneus is concerned specifically with Meleager's attraction to Atalanta, who is throughout the play presented as a somewhat masculine girl, a worshiper of the goddess of chastity. To Oeneus, Meleager's devotion to Atalanta is somehow unnatural, and no good can come of it. Toxeus and Plexippus also question Meleager's sexuality, though in a much more derisively confrontational manner. To them, Meleager's feelings for Atalanta are unmanly, as is his awarding of the hunting trophies to the chaste huntress. Meleager kills his uncles as much in overzealous defense of his manhood as in defense of Atalanta.

The drama received almost universal acclaim upon its publication, giving Swinburne a popular acceptance that he would never again enjoy. Despite its reputation as a masterpiece, however, *Atalanta in Calydon* is a rather dull poem and a very inadequate piece of drama. The plot is difficult to follow, and the dramatic business of the play is handled ineptly. Except for Althaea, no character is fully enough realized to be convincing; Atalanta in particular is a remarkably shallow creation. The metric adeptness that characterizes Swinburne's best poems is present in *Atalanta in Calydon*, but it does not always lend itself to dialogue. One wonders if the play has not received so much attention because it is for the most part "clean," capable of being discussed without indelicacy. At any rate, it is unhappily short on the Swinburnian genius that the Victorians considered perverse.

Swinburne's Mary Stuart trilogy is, as has been noted, more the work of a scholarly poet than of a playwright. Swinburne's obsession with the queen got the better of him in these plays: He seems to have been intent on providing the artistic final word on her life and legend, an intention that becomes most grotesquely obvious in *Bothwell*, the second installment of the trilogy, an interminable play of surpassing dullness. By far the most interesting of the three is the first, *Chastelard*, which treats the love triangle between Mary, her future husband Lord Darnley, and the courtier Chastelard. Quite possibly Swinburne wrote the play as an attack on conventional Victorian morality, and as such it succeeds. The love between Mary and Chastelard is as unconventional as the love described in the most daring of Swinburne's lyric poems. Passionate, highly sexual, and reckless in the extreme, the relationship between the courtier and his queen is a prime example of *amour fou*, a mad love whose element of danger is irresistibly attractive to the lovers. Mary is treated as a beautiful, dangerous woman, a direct descendant of Keats's "La Belle Dame Sans Merci." Chastelard, one of the most compelling characters in Swinburne's dramatic canon, is a reckless swain, willing to sacrifice all for the sake of passion. It is Swinburne's most decadently Romantic play, brimming with suggestions of sadomasochism and sexual cruelty: Parts of it, in other words, are pure Swinburne. Predictably, however, the drama was misunderstood. A reading public that had approved of the neoclassical pomp of *Atalanta in Calydon* was scandalized by *Chastelard*, and Swinburne's reputation as an amoral deviant—a reputation finally and incontrovertibly established by the *Poems and Ballads* of 1866—was well under way.

Swinburne's remaining poetic dramas deserve only passing mention, flawed as they are in various ways. *Marino Faliero*, a deliberate answer to Byron's play of the same name, is a revenge tragedy set in Renaissance Italy; it is of interest solely as a testimonial to Swinburne's sustained championship of Italian Republicanism. *Locrine* is another reworking of a myth, this one concerning a love triangle between a king, a queen, and the king's mistress. It is fascinating as an exercise in prosody, employing nearly every English stanza form, from the heroic couplet to the Shakespearean sonnet; as a dramatic work, it is embarrassingly bad. *Erechtheus*, like *Atalanta in Calydon* an imitation of the Greeks, is too stately and solemn for its own good.

The Sisters is Swinburne's only attempt at dramatic realism. Set in 1816, it explores yet another love triangle, this one involving two sisters, both of whom are in love with the same man. When the hero, Reginald Clavering, becomes promised to one, the other poisons them both. Swinburne admitted that the play was autobiographical, with Reginald Clavering a direct attempt to portray himself as a dramatic character. *The Sisters* is at its best a provocative study of love, rejection, and jealousy, but it is more often an awkward tale of courtship among the upper classes. The last dramatic work that Swinburne published was *The Duke of Gandia*, a perverse playlet about murder, incest, and intrigue in the court of the Borgia pope, Alexander VI. In it, one sees flashes of the old Swinburne, for the play is deliberately and violently irreligious. It is perhaps telling that so late in life Swinburne chose to write and to publish a play that is monstrous in its view of religion, authority, and familial love. *The Duke of Gandia* serves as a reminder that Swinburne never lost the decadent rebelliousness that had made him famous during the reign of Queen Victoria.

Other major works

NOVELS: *Love's Cross-Currents*, 1901 (originally in serial form as *A Year's Letters*, 1877); *Lesbia Brandon*, 1952 (written sporadically in the 1860's).

POETRY: *Poems and Ballads*, 1866; *A Song of Italy*, 1867; *Ode on the Proclamation of the French Republic*, 1870; *Songs Before Sunrise*, 1871; *Songs of Two Nations*, 1875; *Poems and Ballads: Second Series*, 1878; *Songs of the Springtides*, 1880; *The Heptalogia*, 1880; *Tristram of Lyonesse and Other Poems*, 1882; *A Century of Roundels*, 1883; *A Midsummer Holiday and Other Poems*, 1884; *Gathered Songs*, 1887; *Poems and Ballads: Third Series*, 1889; *Astrophel and Other Poems*, 1894; *The Tale of Balen*, 1896; *A Channel Passage and Other Poems*, 1904; *Posthumous Poems*, 1917; *Ron-*

deaux Parisiens, 1917; *Ballads of the English Border*, 1925.

NONFICTION: *Byron*, 1866; *Notes on Poems and Reviews*, 1866; *William Blake: A Critical Essay*, 1868; *Under the Microscope*, 1872; *George Chapman*, 1875; *Essays and Studies*, 1875; *A Note on Charlotte Brontë*, 1877; *A Study of Shakespeare*, 1880; *Miscellanies*, 1886; *A Study of Victor Hugo*, 1886; *A Study of Ben Jonson*, 1889; *Studies in Prose and Poetry*, 1894; *The Age of Shakespeare*, 1908; *Three Plays of Shakespeare*, 1909; *Shakespeare*, 1909; *Contemporaries of Shakespeare*, 1919.

MISCELLANEOUS: *The Complete Works of Algernon Charles Swinburne*, 1925-1927 (20 volumes), 1968 (reprint).

Bibliography

Cassidy, John. *Algernon C. Swinburne.* New York: Twayne, 1964. In this excellent collection of critical essays, the author's purpose is to shed as much light as possible on Swinburne's literary work. The biography enters the discussion only where it is indispensable to a full understanding of the texts. Raphaelitism, positivism, and French aestheticism are discussed extensively in connection with Swinburne's tendencies toward the sadistic and masochistic. Contains a chronology and a useful bibliography.

Henderson, Philip. *Swinburne: Portrait of a Poet.* New York: Macmillan, 1974. Drawing upon Swinburne's voluminous and uninhibited correspondence, the autobiographical novels, memoirs, and private journals, Henderson presents a vivid portrait of Swinburne the man and poet. He discusses the strange charm and complexity of Swinburne's personality and argues for a reappraisal of Swinburne as poet and critic. Included in the biography are lengthy excerpts from Swinburne's writings as well as observations about him by many of his contemporaries. Illustrations.

Hyder, Clyde K., ed. *Swinburne as Critic.* Boston: Routledge & Kegan Paul, 1972. The selections in this book illustrate various aspects of Swinburne's literary criticism and include his best and most representative work. The work contains three main divisions: poetry and art, fiction, and drama. Twenty-five major selections cover some of the most important writers in English literature, including Geoffrey Chaucer, Lord Byron, Charles Dickens, and the Brontës. The introduction contains numerous quotations from Swinburne's critical prose and letters in order to illustrate his ideas and methods and to appraise his achievement.

Peters, Robert L. *The Crowns of Apollo, Swinburne's Principles of Art and Literature: A Study in Victorian Criticism and Aesthetics.* Detroit: Wayne State University Press, 1965. The aims of this study are to rescue Swinburne's contributions to the aesthetics of his time and to provide a more detailed arrangement and evaluation of his principles of literature and art than previously considered. The first chapter discusses the most obvious defects and merits of Swinburne's criticism; subsequent chapters present specific aspects of his theories. Illustrations and a bibliography.

Reide, David G. *Swinburne: A Study of Romantic Mythmaking.* Charlottesville: University Press of Virginia, 1978. In this excellent study of Swinburne's criticism, poems, and plays, the author argues that Swinburne is the link between the first English Romantics and the modern Romantics. Traces Swinburne's development from unthinking acceptance of earlier modes to creative affirmation, reflecting the development of a literary tradition insisting on the creative continuation of tradition itself as the one certainty against meaninglessness.

Thomas, Donald Serrell. *Swinburne: The Poet in His World.* 1st ed. New York: Oxford University Press, 1979. The purpose of this volume is to depict Swinburne in relation to the society in which he lived. Neither an essay in psychoanalysis nor a linguistic analysis of Swinburne's work, this book is an insightful biography of what the author deems to be one of the most eccentric and original writers of the Victorian period. Thomas' study offers a new critical discussion of Swinburne's work in the light of its influence on the development of English literature. Contains illustrations and a select bibliography.

J. D. Daubs
(Updated by *Genevieve Slomski*)

JOHN MILLINGTON SYNGE

Born: Rathfarnham, Ireland; April 16, 1871
Died: Dublin, Ireland; March 24, 1909

Principal drama

When the Moon Has Set, wr. 1900-1901, pb. 1968; *Luasnad, Capa and Laine*, wr. 1902, pb. 1968; *A Vernal Play*, wr. 1902, pb. 1968; *The Tinker's Wedding*, wr. 1903, pb. 1908, pr. 1909; *In the Shadow of the Glen*, pr. 1903, pb. 1904 (one act); *Riders to the Sea*, pb. 1903, pr. 1904 (one act); *The Well of the Saints*, pr., pb. 1905; *The Playboy of the Western World*, pr., pb. 1907; *Deirdre of the Sorrows*, pr., pb. 1910; *The Complete Plays*, pb. 1981.

Other literary forms

John Millington Synge's nondramatic works—autobiographical sketches, essays, reviews, and diaries—document the proposition that his dramatic career began with his response to William Butler Yeats's advice to abandon Paris for Ireland's remote regions. Synge's observations of the lives of the country people of Aran, Connemara, Kerry, and Wicklow indicate that until he lived in these repositories of folk tradition, he had not found either theme or style. The diaries and essays from these visits report Synge's compilation of dramatic incidents, details of local color, images, and turns of speech, and show an understanding of that way of life that encompassed its dialect, character, and fatalism. Although these accounts show an acute eye for the dramatic, they have less-than-scientific reliability, permeated as they are with Synge's nature mysticism, his brooding remove from social engagement, and his lack of sympathy with the religious traditions of the people. Synge's direct, precise prose is chiefly valuable as a record of the sources for his plays and of his developing creative consciousness.

With a few exceptions—"In Kerry," "Queens," and "Danny"—Synge's poetry merits the same judgment. Ironic, romantic, and morbid, it is rich with Celtic and folk reference; it also shows, however, the influence of various European poets—François Villon, Giacomo Leopardi, Petrarch—whose works Synge translated. There is some evidence that Synge's direct idiom contributed to Yeats's abandonment of romantic idealism after 1902.

Synge's photographs (*My Wallet of Photographs*, 1971) are valuable documents of turn-of-the-century life on the Irish seaboard. His *Letters to Molly* (1971) and *Some Letters of John M. Synge to Lady Gregory and W. B. Yeats* (1971) are equally valuable in coming to an appreciation of Synge's personal and business struggles in his final and more creative years.

Achievements

The Irish Literary Revival was the result of the collective efforts of diverse talents in the fields of translation, folklore, fiction, poetry, and drama. Under the leadership of the Olympian W. B. Yeats, the movement counted the folklorist Douglas Hyde, the novelists James Joyce and George Moore, the translator and dramatist Lady Augusta Gregory, and the poet and editor George Russell (whose pseudonym was Æ) among its contributors. These writers shared the desire for the establishment of a national literature that would express what they considered distinctive about the Irish imagination. Each contributed to the dramatic literature presented on the stage of the Abbey Theatre, but John Millington Synge is the only one of this group whose contribution lies mainly in the drama. Indeed, Synge is generally regarded as the most distinguished dramatist of the Irish Literary Revival.

This reputation rests on the output of his final seven years: six plays, two of which, *Riders to the Sea* and *The Playboy of the Western World,* are masterpieces. These plays in particular exhibit the characteristic qualities of intense lyric speech drawn from the native language and dialects of Ireland, romantic characterization in primitive settings, and dramatic construction after the classics of European drama. Three central theses dominate Synge's work: the enmity between romantic dreams and life's hard necessities, the relationship between human beings and the natural world, and the mutability of all things. These plays are the expressions of a complex personality, formed by Synge's early musical training, his alienation from his own Anglo-Irish roots, his love for the landscapes and country people of Ireland, the tension between romantic impulse and realistic imperatives, and his persistent morbidity and personal loneliness.

Synge has had considerable influence in shaping the style and themes of subsequent Irish dramatists, such as George Fitzmaurice and M. J. Malloy, and some influence outside Ireland, most notably in the work of Federico García Lorca and Eugene O'Neill.

Biography

Edmund John Millington Synge was born April 16, 1871, in Rathfarnham, County Dublin, the youngest of the five children of a comfortable Anglo-Irish Protestant family. His schooling was mostly private until, at the age of seventeen, he entered Trinity College, Dublin, where he won prizes in Irish and Hebrew even though he put most of his energy into the study of the piano, violin, and flute. During his youth, he developed a strong reaction to his mother's religiosity and an enthusiasm for the antiquities and natural beauty of the Irish countryside. He went to Germany in 1893 to study music but the following year abandoned his plans to move to Paris and attend lectures in European language and literature at the Sorbonne. Instead, he traveled through Germany, Italy, and France between 1894 and 1896; he wrote some poetry and dramatic fragments, gave lessons in English, and studied French and Italian, returning during the summers to Dublin, where he furthered his interests in the Irish language and Irish antiquities.

In December, 1896, Yeats encountered Synge in Paris and discerned a literary talent in search of a subject. He advised Synge to go to the Aran Islands off the Atlantic coast of Ireland, where the people spoke Irish and still led lives free of modern convention. Synge complied, and for a portion of each summer from 1898 to 1902, he lived among the fisherfolk and recorded his observations with notebook and camera. He continued to write dramatic sketches and literary reviews and edited his notes under the title *The Aran Islands* (1907). His first plays, *When the Moon Has Set*, written in prose, and *A Vernal Play* and *Luasnad, Capa and Laine*, written in verse—although apprenticeship works—exhibit fragmentary characteristics of his mature work. This maturity came rapidly, for during the summer of 1902, he wrote *Riders to the Sea* and *In the Shadow of the Glen* and began *The Tinker's Wedding. Riders to the Sea* was the first of Synge's plays to be published (October, 1903), but *In the Shadow of the Glen* was the first to be produced on the stage—by the Irish National Theatre Society (October, 1903). An acrimonious public debate over the play's depiction of Irish life followed this production, a debate to which its author contributed little. When *Riders to the Sea* was produced, Synge's reputation improved, especially following the London presentation of the two plays in March, 1904.

When the Abbey Theatre opened in December of 1904, Synge was appointed literary adviser and later director, along with Lady Augusta Gregory and W. B. Yeats. The following February, *The Well of the Saints* was produced there, though it was poorly received. Meanwhile, Synge was visiting Counties Kerry, Galway, and Mayo and was working on his masterpiece, *The Playboy of the Western World.* As he drafted and revised this play throughout 1906, a romantic relationship was growing with Molly Allgood (known onstage as Máire O'Neill), the Abbey actress who played the role of Pegeen Mike in the first production, on January 26, 1907. The play offended Irish sensibilities, provoking a week of riots and a bitter public debate over the play and freedom of expression on the stage. Again, Synge took little part in the argument, leaving the burden of defending his work to Yeats.

Synge commenced his last play, *Deirdre of the Sorrows*, which is based on a story of the Sons of Usnach from the Ulster cycle of Celtic tales, during 1907. During this same year, the symptoms of Hodgkin's disease, which had first manifested themselves in 1897, reappeared. The resultant operations interfered with Synge's revisions of the play, caused the postponement of his wedding, and failed to arrest the disease. He died on March 24, 1909. In January, 1910, *Deirdre of the Sorrows* was first performed, with Molly Allgood in the title role.

Analysis

When, in 1893, John Millington Synge was choosing between musical and literary careers, two seminal documents were published which would profoundly affect his decision and form the character of his subsequent work. These were Stopford Brooke's lecture "The Need of Use of Getting Irish Literature into the English Tongue," and Douglas Hyde's *Love Songs of Connaucht* (1893). Brooke's lecture identified four tasks essential to the development of an Irish national literature: the translation of ancient Irish texts, the molding of the various mythological and historical cycles into an imaginative unity, the treatment in verse of selected episodes from these materials, and the collection of folk stories surviving in the Irish countryside. Some of these tasks had already been undertaken, but none had an impact on the developing revival to equal that of Hyde's slim volume of the same year. He showed that the living song tradition in the Irish Gaelic-speaking areas was rich, complex, and sensitive; that a strong link with an ancient cultural tradition still persisted; and that a translation of these songs into Hiberno-English opened new avenues of expression to the literary artist.

By the early 1890's, Yeats was already committed to some of the tasks outlined by Brooke, and he also greeted Hyde's work enthusiastically. Yeats wrote in an 1893 issue of *The Bookman*: "These poor peasants lived in a beautiful if somewhat inhospitable world, where little has changed since Adam delved and Eve span. Everything was so old that it was steeped in the heart, and every powerful emotion found at once noble types and symbols for its expression." When Yeats encountered Synge in Paris three years later, it was with these principles and sentiments that he persuaded him to abandon the French capital for the Aran Islands. The plays that resulted do indeed constitute a distinguished translation of folk and heroic materials to the modern stage.

Riders to the Sea was the first play Synge wrote, and it draws most heavily and directly on his experience of life on the Aran Islands; many of the details, along with the main incident on which the play is based, can be found in the journals Synge kept during his visits there. It was Synge's first successful use of Hiberno-English to serve his own dramatic and poetic purposes, and it is regarded by most commentators as one of the finest short plays in that literature.

The action of the play is simple and highly compressed. An old woman of the Aran Islands, Maurya, has lost her husband, father-in-law, and four sons to the sea. She now awaits news of the fate of Michael, another son, as her last and youngest son, Bartley, prepares to make the crossing to Galway with two horses. Maurya's two daughters have just received a bundle of clothes which they identify as those of Michael. As the young women attempt to keep the news from her, she attempts to dissuade Bartley from the hazardous journey—in vain, for just as Bartley must play the provider's part, Maurya's timeworn experience has taught her to anticipate the truth. While her daughters find confirmation of Michael's death in the bundle of clothes, Maurya sees a vision of what is about to happen: Bartley's drowning. As the daughters tell Maurya of Michael's death, the neighbors carry in Bartley's body. The play climaxes with Maurya's lament for these and all her menfolk, ending with a prayer for all the living and the dead.

Although it requires less than thirty minutes to perform, the play encompasses a succession of moods and a universe of action. By contrasting the young women's particular, objective attitudes (their preoccupation with the physical evidence of Michael's death) with Maurya's subjective, universal, even mystical, consciousness (her forgetting the blessing and the nails, and her visionary experience), Synge establishes a pattern of dramatic ironies. Maurya's feelings in regard to the external action of the play, moreover, are seen to evolve from a subdued disquiet, to a higher anxiety, to a visionary sympathy with her last two sons, and finally to a threnody of disinterested compassion for the mothers and sons of all humankind. Maurya is, therefore, not only a credible individual character but also an archetypal figure: She is cast among domestic details yet is inattentive to them because her awareness of commonality and community eventually obscures particular concerns. Only her indomitable attitude in those eloquent, passionate speeches offers a nearly adequate human response to the implacable antagonist, the sea.

The sea which surrounds the bare islands is both the islanders' source of sustenance and their principal natural enemy; in the play, it insistently reminds the characters that, contend with it or not, they are doomed. Synge has carefully selected the domestic details to develop his themes—the bread, the nets, boards, knife, rope, and knot—details which establish a practical and symbolic relationship between the smaller and larger worlds of action, onstage and offstage, practical and moral. Other elements in the play act as religious or mystical allusions: the apocalyptic horses, the fateful dropped stitches, the ineffectual young priest, the omens in the sky and in the holy well. Many aspects of the setting—the door, the colors, the blessing—repeat and reverse themselves as images of the life-and-death ritual which sets Maurya and the sea against each other again and again. Maurya's maternal mysticism is solemnly expressed by her prayers, blessings, gestures, litanies, and pitiful elegy for the cavalcade of death.

Although Maurya's speeches are interlaced with Christian invocation, her response to the catastrophe does not, at its most profound depths, derive from conventional Christian feelings. Maurya confronts a system of natural elements which confounds all human aspirations, and her response is in the tradition of characters from grand tragedy. Thus Synge has written a play that combines elements from Greek tragedy (it reminded Yeats of the plays of Aeschylus), the attitudes of primitive Gaelic society (its fatalism and impersonality), and the modern world, with its nihilism and cultivation of a sense of the absurd. There has been considerable argument over the compatibility of these ethics with one another, but there is no disagreement over the intensity and complexity of the emotions engendered by the play, whether read or staged.

Synge's second play, *In the Shadow of the Glen* (written under the title *The Shadow of the Glen*) is set in the Wicklow Mountains south of Dublin, a remote area familiar to Synge, in which he had a cottage and about which he had written several essays gathered under the title *In Wicklow* (1910). The play shows the influence of Henrik Ibsen's *A Doll's House* (pr. 1879), but its direct source is "An Old Man's Story," which Synge had heard from the Aran Island shanachie Pat Dirane; it is found in Synge's prose work *The Aran Islands*. The question of the play's origin is significant because it was immediately attacked for its depiction of an unfaithful wife and its unfair portrayal of Irishwomen. Synge unquestionably took considerable liberty with his raw materials—drawing, for example, on an episode from Petronius' *Satyricon* (c. A.D. 60), "The Widow of Ephesus"—and the result was an original, concise, complex comedy.

A "Tramp" is admitted to a lonely cottage by one Nora Burke, whose husband is laid out as if for a wake. Conversation between the two reveals that Nora has been living unhappily with her relatively well-off but aged husband, a situation that has led to a number of dalliances with other men, including the now deceased Patch Darcy. Nora then exits to rendezvous with another young man, Michael Dara, leaving the Tramp to maintain the wake. The Tramp, however, is soon shocked to find that Nora's husband, Dan Burke, is feigning death in order to trap his wife and either bring her to heel or eject her from his house. No sooner has the Tramp agreed to cooperate with Dan's scheme than Nora returns with Michael Dara. The pair discuss their prospects of marriage now that Nora is apparently free. Suddenly Dan springs from the bed to confront the pair. Michael Dara backs off immediately, and Nora is left to face her husband alone; at this point, the Tramp reintroduces himself with renewed eloquence, offering Nora a romantic life with him outside material security. This appeal finally releases Nora's imaginative energies, and she departs with him, leaving Dan Burke and Michael Dara to share a bottle of whiskey.

In the Shadow of the Glen offered the first explicit treatment of sexual frustration on the modern Irish stage; at the same time, the play's symbolic setting and the rich imagery of its language enlarge its reference to register a protest against the constraints of time and space (represented by the mists moving up and down the Wicklow glen). Synge sympathizes with Nora and identifies with the Tramp, the two developing characters in the play, in opposition to their static counterparts, Dan Burke and Michael Dara. The Tramp's sympathetic nature and colorful talk awaken hitherto untapped imaginative reserves in Nora, so that the surroundings of mountain mist and road become reinvested with their primary magic. The play thus dramatizes Synge's central preoccupations: the conflict between actuality and human aspirations, the awareness of human mutability, and human beings' intimate relation with the natural world.

In the Shadow of the Glen dramatizes life-and-death issues in many ways, both literally and metaphorically, and on different levels of seriousness and comedy: Daniel Burke appears dead but rises twice. His ploy is to test the convention of life (his wife's fidelity) with the perspective of death, and he succeeds in exposing it as illusory. The audience begins with a conventional view of death; proceeds, after Dan's first resurrection (through the sharing of his vantage point, but not his point of view), to a seriocomic view of life; and ends, after his second resurrection, with a romantic sharing of the Tramp's vantage point and point of view on both life and death. As its sympathies shift, the audience proceeds from an ironic view of Nora's infidelity to an ironic view of Dan's righteousness. The first revelation is that the conventional phenomena of death are deceptive; the final revelation is that the conventional phenomena of life are equally deceptive; the playgoer begins by believing Dan to be dead in body and ends by believing him dead in soul. These ambiguities and shifts in the plot are reflected in the language and imagery of the play, which propose states of animality, madness, and age as relative conditions between life and death.

It is clear, for example, that Nora's memories of Patch Darcy condition her response to the Tramp, and as the play progresses, the connections between these two male figures multiply, as do the associations of the Tramp with death. Thus, as the image of Patch Darcy (his life-in-death counterpart), the Tramp is at once the antagonist of Dan and Michael, death-in-life counterparts. The Tramp is, in an important sense, the ghost of Patch Darcy, for he is the counterpart, in Nora's consciousness, of her dead lover. She seems to recognize the affinity, at first dimly but with sufficient clarity at the end to follow her Patch into the mists on the mountainside to romance, and probably to madness and death. Thus, the Tramp, as Patch Darcy revenant, is Nora's shadow of the Wicklow glen. By a combination of poetic language, naturalistic action, and farce, the play transforms its source into a small triumph, preparing the way for Synge's greatest achievement, *The Playboy of the Western World.*

The Playboy of the Western World originated in a story, recorded in 1898, about a man named Lynchenaun "who killed his father with the blow of a spade when he was in a passion" and, with the aid of the people of Inishmaan, evaded the police to escape eventually to America. When later (1903-1905) he visited Counties Kerry and Mayo, Synge gathered further materials for this work: observations of the lonely landscapes of the western seaboard; the moodiness and rebellious temperament of the people; their religiosity, alcoholism, and fanciful language. For the next two years, he worked steadily on the play under five successive titles, almost twenty scenarios, and a dozen complete drafts, before it was finally produced on January 26, 1907.

The play develops the Lynchenaun story into that of Christy Mahon, a timorous Kerry farmboy who has fled north from the scene of his parricide to a lonely stretch of the coastline of Mayo. There he happens on a remote public house where he tells his story. The villagers give him refuge, and as he is called upon to retell his story to a succession of curious neighbors, his embellishments become more colorful, and his self-confidence grows in proportion to the hyperbole. The villagers respond to these accounts with increasing admiration, so that Christy is soon regarded as a hero for his passionate deed. He strikes fear in the men and desire in the women, especially in the daughter of the house, Pegeen Mike. She rejects her fiancé, the pious Shawn Keogh, for Christy's attentions which she seeks to retain against the competition of the village women, especially the Widow Quin. All this attention drives Christy to further heights of eloquence—especially in the love scene with Pegeen—and to feats of athletic skill at the village sports.

These triumphs, however, are rudely deflated by the appearance of another, older Kerryman, with a bandaged head: Christy's father, very much alive. He exposes Christy as a coward and a liar, and the crowd, Pegeen included, immediately rejects their erstwhile champion. Christy has been changed, however, and to prove his father wrong and regain his reputation and Pegeen's affections, he attacks his father again, this time laying him low "in the sight of all." Christy, however, has misjudged the effect of such an action on the villagers, who distinguish between the admirable "gallous story" and the shocking "dirty deed," and they capture Christy to bring him to justice. He is disillusioned with all of them and threatens indiscriminate vengeance, whereupon his father again revives, recognizes Christy's newfound character, and invites him back to Kerry as master of the house. Christy agrees, and they depart, casting aspersions on the "villainy of Mayo and the fools in here." Too late, Pegeen realizes that she has lost a true champion.

The play provoked immediate outrage among the Dublin audiences: They considered it an insult to national pride, to Catholicism, and to common decency. Among a people hoping for a fair, if not positive, treatment in support of their long-standing grievance against British rule, the play was a cruel disappointment. For his part, Synge refused to tone down the play's oaths and irreverent allusions, even when appealed to privately by the actors and by his fellow Protestants Yeats and Lady Gregory. The protests, in fact, turned into a full-scale riot with Christy's reference to "a drift of chosen females standing in their shifts," which was considered an intolerable obscenity. In the week that followed, the police protected the stage and players from nightly attack, Yeats defended the freedom of the stage in public debate, Synge himself granted an unfortunate interview to the press, and the newspapers were full of acrimonious argument. In retrospect, it is not difficult to understand why a Dublin audience, sensitive to signs of religious and ethnic derogation, should react so vehemently to the work of a son of the landed class produced at the "national" theater and composed of such an original blend of Rabelaisian humor, lyricism, romance, and exaggeration.

In his preface to the play, Synge anticipates a hostile reaction by praising the "popular imagination that is fiery and magnificent, and tender" that he found among the people of the remote regions. He proposes that the language and images are authentic, "that the wildest sayings and ideas in this play are tame indeed compared with the fancies one may hear in any little hillside cabin." While it is true that Synge's sources—in plot, language, and characterization—are sound, the combination here, more than in his other works, is uniquely his own. Just as the action and characterization lack normal constraints, so, too, is the language compressed and heightened.

The distinctive language of *The Playboy of the Western World* derives from several sources: the Hiberno-English dialects of the West of Ireland, vestiges of Tudor English still found in Ireland, popular sermons, and Synge's own penchant for musical, rhythmic prose. Chief among these is the influence of Irish Gaelic syntax, vocabulary, and idiom, with its rich lode of religious and natural imagery. This convention is particularly effective at the romantic climax in act 3, although it can sound parodic in scenes of less excitement. Even so, Synge's particular artistic use of local dialect is considerably more flexible and expressive than the comparable experiments of Lady Gregory or Yeats.

In this dialect, Synge found an ideal vehicle for his own passionate vision of the lonely outsider. Christy is the poet whose creative gifts are only superficially appreciated by a convention-bound society; Christy not only invests the language with new zest and daring but also unknowingly transforms himself, by the same process of imaginative energy, from a cowering lout into a master of his destiny. His transformation begins as the people of Mayo trust his story and continues as he realizes his own narrative skills; it is completed when, with full moral awareness, he strikes his father down a second time. His father is the first to recognize the new Christy; Pegeen Mike does so, too, but for her it is too late; for the rest, the episode is no more than a subject for gossip.

Christy's path to his apotheosis comes only after an erratic journey of surges and reversals; *The Playboy of the Western World* is exuberant comedy in its action as well as in its language and characterization. It contains moments of farce, satire, tragicomedy, and the mock heroic. As Ann Saddlemyer's standard edition shows, Synge's revisions were vigorous and meticulous, act 3 giving him the most difficulties; some of these difficulties—Pegeen's motivations and the resolution of the Widow Quin's role—arguably remain unresolved. For all of its difficulties, however, this act achieves brilliant closure and includes perhaps the finest dramatic writing to come from the Irish theater.

The power of *The Playboy of the Western World* rests on more than its verbal pyrotechnics and comic structure; as many critics have argued, it exhibits features of the scapegoat archetype, the Oedipus myth, and the Messiah theme. It has relationships with Irish folk legend, with the early Irish Ulster cycle of heroic tales, and with Ibsen's *Peer Gynt* (1867). Whatever the relevance of these sources or analogues to an appreciation of this great play, the play's qualities derive from the happy collaboration of Synge's instinctive sense of the dramatic and the quality of his material. He describes it thus to an admirer: "The wildness and, if you will, the vices of the Irish peasantry are due, like their extraordinary good points of all kinds, to the *richness* of their nature—a thing that is priceless beyond words."

In his unfinished last play, *Deirdre of the Sorrows,* Synge was in the process of making a new departure. He found that the challenge of writing on a heroic theme from the Ulster cycle presented fresh difficulties which he took satisfaction in solving. It is generally conceded that his version humanizes the legend: It is more realistic than the versions by Æ and Yeats, with which it is often compared.

Synge set himself not only against the mystical excesses of the Irish writers of his time but also against the intellectual drama of Ibsen and George Bernard Shaw and produced works of narrow but intense passion. Synge's plays realize, more successfully than those of any of his contemporaries, Yeats's dictum that Irish writers should seek their form among the classical writers, but their language at home.

Other major works

NONFICTION: *The Aran Islands*, 1907; *In Wicklow*, 1910; *The Autobiography of J. M. Synge*, 1965; *Letters to Molly: John Millington Synge to Máire O'Neill, 1906-1909*, 1971 (Ann Saddlemyer, editor); *My Wallet of Photographs*, 1971 (Lilo Stephens, introducer and arranger); *Some Letters of John M. Synge to Lady Gregory and W. B. Yeats*, 1971 (Ann Saddlemyer, editor); *The Collected Letters of John Millington Synge*, 1983-1984 (2 volumes; Saddlemyer, editor).

MISCELLANEOUS: *Collected Works*, 1962-1968 (Anne Saddlemyer and Robin Skelton, editors).

Bibliography

Bourgeois, Maurice. *John Millington Synge and the Irish Theatre.* Bronx, N.Y.: B. Blom, 1965. A later edition of the classic 1913 study of the director of the Abbey Theatre who, along with William Butler Yeats and Lady Augusta Gregory, was a leader in the Irish Literary Revival.

Greene, David H., and Edward M. Stephens. *J. M. Synge, 1871-1909.* Rev. ed. New York: New York University Press, 1989. This volume is a revised edition of an earlier but unsurpassed account of Synge's transformation from a minor literary critic into a genius of Western drama.

Skelton, Robin. *J. M. Synge and His World.* New York: Viking Press, 1971. A short but useful account of Ireland's greatest playwright by a leading authority and poet. It discloses the influence of William Butler Yeats and discusses Synge's repeated visits to the Aran Islands during his brief but productive career as a dramatist.

Stephens, Edward M. *My Uncle John: Edward Stephen's Life of J. M. Synge.* Edited by Andrew Carpenter. London: Oxford University Press, 1974. Provides insights into the playwright's childhood and family life in middle-class Protestant Dublin.

Thornton, Weldon. *J. M. Synge and the Western Mind.* New York: Harper & Row, 1979. A later and trenchant study of Synge's inspiration and his place in European literature.

Cóilín D. Owens
(Updated by *Peter C. Holloran*)

ALFRED, LORD TENNYSON

Born: Somersby, England; August 6, 1809
Died: Near Haslemere, England; October 6, 1892

Principal drama

Queen Mary, pb. 1875, pr. 1876; *Harold*, pb. 1876, pr. 1928; *Becket*, wr. 1879, pb. 1884, pr. 1893; *The Falcon*, pr. 1879, pb. 1884 (one act); *The Cup*, pr. 1881, pb. 1884; *The Foresters*, wr. 1881, pr., pb. 1892; *The Promise of May*, pr. 1882, pb. 1886; *The Devil and the Lady*, pb. 1930 (unfinished).

Other literary forms

Alfred, Lord Tennyson's plays were an interlude in his long and distinguished career as a poet. During his lifetime he published more than fifteen volumes of poetry, which have been collected into the nine-volume *The Works of Tennyson* (1907-1908), edited by his son, Hallam, Lord Tennyson. At the insistence of Sir Arthur Sullivan, Tennyson wrote a song cycle, *The Window* (1870), which Sullivan set to music. Several songs from *The Princess* (1847) were also set to music, one by Benjamin Britten in *Serenade for Tenor, Horn, and Strings*, Opus 31. Tennyson's letters from 1821 to 1892 have been edited by Cecil Y. Lang and Edgar F. Shannon and have been published in three volumes.

Achievements

Tennyson's achievements as a dramatist are of interest primarily for the light they shed on his poetry. Tennyson was the best known and most loved poet of the Victorian period, but his fame and popularity were purchased at a high price. Honors were plentiful: his appointment as poet laureate after William Wordsworth's death, his audiences with the Queen, his peerage, his burial in Westminster Abbey. During his last twenty years, his birthdays were solemnized almost as national holidays. Lakes in New Zealand, agricultural colonies in South Africa, and roses in England were named for him. His views on all subjects were eagerly sought and accepted. With such great expectations, it would take a most exceptional man to resist, and Tennyson, unfortunately, was not exceptional enough. He tried to be the spokesman of his country, and he published more than he should have. Earlier in his career, he showed that he could profit from sound criticism and became a better poet, but once the criticism stopped, he lost his own critical sense.

After his death, the inevitable reaction occurred, and it became so radical a shift that "Tennysonian" became a term of mockery and contempt. Tennyson had been the symbol of his age, and the twentieth century could see nothing worthy of preserving from the Victorian era. Tennyson's ability to inspire and console his age led later readers to denounce him for his moralizing. This "debunking period" was perhaps necessary to achieve a more balanced view of his accomplishments. Modern assessments have emphasized the division within Tennyson, who was caught between the mysticism of the Romantics and the dogmatism of the Victorians. He was a poet who wrote about the eternal tensions of withdrawal and involvement, of doubt and faith, of the fanciful and the real. His technical virtuosity, his impressionistic rendering of scenes, his dedication to the poet's calling, and his place in a tradition all contribute to his reputation as a major poet and assure him a lasting place in the history of English literature.

Biography

Alfred, Lord Tennyson was born in 1809 at Somersby Rectory in Lincolnshire, but his father, the Reverend Dr. George Tennyson, was not the typical Anglican clergyman. As the dispossessed eldest son of a wealthy landowner, he was forced to accept a profession he disliked, but it afforded him time to educate his children. A man of culture and intelligence himself, he noticed early that Alfred, the fourth of his twelve children, had a gift for poetry, which he readily encouraged. Alfred began writing verses during his earliest years, and at twelve he began an epic poem in imitation of Sir Walter Scott. This caused his father to remark: "If that boy dies, one of our greatest poets will have gone." Tennyson was spurred on by this encouragement and by collaboration with his brother Charles; *Poems by Two Brothers* was published when Alfred was still in his teens.

When Tennyson went to Cambridge in 1827, he became associated with a group of brilliant young men who called themselves the Apostles. One of the most gifted of them, Arthur Hallam, became his best friend and chief advocate. This group of friends helped him to overcome his initial shyness (he had had few friends outside his immediate family); they gave him confidence and broadened his experience so that in the next few years he published two volumes of poetry: *Poems, Chiefly Lyrical* (1830) and *Poems* (1832, imprinted 1833).

All seemed to be going well in a promising literary career, but then came a series of shocks. The most traumatic was certainly the sudden death of Hallam in 1833; their friendship had become so close and deep that Tennyson went into a long period of depression following his friend's death. He published very little over the next nine years, but rather than attribute these years of silence completely to Hallam's death, one has to recognize several other serious blows that fell at about the same time. In 1831, two years before Hallam's death, Tennyson's family suffered a series of grievous troubles: Alfred's father died, his brother Edward had to be confined because of insanity, and his favorite brother, Charles, became addicted to opium. Added to these troubles were the hostile reviews of his poetry. For one who had received only encouragement and praise from family and friends, the reviews, which called his poetry "obscure" and "affected" and branded him "the pet of a cockney coterie," were sufficient to cause Tennyson to question his poetic gifts. Though stung by these losses and criticism, he became a much better poet. When he did publish again, in 1842, he showed a remarkable advance over his earlier work, and the critical reception that followed assured him a place in English literature. Even Wordsworth acknowledged, "He is decidedly the first of our living poets." Tennyson followed this triumph with the publication of his long elegy on Hallam, *In Memoriam* (1850), and that same year he was named poet laureate to succeed Wordsworth.

The remaining years of Tennyson's long life were productive. Financially secure, he was able to marry Emily Sellwood, whom he had loved for fourteen years. They purchased a country estate, which freed him somewhat from the public demands that accompanied his growing popularity. After publishing the experimental monologue *Maud* in 1855, he devoted nearly twenty-five years to the twelve books of the epic *Idylls of the King* (1859-1885). During the last third of his life, he published six other volumes of poetry, which contained some good poems and a great number of popular poems. Works such as *Enoch Arden* (1864), full of domestic sentimentality, added to his popularity but detracted from his lasting reputation. It was also during this period that he began writing his verse dramas. Reassured by his almost universal fame and his belief that someone needed to restore the lagging stature of English drama, he disregarded his own lack of knowledge of the theater and wrote seven plays in the hope that someone else would make them acceptable for public performance.

Tennyson remained for fifty years the most popular poet of his age. After he accepted the peerage in 1883, he lived out the last years of his life as beloved poet and respected sage, mostly at his country estate of Aldworth. When he died in October, 1892, he was buried in Westminster Abbey, and a whole nation mourned the loss.

Analysis

The fact that Alfred, Lord Tennyson began writing plays at the age of sixty-five is unusual and perhaps accounts in part for the relative failure of his poetic dramas. His friend Robert Browning had begun his career writing plays, but Browning realized that his gifts were not suited to playwriting, and he shifted with great success to the dramatic monologue and narrative poetry. Tennyson must have felt that he would succeed where Browning and others had failed. English drama during the nineteenth century had reached a low point with facile plots, melodramatic endings, stock characters, bombastic language, and pseudo-Elizabethan techniques. Every major poet of the century recognized the problem and wrote dramas, hoping to resurrect the proud past of the English stage. They, like Tennyson, failed. Tennyson might have had a better chance of success since, writing after others had failed, he could profit from their mistakes.

Drama was not for him a completely new turn. One of his earliest works was a blank-verse drama, *The Devil and the Lady*, which he wrote when he was fourteen or fifteen and which remained unfinished and unpublished until long after his death. His poetry had included dramatic elements, such as his dramatic monologues and the monodrama *Maud*. Moreover, he had an interest in the stage throughout his life—an interest that led to friendships with a number of actors and directors. He believed that he possessed the dramatic instinct and that he was a competent judge of acting and play production. Because of this background, limited though it was, he believed that he could overcome his lack of any real knowledge of stagecraft or the practical necessities of the theater. He expected his plays to be edited for stage production by those who had the special training. Such editing did occur, but his primary difficulty was his inability to portray the subjective action of the characters within the constraints of the dramatic form.

When Tennyson as a boy began writing blank-verse plays, his model was William Shakespeare. It is not surprising that when he later turned to drama, he would again look to Shakespeare, particularly Shakespeare's historical plays. Tennyson, however, was careful to select subjects that had not been used by Shakespeare. He envisioned a trilogy of plays—*Harold, Becket*, and *Queen Mary*—that would portray the making of England. *Harold* centers on the great conflict among Danes, Saxons, and Normans for predominance, the awakening of the English people and the Church from their long sleep, and the forecast of greatness for England's composite race. *Becket* concentrates on the struggle between the Crown and the Church for supremacy, a struggle which continued for hundreds of years. *Queen Mary* portrays the final defeat of Roman Catholicism in England and the beginning of a new age in which freedom of the individual replaced the priestly domination of the past.

Queen Mary, the last in the trilogy, was the first play that Tennyson completed. He became interested in the subject because of the resurgence of Roman Catholicism brought on by the Tractarian movement. Several of his friends had converted, and the pronouncements of the Vatican were alarming to staunch Protestants. Tennyson, as spokesman and sage, believed that he should write a poetic play on the life of Queen Mary and show the fiercest crisis of his country's religious struggle. He was firmly on the side of the Protestants, but he was sympathetic to the tragic life of Mary, who was cast off by her father and treated with shameless contempt before her accession to the throne. Hallam, Lord Tennyson wrote that his father believed that "there was nothing more mournful than the final tragedy of this woman, who, with her deep longing for love, found herself hated by her people, abandoned by her husband, and harassed in the hour of her death by the restlessness of despair."

Although Tennyson set out to relate the tragic story of this misunderstood queen, his desire to be faithful to the historical record caused him to include far more than a play could hold. A summary of the five acts suggests a harmonious pattern. Act 1 opens with Mary's coronation and her decision to reinstate Catholicism, which she will cement through her marriage to Philip. Act 2 introduces the major military challenge to her authority with the unsuccessful rebellion by Thomas Wyatt. Act 3 deals with the marriage of Philip and Mary and the absolution of the members of the English Parliament by Cardinal Pole, the pope's legate. Act 4 is used to present Thomas Cranmer's death, which is the major spiritual challenge to Mary's authority. Act 5 depicts the nation beginning to fall apart because of the military threats from abroad and the religious dissension within—a dissension which Mary, trapped in her marriage to the loveless Philip, is unable to combat. At her death, Elizabeth succeeds her to the throne, and a Protestant England is assured.

What distracts from this harmonious pattern is the loose structure, with capricious changes of scene to include a number of background events and characters that intrude on the main story. The political ploys and stratagems of France and Spain, the rise and fall of minor characters such as Edward Courtenay and Stephen Gardiner, even the major episodes of Wyatt's rebellion and Cranmer's death—all distract from the central character of the play. Tennyson's published version of *Queen Mary* has twenty-three scenes and forty-five speaking characters. Although many of the scenes and characters were omitted in Henry Irving's production of the play, the separate treatment of so many parts causes the reader or the spectator to become confused and lose sight of the central figure in the drama.

Tennyson set out to be fair to the queen, but he almost lost sight of her in the panorama of her struggles. One question that is left unanswered by the play is what caused her to change from the merciful, forgiving queen who could pitifully speak of "good Lady Jane as a poor innocent child who had but obeyed her father" to the vengeful queen who at her wedding wore red shoes, "as if her feet were washed in blood." Not only does she have Lady Jane beheaded, but also she renounces the nobles' plea for Cranmer's exile by saying, "It is God's will, the Holy Father's will,/ And Philip's will, and mine, that he should burn." Her only motive throughout the play is to win the love of Philip, but such a motive is weak because Philip is almost a caricature of the ruthless, self-serving, loveless husband. Moreover, Mary knew this before she ever met Philip; she was told that he is a man "Stone-hard, ice-cold—no dash of daring in him," who lives a "very wanton life." Since Tennyson provides no insight into another, more favorable, side of Philip's character, Mary's devotion to him, which causes her to sacrifice the lives of so many "heretics" and almost causes her to lose her country, seems more pitiable than tragic.

Queen Mary, as Tennyson's first play, is seriously flawed, but it also has some strengths. The multiple scenes and subjects suggest the confused temper of the age. There is also some good characterization, such as that of Thomas Cranmer, who is torn between his fear and his faith, his desire to live and his call to martyrdom, his pride and his humility. The play was not an unmitigated failure; indeed, after major editing, it enjoyed a fairly successful run.

Tennyson, more fully aware of his inexperience in the theater after seeing *Queen Mary* on the stage, read several contemporary plays before he began to write his second play, *Harold*, which would be the first in the completed trilogy. The structural improvement is apparent: He halved the number of scenes to eleven and the number of characters to twenty-three. Nevertheless, this was the only one of Tennyson's plays not to be produced during his lifetime; there was no public performance until 1928.

The action of the play follows roughly the order of events represented on the Bayeux tapestry, which Tennyson had seen in Brittany some years earlier. The tapestry, two hundred twelve feet long and one and a half feet wide, shows Harold's hunting expedition in Flanders, his capture and enforced stay with William of Normandy, his oath to assist William in becoming King of England, the return to England, the death of Edward, the coronation of Harold, and William's invasion and victory at Hastings. Tennyson adds to his play Harold's love for Edith and his political marriage to Aldwyth.

The story has the ingredients to make a fine tragedy. Harold is a strong character who is destined to be king because he had driven out the Normans and brought peace. He is presented in contrast to the other two kings—Edward the Confessor, pious and incompetent, and William of Normandy, strong but deceitful. Harold has both strength and honor, as he shows when he initially refuses to take an oath that he knows he cannot honor: "Better die than lie." He cannot maintain this resolve, however, and he is doomed by fate to lose both the woman he loves and the country he tries to defend. On his deathbed, Edward commands Edith to be a virgin saint, to spend her life in prayer against the curse which Harold brought upon himself and on England when he broke his oath.

Despite these potentially dramatic conflicts, the play is a failure, largely because all the major characters are weakly conceived and developed. Edward's piety and saintliness are overemphasized, as are William's cruelty and deceitfulness. There is nothing in the play to suggest the qualities of one who would unify the country and, in Tennyson's own words, "mold the greatness of our composite race." Edith is a stereotype of the lovely, faithful woman who will sacrifice her own happiness for Harold's safety. Aldwyth, conversely, is the scheming, ambitious female who will destroy her country if it will make her its queen. Even Harold is a confusing portrait. He is presented as a strong leader and man of honor, but his actions too often belie his words. He naïvely believes that he can go to Normandy for a hunting holiday because the Normans certainly have forgotten and forgiven him and his father, who drove them out of England. He pledges his undying love to Edith but then quickly makes a political marriage with Aldwyth. His final defeat is expected and accepted because the inconsistencies in his character have confused the reader and muted the desired sympathy.

Tennyson did not have much better success with the final drama of his historical trilogy, *Becket*. Failing in his initial effort to have the play accepted for production, he published it with the apologetic statement that it "was not intended in its present form to meet the exigencies of our modern theatre." In the last year of his life, it was accepted, and four months after his death it began a successful run of 112 nights.

Tennyson's failure in this play, as in the two earlier plays, was twofold: his inability to control the historical material and his inability to develop character. He had chosen a fitting subject in the confrontation of temporal power with spiritual power, but he was not able to reveal the subjective crises that motivated Henry and Becket. The play opens with a chess game that obviously foreshadows the play's theme. After Becket moves, he says, "Why—there then, for you see my bishop/ Hath brought your king to a standstill. You are beaten." The struggle between Archbishop Becket and King Henry should now begin, but it fails to materialize because of the introduction of a subplot. Rather than allowing the two chess players to discuss the conflict of Church and State that will surely come, Henry urges Becket to help him protect his paramour, Rosamund de Clifford, from his jealous Queen Eleanor. The two plots war against each other throughout the play. Tennyson must have felt that he could not sustain the interest of the audience solely by the spiritual conflict within Becket, and thus he brought in the love triangle with Becket as an unwilling accomplice. The unsatisfactory union of history and romantic legend confuses and distorts the conflict between the two men. Because of the Rosamund story, Becket appears only briefly in the third and fourth acts. The principal distortion is that Rosamund becomes the cause of Becket's death. In Tennyson's version of the story, it is after Eleanor tells Harold a lie, saying "Your cleric has your lady," that Henry utters the famous words, "Will no man free me from this pestilent priest?" The great conflict between Church and State is incidental to the King's love for his paramour.

The subplot also prevents Tennyson from exploring Becket's inner conflict. Becket often mentions his doubts, but whenever he begins to engage in serious introspection, the demands of the plot intrude and the reader cannot experience his spiritual crisis. After Becket is told that he will become archbishop, he begins to doubt his calling, asking, "Am I the man?" Twenty-five lines later, however, he concludes, "I do believe thee, then. I am the man." When he is asked to sign the "customs," which will restrict the power of the Church, he does so impulsively, without introspection, and then, just as quickly, he recants and refuses to seal them. Too often in the play the act of deciding is omitted, and we are left with only the decision itself. Even before his martyrdom, his friends try to persuade him to save himself, but Becket ignores them. Again, the decision is already made.

Tennyson's real success in the play lies in his portrayal of Becket as a man who becomes consumed by his spiritual pride. Once he assumes the robes of the Church, he begins to confuse his will with the will of God. He even uses Christ's words to refer to himself: "Why, John, my kingdom is not of this world," but John answers him: "We are self-uncertain creatures, and we may,/ Yea, even when we know not, mix our spites/ And private hates with our defense of Heaven." It is clear that Tennyson admires Becket, but he sees the fundamental flaw of those who will themselves to martyrdom.

Tennyson was not discouraged by his failure readily to find a producer for his last two plays. He wrote four more plays, but he did not again try to write a history play. His next play, *The Falcon*, was a sentimental comedy in one act based on a tale from Giovanni Boccaccio's *Decameron* (c. 1348-1353). Count Federigo, who has squandered all of his wealth in the vain pursuit of the widowed Lady Giovanni, is forced to live in a cottage with only his falcon to delight him. When Lady Giovanni unexpectedly comes to visit him, he realizes that he has no food to offer her, but he does not hesitate to order the killing of the falcon to provide a suitable meal for her. He then discovers the reason for her visit. Her desperately ill son had begged for the falcon to help him recover. It is a rather touching and mournful story, but the lady is won over by the gentleman's sacrifice, and the play ends as they embrace. Though there is not much substance to the work, it enjoyed a limited success on the stage.

The Cup is a two-act play based on a story in Plutarch, a tale of revenge in which the beautiful Galatian priestess Camma avenges the death of her husband, the victim of the lecherous and devious Synorix. When Synorix pursues her into the temple, she feigns a willingness to yield, but she says they must drink together from one cup. After she has poisoned the cup, she drinks half and gives the other half to her guilty lover, rejoicing that she has been permitted to avenge and then rejoin her dead husband.

The Cup had a long run, but its success was largely the result of spectacular staging. In this lavish production, more than two thousand pounds was spent on costumes and sets, and one hundred beautiful actresses were selected as vestal virgins, Camma's attendants in the temple. A review in *The*

Times of London praised the magnificence of the production and the excellence of the acting, but it found "something shadowy and unreal" in the play.

Tennyson returned to a full-length play with *The Foresters*, an old man's nostalgic dream of Robin Hood and Sherwood Forest. Robin Hood, the ideal outlaw, appears as a dubious shadow of King Arthur, the ideal king; his merry men's efforts to revolt against tyranny are marred by sentimentality and boyish antics. Interestingly, although the play was a failure in England, it was very successful in the United States.

The Promise of May is noteworthy for several reasons: It was Tennyson's only play on a contemporary subject, it is predominantly prose, and it was his last play. It was also a dismal failure on the stage. Tennyson intended to present "a surface man of many theories," but his central character, Philip Edgar, is really an insincere hedonist with no ideology at all. The contrived plot involves an intellectual from the city corrupting and then abandoning a simple country girl, only to be forgiven by her at the end. Tennyson himself realized that it was a failure, and he did not try again to write plays.

As a playwright, Tennyson achieved only a modest popular success, and even that can be attributed to his fame as a poet rather than to the intrinsic merit of his plays. He made no lasting contribution to English drama. Nevertheless, his works for the stage should not be dismissed as mere diversions of an aging poet. The dominant form of Tennyson's later poetry is the monologue, often in a dramatic setting; here one can see the same desire for greater objectivity that inspired his plays.

Other major works

POETRY: *Poems, Chiefly Lyrical*, 1830; *Poems*, 1832 (imprinted 1833); *Poems*, 1842; *The Princess*, 1847; *In Memoriam*, 1850; *Maud and Other Poems*, 1855; *Idylls of the King*, 1859-1885; *Enoch Arden and Other Poems*, 1864; *The Holy Grail and Other Poems*, 1869 (imprinted 1870); *The Window: Or, The Songs of the Wrens*, 1870 (set to music by Sir Arthur Sullivan); *Gareth and Lynette*, 1872; *The Lover's Tale*, 1879; *Ballads and Other Poems*, 1880; *Tiresias and Other Poems*, 1885; *Locksley Hall Sixty Years After, Etc.*, 1886; *Demeter and Other Poems*, 1889; *The Death of Œnone and Other Poems*, 1892.

NONFICTION: *The Letters of Alfred Lord Tennyson*, 1981-1990 (3 volumes; Cecil Y. Lang and Edgar F. Shannon, editors).

MISCELLANEOUS: *The Works of Tennyson*, 1907-1908 (9 volumes; Hallam, Lord Tennyson, editor); *The Tennyson Archive*, 1987-1992 (28 volumes; Christopher Ricks and Aidan Day, editors).

Bibliography

Buckley, Jerome Hamilton. *Tennyson: The Growth of a Poet.* Cambridge,

Mass.: Harvard University Press, 1961. A masterfully succinct study of Tennyson's career. Examines the poems as biographical statements and works of art. Discusses extensively the major works and focuses on the seven plays in a chapter that argues that they show how vigorous Tennyson's imagination continued to be in his old age. Contains notes and an index.

Culler, A. Dwight. *The Poetry of Tennyson*. New Haven, Conn.: Yale University Press, 1977. Using previously unavailable letters and papers, Culler traces Tennyson's interest in the power of language to create trancelike experiences. Mediating between human and divine visions, Tennyson's poetry moves dialectically between apocalyptic and elegiac modes of expression. Devotes chapters to analyses of *The Princess*, *In Memoriam*, and *Idylls of the King*. Notes, index.

Kozicki, Henry. *Tennyson and Clio: History in the Major Poems*. Baltimore: The Johns Hopkins University Press, 1979. Explains Tennyson's poetic success as the product of his philosophy of history in which divinity governs the process of human experience. This philosophy developed through six stages in Tennyson's career, each reflected in the thematic structures of major poems. A thoughtful and lucid analysis despite the mechanical outline. Includes footnotes, a bibliography, and an index.

McGhee, Richard D. "Tennyson." In *Marriage, Duty, and Desire in Victorian Poetry and Drama*. Lawrence: Regents Press of Kansas, 1980. Analyzes Tennyson's poems and dramas as expressions of Victorian pressure to reconcile conflicting values of social duty and private desire through symbolic images and ritual of marriage. The final works are presented as evidence that Tennyson could not maintain faith in poetry as a means of achieving this reconciliation. Notes, index.

Pattison, Robert. *Tennyson and Tradition*. Cambridge, Mass.: Harvard University Press, 1979. Proposing that Tennyson developed a paradigm of process using traditional genres, Pattison focuses on the idyll, from its classical sources to Tennyson's early experiments in the idyllic tradition and finally to his visionary epic in *Idylls of the King*. A learned and clear account with an economy of expression. Includes ample notes and an index.

Shaw, W. David. *Tennyson's Style*. Ithaca, N.Y.: Cornell University Press, 1976. Examines Tennyson's stylistic experiments in ballads, sonnets, and blank-verse monologues. Devotes some chapters to studies of the Victorian context, elegiac modes, narrative and dramatic indirection; others focus on single works, such as *In Memoriam*, *Maud*, and *Idylls of the King*. Contains footnotes, a substantial bibliographical essay, and an index.

Edwin W. Williams
(Updated by *Richard D. McGhee*)

MEGAN TERRY

Born: Seattle, Washington; July 22, 1932

Principal drama

Ex-Miss Copper Queen on a Set of Pills, pr. 1963, pb. 1966; *Calm Down Mother*, pr. 1965, pb. 1966; *Keep Tightly Closed in a Cool Dry Place*, pr. 1965, pb. 1966; *Comings and Goings*, pr. 1966, pb. 1967; *The Gloaming, Oh My Darling*, pr. 1966, pb. 1967; *Viet Rock: A Folk War Movie*, pr., pb. 1966 (music by Marianne de Pury); *The Magic Realists*, pr. 1966, pb. 1968; *The People vs. Ranchman*, pr. 1967, pb. 1968; *Megan Terry's Home: Or, Future Soap*, televised 1968, staged 1974, pb. 1972; *Massachusetts Trust*, pr. 1968, pb. 1972; *The Tommy Allen Show*, pr. 1969, pb. 1971; *Approaching Simone*, pr. 1970, pb. 1973; *Three One-Act Plays*, pb. 1970; *Couplings and Groupings*, pb. 1973; *Nightwalk*, pr. 1973, pb. 1975 (with Sam Shepard and Jean-Claude van Itallie); *Babes in the Bighouse*, pr., pb. 1974; *Hothouse*, pr., pb. 1974; *The Pioneer, and Pro-Game*, pr. 1974, pb. 1975; *100,001 Horror Stories of the Plains*, pr. 1976, pb. 1978 (with Judith Katz, James Larson, and others); *Brazil Fado*, pr., pb. 1977; *Willa-Willa-Bill's Dope Garden*, pb. 1977; *American King's English for Queens*, pr., pb. 1978; *Attempted Rescue on Avenue B: A Beat Fifties Comic Opera*, pr., pb. 1979; *Goona Goona*, pr. 1979, pb. 1981; *Advances*, pb. 1980; *Mollie Bailey's Traveling Family Circus: Featuring Scenes from the Life of Mother Jones*, pr. 1981, pb. 1983; *Family Talk*, pr., pb. 1986; *Sea of Forms*, pr. 1986, pb. 1987 (with JoAnn Schmidman); *Walking Through Walls*, pr., pb. 1987; *Dinner's in the Blender*, pr., pb. 1987; *Retro*, pr. 1988; *Amtrak*, pr. 1988; *Headlights*, pr., pb. 1990; *Do You See What I'm Saying?*, pb. 1991.

Other literary forms

Megan Terry authored lyrics for *Thoughts* (1973), a musical by Lamar Alford, and she has contributed prose pieces to *The New York Times* and *Valhalla: A Modern Drama Issue*. She has also written teleplays and radio plays.

Achievements

One of the most prolific playwrights of the "New Theater" in the United States, Terry is linked with the Open Theatre, which she helped form with Joseph Chaikin and Michael Smith in 1963. The work which brought international attention to Terry is *Viet Rock*, the first well-publicized play about Vietnam to be produced in the United States. Terry and the Open Theatre created an improvisational workshop atmosphere, in which actors, directors, and playwrights could form a living theater experience, disorienting audience expectations through "transformations" in which actors, settings, times, or moods may alter without transition or apparent logic. While some critics find this experience alienating or confusing, others hail the technique as a significant contribution to the development of a truly living theater experience. Her plays' earthy language, sexual and political content, musical segments, humor, and vaudeville touches all blend to create lively, dynamic experiences for audiences. Her innovative work has received numerous awards, including the Stanley Drama Award (1965), WGBH Award (1968), Latin American Festival Award (1969), Obie Award (1970), Earplay Award (1972), Dramatists Guild Award (1983), and grants from the National Endowment for the Arts, Creative Artists Public Service Grant, Rockefeller Foundation, and the Guggenheim Foundation. In 1971, she became resident playwright at the Omaha Magic Theater.

Biography

Megan Terry was born in Seattle, Washington, on July 22, 1932, and was named Marguerite Duffy. Throughout grade school, Terry was fascinated with the theater, and she was exposed at an early age to the influence of the Seattle Repertory Playhouse. In 1951, the theater closed under pressure from a state committee investigating so-called un-American activities, an event which both radicalized the young Terry and confirmed her in her view of the theater as a powerful political tool. Terry received a B.Ed. from the University of Washington, and she taught at the Cornish School of Allied Arts. She traveled to New York, where she became involved with the Playwrights' Unit Workshop, which included Edward Albee, Richard Barr, and Clinton Wilder, in the 1963 production of *Ex-Miss Copper Queen on a Set of Pills*, a work based on her fascination with a pill-popping prostitute who had once been a beauty queen. Terry's career includes several attempts at realistic drama, including *Hothouse* and an early version of *Attempted Rescue on Avenue B*, but she found that she wanted to create new techniques for conveying her messages about the destructiveness of the United States' economic and political power structures. In working with the Open Theatre on *Calm Down Mother* and *Keep Tightly Closed in a Cool Dry Place*, Terry created two of her most successful one-act transformation plays. Using three female actors, *Calm Down Mother* explored what is possible for women and what role limitations women encounter in society. In a similar fashion, *Keep Tightly Closed in a Cool Dry Place* used three male actors, whose characters begin in a prison setting and transform from gangsters to drag queens to soldiers, testing various kinds of enclosures, both imagined and real. Her fascination with sexuality appeared in another transformation play entitled *Comings and Goings*, which stretched actors' technique and delighted its original audiences, many of whom were actors themselves. The first collaboration play to be created in a workshop situation was also Terry's most renowned, *Viet Rock*. Gerome Ragni was among the actors in the workshop, and he later collaborated with James Rado to produce *Hair* in 1967. *Viet Rock* created a number of firsts, including the combination of rock music with the traditional musical-theater genre, treatment of the controversial Vietnam war theme, and the intrusion of actors touching and interacting with audience members.

After receiving an American Broadcasting Company "Writing for the Camera" Fellowship from Yale, Terry wrote *The People vs. Ranchman*, a work dealing with the creation of stars out of people such as Charles Manson and Angela Davis. After receiving negative reviews for this work, Terry went on to produce *Megan Terry's Home*, a futuristic play commissioned by Channel Thirteen's "New York Television Theater," the first commissioned play ever presented on National Educational Television (NET) Playhouse. With an increasing interest in feminist issues, Terry wrote *Approaching Simone* (winner of the Obie Award for Best New Play of 1969-1970) in 1970, studying the life of Simone Weil, a Jewish-French philosopher who starved herself to death in protest over the World War II soldiers who were starving at the front. Turning again to historical sources, Terry created *100,001 Horror Stories of the Plains* in 1976 from the accounts of family stories, poems, and songs collected while Terry was playwright-in-residence for the Magic Theater in Omaha, Nebraska. Another controversial work combining her concern over violence and women's rights was *Goona Goona*, a burlesque treatment of child abuse and wife abuse in the imaginary Goon family. Terry further explores feminist themes in *Mollie Bailey's Traveling Family Circus*, first produced in 1981 at the Mark Taper Laboratory Theater of Los Angeles, a play dealing with real and imagined events in the lives of Mollie Bailey and Mother Jones.

After Terry became playwright-in-resident at the Omaha Magic Theater, she became increasingly well known as a feminist playwright. Her work continued to deal with such domestic issues as family violence, illiteracy, and alcoholism, but she also expanded it to include musical collaborations, in such works as *Sea of Forms*, *Walking Through Walls*, and *Headlights*, which was produced in 1990.

Analysis

Megan Terry's works, although varied in structure, length, technique, and subject matter, are linked by a dynamic emphasis on emotion over reason; a lively use of earthy language, humor, music, metaphors, and symbols; a fearless treatment of timely controversial subjects; and a dedication to collaboration and spontaneity in acting and production. Because of her quickness to address controversial issues, some of her most noted works may not be her best plays, but rather those works which elicited the strongest public reaction at the time of first production. *The Magic Realists* drew sharp criticism and publicity for its failure to touch ground with some realistic setting or situation, but it merits analysis in that it marks the beginning of Terry's shift to her own distinctive theatrical style, rooted in the traditions of vaudeville and early film comedy. *Viet Rock*, while characterized by some critics as naïve and simplistic, clearly captures the spirit of early protest reactions to the war in Vietnam, and as such it is Terry's best-known play. Two of her most representative works, *Keep Tightly Closed in a Cool Dry Place* and *Megan Terry's Home*, explore the theme of enclosure and entrapment, at both personal and cultural levels. *Mollie Bailey's Traveling Family Circus* represents yet another phase in the development of Terry's playwriting, combining her love of music and strong female characters with a deep commitment to exploring ethical and political issues.

The Magic Realists premiered in 1966 at La Mama Experimental Theatre Club in New York, and drew sharp criticism from *Village Voice* reviewer Michael Smith for its lack of connection to any outside reality. Terry's first break from realistic theater styles, *The Magic Realists* presents a combination of obscure dialogue and stereotyped characterizations. The action of the play centers on T. P. Chester's attempts to find a clone of himself who can carry on his nonstop wheelings and dealings. He chooses Don, a teenage escaped convict, in whom he recognizes the same total lack of scruples and the same "hunger" that have brought him to his esteemed position in the world of high finance. Occasionally, a "person" enters the stage, representing one of his numerous children, whom Chester views solely as tax exemptions. When a beautiful black woman named Dana arrives on the scene, she manages to seduce Don from Chester's influence. Dana, a Japanese American, and an American Indian, who all turn out to be secret agents, attempt to arrest Chester, but one of Chester's offspring persons appears to rescue him with a submachine gun. At last united, the father and child inadvertently gun down the secret agents as the weapon is held between them in a wild, whirling embrace.

The action demonstrates in vaudeville style how the capitalist economic power structure creates machinelike human beings whose sense of family, justice, and human emotion are entirely subordinated to the drive for money. While the plot and characterizations are admittedly thin, this early work reveals several of Terry's strong points. She captures natural speech rhythms and the comedy inherent in juxtaposition of radically differing character types. The combined elements of violence and sexuality create lively slapstick comedy and a few thought-provoking insults to the status quo.

In a similar vein, *Viet Rock* garnered much attention but little praise for its earnest, naïve attack on the brutality and absurdity of the Vietnam War. The play uses all the familiar clichés about honor, duty, and love of country to demonstrate that the soldiers who deliver these lines are basically automatons. Women in the play share responsibility for creating males who are infantile, obedient, and easily manipulated by brainless sentimentality. *Viet Rock* depicts events as varied as senate hearings and soldiers writing home to mothers and sweethearts in a collection of vignettes linked by few or no transitions. Although the music and satire received negative reviews for failure to achieve depth or complexity, Terry also drew admiration for her canny sense of theater and her ability to create a "happening" that captured the current mood of public outrage. Critics argued, however, that the play did very little to deepen anyone's understanding of issues or to undermine self-satisfaction, two principal aims of satire. The play may not be notable for its depth, but its innovative use of rock lyrics and interaction between actors and audience broke ground for the creation of *Hair*, one of the best-known rock musicals to come out of the Vietnam War era.

Receiving much more critical acclaim but less publicity, *Keep Tightly Closed in a Cool Dry Place* premiered at the Sheridan Square Playhouse in 1965 under the aegis of the Open Theatre. Dedicated to Joseph Chaikin, one of the founders of the group, the play typifies the concept of "transformation," a theater style in which actors, setting, and mood metamorphose, often without transition. The play has only three characters: Jaspers, an intellectual lawyer; Michaels, a burly type; and Gregory, a bewildered, handsome young man destined to become victim of the other two characters. In jail, Jaspers and Michaels consider how to undermine Gregory's confession, which has revealed that Jaspers hired Michaels to get Gregory to kill Jaspers' wife. The first transformation turns Jaspers into General George Armstrong Custer, with Michaels as one of his soldiers, whom he instructs to kill Gregory, now a "redskin." Just as abruptly, the characters become themselves again, and Gregory dreams of rape, achieving orgasm as Jaspers and Michaels berate him for his lack of control, his ineptitude, and his unprofessionalism.

If the audience members believe that they understand the character types established in the opening, the remainder of the play shatters these assumptions. The three men join to become a machine, apparently a gun, and each actor describes a part of the machine's features. In the next transformation, Jaspers becomes a dying English soldier under Captain John Smith, alias Gregory. Later, Jaspers becomes mother to Michaels, then victim of a murderer, then an evangelist, and finally father to Michaels and Gregory. The play closes with a dancing chant in which the three form a human wheel, with Jaspers offering the closing line, "This side should face you!" Although the unexpected transformations are jarring and disorienting, the play offers the unifying notion that all human beings go through a series of roles, presenting different facets of human behavior, as dictated by society and circumstance. The prison setting suggests that people are locked into these roles, just as unwillingly and randomly as prisoners are incarcerated.

Another play examining confinement, this time in a futuristic setting, is

Megan Terry's Home, originally created for Channel Thirteen in New York and later commissioned for NET and nationally broadcast in January of 1968. The principal characters, Mother Ruth, Cynthia, and Roy, constitute part of a unit of nine people, forced by overpopulation to live and die together in a room smaller than a jail cell. Central Control, the governing body, ministers to their physical, spiritual, and psychological needs, through the total organization of their sleeping and waking time. They pop pills for nourishment and psychological well-being, watch multiple television screens for news of past and present, and dream, chant, and perform isometrics for social and physical interaction.

The central conflict of the play rests in Cynthia and Roy's desire to marry and have their own real baby for the group, a privilege rarely granted to units, regardless of how obedient, efficient, or patient they are. When the air-venting system temporarily breaks down, allowing another human to enter their cell, Ruth panics, overrides her socialization, and kills the intruder. The group of nine quickly disposes of the body and the marriage ceremony of Roy and Cynthia continues, with all nine hoping that they may one day be allowed by the state to have a baby of their own.

Terry's play cleverly creates an alternative world, complete with values, customs, and mannerisms convincingly appropriate to a highly technological civilization coping with overpopulation and limited resources. It confronts the idea that human instincts for survival may be exactly the impulses that will lead to self-destruction. The overcrowded society places a premium on cooperation, self-sacrifice, obedience, and nonviolence, but it is unable to overcome the women's urges to become mothers to their own children. One of her most sophisticated and intellectually complex works, *Megan Terry's Home* calls on audiences to question human nature, media culture, religious values, and Western notions of progress. The action of the play suggests the possibility that brutality in the name of survival may be unavoidable, and it does so in a way that creates dramatic suspense and empathy for believable characters. Terry effectively exploits the medium of television, but stage directions make the work easily adaptable for live presentation as well.

Terry's dedication to feminism appears in numerous plays, nowhere more openly than in *Mollie Bailey's Traveling Family Circus*. This piece, dedicated to Mollie Bailey and Mother Jones, alternates between scenes of Mollie and Gus Bailey and children and the life of Mother Jones. As with some of her earlier work, this play is at times heavy-handed in its delineation of good and evil, with heartless capitalists and their flunkies as adversaries to Mother Jones, who bravely seeks justice and protection for victimized children. Women are portrayed as the preservers of civilization, of all that is good and brave and true, and males appear in the play as little more than sperm banks. Music and humor carry the play, however, creating an entertaining spectacle with the timely obsessions of contemporaneous culture at its heart.

Terry continued with her interest in music, humor, and family issues in such works as *Family Talk*, a play that dramatizes the breakdown in communication within the family. Showing how television acts as a substitute for real communication, this play demonstrates what happens when Mother Kraaz unplugs the television. The seven family members literally and figuratively stumble and grope as they attempt to communicate with one another without the escape hatch of the huge, centrally located television set. Dian Ostdiek's stage design includes a monopoly board setup with such location markings as "Danger—Mom at Work" or "Stargazing Strip," where family members retreat when the stress of communication becomes too great. The music and lyrics, by Joe Budenholzer and John J. Sheehan, range from Andrews Sisters style, to country-western or folk rock, to sound effects in the tradition of John Cage. While the vision is at times grim, the humor and musical play of *Family Talk* suggest healing and reconciliation.

In a similar vein, *Headlights* presents an alarming portrait of American society, pointing out that one of every eight Americans cannot read and then focusing on solutions to illiteracy. The play uses music, choral speech, multiple actors for single characters, and standard dialogue to relay the devastating effects of illiteracy. Multimedia presentations of slides and collages combine with props—fluorescent tubes, rings, rubber balls, and lampshade hats that illuminate when a character is "enlightened"—to illustrate how the system fails to educate. At the same time, the play's portrayal of individual characters learning to read serves as an inspiration to nonreaders and teaching volunteers alike. As with *Family Talk*, the subject matter for *Headlights* came from interaction with audiences encountered by the Omaha Magic Theater's touring group.

Megan Terry's work demonstrates adaptability, variety, and a consistent dedication to political and ethical ideals, qualities that provoke criticism as well as praise. Analysis of the body of her work reveals a prolific and imaginative mind at work, constantly striving and reworking themes as old as drama: family and gender roles, violence and pacifism, individual and social welfare, subordination and freedom. Her plays, numbering more than seventy-five, represent a substantial contribution to American drama, both in their innovative forms and in their political and philosophical substance.

Other major works

TELEPLAYS: *The Dirt Boat*, 1955; *One More Little Drinkie*, 1969.

RADIO PLAYS: *Sanibel and Captiva*, 1968; *American Wedding Ritual Monitored/Transmitted by the Planet Jupiter*, 1972.

Bibliography

Babnich, Judith. "Family Talk." Review of *Family Talk. Theatre Review* 39 (May, 1987): 240-241. While this article is only a brief review of one play, it reveals important details about how many of Terry's works are produced through collaboration with psychologists, social workers, artists, and community activists. Babnich points out how Terry uses music, multimedia effects, and comedy to achieve serious social criticism and a call for action and social healing.

Bermel, Albert. "Cutting Up in Time and Space." *The New Leader* 50 (September 11, 1967): 23-24. Bermel explores Terry's use of time and space in analyses of *Viet Rock*, *Comings and Goings*, *The People vs. Ranchman*, and *Keep Tightly Closed in a Cool Dry Place*. He views the energy of her work with the Open Theater as probably inimitable, and he compares her work with that of Eugène Ionesco and Samuel Beckett, thus placing it within a past and future theater tradition.

Kerr, Walter. "Togetherness: I." In *God on the Gymnasium Floor and Other Theatrical Adventures*. New York: Simon & Schuster, 1971. In this section, Kerr describes the shortcomings of avant-garde theater, using his viewing of Terry's and Café La Mama's collaborative improvisation, *Massachusetts Trust*, as a focus. He argues that experimental theater makes it impossible to distinguish between good and bad drama or acting. The more it tries to become public, the more private and idiosyncratic it becomes.

Keyssar, Helene. "Megan Terry: Mother of American Feminist Theatre." In *Feminist Theatre*. New York: Grove Press, 1985. This article details the contributions of Terry to the development of a collaborative feminist theater in the United States. In addition to providing thorough bibliographic information and notes, this essay offers a valuable overview and analysis of Terry's vital impact on American drama, from her early work as a founding member of the Women's Theatre Council in 1971 to her community-based collaborative playwriting techniques, developed with the Omaha Magic Theater.

Klein, Kathleen Gregory. "Language and Meaning in Megan Terry's 'Musicals.'" *Modern Drama* 27 (December, 1984): 574-583. Focusing on the plays *American King's English for Queens*, *Babes in the Bighouse*, *Brazil Fado*, and *The Tommy Allen Show*, Klein details how Terry's work elucidates the relationship of language to gender. This insightful article draws connections between Terry's work and the traditions of B-movie musicals, television, and popular culture, with an emphasis on the language of Terry's musicals.

Natalle, Elizabeth. *Feminist Theatre: A Study in Persuasion*. Metuchen, N.J.: Scarecrow Press, 1985. This survey of feminist theater features a ten-page bibliography, an index, and nine pages of analysis of Terry's role in the development of feminist theater. The discussion focuses primarily on *American King's English for Queens* and *Babes in the Bighouse*, placing them in the context of feminist concerns. Unlike Dinah L.

Leavitt's *Feminist Theatre Groups* (1980), which scatters anecdotal references to Terry throughout the book, or Judith Olauson's *The American Woman Playwright* (1981), which looks primarily at critical responses to *Viet Rock*, Natalle's work offers scope and somewhat detailed thematic analysis.

Rebecca Bell-Metereau

STEVE TESICH

Born: Titovo Užice, Yugoslavia; September 29, 1942

Principal drama

The Carpenters, pr. 1970, pb. 1971 (one act); *Lake of the Woods*, pr. 1971, pb. 1981 (one act); *Baba Goya*, pr. 1973, pb. 1981 (also published as *Nourish the Beast*, 1974); *Gorky*, pr. 1975, pb. 1976 (musical); *Passing Game*, pr. 1977, pb. 1978; *Touching Bottom*, pr. 1978, pb. 1980 (includes the one-acts *The Road*, *A Life*, and *Baptismal*); *Division Street*, pr. 1980, pb. 1981; *The Speed of Darkness*, pr., pb. 1989; *Square One*, pr., pb. 1990.

Other literary forms

Steve Tesich is best known as a screenwriter because of the critical and popular success of his first screenplay, *Breaking Away* (1979). He had five screenplays produced in the 1980's, the most successful of which was *The World According to Garp* (1982), an adaptation of John Irving's novel. Tesich has also published the novel *Summer Crossing* (1982), a coming-of-age story set in East Chicago, Indiana. Both the screenplays and the novel draw heavily upon his own experiences and have been praised for their intriguing characters.

Achievements

Tesich has been called the United States' cheerleader because of the optimism expressed in his early absurdist comedies for the land "where anything is possible." He demonstrates a unique ability to create fully developed, if eccentric, characters, individualized dialogue, and outrageous situations. His early plays are significant as commentaries on the faith of the United States' promise in the 1970's and his later plays on the outrage of that nation's unrealized promise in the late 1980's. He has received many awards including the Vernon Rice Award and Drama Desk Award for *Baba Goya*; the Writer's Guild Award, the New York Film Critics Circle Award, the National Society of Film Critics Award, and the Academy of Motion Picture Arts and Sciences "Best Original Screenplay" Award for *Breaking Away*; and the National Board of Review "Exceptional Film" Award for *The World According to Garp.*

Biography

Steve (Stoyan) Tesich was born September 29, 1942, in Titovo Užice, Yugoslavia, where he learned the art of storytelling from his mother, Gospava (Bulaich) Tesich. His favorite boyhood theme was going to the United States to find his father, Radisa, who was missing in the war. Eventually,

Radisa contacted his family from England, where he turned up after fleeing Yugoslavia to join its government in exile. The Tesich family was finally reunited in 1957, but in the United States, because Stoyan had led a family revolution against going to England: He wanted to go to the land "where anything could happen." Therefore, at age fourteen, Stoyan became Steve, living in East Chicago, Indiana, where his machinist father found work in the steel mills. Although the unrelenting red glow of the smokestacks was not the great American West that he had learned to love in motion pictures, he optimistically believed that he had found the "frontier of possibility." Tesich quickly learned English and was assimilated into the high school culture of the late 1950's. He won a wrestling scholarship to Indiana University, where he made Phi Beta Kappa, won the Little Five Hundred bicycle race, and was graduated in 1965. Tesich has often used his Indiana years as the background for his stories.

After Columbia University awarded Tesich with a graduate scholarship, he moved to New York City to study Russian literature, with the notion that he might become an academic. As he began to understand the characters in Russian novels, however, he began to get excited about the idea of becoming a writer, and he augmented his literary studies with writing classes. He also met Rebecca Fletcher, who encouraged him in a writing career. Tesich was graduated from Columbia University with his master of arts degree in Russian in 1967 and married Fletcher on May 24, 1971. He worked briefly as a caseworker for the Brooklyn Department of Welfare while he tried his hand at novels and scripts. The American Place Theatre agreed to produce *The Carpenters* in 1970. Over the next eight years, the American Place Theatre actively supported his playwriting by producing several of his plays. The most successful of these was *Baba Goya* (later retitled *Nourish the Beast*), which won the 1973 Vernon Rice and Drama Desk awards and was produced on public television.

Tesich had also been writing screenplays during this time, with no success. Director Peter Yates suggested that he merge two of his scripts, one about four college-town locals, the other about the Little Five Hundred bicycle race. The result was the award-winning *Breaking Away*, which established Tesich as a major American writer. He immediately returned to the theater in 1980 with the political farce *Division Street*. The play was first staged in Los Angeles at the Mark Taper Forum, where it was a resounding success. It then became his first Broadway production, where it was savaged by New York critics.

Tesich did not return to the theater for almost ten years during which time five of his screenplays were filmed and his novel *Summer Crossing* was published. He was not "lured away by Hollywood" or disgruntled by all the criticism. He simply intended to stay away from the theater until he could approach playwriting from a new angle. In 1989, Tesich emerged with a daughter, Amy, and two new plays, *The Speed of Darkness* and *Square One*, which do present a new Tesich vision of his adopted homeland. Instead of his personal perspective, he has developed the ability to write from a societal perspective, to write about moral issues in the dramatic form.

Analysis

Steve Tesich's plays are divided into two groups by a ten-year, self-imposed exile from the theater. The early plays, beginning with *The Carpenters* and ending with *Division Street*, share the personal viewpoint of "immigrant optimism," an America where anything is possible, where a Yugoslavian teenager who does not speak English can win an Academy Award before his fortieth birthday. The later plays, beginning with *The Speed of Darkness*, are based on a social viewpoint that mourns for an America that has not lived up to its promise. The early plays are noted for their bizarre portraits of family life full of eccentric characters, outrageous comedy, wordplay, and individualized dialogue, as well as for their extensive, often burdensome symbolism. The later plays demonstrate the unique comic perspective and symbolism together with the vivid characterization, dialogue, and extreme situation of the early plays, while charting new dramatic territory dealing with moral issues. As he is an intensely personal writer, the plays are a commentary on Tesich's life.

Tesich has always experimented with dramatic forms, most prevalently the absurdist worldview. *The Carpenters* depicts a dysfunctional American family living in a house that is breaking down around them, just as their family relationships are breaking down. The father tries but is unable to understand his existence. *Lake of the Woods* shows another family, on vacation in America's wonderlands. When they reach their scenic destination, however, they find only a desolate wasteland. Their intentions are hobbled, their mobile home and car are vandalized, and it seems as though their hardships will kill them. Instead of giving up, however, the father rallies his family and sets out on an optimistic trek, away from the lapidation of modern urbanism toward a wilderness of happy people. Both plays have moments of brilliance, with clever dialogue and surprise comic twists, but they are often self-conscious and deteriorate into heavy-handed symbolism that becomes preachy and banal.

The absurdist comedy *Baba Goya* is Tesich's most successful early play. Often called a 1970's *You Can't Take It with You* (pr. 1936, pb. 1937, by George S. Kaufman and Moss Hart), it depicts another outlandish family, this time headed by a raunchy mother who is intent on making every screwball who darkens her door a member of her family. In the mistaken belief that he is dying, her fourth husband, Mario, takes out a newspaper advertisement to find his replacement. Baba interviews applicants as she tries to help her depressed son and disparaged daughter develop enough strength to leave her nest. Baba can forgive her daughter for divorcing her liberal husband who talked her into getting pregnant just so an abortion law could be tested. She can forgive her daughter's starring in a pornographic film, selling drugs, and becoming a thief, but never her voting for Richard M. Nixon. Detractors of *Baba Goya* condemn it as a silly and pointless contrivance of sight gags and clever one-liners. They are, however, blind to this play's subtler symbolism. Baba Goya is Tesich's America, taking in all no matter what their idiosyncrasies or problems and helping them to stand on their own two feet, becoming productive members of the family.

Tesich's next effort was a musical, *Gorky*, based on the life of the Russian writer Maxim Gorky. In what has become a recurring pattern, the play was resoundingly criticized by some but highly praised by others. Tesich had become an acknowledged voice in the theater but one that struck either a nerve or a chord. *Gorky* is one of his least successful efforts, with not enough facts to be a biography and hardly enough opinion to be a political commentary. What remains is a conversation between three actors depicting Gorky as an innocent youth, a passionate revolutionary, and a disillusioned victim of a Stalin purge. Tesich returned to his absurdist viewpoint in *Passing Game* and *Touching Bottom*, the latter containing three one-act plays in the tradition of Samuel Beckett. Both plays return to the skewed lives that have become the hallmark of his plays. He also returned, however, to his heavy-handed symbolism.

Division Street, the last of Tesich's early plays, combines all of his most successful elements into a political farce that emphasizes character and plot over symbolism. A metaphor borrowed from Studs Terkel, *Division Street* is the story of Chris, an aging radical from the 1960's, who has sold out to the establishment and is intent on starting a career. As chance would have it, however, he is served a putrid cabbage in a Yugoslavian restaurant and is photographed regurgitating on the street. The picture makes the newspaper, and his past gallops unwanted to his door. What follows is a brilliant farce complete with slamming doors and windows, mistaken identities, reunited orphans, outrageous characters and situations, and clever dialogue full of Tesich wordplay, one-liners, and repartee. The script is filled with radicals who have no place in the "Me" generation but who long for the good old days of "the movement." The original, published version has a weakly resolved ending, with Chris once again leading the displaced radicals in a new movement and a patriotic rendition of "America the Beautiful." A revised production eliminated the song, along with two characters, but still ended in sentimental patriotism. Tesich did not intend for the characters to be perceived as shallow hippies without a cause, as it is sometimes interpreted, becoming a mindless romp, a shallow farce and nothing more. When it is understood that Tesich intended the play to be a remembrance of his own college activist days ending with a call to continued activism, to find and eliminate injustice, the play becomes a comedy of ideas.

Even when Tesich is criticized, he is praised for his ability to create fascinating characters and intriguing dialogue. This talent is the result of his mastery of American English, his keen ear for the ways people speak, and his unusual approach to creating characters first, and then situation and conflict. When studying Russian literature, he recognized how he felt about the United States as he observed what happened when Russian characters with differing ideologies bumped into each other. In the Russian novels, the ideas and beliefs were heavy burdens; in the United States the divergent ideas were energizers. This notion of interacting and reacting ideas evolved into the methodology of Tesich's writing. He begins by writing character notes: anecdotal biographies, snatches of dialogue, and philosophical questions, often accumulating as much as a hundred pages of background material. Next, he begins to write about his characters, to explore and see what they do. As the divergent characters collide, something happens, and *that* is what he writes about. He discards the preliminary material and writes the story of what happens when his intricately delineated, conflicting, and contradicting characters collide.

When Tesich returned to the theater after almost ten years of absence, that method was still in evidence. Even though his perspective and motivation for writing changed, his later plays are based squarely on character. While the early plays sprang from his own perspective, emanating from his own experience, in his later plays he writes from the experience of others. He is the disappointed American, still loving the United States for what it should be, but he is outraged at the moral bankruptcy that he sees around him. *The Speed of Darkness* was written in response to what he perceived as creeping revisionism in the United States' memory of the Vietnam War. Tesich has adopted a traditional dramatic structure that goes back to Henrik Ibsen's plays, where the present is jeopardized, if not destroyed, by the secrets of the past. Joe and Lou are emotionally destroyed by the war. Angry and bitter, they return to the United States with no hopes or dreams. They vent their anger by getting drunk and illegally disposing of toxic waste on a bluff outside a South Dakota town. Their lives part, however, when Joe meets Anne, falls in love, and finds some meaning in life. Eighteen years later, Joe is being honored as the state Man of the Year at the same time that Lou shows up, a dirty, homeless Vietnam veteran, aimlessly carrying his life in a bundle as he follows the traveling Vietnam Memorial from city to city. His return opens the floodgates of guilt for past crimes and infidelities, which lead to tragedy and catharsis for this American family. Earlier Tesich themes of the displaced, the foreign, and the guilt of the past are played out against a new moral backdrop of social commentary. The symbolism is somewhat more successfully integrated into character and action, and the theatricality of the crises is not so gratuitous.

The absurdist comedy *Square One* creates outlandish characters and situations for social comment. It grew out of Tesich's observation that humankind's aspirations have become small and that society satisfies its obligations merely by becoming informed, not by acting upon any indignation or moral outrage. He creates a future world in a dysfunctional society where almost no one acknowledges pain. The masses are emotionally massaged by a constant barrage of entertainment presented by "artists, third class." Tesich's two characters, who never call each other by name, meet, marry, reproduce, and separate against a background where Wagnerian tenors are janitors and where politicians do not appear in public but hire actors to deliver their hollow election promises. The strength of the play is its delicious wordplay. It is the aesthetic counterpart to Larry Gelbart's political and satirical play *Mastergate* (pr. 1989). As it did in the early plays, however, the symbolism takes over, becoming too literal and heavy-handed, overwhelming the fun of the language and the outrageousness of the situation.

Tesich has found a new voice for the theater without giving up the best qualities of his earlier plays. Although he still loves his adopted homeland, he has lost his sense of wonder and has begun to write plays about moral issues. His strength remains his ability to create characters and dialogue that collide, resulting in remarkable situations. His craft in creating the pathos of the Vietnam soldier MIA—"Missing in America"—and the wordplay between the state artist and his wife join with his earlier absurdist comedies to make a significant contribution to the American theater.

Other major works

NOVEL: *Summer Crossing*, 1982.

SCREENPLAYS: *Breaking Away*, 1979; *Eyewitness*, 1981; *Four Friends*, 1981; *The World According to Garp*, 1982; *American Flyers*, 1985; *Eleni*, 1985.

Bibliography

Chase, Donald. "Tesich and Yates." *Horizon* 23 (December, 1980): 26-32. An excellent critical examination, in a popular context, of Tesich as both a screenwriter and a playwright. The essay shows how the themes of his plays can be seen as commentaries on his life and how the plays are darker than the affirmative *Breaking Away.* Also describes how Tesich creates "highly individualized voices." Includes Howard Kissel's review of the Broadway production of *Division Street* as a sidebar and several photographs from *Eyewitness* locations.

Cohen, Barney. "Steve Tesich Turns Memories into Movies." *The New York*

Times Magazine, January 17, 1982, 42-54. The best available source on Tesich's life and the influences on him as a writer. It discusses his approach to writing through notetaking: creating character biographies, beliefs, images, conversations, and then suddenly discovering what it is his characters want, which he then uses to write his stories. Several photographs of Tesich's personal and professional life.

Dudar, Helen. "As One Playwright Strikes Out for the Future . . ." *The New York Times*, February 19, 1990, p. B5, 20. Written on the premiere eve of *Square One*, then the first new Tesich play in New York in ten years, this article briefly describes the "new Tesich." Dudar finds that he is no longer the United States' cheerleader, having lost his sense of wonder, and that he has learned to write from others' experiences, not only from his own. Photographs of Tesich and scenes from *Square One*.

Kramer, Mimi. "Played Out." Review of *Square One*. *The New Yorker*, 66 (March 5, 1990): 89-90. This review of *Square One* describes how Tesich rises above other plays through character and humor. It also describes how the play's literal, instead of figurative, meaning detracts from it.

Rich, Frank. "Turning Back the Clock." Review of *The Speed of Darkness*. *The New York Times*, March 1, 1991, p. C1, 3. Explains how Tesich has defiantly created an old-fashioned drama filled with thunderous emotions. The play is compared to some by Arthur Miller, Edward Albee, Sam Shepard, and David Rabe.

Rothstein, Mervyn. "Morality's the Thing for This Playwright." *The New York Times*, March 12, 1991, p. C11, 13. In response to the relatively successful Broadway opening of *The Speed of Darkness*, Tesich explains how he has changed in the decade since his early plays. He now is concerned with "moral issues," such as this play's decrial of the United States' refusal to deal with the aftermath of the Vietnam War. Photograph.

Simon, John. "The Graying of America." Review of *Division Street*. *New York* 22 (February 16, 1987): 92. This review of *Division Street*'s revival places the play in a political and social context. It also examines the rich sources of its humor. Photograph.

Gerald S. Argetsinger

DYLAN THOMAS

Born: Swansea, Wales; October 27, 1914
Died: New York, New York; November 9, 1953

Principal drama

Under Milk Wood: A Play for Voices, pr. 1953 (public reading), pr. 1954 (radio play), pb. 1954, pr. 1956 (staged; musical settings by Daniel Jones).

Other literary forms

Although Dylan Thomas wrote only a single work for the theater, its originality, importance, and influence are far-reaching. Thomas was above all else a poet. His main collections of poems are *Eighteen Poems* (1934), *Twenty-five Poems* (1936), *The Map of Love* (1939), *New Poems* (1943), *Deaths and Entrances* (1946), *Twenty-six Poems* (1950), *In Country Sleep* (1952), *Collected Poems, 1934-1952* (1952), and *The Poems of Dylan Thomas* (1971), a posthumous collection edited by Daniel Jones.

Thomas was also a writer of prose. With John Davenport, he wrote a novel, *The Death of the King's Canary* (1976), published more than twenty years after Thomas' death. Among his major collections of short stories are *Portrait of the Artist as a Young Dog* (1940) and two collections published posthumously, *A Prospect of the Sea and Other Stories* (1955) and *Adventures in the Skin Trade and Other Stories* (1955). A definitive edition of his short fiction, *The Collected Stories*, was published in 1984.

Particularly germane to a consideration of Thomas the dramatist are his radio scripts. The collection *Quite Early One Morning* (1954) contains twenty-two scripts for broadcast by the British Broadcasting Corporation. Two of these scripts, *Quite Early One Morning* (1944) and *Return Journey* (1947), contributed to the evolution of *Under Milk Wood*. A third radio script, *The Londoner* (1946), also contributed to the evolution of the play and is included in the volume *"The Doctor and the Devils" and Other Scripts* (1966). This volume also contains two film scripts, *The Doctor and the Devils* (1953) and *Twenty Years A'Growing* (1964). Other film scripts by Thomas include three published posthumously: *The Beach of Falesá*, published in 1963; *Rebecca's Daughters*, published in 1965; and *Me and My Bike*, also published in 1965. Thomas also wrote two potboilers, *Three Weird Sisters* (1948), with Louise Birt and David Evans, and *No Room at the Inn* (1948), with Ivan Foxwell for British National.

Thomas' notebooks and letters have also been published: *Letters to Vernon Watkins* (1957), edited by Watkins; *Selected Letters of Dylan Thomas* (1966), edited by Constantine FitzGibbon; *Poet in the Making: The Notebooks of Dylan Thomas* (1967), edited by Ralph Maud; and *Twelve More Letters by Dylan Thomas* (1969), edited by FitzGibbon.

Achievements

Although Thomas wrote in many genres, he was, above all, a poet. He is probably one of the half-dozen most significant poets to have written in English in the twentieth century, although critical opinion about his work has been divided. By the end of his life, Thomas had become a popular poet; the sales of his *Collected Poems, 1934-1952*, published the year before he died, showed that the popularity of his work was unequaled by any other serious modern poet in English. The interest in Thomas was partly a result of the "legend" that developed during his lifetime, fostered by Thomas' eccentric mode of life, his striking originality, and his extraordinary ability to read his poetry aloud. Perhaps in reaction to the Thomas cult, academic critics in Great Britain were slower than were their American counterparts to recognize his status as a major poet.

Although Thomas wrote only one play, its incorporation into the repertory of most theaters was extremely rapid after its initial performance in 1953. More so than the poetic dramas of T. S. Eliot or Christopher Fry, *Under Milk Wood* has become one of the major contemporary challenges to conventional notions of theater. The play is distinguished by the density, sonority, and expressiveness of its language. Although it does not achieve the full Shakespearean synthesis of poetry and drama, *Under Milk Wood* has restored one aspect of that synthesis—the expressive potential of the human voice—to its former prominence. It is likely that *Under Milk Wood* will remain the primary example and measure for future experiments in this important domain of the theater.

Biography

Dylan Thomas was born in Swansea, Wales, in 1914. He had a sister, Nancy, older than he by some eight years. Thomas spoke no Welsh, although both of his parents had spoken Welsh in their childhood homes. Thomas' father had written poetry in his youth; he was a schoolmaster, an atheist, and had deliberately rejected the Welsh language. Thomas attended the Swansea grammar school. When he was seventeen, he became an apprentice reporter and proofreader for the *South Wales Daily Post*, and he did not attend a university. He began to publish his first poems in newspapers in the early 1930's. He was also an amateur actor with the Swansea Little Theatre. (A friend and fellow actor, Malcolm Graham, has written, "The more fantastic the part, the better Dylan was.") It was during these years that Thomas' voice became strong and acquired the resonance that was to make him as famous as his poetry.

In 1934, Thomas moved to London, and in that year his first collection, *Eighteen Poems*, was published. In 1937, Thomas married Caitlin Macnamara, and their first child, Llewelyn, was born in 1939. After the outbreak of World War II, Thomas tried to enlist for military service but was rejected. His second child, Aeron, was born in 1943. The family spent the years from 1940 to 1945 living in or near London, Thomas working on scenarios for documentary films. His first radio broadcast for the British Broadcasting Corporation had been made in 1937, but after 1945 he made more frequent broadcasts for the corporation on a free-lance basis. In 1948, he began the production of feature-length films. During the postwar years, he traveled to Italy and to Prague, Czechoslovakia, and in 1951 he went to Persia with a commission to write a film for the Anglo-Iranian Oil Company. His third child, Colm, was born in 1949.

In 1950, Thomas made his first trip to the United States at the invitation of John Malcolm Brinnin. He read at the Poetry Center at the Young Men's and Women's Hebrew Association in New York, and for three months he visited American colleges, reading his own work as well as that of other nineteenth and twentieth century poets. In 1952, he made his second trip to the United States, and he returned in 1953 for his third visit. In May, 1953, *Under Milk Wood* was given its first performances in Cambridge, Massachusetts, and in New York. In October, 1953, Thomas returned to the United States for a fourth time; on November 9, he died in New York City at the age of thirty-nine. He was buried in St. Martin's Churchyard in Laugharne, Wales.

Analysis

Dylan Thomas' play *Under Milk Wood* was not the product of a career that developed in the theater; rather, it developed from a poet's experience with radio drama. Indeed, one of the most pertinent questions to be asked about *Under Milk Wood* is whether it is really a play at all. Is it, in fact, a radio script (or exotic poem) that has been railroaded by enthusiasts into the dramatic repertory? One must answer emphatically that *Under Milk Wood* is a play, written with a deliberateness and a consciousness of different genres and alternate modes of expression of which few readers are aware. Like many works at the frontier of a medium of expression, it is a synthesis. It had a long and complicated evolution in the author's mind over the course of a decade, ending as "a play for voices" performed by professional actors.

At the time the play was first performed—only a few months before Thomas' death—he was turning away from the more strictly personal, lyric poetry he had written previously, toward a more public form of expression with large-scale dramatic works that would provide scope for his versatility and for his gifts of humor and characterization, as well as for his ability as poet. He had planned to collaborate with Igor Stravinsky on an opera; according to Thomas' concept and in Stravinsky's words, "The opera was to be about the rediscovery of our planet following an atomic misadventure. There would be a re-creation of language, only the new one would have no abstractions; there would only be people, objects, and words." Far from being the eccentric excursion of a poet into the domain of theater, *Under Milk Wood* was to have been the first of a series of large-scale mixed-media productions for the stage. Death intervened, however, leaving only the first work of this projected cycle.

There is a reasonably good text available for *Under Milk Wood* and considerable commentary on it, yet a simple definition of the play is elusive. Its subtitle, *A Play for Voices*, indicates to many that it is not "normal" theater, yet this begs the question of what normal theater is. A tradition of what might be called dramatic realism is very much alive in British and American theater, and plays that do not fit into this mold are often seen as suspect, or not viable commercially, by theater professionals. To stage Thomas' play successfully, a theater company must have actors capable of using their voices to render a dense, highly articulated text, and many groups do not have actors with the necessary ability or training. An actor—the "First Voice"—must be able to speak the following words in a convincing, effective manner:

> It is Spring, moonless night in the small town, starless and bible-black, the cobblestreets silent and the hunched, courters'-and-rabbits' wood limping invisible down to the sloeblack, slow, black, crowblack, fishing-boat-bobbing sea. The houses are blind as moles (though moles see fine tonight in the snouting, velvet dingles) or blind as Captain Cat there in the muffled middle by the pump and the town clock, the shops in mourning, the Welfare Hall in widows' weeds.

For the actor, not only is there the problem of the use of his voice, but also there remains the all-important matter of interpretation. Words such as "hunched," "limping," "muffled middle," and "mourning" must be interpreted and understood before they can be spoken effectively. Many actors and also directors will not be able to perform this basic act of interpretation and consequently will turn with relief to a different kind of play that is less demanding.

Thomas' language is rooted in place, dialect, and province. It is not literary—at least it is not literary in an English sense. The dialect is Anglo-Welsh. There are a certain number of literary additions, largely rhythmic, and there is consonance, assonance, and alliteration, but Thomas has the advantage that his dialect, or the voices he knows, can make use of these devices without becoming stilted or artificial; hence, they are not literary, strictly speaking.

Perhaps more than any other twentieth century play, *Under Milk Wood* poses the question: What is the function of language in theater? For those who instinctively reply that its function is to be the most economic vehicle for the plot, *Under Milk Wood* will be a disappointment. Yet the theater is always subject to historical evolution, and for long periods in the past, poetry and drama were combined. In the late nineteenth and early twentieth centuries, they were kept separate, but it could be argued that this span was atypical. The British critic Raymond Williams has observed that "many of our deepest and richest experiences are unlikely to be reducible to conversational terms, and it is precisely the faculty we honor in poets that, by means of art, such experiences can find expression." An important function of the older pieces in the theatrical repertory, especially those of William Shakespeare and the Elizabethans, is that their language keeps this broader sense of realism alive. Perhaps it is the deprivation of this older tradition that accounts in part for the revolt against the naturalism of the past fifty years and also for the special sense of discovery that the experience of poetic drama can offer—for example, the poetic drama of Federico García Lorca, or that of Dylan Thomas and *Under Milk Wood*.

What is the main dramatic action of *Under Milk Wood*? As in the first act of Thornton Wilder's *Our Town* (pr. 1938), it is a day in the life of a small town, in this case Llareggub, modeled after Laugherne on the coast of Southern Wales. The notion of the single day's span might have derived from James Joyce's *Ulysses* (1922); at any rate, the drama of a town waking in the morning was prefigured in Thomas' radio script *Quite Early One Morning*, and a full day served as the frame of his radio script *The Londoner*. Wilder had felt that one day was not enough for all three acts of his play, and he introduced huge lapses of time between acts to dramatize his characters growing, aging, and dying—this is what "happens" in his play. In *Under Milk Wood*, there is a constant process of what might be called the exposition of character, but this exposition is in no way abstract, purely informative, or staid; rather, each character is in a state of uniquely dynamic flux. This applies to their dreams at the beginning of the play (the first twenty-five pages are dreams), and to the movement of time itself, with dawn finally lifting: "The principality of the sky lightens now, over our green hill, into spring morning larked and crowed and belling."

Is it enough, as one listens to the various characters of the play (who are quite unusual), to wonder what they will do next, and how they will act? For example, will Mr. Pugh give expression to his desires and poison Mrs. Pugh? Will Polly Garter, once again, be unable to say no; will the ghosts of Ogmore and Pritchard live on in obedience to Mrs. Ogmore-Pritchard, or will they disappear; will the clock collection of Lord Cut-Glass continue to tick and multiply; will the two Mrs. Dai Breads continue living with the same husband? Why cannot Mog Edwards and Myfanwy Price marry and live together; what will happen to Lily Smalls and Rose May Cottage (will they sail into the spring sky?); what will happen to the blind Captain Cat as he sails among the drowned; will *all* the dead come out in the end? One of the unique features of the play is that all of these characters and many more (sixty-three are included in the cast) are acting simultaneously, and their voices are skillfully interwoven to flow naturally and unexpectedly into one another. For example, the First Voice is describing the afternoon:

> First Voice: Clouds sag and pillow on Llareggub Hill. Pigs grunt in a wet wallow-bath, and smile as they snort and dream. They dream of the acorned swill of the world, the rooting for pig-fruit, the bagpipe dugs of the mother sow, the squeal and snuffle of yesses of the women pigs in rut. They mud-bask and snout in the pig-loving sun; their tails curl; they rollick and slobber and snore to deep, smug, after-swill sleep. Donkeys angelically drowse on Donkey Down.
>
> Mrs. Pugh: Persons with manners,
>
> Second Voice: snaps cold Mrs. Pugh
>
> Mrs. Pugh: do not nod at table.
>
> First Voice: Mr. Pugh cringes awake. He puts on a soft-soaping smile: it is sad and gray under his nicotine-eggyellow weeping walrus Victorian moustache worn thick and long in memory of Doctor Crippen.
>
> Mrs. Pugh: You should wait until you retire to your sty,
>
> Second Voice: says Mrs. Pugh, sweet as a razor. . . .

Throughout the play, transitions between voices are handled with great dexterity, as with the repetition of the pig motif in a totally unexpected place. The voices interweave, break away from one another, and suddenly flow back together again when least anticipated. It has been said that the characters in the play are "eccentrics," but this is not quite correct. They are held in a very dynamic imbalance that becomes, as the play progresses, a strange type of dramatic balance constantly undone and reestablished again. The dynamism is such that one does not perceive a static day at all; rather, one sees the people growing and dying and hears the dreams and voices of both the living and the dead.

Toward the end of the play the First Voice says:

> Dusk is drowned forever until tomorrow. It is all at once night now. The windy town is a hill of windows, and from the larruped waves the lights of the lamps in the windows call back the day and the dead that have run away to sea. All over the calling dark, babies and old men are bribed and lullabied to sleep.

The play deals with multiplicity, a carefully worked out multiplicity of diverse characters who are drawn with sharpness and exuberance and who obey a large variety of types of motivation. There is, for example, much ribaldry, reaching its peak with the song near the end, addressed to the "chimbley sweep." The abundant sexual fantasy in the play has been censured by Thomas' dourer critics; two observations may clarify the function of this element. The lines expressing sexual fantasy are filled with humor and verbal life, and regardless of whether they are to the actor's or to the audience's taste, they must be spoken so that they communicate these qualities. They are not all of the same mold (Mae Rose's, Lily's, Captain Cat's, Mr. Waldo's); clearly it is a mistake to attribute them to the author. Perhaps the soundest approach to this aspect of the play is to see it as analytical, similar, for example, to the endeavor of Arthur Schnitzler, who probed behind the repressive mechanisms of his characters and described their private, outlandish fantasies and illusions.

As the voices weave in and out of one another, a major problem remains: How is the play to be visualized? Thomas provided only a minimum of stage directions, and it is far from clear, especially for actors brought up on domestic naturalism, how they should position themselves. *Under Milk Wood* is not a radio play with disembodied voices invisible behind a microphone. On the contrary, the "voices" must be fully visible and the actors are the focus of attention, lit on the stage. It is a mistake to have the actors sit—they must be choreographed. Many cues will be found in the language, yet there is much room for the creative imaginations of the director and the actors. The present writer saw a particularly resourceful version of the role of Lord Cut-Glass (performed in 1968 by the American Conservatory Theater in San Francisco; the actor was René Auberjonois) in which the actor moved from clock to clock to clock onstage, performing a hilarious dumb show that lasted several minutes. Not a single word was spoken. The audience left the theater thinking, perhaps, that Lord Cut-Glass was one of the most effectively drawn characters in the play. This, however, was an illusion of creative staging, for there are many characters with longer or more important roles. Thomas himself did not spell out these stage directions; their absence, when combined with an unimaginative director, can lead to a production that is a resounding failure. This represents a potential weakness of the play; the language, however, contains innumerable possibilities for action, movement, and gesture. *Under Milk Wood* provides maximum challenge, and freedom, for a resourceful director.

The question remains: What is the structure or plot of *Under Milk Wood*? The play is not divided into acts or scenes in the traditional manner; the introduction of each new voice—and personage—brings with it a new "scene." As indicated above, this is, in itself, a structural feature of the play, and the fluidity, the simultaneous presence, of all the inhabitants of the town is rendered by the play's language. Some critics have argued that Thomas had no talent for structure. Thomas' biographer Paul Ferris, generally objective and sympathetic, writes: "His gift was for dialogue; when he had to construct a story, he was in difficulties. His idea of a plot was a straight line moving forward in time, as in *Under Milk Wood*." John Davenport has written that Thomas was "incapable of dramatic structure." No doubt Thomas' main talents were for sound, rhythm, and dialogue: the spoken voice. Yet if one reads his film scripts, one sees that he paid meticulous, practical attention to visual detail when required to do so: ample directions for the camera, to "dissolve and track downwards," "pan up" or "pan down," or the carefully imagined "close-ups." He made everything painstakingly visual.

During one stage of the composition of *Under Milk Wood*, Thomas considered introducing an action and plot into the play that was to have been highly dramatic in the traditional or naturalistic sense. According to Thomas' project of 1943, the town was to be literally put on trial, with Captain Cat as Counsel for the Defense. This was to highlight the contrast between the town and the outside world. The trial was to have a surprise ending: The final speech of the Prosecution was to prescribe an ideally sane town, and when the inhabitants of Llareggub heard it, they were to withdraw their defense, begging to be cordoned off from the "sane" world as soon as possible. Thomas' working title for the play at this time was "The Town Was Mad." At least one critic (Raymond Williams) thinks it unfortunate that Thomas abandoned this plan. Later, in 1944-1945, Thomas had new ideas for the play; according to Constantine FitzGibbon,

> After the revelations of the German concentration camps, Dylan outlined the idea to me one afternoon in an underground drinking club called the Gateways. The village was declared insane, anti-social, dangerous. Barbed wire was strung about it and patrolled by sentries, lest its dotty inhabitants infect the rest of the world with their feckless and futile view of life. They do not mind at all, though they grumble about the disappearance of the buses. The village is the only place that is left free in the whole world, for the authorities have got it wrong. This is not a concentration camp; the rest of the globe is the camp, is mad, and only this little place is sane and happy.

FitzGibbon adds that he thinks Thomas rightly discarded all of this superstructure when he wrote the play, for he was "far too skilled a writer to underline his plots."

For several years after the war, Thomas continued to be uncertain about the direction his play should take. According to Daniel Jones, Thomas was unable to decide upon the form of the work: "There was much discussion with friends about a stage play, a comedy in verse, and a radio play with a blind man as narrator and central character. The blind man, a natural bridge between eye and ear for the radio listener, survives in *Under Milk Wood*, with the difference that Captain Cat is made to share his central position with two anonymous narrators." By the time the play appeared in *Botteghe Oscure* in 1952, Thomas had partly returned to the plan of *Quite Early One Morning*, limiting the picture to the town itself, with hardly a suggestion of a world beyond the town, and the time sequence was extended to form a complete cycle. Yet Thomas was not writing another radio play, and he was developing the project in a specific direction. As Aneirin Davies, Thomas' employer for the British Broadcasting Corporation, has written, "By leaving the stage himself, the poet has taken the step from dialogue to drama." Another British Broadcasting Corporation producer, Douglas Cleverdon, has written that Thomas found the form of the radio play too confining. He thinks that Thomas developed the structure of

"The Town Was Mad" with a full-length radio play in mind, but that he switched to the form of the "radio feature" because of its relative freedom: "It has no rules determining what can or cannot be done. And though it may be in dramatic form, it has no need of dramatic plot. Consequently, when the development of *The Village of the Mad* proved complicated, it was natural that Dylan should turn to the more fluid form of the feature."

Slowly, yet deliberately and consciously, Thomas rejected the plot of "Madtown"; as Cleverdon has noted, he seemed relieved when the decision was finally made. At the same time, he was also moving away from the form of the radio feature. By October, 1951, he had written to Countess Caetani saying he had abandoned one play ("Madtown") because "the comedy was lost in the complicated violence of the words." The new play was described as "a piece, a play, an impression for voices, an entertainment out of the darkness of the town I live in."

Thomas continued to work on the play until the last moment before its reading on May 3, 1953, at the Fogg Museum at Harvard, and he continued to write additional material until the production of the play in New York eleven days later. An hour before the play was to begin, he still had not written the conclusion. As John Malcolm Brinnin has recorded:

> But in these last minutes he devised a tentative conclusion that would serve. Twenty minutes before curtain time, fragments of *Under Milk Wood* were still being handed to the actors as they applied make-up, read their telegrams and tested their new accents on one another. Some lines of dialogue did not actually come into the hands of the readers until they were already taking their places on stage.

Thomas himself took the parts of the First Voice and the Reverend Eli Jenkins. At the end of the performance, when the lights had faded, the thousand spectators sat as if stunned. "But within a few moments," Brinnin goes on, "the lights went up and applause crescendoed and bravos were shouted by half the standing audience while the cast came back for curtain call after curtain call until, at the fifteenth of these, squat and boyish in his happily flustered modesty, Dylan stepped out alone."

More than anything else, the evolution of the play shows that traditional plot was found to be awkward and unsuitable. By a deliberate decision it was rejected, and only after this was Thomas able to write the play that now exists. The rejection was both conscious and subconscious. For years he had worked on the version with the plot, trying to reconcile it with his new ideas and conceptions, but artistically they proved to be irreconcilable. One can assume that if he had lowered his standards and tried to produce a version that would "work," analogous to his film scripts, he would have had no difficulties, but he was aiming much higher. The answer to the question of what "happens" in the play is clear. No traditional, naturalistic plot, with an orderly sequence of delimited actions, "happens." Something much more happens: An entire town, represented by more than sixty characters onstage, acts out all of its innermost desires, intentions, thoughts, and dreams—often highly contradictory—and these take place as close to simultaneously as the medium permits. The characters are interwoven in a seamless web—or, if there are seams, they are interconnected with an astonishingly high degree of art. The characters develop, age, and are engaged in the act of dying as the audience sees and listens to them. The process might be called "dynamic integration"—it constantly threatens to become undone, and it is intensely dramatic. At the same time, the play is one of the most demanding in the repertory: The voices must be skillful and highly trained, and more than in any other play the director is required to find visual counterparts, onstage, for words and their voices.

Other major works

NOVEL: *The Death of the King's Canary*, 1976 (with John Davenport).

SHORT FICTION: *Portrait of the Artist as a Young Dog*, 1940; *Selected Writings of Dylan Thomas*, 1946; *A Child's Christmas in Wales*, 1954; *Quite Early One Morning*, 1954; *A Prospect of the Sea and Other Stories*, 1955; *Adventures in the Skin Trade and Other Stories*, 1955; *Early Prose Writings*, 1971; *The Followers*, 1976; *The Collected Stories*, 1984.

POETRY: *Eighteen Poems*, 1934; *Twenty-five Poems*, 1936; *The Map of Love*, 1939; *New Poems*, 1943; *Deaths and Entrances*, 1946; *Twenty-six Poems*, 1950; *In Country Sleep*, 1952; *Collected Poems, 1934-1952*, 1952; *The Poems of Dylan Thomas*, 1971 (Daniel Jones, editor).

NONFICTION: *Letters to Vernon Watkins*, 1957 (Vernon Watkins, editor); *Selected Letters of Dylan Thomas*, 1966 (Constantine FitzGibbon, editor); *Poet in the Making: The Notebooks of Dylan Thomas*, 1967 (Ralph Maud, editor); *Twelve More Letters by Dylan Thomas*, 1969 (FitzGibbon, editor).

SCREENPLAYS: *Three Weird Sisters*, 1948 (with Louise Birt and David Evans); *No Room at the Inn*, 1948 (with Ivan Foxwell); *The Doctor and the Devils*, 1953; *The Beach at Falesá*, 1963; *Twenty Years A'Growing*, 1964; *Rebecca's Daughters*, 1965; *Me and My Bike*, 1965.

RADIO PLAYS: *Quite Early One Morning*, 1944; *The Londoner*, 1946; *Return Journey*, 1947; *Quite Early One Morning*, 1954 (twenty-two radio plays).

MISCELLANEOUS: *"The Doctor and the Devils" and Other Scripts*, 1966 (two screenplays and one radio play).

Bibliography

Ackerman, John. *Dylan Thomas: His Life and Work.* London: Oxford University Press, 1964. This standard and popular biography of the poet was written only a decade after his death.

Ferris, Paul. *Dylan Thomas: A Biography.* London: Hodder & Stoughton,

1977. This volume presents a later and readable account of the playwright's upbringing in Swansea, Wales, his education, his move to London and marriage, his travels during the postwar years, and his drama. The book is supplemented by a wide-ranging bibliography that includes later sources.

Fitz Gibbon, Constantine. *The Life of Dylan Thomas.* Boston: Little, Brown, 1965. Although somewhat dated, this well-illustrated study is still useful, especially for Thomas' complex imagery and robust humor.

Gaston, George, ed. *Critical Essays on Dylan Thomas.* Boston: G. K. Hall, 1989. Gaston provides a later and comprehensive selection of modern scholarship on the Welsh poet and places him in historical and literary contexts.

Moynihan, William T. *The Craft and Art of Dylan Thomas.* Ithaca, N.Y.: Cornell University Press, 1966. This volume focuses on the largely autobiographical prose of Thomas.

Sinclair, Andrew. *Dylan Thomas, No Man More Magical.* New York: Holt, Rinehart and Winston, 1975. Sinclair's book is still the most popular biography on Thomas. It captures the spirit of Wales and the great poet's drive toward madness.

John Carpenter
(Updated by *Peter C. Holloran*)

CYRIL TOURNEUR

Born: Unknown; c. 1575
Died: Kinsale, Ireland; February 28, 1626

Principal drama

The Revenger's Tragedy, pr. 1606-1607, pb. 1607; *The Atheist's Tragedy: Or, The Honest Man's Revenge*, pr. c. 1607, pb. 1611; *The Plays of Cyril Tourneur*, pb. 1978.

Other literary forms

Cyril Tourneur's only noteworthy work in addition to his plays is *The Transformed Metamorphosis* (1600), an obscure allegorical verse satire on religion in a Metaphysical style. He also wrote three elegiac works on prominent figures. A few short prose works and occasional verses, signed only "C. T.," have been attributed to him without further evidence of his authorship.

Achievements

If Tourneur was the author of *The Revenger's Tragedy* (its authorship is still a matter of debate), his achievement is considerable: He ranks among the chief Jacobean dramatists for a brilliantly structured drama which rings interesting changes on all the conventions of revenge tragedy and dexterously fuses irony, satire, burlesque, and moral purpose in its characterizations. The language of the play is remarkable for its concentrated imagery and its sense of frenzied intensity and haste. If he wrote only *The Atheist's Tragedy*, he must be recognized as the talented author of a well-structured and interesting variant of the revenge tragedy. In this thesis play, Tourneur creates a memorable villain and several interesting minor characters, shows a deft hand at the farcical twist, and daringly and successfully blends medieval structural devices with more modern ideological concepts.

Biography

There is no documentation relating to Cyril Tourneur's birth or early life. Allardyce Nicoll plausibly conjectures his connection with the Tourneur family of Great Parndon, Essex, suggesting that he might have been son to Edward Tourneur, a Middle Temple barrister. Nothing is known of Cyril Tourneur's education. He might have accompanied the Cadiz expedition of 1596, perhaps under the command of Sir Christopher Heydon, to whom he dedicated his first published work, *The Transformed Metamorphosis*. He served as secretary of Sir Francis Vere, on whose death in 1609 he wrote a funeral elegy. *The Atheist's Tragedy* depicts in its hero Charlemont a character resembling Vere in some respects. A lost tragicomedy by Tourneur, *The Nobleman*, was entered in the Stationers' Register in 1612. As far as is known, the play was never printed, but it was performed, as was *The Revenger's Tragedy*, by the King's Men. Tourneur's elegiac works on Robert Cecil, Earl of Salisbury (wr. 1612), and Prince Henry (1613) complete the recorded corpus of his work, except for a 1613 reference to his being given an act of "The Arraignment of London," a play of which no other record exists, to write for Philip Henslowe's company. Some critics have tried to credit Tourneur with the composition of, or at least his hand in, other plays, but without significant evidence.

A career in military and public service surrounded Tourneur's short period of literary activity. He served the Cecils and carried official letters to Brussels in 1613 and seems later to have been employed in Holland, where he saw military service in 1614. In 1617, Tourneur was arrested—on grounds that are not known—and released on the bond of Sir Edward Cecil, whom he accompanied as Secretary of the Council of War and the Marshal's Court on a voyage to raid Spanish treasure ships at Cadiz in 1625. On the way home from this abortive expedition, he died in Kinsale, Ireland, of an illness which attacked many of the crew. The petitions of his wife, Mary, after his death show that he died destitute.

Analysis

Anyone approaching the study of Cyril Tourneur's work encounters two major debates. The first is the problem of whether he wrote *The Revenger's Tragedy.* No author's name is given in the Stationers' Register entry, and this uncertainty is complicated by the play's being coupled in double entry with *A Trick to Catch the Old One* (pr. c. 1605-1606), known to be by Thomas Middleton. *The Revenger's Tragedy* was not ascribed to Tourneur until 1656, when it appeared in Edward Archer's play lists; ascription to Tourneur was repeated in Francis Kirkman's lists of 1661 and 1671. These lists are not invariably accurate, but their tendency in erroneous ascriptions is to attach inferior plays to well-known authors, not major plays to lesser-known ones.

Since there is so little external evidence of authorship, studies have been made on internal evidence to identify the author, the favored alternative candidate being Middleton, whose chief supporters include E. H. C. Oliphant, Samuel Schoenbaum, and Peter Murray. The arguments include differences in style and phraseology from *The Atheist's Tragedy*, of which Tourneur's authorship is unquestioned, and similarities to Middleton's. The former, however, may be explained by the normal variations and developments in a single author's style, and the latter by influence. That two independent but concurrent studies of imagery, by Marco Mincoff and by Una Ellis-Fermor, conducted on the same principles, produced precisely opposite results—one ascribing the play to Middleton, the other to Tourneur—illustrates the subjectivity of such examinations. Studies of versification are at the mercy of compositors' and editors' mislineation. While studies based on preferred spelling and word forms are more objective, there is not enough of Tourneur's writing extant to apply them confidently, and they can do little more than suggest that Middleton may have supplied the copy from which the play was printed, not that he wrote the play.

Among the chief supporters of Tourneur's authorship are R. A. Foakes, Irving Ribner, and Inga-Stina Ekeblad (later Ewbank). Against Middleton's authorship may be cited the fact that his work before 1607 and for some time after included only city comedies for boy companies; he did not begin writing tragedies until fifteen years later. The title page of *The Revenger's Tragedy* claims it to have been acted by the King's Men, for whom Tourneur is known to have written. In favor of Tourneur's authorship, there are similarities in tone, theme, and imagery between *The Revenger's Tragedy* and *The Transformed Metamorphosis*; between *The Revenger's Tragedy* and *The Atheist's Tragedy*, there seems to be a thematic development, a common moral view, and a similar use of medieval dramatic concepts and techniques. There are other minor similarities between the two plays, in the characters' type-names based on Italian words (something Middleton and other dramatists also did), the central use of a skull, and the debts of both to John Marston and William Shakespeare. Foakes sees a stylistic development, arguing that while *The Revenger's Tragedy* gains atmosphere by swift alternation of dialogue and of verse and prose, *The Atheist's Tragedy* contains more varied verse. Because the slim external evidence points to Tourneur while the internal evidence which might point to Middleton is inconclusive, there seems no choice but to continue ascribing the play to Tourneur—a perfectly plausible ascription. As Allardyce Nicoll points out, the uncertainty of authorship may be an advantage, because it directs critical attention to the play's artistry and to its position in the Jacobean age.

The second debate concerns the worldview of *The Revenger's Tragedy.* The arguments range from that of T. S. Eliot—who sees the play as affirming evil—to that of John Peter, who sees Tourneur's mind as a moral one, which guides the characters' natures and their fates, the action, in its series of peripeteia, the irony and satire, and the references to moral and religious norms throughout the play to a moral conclusion. This dichotomy in critical opinion has arisen largely from an inability to distinguish Vindice's voice from his author's (on the surface, this distinction may not be easy, since the play is seen from Vindice's point of view), from a failure to see the firm authorial control in the irony of language and action, and from lack of attention to the moral elements in both language and action. These failures result in part from a neglect of the theatrical situation. Stage production makes quite clear the variations in Vindice's voice, especially his asides, which, in the scenes with Lussurioso and with Castiza and Gratiana, express an anguish and a bitter sarcasm which contrast with the energetic amorality and insinuation of the pander he is pretending to be. Vindice's close relationship to the audience reveals how the author has judged him by making him the ironic butt of many of his own remarks. Those who see in *The Revenger's Tragedy* an amoral world also fail to give the moral action of Gratiana's fall and conversion the full force and emphasis which they attain in the theater.

The play's sources are to be found in several areas. Some of the main plot elements derive from tales of the houses of Este and Medici told in the Italian *novelle*, and especially from the revenge of Lorenzo de' Medici on his cousin Alessandro, Duke of Florence, as told in *The Heptameron* (1559) of Marguerite de Navarre, translated into English in William Painter's *Palace of Pleasure* (1566): The cruel and licentious duke asked Lorenzo to supply his own sister as a mistress, whereupon Lorenzo set up an assignation at which he had Alessandro killed. (The story was later treated by Alfred de Musset in his play *Lorenzaccio*, pb. 1834.) The Italian setting was popular in English Renaissance tragedy, stage Italy being a land of sophisticated perversion, revenge, murder, and intrigue. The Italian setting and satiric vein recall John Marston, who clearly influenced *The Revenger's Tragedy.* Tourneur seems to be answering Marston with a more moral approach to similar problems. In Marston's *Antonio's Revenge* (pr. 1599), the perpetrators of a horrible revenge go unpunished, while in his *The Malcontent* (pr. 1604), Duke Altofronte appears disguised in the court of the man who usurped his dukedom and emerges undisillusioned and untainted by participation in intrigue to win it back. Vindice is a variant of Marston's malcontent, disguised among his enemies, in a position to comment as a satirizing observer.

Distancing the action of their plays to Italy left dramatists free to comment on English life. Here, there may be reference intended to the court of James I, famous for its banquets, for its promiscuity, and for its costly attire. Leo Salingar, in his famous article "*The Revenger's Tragedy* and the Morality Tradition," interprets Tourneur as equating the decay of moral order with the manorial system, as capitalism replaced divine providence.

Several critics have noted *The Revenger's Tragedy*'s dependence on the medieval morality tradition. Its opening action follows that of such plays as Henry Medwall's *Nature* (pr. c. 1500), a journey of mankind to the world, where he loses his virtue: Vindice, the Everyman character, leaves the abode of Grace (Gratiana) and Chastity (Castiza) and journeys to the court of the World ("for to be honest is not to be in the world"), where he attires himself as "a man of the time" and mingles with characters whose names and actions recall the morality Vices. In addition to the allegorical formalization of characters and action, the medieval grounding of the play is evident in the *contemptus mundi* and *memento mori* elements. The skull stands as the play's central symbol, stressing—as does the series of peripeteia—the futility of human plans and acquisitions: "O, thou terror to fat folks,/ To have their costly three-pil'd flesh worn off/ As bare as this." The hectic violence of the play-world's pleasures and vices and its verbal rhythms remind Samuel Schoenbaum of *danse macabre* iconography, with its combination of the horrible and the humorous, its sensuality, and its banquets and revelry, which are indulged in to divert minds from death.

Tourneur adapts and blends these medieval elements with the various motifs of a newer tradition, the revenge tragedy, which had established itself from Thomas Kyd's *The Spanish Tragedy* (pr. c. 1585-1589) through William Shakespeare's *Hamlet* (pr. c. 1600-1601). The court setting, the delayed vengeance, the complicated intrigues, and the spectacular catastrophe, familiar from Kyd and his followers, are all there, as are, in some form, the emissary from beyond the grave and the revenger's insanity. The delay, which normally gains sympathy for the revenger by showing his internal conflict, has already occurred when the play opens. *The Revenger's Tragedy* focuses on the mind's decay from the point of decision to its self-destruction in excessive addiction to violence, and even more on the moral problem of revenge, not—like *The Spanish Tragedy* and *Hamlet*—on the conflict leading up to the point where passion takes control. Thus, the murder has taken place nine years earlier, and Vindice, who has brooded on it all that time, has had the balance of his mind tipped before the play begins: Love has already turned to poison ("My poison'd love," as he addresses the skull, has a double sense), and his anger to vengeful plotting.

Vindice's deterioration is delineated in several ways. The most dramatic is through his disguise, his dangerous toying with his own identity. He begins with a self-hatred evident in his contempt for men ("the uprightest man [if such there be/ That sin but seven times a day]") and in depression ("since my worthy father's funeral,/ My life's unnatural to me, e'en compell'd/ As if I liv'd now when I should be dead"). He resolves to "turn into another," thinking that he can do so temporarily ("for once"). Still somewhat tentative about his disguise as a pander, he asks Hippolito, "Am I far enough from myself?" Like Lady Macbeth, he must conjure a warping of his nature, praying to "Impudence" to mask his real feelings, and like Macbeth, he prays that he may avoid seeing himself: "O suff'ring heaven, with thy invisible finger,/ . . . turn the precious side/ Of both mine eyeballs inward, not to see myself."

In time, his embarrassment and his anguish both vanish as he loses himself in the cleverness of his exquisitely plotted revenge ("I'm lost again, you cannot find me yet"), and in his enjoyment of bloodshed, he begins to see himself as an instrument of God's justice in the purgation of the sinful state. He takes on a new disguise, that of a dangerous, malcontent revenger, which is what, ironically, he has actually become. His task in this role is to kill "himself" in his previous role as pander. The most poignant irony in this progressive loss of self comes when the blessing he feels in Gratiana's conversion leads him momentarily to forget his vengeance: "Joy's a subtle elf;/ I think man's happiest when he forgets himself"—which in a religious sense is true; unfortunately, Vindice has here confused "self" with his (self-congratulatory) revenge pursuit. For a moment, there seems to be a chance for his salvation, but he takes leave of his mother to pursue his role as avenger. The self-destructiveness in these rejections of identity culminates in the compulsive confession which condemns him to death, the ultimate loss of personal identity.

The skull takes the place of Hamlet's ghost in keeping the image of the offense before Vindice's mind. This is a particularly interesting variant of revenge tragedy motifs, showing that the impulse to revenge arises from *inside* the revenger, since, inanimate and without a will of its own, the skull can only reflect the thoughts of its observer. The skull is a unifying symbol, drawing together the imagery of disguise, dissimulation, and transformation, and also serving as a *memento mori*. It also proves Vindice's abnormality of mind at the beginning of the play and is an index of the deterioration in his worldview. When he first addresses it, he is aware of Gloriana's rare chastity and appreciates her natural beauty. After Gratiana's fall has shaken his faith in chastity altogether, he sees Gloriana's beauty as artificial, too, covering only the unsightliness of the skull: "see, ladies, with false forms/ You deceive men, but cannot deceive worms." In keeping with this jaundiced view, he makes the skull serve as a whore. The revenger's traditional madness is realized in Vindice's macabre sensibility and his growing obsession with lust. Recognizing this, it can be seen that the jaundiced vision is Vindice's, not Tourneur's; since Vindice is the play's presenter, it is his mind that the play reflects; his is the "intense and unique and horrible vision of life," as T. S. Eliot describes it.

As Charles and Elaine Hallett explain in *The Revenger's Madness* (1981), when the revenger's insanity reaches its height, it takes him out of the real world into a play-within-a-play, and in a closed room, where he assumes complete control, he acts out his own rough and poetic justice. Tourneur rings various changes on the play-within-a-play technique, first having *The Revenger's Tragedy* itself begin as one, with Vindice as presenter introducing a procession of the vicious court characters bodied forth by his imagination. It appears again in the theatrical disguise motif, in the dramatic imagery surrounding the duke's murder, and finally in the concluding masque. In the end, Vindice's pageant fades, leaving him to face both earthly justice—flawed at best—and divine justice, whose law he has transgressed in committing murder.

The play contrasts divine with earthly justice. The revenger's tragedy lies in the conflict between the Christian view, in which murder is strictly forbidden, and an older tradition, still privately recognized, which urged personal vengeance for the death of kin. The revenger's downfall lies in his denial of God's providence, his distrust of heaven's efficacy, shown by his taking vengeance into his own hands. The audience sympathizes with the revenger's wrong, his grief, his indignation against the murderer, his search for justice and order, and the dilemma he faces when human justice provides no remedy and divine and civil law prohibit action. That the audience, carefully guided by the author to view the play's inherent order, can see a world order beyond Vindice's ken and that they can see the failure of his insight to comprehend his own error does not inhibit their sympathy with Vindice. His energy, his intelligence, his direct address to them draw them to him. In the very minute of his sadistic fury, they may experience vicariously their own fantasies of wreaking poetic justice on their own offenders. To say, as many critics have done, that the audience cannot sympathize with Vindice is to deny a major aspect of the play's theatrical technique and moral function. Vindice bridges good and evil, play and real world. The audience, having indulged their passion vicariously, may be recalled from their participation with Vindice by Antonio's voice of sanity, standing back while their scapegoat goes to execution. Vindice's death is necessary on one level because the audience needs to impose control on its own urge to unbridled passion. (This may, of course, be the reason that so many critics protest the impossibility of sympathizing with Vindice at all.) On another level, his death is essential because he has taken God's authority into his own hands, seeing himself as God's instrument (he hubristically interprets the thunder as a sign of God's approval), thus disrupting God's order and questioning God's justice.

As the duke's excess of passion leads to his death and Junior's to his, so Vindice's leads to his. Antonio survives. Many critics see Antonio as a cynical comment on human justice. Indeed, his justice is imperfect, for he condemns to death a masquer whom too many readers mistake for innocent. In fact, this particular masquer, though innocent of Lussurioso's death (Antonio condemns him as "Dipp'd in a prince's blood"), has committed murder: By his own admission, he has killed Spurio. This is simply another illustration of the play's main theme, first illustrated by Junior's trial at the beginning and Junior's death through other means: Though human justice is imperfect and unreliable, God's justice is not. God has used Antonio to punish sin: It is God, not Antonio (as Antonio acknowledges), who is in control. Antonio's own fortune in contrast to Vindice's figures this pattern. Like Vindice, Antonio begins as a discontented nobleman. Discontent is the frame of mind most open to temptation. Like Vindice, Antonio has lost his wife through the ruling family's viciousness, and, having sought human justice, has not found it. He is privy to an oath of vengeance—which he does not initiate—but this vengeance is to wait for the outcome of the next judicial sitting. The sitting never takes place: Justice on Junior comes instead through Supervacuo and Ambitioso's misguided machinations. Antonio's patience is rewarded with state power at the end of the play.

Tourneur carefully shows the audience how each of Vindice's grievances would have righted itself without his intervention. Instead of waiting for God to dispense justice, however, Vindice has taken it into his own hands, and thus, according to poetic, divine, and human justice, he is deprived of all power. In sentencing Vindice and Hippolito to death, Antonio passes the only judgment he can. Murder must be condemned by law. Antonio's words, "You that would murder him would murder me," are not egocentric but politic: In murdering a ruler—it is irrelevant how evil the ruler—Vindice has committed treason and disrupted the social order.

To emphasize the play's moral view, several other characters are given revenge motives: Ambitioso and Supervacuo against Spurio, the duchess and Spurio against the duke, Lussurioso against Piato. Their pettiness and failures, the incredible series of ironic reversals in which their plans rebound on themselves, point to the moral of the play and show that personal vengeance is ineffectual (farcically so in the case of Ambitioso and Supervacuo), evil, and self-defeating. In the end, evil has destroyed itself. The play's pervading moral view is upheld by Vindice, whose asides, more profusely toward the beginning of the play before he usurps God's function, have as their basis conventional moral and religious standards—even his cynical remarks, such as "Save Grace the bawd, I seldom hear grace nam'd!" ("Grace" is the name of a major character in the play.) Though temporarily obscured, tempted through human frailty made frailer by poverty, Gratiana, whose name means Grace, is redeemed. Castiza, except when pretending in a ploy to test her mother's penitence, is true to her allegorical name. It is these two, with the values they represent, whom Vindice recalls in his final words, when he has cast off his roles as Piato, Vindice, murderer, masquer, and returned to an impoverished self—which, cherishing these values, proves not so impoverished after all. Acknowledging the order these values imply, he is able to accept death.

Foakes postulates in his edition that the play and the central character's lack of "the common touch" may account for neglect by theater professionals from 1607 to 1965. Yet in a play which presents a gallery of enviable roles, Vindice is one of the most satisfying roles for an actor, for he himself is so highly theatrical. The range of the part in its various disguises demands immense virtuosity of imagination, voice, and body, and the subtle variety of the language, the range from poetry to prose in countless moods and variations, requires a sensitive and practiced speaker. In constructing the duke's murder, Vindice is inventing a work of dramatic art, aesthetic motives having for him entirely displaced moral ones. Portraying his orgiastic involvement in the execution of this vengeance and his satisfaction with it, the actor is playing his own excitement with his own artistry in a manner rarely offered him by any playwright. The fact that in doing so he is performing a dramatic role absolves him from hubris. The play has been performed increasingly in the twentieth century, first by universities, finally in 1965 by the Pitlochry Festival Theatre, and then in 1967 by the Royal Shakespeare Company in a brilliant and memorable several-year run. To the list of productions Foakes cites can be added those of the Theatre West Four (London) in 1971, A Group of Oxford Players in 1973 (Arthur Kincaid as Vindice), the University of Bristol in 1976, and St. John's Mummers with the Oxford-Cambridge Shakespeare Society in 1978.

The Atheist's Tragedy is an idea play, a moral exemplum demonstrating the failure of faith in nature instead of faith in God. It shows also that human striving is vain and that God's justice prevails effectively. The play uses the medieval *de casibus* structure, substituting Providence for Fortune, paralleling the rise and fall of the atheist d'Amville (the atheist's tragedy) with the fall and rise of the patient Christian Charlemont (the honest man's revenge). The moral premise is the same as that of *The Revenger's Tragedy*: that vengeance belongs to God, who will punish those who disturb His order and reward those who suffer patiently. Some of the methods are the same, particularly the use of symbolic rather than naturalistic characters. The structure, like that of *The Revenger's Tragedy*, shows the influence of the morality tradition, as Peter Murray demonstrates in his comprehensive analysis of the play: Man is shown as he should be in an ordered patriarchal society headed by Montferrers and Belforest, is led away from God during d'Amville's amoral machinations (which destroy the social order by attacking primogeniture while at the same time questioning the fatherhood of God), and then is restored in Charlemont's self-conquest, which achieves a right relationship of man with God. As in the morality play, characters are sharply divided into good and evil, and the vicious characters, more energetic than the virtuous, are more interesting to the audience.

The play was probably composed as an answer to George Chapman's *The Revenge of Bussy d'Ambois* (pr. c. 1610), as *The Revenger's Tragedy* seems to answer Marston. The names Charlemont and d'Amville echo those of Clermont and Bussy d'Ambois, Chapman's passive revenger and supreme individualist. Tourneur refutes Clermont's self-sufficient stoicism by showing the failure of d'Amville's self-sufficiency, on the one hand, and the success of Charlemont's positive Christianity, on the other.

As a revenge-play variant, *The Atheist's Tragedy* is daringly experimental. It calls attention to this fact by recalling *Hamlet* in the two appearances of the ghost and in the graveyard scene. Its ghost, however, is used to urge a son *not* to revenge. This results in a dramatic problem: how to maintain sympathy for a passive hero. Tourneur attempts to solve this, first by having the ghost—unlike that which appears to Clermont d'Ambois—give reasons for not avenging, and then by arranging for Charlemont almost to give way to passion once and be restrained by the ghost, after which he is under physical restraint throughout most of the rest of the play so that he *cannot* act. In addition, Charlemont is given a clear moral development, learning to balance passion and reason and submit both to God.

Since this play has no stage history (all that is known from its title page is that it had been performed in "diuers places"), it has not been possible to see how successful Tourneur was in his experimentation. D'Amville, unquestionably the more active character, dominates the play's interest, manipulating most of its plot. His tragedy, like Vindice's, springs from his lack of trust in God. The intellectual position he represents is that nature is simply a mechanism to be manipulated by man's reason to his own advantage, and that in the absence of moral sanctions, the only rational aims of life are pleasure and wealth. For spiritual immortality, d'Amville substitutes immortality through posterity, and all his schemes are directed to making his posterity rich. Thus, he is ironically undermined from the very start, as can be seen in the vanity of his efforts. When he prides himself on the power of his reason to provide against all accidents, he neglects to consider the possibility of his posterity's demise. At the same time, his imagery undermines him, for it traditionally describes not the relationship of earthly father to son so much as that of God to man, a relationship he rejects:

> And for my children, they are as near to me
> As branches to the tree whereon they grow,
> And may as numerously be multiply'd.
> As they increase, so should my providence,
> For from my substance they receive the sap
> Whereby they live and flourish.

All aspects of the play coherently and economically work to show the folly of denying God. The verse, precise and regular, accords with d'Amville's rationalism. The main image, that of building, suggests the transitory nature of man's works, and the presence of the stars symbolizes God's presence, even though d'Amville, like Shakespeare's Edmund, scoffs at their power and tries to substitute the power of gold. Other characters, particularly Levidulcia and Snuffe, underscore particular aspects of d'Amville's nature or serve as extensions of it. Whereas he is a rational atheist, Levidulcia is a sensual atheist, led only by physical lust, which she justifies by nature. She dies when her lust betrays her, as d'Amville does when his reason betrays him. Both experience a revelation of the truth before they die. Snuffe, the Puritan hypocrite, parodies d'Amville, especially in the graveyard scene where his seduction of Soquette, gone ludicrously wrong, sends up d'Amville's attempted murder and rape. The association also stresses d'Amville's Puritan traits. The minor characters' obscenity and wit caricature his materialism and rationalism.

The final ironic reversal shows the man who tried to destroy others destroying himself. Although naturalistically not as farfetched as critics have claimed (it is remarkably easy to deal oneself such a blow, and under the influence of wine it would be more so), the final scene is intended symbolically, to show God's justice in all its appropriateness.

The play is carefully patterned, with a major debate between nature philosophy and Christian patience (since the characters speak these ideas formally, Ribner compares their expression to a medieval *débat*) and a subsidiary debate between chastity and lust. The characters' ideas and experiences are increasingly closely paralleled, d'Amville losing his reason as Charlemont gains in certainty of his faith, d'Amville's increasing fear of death contrasted to Charlemont's contempt for it.

Though it lacks the intensity of *The Revenger's Tragedy*, *The Atheist's Tragedy* has considerable stage potential. D'Amville, the stage Machiavel, is a marvelous role: His energy, manipulativeness, variety of action, and power of poetry—particularly at points where his reason is giving way—recommend him to a powerful actor and should have challenged the actor-managers of the nineteenth century. The role contains numerous theatrical effects: a ghost, a murder onstage, a suicide before the eyes of the audience, a formal funeral, seductions, an attempted rape, a duel, farcical concealment of lovers, and a graveyard romp. Several of the subsidiary characters are tempting to an actor, especially Snuffe, and the likable and surprisingly moral sensualist Sebastian, whose lines inject an element of humor similar to that provided by Spurio in *The Revenger's Tragedy.* As in *The Revenger's Tragedy*, Tourneur shows a very sure grasp of humor, which has not dated, and this would virtually ensure stage success. The play is certainly more inviting to production than many of the equally or more obscure plays that have been produced in the twentieth century, and not until it has been staged, preferably compared in different productions, will it be possible to judge the extent of its success as drama. It is likely that this would also provide critics further insight into the question of the two plays' common authorship, as well as a more comprehensive view of the art of Cyril Tourneur.

Other major works

POETRY: *The Transformed Metamorphosis*, 1600.

MISCELLANEOUS: *The Works of Cyril Tourneur*, 1929, 1963 (Allardyce Nicoll, editor).

Bibliography

Camoin, François A. *The Revenge Convention in Tourneur, Webster, and*

Middleton. Salzburg: Institut für Englische Sprache und Literatur, Universität Salzburg, 1972. Stresses the complexity of moral views among Jacobean playwrights, which led to the questioning nature of their works. Emphasizes the different techniques of Elizabethan and Jacobean playwrights writing revenge plays. The chapter on Tourneur is the most substantial of any on an individual author. Finds that *The Atheist's Tragedy* offers a more frightening view of the conditions of mortals than Tourneur's earlier *The Revenger's Tragedy.*

Jacobson, Daniel J. *The Language of "The Revenger's Tragedy."* Salzburg: Institut für Englische Sprache and Literatur. Universität Salzburg, 1974. Jacobson investigates such aspects of Tourneur's language as antithesis, irony, and paradox. The sections on imagery relate it to function and theme, finding great thematic emphasis on corruption and damnation. Discusses metaphor, metonomy, and metalepsis as elements of the play's figurative language.

Murray, Peter. *A Study of Cyril Tourneur.* Philadelphia: University of Pennsylvania Press, 1964. This full-length study of Tourneur provides a definitive discussion of the authorship question for *The Revenger's Tragedy.* Tourneur's two plays are analyzed in detail for their art and thought. Murray also gives considerable attention to *The Transformed Metamorphosis* but little or no attention to other minor works.

Ribner, Irving. Introduction to *The Atheist's Tragedy: Or, The Honest Man's Revenge.* Cambridge, Mass.: Harvard University Press, 1964. This excellent introduction to a later edition of the play covers with sufficient depth such elements as date, text, and sources before analyzing Tourneur's moral viewpoints and the play's themes. Includes an interesting section relating Tourneur to Christopher Marlowe, George Chapman, and William Shakespeare. Glossarial index.

__________. *Jacobean Tragedy: The Quest for Moral Order.* New York: Barnes and Noble Books, 1962. Ribner finds Tourneur unique, with his answer to the problems of his age lying in a return to medieval Christianity and its concept of *de contemptu mundi.* Tourneur requires human beings to suffer through the evils of their existence in order to receive their final reward.

Tomlinson, T. B. *A Study of Elizabethan and Jacobean Tragedy.* Melbourne: Melbourne University Press, 1974. Tomlinson sees Tourneur as a key link between Elizabethan and Jacobean tragic periods, for Tourneur continued the study of the morality of revenge present in the Elizabethans but also ushered in the new questioning age of cynicism, which led ultimately to John Webster and Thomas Middleton. Contains an interesting chapter on Tourneur's critics.

Arthur Kincaid
(Updated by *Howard L. Ford*)

ROYALL TYLER

Born: Boston, Massachusetts; July 18, 1757
Died: Brattleboro, Vermont; August 16, 1826

Principal drama

The Contrast, pr. 1787, pb. 1790; *Four Plays by Royall Tyler*, pb. 1941 (includes *The Island of Barrataria*, *Joseph and His Brethren*, *The Judgement of Solomon*, and *The Origin of the Feast of Purim: Or, The Destinies of Haman and Mordecai*).

Other literary forms

Royall Tyler is recalled in contemporary anthologies of American literature principally as the author of the first professionally performed comedy by an American; this play, *The Contrast*, is one of five extant plays by Tyler. Readers of his own day, however, probably knew Tyler best as the witty and energetic author of the Spondee essays and poems, which he, along with his longtime friend Joseph Dennie, known as Colon, submitted for several years to various journals, gentlemen's magazines, and newspapers. In these Spondee pieces, collected by Marius B. Péladeau in *The Prose of Royall Tyler* (1972), Tyler addressed himself to such contemporary subjects as current artistic tastes or preferences, social mores, slavery (to which he was vehemently opposed), his staunch support of Federalist politics, and attacks on the French experiment in democracy. His position in regard to these subjects was almost invariably that of the satirist. In a not so subtle critique of the several modes of government, for example, Tyler, as Spondee, defines a mobocracy as "only a species of Democracy—I say again, heaven preserve us from all ocracies."

Tyler and Dennie, as Spondee and Colon, carried on a compatible, if sometimes strained (by geographic separation), literary partnership from 1794 until 1811. The pair often found themselves imitated by other literary partners who assumed such arresting signatures as "Messrs. Dactyl and Comma," "Quip, Crank and Co.," "Messrs. Verbal and Trochee," and "The Shop of Messrs. Anapoestic and Trochee." Tyler's substantial, autobiographical work, *The Bay Boy*, remained in manuscript until Péladeau's publication of it in *The Prose of Royall Tyler*. Tyler apparently worked on *The Bay Boy* off and on throughout his later years; the manuscript, left incomplete at his death, is particularly important to a study of Tyler as a dramatist because of two brief descriptions the author gives of his encounter with dramatic performances attempted within Puritan Boston's unsympathetic boundaries.

One details a homespun attempt to render Joseph Addison's *Cato* (pr. 1713) into dramatic representation, and the other records the witnessing of a "forlorn fragment of monkish mysteries." Addison's *Cato* was performed under cover of night in a store emptied of all merchandise "excepting one or two counters and several empty hogsheads, barrels and boxes which served as pit, box and gallery for the spectators"; Tyler's description suggests a makeshift Globe Theatre. Actors and spectators stealthily assembled after "Mater, Pater or guardian" were all safely asleep. Tyler next describes the exact procedure for securing the "theater" from unsympathetic passersby:

> The front door of the store was closed and every crack and keyhole carefully stopped with paper or cotton that no glimmering light might alarm the passing watchman. The entrance was through a bye lane into a door in the backyard, and such was the caution observed that but one person was admitted at a time, while two, one at each end of the lane, were on the watch to see if the person to be admitted had been noticed. No knocking was permitted but a slight scratch announced the approach of the initiated.

Tyler then says that the thrill of this sort of performance was never equaled by public performances in New York's public theaters.

Tyler's depiction of the "monkish mystery" is a bit less spectacular, but it does express a persistent need for the dramatic despite puritanical restrictions. On a certain Christmas Eve during the Bay Boy's youth, the house wherein he found himself was visited quite suddenly by a group of traveling players who enacted a brief dueling scene which was most realistic but for the grotesque attire and masks of the players. Tyler calls this representation a "masque" and at the same time somewhat satirically refers to it as reminiscent of early Church mystery plays. Tyler's early familiarity with mystery plays, as well as with such a contemporary drama as Addison's *Cato*, suggests a dramatic background of some sophistication, belying the myth that Tyler wrote *The Contrast* some two weeks after having been initiated into the English comedy of manners during a brief stay in New York, when he was an adult of almost thirty. In these two instances, Tyler also gives present-day readers a rare glimpse of how drama exerted itself even in a period during which it had been outlawed (stage plays in Boston, the place of Tyler's birth and youth, were forbidden by a law enacted in March of 1750).

Among Tyler's other works is the two-volume *Reports of Cases in the Supreme Court of Vermont* (1809-1810); these volumes resulted from Tyler's tenure as Chief Justice of Vermont's supreme court. Tyler also published a single novel, *The Algerine Captive* (1797), which enjoyed a modicum of success and became one of the first novels by an American to be reprinted in London (in 1802 and again in *Lady's Magazine* in 1804). As is the case throughout *The Contrast*, Tyler is much concerned in *The Algerine Captive* to plead the cause of American literary independence. In his picaresque account of the adventures of one Updike Underhill, the author delivers a severe indictment of slavery, satirizes various American social customs, and attacks ostensible American and British toleration of the many Algerian assaults on their navies in the Mediterranean. In their book-length study of Tyler, Ada Lou Carson and Herbert L. Carson point out that the original Algerian captive was Royall Tyler's ancestor Thomas Tyler, who was seized by Barbary pirates in 1703 and was never heard from again; hence, Tyler's interest in the topic must have been intensely personal.

Drama and prose were not the only modes of literary expression in which Tyler distinguished himself. He also wrote quite a few poems, collected by Marius B. Péladeau in *The Verse of Royall Tyler* (1968). Such poems as "Ode Composed for the Fourth of July," "Spondee's Mistresses," "Choice of a Wife," and "The Chestnut Tree" display Tyler's penchant for witty satire; at the same time, these poems, especially "The Chestnut Tree," demonstrate the poet's underlying serious concerns.

Achievements

Although Royall Tyler is remembered today almost exclusively as the author of *The Contrast*, the first American comedy to be professionally produced (on April 16, 1787, at the John Street Theatre in New York City), his achievements as a literary artist were much more extensive than is currently recognized. Four others of Tyler's estimated nine or ten plays have been published in the twentieth century, and several of the lyrics of his no longer extant *May Day in Town: Or, New York in an Uproar* (pr. 1787)—perhaps the first musical written and produced by an American—were discovered and published in 1975. Tyler's contribution to American literature, however, does not end with his dramas. *The Algerine Captive* was one of America's first native novels, as well as one of its first to be printed abroad, while Tyler's collaborative efforts with Joseph Dennie on the Spondee and Colon pieces constitute one of the first American newspaper columns. His autobiographical *The Bay Boy* contains material of intrinsic interest to students of American drama and of American culture at large. Certainly his poetry, which is both witty and serious, deserves to be more extensively studied and anthologized. An all-around man of letters, Tyler distinguished himself as one of America's first authors who self-consciously wrote as an American.

Biography

Born William Clark Tyler on July 18, 1757, in Boston, Massachusetts, Royall Tyler adopted his father's name upon the latter's death in 1771. Tyler's older brother, John Steele Tyler, had fallen out of favor with both parents and was disinherited; hence, most of the Tyler estate reverted to the young Royall. In 1772, Royall Tyler entered Harvard, from which he was graduated in 1776, the year of the Declaration of Independence. To be sure, Tyler and his classmates were much caught up in the rhetoric and ideas of revolt which led to independence.

Tyler's days at Harvard were hardly, then, devoted entirely to disputation, to the study of the Latin and Greek authors, or to the pursuit of philosophy, theology, and mathematics. Indeed, at one point in his Harvard studies, Tyler, along with his roommate, was suspended for relieving the college president of his wig by means of a book dropped from their dormitory window. This incident did not mark the end of Tyler's collegiate escapades. During the period of his attendance at Harvard, the college had a strict rule that, on penalty of expulsion, no student could have anything to do with directing, staging, or acting in plays. Certain incidents related in the autobiographical *The Bay Boy*, concerning the clandestine performance of drama in Boston, suggest that the future dramatist violated this restriction as well.

Shortly after Tyler began to pursue his vocation as a lawyer, he struck up a courtship with the young Abigail Adams, daughter of Abigail and John Adams, who were later to become the First Family of the United States. Evidently, the father of seventeen-year-old Abigail heard rumors of the enthusiastic young Tyler (who in 1777 was accused of wayward conduct), for, not too long after Tyler let Abigail know of his intention to marry her, John Adams demanded that his wife and daughter join him in London, where the future second president of the United States was negotiating the peace treaty between America and Britain.

Tyler's abortive romance with Abigail, who was nicknamed "Nabby," also has its irony. While Nabby was in London with her parents, she met and eventually married a Colonel William Stephens Smith, an attaché of the American contingency and one of George Washington's protégés. While Adams was president, he remarked of his son-in-law, "All the actions of my life and all the conduct of my children have not yet disgraced me as much as this man. His pay will not feed his dogs; and his dogs must be fed if his children starve. What a folly!"

Tyler went on to wed Mary Palmer of Boston in 1794, to adopt the state of Vermont as his permanent residence, and subsequently to become one of that state's leading citizens. It is improbable that President Adams would have been disappointed in having Tyler as his son-in-law. Tyler's activities prior to his marriage to Mary Palmer, however, most likely would have disappointed Adams. In 1787, while on a diplomatic mission on behalf of his future state, Tyler was in New York, where he not only flouted the old Harvard restrictions concerning association with plays but also enacted total rebellion against those restrictions by writing *The Contrast*, performed on April 16. This success Tyler immediately followed with *May Day in Town*, produced on May 19. *May Day in Town* was America's first musical comedy; regrettably, only the lyrics of the musical numbers survive.

Later, in Vermont, Tyler established a prosperous legal practice. He was elected an assistant judge of Vermont's supreme court, and in 1807 was elected Chief Justice of the Vermont supreme court. These distinctions were followed in 1811 by his appointment as Professor of Jurisprudence at the University of Vermont. Tyler's middle years of success were also marked by his collaboration with Joseph Dennie on the Colon and Spondee series of newspaper and magazine articles, by the publication in 1797 of the novel *The Algerine Captive*, by the production in that same year of *The Georgia Spec: Or, Land in the Moon* (a play now lost), and by the publication of several poems on public events and prose works of legal commentary.

Shortly after 1820, however, Tyler's fortunes began to decline rather rapidly. About this time, Tyler began to develop a cancerous growth on his face; this health problem and his advancing age limited his capacity to practice. Eventually, he and his wife became totally dependent on the benevolence of their children and neighbors. It is to Tyler's credit that he attempted, during these declining years, to return to his pen. Between 1824 and his death on August 16, 1826, he wrote (usually with the assistance of amanuenses) three biblical dramas, as well as *The Bay Boy*, "The Chestnut Tree," and "Utile Dulci," which is a collection of miscellaneous writings devoted to moralistic instruction (intended for children) and to explication of his ideas on marriage. It is also to Tyler's credit that certain passages among these last works are among his best and his most intense.

Analysis

Although Thomas Godfrey's *The Prince of Parthia* (pr. 1767) must be acknowledged as the first American play to be produced on an American stage, Royall Tyler's *The Contrast* remains a play whose production on April 16, 1787, marked several firsts. The first American comedy, it also introduced to the American stage the prototype of the Yankee in the character of Jonathan and featured the first stage singing of "Yankee Doodle." *The Contrast* was also the first American drama to receive a press review. Finally, Tyler's play was, before 1916, the most commercially successful play written by an American.

Several of Tyler's other dramatic works have survived, including one farce, *The Island of Barrataria*, and three biblical closet dramas. Some of the lyrics of Tyler's *May Day in Town*, perhaps America's first comic opera, have been found; when these lyrics are combined with information Tyler wrote in a letter to James Madison wherein a performance of the play is described, its plot can be almost wholly reconstructed. Three additional plays of which no copies are known to exist have been attributed to Tyler; these include *The Medium: Or, The Happy Tea-Party* (pr. 1795), *The Farm House: Or, The Female Duellists* (pr. 1796), and *The Georgia Spec*. Thus,

Tyler is the author of at least nine plays.

Of Tyler's five extant plays, *The Island of Barrataria* is, next only to *The Contrast*, the most appealing and the most actable. The three blank-verse closet dramas are based closely on stories from the Old Testament; though too constrained and formal for performance, they contain some of Tyler's best poetry. By far the most significant of these five plays is *The Contrast*, and it is this drama which most clearly demands the attention of critics.

Indeed, so popular does *The Contrast* remain that it not only appears in every standard collection of early American literature but also has enjoyed the distinction of being adapted as a musical. On November 27, 1972, *The Contrast: A Musical*, adapted by Anthony Stimac, premiered at New York City's Eastside Playhouse; Don Pippin composed the music, while the lyrics were by Steve Brown. Tyler's play itself can hold the interest of today's readers and audiences primarily because of its steadfast censure of affectation at all social levels, because of its avowed concern to emphasize the corrective function of Thalia (the Comic Muse), because of its intelligent yet humorous depiction of human behavior in terms of seemingly interminable contrasts, and because of its refusal to fit easily within the bounds of a single comedic genre.

Commentators on *The Contrast* frequently emphasize the charge of the play's opening lines: "Exult, each patriot heart!—this night is shown/ A piece, which we may fairly call our own." To be sure, Tyler is, in many of his works, pointedly moved to encourage the quest for American literary independence. In their attempts to ferret out the play's "patriotic gore," however, commentators often obfuscate many other possible themes. Indeed, the prologue asserts other intentions for the play; it is on these additional intentions that the following discussion of *The Contrast* focuses. Investigation of these additional intentions reveals that Tyler endeavored to produce not simply a play by an American or a distinctly American play, but a play which bears the signature of Royall Tyler.

Throughout Tyler's prose and poetry runs the forceful strain of a moralist—though it must be observed that he stops just short of adopting the role of a didactic prescriber of conduct. In *The Contrast*, Tyler most clearly manifests this moral strain in his summary condemnation of affectation and insincerity at all levels of human behavior. In the ninth couplet of the verse prologue, the playwright asserts that "our free-born ancestors" despised the "arts" of the fashions or follies of their age: "Genuine sincerity alone they priz'd." The major theme of the play is the playwright's desire to reject the behavior of "modern youths, with imitative sense,/ [who] Deem taste in dress the proof of excellence" and to reclaim the refined, though unadorned, "native worth" which is the "solid good" of the virtuous American's heritage. Tyler condemns what he sees as the corrupting influx of European affectation and strongly endorses the "honest emulation" of the behavior and customs which characterized those who struggled for American independence.

Billy Dimple, whose effete-sounding name signals his character, most fully embodies the postrevolutionary American who has embraced the European "Vice," which "trembles, when compell'd to stand confess'd." To such an extravagant expression have Dimple's affectations brought him that he stoops to all manner of deceit in order to dupe the young, desirable, and wealthy Maria Van Rough into a marriage of convenience—so that Dimple can carry on in his excessive and profligate manner, thereby avoiding bankruptcy yet experiencing no interruption of his many affairs of lust. When Dimple attempts to seduce Charlotte, sister of Colonel Manly, Dimple's antithesis, he and his "Vice" do indeed tremble before Manly's capable sword. The insipidity of insincere affectation, whether European, American, or extraterrestrial, is vividly "confess'd" by Jessamy, Dimple's valet, to Jonathan, Manly's "waiter." In a lively and hilarious scene derived from the classical subplot of the servants whose behavior both mirrors and comments on the behavior of their "betters," Jessamy presumes to instruct Jonathan in the "art" of proper display of amusement at the theater. Jessamy even points out how his master has clearly marked the texts of plays as to the precise juncture when the spectator should titter a "piano" or laugh a "fortissimo."

This sort of affected behavior Tyler aspires gently to correct by means of Thalia, the Comic Muse: "the wisdom of the Comic Muse/ Exalt your merits, or your faults accrue./ But think not, 'tis her aim to be severe." Tyler does not intend to offend his audience; rather, he hopes to "amend" human foibles. Throughout the history of the drama, the intention of the writer of serious comedy has always been constructive and corrective.

Tyler's seriocomic intentions are much in evidence in the first scene of act 2. Charlotte and her friend Letitia, who is another of Dimple's targets, are engaging in prattling banter about the nature of insincerity in friendship. Charlotte seizes this opportunity to expound her theory of the virtues of scandal. After admonishing Letitia not "to turn sentimentalist," Charlotte continues, "Scandal, you know, is but amusing ourselves with the faults, foibles, and reputations of our friends." Ironically, the process Charlotte describes strikingly parallels the action of the play itself; that is, Tyler's audience is engaged in the process of amusing itself "with the faults, foibles, follies, and reputations" of these characters on the stage. Charlotte has further suggested that such a process cannot attend the sentimentalist. She then reinforces her judgment by making this antisentimentalist remark: "Indeed, I don't know why we should have friends, if we are not at liberty to make use of them."

This remark is indeed hardly that of a sentimentalist; neither is it that of a moralist. Within comedic limits, Charlotte's assertion of immorality—

wanton abuse of one of the most sacrosanct of human institutions, friendship—is simply too ludicrous to be taken seriously; hence, the audience's response is inevitably one of amusement. Within the constraints of Tyler's avowed hope to correct such foibles, however, his motive is at its most serious. Tyler's implicit acknowledgment here of the value of sincere friendship is intensely moral, yet his casting of this moral instruction within the mold of comedy prevents its becoming oppressively didactic.

No less instructive but, happily, more amusing are the many contrasts that pervade the play. Tyler has created the foppish Dimple, who appears to have much in common with the insidious Charlotte. Charlotte, as does Dimple, contrasts dramatically and often according to her own words with her somber, painfully moral brother, Colonel Manly. Maria Van Rough, who is betrothed to Billy Dimple, ironically seems perfectly fitted to become the partner in life to Colonel Manly. Charlotte recognizes the affinity of Maria for Manly when she exclaims to Letitia, "Oh! how I should like to see that pair of penserosos together." Tyler quite cleverly includes a subplot in which the servants of Dimple and Manly imitate somewhat questionably the actions of their masters. This scene, which opens the fifth act, strongly suggests that the playwright recommends, as preferred conduct, neither Manly's melancholic disposition nor the foppishness of Dimple; rather, Tyler bridges these two extremes when he holds up each for ridicule, thereby advancing a golden mean between them.

The scene opens as Jessamy and Jonathan discuss the success (or lack of it) which Jonathan has experienced in his endeavor to seduce Jenny, waitress to Maria. Much as would her mistress, Jenny has soundly rebuffed Jonathan's advances. Jessamy's promise to Jonathan of "cherubim consequences" has, alas, been shattered. Jessamy appears at a loss as to how to explain Jonathan's failure to seduce Jenny, much as Dimple is later dumbfounded that his consistent exercise of all of his arts, prescribed for him in Lord Chesterfield's letters to his son, gets him nowhere but in a court of law for bankruptcy and in a possible duel with Manly for his lustful intemperance. In a state of consternation (one which typifies much of the play), Jessamy concludes that Jonathan's failure can only be attributed to his lack of "the graces." Significantly, Jonathan misunderstands the use of the word "graces" and exclaims, "Why, does the young woman expect I must be converted before I court her?" In this exclamation, Jonathan reveals that, though he is certainly familiar with the rhetoric of Protestant conversion, he has not himself capitulated to it. Hence, Jonathan is every inch an American, who, though schooled in the doctrines of John Calvin, has refused to allow himself to become a saint; rather, he retains the proverbial Yankee independence.

Jessamy next attempts to instruct Jonathan in the art of acting natural—that is, appearing sophisticated while at the same time behaving with artless grace. The aspiration is itself a noble one, but Baldassare Castiglione's *sprezzatura* has here become woefully corrupt. First, Jessamy reproves Jonathan for having laughed too naturally at the theater. Jonathan retorts with a most sensible rhetorical question, "What does one go to see fun for if they can't laugh?" Undaunted, Jessamy explains to Jonathan, whom he perceives to be a sort of country bumpkin, that he must affect "natural motions . . . regulated by art." The explicit contradiction here is hardly lost on the not-so-dumb Jonathan. Then Jessamy details so unnatural a gamut of "artful" audience response to comedic action that, if such descriptions were drawn out on the stage, they would approach some of the distorted, contorted figures of Dante's *Inferno*. Picture an entire audience with mouths twisted "into an agreeable simper." How does one "twist" oneself into an agreeable anything?

Nevertheless, so misshapen is Jessamy's conception here that he sees such a scene to resemble a "chorus of Handel's at an Abbey commemoration." Jonathan, however, is not persuaded; he responds much as the audience of Tyler's own time doubtless did: "Ha, ha, ha! that's dang'd cute, I swear." As Colonel Manly is not at all convinced by the pseudosophisticated behavior both of his sister and of Dimple, Jonathan does not for a moment seriously consider adopting Jessamy's counsel concerning the proper response to comedy. Indeed, he has allowed himself to be advised by Jessamy in his approach to Jenny, which has proved most unrewarding. Now he joins the audience, and the comic spirit, in his gentle but definitely unapproving laughter at poor Jessamy, who is diseased with most foolish affectation.

This scene exposes affectation for what it is, insincere behavior that only the most lamentably foolish can long sustain in a world which always prefers reality to falsehood. It also predicts Dimple's inevitable exposure, Charlotte's reform, and Manly's triumph. One essential difference between Jonathan and his master, however, must be pointed out. Unlike Jonathan, who achieves a measure of disinterestedness and aloofness from the action and who learns not to be so gullible, Manly remains relatively static. Even before the action of the play begins, Charlotte tells Letitia that her brother once instructed her that "the best evidence of a gentleman" was that he "endeavor in a friendly manner to rectify [the] foibles" of his lady. At the crucial moment when he realizes that he loves Maria and she loves him but her betrothal to Dimple prevents their happiness, he finds solace in his injunction to Maria and to himself that their respective virtues merit that "we shall, at least, deserve to be" happy. Maria and Manly overcome this obstacle. The point here, however, is to emphasize the difference between master and servant; in keeping with the Roman comedies of Plautus and Terence, the servant is actually the superior of the master. Jonathan's gentle laughter at Jessamy's specious logic firmly grounds *The Contrast* in the real world, while Colonel Manly continues to reside within a world of morose idealism.

Though virtue wins and vice pays the price of depravity, the Comic Spirit who instructs by means of gentle laughter appears still to have the upper hand in *The Contrast*. In good-naturedly correcting excessive behavior, Tyler has created comedy of neither manners nor sentiment, nor of morals. What he has created is a play which bears his own signature—one characterized by an easily recognizable morality but stamped with the gentle judgment of a comedic spirit which anticipates that of George Meredith.

Other major works

NOVEL: *The Algerine Captive*, 1797.

POETRY: *The Verse of Royall Tyler*, 1968 (Marius B. Péladeau, editor).

NONFICTION: *Reports of Cases in the Supreme Court of Vermont*, 1809-1810 (2 volumes); *The Prose of Royall Tyler*, 1972 (includes *The Bay Boy*; Marius B. Péladeau, editor).

Bibliography

Carson, Ada Lou, and Herbert L. Carson. *Royall Tyler.* Boston: Twayne, 1979. This volume offers the most convenient and available account of this early American lawyer, law professor, judge, and scholar.

Silverman, Kenneth. *A Cultural History of the American Revolution: Painting, Music, Literature, and the Theatre in the Colonies and the United States from the Treaty of Paris to the Inauguration of George Washington, 1763-1789.* New York: Thomas Y. Crowell, 1976. The most comprehensive survey of Tyler's life and times. Silverman places Vermont's first scholar in a historical and cultural context.

Tanselle, G. Thomas. *Royall Tyler.* Cambridge, Mass.: Harvard University Press, 1967. This volume has become the standard source on this early American playwright, poet, and novelist.

Tyler, Royall, *The Prose of Royall Tyler.* Edited by Marius B. Péladeau. Montpelier: Vermont Historical Society, 1972. A definitive collection of Tyler's essays, stories, and other work, edited by the leading Tyler authority.

___________. *The Verse of Royall Tyler.* Edited by Marius B. Péladeau. Charlottesville: University Press of Virginia, 1968. A thoughtful collection of Tyler's poetry by the leading authority on this often overlooked early American poet.

John C. Shields
(Updated by *Peter C. Holloran*)

NICHOLAS UDALL

Born: Southampton, England; December, 1505(?)
Died: London, England; December, 1556

Principal drama

Ralph Roister Doister, pr. c. 1552, pb. 1566(?).

Other literary forms

Nicholas Udall is known today almost exclusively as the author of the first regular English comedy, *Ralph Roister Doister*. He was better known in his own time, however, as a scholar and translator. Aside from a few occasional verses and a medical book (*Compendiosa totius anatomie delineatio*, 1552), the balance of Udall's work consists of translations of Latin authors. In 1534, he published *Floures for Latine Spekynge*, a translation into idiomatic English of selected parts of Terence. Two translations of the great Humanist Desiderius Erasmus followed, *Apopthegmes* in 1542 and *The Paraphrase of Erasmus upon the New Testament* in 1549. Finally, in 1550, Udall published a translation of Peter Martyr's Protestant disputation with Roman opponents, *Tractatie de Sacramente* (1549); Udall's work is entitled *A Discourse or Tractise of Petur Martyr.*

Achievements

Udall's literary efforts are almost exclusively connected to his work as a scholar and teacher. Except for a few verses written to celebrate the coronation of Anne Boleyn, the famous wife of Henry VIII and mother of Queen Elizabeth, the translations and plays credited to him were produced to aid him in his profession. Even the play which secured his reputation, the innovative and delightful *Ralph Roister Doister*, was likely composed as a Christmas comedy for a boys' school in London.

The *Floures for Latine Spekynge* is a work written by a schoolmaster for schoolchildren. Udall's work was used in a Latin-English dictionary published in 1548 by Thomas Cooper: *Bibliotheca Eliotae*. Cooper praises "the learned man Udall, by whose scholarly annotations our labors have been lightened in many places, give deserved praise and gratitude."

Udall's purpose in *Floures for Latine Spekynge* was to give students selected Latin passages from Terence as exercises. Udall best explains his intent on the title page: "*Floures for Latine Spekynge* selected and gathered out of Terence, and the same translated into Englyeshe, together with the exposition and settynge forthe as welle of such latyne words, as were thought nedeful to be annoted, as also of dyvers grammatical rules, very profytable and necessary for the expedite knowledge in the latine tongue: Compiled by Nicholas Udall."

In his preface, Udall notes, "I have added wherever it seemed necessary certain scholia as it were, in which both the sense of the poet is explained and the words themselves not a little more clearly declared." The "scholia" were intended to help the neophyte student understand not only the ideas of Terence but also the difficult task of translating those ideas from Latin into English. Instead of translating idioms literally, Udall uses equivalent English idioms, so that the resulting translation is both faithful to the sense of the Latin and at the same time a good English composition. The work was used by hundreds of English schoolchildren to gain an understanding of and an appreciation for classical ideas and language.

More important than *Floures for Latine Spekynge* for Udall's reputation, for both his own generation and the succeeding generation, was his *The Paraphrase of Erasmus upon the New Testament*. Erasmus had popularized scholarly annotations on the New Testament, maintaining the scholarly quality of the commentaries while omitting the jargon and apparatus peculiar to scholarship. Udall employed his skills as an accomplished translator to provide for English readers a clear, lively rendering of the important commentaries.

So important was Udall's translation thought to be to the Protestant clergy, many of whom were ill-prepared as scholars, that royal injunctions in 1547 and 1559 insisted "that every parson, vicar, curate, chantry-priest, and stipendary, being under the degree of bachelor of divinity, shall provide and have of his own . . . the New Testament both in Latin and English, with the Paraphrase upon the same of Erasmus, and diligently study the same, conferring the one with the other. . . ." William L. Edgerton, in his analytical and critical book *Nicholas Udall* (1965), reports that "as late as 1843 a copy of the *Paraphrase of Erasmus* was still chained in two churches in England."

Whether Udall's *Ralph Roister Doister* was as important and influential as his translations is a question not easily answered. The play clearly cannot be considered in the same category as comedies by Ben Jonson or William Shakespeare. Udall's comedy does not develop a complete plot, analyze a significant idea, or probe the psychology of human emotions or foibles, but it does blend classical Roman and native English elements in an English comedy in a way which forms a foundation for the author's more famous successors. Udall is not unreasonably considered the father of English comedy.

Biography

Nicholas Udall (or Udal, Owdall, Uvedale, Owdale, Dowdall, Woodall, Woddell, or Yevedale) was born during the Christmas season, probably of 1505, in Southampton, Hampshire, England. Little is known of his family, but some scholars speculate that the future playwright was a member of the prominent Uvedale family in Hampshire. No record exists of Udall's ever having been married.

In 1517, Udall can be placed in residence at St. Mary's College, Winchester, a school noted for rigorous studies, long days, and few holidays. At Winchester, where Latin was the language both of studies and of daily life, Udall would have studied the works of Vergil, Cicero, Terence, and other Latin authors, but especially Terence, whose subjects and Latin style are accessible to students. Udall's later devotion to the works of Terence can reasonably be traced to his early days at Winchester.

In 1520, Udall was admitted to Corpus Christi College, Oxford, the center for Humanistic studies. Under the tutelage of Thomas Lupset, lecturer and friend of the Humanists Sir Thomas More and Erasmus, the young Udall, in company with his friend John Leland, embraced Humanistic ideas and skills to such an extent that Udall and Leland are usually considered to be "second-generation Humanists." It was at Corpus Christi College also that Udall met Edward Wotton, lecturer in Latin and Greek and a scholarly English physician. Udall's later *Compendiosa totius anatomie delineatio*, an illustrated digest of anatomy, may be traced to his association with Wotton.

At Oxford, Udall likely studied under the Spanish Humanist and Latin lecturer Juan Luis Vives. From Vives, Udall would have been introduced to such Humanistic concepts as the importance of education for women, the importance of the vernacular, and reasonable arguments for morality. Although Vives adopted Plato's opinion of poetry, especially of drama, the Humanistic principles he espoused can be found in Udall's *Ralph Roister Doister*. A clearly English play, written in the vernacular, it has a strong, well-educated heroine in Dame Christian Custance. Furthermore, it is free of the more earthy, obscene, and immoral thoughts, actions, and language of Latin comedies.

The exciting intellectual atmosphere at Oxford might well have led the young scholar-author close to his first scrape with the law. He had received his bachelor of arts degree in 1524 and immediately became a probationary fellow of the college. By 1526, he was a full fellow and lecturer in Greek. In 1527, the English authorities arrested several Oxford men for circulating Lutheran works and the outlawed Tyndale Bible. Apparently Udall was one of several men who were admonished to avoid even the appearance of heresy. Surely the curiosity of these young men, thriving in the center of Humanistic learning, had been drawn to the ideas of the Protestant Reformation.

Udall's whereabouts from 1529, when he left Oxford, until 1533 are not known. Some evidence exists to suggest that he may have traveled in France and Germany, where school drama enjoyed great popularity. By 1533, he was in London, where he and John Leland, his friend from Oxford, wrote verses for the coronation of Anne Boleyn. Using the "Judgment of Paris" theme from Homer and Ovid, Udall and Leland praise the new queen as more beautiful than the three goddesses Hera, Athene, and Aphrodite. The verses are at once hyperbolic and rather dull.

In 1534, Udall turned his attention from polite flattery to scholarship with his *Floures for Latine Spekynge*, a work used for many years to teach Latin to English schoolboys. In June, 1534, soon after the publication of this pedagogical work, Udall was appointed headmaster of Eton. A stern master, one who did not spare the rod, Udall was nevertheless praised for his devotion to the subjects he taught and for his effectiveness as a teacher.

Udall's tenure as headmaster at Eton, however, was not without problems. While his work as a scholar and teacher was without blemish, he did run afoul of the law in his personal life. In 1541, he was charged with complicity in the theft of "certain images of silver and other plate" (according to *Proceedings and Ordinances of the Privy Council of England*, 1834-1837; Harris Nicolas, editor) and was sent to Marshalsea. The *Proceedings* also reports that while "Nic. Vuedall, Schoolmaster of Eton" was being questioned about "other felonious trespasses," he confessed "that he did commit buggery with the said Cheney," Thomas Cheyney, an Eton scholar.

Certainly conviction of such crimes, especially that of buggery, would have been more than serious enough to end the career of any scholar-teacher. Whether it was a case of an error in the records ("buggery" written for "burglary") or of Udall's having powerful friends (namely, Thomas Wriothesley, on the Privy Council) or of his having written a moving letter of apology addressed to "Right Worshipfull and My Singular Good Master," Udall was soon released from custody.

Udall continued his scholarship, publishing in 1542 *Apopthegmes*, a translation of the oral sayings of the ancients collected by Erasmus. That he was, in 1543, appointed to direct a group of scholars in translating *The Paraphrase of Erasmus upon the New Testament* indicates that Udall had escaped the stigma of his conviction and suggests that it was not, after all, buggery for which he was convicted. After devoting several years to this translation and several more years working in a scholarly fashion for the Protestant government, Udall was, in 1549, appointed tutor to Edward Courtenay, then a royal prisoner in the Tower. By 1552, Udall's career was fully recovered from his earlier troubles. He had, during the previous year, been appointed canon of St. George's Chapel at Windsor Castle, and when Edward VI was in residence at Windsor during September of 1552, Udall very likely presented his play *Ralph Roister Doister* for the first time.

When Mary came to the throne in 1553, Udall's work as a Protestant-Humanist scholar was over. By June of 1554, he was replaced as canonary at Windsor, and no more translations of the great Humanists appeared. Extant records show that his reputation as a dramatist was still good: Warrants from Queen Mary indicate that Udall received payment for dramatic entertainment performed in the royal presence.

In December of 1555, Udall was appointed headmaster of St. Peter's Grammar School, Westminster. The year he spent in residence at Westminster seems to have been uneventful; in any case, there are no records of translations, plays, or lawsuits during this period. Udall was never able to resume his important scholarly activities, perhaps because of the Catholic reign of Queen Mary, perhaps because he was ill. What is known is that slightly more than a year after his appointment as headmaster at Westminster, Nicholas Udall died. Under the name "Nicholas Yevedale," he is listed as having been buried on December 23, 1556, at St. Margaret's Church, Westminster.

Analysis

Nicholas Udall would almost certainly have seen mystery and morality plays presented in his community as he was growing up. Traveling companies brought English drama to communities throughout England, including Southampton. When, beginning at the age of twelve, he attended St. Mary's College, Winchester, he likely would have studied the *Poetics* of Aristotle, the major plays of the Greek dramatists, and the Roman comedies of Plautus and Terence, especially those of Terence. While no records exist to indicate specifically which plays might actually have been performed at Winchester while Udall was a student, we do know that Greek and Roman plays were presented at other grammar schools in England at that time, and we know that later in his life Udall demonstrated an analytical knowledge of the works of Terence. Further familiarity with the elements of drama would have come from his participation in, or at least his knowledge of, the ceremony of the Festival of the Boy Bishop, which was celebrated annually at Winchester. The ceremony involved having students take the parts of ecclesiastical officials in presenting divine services at the school. If Udall did not actually participate in such ceremonies, he would certainly have observed them.

It is likely that Udall wrote a number of plays presented during and after his lifetime both in the schools as pedagogical exercises and at court for entertainment; John Bale, the notable Protestant spokesman, credits Udall with *commaediae plures* (many comedies). The only play that, in addition to *Ralph Roister Doister*, can definitely be attributed to Udall is *Ezechias* (c. 1546), a play acted before Queen Elizabeth at Cambridge in 1564, but no longer extant. In this play, which perhaps belonged to Udall's Eton period, Hezekiah was portrayed as a reformer sent by God "to roote up al Idolatry," as Udall wrote in *The Paraphrase of Erasmus upon the New Testament*, comparing King Henry VIII to Hezekiah in that regard.

Two other plays are sometimes thought to be by Udall, but inadequate evidence exists to make such an assertion: *Thersites* (1537), an interlude whose title character is a braggart soldier in the vein of *Ralph Roister Doister*, and *Respublica* (wr. 1553, pb. 1866), a piece of dramatic propaganda illustrating how Roman Catholicism is beneficial to a nation. Still two more plays are occasionally mentioned in connection with Udall, mainly because the authors are unknown and because the plays resemble *Ralph Roister Doister* in some ways. In *Jacob and Esau* (entered in the Stationers' Register in 1557), the household servants of Esau are reminiscent of those in the household of Dame Christian Custance in *Ralph Roister Doister*. In *Jack Juggler* (pb. 1562), a Plautine plot is given English dress, again as in *Ralph Roister Doister*.

Most scholars believe that *Ralph Roister Doister* was written in 1552, at the time the author was canon of St. George's Chapel at Windsor Castle. Udall's purpose was apparently to provide a Christmas comedy for the students of some London school. The plot of the play is simple enough. Ralph Roister Doister is a roistering, bullying coward who, like Shakespeare's Sir Andrew Aguecheek in *Twelfth Night*, is nothing but bluster. He is constantly in love with some woman or another. As the play opens, he is infatuated with Dame Christian Custance, a rich and virtuous widow betrothed to Gawin Goodluck, a merchant who is away on business. Ralph sees himself, quite inaccurately, as God's gift to women and sees no reason why Dame Christian should not be delighted to wed him. In his misapprehension, Ralph is aided by the sycophantic Matthew Merrygreek, who avows that people often mistake Ralph for Launcelot, Guy of Warwick, Hector of Troy, Sampson, Alexander, and others. Merrygreek assures Ralph that he is indeed "the tenth worthy." Thus encouraged, Ralph sends a love letter to Dame Christian.

Using flattery and promises of gifts, Ralph persuades Dame Christian's servant Madge Mumblecrust to take the letter to her mistress. Dame Christian refuses even to open the letter, however, and chastises Madge, ordering her to bring "no mo letters for no man's pleasure." When Dobinet Doughty, Ralph's servant, brings a ring as a present for Dame Christian, Madge, therefore, refuses to deliver it. Dobinet turns to other servants: Tom Truepenny, Tibet Talkapace, and Annot Alyface, who are anxious to take the gift to their mistress. Their reward, however, is a severe scolding from Dame Christian.

Sent by Ralph to learn the effects of his letter and gifts, Merrygreek praises Ralph to Dame Christian, who rejects Ralph utterly, calling him "a very dolt and lout." When he hears of the rejection, the courtly lover Ralph insists that he will surely die. Merrygreek holds a mock funeral, with Ralph interrupting from time to time. Merrygreek advises Ralph "for a while to revive again," in order to get even with Dame Christian, who has caused his death.

When Ralph meets Dame Christian, he again declares his love for her. The virtuous widow, angered at being pestered, tells him plainly: "I will not be served with a fool in no wise; When I choose a husband, I hope to take a man." Reminded that Ralph has sent her tokens of his love and a true love letter, the widow produces the letter and allows Merrygreek to read it. The parasite so alters the punctuation that the letter consistently says the opposite of what Ralph intended it to say. Ralph threatens to avenge himself on the scrivener who wrote the letter for him, but when the scrivener arrives, he so bullies the cowardly Ralph that no revenge is attempted. Merrygreek agrees to explain the misunderstanding to Dame Christian.

Sim Suresby, servant to Goodluck, arrives to see how Dame Christian is getting along. As he and the widow talk, Ralph and Merrygreek come back to explain the love letter. Sim hears enough to arouse his suspicions and leaves to report to his master. Angered at having her good reputation stained, Dame Christian sends Ralph and the mischievous Merrygreek packing; Ralph threatens to burn down her house. Dame Christian sends for her Tristram Trusty to protect her and arms her servants with brooms, clubs, and distaffs to defend herself against the threat. Trusty arrives and assures her that she has nothing to worry about from the cowardly Ralph and the practical joker Merrygreek. When Merrygreek returns, they enlist him as an ally against Ralph.

Ralph returns ready to battle the woman who spurned him and is advised by Merrygreek to show Dame Christian that he is a real man. When she sees Ralph, the widow, as agreed, runs away pretending to be afraid. Even so, Ralph decides to retreat, claiming that he has forgotten his helmet, but Merrygreek gives him a stewpot for his head and urges him forward. With drums beating and flags waving, Ralph inches his way into battle. Dame Christian returns to take on Ralph, while her servants take revenge upon Dobinet for his earlier behavior.

Merrygreek, arguing that he is protecting his valiant friend by striking at the widow, actually pummels Ralph with every blow. Thoroughly battered and defeated, Ralph swears that Dame Christian is an Amazon and wagers that she must have killed her first husband. Shouting "Away, away, away! She will kill us all, " Ralph drops ceremony and runs for his life.

In the meantime, Sim Suresby has reported his suspicions to his master, who has returned home. After talking with his friend Tristram, Gawin Goodluck is reconciled with Dame Christian. To celebrate, Goodluck invites all of his friends to supper. After Merrygreek apologizes for his mischief, Goodluck asks both the parasite and the braggart soldier to join the party. The play ends with a song in praise of the queen.

The plot of *Ralph Roister Doister* is clearly based on the classical Roman model of comedy that Udall knew well from his study of Plautus and Terence. The unities of place and action are strictly adhered to, and the unity of time is not much warped. The scene is consistently simple, a village street. The action, occurring in only slightly more than a day, has a clear beginning, middle, and end.

The character of Ralph Roister Doister is easily traceable to the *Miles Gloriosus* (c. 206 B.C.) of Plautus and Terence's Thraso in *Eunuchus* (pr. 161 B.C.). Ralph's opinion of himself as a great man, one whom love has weakened, is established early in the play and developed consistently throughout the work. Matthew Merrygreek is also a character suggested by the traditional parasite of Roman comedy. Like Diccon of *Gammer Gurton's Needle* (pb. 1575), Merrygreek is an opportunist who depends upon his wit for his livelihood.

As dependent as both Ralph and Merrygreek are on their Roman models, however, both are also distinctively English. Plautus' braggart soldier is brasher, less sociable than Ralph. Terence's Thraso is overweening in his pride; Ralph is merely stupid—agonizingly, painfully, pitifully stupid. Terence's parasite fools Thraso more to further his own interests than in an attempt to increase the festivities of the play. Merrygreek, on the other hand, intends no one any lasting harm. More important than his own gain is the intrinsic humor of the situation of the blockhead, Ralph, in love with a woman whose name he cannot even remember. Merrygreek says early in the play,

> But such sport have I with him as I
> would not leese,
> Though I should be bound to live with
> bread and cheese.

He is more nearly the father of the buffoons who appear in the later English comedies than the son of Roman parasites; in truth, he is both.

Dame Christian Custance can also be traced to Roman comedy. Terence regularly presents heroines in distress who are rescued from dire financial, physical, or social straits. Such a woman is Dame Christian Custance. At the same time, she recalls Geoffrey Chaucer's Constance in "The Man of Law's Tale": Both are women in distress, and both pray to the God who "didst help Susanna wrongly accused." Udall's Custance is distinctive, however, as an English woman beset with local problems and surrounded with English servants.

Perhaps Dame Christian's servants are the most English element in the play. Unlike the servants of Roman comedy, who can never be anything but servants, no matter if they be wiser than their masters, Udall's servants act as though they are all pretenders to the middle class. Dame Christian's servants are clearly not wiser than their mistress, as she often explains to them, but they have a kind of independence unknown to Roman servants.

Madge Mumblecrust does not hesitate to kiss Ralph, who she thinks has come to woo her mistress. Tibet and Annot leap at the chance to take Ralph's love tokens to their mistress because they believe that as soon as Dame Christian is marrried,

> . . . we shall go in our French hoods
> every day,
> In our silk cassocks, I warrant you,
> fresh and gay.

In sum, Udall did not merely translate Plautus and Terence, as Sir Thomas Wyatt and Henry Howard, Earl of Surrey sometimes did Petrarch; rather, Udall added to his classical models elements of native English drama and of life on sixteenth century English streets. All English comedies that followed—those by Shakespeare, Jonson, Thomas Dekker, and even *Gammer Gurton's Needle* (written shortly after *Ralph Roister Doister*)—show great improvements in the genre, but *Ralph Roister Doister* established the type by combining Roman and English elements into a new formula whose total is greater than the sum of its parts.

Because *Ralph Roister Doister* has a secure place in history as the first regular English comedy, scholars sometimes give it more credit than it is due. Although it provided the foundation for the later great English comedies, no one can reasonably discuss it alongside the significant plays of Jonson, Shakespeare, and others. Udall's purpose, as the prologue declares, was to use "mirth with modesty." Who, the audience is asked, would not like to have a story told

> Wherein all scurrility we utterly refuse,
> Avoiding such mirth wherein is abuse,
> Knowing nothing more commendable for
> man's recreation
> Than mirth which is used in an honest
> fashion?

Other major works

NONFICTION: *Compendiosa totius anatomie delineatio*, 1552.

TRANSLATIONS: *Floures for Latine Spekynge*, 1534 (of Terence); *Apopthegmes*, 1542 (of Erasmus); *The Paraphrase of Erasmus upon the New Testament*, 1549 (of Erasmus); *A Discourse or Tractise of Petur Martyr*, 1550 (of Peter Martyr's *Tractatie de Sacramente*).

Bibliography

Bevington, David. *Tudor Drama and Politics: A Critical Approach to Topical Meaning.* Cambridge, Mass.: Harvard University Press, 1968. Discusses Udall under the heading "England Returns to Catholicism." Suggests that *Ralph Roister Doister* was written for performance before Queen Mary with the strength of the woman character Christian Custance designed to please the woman who wore the crown. Provides a comparison with *Respublica*, where male vices also oppose female virtues. Sees *Respublica* as an attack of young Edward's counselors: Authority must lie in the hands of one, not of many. Mary is seen as Nemesis.

Boas, Frederick F. *An Introduction to Tudor Drama.* Reprint. Westport, Conn.: Greenwood Press, 1977. An attractive reprint of the 1933 original edition. Contains basic facts about Udall and his works, including his relationship with Queen Mary and a lawsuit against him in the early 1500's. Offers a comment on the classical influences on Udall, the "most representative" English playwright in the three decades between John Heywood and the major Inns of Court dramas of the 1560's.

Edgerton, William. *Nicholas Udall.* New York: Twayne, 1965. The biographical sections are enlarged by references to major historical events. *Respublica* is dismissed as probably not by Udall. The longest chapter is devoted to *Ralph Roister Doister*, with emphasis on the dating problem and on the presence of Latin influence in the comedy. *Ezechias*, though now lost, is examined for its importance to Tudor England. Annotated bibliography.

Schelling, Felix. *Elizabethan Drama, 1558-1642.* 2 vol. Boston: Houghton Mifflin, 1908. Udall is mentioned passim in volume 1. Provides a lengthy, comprehensive survey of Elizabethan and Stuart drama, with significant attention to Udall, presenting some information not usually covered in shorter surveys or in other works dealing with the writer. Stresses the historical significance of Udall.

Wilson, F. P. *The English Drama, 1485-1585.* New York: Oxford University Press, 1969. A general study of an important century of development in English Renaissance drama, with major points about Udall's life and the four plays attributed to him. Discusses the importance of Plautus in England in the 1500's and the use Udall made of Plautine comedies.

Eugene P. Wright
(Updated by *Howard L. Ford*)

LUIS MIGUEL VALDEZ

Born: Delano, California; June 26, 1940

Principal drama

The Theft, pr. 1961; *The Shrunken Head of Pancho Villa*, pr. 1965, pb. 1967; *Las dos caras del patroncito*, pr. 1965, pb. 1971; *La quinta temporada*, pr. 1966, pb. 1971; *Los vendidos*, pr. 1967, pb. 1971; *Dark Root of a Scream*, pr. 1967, pb. 1973; *La conquista de México*, pr. 1968, pb. 1971 (puppet play); *No saco nada de la escuela*, pr. 1969, pb. 1971; *The Militants*, pr. 1969, pb. 1971; *Vietnam campesino*, pr. 1970, pb. 1971; *Huelguistas*, pr. 1970, pb. 1971; *Bernabé*, pr. 1970, pb. 1976; *Soldado razo*, pr., pb. 1971; *Actos*, pb. 1971 (includes *Las dos caras del patroncito*, *La quinta temporada*, *Los vendidos*, *La conquista de México*, *No saco nada de la escuela*, *The Militants*, *Vietnam campesino*, *Huelguistas*, and *Soldado razo*); *Las pastorelas*, pr. 1971 (adaptation of a sixteenth century Mexican shepherd's play); *La Virgen del Tepeyac*, pr. 1971 (adaptation of *Las cuatro apariciones de la Virgen de Guadalupe*); *Los endrogados*, pr. 1972; *Los olivos pits*, pr. 1972; *La gran carpa de los rasquachis*, pr. 1973; *Mundo*, pr. 1973; *El baille de los gigantes*, pr. 1973; *El fin del mundo*, pr. 1975; *Zoot Suit*, pr. 1978, pb. 1992; *Bandido!*, pr. 1981, pb. 1992; *Corridos*, pr. 1983; *"I Don't Have to Show You No Stinking Badges!*, pr., pb. 1986; *Luis Valdez—Early Works: Actos, Bernabé, and Pensamiento Serpentino*, pb. 1990; *Zoot Suit and Other Plays*, 1992.

Other literary forms

Although Luis Miguel Valdez is known primarily for his plays, his writing on Chicano culture has had a significant impact. In a number of essays in the 1960's and 1970's ("Theatre: El Teatro Campesino," "Notes on Chicano Theatre," and several others), he elaborated an aesthetic based on what he believed to be the special features of Chicano reality: bilingualism, *mestizaje* (mixed race), and cultural disinheritance. Valdez's commitment to Chicano nationalism is reflected in two important works of nontheatrical writing—*Aztlan: An Anthology of Mexican American Literature* (1972; coedited with Stan Steiner), whose lengthy introduction recounts the history of the Chicano people as the original inhabitants of "Aztlan" (the contemporary American Southwest), and *Pensamiento Serpentino: A Chicano Approach to the Theatre of Reality* (1973), which explores the influence of Aztec and Mayan spirituality on Chicano art and thought. It is in this latter book that all of Valdez's published poetry can be found.

Achievements

Without Valdez, the Chicano theater would not exist in its present vibrant form. At the age of twenty-five, in the fields of rural California, without financial backing and using farm laborers as actors, Valdez single-handedly created a movement that has since become international in scope, leading to the founding of Chicano theater troupes from Los Angeles, California, to Gary, Indiana. Although not usually mentioned in the company of revered American playwrights of his generation, such as Sam Shepard, David Mamet, and Richard Foreman, he is in many ways as distinguished and as well-known internationally, both in Europe and in Latin America.

In one respect especially, Valdez has accomplished what no other American playwright has: the creation of a genuine worker's theater, completely indigenous and the work of neither university intellectuals nor producers of a commercialized "mass culture." He has made "serious" drama popular, political drama entertaining, and ethnic drama universal.

Valdez has won acclaim in two parallel but distinct artistic communities. If his early career fits neatly within the contours of the cultural nationalism of the Civil Rights movement (whose Chicano forms in the American Southwest are perhaps less well-known than the African-American forms of the South), he found a hearing also in more established circles. One of the original organizers for the United Farm Workers Union, a tireless propagandist for Chicano identity, and a founder of a still-flourishing annual cultural festival in Fresno, California, he has also been a founding member of the California Arts Council. In addition to this, he served on a congressional subcommittee of the National Endowment for the Arts and on the board of directors of the Theatre Communications Group, and he acted in teleplays and films based on his own work. Winning an honorary Obie Award in 1968 for his work on the West Coast, he appropriately was the first, ten years later, to produce a Chicano play on Broadway, the highly acclaimed *Zoot Suit.*

He cannot, however, be seen simply as a major playwright. His fortunate position as a public figure at the first serious outbreak of Chicano nationalism in the mid-1960's—which he helped articulate, and which helped articulate him—makes him also an emblematic representative of American cultural politics, especially as it regards the important (and often forgotten) Latino community.

Crucial in this respect is his groundbreaking book, *Aztlan*, which brings together documents from the pre-Columbian period to the late twentieth century, sketching a picture of Chicanos as a distinct people with a long tradition and an active history. Valdez's passionate commitment to Chicano nationalism must be seen as a driving force of his art. If *Aztlan* defiantly underlines the uniqueness of the Chicano in an alienating landscape of oppressive "Anglo" institutions, his next book, *Pensamiento Serpentino*, emphasizes the evils of artificially separating peoples on the basis of race and culture; it argues for a common North American experience in a spirit of forgiveness and mutual cooperation and derives its moral approach to contemporary social problems from Aztec and Mayan teachings.

The rarity of someone from Valdez's background and interests finding so distinctive a public voice cannot be underestimated. Nevertheless, his greatest work is probably the legacy he leaves to Chicano culture itself. The Centro Campesino Cultural, a nonprofit corporation which he founded in Del Rey, California, in 1967, became a clearinghouse for Chicano artists around the country and operated film, publishing, and musical recording facilities for their use. Inspired by the success of Teatro Campesino, many other groups have come into being. Some of the most important are Teatro Urbano, El Teatro de la Esperanza, El Teatro de la Gente, and El Teatro Desengañó del Pueblo. It is the pioneering work of Valdez that has allowed these vital regional theaters to operate in a coordinated and organized fashion under a national network known as TENAZ (El Teatro Nacional de Aztlan), a direct offshoot of the Centro Campesino Cultural.

Biography

Luis Miguel Valdez was born on June 26, 1940, in Delano, California, the second of ten brothers and sisters. His father and mother were migrant farmworkers. Already working in the fields by the age of six, Valdez spent his childhood traveling to the harvests in the agricultural centers of the San Joaquin Valley. Despite having little uninterrupted early schooling, he managed to win a scholarship to San Jose State College in 1960.

Soon after his arrival at college, he won a regional playwriting contest for his first one-act play, *The Theft*. Encouraged by his teachers to write a full-length work, Valdez complied with *The Shrunken Head of Pancho Villa*, which was promptly produced by the San Jose State Drama Department. Graduating with a bachelor's degree in English in 1964, Valdez spent the next several months traveling in Cuba; upon his return, he joined the San Francisco Mime Troupe under Ron Davis, where he worked for one year, learning from the troupe's *commedia dell'arte* techniques, which he was later to adapt in new ways.

Partly as a result of the sense of solidarity which he gained from his experiences while in Cuba, Valdez returned home to Delano, where the United Farm Workers Union was then being formed under the leadership of César Chávez. Amid a strike for union recognition, the union officials responded enthusiastically to Valdez's offer to create an educational theater group. Using volunteer actors from among the strikers, he formed the Teatro Campesino in 1965. Traveling on a flatbed truck from field to field, the troupe produced a series of one-act political skits dubbed *actos* (actions, or gestures), performing them in churches, storefronts, and on the edges of the fields themselves.

Enormously successful, the plays soon won outside attention, and led to a United States tour in the summer of 1967. Later that year, Valdez left the fields to found the Centro Campesino Cultural in Del Rey, California. Similar recognition followed, with an Obie Award in New York in 1969 for "creating a workers' theater to demonstrate the politics of survival" and an invitation to perform at the Theatre des Nations festival in Nancy, France—one of four tours to Europe between 1969 and 1980. Later in 1969, Valdez and the troupe moved to Fresno, California, where they founded an annual Chicano theater festival, and Valdez began teaching drama at Fresno State College.

The Centro Campesino Cultural relocated once again in 1971 to San Juan Bautista, a small rural California town, where it would stay for the next several years, rooting itself in the community and transforming its dramaturgy to reflect local concerns—particularly through its adaptations of earlier devotional drama dating from the Spanish occupation. Teatro Campesino there underwent a fundamental transformation. Living more or less in a commune, the group began increasingly to emphasize the spiritual side of their work, as derived not only from the prevalent Christianity of the typical Chicano community but also from their own newfound Aztec and Mayan roots. This shift from the agitational *actos* to a search for spiritual solutions was met with anger by formerly admiring audiences at the Quinto Festival de los Teatros Chicanos in Mexico City in 1974.

From its base in San Juan Bautista, the Centro Campesino Cultural continued to flourish, touring campuses and communities on a yearly basis; giving financial support, training, and advice to other theater troupes; and hosting visitors such as English director Peter Brook, who brought his actors from the International Centre of Theatre Research in 1973. After a career of refusing to participate in the commercial theater, Valdez determined finally, in 1978, to try reaching a middle-class audience. The result was *Zoot Suit*, a polished, full-length dance-musical based on the "Sleepy Lagoon" murder trial of 1943. It premiered at the Mark Taper Forum in Los Angeles in 1978 and ran for eleven months. The play opened at the Wintergarden Theatre on Broadway in 1979 but was forced to close after a month because of bad reviews. A film version of the play was made in 1981. In 1985, *Soldado razo* and *Dark Root of a Scream* were performed for the first time in New York at the Public Theater as part of a Latino theater festival.

Valdez brought Tony Curiel into the Teatro Campesino in 1985 to help run the company. Valdez's play *"I Don't Have to Show You No Stinking Badges!"* (a famous line from the 1948 film *The Treasure of the Sierra Madre*) was coproduced with the Los Angeles Theatre Center in 1986. The film *La Bamba* (1987), written and directed by Valdez, was the first major release to celebrate the urban Hispanic youth life-style.

In 1991, a trio of *actos* from earlier Teatro Campesino projects were presented in Dallas at the South Dallas Cultural Center; reviewers noted that they remained "remarkably fresh and quick-witted." *Soldado razo*, a

1970's play of protest about Chicano involvement in the Vietnam War, was revived in San Jose, California, in 1991.

El Teatro Campesino began the process of restructuring in 1988, learning to work more independently of Valdez, although his commitment to it remained substantial. On July 29, 1990, in a retrospective in the *Los Angeles Times* in celebration of Valdez's fiftieth birthday ("Luis Valdez at 50: The Rage Has Cooled"), the playwright, firmly established in Hollywood, admitted: "I couldn't turn around and kiss the teatro good-bye . . . without ruining my chances in Hollywood . . . my roots would dry up. I need to be true to what I set out to do."

Analysis

Luis Miguel Valdez's genius was to reach an audience both Chicano and working-class, not only with political farces about strikers, "scabs," and bosses in a familiar street-theater concept but also by incorporating the popular theatrical forms of Latino America itself—the *carpas* (traveling theater shows), *variedades* (Mexican vaudeville), *corridos* (traditional Mexican folk ballads), and others. It is a unique combination to which Valdez added his own distinctive forms. Appraising Valdez's work is, however, different from appraising that of most other playwrights of his stature. By political conviction and by necessity, much of his oeuvre is a collective product. While he has always been Teatro Campesino's major creative inspiration, and although entire passages from the collective plays were written by him alone, Valdez's drama is largely a joint project under his guidance—a collective political and religious celebration.

The starting point for all of Valdez's work is his evocation of what he calls *la plebe*, *el vulgo*, or simply *La Raza*, that is, the Chicano people. It is from this outlook that the first *actos* were created—a genre very close to the Brechtian *Lehrstück* (teaching piece), with its episodic structure, its use of broad social types, its indifference to all but the most minimal of props and scenery, and its direct involvement of the audience in the solving of its dramatized social problems. In Valdez's words, the *actos* "must be popular, subject to no other critics except the pueblo itself, but it must also educate the pueblo toward an appreciation of *social change*, on and off the stage."

According to various accounts, the form was first developed in a Delano storefront, where Valdez had assembled his would-be performers from among the strikers. He hung signs around their necks which read: *huelguista* (striker), *esquirol* (scab), and *patroncito* (little boss) and then simply asked them to show what had happened that day on the picket line. After some hesitation, the actors performed an impromptu political play, alive with their own jargon and bawdy jokes and inspired by the passions of the labor dispute within which they found themselves.

One exemplary early *acto* is *Las dos caras del patroncito* (the two faces of the boss), in which a typical undocumented worker, recruited fresh from Mexico by a California landowner in order to scab on the strike, exchanges roles with his *patroncito*. Dressed in a pig mask and speaking in an absurd Texas drawl, the *patroncito* playfully suggests that he temporarily trade his own whip for the *esquirol*'s pruning sheers. The two quickly assume the inner reality of these symbolic outward forms. The climactic moment occurs when the owner removes his mask, at which point the *esquirol* has the revelation that worker and boss look (and therefore are) the same. Calling now for help, the boss is mistaken by the police for a troublemaker and is hauled offstage, shouting for César Chávez and declaring his support for *La huelga* (the strike). The social tensions and contradictions of this role-reversal are central to all the *actos*. If the boss is brought down to a vulnerable stature and the worker is shown to be capable of leadership, there is no simplistic identification of one or the other as totally good or evil.

In the next stage of his career, Valdez explored the legends and myths of the Chicano's *indio* past. *Bernabé* is perhaps Valdez's most fully realized *mito* (myth-play). The hero is a thirty-one-year-old village idiot who has never had sexual relations with a woman. At the same time, he is a symbolic embodiment of the Chicano who possesses what Valdez calls "divinity in madness." After a series of taunts by the village toughs and an embarrassing encounter with Consuela, the local prostitute, Bernabé flees to a favorite hiding place in the countryside, where he has dug a gravelike hole in which he frequently masturbates in a kind of ritual copulation with *La Tierra* (the earth).

The climactic scene occurs when the elemental surroundings take on the forms of an Aztec allegory. *La Luna* (the moon) appears dressed as a *pachuco* (an urban Chicano zoot-suiter), smoking marijuana and acting as a go-between for his sister *La Tierra*, who then enters in the costume of a Mexican revolutionary camp follower (the proverbial "Adelita"). In the interchange, *La Tierra* questions the extent of Bernabé's love for her—whether he is "Chicano" enough to kill and to die for her. It is precisely his status as *loco* (crazy) that gives him the courage finally to say yes, and *El Sol* (the sun), as father, is pleased. As if mimicking the sacrifices to the Aztec sun god, Huitzilopochtli, Bernabé offers his physical heart to *La Tierra* and immediately ceases being the village idiot he was before, buried now within the earth but living on as a lesson to his people.

Valdez was to refine further this allegorical (and less immediately political) approach to Chicano identity in his plays throughout the 1970's, particularly in *La gran carpa de los rasquachis* (the great tent of the underdogs) and *El fin del mundo* (the end of the world), which further developed the use of the Mexican *corrido* (musical ballad), the split-level staging designed to evoke a mythical and suprahistorical realm of action, and the traditional images from Spanish American religious drama—particularly the *calavera* (skeleton) costume. In *El fin del mundo*, his play had become a full-scale allegorical ballet—a great dance of death.

With his first deliberate turn to the commercial theater in 1978, Valdez incorporated the *mito*, *acto*, and *corrido* in the unlikely framework of a play about the urban Chicano of the 1940's. *Zoot Suit*—filled with stylized scenes from the Los Angeles barrio—was a drama about a celebrated murder trial and the racist hysteria surrounding it. A panorama of American life of the time, the play deliberately adopted many of the outward features of the "professional" theater, while transforming them for its purposes. It displayed immense photographic projections of newspaper headlines, slickly choreographed dances and songs, and the overpowering central image of the narrator himself, dressed in a zoot suit—the mythical *pachuco*. To an extent greater than in any other of his plays, the work addressed Americans as a whole, reviving for them a historical moment of which they had never been aware and bringing them face-to-face with their latent prejudices.

"I Don't Have to Show You No Stinking Badges!," Valdez's most celebrated play, concerns a middle-class Chicano family's attempts to blend into the American cultural mainstream. The family's parents, Buddy and Connie Villa, are middle-aged bit-part actors who play stereotyped Latino roles in television and films; their son, Sonny, is a law student who disapproves of his parents' work, which he finds demeaning. The play's mixture of the themes of generational and cultural conflict drew wide praise, and the work confirmed Valdez's standing as an important contemporary dramatist.

Valdez's theatrical vision is inseparable from the conditions under which he founded the Teatro Campesino in the farmworkers' strike of 1965. Born in struggle, his early plays all have a vitality, directness, and urgency that cannot be divorced from their lasting appeal. His achievement blossoms finally with his successful incorporation of the deep cultural roots of the Chicano nation, which are found in the religious imagery of the *indio* past. Both facets of his career have been widely copied by other Chicano directors and playwrights and admired widely outside the Chicano community as well.

Other major works

SCREENPLAYS: *Zoot Suit*, 1982; *La Bamba*, 1987.

TELEPLAYS: *Fort Figueroa*, 1988; *La Pastorela*, 1991.

ANTHOLOGY: *Aztlan: An Anthology of Mexican American Literature*, 1972 (with Stan Steiner).

MISCELLANEOUS: *Pensamiento Serpentino: A Chicano Approach to the Theatre of Reality*, 1973.

Bibliography

Flores, Arturo C. *El Teatro Campesino de Luis Valdez.* Madrid: Editorial Pliegos, 1990. This five-chapter study, unfortunately as yet not translated from the Spanish, examines the importance, gradual development, theoretical considerations, touring and "return to identity," and the "steps to commercialization (1975-1980)" represented by *Zoot Suit.* A strong study with a bibliography; no photographs.

Huerta, Jorge A. *Chicano Theatre: Themes and Forms.* Ypsilanti, Mich.: Bilingual Press, 1982. This well-written and well-illustrated study begins with Valdez's experiences in Delano in 1965. It contains an excellent immediate description with dialogue of these first energies and is written in the present tense for immediacy and energy. Provides some discussion of the beginnings of the San Francisco mime troupe and strong description of the *actos* and their literary history in Europe. Highly descriptive and lively. Valuable bibliography and index.

__________. "Labor Theatre, Street Theatre, and Community Theatre in the Barrio, 1965-1983." In *Hispanic Theatre in the United States*, edited by Nicolas Kanellos. Houston: Arte Publico Press, 1984. Placed at the end of a longer study of Hispanic theater history, this essay takes on more importance by indicating that Valdez's contribution belongs in a continuum of history. Under the wing of César Chávez's farm labor-union, the playwright used the workers in a manner reminiscent of Clifford Odets' *Waiting for Lefty* (pr., pb. 1935). Good on contemporaries of El Teatro Campesino; strong bibliography.

Kanellos, Nicolas. *Mexican American Theater: Legacy and Reality.* Pittsburgh: Latin American Literary Review Press, 1987. Begins with an examination of Valdez's transformation from director of El Teatro Campesino, in league with the rural farm worker, to the urban commercial playwright of *Zoot Suit* in 1978, "an attempt at addressing a mass audience on a commercial basis." Cites Valdez's contribution to the "discernible period of proliferation and flourishing in Chicano theatres" from 1965 to 1976, then moves on to examine other offshoots of the impulse.

Morales, Ed. "Shadowing Valdez." *American Theatre* 9 (November, 1992): 14-19. An excellent essay on Valdez, his followers, his film plans, his shelved Frida Kahlo project (he was criticized for casting an Italian American in the role of Kahlo), and later productions in and around Los Angeles, with production stills. Includes an essay entitled "Statement on Artistic Freedom" by Valdez, in which he defends his nontraditional casting: "My first objective is to create mutual understanding between Americans and Mexicans, not to provoke more mistrust and suspicion."

Orona-Cordova, Roberta. "*Zoot Suit* and the Pachuco Phenomenon: An Interview with Luis Valdez." In *Mexican American Theatre: Then and Now*, edited by Nicolas Kanellos. Houston: Arte Publico Press, 1983. The opening of the film version of *Zoot Suit* in 1982 prompted this interview, in which Valdez reveals much about his motives for working, his view of Chicano literature and art, and his solutions to "the entrenched attitude" that will not allow Chicano participation in these industries. Much on Pachuquismo from an insider's point of view.

Pottlitzer, Joanne. *Hispanic Theater in the United States and Puerto Rico: A Report to the Ford Foundation.* New York: Ford Foundation, 1988. This volume provides a brief history to 1965 and discusses the Hispanic theater during the upheaval of the Vietnam War. Also examines the theater's activities and budget, and pays homage to the inspiration of El Teatro Campesino and Valdez. Supplemented by an appendix and survey data.

Timothy Brennan
(Updated by *Thomas J. Taylor*
and *Robert McClenaghan*)

SIR JOHN VANBRUGH

Born: London, England; January 24, 1664 (baptized)
Died: London, England; March 26, 1726

Principal drama

The Relapse: Or, Virtue in Danger, pr., pb. 1696; *Aesop*, *Part I*, pr. 1696, pb. 1697, *Part II*, pr., pb. 1697 (based on Edmé Boursault's play *Les Fables d'Ésope*); *The Provok'd Wife*, pr., pb. 1697; *The Country House*, pr. 1698, pb. 1715 (based on Florent-Carton Dancourt's play *La Maison de Campagne*); *The Pilgrim*, pr., pb. 1700 (based on John Fletcher's play *The Pilgrim*); *The False Friend*, pr., pb. 1702 (based on Alain-René Lesage's play *Le Traître puni*); *Squire Trelooby*, pr., pb. 1704, (with William Congreve and William Walsh; adaptation of Molière's play *Monsieur de Pourceaugnac*); *The Confederacy*, pr., pb. 1705 (based on Florent-Carton Dancourt's play *Les Bourgeoises à la mode*); *The Mistake*, pr. 1705, pb. 1706 (based on Molière's play *Le Dépit amoureux*); *The Cuckold in Conceit*, pr. 1707 (adaptation of Molière's play *Sganarelle: Ou, Le Cocu imaginaire*); *A Journey to London*, pb. 1728 (unfinished; also as *The Provok'd Husband*, pr., pb. 1728, with revisions by Colley Cibber).

Other literary forms

Sir John Vanbrugh also wrote *A Short Vindication of "The Relapse" and "The Provok'd Wife"* (1698). The standard edition of Vanbrugh's dramatic and nondramatic works is the four-volume edition prepared by Bonamy Dobrée and Geoffrey Webb (1927-1928).

Achievements

Despite his numerous translations and adaptations of others' plays, Vanbrugh's fame rests on his two complete original plays, *The Relapse* and *The Provok'd Wife*. These comedies reflect the transition from the Restoration comedy of manners to the sentimental comedy that dominated the theater of the eighteenth century. Vanbrugh's plays are transitional only in a very limited sense, however, because the species of comedy Vanbrugh developed, a comedy that presents problems realistically but rejects both cynicism and simplistic solutions to complex problems, did not prosper.

Vanbrugh's primary interest was in the treatment of serious moral issues through careful and consistent characterization. His plays focus primarily on problems that can arise after marriage, rather than on those of courtship, and they explore the relationship between marital incompatibility and infidelity. While Vanbrugh's comedies neither approve nor excuse adultery, they indicate the ways in which husbands can unintentionally encourage their wives to be unfaithful. Although Vanbrugh employs many of the stock character-types of the comedy of manners, he endows them with a new freshness and significance by combining types and by presenting these types in new contexts. Moreover, in Vanbrugh's plays, in contrast to Restoration comedy, characters may be evaluated according to their exercise of charity and common sense rather than simply according to the quality of their wit. Although wit provides much of the humor in Vanbrugh's plays, the dialogue is remarkable more for realism and vigor than for aphoristic polish. Characters also express emotion, especially sexual passion, physically as well as verbally onstage, and this physical element provides some additional humor in the form of farce.

Although some characters in *The Relapse* and *The Provok'd Wife* experience genuine moral struggles and speak of virtue with veneration and without cynicism, Vanbrugh's plays cannot be classified as sentimental comedies. Unlike sentimental comedies, Vanbrugh's plays do not present a facile reformation of immoral characters; rather, they maintain consistency of characterization and thus fail to offer entirely happy conclusions. *The Provok'd Wife* and *The Relapse* are criticized most often for their failure to resolve all the problems each raises.

Biography

Sir John Vanbrugh's parents were Giles Vanbrugh, a prosperous London sugar refiner, and Elizabeth Barker Carleton, a wealthy heiress and widow. His exact birth date is not known; however, he was baptized January 24, 1664. Vanbrugh was probably educated at the King's School in Chester, and, in 1683, he visited France, possibly to study architecture. He did not immediately start his architectural career but obtained a commission in the Earl of Huntingdon's Regiment of Foot. He resigned this commission in August of the same year, and his whereabouts for the next five years are uncertain. In September, 1688, Vanbrugh was arrested in France for his support of William of Orange. He remained imprisoned in France on charges of espionage until 1692, spending the last seven months of his captivity in the Bastille, where he composed an early draft of *The Provok'd Wife*.

Upon his release from the Bastille in November of 1692, Vanbrugh returned to England, where he briefly resumed a military career, only to abandon it again, this time for dramatic pursuits. Encouraged by the success of *The Relapse*, the first of his plays to be produced, he brought to the stage *Aesop, Part I* in December, 1696; *Aesop, Part II* in March, 1697; and *The Provok'd Wife* in April, 1697. *The Provok'd Wife* was the last original play Vanbrugh completed: After responding in an essay to the attacks made upon his plays by Jeremy Collier's *A Short View of the Immorality and Profaneness of the English Stage* (1698), Vanbrugh directed his dramatic gifts toward translating and adapting the plays of others. The one additional original comedy he attempted, *A Journey to London*, was unfinished at the time of his death. After Vanbrugh's death, his old friend Colley Cibber revised and completed the play, which was presented in 1728 as *The Provok'd Husband*.

At about the same time as Collier launched his attack, Vanbrugh's career in architecture suddenly blossomed. By 1700, Vanbrugh was already at work on his first commission, Castle Howard, which Charles Howard, third Earl of Carlisle, commissioned him to build. Vanbrugh's work so pleased Carlisle that he helped Vanbrugh become Comptroller of the Board of Works in 1702. Vanbrugh was thus involved in the building of many public buildings as well as country homes, and he became one of the foremost English architects of the eighteenth century. His most famous architectural achievement is Blenheim Palace, a project that was a source of great political, legal, and financial trouble for him. Vanbrugh also designed and, with William Congreve, managed the Queen's Theatre in Haymarket, which opened in 1705. The theater was not a success, largely because Vanbrugh's massive design caused serious acoustical problems, making it unsuitable for the production of either plays or operas, which Vanbrugh had vainly hoped to popularize in England. In 1708, Vanbrugh sold his interests in this enormous drain on his spirit and pocketbook.

Vanbrugh married only once, happily, to Henrietta Yarborough in 1719. On March 26, 1726, in the Whitehall home that he had designed and that Jonathan Swift had dubbed Goose-Pie House, Vanbrugh died of a quinsy.

Analysis

Although *The Provok'd Wife* was the first play that Sir John Vanbrugh wrote, the first of his comedies to be produced was *The Relapse*. Written in six weeks as part response, part sequel, to Colley Cibber's *Love's Last Shift* (pr. 1696), *The Relapse* was an immediate popular and critical success. The play was performed by the Drury Lane Company, the same company that had presented *Love's Last Shift*; the original cast included John Verbruggen (as Loveless), Susanna Verbruggen (as Berinthia), George Powell (as Worthy), and, in a "breeches part," Mary Kent as Young Fashion. The choice role of Lord Foppington went to Colley Cibber, who had acted as well as created Lord Foppington's original, Sir Novelty Fashion. Although Vanbrugh adopted Cibber's double-plot structure, he retained only the main characters from the original play; Young Fashion and Lord Foppington (in Cibber, Sir Novelty Fashion) appear in *Love's Last Shift*, but Young Fashion's personality and the relationship between the brothers bear very little resemblance to those of the corresponding characters in *The Relapse*.

In writing *The Relapse*, Vanbrugh explored the comic and psychological possibilities suggested by the sudden reformation of the rake Loveless at the end of *Love's Last Shift*. *The Relapse* does not ridicule the idea that a rake can reject vice because of the influence of a virtuous woman—indeed, *The Relapse* itself presents such a rapid reformation in the rake Worthy. Rather, Vanbrugh's play explores the extent to which one's attempt to be virtuous, however sincere, can withstand temptation. Further, in *The Relapse* the moral complexity of the situation is deepened, for Amanda, too, experiences real temptation and undergoes a genuine moral struggle.

Like most English comedies, *The Relapse* presents not one but two plots: Scenes focusing on the concerns of Loveless and Amanda alternate with scenes centering on Lord Foppington and Young Fashion. These two plots are very tenuously connected by a single visit from Lord Foppington to Loveless and Amanda. Because each plot seems to be afforded equal emphasis and development, readers have not always accepted Vanbrugh's assertion in *A Short Vindication of "The Relapse" and "The Provok'd Wife"* that the Loveless-Amanda plot is the central concern of the play.

The Relapse opens with the reformed Loveless expounding in irregular blank verse his contentment with his wife and his quiet, virtuous life in the country. Although Amanda is pleased by her husband's dedication to virtue, she is apprehensive at his insistence that he is capable of withstanding any temptation the city may offer during their forthcoming visit. Her fears deepen after they arrive in London, when Loveless confesses his attraction to a young woman he noticed at the playhouse. Although Loveless' strong sexual appetite is typical of the rake-hero of Restoration comedy, his pride in his chastity (however short-lived) and his verse panegyric to virtue certainly are not.

Whereas in Restoration comedy the wife who contemplates adultery typically concerns herself only with pragmatic considerations and is an object of derisive laughter, Amanda undergoes a real moral struggle and elicits our sympathy and admiration. Unaware that her cousin is the object of her husband's desire, she confesses to Berinthia her contrary emotional responses to Lord Foppington's and Worthy's unsuccessful attempts to seduce her. In response to Berinthia's inquiry whether she will remain chaste should Loveless again betray her, Amanda predicts that, despite her consequent loss of love for him, she will retain her virtue. Amanda vehemently rejects Berinthia's suggestion that she avenge herself on a straying Loveless by cuckolding him, innocently dismissing Berinthia's wholly serious suggestion as mere wit. In the scenes in which Berinthia—not, as in Restoration comedy, a potential lover—tries to persuade Amanda to allow herself to be seduced, Berinthia's cynicism concerning love and marriage becomes evident. Berinthia's wit and her cynical and exploitative conception of human relationships align her with the characters of Restoration comedy, just as Amanda's implicit faith in her husband and often vocalized dedication to virtue anticipate the qualities of the heroine of sentimental comedy.

Eager to conceal the affair she wishes to have with Loveless, Berinthia agrees to Worthy's scheme to distract Amanda by entangling her in an affair with Worthy. Aware that Amanda will be more receptive to Worthy's attentions if she feels abused and betrayed by Loveless, Berinthia offers to confirm Amanda's suspicions concerning Loveless' fidelity by enabling Amanda to observe him meeting his mistress. In addition to informing Amanda of Loveless' betrayal, Berinthia also repeatedly tells her of Worthy's devotion.

Amanda's convictions are put to the test when she sees Loveless meet his mistress (whom she never recognizes as Berinthia) for a rendezvous. Although she knows that Loveless truly cares for her, that he only "runs after something for variety," Amanda is so deeply disturbed at finding him relapsed into rakehood that she momentarily considers duplicating his sin. Immediately, however, Amanda rejects such moral relativism, declaring in a lengthy verse speech that her husband's fall would in no way excuse her own. Though her love for him has died, her love for virtue is unaltered. Thus, despite Amanda's intense attraction to him, Worthy's advances fail utterly. Resisting his attempts to seduce her at first with words and later with force, she insists that the only proof of Worthy's love that she will accept is his not tempting her virtue. Amanda leaves the awed Worthy alone onstage to confess the profundity of his admiration and love for Amanda and for virtue. As Loveless once had, he now dedicates himself to virtue, though he realistically prefaces his announcement of his reformation with "How long this influence may last, heaven knows. . . . "

This last section of the Loveless-Amanda plot, like the first, is written entirely in blank verse, perhaps to emphasize the high seriousness of the ideas. Nevertheless, the conclusion of this plot is at best partial, for several serious problems remain unresolved: Loveless has not reformed, and there is no suggestion that he will reform or that Amanda's love for him will be rekindled; even at the moment of his repentance, Worthy admits the fragility of his love for virtue; and Amanda's only reward for her chastity is her not being raped by Worthy. Worthy's attempted rape of Amanda, like Loveless' mock-rape of the softly protesting Berinthia, is also significant in that in these scenes, passion is presented onstage in an overtly physical rather than in a detached, intellectualized manner, as was the case in Restoration comedy.

Like the Loveless-Amanda plot, the Lord Foppington-Young Fashion plot also employs and adapts the elements of Restoration comedy. The humor in this plot, unlike that of the other, comes largely from farce, though Lord Foppington also provides humor of wit. Having expended his small inheritance, Young Fashion unsuccessfully appeals for money to his wealthy, wasteful, and selfish brother, Lord Foppington, and ultimately relieves his financial distress by stealing his brother's bride, Miss Hoyden.

Although Young Fashion shares the Restoration rake-hero's refined tastes and insight into human nature, he has a more fully developed conscience than does the rake, for he gives his brother several opportunities to avert being duped by exercising even minimal generosity.

Young Fashion's brother, Lord Foppington, is unquestionably the wittier of the pair, but it is clearly not he with whom the audience is intended to sympathize. In Lord Foppington, Vanbrugh transforms the intellectually deficient, self-deluded fop of Restoration comedy into a heartless yet self-aware egotist. Unlike his predecessors, Lord Foppington is not a fop because he lacks sufficient wit to establish proper values: An intelligent but unscrupulous man, he deliberately adopts contemptible values and displays ludicrous behavior because he knows that those who do so prosper most in society. Cruelly selfish, he advises his brother to become a highwayman and thus obtain relief from his problems through theft or hanging. Lord Foppington's awareness of and indifference to the consequences of his distorted priorities provide a novel and serious undercurrent to the traditional fop scenes. Such concern with the moral implications of a fool's actions, rather than mere laughter at the fool's expense, indicates Vanbrugh's movement away from the Restoration comedy ethos and toward that of sentimental comedy.

Another character who is based on a Restoration comedy type is Miss Hoyden, a virginal but sexually precocious country girl. Hoyden's virtue is merely technical, having been preserved only by the watchfulness of her overly protective father, also a Restoration comedy country type. Moral questions do not trouble Hoyden: Unconcerned about committing bigamy, she readily marries the real Lord Foppington after having just married an impostor. Hoyden ultimately rejects her second spouse and retains her first not because of any promptings of conscience or affection but because she finds Young Fashion more attractive physically and because she expects he will be less likely to restrict her spending than would his brother.

Though Young Fashion is pleased to have stolen Miss Hoyden for himself, he is aware of her moral shortcomings, including the likelihood that, once in London, she will be successfully pursued by young beaux. Young Fashion does not contemplate his imminent cuckoldom with much distress, however, assuring himself that the size of Hoyden's estate will provide him with sufficient consolation. Certainly in this plot, unlike the other, marriage and adultery are not weighty concerns; marital compatibility and virtue are of no importance to either party; the ultimate priority for these characters is financial. Thus, though Young Fashion's reluctance to deceive his brother suggests that he has a conscience, he is nevertheless not a typical hero of sentimental comedy; his complacency about marrying and being cuckolded solely for money indicates that he does not share their veneration of virtue.

From its opening at the Lincoln's Inn Fields playhouse early in 1697 through the middle of the eighteenth century, *The Provok'd Wife* enjoyed an even more frequent production than did *The Relapse*. Sir Thomas Betterton, the head of the company, was the first actor to play Sir John Brute, a role that became a favorite of eighteenth century actors, including Colley Cibber and David Garrick. Because of its occasional coarseness in dialogue and action and its ambiguous moral stance concerning adultery, the popularity of *The Provok'd Wife* declined during the latter half of the eighteenth century, despite the revision of material that the new audience would have found objectionable. Even more than *The Relapse*, *The Provok'd Wife* is concerned with problems between couples after marriage, but whereas *The Relapse* focuses on the effects of adultery, *The Provok'd Wife* focuses on its causes. In *The Provok'd Wife*, as in *The Relapse*, there is a secondary plot involving a courtship, but the more carefully unified structure of *The Provok'd Wife* makes it evident that the Sir John-Lady Brute-Constant plot rather than the Heartfree-Bellinda-Lady Fancyfull plot is the main concern of the play.

The Provok'd Wife opens with Sir John Brute voicing in soliloquy his contempt for marriage and for his wife. Despite his awareness of her attractiveness and virtue, he never loved Lady Brute but married her only in order to satisfy his sexual desire for her. His irrational hostility in response to Lady Brute's polite inquiry whether he will be dining at home is typical of his treatment of her throughout the play. Although antipathy toward marriage typifies the Restoration rake-hero, Sir John's poor manners, his disregard for his appearance, his belligerence, cowardice, coarse language, and lack of wit and self-control certainly are not. Thus, with Sir John, Vanbrugh put the cynical sentiments of the Restoration comedy rake-hero into the mouth of a despicable character.

Although, like Amanda, Lady Brute is a mistreated wife who elicits the sympathy of the audience, unlike Amanda, she is partly to blame for having entangled herself in such an unhappy match, as she admits in her soliloquy. Though forewarned of the problems that would arise between them, she married Sir John not for love but for money, vainly assuming that she could control his behavior through her sexual charms. Nevertheless, it is she who most earns sympathy because, unlike Sir John, she tries to make the best of this unfortunate union and struggles to remain a pleasant and virtuous companion to her husband. Despite her unwillingness to cuckold Sir John, Lady Brute does not derive the same degree of satisfaction from maintaining her virtue that Amanda does, nor does she always discuss virtue with Amanda's deep seriousness. For Lady Brute, chastity is a source of frustration rather than of comfort, and though she fails to convince herself of the justice of discarding her marriage vows, she cynically questions accepted assumptions about the rewards of virtue. Lady Brute is thus not the model of self-restraint Amanda is, but she is decidedly the more human of the two women.

At the end of her soliloquy, Lady Brute is joined by her cousin and confidante, Bellinda, who is aware of the mutual attraction between Lady Brute and Constant. Unlike Amanda's confidante, Berinthia, Bellinda is virtuous and does not try to manipulate her friend into committing adultery. Lady Brute's and Bellinda's witty discussion of sexual matters is reminiscent of Restoration comedy, but here, as in *The Relapse*, the discussion is between two women rather than between a woman and her would-be lover. Unlike Amanda's, Lady Brute's wit is as sharp as is that of her confidante, and throughout their conversation, the intelligence, perceptiveness, and fundamental virtuousness of both women are emphasized.

Attention is next directed to Lady Fancyfull, a female fop also drawn from the Restoration comedy tradition, whose vanity and affectation emphasize by contrast Lady Brute's and Bellinda's self-awareness and naturalness. Like that of Lord Foppington of *The Relapse*, Lady Fancyfull's foolishness is the result of conscious effort. So adamant is Lady Fancyfull in her self-delusion that she rejects without reflection the constructive criticism Heartfree offers her as a prerequisite for his love, despite her attraction to him.

Having failed to rescue Lady Fancyfull from her vanity, Heartfree wittily examines woman's nature with his friend Constant, who has been attempting to seduce Lady Brute since he first met her at her wedding two years earlier. Half rake and half sentimental comedy lover, Constant simultaneously praises Lady Brute for her virtue and complains that she will not commit adultery with him. After accepting the unsuspecting Sir John's invitation, Heartfree encourages Constant to persist in his seduction, believing that Sir John's ill usage may prompt Lady Brute to cuckold him to gain revenge.

Awaiting his visitors, Sir John deliberately annoys Lady Brute and Bellinda by smoking his pipe. Determined not to allow him to force them from the room, Lady Brute and Bellinda wittily tease him about its unpleasant smell. When Bellinda suggests that men who deliberately offend their wives deserve to be cuckolded, the enraged Sir John hurls his pipe at them and chases them out of the room; while running from her husband, Lady Brute runs, symbolically, into Constant's arms. The emphasis on physical action and the violence in this scene mark another departure from the detached intellectualism of Restoration comedy.

Having drunk with Heartfree and Constant, Sir John departs to carouse with his friends, leaving the young men alone with Lady Brute and Bellinda. After some witty banter between the couples in the manner of Restoration comedy, Lady Fancyfull arrives, and she mockingly reviews Heartfree's criticisms of her. To make Lady Fancyfull jealous, Bellinda flirts with Heartfree, inviting him to offer criticism of her character. Charmed by Bellinda, Heartfree ignores Lady Fancyfull, who follows Constant and Heartfree out as they leave, vowing vengeance on Bellinda.

Once Lady Fancyfull has gone, Constant reenters and, encountering Lady Brute alone, assures her that he left only to safeguard her reputation. Like the Restoration comedy rake, he attempts to seduce her with witty sophistry, and like a Restoration comedy heroine, Lady Brute exposes the fallaciousness of every argument he offers until, feeling her resistance abate, she terminates the conversation. The essential difference between this wit-battle between the sexes and that found in the typical Restoration comedy is, of course, that this witty, virtuous lady is married.

With mutual trust not usually found between women in Restoration comedy, Lady Brute and Bellinda wittily discuss men's and women's mutual deception and abuse. They agree that men are the ultimate source of pleasure in all arenas of a woman's life, and they laugh at the affectation and folly which they themselves cultivate, along with the rest of their sex. Although many women in both Restoration and sentimental comedy are self-aware, only the former are likely to find an assessment of their faults and virtues a source of amusement. In the course of their conversation, Lady Brute also tells Bellinda that she is weakening toward Constant. Aware of Sir John's abuse of her cousin, Bellinda sympathizes with Lady Brute and neither criticizes her for contemplating adultery nor sermonizes about the rewards of virtue. At the end of their conversation, Bellinda and Lady Brute devise a stratagem typical of Restoration comedy: In order to meet Heartfree and Constant again, they will invite the men anonymously to a rendezvous in Spring Garden and meet them there in disguise.

The scene then shifts to Sir John and his friends, who drunkenly lament that a man whom they have attacked is not dead; they next threaten a tailor and steal the parson's gown he carries, which Sir John puts on, adding to the farce. When the Constable comes to investigate the disturbance, Sir John swears and strikes the Constable and, as his friends run off, is taken into custody. Once again, the violence and coarseness of the scene mark a departure from the comedy of manners. Because Sir John has donned the parson's gown, his captors assume that he is a clergyman and thus lock him up not in jail but in the Constable's roundhouse. Later, when he is brought before the justice of the peace, he remains sullen and abusive but is again given preferential treatment and released without penalty because he wears the garb of a cleric. Anticipating an unfavorable response to the satire on the clergy in this scene at the 1726 revival of the play, Vanbrugh revised it extensively, refining Sir John's coarse language and eliminating the clerical satire by substituting one of Lady Brute's dresses for the cleric's gown.

When the anonymous invitation to a rendezvous arrives, Heartfree, now in love with Bellinda, very reluctantly agrees to accompany Constant. On their way to Spring Garden, they are followed by Mademoiselle and Lady

Fancyfull, who conceal themselves in order to eavesdrop on the conversation between the men and Lady Brute and Bellinda. The ladies are forced to reveal their identities to the men when Heartfree and Constant agree to Sir John's request of the favors of their two "whores." After Sir John leaves, angered by his friends' apparent selfishness, Lady Brute and Bellinda express their gratitude, and then each speaks privately with her suitor. With the reluctance to wed typical of a Restoration wit, Heartfree confesses to Bellinda that he could love her "even to—matrimony itself a'most." Bellinda's response is, likewise, in the Restoration comedy tradition: She inquires of him whether he would continue to love her after they were married.

While Bellinda and Heartfree go off for a walk alone, Constant continues his efforts to seduce Lady Brute, reminding her of Sir John's cruelty and of his own constancy. In another scene that departs from Restoration comedy in its emphasis on the physical aspects of love and in its use of physical action onstage, Constant kisses Lady Brute repeatedly and tries to pull her into the arbor to complete his seduction. Unlike Amanda, Lady Brute is saved not by her virtue but by her fear for her reputation, when Lady Fancyfull and Mademoiselle noisily make their presence known. Terrified that she has been recognized, Lady Brute insists that Heartfree and Constant bring her and Bellinda home.

Upon their return to Sir John's house, Lady Brute invites the men to play cards with her and Bellinda because she does not expect Sir John for hours. When Sir John suddenly arrives, however, Heartfree and Constant conceal themselves in the closet. Unaware of their presence, the filthy, blood-covered Sir John makes coarse, drunken sexual advances toward Lady Brute, her revulsion only augmenting his desire. Distracted momentarily by his thirst, Sir John insists on drinking some of the tea in the closet before having sexual relations with Lady Brute, and, kicking in the jammed closet door, he discovers Heartfree and Constant. Although Sir John assumes that Lady Brute has cuckolded him, his drunkenness prevents him from taking any action, and after a few coarse remarks, he passes out.

To avert Sir John's wrath, Lady Brute and Bellinda agree that, if Constant and Heartfree are willing, they will tell Sir John that Constant had merely accompanied Heartfree on a visit to Bellinda, whom he wishes to marry; Bellinda will readily break off the engagement, if Heartfree wishes, once Lady Brute's good name has been restored. Despite her awareness that she could find a wealthier husband than this younger brother, Bellinda is nevertheless willing to marry Heartfree. Unlike the heroines of sentimental comedy, Bellinda does not romanticize suffering: She assures Lady Brute that she would not join Heartfree to live in utter poverty on love alone. Bellinda is, nevertheless, an idealist in that love is her highest consideration in choosing a spouse; she prefers to marry a man of moderate means whom she loves than a wealthy man whom she does not. As a realist, Bellinda acknowledges the truth of Lady Brute's warning that she may end up unhappy and poor rather than unhappy and rich, but she resolves to trust to Heartfree's sense of honor and good nature.

When the ladies' proposal arrives, Heartfree is very reluctant to marry Bellinda despite his love for her, for he fears that some man may eventually cuckold him just as his friend Constant intends to cuckold Sir John. Although Heartfree and Constant agree that women usually remain faithful to their husbands unless they are abused, Heartfree fears that he might indeed turn into a Sir John in time, arguing that men, not women, are the more likely to change. Agreeing with Constant that marriage is "the only heaven on earth," Heartfree expresses the very unrakish sentiment that "to be capable of loving one, doubtless is better than to possess a thousand." Still questioning his capacity for love, he does not decide to marry Bellinda until, wielding the wit he has found so attractive, she asks his intentions, drawing her imagery from warfare.

Despite Heartfree's engagement to Bellinda, Sir John remains convinced that he has been cuckolded; he hypocritically declares love for and trust in Lady Brute only to avoid fighting a duel for her honor with Constant. Just as Lady Brute's honor is being restored, however, Lady Fancyfull enters in disguise, intending to sully Bellinda's and Heartfree's reputations and thus to prevent their marriage. Lady Fancyfull informs Bellinda that she is Heartfree's wife whom, she says, he married for money (thus playing on one of Bellinda's fears) and whom he has reduced to poverty and threatened with murder. Meanwhile, Lady Fancyfull has also sent a letter to Heartfree, informing him that Bellinda has already had one illegitimate child and that she is anxious to marry because she is pregnant with another. Both Bellinda and Heartfree are thoroughly deceived, and each hurls veiled accusations at the other until Rasor, Heartfree's servant, confesses his part in the plot and forces Lady Fancyfull and Mademoiselle to admit theirs. Having begged each other's pardon, Heartfree and Bellinda once again agree to marry, and the play ends with Bellinda warning Heartfree of the fate of surly husbands.

In *The Provok'd Wife*, as in *The Relapse*, Vanbrugh does not resolve the questions that he raises; he does not employ a facile happy ending at the expense of the consistency of the characterization. Sir John and Lady Brute remain yoked together with no suggestion that their relationship will improve; Lady Brute can—and probably will—find physical and emotional satisfaction only through an extramarital affair; and although Heartfree and Bellinda will marry, the readiness with which they believe profound ill of each other does not bode well for their future happiness.

Although Vanbrugh never completed another original play, he did draft a little more than three acts of *A Journey to London*. Here, again, Vanbrugh employs a double-plot structure but does not adequately integrate the elements of the two plots. The play's minor plot satirizes the Headpieces, a family of country bumpkins who visit London, while the main plot focuses on the incompatibility of Lord and Lady Loverule. In *A Journey to London*, however, unlike *The Relapse* and *The Provok'd Wife*, the husband rather than the wife is the more sensible and sympathetic character, and gambling, not adultery, is the main source of conflict. Although Vanbrugh did not complete this play—with Cibber's revisions, it became *The Provok'd Husband*—he told Cibber that the main plot would conclude with Lord Loverule's turning out Lady Arabella for her refusal to mend her ways. Thus, Vanbrugh intended once more to reject the unrealistic fifth-act reformation and falsely happy ending of sentimental comedy.

The Relapse and *The Provok'd Wife* are also important in theatrical history because they were among the main targets of Jeremy Collier's famous attack on contemporary theater, *A Short View of the Immorality and Profaneness of the English Stage*. Vanbrugh drew Collier's fire not only because of his treatment of adultery but also because of his satire on the clergy, which appears not only in the plays but in their prefatory material as well. Collier accused Vanbrugh of both moral and artistic irresponsibility, humorlessly condemning Vanbrugh's presentation of flawed characters. Vanbrugh argues in his response, *A Short Vindication of "The Relapse" and "The Provok'd Wife,"* that Collier understands neither the nature nor the function of satire but wrongly assumes that to present behavior onstage is to recommend it. Nevertheless, Collier does offer some valid criticism of *The Relapse*: The blank verse is indeed poor, the plot is improbable, and the play's awkward structure does obscure its focus.

Collier's attack is important, however, not so much because he provided literary insight into the plays but because his attitude reflected the shift in public taste away from Restoration comedy and Vanbrugh's more realistic comedy toward sentimental comedy. Gradually, Vanbrugh's audience came to share Collier's disapproval of the character-types, dialogue, and plots that were typical of Restoration comedy and to demand a more morally self-conscious theater.

Other major works

NONFICTION: *A Short Vindication of "The Relapse" and "The Provok'd Wife,"* 1698.

MISCELLANEOUS: *The Complete Works of Sir John Vanbrugh*, 1927-1928 (4 volumes; Bonamy Dobrée and Geoffrey Webb, editors).

Bibliography

Bruce, Donald. *Topics of Restoration Comedy.* New York: St. Martin's

Press, 1974. Mentions Vanbrugh passim, particularly in a chapter entitled "Sons of Belial," which concerns the attack on the stage by Jeremy Collier, who was angry over Vanbrugh's *The Provok'd Wife*, in which Sir John Brute, disguised as a clergyman, ran drinking and whoring throughout. Bruce discusses Vanbrugh's Lord Foppington in a chapter on Epicureans and considers Lord Foppington the supreme egotist, having utter disregard for the opinions and values of others. Includes an interesting discussion of Charles Baudelaire's comments on the Epicurean dandy, many of which fit Lord Foppington well.

Harris, Bernard. *Sir John Vanbrugh.* London: Longmans, Green, 1967. Contains brief but effective analyses of characters and plots in Vanbrugh's two independent plays, *The Relapse* and *The Provok'd Wife.* Harris praises Vanbrugh's skill in creating dialogue. Four illustrations.

Husebee, Arthur R. *Sir John Vanbrugh.* Boston: Twayne, 1976. Husebee interprets *The Relapse* not as a correction of Colley Cibber's psychological weakness in the characterizations of *Love's Last Shift* but as an effort to take advantage of the popularity of Cibber's play by creating its sequel. He treats *The Provok'd Wife* in a separate chapter. Contains good general information on Vanbrugh's life, his translations of French works, and his critical reception to 1913. Annotated bibliography, index.

Johansson, Bertil. *The Adapter Adapted: A Study of Sir John Vanbrugh's Comedy "The Mistake," Its Predecessors and Successors.* Stockholm: Almqvist & Wiksell International, 1977. This study of the relationship between Vanbrugh's play and Molière's *Le Dépit amoureux* (pr. 1656, pb. 1663) concludes that *The Mistake* should be termed an adaptation rather than a translation of Molière's play. Analyzes plot, characters, and style, and includes a lengthy chapter on two adaptations of *The Mistake.* Bibliography but no index.

Vanbrugh, John, Sir. *The Complete Works of Sir John Vanbrugh.* Vol. 1 Edited by Bonamy Dobrée. Bloomsbury, England: Nonesuch Press, 1927. Volume 1 introduces Vanbrugh's life and work and compliments his personal nature and artistic abilities. His plays are judged as invigorating and having genuine literary quality, and they are compared with those of Thomas Shadwell and several others, including favorable comparisons with those of Richard Brinsley Sheridan.

Laurie P. Morrow
(Updated by *Howard L. Ford*)

GEORGE VILLIERS

Born: London, England; January 30, 1628
Died: Kirkby Moorside, England; April 16, 1687

Principal drama

The Chances, pr. 1667, pb. 1682 (revision of John Fletcher's play); *The Rehearsal*, pr. 1671, pb. 1672; *The Battle of Sedgmoor*, wr. 1685, pb. 1704; *The Militant Couple: Or, The Husband May Thank Himself*, wr. 1685(?), pb. 1704; *The Restauration: Or, Right Will Take Place*, wr. 1685, pb. 1704 (revision of Francis Beaumont and Fletcher's play *Philaster*).

Other literary forms

George Villiers has left his mark on English literature solely with his contribution to the drama; his remaining miscellaneous works are obscure. His letters have not been collected, although Tom Brown, Villiers' editor, included a number of them in *The Works of His Grace, George Villiers, Late Duke of Buckingham* (1715). The published letters appear to hold more interest for the biographer and historian than for the student of literature.

Only a few of Villiers' poems were published during his lifetime, and his total poetic output is small. Brown's edition includes twenty-odd poems largely occasional verses, songs, verse epistles, satires, prologues, and epilogues. The verses reveal that Villiers never achieved the smoothness and polish found in the works of the best courtier poets during the reign of Charles II. Poets such as the Earls of Dorset and Rochester, taking to heart the maxims of Horace and following the example of Ben Jonson, produced verses of lyric smoothness and elegance. Villiers lacked either the ear to detect or the patience to produce pleasing rhythm, and his poems do not achieve memorable figures of speech or scintillating wit. Thus, editors of anthologies of his period omit his poems from their collections.

Achievements

Time has not dealt kindly with either Villiers' life or his works. In his public and private life, he is remembered more for his eccentricities than for his achievements, and only one of his literary works is read today. One reason for this is that he took only a passing interest in literature. Another reason is that he possessed a talent narrow and ill-suited to some of the projects he undertook. Defending his ministry before the House of Commons in 1674, Villiers declared that he could hunt the hare as well as any man with a pack of hounds, "but not with a brace of lobsters," a reference to the king and the Duke of York. This preposterous comparison proved more shocking than effective, but it indicates his ready wit, his willingness to take risks for a jest, and his sense of the ridiculous. This talent for oblique wit enabled him to produce brilliant parody. It represents one gift that can lead to brilliant satire, yet more is required—knowledge and skill in the craft of poetry, balance, an idealistic vision or a sense of a norm, and a genuine desire to reform. Villiers achieved the full potential of his limited talent only in *The Rehearsal*.

Biography

George Villiers, second Duke of Buckingham, devoted little of his active and irregular life to literature, a matter to him of amateur interest. Instead, he turned his major efforts to the pursuits of pleasure and statecraft, two interests that came naturally to him because of his birth and rearing. He was the oldest son of the first Duke of Buckingham, who was a favorite courtier of James I and Charles I. Assassinated by a fanatic at the height of his power and fame, the duke left three children—two sons and a daughter. Out of respect for the father, King Charles I took the two boys as his wards and reared them as his own, allowing them to spend much of their time with the royal princes. Provided with the best education and with financial security, Villiers developed a strong attachment to the house of Stuart. From his father he inherited vast estates, treasures of art, and other properties. After the Restoration, his estates made him for a time the wealthiest man in England, ensuring him a base of support for his ambitions and his pleasures.

After the death of Charles I, Villiers attached himself closely to Prince Charles, sharing with him the adventures and dangers involved in his attempts to advance his claim to the throne. Villiers' military exploits were marked by audacity, gallantry, and a total disregard of his own safety. During the period when he was assuming the role of military commander, he was also developing his political abilities. In the role of adviser to the prince, he revealed his mercurial nature, his intelligence, a certain instability, and a penchant for intrigue. Further, in some of his exploits he showed himself a master of mimicry and disguise.

When the hopes of toppling the government of Oliver Cromwell collapsed following the Battle of Worcester, the prince and Villiers sought refuge on the Continent. Villiers, restless in inactivity, returned to England and there married Mary Fairfax, daughter of the parliamentary general Lord Fairfax. This alliance failed to reassure Cromwell of Villiers' loyalty, and he had the duke imprisoned in the Tower of London, where he remained until Cromwell's death. Following his release, he involved himself in intrigues intended to restore the Stuart monarchy and stood among the first to greet Charles II upon his return in 1660.

The king appointed Villiers to the ruling Privy Council, a group of thirty ministers then under the leadership of the Lord Chancellor, the Earl of

Clarendon. Jealousies, rivalries, and intrigues among the king's ministers proved the order of the day, and Villiers allied himself with those ministers opposed to Clarendon. After the fall of the Lord Chancellor, Villiers became one of the five ministers known as the Cabal—Lord Clifford, Lord Arlington, Villiers, Anthony Ashley Cooper, and Lord Lauderdale—who led in matters of state for seven years. During much of the period, Villiers remained the most powerful among them. He was entrusted with important foreign affairs and missions, carrying on negotiations in France and Holland, yet the king did not repose his entire trust in his childhood companion, for in his public career, Villiers consistently pressed two important principles that did not always suit the king's purposes—religious freedom and English sea power. It was Villiers' private life, however, that proved to be the pretext for his fall from power.

While serving as a minister of state, Villiers pursued a variety of interests and avocations. A frequenter of the theater and an amateur musician, he pursued numerous other interests as well—the manufacture of glass, chemistry, astrology, and architecture. His usual associates were the king, the ladies of the court (through whom he exerted influence), and the Court Wits, the brilliant and profligate young lords who attached themselves to the king after the Restoration. Frequently seen in the theater, Villiers, like the other Court Wits, became the subject of gossip, anecdotes, and scandal. Having been reared as a royal ward, he seemed not to understand that the degree of license in behavior tolerated in the king did not apply equally to him.

Villiers' duchess, Mary Fairfax, fell far short of the beauty and charm that Andrew Marvell praised so highly in his poem "Upon Appleton House," though what she lacked in these qualities she made up for in her patience with and endurance of her philandering husband. Like the queen, she was barren, a fact that Villiers took as an excuse for his numerous infidelities. In 1667, he fell passionately in love with Anna Maria, Countess of Shrewsbury, whose languid and voluptuous beauty lives today in her portraits by Sir Peter Lely. They appeared in public together on numerous occasions, and one evening at the theater, Harry Killigrew, her previous lover, insulted the countess. When Villiers sought an apology, Killigrew struck Villiers across the head with the flat of his sword, whereupon the enraged duke drove Killigrew from the theater, creating a furor. The earl of Shrewsbury, husband of the countess, took this public display as an insult and felt compelled to issue Villiers a challenge, Killigrew having fled to France. In the ensuing duel, Villiers ran the earl through, not killing him outright but causing his death some three months afterward. Thereafter, Villiers installed the widowed countess in his London home as his mistress for seven years, a situation accepted by his duchess. When the countess bore him an illegitimate son, Villiers managed to obtain for him the hereditary title Earl of Coventry. Following the death of his son during his first year of life, Villiers had the infant interred with ceremony and pomp in Westminster Abbey. This flagrant disregard of convention was remembered when Villiers' enemies grew strong enough to topple him from power. In 1674, Parliament forced him to resign all of his offices and swear never to cohabit with the countess again. She married another man shortly after the duke's fall, and the duke joined the opposition to the court party, led by Anthony Ashley Cooper, first Earl of Shaftesbury, with whom he had served on the Cabal. For the next few years, his efforts in politics were devoted to the vain attempt to exclude James, Duke of York, from the throne.

In an exceptionally active and eventful life, literature represented for Villiers only one interest among many. He associated with poets and dramatists and became the patron of a few, though he did not rank as one of the great literary patrons of the age. Abraham Cowley enjoyed his support and hospitality for a time, as did Thomas Sprat, who wrote the history of the Royal Society. While Villiers could match the brilliance of his fellow Court Wits in conversation, he was not their equal in poetry. It is remarkable that John Dryden, whom he satirized so effectively in *The Rehearsal*, left in response verses on Villiers which capture, strikingly and somewhat unfairly, the contradictions inherent in his character. In his political satire *Absalom and Achitophel* (1681), Dryden produced a character based on Villiers named Zimri. By a cruel irony, these lines usually represent what students of literature remember about George Villiers, if they take note of him at all:

> A man so various that he seem'd to be
> Not one, but all mankind's epitome.
> Stiff in opinions, always in the wrong,
> Was everything by starts and nothing long,
> But in the course of one revolving moon,
> Was chemist, fiddler, statesman, and buffoon;
> Then all for women, painting, rhiming, drinking,
> Besides ten thousand freaks that di'd in thinking.
> Blest madman, who could every hour employ
> With something new to wish or to enjoy!
> ....
> Begger'd by fools, whom still he found too late,
> He had his jest, and they had his estate.

During the final period of Villiers' life, King Charles was reconciled to his old companion, and Villiers spent many enjoyable hours with the king, but he was not trusted to wield power. With the accession of James II, shunned by his former allies and no longer able to pay his debts or appeal to his friends, Villiers left London and established himself at one of his remaining estates, the ruined Helmsly Castle in Yorkshire, where he spent most of his time racing and riding to the hounds. Following one outing, he grew suddenly ill and took refuge in Kirkby Moorside, an obscure village near York, where he died quietly within two days. His debts consumed his entire estate at his death. King James II, his old adversary, boasted that the Duchess of Buckingham would have been destitute without his support, but the king's boast was not entirely correct, for the duchess retained her father's estate, Nun Appleton, in her own right.

Villiers' restless, unstable nature urged him to live at a fast pace and to play for high stakes. He would no doubt have justified his risk-taking with the potential rewards, yet despite a few successes, notably the manufacture of glass in England, he lost in most of his ventures. His achievements in statecraft and literature, with the exception of *The Rehearsal*, do not rise above mediocrity.

Analysis

During the Restoration, scores of plays by Elizabethan dramatists, including William Shakespeare, Ben Jonson, and Beaumont and Fletcher, were revised for theater audiences. George Villiers' first significant effort as a playwright was a revision of Fletcher's comedy *The Chances*, which saw a successful production in 1667. He retouched Fletcher's first three acts and rewrote entirely the final two acts, rendering the blank verse of the original into prose while leaving the first three acts largely in blank verse.

The play features a tangled plot which turns on coincidence and confusion of identities. Two women named Constantia, one a duke's mistress and the other the unwilling mistress of an older lover who proves to be impotent, decide to leave their lovers at the same time. Both seek help from Don John, a young rake, and his friend Don Frederick. Meanwhile, Petruchio, brother of the duke's mistress, seeks to avenge her loss of honor and sends the duke a challenge, only to learn that the duke has married her. After confused brawling in the street and several mistakes in efforts to straighten matters out, the play ends with the first Constantia restored to the duke and with the younger Constantia beginning a relationship with the reformed rake Don John, after her lover Antonio has reclaimed the money she took from him in order to flee.

The play features a number of witty exchanges and maintains a realistic tone throughout, successfully avoiding sentimentality, but it relies too heavily on confused identity and improbable circumstances in the plot, and it lacks the brilliant repartee of the later Restoration comedies of manners. Oddly, very few of the speeches are between the paired lovers. Villiers ties up the loose ends of the plot and sets a moral tone regarding love somewhat above that of the comedy of manners, yet apart from the lively character Don John, the play holds little attraction.

The only drama by Villiers well-known today is *The Rehearsal*, a burlesque of the theater first produced in 1671. In its composition he probably had the assistance of Samuel Butler, Martin Clifford, and Thomas Sprat. The work achieved enormous popularity during its day. It belongs in the literary tradition of such drama burlesques as Beaumont and Fletcher's *The Knight of the Burning Pestle* (pr. 1607), Henry Fielding's *Tom Thumb: A Tragedy* (pr. 1730), and Richard Brinsley Sheridan's *The Critic* (pr. 1779). The object of its satiric attack is the heroic play, a dramatic genre that developed following the Restoration, and its most successful practitioner, John Dryden.

Largely influenced by French tragedy, which attracted the king's interest during his exile, the heroic play originated in England during the early 1660's. Dramas of this type were written in rhymed heroic couplets, a distinctive feature which rendered the dialogue artificial. The speeches were often long, consisting of debate and ratiocination, often marked by bombastic language. The dramas typically presented a swashbuckling hero drawn into a conflict between love and his sense, or code, of honor; his task was to resolve the conflict without compromising either emotionally charged value. He was surrounded by a group of stock characters drawn primarily from the drama of Beaumont and Fletcher—characters such as the weak king, the faithful friend, the sentimental maiden, the evil woman, and the Machiavellian villain. The plays usually had remote or exotic settings, strange names, violent action, somewhat disjointed plots, and elaborate scenery and costuming.

As a counterweight to the excesses of the heroic play, *The Rehearsal* introduces two characters who might be considered naïve observers. Smith, who has just arrived at the theater from the country, seeks out Johnson, a city man who can explain to him the current fashion and taste of the city. They create a kind of commonsense perspective that illuminates the absurdities of the popular drama. As they are talking, John Bayes, a dramatist, walks across the stage, and they engage him in conversation about the theater. He invites them to remain for a rehearsal of his new play, *The Two Kings of Brentford.*

Although Bayes is something of a composite, reflecting certain qualities of Sir William Davenant and using speech mannerisms of Edward Howard, he is intended chiefly as a caricature of John Dryden. Villiers himself coached the actor John Lacy, who played the role, so that he might accurately mimic Dryden's mannerisms and speech. Often the dialogue incorporates brief passages from Dryden's critical writings, and some of the expressions—"nick," used as a verb, and "igad"—were habits of speech identified with Dryden. As a character, Bayes comes alive, proving himself interesting and memorable, if not well-rounded. One finds Smith and Johnson reacting with incredulity and bewilderment to the absurd parodies and dramatic conventions of the play being "rehearsed," yet Bayes takes the two into his confidence and proudly explains all that is going on with genuine and naïve enthusiasm. With disarming candor, he reveals his tricks of plotting, which amount to plagiarism, unaware that they will be viewed with disfavor. Frequently he praises his work without waiting for response, commenting to the observers after one scene, "I'm afraid this scene had made you sad, for, I must confess, when I writ it, I wept myself." The only explanation that occurs to him for the failure of some to appreciate his work is that they lack taste, and when the actors refuse to continue the rehearsal, Bayes threatens to sell his work to a rival theater. Throughout, he maintains a kind of irrepressible optimism and oblivious good humor.

In its multiple parodies and wide-ranging allusions, *The Rehearsal* satirizes at least seventeen plays, the majority being heroic plays, though not all by Dryden. The primary vehicle for satire is the play-within-the-play, Mr. Bayes's *The Two Kings of Brentford*. The chaotic and disjointed plot concerns the deposing of the two kings by their physician and a gentleman usher. Following the deposition, Prince Pretty-man, Prince Volscius, and the swashbuckling hero Drawcansir appear, each in his turn, and introduce separate and unrelated themes. The "heroines," Chloris, Parthenope, Lardella, and Amaryllis, provide opportunities for developing the theme of love. Following an elaborate procession involving four cardinals, the two kings are restored, descending from the clouds, and the usurpers steal away. Then a battle takes place, stopped suddenly by an eclipse. Afterward, the fighting resumes and Drawcansir enters slaying all the participants, friend and foe alike. This devastation concludes the fourth act of the play-within-the-play. For the final act, Bayes reads a synopsis, a digression involving a tragic ending to the love of Chloris and Prince Pretty-man. Before the reading, Smith and Johnson steal away, and afterward the actors follow their example, leaving Bayes to express his frustration to the stage keeper.

To appreciate fully the exquisite parody found in *The Rehearsal*, one needs to recognize the echoes from now obscure heroic plays. With only slight changes of phrasing, it was possible to reduce the exaggerated and artificial expressions of emotion in heroic couplets to absurdity. In Dryden's *The Conquest of Granada by the Spaniards* (pr. 1670, 1671), the hero Almanzor steals to the queen's chamber to profess his love for her. When asked his identity, he thus explains: "He, who dares love, and for that love must die,/ And, knowing this, dares yet love on, am I." Villiers parodies this episode by having Drawcansir, a similar hero, enter upon a banquet held by the two usurping kings and identify himself in the following manner:

KING PHYSICIAN: What man is this that dares disturb our feast?
DRAWCANSIR: He that dares drink, and for that drink dares die;
And, knowing this, dares yet drink on, am I.

In numerous other passages, the bombast of the heroic play is captured with withering effect. A lieutenant general addresses the eclipse which has stopped the battle: "Foolish Eclipse, thou this in vain hast done;/ My brighter honour had eclips'd the sun./ But now behold eclipses two in one." At times, the prosaic content of the heroic couplets, when expressed in heightened style, produced bathos, an effect parodied in this speech by the first king as he seeks safety from the battle: "Let us for shelter in our cabinet stay;/ Perhaps these threat'ning storms will pass away." More often, however, the inflated and sometimes inpenetrable language of the heroic plays forms the target, as in Prince Pretty-man's lament: "The blackest ink of fate was sure my lot,/ And when she writ my name she made a blot." Prince Volscius, smitten by love for Parthenope, experiences the love-honor conflict, a thematic commonplace, when he is called to meet his army outside town. Putting on one boot, he sees that leg as representative of honor—the bootless one symbolizing love. His will being paralyzed by the conflict, he hobbles out wearing only one boot.

The gaiety, energy, and mirth of burlesque and parody are sustained throughout Villiers' comic masterpiece. He refrains from satirizing those elements of the heroic play that would detract from the lighthearted parody. There are no Machiavellian plotters or evil women—even his villains are comic. Although the work achieved acclaim and had an unusually successful run in the theater, it did not drive the heroic play from the stage. London audiences laughed at the absurdities with Villiers, yet they enjoyed the pageantry, liveliness, novelty, and variety of the heroic drama until the vogue wore itself out approximately a decade later.

Other major work

MISCELLANEOUS: *The Works of His Grace, George Villiers, Late Duke of Buckingham*, 1715 (2 volumes; Tom Brown, editor); *Buckingham, Public and Private Man: The Prose, Poems, and Commonplace Book of George Villiers, Second Duke of Buckingham (1628-1687)*, 1985 (Christine Phipps, editor).

Bibliography

Burghclere, Winifred. *George Villiers, Second Duke of Buckingham, 1628-1687.* Port Washington, N.Y.: Kennikat Press, 1971. Lady Burghclere blends her biographical narrative of Villiers with a historical account of his time. She emphasizes his aristocratic family background, his close association with the Stuart monarchy, and his inconsistencies as a powerful courtier.

Chapman, Hester. *Great Villiers.* London: Martin Secker & Warburg, 1949. Chapman provides a detailed account of Villiers' family background and his early development. Although her biography stresses the subject's public career as courtier and cabinet minister, she assesses his literary works and offers a synopsis of *The Rehearsal.*

MacMillan, Dougald, and Howard Mumford Jones, eds. *Plays of the Restoration and Eighteenth Century.* New York: Henry Holt, 1931. This anthology on English drama of the period includes a sparkling introduction to Villiers' *The Rehearsal* and numerous footnotes explaining the numerous allusions in the drama. The notes identify passages in contemporary dramas such as those of Dryden that are the objects of devastating satire. Also includes a generous selection of the plays satirized in Villiers' drama.

Wilson, John Harold. *The Court Wits of the Restoration.* Princeton, N.J.: Princeton University Press, 1948. Wilson explores Villiers' role as a member of the Court Wits during the reign of Charles II. The loosely associated group, led by John Wilmot, Earl of Rochester, was noted for the licentious behavior of its members, their patronage of drama and poetry, their writings, and their sometimes scandalous escapades. Wilson includes a detailed chronology of Villiers' life in an appendix.

____________. *A Rake and His Times: George Villiers, and Duke of Buckingham.* New York: Farrar, Straus, and Young, 1954. After a brief account of Villiers' family background, Wilson centers this biography on Villiers' political career, devoting special attention to his intrigues and his complicated rivalries among political leaders of the time. Although he gives only brief attention to *The Rehearsal*, Wilson devotes some attention to the lesser known writings.

Stanley Archer

THE WAKEFIELD MASTER

Born: Wakefield, England; c. 1420
Died: Unknown; c. 1450

Principal drama

Mactacio Abel (commonly known as *The Killing of Abel*); *Processus Noe cum Filiis* (commonly known as *Noah*); *Prima Pastorum* (commonly known as *The First Shepherds' Play*); *Secunda Pastorum* (commonly known as *The Second Shepherds' Play*); *Magnus Herodes* (commonly known as *Herod the Great*); *Coliphizacio* (commonly known as *The Buffeting*). These plays are among the thirty-two surviving pageants of the Towneley (also known as the Wakefield) mystery cycle and are included in *The Wakefield Pageants in the Towneley Cycle*, pb. 1958 (A. C. Cowley, editor).

Other literary forms

A few scholars have perceived a relationship between the style of verse used in the plays of the Wakefield Master and the fifteenth century poems *The Northern Passion* and *The Turnament of Totenhamm*. The relationship is tenuous, however, and most scholars believe it to be specious.

Achievements

The mystery pageants of medieval Europe did not follow classical dramatic form. They were indigenous Western European plays that evolved out of religious ritual. The plays of the Wakefield Master are the finest surviving examples of this genre. His work is notable for its humor, its structural sophistication, its unusually fine use of dialect, and its finely developed character. In the mystery pageants of the Wakefield Master, one can find the elements of a uniquely English drama that blossomed in the works of the great Elizabethan and Jacobean playwrights. The dramatic force of his plays, the exuberance of his language, and the insight of his characterizations make the Wakefield Master a significant contributor to the development of Western drama.

Biography

The Wakefield Master is a mysterious figure, and the high literary value of his work has enticed many scholars into speculating about who he may have been. The dialects used by the Wakefield Master are from the general area of Wakefield, England; the Master's plays also refer to places in and around Wakefield. Thus, he probably wrote while living in or near the town. Evidence that the town staged mystery pageants indicates that the Master's work was composed specifically for Wakefield; the signs of his style in revisions of various portions of the cycle as well as the neatness with which his plays fit into the cycle have led some scholars to conclude that all the plays in the Towneley manuscripts were performed in Wakefield. Such a conclusion is reasonable and accounts for many scholars calling the cycle the "Wakefield Mystery Plays."

Drawing on what is known of the York and Chester cycles, scholars have speculated that the Wakefield Master was a cleric, perhaps a monk. He was probably a man, although not necessarily so. Custom and known practice indicate that women were excluded from participation in the writing of such works as the Wakefield pageants. He almost certainly had an occupation other than writing; his plays were probably commissioned, as was his editing of other plays in the Towneley Cycle. Learned members of the clergy were often expected to be able to contribute writings to public religious activities. The variety of dialects in his plays indicates that the Wakefield Master may have traveled in the Midlands area of England; the dominant dialect indicates that he was native to the Wakefield area.

Analysis

In order to appreciate the Wakefield Master's work, one needs to understand the nature of the mystery pageants, which were specialized religious dramas with staging and format requirements different from those of modern drama. Part of what elevates the Wakefield Master's plays above the ordinary is his manipulation of the limitations of his dramatic form to obtain sophisticated dramatic effects. His actors were shopkeepers and laborers; his employers undoubtedly expected him to follow carefully the well-known biblical stories; his stage was limited in the props and scenery it could contain. The Wakefield Master made these limitations into assets; he used them to heighten the effect on his audience of the characters and events in his plays.

A medieval mystery pageant is a play that deals with the Christian concept of the universe. The creation of the world, the sacrifice of Christ, and the Judgment are parts of the mystery, with the life of Christ being central to all the events. Thus, in a mystery cycle, the creation of the world is related to the life of Jesus, as are the biblical events that precede his birth; events that follow His Ascension to Heaven are shaped by His life, with the end of the world coming as a logical consequence of Christ's life. The word "cycle" has a double meaning: It refers to the medieval Christian concept of God's Creation as a unified whole, which the mystery cycle portrays with plays depicting Christian history beginning with God before the act of Creation and ending with the final Judgment; "cycle" also refers to the medieval tradition of viewing life as cyclical. Therefore, a mystery cycle is a dramatic representation of the medieval Christian's view of the universe; the mystery cycle presents the beginning and end of the world, unified and given their meanings by Jesus Christ.

Mystery plays are sometimes called Corpus Christi pageants because of their association with the spring Corpus Christi festival. The mystery cycles seem to have evolved as part of the public celebrations held after Easter, but their performances were held not only during Corpus Christi celebrations but also at other times, notably during Whit week. Regardless of whether they coincided with the Corpus Christi observances, these plays were springtime events and were profoundly religious in purpose. Their origins were both religious and secular, a blend that resulted in the mysteries of God's work becoming powerfully accessible to lay audiences. Liturgical drama began in the early Middle Ages as a way to teach biblical ideas to illiterate audiences who could neither read their vernacular languages nor understand Latin. Such early plays probably were staged inside churches and were part of significant religious holidays. Late medieval performances of the Lincoln Corpus Christi plays were probably still staged at the Lincoln cathedral—although outside—long after liturgical drama had evolved into the complex mystery cycles and miracle plays (the miracle plays focused on the lives of saints, not on Christ). By the time the Wakefield Master wrote his plays, mystery cycles were well-established religious celebrations, with rules and audience expectations that he had to fulfill. The rules involved inclusion of important aspects of Christian faith, and the expectations were based not only on the biblical accounts themselves but also on Christian tradition. For example, tradition had it that the wife of Noah was a shrew: She was anticipated comic relief in the mystery cycle.

Indeed, extrabiblical tradition played a large role in the development of the mystery cycles and was an important influence on the Wakefield Master. The medieval audience rarely read the Bible; it developed embellishments and twists for biblical stories. Some of the embellishments linger in modern tradition: Satan with horns, hooves, and a tail; the Apostle John as Jesus' closest friend; the apple as the forbidden fruit of which Adam and Eve eat in the Garden of Eden. The satire and ribald humor in the Wakefield Master's plays reflect the influence of folk dramas such as the Feast of Fools, in which Church ritual was mocked. In addition to popular biblical traditions and folk dramas, the mystery cycles reflected some of Western Europe's most significant secular—sometimes even pagan—myths. The death and rebirth of Christ is informed by old myths of hero-gods of the pre-Christian era; the legends of King Arthur and Roland reflect the old myths of heroes rising from their graves to help their people in times of peril. Christ was thus a secular hero-figure as well as a messianic one.

The Wakefield Master had to fulfill the basic purposes of the mystery plays, the foremost of which was to teach the audience about fundamental Christian doctrines. In *Noah*, he must communicate the idea of the Great Flood as God's response to the sins of humanity, and must be sure to tell his audience how animals and the human race were preserved. In the shepherds' plays, he must convey the importance of the birth of Christ. In *The Buffeting*, the belief that Christ suffered as a surrogate for all people, past and future, is important.

In addition to meeting such expectations, the Wakefield Master had to work within the peculiar stage conventions of the mystery pageant. No one knows exactly how the Towneley Cycle was staged in the era in which the Wakefield Master flourished, although many scholars assume that the Wakefield plays were staged in a manner similar to the staging of the York Cycle, about which more is known. There were crucial differences between York and Wakefield that make some of the York practices unlikely for Wakefield, but York represents the broad pageant tradition in which the Wakefield Master worked. York was a relatively large and prosperous medieval city, with a large mercantile class. The mercantile class was divided into trades, and each trade was represented by a guild. Each guild was responsible for the performance of a particular play in the York Cycle. The effect of this is a fragmentation in the cycle; each play had to suit the available players in a given guild and would be altered to suit changes in the membership of the guild. Thus the continuity found in the Towneley Cycle is not found in the York Cycle. Further, the cycles were associated with a processional tradition that was part of the Corpus Christi celebrations. The procession, a kind of parade, would involve an entire community; the guild actors would participate in their roles. Eventually the procession and the performances split, because the cycles became too complex to be performed on the same day as the procession took place. In York, twelve to sixteen stations were designated along a processional route; at each station, a single audience could see all the plays. The stages were on large carts that were pulled by horses or oxen, and each stage belonged to a particular guild that was responsible for a particular play. Thus, Jesus, who would appear in several plays, would be performed by a different actor in each play; there was no continuity of actors from one play to the next. The York Cycle grew so long that it probably had to be performed on two or three consecutive days, because of the time needed to move the stages from one station to the next.

The manner of the York Cycle's presentation is generally believed by literary historians to be the standard one for mystery cycles, but Wakefield differed from York in ways that might have made the presentation of the Towneley Cycle significantly different from that of the York Cycle. Wakefield was relatively small; it probably did not have the large number of guilds that York had. The Towneley Cycle is believed to have included at least thirty-two known plays; missing numbered leaves from its manuscript indicate that it comprised even more plays in the Wakefield Master's day. The city of Wakefield may have been too small to have the necessary number of guilds; it might even have had trouble finding enough actors for the multitude of roles if its plays were to have separate companies as in the York performances. In *The Wakefield Mystery Plays*, published in 1961, Martial Rose suggests that the Towneley Cycle was performed on one stage with the same actors playing the major roles throughout.

There is much to recommend the theory that the Wakefield plays were performed in a single location, probably in a theater-in-the-round. The Towneley Cycle was edited, perhaps by the Wakefield Master himself, to give it a continuity in structure and theme not found in the York Cycle. A continuity of actors and a minimum of guild plays would allow for such consistency. Also, the few records that exist indicate that the plays began and ended in one day; if they were performed in one place, they could have fit into the dawn-to-dusk schedule required by daylight performances (dusk was customarily the legal curfew). The Church, as with the Corpus Christi procession, could have had principal responsibility for staging the cycle, instead of the guilds, although there is evidence that, after the Wakefield Master's day, at least a few guilds were given specific plays. This would explain the consistent editing that is evident throughout the cycle; the plays could have been the responsibility of a central group rather than many.

The theater-in-the-round was used by traveling companies; *The Castle of Perseverance* (c. 1440), one of the great medieval morality dramas, was roughly contemporaneous with the Towneley Cycle and was performed in an outdoor theater. The use of such a theater by traveling troupes indicates that this kind of stage could be quickly set up in a field; an easily set up outdoor theater would have been well suited to the needs of Wakefield and the annual nature of the performances of its cycle. The stage would enable the Wakefield Master to use multiple exits and entrances, to and from which his actors would pass through their audience. The stage's limitations would resemble those of the York Cycle's processional arrangement; there would be no curtains and thus no changes of scenery during a given play, the actors would be surrounded on all sides by their audience, and the actors would be local people, not professionals. The Wakefield Master may have solved some of his problems by designating different areas of his stage as different dramatic locales; when an actor moved from one area of the stage to another, he moved from one imagined locale to another. The Wakefield Master also handled his staging problem by implying much of the action; unable to build an ark onstage in *Noah*, he has the action take place in Noah's home with references to the work on the ark.

Like many medieval writers, the Wakefield Master did not view time as linear. It was, instead, eternal; in the Christian universe of his day, God was everywhere in time as well as space. Thus, it was reasonable that the shepherds should be like local ones and that Cain should speak of being buried locally; the Wakefield Master would have perceived little incongruity in having English tradesmen portray biblical figures. Part of the message of the cycles, indeed, was that Christ's sacrifice involved people from all eras. This treatment of time based on the universality of human experience enhances the appeal of the Wakefield Master's plays to modern readers.

The Killing of Abel was probably edited and rewritten by the Wakefield Master. His typical nine-line stanza—found in his other plays—is possibly uniquely his; elements of the stanza have been detected by some researchers among the couplets of *The Killing of Abel*. The play also shares themes of human and divine relationships and a distinctive comic style with his other plays. The Wakefield Master has in common with other great playwrights the ability to mix pathos and humor; as in William Shakespeare's plays, tragedy is leavened with humor, and comedy with the tragic.

The plot of *The Killing of Abel* is that of the familiar biblical story: A jealous Cain commits the first murder by slaying his brother Abel; after lying to God about his deed, he is exiled by God. In this story, the Wakefield Master incorporates themes of the relationships between masters and servants, the nature of good and evil, and the universality of sin. Some critics assert that the themes of the play are too complex for its intended audience of farmers, tradespeople, and the general citizenry of Wakefield; others note that the play is loose and disorganized. Neither negative criticism is fair to the play. The first one underestimates the audience; the middle and lower classes of medieval England were deeply inculcated with religious doctrine. Nearly everything they did could have religious significance; John Gardner points out in *The Construction of the Wakefield Cycle* (1974) that the intended audience of *The Killing of Abel* would have been able to recognize in Cain, the plowman, the symbol of "the assiduous Christian." The audience would have understood the Christian symbolism and much of the basic theology. Medieval England of the Wakefield Master's day was not untouched by the Humanist revolution—as the secular themes of the Master's plays indicate—but religion still gave life and its events their meanings for the Towneley Cycle's audience. Such an audience would have perceived, for example, in the relationship between Garcio and his master Cain the relationship between God and Christian, and Satan and sinner. Gardner asserts that if Garcio is understood to be a demon, then *The Killing of Abel*'s seemingly confused structure makes sense. Simply put, if Garcio is a demon and servant of Cain, then Cain is the servant of Satan, although he may not know whom he serves. The role of Garcio need not be demoniac, though, to serve its purpose. He remarks early in the play that "Som of you ar his [Garcio's master's] men." Gardner takes Garcio's master to be not only Cain but also Satan, thus making members of the audience servants of Satan; this is a good reading, but not one that would be readily picked up by an audience during the rush of the play's events. Cain's entrance is enough to lend meaning to Garcio's assertion; he enters while driving a plow team before him. The comparison of men with animals was common in medieval literature, and like the animals, some of the audience would be servants of sin—of the first murderer, Cain. Such an image is consistent with the Wakefield Master's work; its wit is biting. Cain is the focus of the play, the representative of the universality of sin.

The sophistication of imagery and theme in *The Killing of Abel* is typical of the Wakefield Master's work. That he should turn the story of Cain and Abel into one that involves his audience typifies his efforts to stretch the subjects of his plays to encompass universal truths. *Noah* continues the themes of master-and-servant relationships, with the relationship between God and Noah opposed to that between Noah and Uxor. Noah is a near-perfect servant; God commands, and he obeys. In his role as servant of God, Noah is Christlike—a notion that would have been immediately comprehended by a medieval audience because Noah was commonly used as a Christ figure in religious teachings. The serious theme of Noah as a type of Christ is wonderfully blended with Noah's comic relationship with Uxor, his wife. Like Christ, Noah gathers his flock from the world; the ark was often treated as a symbol of the body of Christ by medieval biblical commentators, and thus Noah gathers the world to the symbol of the body of Christ, much as the Word of Christ is supposed to do. When Noah deals with Uxor, he is sometimes confounded by her cantankerous refusals to cooperate with him; when the great storm comes, she sits at her spinning wheel and ignores all entreaties to board the ark until the water rises near her. Her behavior at home and in the ark is amusing; it also represents the cantankerous, mulish, and foolish behavior with which Christ must contend in His Christian servants. The Wakefield Master blends biblical story, Christian tradition, and earthy humor into a play that tells Noah's story, shows the relationship between human beings and God, and presages the coming of Christ later in the cycle.

The Wakefield Master contributed two plays about the coming of Christ to the Towneley Cycle, *The First Shepherds' Play* and *The Second Shepherds' Play*. Some scholars suggest that *The First Shepherds' Play* was meant to end a day's series of performances and that *The Second Shepherds' Play* was meant to begin the next day's performances. Another possible explanation for two shepherds' plays is that the first one gave the Wakefield Master inspiration for the second, better play, and he chose to preserve both. *The First Shepherds' Play* focuses on three pastors or shepherds who begin as comic figures incapable of understanding the spiritual world and who end with enough wisdom to perceive the divine nature of the Christ child. John Gardner calls the shepherds "clowns (in the modern sense)" and his argument that the play's farcical elements represent Old Jerusalem, body, and earth, and that the coming of understanding represents New Jerusalem, spirit, and heaven, is persuasive. A less traditional view is taken by Jeffrey Helterman in *Symbolic Action in the Plays of the Wakefield Master*, published in 1981, in which he asserts that the play portrays the growth of imagination—that the shepherds begin by perceiving their world only in literal terms and that, as their imaginations grow, they come to perceive the greater reality of the spirit. *The First Shepherds' Play* is impressive in the sophistication of the readings it allows; the Wakefield Master grapples with difficult and important questions about the human spirit and humanity's ability to comprehend the divine. The play also is good entertainment; Gardner compares the shepherds to the twentieth century's Marx Brothers, and when one reads the shepherds' argument over nonexistent sheep, the comparison seems apt.

The Second Shepherds' Play is the Wakefield Master's best play and is one of the masterpieces of world drama. It exhibits the Wakefield Master's control of form; it is carefully structured to reflect the Holy Trinity, containing three shepherds, three gifts to the Christ child, and three dramatic movements, among other sets of three. The characters of the shepherds—Coll, Gyb, and Daw—are well defined and realistic. In fact, the realism of the characters, combined with the realistic earthiness of their humor, has encouraged some critics to discuss *The Second Shepherds' Play* as if it were a modern play instead of the medieval pageant it is. The Wakefield Master's genius is revealed in the combination of realistic characterization and tone with medieval Christian traditions; he anticipates the sophistication of later English drama but remains rooted in the concerns natural to the subject of the play.

The three shepherds are oppressed by misbehaving gentry and a cold and almost barren world. Their joking and singing are intended to fend off despair. When Mak enters the stage, the shepherds have shown their spiritual unreadiness to know of the birth of Christ. The subsequent farcical scenes with Mak prepare them for seeing the Christ child. Mak, dressed as if one of the gentry, dupes the shepherds and steals one of their sheep. In order to hide his crime, he and his wife, Gyll, hide the sheep in a cradle. When the shepherds come to look for their sheep, Mak claims that the cradle holds his new child. The shepherd Daw's anger changes to friendly interest; he likes children. Coll and Gyb are similarly moved. They are willing to set aside their suspicions. The discovery of the sheep and the tossing up and down of Mak are moments of boisterous comedy that might distract from the significance of what has happened. The shepherds have matured from complainers to doers—from uncharitable people to ones who wanted to visit kindnesses on Mak's putative son. The parallel between the sheep in the cradle and Christ, the Lamb of God, is obvious, and the three shepherds' readiness to offer gifts to the sheep-child represents their preparedness to give to Christ. Less obvious is the notion put forward by some scholars that Mak is an anti-God figure. Perhaps the Wakefield Master intended Mak and the stolen sheep to be antitheses of God and Christ, but their roles make good sense without heavily allegorical interpretations: Mak, Gyll, and the sheep provide a rehearsal for the three shepherds.

The play lends itself to allegorical interpretations that enhance its literary sophistication, but its dramatic success is the growth of the shepherds, and the careful development of events and form is wonderful. The play is not, as some might contend, two plays: one of Mak and the shepherds and another one attached, like a coda, of the shepherds visiting Christ. It is a careful rendering of three steps in the lives of Coll, Gyb, and Daw. They begin as lost souls in a universe whose order they do not understand; they move into the world of disorder, in which sheep are babies, in which the wife, Gyll, rules the man, Mak, and good and evil are confused; and they mature to an understanding of the importance of the birth of Christ, to Whom they bring with open hearts gifts they can happily give. Christ is the restoration of God's order and the negation of oppression, disorder, evil, and despair. *The Second Shepherds' Play* is a blend of comedy and pathos worthy of a great playwright; it is a dramatic gem that speaks of hope.

Herod the Great is possibly the Wakefield Master's best allegory. Herod, the slaughterer of the Innocents, was traditionally a satanic figure. Some critics view the Wakefield Master's Herod as a satanic parody of God; Herod is called "kyng of kyngys" and is ruler over all the world. He and his court are ostentatious and loud; he is prone to claiming powers for himself that are God's alone. He represents the old order—the world before the new age Christ brings to Earth. As such, he represents satanic perversion of order and virtue: Bragging substitutes for deeds, the master rules by fear instead of love, and courage is manifested by the butchering of infants. The Wakefield Master's comedy, open and earthy in the shepherds' plays, is dark and terrible in *Herod the Great*. The strutting Herod and his moronic sycophants are ridiculous; their absurdity is laughable, yet the results of their hellish views of the world are awful. The absurd Herod becomes a monster when, onstage, his troops pull babies from their mothers and stab the infants: "His hart-blood shall thou se," declares a soldier to a mother. The language indicates that the audience is shown stage blood; swords are reddened and babies are then displayed to their mothers. Rarely in literature is humor so turned in on itself; the silly king arrogates to himself the prerogatives of God in a contest between himself and the Lord. Thematically, Herod is Satan lashing out at the newborn Christ.

The Wakefield Master is admired by many critics for his comedy rather than for his other dramatic traits, perhaps because his comedy presages modern dramatic techniques and was innovative for his era. His comedy can provide a modern reader with an exciting sense of seeing postmedieval drama being invented. Often, however, critics ignore his other achievements because of their interest in his comedy, missing the pathos in *The*

Killing of Abel and the shepherds' plays. His skill encompassed the major elements of good drama, and in *Herod the Great* he actually turned his comic skills into evocations of horror and palpable evil.

In *The Buffeting*, he used his talent for creating lively, bantering dialogue to convey, not comedy, but brutal insensitivity. Christ is tried by Cayphas and Anna in a mockery of a trial; one of His torturers says "wychcraft he mase" (he makes witchcraft), accusing Christ of witchery. *The Buffeting* features another of the Wakefield Master's reversals; the evildoers accuse Christ of evil. They derogate his teachings, subject him to an insane trial and to torture. The play seems peopled by madmen, with Christ like a rock of serenity in the middle of a world gone crazy. Jeffrey Helterman argues powerfully for Jesus' silence as a sign of the Wakefield Master's genius, suggesting that the Wakefield Master turns Christ's silence into words, that in the context of the cycle as a whole, the play's audience would speak Christ's words for Him as they helplessly watched lying witnesses try to degrade Him. The easy conversation of the torturers, Cayphas, and Anna, with their smiles and jokes and their almost serene confidence in merciless law, is disquieting, not amusing. Christ's silence provides answers to their gibes and accusations; these are people who are out of touch with the new world Christ has brought with Him. Christ is sanity amid the insane; the lies of His accusers attest His truth. They answer themselves by revealing the emptiness of their beliefs. *Herod the Great* was disquietingly horrific; *The Buffeting* is disquieting through the contrast between worldly values and heavenly ones. Christ need not even speak; His presence alone answers His enemies.

The Wakefield Master was an unusually talented playwright. He used tradition and the Bible to create plays that make insightful comments on humanity. Although he was very much a medieval Christian, his authorial techniques presaged the outburst of English Humanism that occurred only two or three generations after he wrote. Notable for his wit and skill with language, he was also a highly skilled dramatist who took best advantage of what the form of the mystery pageant offered him. Characterization, format, theme, and staging—in these and the other major facets of drama he was superbly accomplished. He was therefore not only a good writer of mystery plays, nor only a good medieval dramatist, but also a great dramatist for any age. Perhaps the strongest impression one retains after reading his plays is that of a writer who knew people and knew how to show them truthfully onstage, one who understood the problems that afflict every generation.

Bibliography

Gardner, John. *The Construction of the Wakefield Cycle.* Carbondale: Southern Illinois University Press, 1974. This general discussion of the cycle contains close analysis of the more important individual plays and the key connections among them. Credits the Wakefield Master as the controlling hand in the design of the cycle. Gardner analyzes the Wakefield Master's connection with the *Mactacio Abel* and investigates the comparison made with the York poet.

Helterman, Jeffrey. *Symbolic Action in the Plays of the Wakefield Master.* Athens: University of Georgia Press, 1981. In this full-length study of the playwright, Helterman states his belief that the Wakefield Master rewrote existing plays in the final third (the "passion group") of the cycle and that the success led to the composition of six new plays (including *Mactacio Abel*), each of which is discussed in a substantial chapter. The Wakefield Master has a special talent in all of his works for creating villains who are colorful and memorable. Excellent bibliography.

Kahrl, Stanley J. *Traditions of Medieval English Drama.* Pittsburgh: University of Pittsburgh Press, 1975. The Wakefield Master's great originality is evident in the *Coliphizacio* in characterizing those who interrogate and torture Christ. The high priest, Caiphas, is shown as a bully; his son-in-law, Annas, is shown as a sadist. Kahrl contends that, in general, medieval playwrights insert contemporary stereotypes into biblical periods: Cain, for example, is shown as an English farmer abusing servants and failing to tithe.

Meyers, Walter E. *A Figure Given: Typology in the Wakefield Plays.* Pittsburgh: Duquesne University Press, 1970. Argues that the types of dramatic unity that are praised in *Secunda Pastorum* appear in five other Wakefield plays and that this results "from a particular theory of time arising from the typological method of exegesis." Views Mak as a type of Satan and compares *Secunda Pastorum* and *Prima Pastorum* on key points. Indebted to Homer A. Watt's study (below).

Stevens, Martin. *Four Middle English Mystery Cycles.* Princeton, N.J.: Princeton University Press, 1987. Stevens considers the Wakefield Cycle to have been constructed as a unit and asserts that the Wakefield Master was the guiding mind in the creation of this unit. Evidence for this interpretation is found in the "Wakefield Stanza." Illustrations.

Watt, Homer A. "The Dramatic Unity of the *Secunda Pastorum.*" In *Essays and Studies in Honor of Carleton Brown.* New York: New York University Press, 1940. This groundbreaking study finds the two major divisions of the play linked by parallel episodes: Mak's insistence that a sheep is his son is parallel to the final scene, wherein Mary's son is seen as the Lamb of God. This pseudo-Nativity scene was added to the biblical story to create a burlesque of the Nativity scene.

Kirk H. Beetz
(Updated by *Howard L. Ford*)

DEREK WALCOTT

Born: Castries, St. Lucia, West Indies; January 23, 1930

Principal drama

Henri Christophe: A Chronicle, pr., pb. 1950; *The Sea of Dauphin*, pr., pb. 1954; *The Wine of the Country*, pr. 1956; *Drums and Colours*, pr. 1958, pb. 1961; *Ti-Jean and His Brothers*, pr. 1958, pb. 1970 (music by Andre Tanker); *Dream on Monkey Mountain*, pr. 1967, pb. 1970; *Dream on Monkey Mountain and Other Plays*, pb. 1970; *In a Fine Castle*, pr. 1970; *The Joker of Seville*, pr. 1974, pb. 1978 (adaptation of Tirso de Molina's *El burlador de Sevilla*; music by Galt MacDermot); *O Babylon!*, pr. 1976, pb. 1978; *Remembrance*, pr. 1977, pb. 1980; *The Joker of Seville and O Babylon!: Two Plays*, pb. 1978; *Pantomime*, pr. 1978, pb. 1980; *Marie LaVeau*, pr. 1979; *Remembrance and Pantomime*, pb. 1980; *Beef, No Chicken*, pr. 1981; *Three Plays*, pb. 1986; *Steel*, pr. 1991 (music by MacDermot).

Other literary forms

Derek A. Walcott began writing poetry and poetic drama while he was still a teenager. First on street corners in Castries, then in regional journals, and ultimately through major publishing houses in England and the United States, his poetry has gathered a following until he now enjoys international recognition. His early affinity for the Metaphysical poets is abundantly clear in his first collection, *In a Green Night* (1962). Since then, his travels and his interest in a variety of cultures have added considerable variety and depth to successive volumes: *The Castaway and Other Poems* (1965), *The Gulf and Other Poems* (1969), the semiautobiographical *Another Life* (1973), *Sea Grapes* (1976), *The Star-Apple Kingdom* (1979), *The Fortunate Traveller* (1981), and *Midsummer* (1984). In addition to his duties as founding director of and chief writer for the Trinidad Theatre Workshop from 1959 to 1977, Walcott contributed steadily as a columnist on the arts to the *Trinidad Guardian*. A recording of Walcott reading selections from his own work may be found on Caedmon's *Poets of the West Indies Reading Their Own Works* (1971); Semp Studios Ltd. (Port of Spain) has recorded the sound track for Walcott's play *The Joker of Seville* (score by Galt MacDermot in 1975). His poems collected in *Omeros* (1990), based on Homer's epics, were instrumental in his winning the Nobel Prize in Literature in 1992.

Achievements

Recognition of Walcott's promise as a playwright came early, when in

1958 he received a Rockefeller Foundation grant to work with theater in New York. What was to have been an extended period of study was cut short, however, when the scarcity of serious plays with major parts for black actors drove him to return to the West Indies, where he established the Trinidad Theatre Workshop in 1959. In the short time that he had been away, he had been selected to write a play *(Drums and Colours)* to commemorate the opening of the first Federal Parliament of the West Indies on April 23, 1958. The Negro Ensemble Company performance of his *Dream on Monkey Mountain* garnered an Obie Award in 1971. The Royal Shakespeare Company commissioned Walcott to write an adaptation of Tirso de Molina's *El burlador de Sevilla*, which became *The Joker of Seville* in 1974.

Walcott's poetry has also been well received, winning a number of awards: the Guinness Award for Poetry in 1961, the Royal Society of Literature Award for *The Castaway* in 1965, the Cholmondeley Award for *The Gulf* in 1969, the Jock Campbell New Statesman Award for his autobiographical *Another Life* in 1973, the Welsh Arts Council's International Writer's Prize in 1980, and a John D. and Catherine MacArthur Award in 1981. He won the Queen Elizabeth II Gold Medal for Poetry in 1988 and the Nobel Prize in 1992.

Because drama is performed live before an audience, its impact is more immediate and of a more communal nature than that of fiction and poetry. Walcott's major contribution to West Indian literature may be his dramatic re-creation of the scenes, the people, and the language of his native region. On a larger scale, his Trinidad Theatre Workshop tours, as well as performances of his plays by foreign companies, have brought West Indian life to the attention of audiences on virtually every continent.

Drawing from St. Lucia, Trinidad, Jamaica, and other islands, Walcott uses the patchwork history of his Caribbean people to focus on problems that relate to all humankind. The child of mixed blood, he embodies the cultural heritage of Europe and the New World. Translating this legacy to the stage, he re-creates conquistadors, slaves, indentured servants, colonialists, and the unheralded common men and women who may be the most interesting figures of all—for their ingenuity in simply surviving.

The culture of Western Europe lends a shaping hand to Walcott's polyglot material. Over the years, he has been indebted to sources as diverse as the Jacobean dramatists, the Spanish Golden Age, John Millington Synge, T. S. Eliot, Bertolt Brecht, the Japanese Nō theater, and the Greek classics. Conveniently for Walcott, Trinidad's fabulous carnival provides the raw material and inspiration he needs—masquerades, pantomime, satiric calypso, massive choreography, the meeting of disparate cultures in one gigantic bacchanal—for blending all the disparate ingredients of his native background.

Biography

In Castries, capital of the small Caribbean island of St. Lucia, Derek Alton Walcott and his twin brother, Roderick, were born January 23, 1930. Their mother, Alix, was a teacher in a Methodist primary school, while their father, Warwick, was a civil official and a gifted artist. Although Walcott lost his father when he was hardly a year old, fatherly guidance was provided by the St. Lucian painter Harold Simmons, the mentor commemorated in Walcott's autobiographical poem *Another Life*.

Being of mixed blood—his grandfathers were white Dutch and English, his grandmothers black—and the son of Protestants in a predominantly Catholic island, Walcott experienced from an early age the schizophrenia of New World blacks in an alien environment. While childhood in a colonial backwater island might seem disadvantageous, Walcott believes that his classroom exposure to traditional Western culture—Greek, Roman, and British—was vitally enriching. Combining this with his informal contact with African slave tales and life in the streets, he learned to admire both currents of his dual heritage. Early evidence of his gift for cultural synthesis appears in one of Walcott's first plays, *Henri Christophe*. This dramatization of the famous black rebel general is couched in the poetic images and the elaborate language of Elizabethan England.

In order to provide an outlet for his drama, Walcott and his brother founded the St. Lucia Arts Guild in 1950, the same year in which Walcott was awarded a scholarship to pursue advanced education at the University of the West Indies in Mona, Jamaica. His graduation in 1953 was followed in 1954 by his marriage to Faye Moyston. Four years later, as a result of a Rockefeller Foundation grant to study theater in New York, Walcott reached a major turning point in his career.

Two specific influences in New York seem to have given Walcott the impetus to launch his professional career. First was his discovery, through Bertolt Brecht, of Oriental theater. In Brecht there were precedents for using the ritual, mime, symbolic gestures, rhythmic movement, and music of Walcott's native background. Second was Walcott's realization that there were precious few major roles for black actors in the standard repertoire. Thus, he resolved to return to the islands and create a style of drama that would be suited to the multifarious elements of the West Indian character: an indigenous drama.

Walcott's creation of the Trinidad Theatre Workshop came in 1959, the same year as his divorce from his first wife, after which he remarried, went through a second divorce, and married again. From the first two marriages there are three children, two daughters and a son. Indications of his struggle to maintain himself as a creative writer and continue living in the Caribbean may be seen in many of the articles he wrote for the *Trinidad Guardian* in the 1960's and early 1970's. His column often served as a forum for arguing the cause of a national theater. After his second divorce and his resignation from the Trinidad Theatre Workshop in 1977, Walcott began dividing his time between the New York area and Trinidad. In 1982, he established a new theatrical company, Warwick Productions. Thereafter, he and his wife, Norline Metivier, a Trinidadian actress, moved to Brookline, Massachusetts, where Walcott combined teaching at Boston University with writing poetry and plays and occasionally directing theater productions; he travels between Boston and the Caribbean.

Walcott's musical *Steel*, with music by Galt MacDermot, opened in Boston in April, 1991, and moved to Philadelphia in May of the same year.

In 1992, Walcott was honored with the Nobel Prize in Literature for his lifelong work in drama and poetry, from *Henri Christophe* and *Steel*, to his breakthrough poems in *In a Green Night*, to the publication of his poetic work, *Omeros*, a sixty-four-chapter Caribbean epic. The Swedish Academy said of Walcott: "In him West Indian culture has found its great poet."

Analysis

Prior to his formative experience in New York in 1958, Derek A. Walcott's playwriting suffered from his failure to integrate his folk subjects with borrowed European forms. Alongside *Henri Christophe*'s Elizabethan verse is *The Sea at Dauphin,* with deliberate echoes of John Millington Synge's *Riders to the Sea* (pb. 1903): peasant fishermen enduring their fate with unassuming nobility. *Drums and Colours,* with its extensive pageantry and broad range of characters (from the days of discovery up to the 1958 West Indian Federation) may be said to have settled any debt Walcott owed to West Indian history. In the year of the initial performance of *Drums and Colours,* he also put into production *Ti-Jean and His Brothers,* his first stylized West Indian play.

In an interview entitled "Meanings: From a Conversation with Derek Walcott," Walcott explains the type of dynamic fusion that West Indian drama requires. Studying Brecht in New York, he came to the conclusion that the besetting sin of most Caribbean theater was its self-indulgent exuberance. Brecht's adaptation of highly ritualized Oriental techniques offered the model Walcott needed. Without stifling the vitality of West Indian folk spirit, he sought to instill discipline. Since his culture is an amalgam of the African, the Oriental, and the Occidental, Walcott draws from them all. From Europe, he takes classical conventions of language and structure; from Africa and parts of the East, he adopts ritual ceremonies involving dance, mime, and narrative traditions; from the Kabuki and Nō plays, he takes expressive power and beauty in restrained gesture and formalized rhythm.

A St. Lucian folktale with vestiges of African animal fable provides the story of Ti-Jean, a young black man who outsmarts the plantation-master devil. Dialogue is spiced with fast-paced puns, metaphors, and verbal play. Movement is carried by music, dance, mime, abrupt pauses, asides to the audience, and intervals of conversation among the animal chorus about human affairs. Pleased as Walcott was with the blend of discipline and folk life in *Ti-Jean and His Brothers,* this work was but a prelude to the more profound and highly imaginative *Dream on Monkey Mountain.*

Completed especially for the Trinidad Theatre Workshop's first tour outside the Caribbean, *Dream on Monkey Mountain* appeared in Toronto in 1967. Subsequent productions in the United States and on NBC television in 1970 garnered the prestigious Obie Award for the best foreign play of 1970-1971. Multiple themes and the dream framework account for only a fraction of the play's complexity. Characters exchange parts, glide into symbols, are revived from death; the plot develops in fragments as the hero, Makak, tries to explain his vision of a white goddess. The very names of characters imply allegory: Makak, the monkey, is an ugly charcoal burner who must come to grips with his awareness of being black; Lestrade, neither black nor white, is an ambivalent straddler.

Lestrade's stereotypical house-Negro prejudices surface in the prologue, when he ridicules Makak's apelike appearance and his obsessive dream of a white woman. The first scene is a flashback to Makak's first vision, where he reveals that he has been called back to Africa, to his true place as a lion-king. Armed with his new racial identity, Makak is able to heal the sick while crowds pour in to hear his words. Unfortunately, Moustique, his traveling companion, is quick to exploit opportunity; like many a trickster character of West Indian folklore, he turns faith and trust into profitable enterprise. When his tricks are discovered, he is killed by a mob, only to return to life again in later scenes.

Although the play is cast in terms of black consciousness, the action continually pushes the meaning of the narrative to a broader plane. In his dream, Makak escapes and establishes his African throne. Corporal Lestrade, in pursuing the rebels, goes native and ultimately becomes Makak's most fanatic convert, a blind advocate of black supremacy. Caught up in the frenzy for power and revenge, Makak is helpless to avert the internecine bloodletting and the execution of all symbols of whiteness that follow. Moustique, for example, is resurrected only to be killed a second time because of his violation of the original dream.

Paradoxically, Makak's beheading of the white goddess finally frees him from his obsession with blackness. By doing away with his illusion, Makak is free to become himself; he completes the journey by recognizing the possibility of beauty in his own black body, by reclaiming his birthright in Africa, and ultimately by discarding his racial crutch. In his introduction to *Dream on Monkey Mountain and Other Plays*, Walcott argues that once blacks have given up the wish to be white, they assume the longing to be black; the difference is clear, but both pursuits are careers. He adds that the depth of a person's roots is related to the shallowness of his "racial despair."

In the epilogue, then, Walcott leads his protagonist to his essential being through the act of understanding. Makak's first recollection after the dream is his real name, Felix Hobain. Upon his release after the night that he has spent in jail, he determines to establish himself on his mountain and fulfill his chosen destiny—neither white nor black, but a West Indian with a home, a job, and self-esteem. Even Moustique recognizes that Makak is a new man.

Thus, the final image of *Dream on Monkey Mountain* is not the beheading of a white goddess but rather a hopeful vision of a man's accommodation to his environment, a fact easily overlooked by critics seeking racial conflict. Despite the narrative's violent overtones, the resolution focuses on personal needs. Within its blending of dream and reality, its stylized movement, and its humor, the play offers a serious prescription for evolutionary development.

Because of the vital Spanish background of Trinidad's culture and because of the society's predilection for the flamboyant male, Walcott may seem well-suited to revive the ancient legend of Don Juan. This, at any rate, was the decision of the Royal Shakespeare Company when they commissioned him in 1974 to write a modern version of Tirso de Molina's *El burlador de Sevilla.* Don Juan the aristocratic violator of maidenhood is a departure from Walcott's peasant heroes, yet he is a rich vehicle for some of Walcott's primary themes. Juan is the archetypal lover, the arch-rebel, the trickster, the Dionysian liberator, and, in Walcott's version, the sacrificial god. Rather than alter these dimensions, Walcott prefers to amplify certain characteristics and expand the field of action to include the New World.

While Tirso places Juan's second scene of seduction (of Tisbea) in a Spanish coastal village, Walcott's *The Joker of Seville* sends him across the Atlantic to a Caribbean island. Whether in the Old or New World, however, Juan's adventures lead to death and immortal legend. He embodies an irrational force—the subconscious impulse to defy the prohibitions that were first imposed in Eden and then in society. As it turns out, the men he outwits learn to see vicarious fulfillment, through him, of their own suppressed drives. While they despise him and the dark elements their consciences attempt to keep under control, they secretly relish his freedom. Ironically, having selected his inhuman role, Juan denies himself all the pleasures of ordinary life. He admits that he cannot feel love. Instead, like Dionysus, he presents to humankind the possibility of uninhibited pleasure and pain, but he ultimately suffers and returns to the cold earth.

Death, nevertheless, does not have the final word. Juan's corpse is carried off to the insistent calypso beat of a song of resurrection. Juan's compensation, like Makak's in *Dream on Monkey Mountain,* is to attain the status of a dream image. Unlike Makak, however, Juan does not have the privilege of descending from the realm of legend to the earthly plane of day-to-day living.

The lively music and expressive dance that animate *The Joker of Seville* again attest Walcott's inventive use of West Indian culture. The same may be said of his next major play, *O Babylon!*—the music in the play is based on the reggae of Jamaica's Rastafarian cult. This cult also is the logical source of the play's ritualistic elements: the "four horsemen of the apocalypse" and the visions. At the center of the plot is a conflict between the temptations of material gain and human beings' yearning for spiritual fulfillment. Land developers with Mafia ties plan to acquire an area settled by a Rastafarian community. The corporation buys the support of politicians, social workers, and weaker members of the settlement. Aaron, the protagonist, and Sufferer, one of the older brethren, hold out against official harassment, physical abuse, and bribery. Matters are forced to a climax by the news that the Rastafarians' god in the flesh, Haile Selassie, is arriving. (The play is set in 1966 to coincide with Selassie's actual visit to Jamaica.)

Problems arise when Aaron and a few others are prohibited from accompanying their leader back to Africa. Frustrated, Aaron commits arson; arrested, tried, and jailed, he is deprived of his one chance to see Selassie. His lawlessness comes close to driving his girlfriend away; more important, it costs the brethren their land. Those who are left behind after their friends sail for Ethiopia must return to the Babylon of corrupt Kingston or begin anew in the mountains.

Despite the losses, Walcott concludes with a triumphant vision of a heavenly Zion. The final scene is rescued from escapism by explicit passages that show Aaron gaining a sense of his own belonging. In two days of meditation in the quiet mountains, Aaron finds peace with his homeland and within himself—the place, Walcott implies, where one must seek one's authentic identity.

Remembrance and *Pantomime* seem subdued in comparison with the exuberant music and action of their immediate predecessors. *Remembrance* was first performed in St. Croix in April, 1977. Albert Jordan, a retired schoolteacher, reminisces for a local newspaper reporter about the independence and Black Power movements that swept through Trinidad and interfered with the life he would have preferred to live in peace.

At first recalling only mistakes, Jordan contends that his efforts as teacher, husband, father, and amateur writer have been futile. Students called him "Uncle Tom" because of the standards he asserted in the classroom. His wife constantly chided him about his get-rich-quick lottery tickets. The police killed one son during a Black Power confrontation. His younger son is risking a slower death by undertaking the life of an artist in the lost and forgotten colony of Trinidad.

Contrary to his own assessment, Jordan is worthy of the credit he only grudgingly allows himself for having raised his students' consciousness to the point where Black Power found receptive imaginations. Both sons' independent choices might seem futile to him, yet they reveal the strength of character to undertake ambitious destinies. Others who know Jordan—his wife and son, the editor of the *Belmont Bugle*—respect what he stands for in spite of his own self-criticism. Had he really been a weakling, he would not have called for reason against the furious rhetoric and blind revolutionary action that surrounded him. Jordan's life is the stable factor blending the episodes reenacted on the stage. At the close of the final curtain, he has come to terms with himself and he is ready to begin the review of his eventful career.

Pantomime involves no reverie, but it draws on history to accomplish an enlightening as well as entertaining tour de force. The action involves an agreement—between Harry, an Englishman managing a second-rate tourist hotel, and Jackson, a struggling calypsonian—concerning a skit to be performed before the hotel's patrons. After much argument about the propriety of the skit, the two undertake a reversal of the Robinson Crusoe and Friday roles.

Harry tries to play his part at first, but balks at the extreme idea of having African culture and gods imposed on a civilized Christian. Jackson, who is quick to convert to the inversion, seizes the opportunity to note that Harry's refusal is precisely the history of colonialism. At the point when a native asserts equality with his master, the dominant power wants to revert to the old order.

In act 2, Harry is more willing to pursue the implications of racial and cultural equality, and Jackson instructs him in the characteristics of a more mature version of Robinson Crusoe. His West Indian Crusoe would be a practical man, not Harry's lonely romanticist yearning for his distant wife and son. The New World Crusoe would come to grips with the raw material of his environment. Jackson sees him as the original Creole because of his faith and effective action. The immediate application of this new version is to Harry's personal situation. With Jackson's encouragement, he acts out some of his frustrations over his failures as an actor and as a husband. Living through the experience, Harry gains deeper understanding, and both men achieve a more equitable relationship.

After the publication of *Remembrance and Pantomime* (the two plays appeared together in the same volume), Walcott produced *Marie LaVeau* and *Beef, No Chicken*, both set in the West Indies. *Steel*, a musical Walcott wrote in collaboration with Galt MacDermot, focused on the birth of the region's steel-drum music. Walcott has neither abandoned his native islands nor adopted the trappings of a nationalist. Synthesizing one influence after another, he has imposed his own stamp on the literature of a multifaceted New World culture. Not only are the West Indies enriched by his lucid dramatization of human complexities, but the mainstream of Western literature is greatly expanded as well.

Other major works

POETRY: *In a Green Night*, 1962; *Selected Poems*, 1964; *The Castaway and Other Poems*, 1965; *The Gulf and Other Poems*, 1969; *Another Life*, 1973; *Sea Grapes*, 1976; *The Star-Apple Kingdom*, 1979; *The Fortunate Traveller*, 1981; *Midsummer*, 1984; *Collected Poems, 1948-1984*, 1986; *The Arkansas Testament*, 1987; *Omeros*, 1990.

NONFICTION: "Meanings: From a Conversation with Derek Walcott," 1970 (in *Performing Arts*).

Bibliography

Hamner, Robert D. *Derek Walcott*. Boston: Twayne, 1981. An analytical appreciation of the poet and dramatist in midcareer. Although out of date, it is valuable for the balance of poetic discussion and dramatic analysis, and the placement of Walcott in St. Lucian literature as well as Third World literature in general. Includes a strong discussion of *Dream on Monkey Mountain*, a chronology, a good bibliography, and an index.

Kelly, Kevin. "Man of *Steel*." *Globe* (Boston), March 31, 1991. The musical *Steel*, first written as a film, is previewed before its Boston opening at the American Repertory Theatre. Walcott discusses Trinidad, American preconceptions about Caribbean culture, his collaboration with Galt MacDermot, and the possibilities of *Steel* reaching Broadway.

Ross, Robert L., ed. *International Literature in English: Essays on the Major Writers*. New York: Garland, 1991. Robert D. Hamner contributes an essay on Walcott, taking his biography up to the Catherine MacArthur Award in 1981. Counts fourteen books of poetry (to *The Arkansas Testament*, 1987) and four volumes of plays, and discusses the "chiaroscuro" of Walcott's aesthetic choices, which "creates the illusion of bulk and depth for three-dimensional objects in a two-dimensional plane."

Rule, Sheila. "Walcott, Poet of Caribbean, Is Awarded the Nobel Prize." *The New York Times*, October 9, 1992, pp. A1, B6. A good overview of Walcott's accomplishments, with a chronology of his poems and plays and an "appreciation" by James Atlas that includes several Walcott quotations. The Swedish Academy of Letters cites his "historical vision, the outcome of a multi-cultural commitment," referring to "the Caribbean where he lives, the English language, and his Africa origin." Two photographs.

Walcott, Derek. "An Interview with Derek Walcott." Interview by David

Montenegro. *Partisan Review* 57 (1990): 202-214. This long interview begins with analyses of Walcott's poems and discusses climate changes from St. Lucia to Boston, as a metaphor for general misplaced attitudes about the Caribbean. Walcott's philosophical overview of American theater is that it is "closeted and chambered and dark and small." He believes that American playwrights "aren't wild enough." Discusses Rainer Maria Rilke, suffering, and the "deadening" loss of communication. Not a biographical account—more an intellectual discussion with the interviewer.

Robert D. Hamner
(Updated by *Thomas J. Taylor*)

WENDY WASSERSTEIN

Born: Brooklyn, New York; October 18, 1950

Principal drama

Any Woman Can't, pr. 1973; *Happy Birthday, Montpelier Pizz-zazz*, pr. 1974; *When Dinah Shore Ruled the Earth*, pr. 1975 (with Christopher Durang); *Uncommon Women and Others*, pr. 1975 (one act), pr. 1977 (two acts), pb. 1978; *Isn't It Romantic*, pr. 1981, pr. 1983 (revised version), pb. 1984; *Tender Offer*, pr. 1983 (one act); *The Man in a Case*, pr., pb. 1986 (one act; adapted from Anton Chekhov's short story of the same title); *Miami*, pr. 1986 (musical); *The Heidi Chronicles*, pr., pb. 1988; *The Heidi Chronicles and Other Plays*, pb. 1990; *The Sisters Rosensweig*, pr. 1992.

Other literary forms

Wendy Wasserstein, though best known for her plays, is the author of several teleplays, including *The Sorrows of Gin* (1979), an adaptation of John Cheever's short story. She has written several unproduced film scripts, among them an adaptation of her play *The Heidi Chronicles.* Her essays, which have appeared in numerous periodicals, including *Esquire* and *New York Woman*, have also been published in a collection entitled *Bachelor Girls* (1990).

Achievements

Wasserstein has been hailed as the foremost theatrical chronicler of the lives of women of her generation. Her plays, steeped in her unique brand of humor, are nevertheless moving, sometimes wrenching explorations of women's struggle for identity and fulfillment in a world of rapidly shifting social, sexual, and political mores. Most often against the backdrop of the burgeoning feminist movement, her characters navigate through obstacle courses of expectations—those of their parents, their lovers, their siblings, their friends, and, ultimately, themselves. They seek answers to fundamental questions: how to find meaning in life, and how to strike a balance between the need to connect and the need to be true to oneself. Wasserstein's works, which deftly pair wit and pathos, satire and sensitivity, have garnered numerous honors for her work, including the Pulitzer Prize, the Tony (Antoinette Perry) Award, the New York Drama Critics Circle Award, the Outer Critics Circle Award, and the Susan Smith Blackburn Prize.

Biography

Wendy Wasserstein was born on October 18, 1950, in Brooklyn, New York. She was the fourth and youngest child of Morris W. Wasserstein, a successful textile manufacturer, and Lola (Schleifer) Wasserstein, a housewife and nonprofessional dancer, both Jewish émigrés from central Europe. When she was thirteen, Wasserstein's family moved to Manhattan, where she attended the Calhoun School, an all-girl academy at which she discovered that she could get excused from gym class by writing the annual mother-daughter fashion show. Some years later, at Mount Holyoke, an elite Massachusetts women's college, a friend persuaded Wasserstein, a history major, to take a playwriting course at nearby Smith College. Encouraged by her instructor, she devoted much of her junior year, which she spent at Amherst College, performing in campus musicals before returning to complete her B.A. degree at Mount Holyoke in 1971.

Upon graduating, Wasserstein moved back to New York City, where she studied playwriting with Israel Horovitz and Joseph Heller at City College (where she later earned an M.A.) and held a variety of odd jobs to pay her rent. In 1973, her play *Any Woman Can't* was produced Off-Broadway at Playwrights Horizons, prompting her to accept admission to the Yale School of Drama, turning down the Columbia Business School, which had simultaneously offered her admission.

It was at Yale University, where she earned her M.F.A. degree in 1976, that Wasserstein's first hit play, *Uncommon Women and Others*, was conceived as a one-act. Ultimately expanded, it was given a workshop production at the prestigious National Playwrights Conference at the O'Neill Theater Center in Connecticut, a well-known launching pad for many successful playwrights. Indeed, in 1977, the Phoenix Theater's production of *Uncommon Women and Others* opened Off-Broadway at the Marymount Manhattan Theater. Although some critics objected to the play's lack of traditional plot, most praised Wasserstein's gifts as a humorist and a social observer.

By 1980, Wasserstein, established as one of the United States' most promising young playwrights, was commissioned by the Phoenix Theater to write *Isn't It Romantic* for its 1980-1981 season. The play's mixed reviews prompted Wasserstein to rework it under the guidance of director Gerald Gutierrez and André Bishop, artistic director of Playwrights Horizons. There, with a stronger narrative line and more in-depth character development, it opened in 1983 to widespread praise.

In the meantime, Wasserstein had been at work on several new pieces—among them a one-act play, *Tender Offer*, which was produced at Ensemble Studio Theater, and, collaborating with Jack Feldman and Bruce Sussman, a musical, *Miami*, which was presented as a work-in-progress at Playwrights Horizons in 1986. In 1988, one of Wasserstein's most ambitious works, *The Heidi Chronicles*, which had been previously performed in workshop at the Seattle Repertory Theater, had its New York premiere at Playwrights Horizons. It moved quickly to the larger Plymouth Theater on

Broadway, where it opened to mostly positive critical response. The play earned for Wasserstein the Pulitzer Prize, the Tony Award, and virtually every New York theater award. Wasserstein's eagerly awaited *The Sisters Rosensweig* opened at the Mitzi E. Newhouse Theater at Lincoln Center in the fall of 1992. Receiving widespread critical acclaim, the piece augmented her already prominent presence on the American dramatic scene.

Analysis

Wendy Wasserstein's plays are, for the most part, extremely consistent in their emphasis on character, their lack of classical structure, and their use of humor to explore or accompany serious, often poignant themes. Throughout her career, Wasserstein's central concern has been the role of women—particularly white, upper-middle-class, educated women—in contemporary society. Though her plays are suffused with uproarious humor, her typical characters are individuals engaged in a struggle to carve out an identity and a place for themselves in a society that has left them feeling, at worst, stranded and desolate and, at best, disillusioned. This is not to say that Wasserstein's worldview is bleak. Rather, the note of slightly skewed optimism with which she characteristically ends her works, along with her prevailing wit, lends them an air of levity and exuberance that often transcends her sober themes.

These themes—loneliness, isolation, and a profound desire for meaning in life—are examined by Wasserstein chiefly through character. One of the playwright's great strengths is her ability to poke fun at her characters without subjecting them to ridicule or scorn. Her women and men, with all their faults and foibles, are warmly and affectionately rendered. They engage their audience's empathy as they make their way through the mazes of their lives, trying to connect and to be of consequence in the world.

Wasserstein is best known for her four full-length, professional plays, *Uncommon Women and Others*, *Isn't It Romantic*, *The Heidi Chronicles*, and *The Sisters Rosensweig*. The first three plays have in common their episodic structure and non-plot-driven narrative. In each of the three, scenes unfold to reveal aspects of character. *Uncommon Women and Others*, for example, begins with five former college friends assessing their lives as they reunite six years after graduation. The body of the play is a flashback to their earlier life together at a small women's college under the often conflicting influences of the school's traditional "feminine" rituals and etiquette and the iconoclasm of the blossoming women's movement. In each of the two time frames, events are largely contexts for discussions in which Wasserstein's women use one another as sounding boards, each one testing and weighing her hopes, fears, expectations, and achievements against those of her friends. Similarly, in *Isn't It Romantic*, two former college friends, Janie Blumberg, a free-lance writer, and Harriet Cornwall, a corporate M.B.A., move through their postcollege lives, weighing marriage and children against independence and the life choices of their mothers against their own. The play climaxes at the point where the two women diverge, Harriet, who has formerly decried marriage, accepting a suitor's proposal out of fear of being alone, Janie choosing to remain unattached and to seek happiness within herself.

The Heidi Chronicles, though more far-reaching in scope, is also a character-driven play. Here, Wasserstein narrows her focus to one woman, Heidi Holland, but through her reflects the changing social and political mores of more than two decades. From the mid-1960's to the late 1980's, Heidi, like Wasserstein's earlier characters, struggles to find her identity. Moving through settings ranging from women's consciousness-raising meetings and protests to power lunches in trendy restaurants and Yuppie baby showers, Wasserstein's Heidi functions as, in her words, a "highly-informed spectator" who never quite seems to be in step with the prescribed order of the day. In a pivotal scene, Heidi, now an art-history professor, delivers a luncheon lecture entitled "Women, Where Are We Going?" Her speech, which disintegrates into a seeming nervous breakdown, ends with Heidi confessing that she feels "stranded": "And I thought the whole point was that we wouldn't feel stranded," she concludes, "I thought the whole point was that we were in this together."

Isolation and loneliness and, contrastingly, friendship and family are themes that run throughout these three earlier plays. Heidi's wish, expressed in that luncheon speech, is for the kind of solidarity that exists among the women in *Uncommon Women and Others*, who, while constantly comparing their lives, are not competitive in the sense of putting one another down. On the contrary, they are fervent in their praise and support of one another, a family unto themselves. Janie and Harriet, in *Isn't It Romantic*, share a relationship that is much the same until something comes between them, Harriet's decision to marry a man she hardly knows because he makes her feel "like [she has] a family." Heidi, on the other hand, at the point when she makes her speech, has no close women friends. Presumably, they are all off having babies and/or careers. Her decision, at the play's end, to adopt a Panamanian baby girl, thereby creating a family of her own, is much akin to Janie Blumberg's decision finally to unpack her crates in her empty apartment at *Isn't It Romantic*'s end and make a home for herself.

This desire on the part of Wasserstein's characters for a family and a place to belong has at its root the desire for self-affirmation. It is evident in the refrain that echoes throughout *Uncommon Women and Others*, "When we're twenty-five [thirty, forty, forty-five], we're going to be incredible," as well as in Janie Blumberg's invocation, "I am," borrowed from her mother, Tasha. Though failures by the standards of some, Janie, Heidi, and the others can be seen as heroic in their resilience and in the tenacity with which they cling to their ideals—however divergent from the reality at hand.

This aspect of Wasserstein's writing—that is, her tendency to create characters who resist change—can exasperate audiences, as her critics have noted. The women, in particular, who people her plays are often, like Janie with her unpacked crates of furniture, in a state of suspension, waiting for life to begin. In *Uncommon Women and Others*, there is a constant look toward the future for self-substantiation, as there is, to some extent, in Heidi's persistent state of unhappiness. Still, Heidi does ultimately make a choice—to adopt a baby, a step toward the process of growing up, another of Wasserstein's recurrent themes.

One of Wasserstein's greatest gifts is her ability to find and depict the ironies of life. This is evident in each of the three plays' bittersweet final images: the "uncommon women," their arms wrapped around one another, repeating their by now slightly sardonic refrain; Janie, tap-dancing alone in her empty apartment; and Heidi, singing to her new daughter "You Send Me," the song to which she had previously danced with her old flame, Scoop, at his wedding reception. These images are pure Wasserstein. In the face of disappointment, even the disillusionment, of life, her characters manifest a triumph of the spirit and a strength from within that ultimately prevails.

Wasserstein's *The Sisters Rosensweig* is a departure from her earlier plays in a number of ways. Most overt among these differences are the play's international setting (the action takes place in Queen Anne's Gate, London) and its concern with global issues and events. Also of note is the playwright's uncharacteristic use, here, of classical, nonepisodic structure, maintaining unity of time and place: in this case, several days' events in the sitting room of Sara Goode, the play's main character and the eldest of the three sisters for whom the play is named.

Sara shares many of the characteristics of Wasserstein's earlier protagonists—that is, her gender (female), ethnic group (Jewish), social class (upper-middle to upper class), and intelligence quotient (uncommonly high). She is, however, considerably older than her forerunners. *The Sisters Rosensweig* centers on the celebration of Sara's fifty-fourth birthday. This is significant in that Sara, a hugely successful international banker who has been married and divorced several times, does not share the struggle for self-identity carried out by such Wasserstein heroines as Heidi Holland and Janie Blumberg. With a lucrative, challenging career (noteworthily, in a male-dominated field) and a daughter she loves, Sara has achieved, to some degree, the "meaning" in her life that those earlier characters found lacking and sought.

As the play progresses, however, it is revealed that Sara, despite her self-confidence and seeming self-sufficiency, shares with Heidi, Janie, and the others a deep need to connect—to find, create, or reclaim a family. As she fends off and at last gives in to a persistent suitor, Merv Kant, a false-fur dealer, and plays hostess to her two sisters (Pfeni Rosensweig, a sociopolitical journalist-turned-travel-writer, and "Dr." Gorgeous Teitelbaum, who hosts a radio call-in show), Sara manages, at last, to peel back the layers of defense and reserve that have seen her through two divorces and the rigors of her profession and to rediscover the joys of sisterhood and the revitalizing power of romantic love.

It is not Sara alone who serves Wasserstein in her exploration of her characteristic themes of loneliness, isolation, and the search for true happiness. Pfeni, forty years old, the play's most seemingly autobiographical character, a writer who has been temporarily diverted from her true calling, has been likewise diverted from pursuing "what any normal woman wants" by remaining in a relationship with Geoffrey, a former homosexual. Jilted, and distraught over the havoc that acquired immune deficiency syndrome (AIDS) has played with the lives of his friends, Geoffrey has wooed and won Pfeni, only to leave her in the end to follow his own true nature. Pfeni's ceaseless "wandering" as well as her self-confessed need to write about the hardships of others to fill the emptiness in her own life is much akin to Heidi Holland's position as a "highly-informed spectator," waiting for her own life to begin.

The Sisters Rosensweig harks back to Wasserstein's *Isn't It Romantic* in its concerns with the profound role that both mothers and Judaism play in shaping women's lives. Here, Sara rejects, and attempts to cast off, the influences of both. An atheist expatriate in London, she has reinvented her life, purging all memories of her Jewish New York upbringing and her deceased mother's expectations as firmly as she has embraced the habits and speech patterns of her adopted home. Sara's eventual acquiescence to Merv, a New York Jew, along with the rekindling of her emotional attachment to her sisters, represents, at the play's end, an acceptance and embracing of the past that she has worked so hard to put behind her.

Like all Wasserstein's works, *The Sisters Rosensweig* presents characters whose spirit triumphs over their daily heartaches and heartbreaks. While they long to escape the tangled webs of their lives ("If I could only get to Moscow!" Pfeni laments, in one of the play's several nods to Anton Chekhov's *The Three Sisters*), they manage to find within themselves and in one another sufficient strength not only to endure but also to prevail.

As in *Uncommon Women and Others*, *Isn't It Romantic*, and *The Heidi Chronicles*, there is a scene in *The Sisters Rosensweig* in which women join together to share a toast, affirming and celebrating their sisterhood and themselves. Be they blood sisters, sorority sisters, or sisters of the world, Wasserstein has made sisters her province. With *The Sisters Rosensweig*, she adds three more portraits to her ever-growing gallery of uncommon women, painted, as always, with insight, wit, and compassion.

Wasserstein is a unique and important voice in contemporary American theater. As a woman writing plays about women, she has been a groundbreaker, though never self-consciously so. Despite her often thin plot lines, she finds and captures the drama inherent in the day-to-day choices confronting the women of her generation. As a humorist, too, Wasserstein is unquestionably a virtuoso. Her ability to see the absurdity of even her own most deeply held convictions, and to hold them deeply nevertheless, is perhaps the most engaging and distinctive of her writing's many strengths.

Other major works

NONFICTION: *Bachelor Girls*, 1990.

TELEPLAY: *The Sorrows of Gin*, 1979 (from the story by John Cheever).

Bibliography

Bennetts, Leslie. "An Uncommon Dramatist Prepares Her New Work." *The New York Times*, May 24, 1981, p. C1. Written as *Isn't It Romantic* was being previewed, this two-page piece provides a look at Wasserstein's entry into writing and theater during her high school and college years. Wasserstein discusses feminism and women's difficulty in making choices in life. Contains photographs of Wasserstein and Steven Robman, the director of *Isn't It Romantic.*

Berman, Janice. "The Heidi Paradox." *Newsday*, December 22, 1988. This two-page article, in which Wasserstein defines herself as a "feminist," discusses the male and female characters in *The Heidi Chronicles* and refers to Wasserstein's earlier plays. Contains photographs of the playwright, of Joan Allen in *The Heidi Chronicles*, and of Christine Rose and Barbara Barrie in *Isn't It Romantic.*

Nightingale, Benedict. "There Really Is a World Beyond 'Diaper Drama.'" *The New York Times*, January 1, 1984, p. C2. This two-page piece discusses *Isn't It Romantic* in the context of plays that focus on adult children struggling to sever ties with their parents. It compares Wasserstein's play with those of Tina Howe and Christopher Durang. Includes a photograph of the "mothers" in *Isn't It Romantic.*

Rose, Phyllis Jane. "Dear Heidi—An Open Letter to Dr. Holland." *American Theater* 6 (October, 1989): 26. Written in letter form, this essay is a provocative, in-depth feminist critique of the images of women as presented in *The Heidi Chronicles.* Rose emphasizes Heidi's complicity in surrendering her independence to men, referring to Aeschylus' Oresteia trilogy as a means of furthering her point. Contains numerous photographs of scenes from *The Heidi Chronicles.*

Shapiro, Walter. "Chronicler of Frayed Feminism." *Time* 133 (March 27,

1989): 90-92. Written shortly after *The Heidi Chronicles* moved to Broadway, this two-page article provides insight into Wasserstein's impetus for writing the play. Shapiro offers a brief look at the feminist subtext throughout Wasserstein's work, as well as a more lengthy examination of her New York roots and family. Contains a full-page photograph of Wasserstein.

Wallace, Carol. "A Kvetch for Our Time." *Sunday News Magazine*, August 19, 1984, 10. In this two-page-plus article, Wallace focuses on *Isn't It Romantic* as a chronicle of the women of Wasserstein's generation. She also discusses Wasserstein's overachieving siblings, her New York youth, and her years at Mount Holyoke College. Includes a photograph of the playwright.

Anne Newgarden

JOHN WEBSTER

Born: London, England; c. 1577-1580
Died: London, England; before 1634

Principal drama

Westward Ho!, pr. 1604, pb. 1607 (with Thomas Dekker); *Northward Ho!*, pr. 1605, pb. 1607 (with Dekker); *The White Devil*, pr. c. 1609-1612, pb. 1612; *The Duchess of Malfi*, pr. 1614, pb. 1623; *The Devil's Law-Case*, pr. c. 1619-1622, pb. 1623; *A Cure for a Cuckold*, pr. c. 1624-1625, pb. 1661 (with William Rowley); *Appius and Virginia*, pr. 1634(?), pb. 1654 (with Thomas Heywood).

Other literary forms

John Webster wrote a few short poems, including commendatory verses to accompany publications by other poets and an elegy on the death of Prince Henry, heir to the English throne, entitled "A Monumental Column." In prose, he is believed to have written the thirty-two new character sketches that appeared in Sir Thomas Overbury's sixth edition of *New and Choice Characters of Several Authors* in 1615, including the famous one entitled "Excellent Actor." He also wrote a pageant, "Monuments of Honor," for the procession of John Gore, the Lord Mayor of London, in 1624.

Achievements

Webster is known for two powerful tragedies, *The White Devil* and *The Duchess of Malfi*, that have sufficiently impressed readers to rank him second only to William Shakespeare as a writer of English Renaissance tragedy. Each play presents an intense penetration into a world of evil, fully displaying Webster's genius for horror in scenes in which characters are tortured to the limits of endurance. Webster's deep psychological studies of ambition, lust, and revenge turn the morbid and macabre into great art. Webster's title characters, unusual for Renaissance tragedy, are women who are different in nature. In *The White Devil*, the murderous intent of Vittoria and her impassioned defense of herself at her trial contrast in *The Duchess of Malfi* with the kind, loving nature of the Duchess and the quiet nobility with which she ultimately faces death. Webster's poetry creates passages of great beauty and power, which in the Duchess' death scene combine to create one of the great moments in world drama.

Biography

In the late 1970's, new information was learned about a family named Webster that lived in London in the parish of St. Sepulcher-Without-Newgate and that is believed to have been the family of John Webster, the tragic dramatist. The head of this family, also named John, was a member of the Merchant Taylors' Company; this information accords with a statement written by the playwright, which mentions that he had been "born free" of the Merchant Taylors', meaning that at the time of his birth his father was an actual member of that guild. The senior Webster became free in 1577 and, having probably expected a sufficient income to allow him to have a family, married Elizabeth Coates probably that same year. The future playwright, probably the eldest son because he bears his father's name, was likely born within the years 1577-1580. The father later became a prosperous coach maker, his coaches frequently carrying the dead to burial; this may explain the playwright's preoccupation with death, which began at an early age.

No records prove that the young Webster went to the famous Merchant Taylors' School, but such an assumption is reasonable. Since his plays show knowledge of the law, it has always been thought that he attended law schools. Records do show, however, that on August 1, 1598, a John Webster was admitted to the Middle Temple from the New Inn.

The earliest record about the playwright's theatrical career comes from 1602, when he, along with four other writers, including Thomas Dekker, received commission from the Lord Admiral's Company to write a play to be known as *Two Shapes*, probably the same play as *Caesar's Fall*, now lost, for which the company paid the playwrights five pounds on May 22. Later that year Webster collaborated on two other plays, being paid in October for *Lady Jane*, which may have been published under a different title, and in November for *Christmas Comes but Once a Year*, now lost. In 1602 and 1604, he wrote minor poems, prefatory verses for works by other poets, among whom was Thomas Heywood. Webster also worked with John Marston, penning the induction to his *The Malcontent* (pr., pb. 1604). He collaborated with Dekker on several plays over the next few years, the most notable being *Westward Ho!* and *Northward Ho!*, both performed by the boy actors at St. Paul's, probably in 1604 and 1605, respectively, and both published in 1607 along with *The Famous History of Sir Thomas Wyatt*, which may be, at least in part, the same play as *Lady Jane*.

Webster married Sara Peniall, probably on March 18, 1605, and their first child, John, was baptized on May 8, 1606. Shortly thereafter, Webster decided to write without collaborators. His first independent play was *The White Devil*, written in 1609 and performed that winter by the Queen's Company at the Red Bull theater; according to Webster himself, this play was not well received. In 1613, Webster published his elegy on the death of Henry, Prince of Wales. Webster's other major play, *The Duchess of Malfi*, was performed before the end of 1614 by Shakespeare's company, the King's Men, at both the Blackfriars and the Globe theaters. Around this time, Webster staged a tragedy entitled *The Guise*, now lost.

Webster's father died in 1614 or 1615. By this time, the playwright had at least four other children. Definite biographical information comes from 1615; on June 19, Webster paid a fee to gain membership in the Merchant Taylors' Company, perhaps so that he could become the official poet of the guild. Also in 1615, the sixth edition of *New and Choice Characters of Several Authors* appeared, containing thirty-two new character sketches believed, on stylistic evidence, to have been written by Webster. In 1617, Webster was attacked in print by a figure of no literary importance, the satiric portrait describing Webster unfavorably and calling his work "obscure."

His last independent play, *The Devil's Law-Case*, was probably performed by the Queen's Men around 1620. He may have collaborated on a few other plays in the next few years, perhaps with an old acquaintance, Thomas Middleton, on *Anything for a Quiet Life* (pr. c. 1621, pb. 1662), and perhaps with William Rowley on *A Cure for a Cuckold* around 1624-1625. He assuredly collaborated with Dekker, Rowley, and John Ford on *The Late Murder in Whitechapel: Or, Keep the Widow Waking* in 1624. Later that year, Webster wrote a show for the Lord Mayor, a member of the Merchant Taylors' Company; it was in his dedication to this work that Webster stated he was "born free" of that company. Webster's name appears frequently in the records of the organization around 1623-1625. One other extant play is attributed to Webster, *Appius and Virginia*, of uncertain date and not published until 1654.

Webster probably died before 1634, since Heywood spoke of him in the past tense in *The Hierarchy of the Blessed Angels* (1635). The dramatist, however, may have been the John Webster whose burial was recorded on March 3, 1638, at St. James, Clerkenwell, where Dekker and Rowley were also buried.

Analysis

John Webster's two greatest plays are *The White Devil* and *The Duchess of Malfi*. They have many points in common. Both are tragedies based on events that occurred in Italy in the sixteenth century. Both carry the audience into a dark and grim world in which evil characters are capable of virtually any atrocity and in which good characters are all too frequently destroyed by murderous plotters, many of whom are of their own family; bonds of kinship and marriage are not enough to protect the innocent from the greed, jealousy, and ruthlessness of husbands, wives, and brothers. The bases of order seem in question. Church and state are both corrupt; evil seems rampant everywhere.

Webster's characters are memorable, particularly the women. Webster creates tragic heroines, Vittoria and the Duchess, women whose lives and deaths make them capable of drawing the admiration and sympathies of author and audience. The three major villains—Brachiano, the Cardinal, and Duke Ferdinand, men of rank in church and state—are creatures of immense selfishness whose will is law. What they desire they must have, even if innocents have to die. Both plays contain melancholics, Flamineo in *The White Devil* and Daniel de Bosola in *The Duchess of Malfi*, and much of Webster's sarcasm appears in their speeches. Both of them are poor, having been scholars who could find no preferment except by joining the service of cruel noblemen. Their low birth and poverty doom them to serve as tools to be used in the iniquity of others. Flamineo takes some pleasure in the villainies he commits, but Bosola is pained by the tortures he is forced to inflict.

The evil master whom Flamineo serves is the Duke of Brachiano, who has been smitten by the great beauty of Vittoria, Flamineo's sister. Flamineo has no qualms about pandering to his own sister; her allure can help him to advance in Brachiano's service. Early in *The White Devil*, Brachiano meets secretly with Vittoria, whom he desires as a mistress. Vittoria indicates her willingness to become his lover, but unfortunately she sees two problems: his wife and her husband. Without ever saying so directly, she indicates that Brachiano should kill both of them. She tells him of a dream in which she was attacked by both of their spouses. Her situation was desperate until a limb from a yew tree fell and crushed both of her attackers. She has let Brachiano know that he is the "you" who must kill to get her. Flamineo, eavesdropping, appreciates the cunning of her invitation to murder.

In staging his plays, Webster greatly favored the device of the dumb show. The deaths of both unwanted spouses are depicted in this way. The murder of Brachiano's wife, Isabella, who loves her husband devotedly, is silently acted out on stage as Brachiano, with the aid of a conjurer who has supplied him with a magic cap, happily watches from a distance. Isabella prepares for bed, saying her prayers and then kissing, as she always does, her husband's picture, which has been anointed with a powerful poison. She dies immediately. Brachiano continues to watch as Vittoria is freed from her unwanted husband, Camillo, in a second show provided by the conjurer. The ambitious and unscrupulous Flamineo commits the murder himself, breaking the neck of his brother-in-law but making the injury appear to be the tragic result of a fall from a vaulting horse. Webster characterizes Brachiano deftly as he praises his henchmen; they provided a good show, and he enjoyed it. Vittoria is his.

Although the death of Isabella is not immediately known, the murderers have made dangerous enemies of two potent figures in church and state. Camillo was a nephew of Cardinal Monticelso, who will become the pope before the play ends. Isabella was a Medici, sister to Francisco, the great Duke of Florence, who resents Vittoria's adultery with his sister's husband. These powerful men prosecute their revenge. Vittoria is brought to trial, and Webster's training in the law creates an impressive scene. Vittoria defends herself against all charges; she is neither a whore nor a murderess. Her spirited defense and her magnificent beauty win over many of the judges but show her to be the white devil of the title, for one meaning of the term is "hypocrite" and the other, something of external beauty that is ugly within. In either case, Vittoria seems a "white devil." She is sentenced to confinement in a religious house.

After the trial, Francisco learns of his sister's murder and plans his revenge. A book exists that contains the names of criminals who would be available for a price. Francisco borrows it from its owner, Cardinal Monticelso, soon to be pope. The next step in Francisco's revenge is to make Brachiano think that he has a rival for Vittoria's love. Brachiano rages at Vittoria, who turns away from him. Afraid of losing her, he takes her away from her house of confinement and marries her. Francisco chortles: He has tricked Brachiano into the disgrace of marrying his whore. Now he will kill him. As Brachiano prepares for a tournament, his assassins put poison inside his helmet. Heat and perspiration activate the poison, which surges through him. His agony is terrible, and his murderers delight in his suffering.

The duke's death is hard for Flamineo to bear. He has risked everything for Brachiano, but the new duke, Brachiano's son, banishes Flamineo from his court. Unless Vittoria, his sister, can rescue him, Flamineo has lost everything. Vittoria will not help him because one of his victims was their own brother, Marcello. The angry dispute between the two is interrupted by the assassins. Flamineo, furious with his sister, volunteers to kill her for them, but the killers strike both together. Vittoria dies bravely, regaining the admiration of her brother. Vittoria's last words voice Webster's view of nobles and their corrupt courts: Those who have never seen a court and have never known a nobleman are truly fortunate.

The Duchess of Malfi is favored above the earlier play by many. The second play does have flaws, but its language is superb, its characterization rich, its themes immensely significant, and its story, from Italian history, well chosen to give Webster frequent opportunity to display his talent for creating horror.

At the court of the Duchess Giovanna of Malfi, five truly interesting characters appear, three of them villains. The coldest of them is the older brother of the Duchess, the Cardinal. The younger brother, Duke Ferdinand, is fiery. Again, Webster shows evil and corruption in the great positions that control power in the state and the church. The third figure is Bosola, the tool villain, used by the other two to carry out their crimes.

The victims of these men are the Duchess herself and Antonio Bologna. At the beginning of the play, Antonio, steward to the Duchess, wins a prize for his equestrian skill. Webster has thus indicated Antonio's worth; in an age that values good horsemanship exceedingly, Antonio, though not of noble birth, has excelled. From such a man, serving as Webster's choric commentator, come the statements that begin the characterization of the other major figures. The Cardinal employs spies and panders to do his bidding; he has even tried to bribe his way into the papal chair. The Duke is like a spider, using the law like a cobweb to entrap his victims. The Duchess, however, is far different from her brothers; she is a gracious lady. As for Bosola, he is too melancholic, but Antonio has sympathy for him, believing that he has been used badly by the brothers and that he will be used by them again.

The situations that create the later crises begin with the brothers instructing their recently widowed sister not to remarry. Although the Duchess promises to obey their wishes, she immediately calls Antonio to her, and in a very affecting scene she tells him that she recognizes his great worth and wishes him to be her new husband. For the Duchess—as for John Webster the iconoclast—there are measures of a person's worth other than birth or titles. They wed immediately in a ceremony that is binding because it occurs in the presence of a witness, her maid Cariola. The Duchess obviously demands to live her own life; for that, many readers admire her. She is acting in a very willful way, however, creating a situation of great danger for all present in the chamber and for any children born from this union; for that, many readers believe that she is at fault.

Her dangers are real and immediate because her brothers hire Bosola to stay at Malfi and spy on her. The Cardinal chooses Bosola, but he persuades Duke Ferdinand to do the actual hiring because the Cardinal does not want his involvement to be known by anyone else. The Cardinal is the Machiavellian villain in the play, preferring to let others do his evil work for him. The scene between Duke Ferdinand and Bosola is remarkably rich. When Duke Ferdinand suddenly offers gold coins to Bosola, he refuses them. Bosola knows that a nobleman would not come to him and offer riches without expecting much in return, and there are some things Bosola is not willing to do for money. Bosola is a villain with a conscience and a soul. Therefore, Duke Ferdinand announces nonchalantly that he has also secured a position for Bosola. Perhaps Bosola has not heard the news yet—Bosola is to be the master of the horse at the castle of Malfi. Again, the value placed by the age upon the horseman is emphasized; the honor just paid to Bosola is, as Bosola fully knows, an incredibly great one. For a nobleman to single out a poor man such as Bosola and gain for him a prestigious court position shocks Bosola. He cannot turn down such a benefactor, but he does not hesitate to give vent to his anguish:

> I would have you curse yourself now, that your bounty
> (Which makes men truly noble) e'er should make me
> A villain.

The next few scenes cover several years. The Duchess has had children. Bosola thinks her foolish and lustful, but he never considers the possibility that Antonio, a man far below the Duchess in rank, could be her husband; the only possibility that occurs to him is that Antonio is the bawd to the Duchess. When he learns that Antonio and the Duchess are actually married, he is amazed to realize that a man may succeed by virtue alone. His virtue will not save either of them now.

The Duchess' death scene, one of the superbly crafted scenes of English drama, constantly shows Webster's theatricality. By this time, the Duchess believes that Antonio and the children, who had stayed with him, are dead. Life is almost more than she can bear. As the scene opens, hideous noises come from outside her chamber; her brother tries to increase her torments by bringing madmen to scream and howl within her hearing. Ironically, this helps her retain her sanity. It is silence that she cannot stand, since it gives her time to think and remember the depth of her loss.

The madmen are described as Webster mixes satire into even the most tragic of his scenes: One of the madmen is an English tailor who lost his mind by trying to keep up with changing fashions; another is an astrologer who predicted that the world would end on a certain day, and when it did not, he went mad from disappointment. Eight madmen enter and sing, the stage directions calling for "a dismal kind of music." The macabre stage business continues with their dance, "with music answerable thereunto," performed right in front of the suffering woman.

Bosola enters. His shame prevents him from coming to her without disguise; he appears as an old man, telling her, "Thou art a box of worm-seed, at best but a salvatory of green mummy." The Duchess speaks of her rank; Bosola says that he knows she is a woman of high authority because her hair has turned gray many years before it should have. She proudly insists: "I am Duchess of Malfi still!" The response comes quickly: "Glories, like glowworms, afar off shine bright, But, looked to near, have neither heat nor light." Bosola knows the Duchess is shortly to die; Ferdinand will have it so. The unexpected element in the scene is that Bosola is concerned that she face death without pride in her position, for her title will not go with her in her passing. Her soul is Bosola's concern. The Duchess learns the lesson. As her assassins approach, she asks only for time to kneel:

Yet stay. Heaven-gates are not so highly arched
As princes' palaces; they that enter there
Must go upon their knees.

Earlier in the play, when the Duchess was tricked into believing her loved ones to have been murdered, she wished to die. Bosola would not let her die in despair. Now he relieves her soul of its burden of pride. She faces death not as a great Italian lady but as a simple mortal being. Never has she shown more nobleness than in her final moments.

The scene is not yet ended. Duke Ferdinand enters to see his murderers' handiwork. The Duchess' children have been killed also, but their deaths are of no interest to him: "The death/ Of young wolves is never to be pitied." It is his sister's body that holds his gaze: "Cover her face! Mine eyes dazzle; she died young." Then, to Bosola's consternation, Duke Ferdinand turns against him; the duke will give him no reward for his service. Bosola protests, but Duke Ferdinand cannot be brought to reason: He speaks of wolves digging up the grave; his sanity is going. Bosola has participated in Duke Ferdinand's atrocities for nothing; he has served a madman.

Commentary on this scene is important. Only here do readers learn that Duke Ferdinand and the Duchess are twins. Realization of their physical closeness reminds readers of earlier lines in which he spoke of her body and of the fury that erupted from him upon Bosola's first report that she had a lover. Duke Ferdinand's incestuous desires for his sister explain many of his earlier actions.

The frequent references to wolves and howling in this and earlier scenes build to a grotesque consequence in act 5. Duke Ferdinand becomes a lycanthrope. He is found coming from a graveyard with a dead man's leg. The man whose cruelties seemed beastly has become a beast.

Many scholars object that the fifth act is anticlimactic because the Duchess plays no part in it. Bosola, however, has been as important a character as Giovanna, and his role continues to develop. He discovers that the Cardinal has been involved in the death of his sister, and he witnesses the Cardinal murder his mistress, having her swear her loyalty to him by kissing a Bible, which he has poisoned. As is true in Isabella in *The White Devil*, the woman literally kisses death. Bosola resolves that this churchman must die. He wounds him but is kept from killing him by the entrance of the mad Duke Ferdinand, who kills the Cardinal himself, just before Bosola kills him. There is symmetry and poetic justice at the end, as Duke Ferdinand turns upon and slays the one who has manipulated him and then is slain in turn by Bosola, the one he has used, abused, and then fatally wounded. Bosola lives long enough to see the brothers die.

The ways in which his characters face death reveal much about Webster's moral views. The evil characters are not certain what will happen to their souls. Vittoria compares her soul to a ship on a stormy sea, driven she knows not where. Flamineo's end comes wrapped in mist. The Cardinal wishes to be buried and then forgotten. Duke Ferdinand's madness continues also to the very end; then he recognizes that what he has done to his sister is the cause of his own destruction. Bosola, like Vittoria, is about to make a voyage; like Flamineo, he finds a mist before his eyes. Bosola, however, has tried to atone; he can accept death. The dignity of the Duchess when facing death contrasts vividly with all the others. Webster still views life in terms of good and evil, sin and redemption, damnation and salvation. For the Duchess, thanks to Bosola, death merely brings her to her home.

Various other aspects of Webster's art have received high compliments from critics. The opening word in *The White Devil* catches attention immediately: "Banish'd!" The speaker is Count Lodovico, who is being banished for his many crimes, including several murders; he indicates the lack of moral value in his diseased world by calling his killings flea bites. He reveals more about his world by naming the gods that rule it: reward and punishment at court.

A human touch appears in the Duchess' concern for her children. She knows she must die shortly, but she asks her maid Cariola to be sure to give her "little boy/ Some syrup for his cold" and have the little girl say her prayers before she sleeps. A small flaw in the play involves one of her children. Webster has mentioned a son by her previous marriage, but then he is forgotten. The existence of this heir makes Duke Ferdinand's statement that he hoped to gain a great fortune by his sister's death implausible.

The echo scene in *The Duchess of Malfi* is famous. Shortly before his death, Antonio walks near an old fortification. He wonders about his wife: "Shall I never see her more?" The echo catches his words and mournfully returns: "*Never see her more.*" Within moments Antonio will be dead, killed in the darkness by accident.

Webster's language is often magnificent. His prose in the satiric passages of his melancholics is caustic and brutal. The slow cadences of his poetry create passages of great beauty, even though sometimes touched with morbidity, as in the scenes of the Duchess' torture and death. In those scenes, the relationship between Bosola and the Duchess is most memorable. He admires his victim, her greatness shows through her pain, and he must not let her despair. When she wishes to curse the heavens, Bosola responds with the famous "Look you, the stars shine still." His message is that even though she is a great duchess, her curses will have no effect on the stars. Duchesses, in their mortality, are slight things when compared to the order of the heavens.

Webster is greatly concerned with order. In the very opening lines of *The Duchess of Malfi*, Antonio, again serving as a chorus, speaks for Webster in lines praising the order being brought to France by the young French king. At the end of both of Webster's tragedies, with evil having been destroyed, young heirs to the power of Brachiano and Malfi appear to symbolize the hope for a better world. In Malfi, the Duchess' eldest son by Antonio is brought in by Delio, one of the few righteous characters in the play, so that he may be established in his mother's authority. In the other play, Brachiano's son, Giovanni, succeeds his father. His first act is to banish Flamineo from his presence, his next to capture four of the assassins, including Lodovico, and send them to prison, threatening punishment for all who have participated in the murders in his court. The courts have been purged, at a heavy price to be sure, but purged nevertheless. Just as Webster saw a new order coming in France, the reader may see a new order dawning at Fortress Brachiano and at the castle of Malfi.

Bibliography

Bliss, Lee. *The World's Perspective: John Webster and the Jacobean Drama.* New Brunswick, N.J.: Rutgers University Press, 1983. Jacobean drama is heavily experimental, with Webster one of its main practitioners as he continues the dramatic experiments of George Chapman and William Shakespeare. Webster's unusual dramatic effects result from his varied and dynamic aesthetic, social, and political concerns.

Bogard, Travis. *The Tragic Satire of John Webster.* New York: Russell & Russell, 1965. The key to understanding Webster lies in the realization that his great plays mix tragedy with satire. In Webster's tragic vision, the world is a place for which he can feel both contempt and pity; the former leads him to satire, the latter to tragedy.

Boklund, Gunnar. *The Sources of "The White Devil."* Cambridge, Mass.: Harvard University Press, 1957. Extensive research into more than one hundred possible sources for the play highly limits the number of probable choices in this predecessor to Boklund's *"The Duchess of Malfi": Sources, Themes, Characters* (1962), which uses source study as a guide to understanding the play as a whole.

Bradbrook, Muriel C. *John Webster: Citizen and Dramatist.* New York: Columbia University Press, 1980. "Citizen" indicates Bradbrook's acceptance of biographical information presented in the late 1970's about the family of one particular John Webster. Bradbrook believes that the new discoveries do relate to the dramatist and that his plays might have been influenced by memories of personages living in his neighborhood, particularly Lady Penelope Rich (Sir Philip Sidney's Stella) and Antonio Perez, the Spanish spy. Map of Webster's neighborhood.

Goldberg, Dena. *Between Worlds: A Study of the Plays of John Webster.* Waterloo, Ontario, Canada: Wilfrid Laurier University Press, 1987. Webster, born into the Elizabethan world, spoke frequently of its institutions and laws. That world was crumbling during the early years of Webster's maturity. The second world is that of revolutionary fervor in the 1640's; Webster, dead before 1640, is a prerevolutionary. He is an iconoclast, but he sees potential for a new order.

Griffin, Robert P. *John Webster: Politics and Tragedy.* Salzburg: Institut für

Englische Sprache and Literatur, Universität Salzburg, 1972. In this volume, one of several on Webster from the Salzburg Institute since 1972, the thesis is that Webster saw conflict existing between the will, which leads to anarchy, and the desire for order. The issues involve morality and politics: Machiavellianism fades: Stoicism returns.

Pearson, Jacqueline. *Tragedy and Tragicomedy in the Plays of John Webster.* Totowa, N.J.: Barnes & Noble Books, 1980. Webster mixed modes in his plays. His tragedies mix tragedy and tragicomedy with something which is here called "anti-tragedy," an element which undermines tragic effect, as in scene 3 of act 3, when the violence the audience expected to occur failed to develop. The fifth acts, where elements of non-tragedy are strongest, receive close analysis. Chapters on frequently overlooked plays, *The Devil's Law-Case* and *A Cure for a Cuckold*, are welcome.

Peterson, Joyce E. *Curs'd Example: The Duchess of Malfi and Commonweal Tragedy.* Columbia: University of Missouri Press, 1978. The Duchess is a bad example of a ruler. In deciding to marry she acts on caprice and whim, and the necessity of keeping the marriage secret damages her reputation. Peterson's extensive reading in Renaissance literature about duties and qualities of ideal rulers fail to convince some scholars.

Ranald, Margaret Loftus. *John Webster.* Boston: Twayne, 1989. This brief, general, and quite readable overview of Webster's life and work contains basic information about dating, sources, and texts. Critical sections are distinguished by the absence of esoteric argument. Lengthy annotated bibliography.

Waage, Frederick O. *"The White Devil" Discover'd: Backgrounds and Foregrounds in Webster's Tragedy.* New York: Peter Lang, 1984. Extremely close readings of the play (the foreground) follow the action carefully. Knowledge of historical events and contemporary publications (the background) contribute to interpretation.

Howard L. Ford

TIMBERLAKE WERTENBAKER

Born: United States; 1946 (?)

Principal drama

This Is No Place for Talullah Bankhead, pr. 1978; *The Third*, pr. 1980; *Second Sentence*, pr. 1980; *Case to Answer*, pr. 1980; *Breaking Through*, pr. 1980; *New Anatomies*, pr. 1981, pb. 1984; *Inside Out*, pr. 1982; *Home Leave*, pr. 1982; *Abel's Sister*, pr. 1984; *The Grace of Mary Traverse*, pr., pb. 1985; *Our Country's Good*, pr., pb. 1988 (based on the novel *The Playmaker* by Thomas Keneally); *The Love of the Nightingale*, pr. 1988, pb. 1989; *Three Birds Alighting on a Field*, pr. 1991, pb. 1992.

Other literary forms

Timberlake Wertenbaker is acclaimed for her translations and adaptations of French dramatic works into English. Her notable contributions in this area include her translations and stage adaptations of plays by Marivaux, *False Admissions* and *Successful Strategies*, both produced in London in 1983 and published along with a radio play as *False Admissions, Successful Strategies, La Dispute: Three Plays* (1989). *La Dispute*, a play by Marivaux that she adapted for radio, was broadcast in 1987. Wertenbaker has also translated *Léocadia*, a play by Jean Anouilh, which she adapted for radio in 1985 and published in 1987 in *Jean Anouilh: Five Plays.* Her other translations include *Mephisto* (1986), of Ariane Mnouchkine's theatrical adaptation based on a novel by Klaus Mann, and *The Thebans: Oedipus Tyrranus, Oedipus at Colonus, and Antigone* (1992), of Sophocles' plays.

Achievements

Wertenbaker's experience as an American who was reared in Europe and settled in London points to a recurring theme in her work: displacement. In her plays, characters are often removed from the familiarity of home and are forced to live in new cultures. From this central theme emerge related themes, including isolation, dispossession, and the problem of forging an identity within a new cultural milieu. In her work, individuals often seem to assume roles, as if identity were a matter of persons performing themselves. Wertenbaker's work also demonstrates a keen awareness that communication occurs through language that often inadequately expresses experience. Her consciousness of language gives her work a lyricism that is antinaturalistic, a style served by the episodic structure of her plays, in which the narrative emerges from precisely crafted moments rather than from causally developed plots.

Wertenbaker has received a number of prestigious awards, including the

Plays and Players Most Promising Playwright Award (1985) for *The Grace of Mary Traverse*, the Laurence Olivier Play of the Year Award and the *Evening Standard* Play of the Year Award (1988), both for *Our Country's Good*, and the Eileen Anderson Central Television Drama Award (1989) for *The Love of the Nightingale.*

Biography

Timberlake Wertenbaker is reluctant to discuss three aspects of her life: her name, her birthplace, and her birthdate. Born Lael Louisiana Timberlake in the United States, she is the daughter of Charles Wertenbaker (a foreign correspondent for *Time* magazine and a novelist) and his third wife, Lael Tucker Wertenbaker, a prolific author of both fiction and nonfiction.

As a young child, Wertenbaker's family moved to the Spanish Basque Provinces, and she was educated at schools near St. Jean-de-Luz, France. She returned to the United States to attend St. John's College in Annapolis, Maryland, graduating in 1966. After a brief career as a journalist in New York and London, she taught French in Greece for one year. During the 1970's, she moved to London, where she settled. It was there that she began her career as a playwright, initially working in the fringe theaters. By 1984-1985, her eminence was recognized by her serving as the resident writer at the prestigious Royal Court Theatre, where many of the original plays for which she is acclaimed—notably *The Grace of Mary Traverse*, *Our Country's Good*, and *Three Birds Alighting on a Field*—have been produced.

Analysis

The focus of Timberlake Wertenbaker's plays is often a woman who has been radically dislocated from the culture into which she was born. This preoccupation is evident in Wertenbaker's first published play, *New Anatomies*, which dramatizes the life of Isabelle Eberhardt, a French woman who, in the early part of the twentieth century, disguised herself as an Arab man and lived among the Algerians as Si Mahmoud. The movement of the narrative between France and Algeria allows Wertenbaker not only to explore the cultural difference within the specific context of colonization but also to examine the relations between men and women as reproducing the colonial relations between imperial center and colony. By disguising herself as a man, Eberhardt appears to escape the constraints imposed on women by European ideals of femininity, and although she achieves a certain kind of freedom through her disguise, she faces tremendous physical risks, which eventually lead to her death.

Her disguise as an Arab man raises important questions about the European "exoticization" of non-Western cultures, which the play explores in a scene set in a Parisian salon catering to a lesbian clientele. The women in the salon regard Eberhardt with fascination, as if she has overthrown the social constraints that doubly marginalize them as women and lesbians. One of the women, Verda Miles, is fascinated by Eberhardt's non-Western, male clothes. This fascination implies a relationship between the women of the salon and men from countries that Europe has colonized, as if the sexuality of each group not only is exoticized but also disrupts the conventional codes of gender: French lesbians appear as masculine, while Algerian men appear as feminine.

Miles's identification of Eberhardt's clothes as costume raises the possibility of gender as a performative that can be altered by the individual refusing to play the socially sanctioned role appropriate to his or her sex. Eberhardt denies this position by stating that she is not "costumed" as a man and that these are her clothes. Her distinction makes clear that within the space of the salon, gender is theatricalized so that a woman dressing as a man emphasizes gender as the construct. In contrast, Eberhardt, traveling in Algeria, is received as a man, not as a woman in male attire.

Like Isabelle Eberhardt, Mary Traverse, the central character in *The Grace of Mary Traverse*, attempts to escape the limitations imposed by the social codes of femininity. Set in eighteenth century London, Mary is born into a life of privilege, where, as a woman, her only value is as the wife of a socially prominent man. The play opens with her father teaching her to make conversation in such a way that she provides opportunities for a man to display his brilliance. By nature a curious young woman who is unsuited to the passive role assigned to women, Mary asks the family's housekeeper, Mrs. Temptwell, to take her into the streets so that she might see life. Quickly, she realizes that the streets of London are brimming with a vitality that, although often violent, is more attractive to her than her life within her father's home. The world outside the home, however, is masculine and decidedly hostile toward women. One of her first experiences in the streets of London is witnessing Lord Gordon raping a young woman by first raising her skirts with his sword and then sexually violating her. (Men's violence against women as a demonstration of their power is explored again by Wertenbaker in two later plays, *The Love of the Nightingale* and *Our Country's Good*.)

Unlike Isabelle Eberhardt, who disguises herself as a man to escape the constraints of European womanhood, Mary Traverse does not disguise herself; rather, she models her behavior after that of men, demanding, for example, sexual satisfaction from a male prostitute. The social milieu of eighteenth century London cannot accommodate this woman who behaves as a man. Disowned by her father and unmarried, she can support herself only by becoming a prostitute. Once outside her father's home, Mary becomes acutely aware of the intersection of gender and class, particularly in terms of social privilege. The society is hierarchical, with upper-class men, regardless of whether they are worthy, enjoying power, while working-class women, who are at the bottom end of the social strata, are powerless. Without a radical restructuring of the world, Mary realizes that, as a woman, she will never enjoy the prerogatives of men, and therefore she sets out to refashion the world by politicizing the working class. Her attempt is a tragic failure, ending with the Gordon Riots, in which hundreds of people die.

The Grace of Mary Traverse, like *New Anatomies*, deals with a woman's attempt to break the constraints of gender, an image for the larger endeavor of creating a new world in which individuals are free. In *The Grace of Mary Traverse*, Wertenbaker begins to address the problematic nature of this endeavor. While Mary is the agent of change, her motives for wanting change are not altruistic but are apparently motivated by her own desire for power. The problem raised by the play is the following: If the motives of the agent of political change are tainted by her experience of oppression, can she envision a Utopian future? Although the play ends optimistically—with Mary standing with her daughter and father, an image of the future that has reconciled with its past—the terms of that future remain unspoken.

Like both *New Anatomies* and *The Grace of Mary Traverse*, *The Love of the Nightingale* is about a woman who is radically displaced from her homeland. The play retells the Greek myth of Procne, daughter of the Athenian king Pandion, who is married to the Thracian king Tereus. Alone in the strange land, unable to comprehend the nuances of a foreign language and culture, Procne lives in isolation. Tereus offers to go to Athens and return with Procne's sister, Philomele, so that Procne will have company. On the voyage back, however, he falls in love with Philomele, whom, after she refuses his advances, he rapes; to silence her, he then cuts out her tongue. As in *The Grace of Mary Traverse*, male power is exercised through the violent subjugation of women. In the context of the play, this point is reiterated through a monologue by an older woman, Niobe, who has been sent from Athens to attend Philomele on her journey. Hearing Philomele's screams during the rape, she comments that this is an experience common to women during times of war, since soldiers conquering a nation brutalize women as the spoils of war.

Like the two earlier plays, *The Love of the Nightingale* explores the possibility of creating a new world. When Procne realizes that Itys, her son by Tereus, has been socialized to equate masculinity with violence, she decides to end Tereus' line by holding their son while her sister cuts his throat. Whereas *The Grace of Mary Traverse* attempts, although unsuccessfully, to envision a new world free of violence, the somber tone of *The Love of the Nightingale* implies that only an act of violence will rid the world of violence.

Our Country's Good is also about a new beginning. An adaptation of Thomas Keneally's novel *The Playmaker*, *Our Country's Good*, which is set in 1788-1789, deals with a group of convicts being transported by ship to what is now Australia, where they mount the country's first theatrical production, *The Recruiting Officer* by George Farquhar. *Our Country's Good* opens with Lieutenant Ralph Clark overseeing the flogging of one of the convicts, Robert Sideway. The next scene, set in the hull of the ship, is a monologue by another convict, John Wisehammer. He expresses the despair of the convicts who have been ejected forcibly from England and their desire to be returned to their homeland. The speech establishes radical dislocation as a thematic preoccupation of this play; unlike Wertenbaker's earlier plays, however, *Our Country's Good* is a decidedly optimistic piece.

Although the play begins grimly with the flogging of Sideway and Wisehammer's articulation of loss, a sense of community begins to develop during the rehearsal for the production of *The Recuiting Officer.* The therapeutic effects of theater are felt in two ways: The convicts realize that each has a responsibility to others in the group if the production is to be mounted, and so a sense of community, built on the interdependence of its various members, develops; and, in this production, which is directed by Lieutenant Ralph Clark (who also takes the male lead), social difference is overcome because, as a community of actors, the distinctions between the convicts and their jailer are erased. Further, by playing the roles of upper-class characters in *The Recruiting Officer*, the convicts begin to imagine that they, too, might be capable of this refined language and behavior.

The humanistic spirit of the play (which posits that all people, when stripped of their social roles, are equal) is realized in two ways. First, through the experience of community in the rehearsal and through performing Farquhar's characters, the convicts and Clark realize that despite their social inequity within the colony, each is a person of inherent dignity and worth. When two officers interrupt a rehearsal and begin systematically to humiliate the women convicts by asking one of them to drop to her knees and bark like a dog and then asking another to raise her skirts, two of the other convicts resist this exercise of masculine authority by rehearsing the scene that includes the line "I shall meet with less cruelty among the most barbarous nations than I have found at home." This moment demonstrates not only the solidarity among the convicts but also the effectiveness of theater as a tool of political resistance and empowerment.

A second manifestation of the humanism underlying *Our Country's Good* is the love affair between Ralph Clark and one of the convict women, Mary Brenham, who is playing Silvia to Clark's Captain Plume. One evening, Clark approaches Mary, who is alone on the beach rehearsing a scene in which Plume indirectly declares his love for Silvia. Clark joins Mary, using the lines from *The Recuiting Officer* to declare his love for her. He, claiming never to have seen the body of a woman, asks her to undress, which she agrees to do but only if he, too, will undress. The image created by Wertenbaker is one of two people who stand before each other stripped of their social roles, signified by the uniform of an officer and the rags of a convict. On the beach, the two are simply a man and a woman who love each other.

While the humanism of *Our Country's Good* is attractive, the production of the play does serve the interests of the ruling class. The governor of the penal colony believes that theater teaches the convicts to be good citizens not only by exposing them to the fine language of great drama but also by making them into an audience that requires patient attentiveness, a social virtue. In short, the governor believes that theater is a tool in building a homogeneous, stable society.

Three Birds Alighting on a Field seems anomalous among Wertenbaker's published work inasmuch as it is set in contemporary London and not in the past. The play, which like her earlier ones explores a woman's sense of isolation and her desire to forge an authentic identity for herself, deals with a woman named Biddy who, divorced from her first husband, is married to her second husband, a tremendously rich Greek nicknamed Yo-yo. As a Greek, Yo-yo believes that he is not fully accepted by the elite of British society and seeks to secure his position by becoming an art collector. While it is his capital that finances the collection, it is Biddy's responsibility to establish it, even though she knows nothing about art.

In some sense, Biddy is an updated version of the woman whom Mary Traverse might have become had she not left her father's house. Biddy's identity initially is based solely on her being the wife of a wealthy man. As Biddy moves through, and learns about, the world of art, Wertenbaker satirizes this world as one in which value is measured only in economic terms, which becomes an image of the bourgeois ethos of Margaret Thatcher's England. In the course of learning about art and establishing her own sense of what constitutes good art, Biddy gains a sense of herself and, in the process, realizes how much of herself she had to relinquish to maintain her identity as someone's wife. After her marriage to Yo-yo fails, she falls in love with Stephen, the one artist in the play who has retained a sense of integrity, even if it means his refusing to allow his work to circulate as a commodity.

Given Wertenbaker's interest in the ways in which a society's culture defines women as secondary to men, the ending of *Three Birds Alighting on a Field* is curious. While Wertenbaker seems to suggest that Biddy's two marriages denied her a chance to be herself because she was defined as someone's wife, her love affair with Stephen is problematic. She becomes his model, his inspiration. The play ends with her proclaiming that her body is beautiful and then Stephen, who has been painting her, moving from behind his easel and fondling her breasts. The idea of Biddy, a woman, as the object of male desire seems somewhat at odds with Wertenbaker's earlier explorations of women who desire knowledge and agency in the world.

Other major works

RADIO PLAYS: *Léocadia*, 1985 (translation and adaptation of a play by Jean Anouilh); *La Dispute*, 1987 (translation and adaptation of a play by Marivaux).

TRANSLATIONS: *Mephisto*, 1986 (of Ariane Mnouchkine's stage adaptation based on a novel by Klaus Mann); *False Admissions, Successful Strategies, La Dispute: Three Plays*, 1989 (of Marivaux's plays); *The Thebans: Oedipus Tyrannus, Oedipus at Colonus, and Antigone*, 1992 (of Sophocles' plays).

Bibliography

Davis, Jim. "Festive Irony: Aspects of British Theatre in the 1980s." *Critical Survey* 3, no. 3 (1991): 339-350. Davis discusses the original production of *Our Country's Good* in the context of contemporary British drama. He concludes that the play is an apology for theater as a medium that can empower, liberate, and educate both practitioners and audience.

Rabey, David Ian. "Defining Difference: Timberlake Wertenbaker's Drama of Language, Dispossession, and Discovery." *Modern Drama* 33 (December, 1990): 518-528. Rabey analyzes a range of Wertenbaker's plays, suggesting that crisis in her work is a consequence of an individual not being able to fit within a defined code and the resulting quest for meaning.

Taylor, Val. "Mothers of Invention: Female Characters in *Our Country's Good* and *The Playmaker.*" *Critical Survey* 3, no. 3 (1991): 331-338. Taylor compares Thomas Keneally's depiction of women characters in *The Playmaker* to Wertenbaker's representation of them in *Our Country's Good.* Concludes that Keneally's women are created from a paternalistic male perspective, whereas Wertenbaker's female characters, written from a feminist perspective, subvert the patriarchal representation of women evident in her source text.

Wilson, Ann. "*Our Country's Good*: Theatre, Colony, and Nation in Wertenbaker's Adaptation of *The Playmaker.*" *Modern Drama* 34, no. 1 (March, 1991): 23-35. In this comparison of Wertenbaker's play to its source, Thomas Keneally's *The Playmaker*, Wilson argues that in the novel, the personal relationships of the officers with the convicts essentially extend their roles as agents of colonization, whereas in the play, these relationships allow each to recognize the other's humanity.

Ann Wilson

ARNOLD WESKER

Born: London, England; May 24, 1932

Principal drama

Chicken Soup with Barley, pr. 1958, pb. 1959; *The Kitchen*, pr. 1959, pb. 1960; *Roots*, pr., pb. 1959; *I'm Talking About Jerusalem*, pr., pb. 1960; *The Wesker Trilogy*, pb. 1960 (includes *Chicken Soup with Barley*, *Roots*, *I'm Talking About Jerusalem*); *Chips with Everything*, pr., pb. 1962; *The Nottingham Captain: A Moral for Narrator, Voices and Orchestra*, pr. 1962, pb. 1971 (libretto; music by Wilfred Josephs and David Lee); *The Four Seasons*, pr. 1965, pb. 1966; *Their Very Own and Golden City*, pr. 1965, pb. 1966; *The Friends*, pr., pb. 1970; *The Old Ones*, pr. 1972, pb. 1973; *The Wedding Feast*, pr. 1974, pb. 1980 (adaptation of Fyodor Dostoevski's story); *The Journalists*, pb. 1975, pr. 1977; *Love Letters on Blue Paper*, pr. 1976 (televised), pr. 1977 (staged), pb. 1977 (adaptation of his short story); *The Merchant*, pr. 1976, pb. 1980, pb. 1985 (revised; based on William Shakespeare's play *The Merchant of Venice*); *The Plays of Arnold Wesker*, pb. 1976, 1977 (2 volumes); *Caritas*, pr., pb. 1981; *Four Portraits of Mothers*, pr. 1982, pb. 1987; *Annie Wobbler*, pr. 1983, pb. 1987 (staged version of the radio play *Annie, Anna, Annabella*); *The Sullied Hand*, pr. 1984; *Yardsale*, pr. 1984 (radio play), pr. 1987 (staged), pb. 1987; *One More Ride on the Merry-Go-Round*, pr. 1985, pb. 1990; *Whatever Happened to Betty Lemon*, pr. 1986, pb. 1987; *One-Woman Plays*, pb. 1989; *Lady Othello and Other Plays*, pb. 1990.

Other literary forms

Although known mainly for his stage plays, Arnold Wesker has also written poetry, short stories, articles and essays, television plays, and film scripts. His poems have appeared in various magazines. Collections of his short fiction include *Six Sundays in January* (1971), *Love Letters on Blue Paper* (1974), *Said the Old Man to the Young Man: Three Stories* (1978), and *Love Letters on Blue Paper and Other Stories* (1980). A number of his articles, essays, and lectures have been published; representative collections include *Fears of Fragmentation* (1970) and *The Journalists: A Triptych* (1979).

Two of Wesker's television plays have been presented by the British Broadcasting Corporation television: *Menace* (1963) and *Love Letters on Blue Paper* (1976, adapted from his short story). Wesker also wrote the script for the film version of *The Kitchen* (1961).

Achievements

Wesker presents the disheartening spectacle of a playwright who was an immense success at first but has since fallen from grace—a Socialist angel with clipped wings, at least in his own country. With John Osborne, Harold Pinter, John Arden, and others, Wesker was a leading figure in the New Wave (or New Renaissance) of English drama centered on London's Royal Court Theatre in the late 1950's and early 1960's. The New Wave quickly swept the provinces and universities. Wesker was a star, for example, of the 1960 *Sunday Times* Student Drama Festival at Oxford University, where he gave an enthusiastic talk and where there was a rousing performance of *The Kitchen*. Wesker was the theatrical man of the political moment—a playwright of impeccable working-class origins whose naturalistic, socialistic drama seemed to define the true essence of the New Wave. In Wesker, a dynamo of commitment incarnate, there was no suspicious vagueness or wishy-washy wavering: The conditions, dreams, and frustrations of the working class were clearly laid out in *The Kitchen* and in subsequent dramas which rolled off of Wesker's pen.

A quieter presence at the 1960 *Sunday Times* festival was Arden, a dominating presence at the next year's festival in Leeds, where a Leeds University production of Arden's *Serjeant Musgrave's Dance* (pr. 1959) won the first prize. Students were beginning to discover Arden, Bertolt Brecht, and even William Shakespeare; Wesker was already fading from memory. As for Wesker himself, his commitment began to take the form of direct social action, ranging from demonstrations against nuclear weapons to management of vast projects to bring the arts to the working class. When new plays finally came from him in the mid-1960's—*The Four Seasons* and *Their Very Own and Golden City*—the old Wesker, who served chips with everything, had disappeared. There was a shock of unrecognition in critics and audiences alike; Wesker's very own and golden moment had ended. The final indignity was Malcolm Page's 1968 article entitled "Whatever Happened to Arnold Wesker? His Recent Plays."

In the mid-1960's, Wesker began struggling to recapture his original success. He tried various kinds of plays—first, plays about interpersonal relationships such as *The Four Seasons*, *The Friends*, and *The Old Ones*, and later, plays based on other literary works such as *The Wedding Feast*, *The Merchant*, and *Love Letters on Blue Paper.* At times he had trouble getting his plays produced in the British professional theater, although productions on the Continent, where his reputation has grown, have usually taken up the slack. He seems to have made a modest come-back in the English-speaking theater with *The Wedding Feast*, *The Merchant*, and *Caritas. Caritas*, about a fourteenth century anchoress who has herself immured in a cell, could be a harrowing allegory of Wesker's own career as a committed playwright.

Despite the ups and downs of Wesker's reputation, there is more continuity in his work than at first appears. He has been both the beneficiary and the victim of theatrical and political fashions. As a new, young playwright, he was at first overpraised, though some early critics, noting his autobiographical material and kitchen-sink realism, accused him of lacking imagination. His writing and stagecraft were also called awkward. Ironically, by the time Wesker developed his imagination, writing, and stagecraft, his reputation had diminished. Wesker has continued to survey the working class in modern Britain, but a working class dissipated and fragmented by the consumer society. He has also continued to explore questions of class conflict and commitment, but with more subtlety—or with a subtlety which was always there, although earlier audiences did not recognize it.

Biography

Arnold Wesker was born May 24, 1932, in Stepney, a working-class neighborhood of sweatshops and immigrants in London's East End. His parents were Joseph Wesker, a Russian-Jewish tailor, and Leah Perlmutter Wesker, a Hungarian-Jewish Communist who often had to work in kitchens to support the family. *Chicken Soup with Barley* draws on this background.

Like other London children, Wesker was evacuated during periods of World War II, living with foster parents in various sections of England and Wales. Failing his eleven-plus examination, which was given to determine whether eleven-year-olds went on to an academic or vocational secondary school, he did some amateur acting.

He left school in 1948 and worked at assorted jobs—as a furniture maker's apprentice, carpenter's mate, and bookseller's assistant. From 1950 to 1952, he was in the Royal Air Force, where he organized an enlisted men's drama group and started writing. A series of letters, which he originally meant to turn into a novel, later provided material for *Chips with Everything.*

From 1952 to 1958, he worked at another string of jobs—bookseller's assistant and plumber's mate in London, farm laborer, seed sorter, and kitchen porter in Norfolk, then as a pastry cook in London and Paris. With his savings, he studied in 1956 at the London School of Film Technique. He had also continued writing, and in 1957 he showed his work to film director Lindsay Anderson, who sent *The Kitchen* and *Chicken Soup with Barley* to George Devine at the Royal Court Theatre. *Chicken Soup with Barley* was produced in 1958 at the Belgrade Theatre, Coventry, then transferred to the Royal Court. *Roots* and *The Kitchen* followed in 1959, *I'm Talking About Jerusalem* in 1960.

Wesker won immediate recognition for his work. In 1958, he received an Arts Council grant of three hundred pounds, on the strength of which he married Doreen Cecile "Dusty" Bicker, whom he had met when they worked together in a Norfolk hotel (she is the prototype of Beatie Bryant in *Roots*). In 1959, he won the London *Evening Standard* Award for the most promising playwright and an *Encyclopædia Britannica* Award, and *Chips with Everything* was voted the best play of 1962.

With recognition also came social involvement. In 1961, Wesker, with philosopher Bertrand Russell and others, demonstrated against nuclear weapons and was sentenced to a month in prison. Also in 1961, Wesker became the founding director of Centre 42, a cultural movement or coalition of artists, trade unionists, and other prominent citizens who hoped to bring the arts to the working class. During the 1960's, with staging of regional arts festivals and management of the Round House (the London performance center), the movement consumed a considerable amount of Wesker's time and energy. The movement also required efforts to raise funds: When the cost of sustaining it became too great, Centre 42 was finally terminated in 1970.

In addition to his writing, Wesker has also directed some of his own plays. He has three children, two sons and one daughter, and he has continued to live in London.

Analysis

Arnold Wesker's central concern has been the fate of the working class in modern Britain, and the developments in his work have by and large grown from this concern. In his early plays, which form a saga of the working class through two generations in city and country, the concern is obvious, and so is Wesker's commitment. A second group of plays examines interpersonal relationships, which were certainly not neglected in the early plays. Most of the characters in this group are of working-class origin. Some of Wesker's plays have dealt with a variety of subjects and themes—journalism, class divisions, responsibility to one's community, commitment. These issues, however, were first raised in Wesker's early work. Wesker has merely shifted the focus of his concern from direct treatment of the working class to treatment of issues closely affecting it.

Besides indicating Wesker's personal growth, the developments in his work also reflect changes in the modern British working class. In Wesker's early plays, the working class is shown in its traditional role: serving the needs of the higher classes and worrying about where its next meal is coming from. Already, though, changes are occurring. With socialism comes more power, better living conditions, and greater opportunity, but these changes bring new problems. The old class solidarity dissipates. Some working people cannot escape their traditional role and grasp the opportunity for richer, fuller lives. Others grasp the opportunity but still find themselves searching for meaning. The Wesker trilogy introduces this stage of socialism, and his plays treating interpersonal relationships explore it further. In an epilogue to *The Four Seasons*, Wesker explicitly connects socialism and interpersonal relationships and defends his shift in emphasis:

> There is no abandoning in this play of concern for socialist principles nor a turning away from a preoccupation with real human problems; on the contrary, the play, far from being a retreat from values contained in my early writing, is a logical extension of them. . . .

In short, building the New Jerusalem is not merely a simple matter of seizing power and satisfying basic material needs.

Food, however, is quite obviously the main symbol in Wesker's plays, changing its meaning from context to context. In *Roots*, the farmers are sweating to grow it, while in *The Kitchen* the cooks are sweating to cook it—they represent the traditional role of the working class. In *Chicken Soup with Barley*, sharing food (particularly the archetypal chicken soup) symbolizes compassion and working-class solidarity. On the other hand, in *Roots* consuming food symbolizes the mindless animal contentment of the welfare state. In *Chips with Everything* (as in fish and chips), the "chips with everything" note on the greasy East End restaurant menu suggests not only familiar working-class identity but also—to the upper-class snob "Pip" Thompson—the indiscriminate potato-like nature of that identity. Throughout Wesker's plays people are constantly preparing food or tea for one another, usually as a token of love, respect, or fellowship. For example, onstage in *The Four Seasons* Adam makes Beatrice an apple strudel, the recipe for which Wesker kindly shares in a note to actors.

The basic introduction to Wesker's work is the Wesker trilogy, consisting of *Chicken Soup with Barley*, *Roots*, and *I'm Talking About Jerusalem*. They do not constitute a trilogy in the strictest sense (the three plays have separate actions and settings and do not follow in entirely chronological order), for each can easily stand alone. They are, however, united by their characters, two generations of the city Kahns and the country Bryants, and by the same general subject: the conditions, aspirations, and frustrations of the British working class. Thematically they are also tied together in a loose thesis-antithesis-synthesis relationship.

Covering the most history is *Chicken Soup with Barley*, which stretches over three decades of life in London's East End. The bustling first act shows militant workers, led by the Communist Sarah Kahn, putting down a Fascist march during the 1930's. Later, one of the young workers, Dave Simmonds, leaves to continue fighting the Fascists in the Spanish Civil War. Even here, however, the idealized solidarity is not complete: A prominent shirker is Sarah's own husband, Harry Kahn, who in the thick of the fight runs off to hide at his mother's home. The second act is set in the 1940's, shortly after World War II, and change is apparent. Deterioration of the one-time solidarity is occurring: Tired out by political activity and war, sick of industrial urban society, Dave Simmonds and Ada, the Kahns' daughter, get married and withdraw to a quiet life in the country. Despite a new Socialist government, capitalists are still finding ways to exploit the workers. By act 3, set in the mid-1950's, the deterioration is complete. The Soviet Union's behavior has exploded Communist ideals, Sarah is now fighting welfare-state bureaucracy, and the old comrades have dispersed. One example is agitator-turned-businessman Monty Blatt, who expresses the prevailing "I'm all right, Jack" philosophy: "There's nothing more to life than a house, some friends, and a family—take my word." Ronnie, the Kahns' son, likewise disillusioned and searching, is embarrassed by the old language of solidarity; words such as "comrade" now seem unreal.

The most interesting characters in *Chicken Soup with Barley* are Sarah and Harry Kahn. Apparently held up for admiration, Sarah is a spunky Mother Courage figure who expounds the play's chicken-soup philosophy and who persists in her ideals even as her world crumbles around her: "you've got to care or you'll die." At the same time, she is a pushy wife and mother and something of a shrew. Poor Harry is already demoralized enough, as a breadwinner who has trouble finding work (it is, after all, the Depression), and Sarah finishes the job of emasculating him. Finally, her nagging gives him a stroke, and thereafter his deterioration mirrors the decline of working-class solidarity, until he becomes the ultimate case of the uninvolved person, paralyzed and unable to control even his bladder and bowels. It is too bad that Sarah does not practice her chicken-soup philosophy more on Harry.

Picking up thematically where *Chicken Soup with Barley* leaves off, *Roots* at the same time provides a strong contrast in setting and characters. It is still welfare-state Britain, now 1959, but the place has switched to the Norfolk countryside, where the rural working class is presented in the persons of the Bryant family. The Bryant men work as pigman, tractor driver, and garage mechanics, and the women are housewives. Although the men are still subject to a mysterious "guts ache" and to being sacked at work, the Bryants are generally fat and complacent. Uneducated, unaware, and conservative, they take no interest in affairs outside their own little circle. Their conversation is about the weather, food, and family, or gossip about the neighbors. They enjoy popular culture (they can hardly wait to get television), but books and classical music are "squit." They represent the members of the working class who have trouble breaking out of the traditional mold and for whom Wesker's Centre 42 project was perhaps intended. They are little better off than poor Harry except that they can move.

There is one exception among the Bryants, the twenty-two-year-old daughter Beatie, who has benefited from living with young Ronnie Kahn for three years in London. Besides cohabiting with him, she has kept his interest by pretending to listen to his ideas, a necessity with which she can dispense once they are married and she starts having babies. The slim plot of *Roots* consists of waiting—while Beatie sings his praises and continuously quotes him—for the great Ronnie to appear and meet the other Bryants. He never does. They prepare a feast for him, but he does not show up. Instead, he sends a letter of regret breaking off his affair with Beatie because she is so uncultured. Ironically, Beatie is not destroyed but is instead shocked into the fluent awareness that Ronnie had always tried to develop in her. Meanwhile, the other Bryants wade into the food lest it go to waste.

Beatie represents the younger generation that is moving to the city and developing "roots" in working-class concerns; she is an embodiment of Sarah Kahn's continuing hope. She also anticipates the concerns of women's liberation, which might partly explain why her role has been a favorite in the contemporary theater. As for Ronnie, he takes after his mother: Politically and culturally correct, he is personally something of a snob and a heel (there is a bit of the father here too). Ronnie gets off too easily in *Roots*, while Wesker is too hard on the country folk. Unfortunately, though Wesker admires D. H. Lawrence, he does not seem to share Lawrence's appreciation for the animal vitality of country people (though it must be admitted that Lawrence wrote about an earlier generation which perhaps was more vital).

Wesker's *I'm Talking About Jerusalem* suggests that his mentor was not D. H. Lawrence but nineteenth century Socialist William Morris, who envisioned a Jeffersonian democracy of independent craftsmen. Picking up a loose end from *Chicken Soup with Barley*, *I'm Talking About Jerusalem* goes to the country with Dave and Ada Kahn Simmonds, who settle a few miles from the Bryants in Norfolk. Their dream is to leave the problems of urban clutter behind and build their own private Jerusalem in the country, where Dave will support them by creating beautiful handmade furniture. He will thereby realize William Morris' vision of the independent craftsman who has a meaningful relationship with his work instead of merely filling a place on a factory assembly line. The Simmonds do enjoy their spacious country freedom, but, after thirteen years, a growing family and economic pressures force them back to the city. The throwaway consumer society does not sufficiently appreciate the worth of handmade items. The point seems to be that people cannot be uninvolved, cannot escape the problems of society, but must work together to bring about the New Jerusalem for everyone.

The annals of British socialism continue in an example of Wesker's later work, *The Old Ones*. From *The Old Ones* it is clear that as the problems of subsistence are solved, the problems of existence come more to the fore. At times *The Old Ones* evokes the Theater of the Absurd as two old brothers, the optimist Emanuel ("Manny") and the pessimist Boomy, quote blasts from William Butler Yeats, Thomas Carlyle, Voltaire, Martin Buber, John Ruskin, the Zohar, and Ecclesiastes at one another. Other characters have similar problems: For example, old Jack goes around ringing a bell and sounding like a mad scene from *King Lear*. Yet the setting and characters are realistic enough—recognizable as contemporary Britain, from the youths who drop out of school and beat up old ladies in the street, to members of the next generation who are approaching middle age and still searching for a career choice, to the old folks who live in comfortable retirement but puzzle over the meaning of it all. It is clear that socialism has not yet solved the problems of old age, death, and the generation gap, much less the meaning of existence.

What is required is a Socialist theology, and Wesker attempts to provide it in the form of the old people's fellowship and Jewish custom. Through their own histories of failed relationships, the old ones have mellowed into tolerance of one another's eccentricities and appreciation of one another's company (even the quarreling brothers seem to need each other). They spend their time calling and visiting back and forth: At this stage, one needs all the moral support one can get. Their fellowship culminates in a revived celebration of Succoth, the Jewish harvest festival. Succoth calls for a symbolic hut in the room (in remembrance of frail humankind's vulnerability and need for God's help) and for a joyful countenance. Although marred by a few quarrels, the old ones' Succoth feast is indeed joyful, ending in a stirring Hasidic dance. Thus, ritual solidarity is achieved in the face of the universe.

As *The Old Ones* suggests, the movement from solidarity to religious fellowship is not as far as it might seem. In the epilogue to *The Four Seasons*, Wesker argues that love must undergird all human interaction, at whatever level: Men and women "need to know and be comforted by the knowledge that they are not alone in their private pain. You can urge mankind to no action by intimidating it with your eternal condemnation of its frailties." In his work, Wesker does not commit the ideological fallacy committed by his characters Sarah and Ronnie Kahn, who voice their love for humankind in the abstract but seem uncaring toward those closest to them. Socialism, so to speak, begins at home.

The Wedding Feast picks up the theme of socialism, returning to Norfolk to do so. The Jewish show manufacturer, Louis Litvanov, tries to put his socialism to work through paternalism, deciding to attend the wedding reception of one of his employees. The often slapstick comedy does not hide his thwarted idealism. Wesker seems to be suggesting that equality is a necessary socialist fiction, rather than an ideal, since, in fact, class divisions need maintaining. Trying to collapse them merely leads to disorientation and disharmony.

In *The Journalists* and *The Merchant*, Wesker moves away from working-class settings and concerns. *The Journalists* works rather like *The Kitchen* in showing the pressures of a hectic working environment undermining the possibility of idealism. The Sunday newspaper staff seem motivated by the need to cut public figures down to size. The central character is a star columnist who was once perhaps an idealist but now adopts a calculated cynicism as a defense against her disillusionment.

In *The Merchant*, Wesker strikes out in a new direction: He takes a Shakespeare play (as did Edward Bond and Tom Stoppard) and rewrites it. He states that he has always found *The Merchant of Venice* insupportable in its anti-Semitism. In his version, Wesker shows Shylock as an idealist, committed to open inquiry, a lover of books, a true Renaissance figure. In opposition to him are Christian "fundamentalists" who attack both the free-market forces of Venice and its toleration of Jews, however limited. The Venetian establishment, holding the political power, is more subtle: It takes a foolish gesture (the signing of the bond between Shylock and his close Gentile friend Antonio) and exploits it to deprive Shylock of his priceless collection of books. His idealism is further shattered by the flight of his daughter, who eventually loses both family and lover.

The play contains rather more plot than is usual for Wesker—the constraints of the original play dictated this. For the play to work, a good knowledge of the original is needed—since it is in the differences that the real force of the play is felt. *The Merchant* is a play where Jewishness is most obviously analyzed for what it is in its most enlightened forms, rather than as a paradigm for social cohesion and motivation.

After critical neglect, the production of *The Merchant* brought Wesker somewhat back into critical focus. The plays that followed, however, did not build on this and showed no clear development. *Annie Wobbler*, the stage version of Wesker's earlier radio drama *Annie, Anna, Annabella*, consists of three character monologues performed by a single actress. *One More Ride on the Merry-Go-Round* focuses on a middle-aged scholar and his wife and the comic results of their mid-life revitalization. Though these and other of his later plays were generally well received, at the end of his third decade in the theater, Wesker had not recaptured his early success.

Other major works

SHORT FICTION: *Love Letters on Blue Paper*, 1974; *Said the Old Man to the Young Man: Three Stories*, 1978; *Love Letters on Blue Paper and Other Stories*, 1980.

NONFICTION: *Fears of Fragmentation*, 1970; *Journey into Journalism*, 1977; *The Journalists: A Triptych*, 1979; *Distinctions*, 1985.

SCREENPLAY: *The Kitchen*, 1961.

TELEPLAY: *Menace*, 1963.

RADIO PLAYS: *Annie, Anna, Annabella*, 1983; *Bluey*, 1985.

CHILDREN'S LITERATURE: *Fatlips: A Story for Young People*, 1978.

MISCELLANEOUS: *Six Sundays in January*, 1971 (stories and plays).

Bibliography

Alter, Iska. "'Barbaric Laws, Barbaric Bonds': Arnold Wesker's *The Merchant.*" *Modern Drama* 31 (December, 1988): 536-547. Traces some of the intertextual ambiguities, especially concerning the insistent use of the law by Shylock. Wesker's historical research is noted to shift the play from Romance to political realism.

Brown, John Russell. *Theatre Language: A Study of Arden, Osborne, Pinter, and Wesker.* London: Allen Lane, 1972. Brown analyzes the language of *Roots*, *The Kitchen*, and *Chips with Everything*, dealing particularly with the way Wesker maintains theatricality by substituting talk for action in his drama. He also shows how he manages to hold theatrical discourse parallel to interpersonal talk in order to make explicit impact didactically. Short bibliography and index.

Hayman, Ronald. *Arnold Wesker.* London: Heinemann, 1970. This volume in the Contemporary Playwrights series includes chapters on each of the plays through *The Four Seasons*, in addition to two interviews with Wesker. A clearly written informative introduction to the earlier Wesker. Bibliography, biographical outline, and photographs.

Leeming, Glenda. "Articulacy and Awareness: The Modulation of Familiar Themes in Wesker's Plays of the Seventies." In *Contemporary English Drama*, edited by C. W. E. Bigsby. New York: Holmes & Meier, 1981. Leeming reviews the development of Wesker's drama from *The Old Ones* through *The Merchant.* She sees particularly an interiorization of a number of themes. The protagonists' awareness of their own suffering is located as the axis for the development.

____________, ed. *Wesker on File.* New York: Methuen, 1985. This invaluable small collection consists both of reviewers' and Wesker's own comments on his plays as well as on his work in general. Chronology and select bibliographies.

____________. *Wesker the Playwright.* New York: Methuen, 1983. This volume is probably the fullest account of Wesker's work written up to the date of its publication. Contains a chapter on each of his plays, an appendix, a select bibliography, an index, and photographs.

Leeming Glenda, and Simon Trussler. *The Plays of Arnold Wesker.* London: Victor Gollancz, 1971. This introduction studies the plays up to *The Friends.* A final chapter seeks to integrate the plays with Wesker's collection of lectures and articles *Fears of Fragmentation.* The book endeavors to move the interest back from biography to the plays themselves, their concerns, and techniques. Three appendices and a bibliography.

Harold Branam
(Updated by *David Barratt*)

PATRICK WHITE

Born: London, England; May 28, 1912
Died: Sydney, Australia; September 30, 1990

Principal drama

Return to Abyssinia, pr. 1947; *The Ham Funeral*, wr. 1947, pr. 1961, pb. 1965; *The Season at Sarsaparilla*, pr. 1962, pb. 1965; *A Cheery Soul*, pr. 1963, pb. 1965; *Night on Bald Mountain*, pr. 1963, pb. 1965; *Four Plays*, pb. 1965 (includes the preceding four plays); *Big Toys*, pr. 1977, pb. 1978; *Signal Driver*, pr. 1982, pb. 1983; *Netherwood*, pr., pb. 1983; *Shepherd on the Rocks*, pr. 1987.

Other literary forms

Patrick White is best known for his novels. In addition, he published numerous short stories and an autobiographical volume that he called a "self-portrait." He also wrote a screenplay based on one of his short stories, "The Night the Prowler."

Achievements

In 1973, White received the Nobel Prize in Literature for his fiction. Thereafter he wrote several more novels, short stories, and plays, which have been staged along with revivals of his earlier plays. Because his dramatic works are not widely known outside Australia, White's international reputation rests on his fiction, which constitutes an astounding achievement. In its grandeur and metaphysical use of the Australian landscape and character, it altered the course of that country's literature, previously marked, for the most part, by self-conscious realism and nationalism. Although many critics in Australia scoffed at his complex philosophical work before he received the Nobel Prize, White had steadily built a following abroad, beginning with the publication of *The Aunt's Story* in 1948. He has often been credited with setting Australian literature into the mainstream, as well as freeing and influencing an entire generation of writers in Australia whose work is now highly esteemed among those bodies of literature written in English. Whether White is a major dramatist may be open to argument; he does, however, deserve attention for a limited but solid achievement in plays characterized by originality in structure, powerful language, and expression of universal concerns. Although a number of Australian dramatists have achieved widespread recognition, White remains one of the first to experiment on the Australian stage. His example posed a challenge in the 1960's, when realistic and provincial plays constituted the few native works that appeared in a country where theatergoers most often looked to Great Britain and the United States for "real plays."

Biography

Although born in London, Patrick Victor Martindale White was the son of wealthy, third-generation Australian landowners, who were visiting England in 1912 but sailed for home six months after their son's birth. He spent his first thirteen years in and around Sydney, then left for Great Britain to attend school in Cheltenham. Returning to Australia in 1929, he worked for three years at a sheep station in the New England area northwest of Sydney before entering King's College, Cambridge. After he took his degree in modern languages, he remained in London to pursue his theatrical and writing ambitions. Travel through Europe and the United States followed, and in 1939 his first novel, *Happy Valley*, appeared. With the outbreak of World War II, he joined the Royal Air Force, serving in North Africa, Alexandria, the Middle East, and Greece. He returned to London after the war and there saw his first play, *Return to Abyssinia*, produced; the manuscript, lost (or destroyed), was never published. At this time, he wrote another play, *The Ham Funeral*, which did not receive a production until 1961. He returned to Australia in 1947 and except for brief trips abroad remained there.

For the next twenty-five years, he wrote novel after novel, all of which gained for him more recognition in Great Britain and the United States than in Australia. Following the award of the Nobel Prize in Literature in 1973 for his impressive achievement as a novelist, he emerged as something of a public figure in Australia, often criticizing his compatriots, voicing his opinion—at one time or another—on politics and politicians, literary criticism and its practitioners, the Australian involvement in the Vietnam War, preservation of natural resources, nuclear disarmament, and the treatment of aborigines. He invested his Nobel Prize money in a fund to assist other Australian writers, established scholarships for aboriginal students, and donated paintings from his extensive private collection to the New South Wales Art Gallery in Sydney. He continued to write both fiction and drama, although he once vowed never to write for the stage again. His plays, which were produced throughout Australia, have yet to be seen elsewhere even though they have appeared abroad in published form. In 1986, one of his most famous novels, *Voss* (1957), was turned into an opera; another Australian novelist, David Malouf, wrote the libretto for the production, which enjoyed tremendous success in Australia. After a long illness, White died at his home in Sydney on September 30, 1990.

Analysis

Patrick White's plays address the same thematic concerns as the novels: the role of the artist, the conflict between the visionary and the materialist, the moral desolation and decay prevailing in modern life. Their language and structure intensify and heighten experience by combining the poetic with the mundane, the experimental with the traditional, the events of ordinary life with the metaphysical quest for truth. In general, the plays owe much to the European tradition of expressionism, which depends on the use of antinaturalistic stage devices; compression of language; symbolic picture sequences achieved through short, unrealized scenes; lofty themes of spiritual regeneration or renewal; and a declamatory tone.

The best known of the plays, *The Ham Funeral*, illustrates these points. The Young Man, the only name given to its major character, reveals in the prologue that he is a poet and, like all poets, knows too much but never enough. He proceeds to explain that the audience must enter with him into the house before which he stands and there learn what it means to be a poet. The scenes that follow bring together the disparate parts of The Young Man's psyche and give him direction as an artist. In the first scene, he lies on his bed in silence, considering "the great poem," when the Landlady interrupts to tell him that her husband has died. He assists in preparation for the funeral, at which the relatives eat the ham the widow has provided to give the funeral class. Later, the Landlady attempts, unsuccessfully, to seduce The Young Man, who returns to his room and carries on a long conversation with The Girl, actually his anima. At the end of the play, The Young Man leaves the house—its back wall dissolving, the stage directions say—and walks into the "luminous night."

Through this fluid series of fragmented scenes, the self-absorbed artist has learned to identify himself with the raw stuff of life: love and lust, hate and compassion, the beautiful and the ugly. Henceforth his poetry will no longer resemble "self-abuse in an empty room" but a discovery of the human condition in all of its forms.

If *The Ham Funeral* may be taken as an autobiographical statement—and there exist substantial grounds for such an interpretation—then The Young Man (White) set his hand to the novel, forsaking poetry altogether and not returning to the drama for almost fifteen years. When he did, he took up in *The Season at Sarsaparilla* the plight of the visionary thrust into a world that is mundane, respectable, conventional, materialistic—but altogether lacking in awareness. An imaginary Sydney suburb, Sarsaparilla, comes to life on the stage through a setting that represents the kitchens and backyards of three adjoining houses. As the action moves from house to house, the families' lives intertwine in the most ordinary of ways, thus giving the outward texture of the play a deceptive air of naturalism. A dog in heat, or in season, interrupts the quiet lives of the three families when she goes under one of the houses, pursued by a pack of excited dogs. This ironic use of "season" in the title extends to the growing awareness of the central character, Pippy, a young girl on the verge of womanhood, who learns through the dogs' natural actions that life embraces passion, violence, birth, death, that it goes through its seasons, as she will hers.

A Cheery Soul takes for its setting the Sundown Home for Old People and centers its action on Miss Docker. This at once comic and bitter portrayal of a cheery soul, the very soul of suburban respectability and morality, offers a superbly drawn character in Miss Docker, who destroys herself and others as she goes about doing good and remaining cheerful in the face of every disaster. The destructive force, which she manifests unknowingly, stems from an absolute belief in the rightness of her actions, an attitude so pervasive that it leaves no room for sensitivity toward other people.

Probably the least successful of all the plays, *Night on Bald Mountain* sets out to portray the disintegration of Western civilization. The means it uses, however, fail to rise to the loftiness of its theme: A woman more devoted to a herd of goats than to humankind, an embittered professor, his alcoholic wife, and a young woman with incestuous longings lack the universal appeal to make convincing so significant a message. Still, the play's artistry in language and structure and its striking use of setting lend it a pure theatrical excitement in spite of the defects.

Disheartened by the reception of his plays, White left the drama for the novel and shunned playwriting for fourteen years. Some critics believe, though, that his early plays, so different from anything native ever produced on the Australian stage, sowed the seeds for the new theater movement that got under way there in 1967, when several young writers demanded that Australian theater make room for the country's linguistic vigor, concern itself with matters contemporarily Australian, and liberate the imagination to experiment with new forms. Whereas these playwrights moved in directions different from White, they surely benefited from his earlier attempts to establish a distinctly Australian drama.

In 1977, *Big Toys* opened in Australia to a new breed of theatergoers, ones who not only took Australian drama seriously but also accepted work that ignored the conventions of theatrical realism. Set in a fashionable Sydney suburb, *Big Toys* depicts the empty lives of Mag and Ritchie Bosanquet, who have what should make life full—wealth, beauty, social position, every imaginable material possession, indeed all the "big toys." As they rise in the material realm, they are actually rushing to their downfall: In White's world, outward success leads to inward failure. *Big Toys* employs the elegant form of comedy of manners and relies on a conflict created by industrial exploitation to draw this bleak picture. Yet the realistic conflict and the stylized form that frames it expand in such a way that they merge into White's earlier devotion to the expressionistic mode. The three characters—as real as those who appear in the daily newspaper with their personal, social, and business connivances—move into abstract and symbolic dimensions to declaim the moral bankruptcy that dominates the lives of those who determine the course of the late twentieth century.

Signal Driver is White's purest dramatic venture into expressionism and one of his most impressive plays. Taking its title from Sydney bus signs that instruct potential riders to "signal driver," the play follows Theo and Ivy Volkes from youth to old age, the telling of their stories amplified by two music-hall characters who serve as the Volkeses' alter egos. The entire action takes place at a bus stop, its environs and conditions changing to show the passage of time. Buses go by, but the Volkeses never board; when old age levels them, they realize that they have metaphorically missed the bus of life. Simplistic though the concept might sound, the talented application of the expressionistic techniques governing language, character development, staging, and handling of theme turns the play into a powerful and memorable statement on the desolate human condition.

Netherwood follows theatrical conventions more closely than *Signal Driver*, at least on the surface. The action takes place in a once-grand Australian country house, called Netherwood, where a group of half-comic, half-mad characters live together on parole from the local mental institution, Bonkers Hall, under the supervision of a couple who are determined to do good. During act 1, the events unfold on a believable level and suggest that this play might be an Australian version of the English manor-house comedy. In the second act, however, all pretense toward representation of reality vanishes. Characters take on multiple identities and serve as one another's alter egos, thereby revealing to the audience their sexual repressions and perversions, their hidden failures, suppressed fears, and inability to grasp life's meaning. When the personal struggles of the characters cannot be solved by a tidy plot, the play ends on an apocalyptic note. Amid gratuitous gunfire, one of the characters says: "Comical bastards, us humans. Seems like we sorter *choose* ter shoot it out . . . to find out who's the bigger dill." At the end, White appears to voice his rising concern with nuclear armament through this statement, so very Australian in its syntax and diction. In Australia, a "dill" is a fool—a condition that suggests White's view of humankind.

White's final play, *Shepherd on the Rocks*, was given a Sydney production in 1987. In the play, described as an "epic religious revue," the action follows the adventures of a priest named Danny Shepherd, who serves an Australian parish called Budgiwank. Through his "Budgiwank Experiment," he plans to convert prostitutes and junkies, then move them to his suburban parish so they can mix with the virtuous parishioners. Shepherd loses his position and moves to Jerusalem, where he becomes a performer in the Jerusalem Easter Show. Although not up to the standards of the earlier plays, *Shepherd on the Rocks* elaborates once more a theme that runs through all White's work when the ruined priest says: "At the gates of death—which is not hell, . . . I hope to shed my doubts, fears, obstinacy, lust. I do not expect an easy transition." So the young poet in the play *The*

Ham Funeral has come to the end of his experience in the "luminous night," still knowing too much but never enough.

Although White's plays will not gain the kind of recognition his fiction has achieved, they should not be discounted or ignored. They stand as accomplished works in their own right, especially in their author's original handling of techniques that made expressionism so vital a force in twentieth century theater. Finally, an understanding of the dramas will lead to a richer appreciation of the novels, for both literary forms show how the artist can meld opposites: symbolism that employs the trivial to clarify the universal; characters who emerge as both real human beings and metaphysical abstractions; settings that rely on the tangible, which are microcosmic, but suggest the elusive, the universal.

Other major works

NOVELS: *Happy Valley*, 1939; *The Living and the Dead*, 1941; *The Aunt's Story*, 1948; *The Tree of Man*, 1955; *Voss*, 1957; *Riders in the Chariot*, 1961; *The Solid Mandala*, 1966; *The Vivisector*, 1970; *The Eye of the Storm*, 1973; *A Fringe of Leaves*, 1976; *The Twyborn Affair*, 1979; *Memoirs of Many in One*, 1986.

SHORT FICTION: *The Burnt Ones*, 1964; *The Cockatoos: Shorter Novels and Stories*, 1974; *Three Uneasy Pieces*, 1987.

POETRY: *The Ploughman and Other Poems*, 1935.

NONFICTION: *Flaws in the Glass: A Self-Portrait*, 1981; *Patrick White Speaks*, 1989.

SCREENPLAY: *The Night the Prowler*, 1976.

Bibliography

Akerholt, May-Brit. *Patrick White.* Amsterdam: Rodopi, 1988. Provides extensive background material on White's published plays, including details on premiere dates, casts, directors, and set designers, as well as plot summaries and information on the plays' origins. Addresses recurrent themes in the plays, comments on their technical innovations, and stresses their satiric bent.

Bliss, Carolyn. *Patrick White's Fiction: The Paradox of Fortunate Failure.* New York: St. Martin's Press, 1986. Although not addressing the drama directly, this study offers an excellent introduction to White's overall thematic concerns. Argues that all White's writing stems from a paradox—that is, the failures so often experienced by the characters can in fact lead to their successful redemption.

Carroll, Dennis. "Patrick White." In *Australian Contemporary Drama, 1909-1982.* New York: Peter Lang, 1985. Focuses on White's use of symbolism, expressionism, and surrealism, and discusses the plays' techniques and stage conventions (through *A Cheery Soul*). Argues that

White's work broke with the realistic Australian drama prior to the 1960's. Sees younger playwrights moving in new directions after White introduced such experimentation.

Marr, David. *Patrick White: A Life.* New York: Alfred A. Knopf, 1992. A lengthy biography covering all facets of White's life, from childhood to death. Provides extensive information on White's lifelong fascination with the theater, the writing and production of the plays, and their origins. Offers a more personal view of White as a playwright than do the formal studies devoted to his drama.

Whitman, Robert F. "The Dream Plays of Patrick White." *Texas Studies in Literature and Language: A Journal of the Humanities* 21, no. 2 (1979): 240-259. Sets out to define White's purpose in the early plays, discover their sources, and examine their themes. Concludes that they are all dream plays: They rely on distorted theatrical conventions, and in this way they uncover elements from the viewers' unconsciousness.

Robert Ross

JOHN WHITING

Born: Salisbury, England; November 15, 1917
Died: Duddleswell, England; June 16, 1963

Principal drama

Paul Southman, pr. 1946 (radio play), pr. 1965 (staged); *A Penny for a Song*, pr. 1951, pb. 1957, pr. 1962 (revised); *Saint's Day*, pr. 1951, pb. 1952; *Marching Song*, pr., pb. 1954; *The Gates of Summer*, pr. 1956, pb. 1969; *The Devils*, pr., pb. 1961 (adapted from Aldous Huxley's book *The Devils of Loudun*); *No Why*, pb. 1961, pr. 1964; *Conditions of Agreement*, pr. 1965, pb. 1969; *The Nomads*, pr. 1965, pb. 1969; *The Collected Plays of John Whiting*, pb. 1969 (2 volumes).

Other literary forms

In 1945 John Whiting completed a novel entitled "Not a Foot of Land," but it was not published. His radio plays, *Paul Southman*, *Eye Witness* (1949), *The Stairway* (1949), and *Love's Old Sweet Song* (1950), were broadcast by the British Broadcasting Corporation (BBC). In 1951, he began writing screenplays that were adaptations of others' works. Of the numerous screenplays Whiting wrote, titles include *The Ship That Died of Shame* (1955, with Michael Relph and Basil Dearden), *The Good Companions* (1957, with T. J. Morrison and J. L. Hodgson), *The Captain's Table* (1959, with Bryan Forbes and Nicholas Phipps), and *Young Cassidy* (1965). His television play, *A Walk in the Desert*, was aired in 1960 and was later published in *The Collected Plays of John Whiting*.

Achievements

John Whiting sharply divided British audiences with his controversial departure from naturalistic drama. Labeled self-indulgent and obscure by critics, Whiting's work was championed by practical men and women of the theater. Actors, directors, and young playwrights found Whiting's structural and thematic density fertile ground for creativity and experimentation, but Whiting's work could not be easily understood in the immediacy of a production, so he alienated his audiences and baffled his critics. In the early 1950's, London audiences were not ready to depart from the standard theatrical diet of plays which were basically reproductions of life and its everyday conflicts. Whiting's way of looking at the world and dramatizing it was too different and too uncompromising to allow him success at the box office. Nevertheless, Whiting's departure from the traditional rules of drama, which require that motive, action, and consequence follow a clearly developed line, significantly expanded the range of drama, and thus he helped prepare the modern audience for such experimental playwrights as Harold Pinter and Samuel Beckett.

In the late 1940's, British drama was in the throes of a poetic renaissance. T. S. Eliot brought accessible verse to the stage and in *The Cocktail Party* (pr. 1949) dramatized a vague spiritual optimism. Christopher Frye's *The Lady's Not for Burning* (pr. 1948) entertained the audience with its whimsical poetry and affirmation of life, and the widely popular plays of Terence Rattigan provided the audience with evenings of well-made plays with easily accessible plots and characterizations. Whiting's work exhibits influences from all three playwrights, but his intellectual vision developed their poetry, comedy, and characterizations into plays with statements the audience did not care to comprehend.

Whiting's plays do not have easily labeled themes and preoccupations. He believed that while the purpose of entertainment was to reassure, the purpose of art was to raise doubts. Whiting claimed allegiance to the tradition of the intellectual elite whose concern was to write difficult plays for a discriminating audience. His recurrent concern with the nature of violence and the limits of personal responsibility anticipated the interests of a younger generation of playwrights who chose to write about similar conflicts, and although Whiting's originality was not recognized until the last years of his life, he is now considered a pioneer of contemporary drama. In 1965, an annual award of one thousand pounds was established—to be awarded to promising young playwrights—in memory of John Whiting.

Biography

Born in Salisbury, Wiltshire, England, John Robert Whiting was the son of an army officer who later became a lawyer. Whiting was educated at Taunton, a public school at Somerset, where he was considered an unremarkable student. When the time came to choose a career, a university education was not even considered an option because his academic standing, as well as his interest, was too low. On the advice of his father and his headmaster, Whiting decided to train to be an actor. As a student at the Royal Academy of Dramatic Art, Whiting was painfully self-conscious and shy, and thus his work suffered in the beginning. While on vacation from school, he was cast in a small part in a provincial theater, and he returned to the academy with much more skill, self-confidence, and determination. He completed his training in 1937 with a positive report of his abilities and chances as an actor. Although acting jobs were scarce, Whiting survived with occasional jobs in radio plays until World War II interrupted his career.

Originally, Whiting registered as a conscientious objector. Shortly after he registered, however, he changed his mind, having been exposed to pacifist groups that he regarded as collections of snobs and aggressive intellectuals. Whiting was also torn by the conflict between loyalty to his father's soldiering tradition and loyalty to his own feeling of repugnance toward war. Finally, Whiting became a reluctant soldier. When he registered in the army, he requested an infantry regiment because his father had been an infantry officer, but the army ignored his preference and put him in artillery. He often told his wife, Asthore Lloyd Mawson, whom he had married in 1940, that the guns he helped fire would never hit anything.

In the army, Whiting began writing as a hobby when he discovered Frederick Rolfe, an author who wrote, under the name Baron Corvo, strange tales in an elaborate pseudomedieval script. The slow, painstaking process of imitating Rolfe's calligraphy influenced more than Whiting's handwriting. The moments of concentration gave Whiting opportunities to think and to absorb an archaic style and a recondite vocabulary. He developed a love for language. Initially, Whiting wrote poems and stories, but his instinctive need for an audience led him to write plays. Several of his early radio plays were broadcast by the BBC, but much of his drama for the stage was kept private or was rejected by theaters.

In March, 1951, his comic *A Penny for a Song* opened at Haymarket Theatre; the much more grim *Saint's Day* was produced the following September and won first prize in the Festival of Britain play competition. *Saint's Day* angered critics and was labeled incomprehensible, but the contest judges remained firm in their support of Whiting as a talented and original playwright. Simple bad luck plagued many of Whiting's plays. Fires, accidents, and illnesses often spoiled premiere productions, and he was rarely well received by audiences and critics.

Finally, in 1961, *The Devils* brought Whiting long-awaited praise from critics. Although his late success brought him many calls for work from major companies and theaters, *The Devils* was his last completed play. In November, 1962, he was diagnosed as having cancer. After years of struggling to support a family, his last year of life was eased by financial and critical success, but his attempts at revisions and new plays were left incomplete when he died in June of 1963.

Like many of his characters, Whiting was forced to accept death when success was just within reach. He became terminally ill just as he was looking forward to a successful and creative future in a theater he could finally call his own. Unlike Pinter and Beckett, who had time to develop an audience, Whiting's audience was just beginning to understand him when his life ended.

Analysis

Deeply influenced by the plays of T. S. Eliot, who had brought philosophical thought as well as verse to the stage, John Whiting showed that heightened prose was more viable than verse. He believed that the easiest way of communicating with an audience was direct speech. Unlike Pinter, who later exploited the colloquialisms of daily speech to the point of absurdity, Whiting combined common language with heightened intelligence and insight, and such a combination often confused his audience. Whereas Eliot never made his characters as interesting as what they said, Whiting created distinctive characters who were articulate, sensitive, and often pathetic in their extreme vulnerability.

The turning points in Whiting's plays involve personality changes which are so basic that they are better labeled conversions. Whiting's characters do not simply change their minds about a person or decision; they dramatically alter their views on life and death. In addition, Whiting never directly dramatizes how his characters change. The audience sees only the beginning and the end of a process, and the actual moments of decision are left obscure. Whiting chooses to dramatize conversions indirectly because to dramatize them too completely would invite didacticism or melodrama.

Whiting's position on the morality of his characters often baffles his audience even more than do his plots. It is futile for the audience to look for motivation or to try to identify with Whiting's characters because they dramatize ideology in action rather than an easily identifiable human need. For example, in *Marching Song*, audiences resist identifying with an ex-army general who brutally killed children as a part of military strategy. When the general is strongly advised to commit suicide to avoid being a further embarrassment to his country, few in the audience care to share in his philosophical dilemma or try to understand Whiting's position. Rather than simple morality, Whiting is concerned with why characters behave the way they do and how their actions affect their worlds. The intellect is Whiting's playground, rather than the emotions, and one can best understand his plays by considering how they raise questions rather than how they stimulate emotions.

Whiting wrote *A Penny for a Song* during a happy period in his life, and the farcical action and the life-loving characters dramatize an optimistic perspective on the world. Set in the garden of the country home of Sir Timothy Bellboys, the tone suggests summer ease and festivities, although the threat of war hovers just beyond the garden: Napoleon and his army are expected to invade. The central characters all have delightfully complicated strategies for survival, and their energy and enthusiasm elevate the farce. The play suggests that war threatens everyday life and therefore that simple domestic moments of peace are fragile and precious.

From the opening moments of the play, when Humpage, the sleeping family lookout, spills his cakes from his post high in a tree and a dignified visitor becomes lost while looking for an outhouse, the audience knows that in this play about war, no one will be harmed. The ineffective, bungling characters with their candid feelings and good intentions charm the audience. Although they caricature a nation of simple people under the threat of war, they invite the audience to share in the real quirks and whims of humankind. The members of this respectable group of family and friends exhibit a childlike innocence in their plans for coping with invasion, and like imaginative children, they accept one another's fantastic schemes. Sir Timothy plans to defeat the French by impersonating Napoleon, tunneling his way to the rear of the invading troops and leading them in a retreat. The audience immediately understands that Sir Timothy does not exhibit a sound method of warfare; rather, he represents the noble human drive to take responsibility for one's countrymen.

In the comic tradition, Whiting's plot is based on confused messages and mistaken identities. When Sir Timothy does not receive the message that the home guard is engaging in a military exercise, he mistakes them for the French, and his potentially dangerous little war is on. Cannons fire, alarms sound, and it appears that real danger threatens these characters who are so intent on preserving life that they might hurt someone. Following the traditional comic plot, however, Whiting contrives timely revelations before serious damage is done.

The theatricality of the action—the sheer entertainment of the clownish characters and slapstick action—prevents the audience from questioning the play's sense. The garden bustles with strangers and relatives coming, going, and getting lost. Doors and windows open and close constantly as servants and family go about their business. In the distance, Sir Timothy flies through the air in a hot-air balloon. His brother Lamprett exhibits his fire-fighting equipment, and Lamprett's wife appears in full armorial regalia as she announces her plans to join the East Anglican Amazon Corps. Throughout the play, Humpage roosts in his tree and, amid the surrounding chaos, tries to hold on to his telescope and cakes.

Hardly a logical argument against war, the play is an affirmation of life and the human will to survive. The implausible plot staggers along as the characters refuse to let logic interfere with their plans to save one another: Whenever a character's ideas are challenged by reasonable remarks, he spontaneously transforms doubt into optimism, or simply changes the subject entirely. Thus, the conversations are often incoherent. For these characters, however, reason stems from a serious perspective, and to be serious would be to admit that Napoleon might win. In a tragic play, such as *Saint's Day*, self-deception leads to self-destruction: In Whiting's serious plays, self-deception always involves the abdication of responsibility to others, and then shame and self-inflicted punishment. In contrast, in *A Penny for a Song*, the characters joyfully assume responsibility for the happiness and safety of others, so their self-deception is redeemed. Still, Whiting does not design the play to end happily simply because the characters have good intentions; many of his tragic characters have good intentions as well. Indeed, the happy resolution depends on inconsequence and implausibility. Disaster is always a possibility in *A Penny for a Song*, and the audience is constantly reminded that the characters survive because Whiting is writing a farce and wants their struggle to end in harmony.

Whiting uses the blind veteran, Edward Sterne, to articulate his view that self-deception is necessary for survival. Sterne comments on the outrageous schemes of the Belleboyses and their visitors:

> And so we escape, childlike, into the illusion. We clown and posture but not to amuse others—no—to comfort ourselves. The laughter is incidental to the tragic spectacle of each man attempting to hide his intolerable self.

Through Sterne, Whiting also comments subtly on the power of the dramatic illusion. While Sterne suggests that he knows the motivations for his own illusions, the playwright insists on a deeper human need to create and participate in dramatic artifice. Edward Sterne knows that his mission to walk to London and tell a mad king to stop the war is futile. He knows that he is deluding himself into believing that his small will can affect the world. Nevertheless, Whiting suggests that purposeful action has a kind of redemptive power, whatever the outcome. When Sir Timothy outlines his ridiculous and dangerous plan to save Britain, he refuses to let reasonable comments intimidate him. He speaks for the playwright when he says, "I may fail—but what of that? It is what we attempt that matters."

Whiting himself remarked that *A Penny for a Song* was simply about Christian charity. In a time of war, a chaotic household of eccentric characters meets, with individual passions ranging from fire fighting to reading a good poem, but in spite of vast differences, harmony prevails. The characters' cross-purposes never result in genuine conflict; the mock war ends with little damage done, and all the self-made soldiers retire to the kitchen to eat and talk of cricket. The successful actions of these charitable characters suggest that the only way to survive the violent onslaught of the world is to throw oneself into it imaginatively and cheerfully.

In *Saint's Day*, Whiting shows a very different response to a world that threatens the individual. The characters respond with self-righteousness, and their cynicism toward others results in self-destruction. They deliberately alienate themselves from family and community. The play's action symbolizes a death wish, with death the ultimate withdrawal into self. Here, Whiting violently dramatizes the dangers of irresponsibility. The characters become so involved in using others for selfish goals that they lose sight of the larger human purpose of survival, and they are destroyed by the inevitable chaos of irresponsible action. After the first scene, set in the living room of the play's main character, Paul Southman, the audience knows that this is no standard drawing-room drama. In his stage directions, Whiting describes Southman's living room as an "architectural freak," noting that the elegant furniture has been neglected and abused. Dirty dishes are piled on an ornate yet filthy tray, and a bicycle lies upstage. The set suggests that normal life has suddenly and radically been interrupted. The audience is uncertain about the tone of the play, and thus Whiting prevents them from assigning labels or drawing neat conclusions.

Whiting uses dialogue to jolt the audience into viewing the play as a symbolic philosophical statement rather than an evening's dramatic illusion. Whereas the drawing-room setting parodies those of popular plays, the dialogue often parodies that of Eliot's poetic drama. Whiting does not use verse, but the audience is forced to perceive language as more than simple communication that moves the plot forward. For sophisticated audiences attuned to his intentions, Whiting's dialogue is dense with meaning, but the casual theatergoer may find it cryptic.

The opening of the play suggests possibilities for fulfillment: Aging writer Paul Southman is about to be honored for his literary achievements; his granddaughter, Stella, is pregnant, and her unsuccessful husband may sell some paintings in town. These possibilities, however, are but glimmers of hope. Images of death and decay permeate the play: The strong old trees outside the house are dying; the family dog mysteriously dies; and young Stella's hair is graying.

Southman himself, once a respected poet and radical pamphleteer, is approaching senility after twenty-five years of self-imposed exile. His literary attacks on society have been reduced to an irrational feud with the nearby villagers, who in turn despise him for his eccentricities. Southman's selfish withdrawal from the world has atrophied his emotions and his intellect. He is cynical about the celebration to be held in his honor. When soldiers terrorize the village, he wants them to be his allies so he can better continue his one-man war. When his granddaughter is killed, he places her death in the context of a bad joke, and when he is finally led to his own hanging, he is so far removed from reality that he believes he is going to his celebration, and thus goes without a struggle. Symbolically, he is dead from the beginning of the play; his execution simply finalizes a process that began when he started his personal war on the world.

For an audience that expects coherent action and characters with identifiable motivations, Whiting's play offers some shocking surprises. The set is confusing; the dialogue, incoherent; and the actions, symbolic. The sequence of events in the play is implausible, but Whiting's purpose is not to present a logical world. Dramatizing the dangerous interrelationships of actions, Whiting illustrates how one careless act can lead to outrageous and deadly consequences.

When the pompous scholar Robert Procathren stupidly and accidentally shoots Stella, Whiting does not intend for the audience to feel sympathy or outrage: The characters are too symbolic and the action too contrived to warrant such emotions. Whiting contrives the shooting to make a statement about the inability of individuals to control themselves and their world.

Although Procathren is innocent of malicious intent, he is guilty of both insensitivity and carelessness.

The audience is forced to consider each character's responsibility as a philosophical problem. Since each action has far-reaching ramifications, the audience must consider how responsible individuals are for their own actions as well as for the actions of others. The accident leads Procathren to alter his view of the value of life, for Stella's death suggests a world where violence is random, where death is not only inevitable but also often occurs as a grim practical joke. He suddenly linked to a violent world, and as a result he begins a course of self-destruction as a way of getting revenge on the world and on himself. When Procathren's plan involves the deaths of Southman and Stella's husband, Whiting suggests that all three are indirectly responsible for Stella's death.

Whiting goes on to show that Procathren's careless act has ramifications beyond the corrupt Southman household. After the accident, Procathren becomes a militant cynic. He takes his bitter revelations to town and convinces the minister that theological books are deceptions and that faith is a lie. Totally convinced, the minister burns his books in a bonfire that rages out of control and destroys the entire town. Following the same logic, the closing scene of the play suggests that no one is innocent. A child from the village who, with her family, seeks refuge in Southman's home, closes the play by ignorantly dancing to music that heralds three hangings just beyond the door. She is immediately shamed when she realizes the impropriety of her actions. The audience learns that the girl's name is Stella, and the link with the dead Stella implies that even the young and innocent are doomed by the irresponsible actions of others and themselves.

In his last completed play, *The Devils*, Whiting even more violently dramatizes the destructive power of human beings' irresponsibility. In the program to the original production, Whiting offered his view of the historical incident that inspired the play—in Whiting's account, the tragedy of a talented and intelligent priest whose downfall was ultimately the result of his own actions. Here Whiting employs Bertolt Brecht's alienation effects to force the audience to consider the horrors that can result from selfishness and vengeful hypocrisy. The play's episodic structure is useful for conveying a wide range of information quickly, but it also continually reminds the audience that they are watching a play, an artifice designed to make a statement.

One of Whiting's typical characters, Grandier the priest, is a sensitive man who is driven toward self-destruction. His struggle toward his own death is a consciously sought redemption for his inability to feel tenderness in physical love. His frequent illicit relationships with women are weak attempts to disguise his sensuality with affection. He romantically enacts a mock marriage to his youngest and most innocent lover, and he says that her naïveté shames him, yet in another scene, when she reveals that she is pregnant, he harshly says that he is finished with her.

Throughout the play, Whiting dramatizes the conflict between human beings' basest drives and their noblest impulses. The nuns are guilty of debasing spiritual passion into lust and vengeance, while Grandier, the great theologian and orator, similarly debases his priestly office by reveling in a sensual life. An almost omnipresent character, the Sewerman, punctuates each act with his presence and reminds the characters and the audience that sewers run through the most official and noble places. Aspirations to love and spiritual redemption are graphically debased by the Sewerman's presence.

Through the destructive hysteria of the nuns, Whiting not only comments on the animalistic drives of people but also raises questions concerning the nature of evil. The sexually frustrated prioress, Sister Jeanne, seeks revenge on the object of her desire, and she incites the nuns to charge that Grandier is a demon who possesses them. As the play progresses, however, the audience sees that Jeanne is not simply pretending. A scene in which she and the demon that possesses her converse and laugh suggests that evil is a real force, but a force made by human beings. The demon is Jeanne's own creation, now all too real, no mere figment of the imagination.

Whiting's vision is essentially tragic. Of his six full-length plays, three end in violent death, and each death is directly or indirectly the fulfillment of self-destruction. Whiting's characters are torn by dual motives to redeem themselves from and to damn themselves for their moral failure. Self-destruction becomes a twisted redemption that also fails. In his plays, the refusal to recognize responsibility leads to a tragic conclusion. The apocalyptic quality of much of Whiting's work, the sense of mortality, and the fear of inconsequence suggest a world that is run by a cruel god who uses death as a practical joke. At best, this awareness of death encourages human beings to grasp at the honest, loving moments of life; at worst, it invites them to enact their own destruction—if only to prove that they have some small measure of control over their lives.

Other major works

SCREENPLAYS: *The Ship That Died of Shame*, 1955 (with Michael Relph and Basil Dearden): *The Good Companions*, 1957 (with T. J. Morrison and J. L. Hodgson); *The Captain's Table*, 1959 (with Bryan Forbes and Nicholas Phipps); *Young Cassidy*, 1965.

TELEPLAY: *A Walk in the Desert*, 1960.

RADIO PLAYS: *Eye Witness*, 1949; *The Stairway*, 1949; *Love's Old Sweet Song*, 1950; *No More A-Roving*, 1975.

MISCELLANEOUS: *The Art of the Dramatist and Other Pieces*, 1969 (short fiction, criticism, lectures; Ronald Hayman, editor).

Bibliography

Goodall, Jane. "*The Devils* and Its Sources: Modern Perspectives on the Loudun Possession." In *Drama and Philosophy*, edited by James Redmond. New York: Cambridge University Press, 1990. The essay shows how Whiting shifts the emphasis from Grandier's villainy to his inner struggle. It also compares the play with Henry de Montherlant's *Port-Royal* (pr., pb. 1954; English translation, 1962) and Jean Genet's *Le Balcon* (pb. 1956; *The Balcony*, 1957).

__________. "Musicality and Meaning in the Dialogue of *Saint's Day.*" *Modern Drama* 29 (December, 1986): 567-579. This essay defends the play against the early charges of abstruseness by demonstrating its underlying logic. It seeks to show the dramatic elements of this logic in terms of the search for revelation. Looks particularly at the play's dialogue.

Hayman, Ronald. *John Whiting.* London: Heinemann, 1969. One of the Heinemann Contemporary Playwrights series, this volume is written by Whiting's own editor. As such, it attempts an introduction to the dramatist and his eight main plays. A brief but effective literary discussion and analysis does take place in most chapters. Short bibliography.

Milne, Tom. "The Hidden Face of Violence." In *The Encore Reader: A Chronicle of the New Drama*, edited by Charles Marowitz et al. London: Methuen, 1965. This review compares *Saint's Day* with Harold Pinter's *The Birthday Party* (pr. 1958) and John Arden's *Serjeant Musgrave's Dance* (pr. 1959) as plays of violence that exploded onto the English stage when first produced.

Robinson, Gabrielle Scott. "Beyond the Waste Land: An Interpretation of John Whiting's *Saint's Day.*" *Modern Drama* 14 (February, 1972): 463-477. Robinson attempts an interpretation of this difficult play by looking at the reworkings of Whiting's drafts, manuscripts, and sources.

Salmon, Eric. *The Dark Journey: John Whiting as Dramatist.* London: Barrie & Jenkins, 1979. Probably the fullest account of Whiting's complete oeuvre. It makes large claims for Whiting, seeing him as prophetic of the drama to come. It traces in particular Whiting's obsession "with the innate tendency of the sensitive towards self-destruction." Four appendices, a full bibliography, and an index.

Trussler, Simon. *The Plays of John Whiting: An Assessment.* London: Victor Gollancz, 1972. A short introduction followed by five chapters, with the last one discussing Whiting's writing on the theater, *The Art of the Dramatist and Other Pieces.* A brief conclusion seeks to place Whiting. Four appendices, including a bibliography.

Jane Falco
(Revised by *David Barratt*)

OSCAR WILDE

Born: Dublin, Ireland; October 16, 1854
Died: Paris, France; November 30, 1900

Principal drama

Vera: Or, The Nihilists, pb. 1880, pr. 1883; *The Duchess of Padua*, pb. 1883, pr. 1891; *Lady Windermere's Fan*, pr. 1892, pb. 1893; *Salomé*, pb. 1893 (in French), pb. 1894 (in English), pr. 1896 (in French), pr. 1905 (in English); *A Woman of No Importance*, pr. 1893, pb. 1894; *An Ideal Husband*, pr. 1895, pb. 1899; *The Importance of Being Earnest: A Trivial Comedy for Serious People*, pr. 1895, pb. 1899; *A Florentine Tragedy*, pb. 1908 (one act, completed by T. Sturge More); *La Sainte Courtisane*, pb. 1908.

Other literary forms

Oscar Wilde's character and conversation were in themselves striking enough to gain for him the attention of the reading public, but, in addition to playwriting, he practiced all the other literary forms. He began writing poetry at an early age, commemorating the death of his sister Isola with "Requiescat" in 1867 and winning the Newdigate Prize for Poetry at Oxford with *Ravenna* in 1878. Wilde's *Poems* appeared in 1881; *The Sphinx* in 1894; *The Ballad of Reading Gaol*, his last literary work, in 1898. His efforts in fiction include "The Canterville Ghost" (1887), which was made into a movie in 1943; *The Happy Prince and Other Tales* (1888); *Lord Arthur Savile's Crime and Other Stories* (1891); *A House of Pomegranates* (1891); and his novel, *The Picture of Dorian Gray* (serialized in *Lippincott's Monthly Magazine* in 1890, published in book form in 1891). Oscar Wilde's best-known essays and literary criticism appear in *Intentions* (1891). *De Profundis*, the long letter the imprisoned Wilde wrote to Lord Alfred Douglas, was published in 1905; his collected letters, edited by Rupert Hart-Davies, appeared in 1962.

Achievements

To accuse Oscar Wilde of anything so active-sounding as "achievement" would be an impertinence that the strenuously indolent author would most likely deplore. Yet it must be admitted that Wilde's presence, poses, ideas, and epigrams made him a potent influence, if not on the English literary tradition, at least on the artistic community of his own day. More visibly than any British contemporary, Oscar Wilde personified the doctrines of turn-of-the-century Aestheticism—that art existed for its own sake and that one should live so as to make from the raw materials of one's own existence an elegantly finished artifice. Wilde's aestheticism, caricatured by W. S. Gilbert and Sir Arthur Sullivan in their operetta *Patience: Or,*

Bunthorne's Bride (1881) and in Robert Smythe Hichens' novel *The Green Carnation* (1894), mingled ideas from his two very different Oxford mentors John Ruskin and Walter Pater with the influence of the French Symbolists and, for a time, certain theories of the American painter James McNeill Whistler; but his Irish wit and eloquence made the articulation of this intellectual pastiche something distinctively his own.

Oscar Wilde's literary works are polished achievements in established modes rather than experiments in thought or form. His poems and plays tend to look across the English Channel to the examples of the Symbolists and the masters of the *pièce bien faite*, though his *Salomé*, a biblical play written in French after the style of the then acclaimed dramatist Maurice Maeterlinck, was to engender a yet more significant work of art, Richard Strauss's opera of the same title. If they are not intellectually or technically adventurous, however, Wilde's works are incomparable for their talk—talk which tends to be Wilde's own put into the mouths of his characters. The outrageous, elegant, paradoxical conversation volleyed by Wilde's languid verbal athletes have given English literature more quotable tags than have the speeches of any other dramatist save William Shakespeare.

Biography

Oscar Fingal O'Flahertie Wills Wilde was born on October 16, 1854, in Dublin, Ireland, to parents who were among the most colorful members of the Irish gentry. His father, Sir William Wilde, one of the foremost Victorian oculists and surgeons, numbered crowned heads of Europe among his patients. He was equally famed for his archaeological research and his amorous adventures. Oscar Wilde's mother was no less remarkable. Born Jane Francesca Elgee, she gained public notice for the patriotic pieces she published under the pseudonym "Speranza." When one of Speranza's essays brought Sir Charles Gavan Duffy, leader of the Young Ireland party, to trial for high treason and sedition, the tall and dramatic authoress rose in court, proclaimed "I alone am the culprit," and on the spot became one of the heroines of Ireland.

This colorful background and his mother's doting attention must have fostered young Wilde's imagination. His mind received more discipline and direction when, through good fortune, he was brought into contact with a series of fine teachers. At Trinity College in Dublin, Wilde's Greek tutor, the Reverend John Pentland Mahaffy, inspired him with a love of Hellenic culture and by his own witty example honed and polished the younger man's conversational talents. Next, having won a demyship to Magdalen College, Oxford, in 1874, Wilde encountered John Ruskin (then Slade Professor of Art), whose social conscience, love of medieval architecture, and belief in the necessary connection between art and life were to become part of Wilde's own creed. Even more important to Wilde's development was Walter Pater, the skeptical latter-day Epicurean famed for his *Studies in the History of the Renaissance* (1873). In the light of Pater's intellectual advice to the youth of the day, most memorably distilled in his observation that "to burn always with this hard, gemlike flame, to maintain this ectasy, is success in life," the Oxonian Wilde's famous ambition, "Oh, would that I could live up to my blue china!" seems a less frivolous objective.

In 1879, Wilde went down to London, where, sharing rooms with the artist Frank Miles, he became one of the central figures of the Aesthetic movement and made the acquaintance of many of the celebrities of the day, particularly the lovely Lily Langtry, whose career as a professional beauty had been launched by Miles's drawings. The tall, heavy, epigrammatic young Wilde was soon known in society for his eccentric dress and his paradoxical wit. Caricatured as Reginald Bunthorne in Gilbert and Sullivan's *Patience*, he became the epitome of Aestheticism for the wider public as well. The shrewd producers of the comic opera, which was to go on an American tour, realized that the presence of Bunthorne's prototype would fan the flames of interest, so with their sponsorship, Wilde embarked on an extended tour of the United States that permitted him to see the notable places, to meet the notable people, and having done so, to conclude, "When good Americans die they go to Paris. When bad Americans die they stay in America."

On his return to England after a short stay in Paris, Wilde launched himself on what was to be his period of eminence. He made friends with the painter Whistler and became engaged to the pretty but conventional daughter of an Irish barrister Constance Lloyd, whom he married in 1883. They had two sons, Cyril and Vyvyan. In need of funds to finance his luxurious mode of life, he cultivated his literary career, if not in earnest, then at least with more enterprise than he would have wished to acknowledge. He lectured, reviewed books, and for a time edited *The Woman's World*. His prose works appeared in rapid succession: short stories (*Lord Arthur Savile's Crime and Other Stories*, *The Happy Prince and Other Tales*, *A House of Pomegranates*), a novel (*The Picture of Dorian Gray*), a collection of critical essays (*Intentions*).

With his fiction, Wilde solidly established his reputation in the world of letters, but his great period of financial success began only when he turned to writing for the popular theater. Although he found the enforced discipline of playwriting difficult and never regarded his social comedies as anything more than well-crafted potboilers, Wilde managed in a span of three years to write four plays that paid him exceedingly well and made him even more famous. *Lady Windermere's Fan* (premiering in February, 1892) was followed by *A Woman of No Importance* (April, 1893), *An Ideal Husband* (January, 1895), and *The Importance of Being Earnest* (February, 1895). After completing *Lady Windermere's Fan*, Wilde went to France, where he wrote *Salomé*, a poetic drama intended to make his artistic reputation on the Continent and at home. Wilde offered the title role in that play to Sarah Bernhardt, who accepted and began rehearsals for a London production that was never to be staged: The Lord Chamberlain banned it for violating the old law forbidding the theatrical representation of biblical characters.

Having reached its zenith, Oscar Wilde's star rapidly sank to oblivion in the spring of 1895. Since 1891, Wilde had been friends, and more than friends, with the handsome, talented, spoiled, unstable Lord Alfred Douglas, a younger son of the eighth Marquis of Queensberry. The relationship was not a discreet one. Lord Alfred took pleasure in flaunting himself in the role of minion to the celebrated Wilde and in flouting the authority of his father. As his letters reveal, Wilde in his turn expressed his feelings for the elegant youth whose "slim gilt soul walks between passion and poetry" with his customary extravagance. Finally, in what was to be one of the most perverse and distasteful interludes in the history of English jurisprudence, Wilde was provoked to sue the ferocious marquis for criminal libel when that rash peer had culminated a campaign of harassment by leaving at Wilde's club a card bearing the words "to Oscar Wilde posing as a somdomite [sic]." For his defense, Queensberry collected a small parade of blackmailers and male prostitutes to testify to the accuracy of his epithet. Unwisely persisting in his suit, Wilde failed, on Queensberry's acquittal, to seize his chance to flee the country. Having lost his battle with the marquis, Wilde in turn was arrested, tried, and ultimately convicted for practicing "the love that dares not tell its name." He was sentenced to two years at hard labor.

Oscar Wilde's twenty-four months of imprisonment was a continuous mortification of body, mind, and spirit. He had lost his honor, his position, his fortune, and his family. Although he was to write one more fine work, *The Ballad of Reading Gaol*, his life was behind him. Released from prison on May 19, 1897, he left England behind him as well. Under the name Sebastian Melmoth, Oscar Wilde resided abroad, principally in France and Italy, until his death in Paris in 1900.

Analysis

Oscar Wilde completed seven plays during his life, and for the purpose of discussion, these works can be divided into two groups. On the one hand are the four social comedies Wilde wrote for the commercial theater of his day, works that brought him money and prestige but not artistic satisfaction: *Lady Windermere's Fan*, *A Woman of No Importance*, *An Ideal Husband*, and *The Importance of Being Earnest*. Then there are the three plays intended as serious works of art: *Vera*, *The Duchess of Padua*, and *Salomé*. None of these three plays gained popular regard, critical acclaim, or theatrical success in Wilde's lifetime. One can disregard the first two and lose little by the omission. *Vera*, published when Wilde was only twenty-five, is an apprentice piece that unsuccessfully mingles revolutionary Russian politics (particularly ill-timed, for Czar Alexander II had recently been assassinated, and the consort of his successor was sister to Alexandra, wife of the Prince of Wales), improbable psychology, creaky melodrama, and what was already Wilde's dramatic forte: witty, ironic speech. *The Duchess of Padua* is a derivative verse drama in the intricate, full-blown style that worked so well in the hands of the Jacobeans and has failed so dismally for their many and often talented imitators. When read, the play has its fine moments, but even at its best, it is nothing more than a good piece of imitation. In *Salomé*, however, Wilde offered the world a serious drama of unquestionable distinction, a work that further enriched Western culture by providing a libretto for Richard Strauss's fine opera of the same title.

The English-speaking public, to whom Wilde's four comedies are familiar enough, is less likely to have read or seen performed his *Salomé*, yet this biblical extrapolation, with its pervasive air of overripe sensuality, is of all of his plays the one most characteristic of its age and most important to the European cultural tradition. Oscar Wilde wrote his poetic drama in France, and in French, during the autumn of 1891. Wilde's command of the French language was not idiomatic but fluent in the schoolroom style; this very limitation became an asset when he chose to cast his play in the stylized, ritualistic mold set by the Belgian playwright Maeterlinck, whose works relied heavily on repetition, parallelism, and chiming effect—verbal traits equally characteristic of a writer who thinks in English but translates into French. Like the language, the biblical source of the story is bent to Wilde's purposes. In the New Testament accounts of the death of John the Baptist (or Jokanaan, as he is called in the play), Salomé, the eighteen-year-old princess of Judea, is not held responsible for John's death; rather, blame for the prophet's death is laid on Salomé's mother, Herodias. Furthermore, as Wilde's literary executor, Robert Ross, and a number of other critics have observed, Wilde's Herod is a synthesis of a handful of biblical Herods and tetrarchs. Although Wilde's license with the language and sources of his play is sometimes deprecated, it should not be faulted. As a poetic dramatist, a verbal contriver of a symbolic ritual, his intention was not to transcribe but to transfigure.

The action of Wilde's *Salomé* takes place by moonlight on a great terrace above King Herod's banquet hall. The simple setting is deftly conceived to heighten dramatic effects. On this spare stage, all entrances—whether Salomé's, and later Herod's and Herodias' by the great staircase or Jokanaan's from the cistern where he has been imprisoned—are striking. In addition, the play's ruling motifs, moonlight and the recurrent contrasts of white, black, and—with increasing frequency as the play moves toward its grisly climax—red, emerge clearly.

As the play begins, a cosmopolitan group of soldiers and pages attendant on the Judean royal house occupy the terrace. Their conversation on the beauty of the Princess Salomé, the strangeness of the moon, and the rich tableau of the Tetrarch and his party feasting within sets a weird tone that is enhanced by the sound of Jokanaan's prophesies rising from his cistern prison. Salomé, like "a dove that has strayed . . . a narcissus trembling in the wind . . . a silver flower," glides onto the terrace. The prophet's strange voice and words stir the princess as deeply as her beauty troubles the young Syrian captain of the guard, a conquered prince now a slave in Herod's palace. At her command, the Syrian brings forth Jokanaan from his prison. The prophet's uncanny beauty—he seems as chaste and ascetic as she has just pronounced the moon to be—works a double charm of attraction and repulsion upon Salomé. His body like a thin white statue, his black hair, his mouth "like a pomegranate cut with a knife of ivory" all kindle the princess' desire. His disgusted rejection of her love only fans the flames of lust. She must have him: "I will kiss thy mouth, Jokanaan," she chants, as the Syrian who adores her kills himself at her feet and the prophet who despises her descends once more to his cistern.

At this point, Herod and Herodias, attended by their court, enter. Their comments on the moon (to Herod, "She is like a mad woman, a mad woman who is looking everywhere for lovers"; to Herodias, "the moon is like the moon, that is all") introduce the significant differences in their equally evil natures. Herod is superstitious, cowardly, obliquely cruel, a tyrannical yet vacillating ruler; Herodias is brutal with the callous directness of an utterly debased woman. Salomé's strange beauty tempts Herod just as Jokanaan's tempts Salomé. Despite Herodias' disapproval and Salomé's reluctance, Herod presses the princess to dance. He offers her whatever reward she may request, even to the half of his kingdom. Having exacted this rash promise of the infatuated despot, Salomé performs her famous dance of seven veils and for her reward requires the head of Jokanaan upon a silver charger. As horrified by this demand as his ghoulish consort is delighted, the superstitious Herod offers Salomé a long and intricate catalog of alternative payments—the rich, rare, curious, and vulgar contents of an Oriental or *fin de siècle* treasure chest. With the sure instincts of the true collector, Salomé persists in her original demand. Unable to break his vow, the horrified king dispatches the Nubian executioner into the cistern. Presently, in a striking culmination of the play's color imagery, the Nubian's arm rises from the cistern. This ebony stem bears a strange flower: a silver shield surmounted by the prophet's bloody head. Delirious with ecstasy, Salomé addresses her passion to the disembodied lover-prophet she has asked for, silenced, and gained. "I have kissed thy mouth, Jokanaan," she concludes as a moonbeam falls upon her and, at Herod's cry, "Kill that woman!" the soldiers rush forward, crushing her beneath their shields.

Even so brief an account as that above demonstrates that the play has potential in sheer dramatic terms, as the great Sarah Bernhardt realized when, though much too old for the title role, she agreed to play the role of Salomé in a proposed London production that was not to be. *Salomé* is a richly fashioned tapestry. The play's prevailing mode, presentation of typically talkative Wildean characters articulating rather than acting upon their emotions, gives way at three powerful moments—when Salomé dances, when the arm bearing Jokanaan's head rises from the cistern, and when the silver shields crush the dancer and her reward—to pure act, unsullied by words.

The play's psychological and symbolic suggestiveness are equally rich. One of Wilde's great contributions to the Salomé story was to provide psychological underpinnings for the sequence of events. To Wilde's invention are owed Salomé's spurned love for the prophet and the mutual hostility that counterbalances the sensual bond between Herod and Herodias. As an expression of love's ambivalence, *Salomé* is "the incarnate spirit of the aesthetic woman," a collector who (much in the spirit of Robert Browning's Duke of Ferrara, it would seem) does not desire a living being but a "love object" handsomely mounted. Richard Ellmann finds something more personally symbolic in the tragedy. Jokanaan, says Ellmann, presents the spirit-affirming, body-negating moral earnestness of Wilde's "Ruskinism"; Salomé, who collects beauty, sensations, and strange experiences, who consummates her love for the prophet in "a relation at once totally sensual and totally 'mystical,'" stands for the rival claims of Pater. Herod, like his creator, vainly struggles to master these opposing impulses both within and outside himself.

Wilde's first three comedies, although each has its particular charms and defects, are sufficiently similar to one another, and sufficienty inferior to his fourth, *The Importance of Being Earnest*, to be discussed as a group rather than individually. Always lazy about writing (which was an arduous process for a verbal artist with his high standards) but perpetually in need of money to pay for the great and small luxuries that were his necessities of life, Wilde agreed in 1891 to write a play for George Alexander, the actor-manager of St. James's Theater. The result was *Lady Windermere's Fan*, a modern drawing-room comedy set in high society and frankly aimed to engage the interest of the London playgoing public. The financial results were gratifying enough to encourage Wilde to write three more plays in the same vein, though he never much respected the form or the products. Only in *The Importance of Being Earnest* was he to overcome the inherent weaknesses of the well-made society play, but each of the other three pieces is fine enough to win for him the title of best writer of British comedies between Richard Brinsley Sheridan and George Bernard Shaw.

Lady Windermere's Fan, *A Woman of No Importance*, and *An Ideal Husband* all center, as their titles suggest, on relationships between men and women, or more precisely between gentlemen and ladies. The plays were up-to-the-minute in providing fashionable furnishings and costumes to charm both segments of their intended audience: Late Victorian society people enjoyed seeing themselves reflected as creatures of such style and wit, while the middle classes delighted at being given a glimpse into the secret rites of the world of fashion. In fact, one might suspect that Wilde's stated concern for the Aristotelian unity of time in these plays springs less from belief in that classical standard than from the opportunity (or even necessity) that placing three acts of high life in a twenty-four-hour period provides for striking changes of costume and set.

In each of these elaborate "modern drawing-room comedies with pink lamp shades," as Wilde termed them, one finds recurrent character types: puritanical figures of virtue (wives in *Lady Windermere's Fan* and *An Ideal Husband*, an heiress soon to be a fiancée in *A Woman of No Importance*), mundanely fashionable hypocrites, and exceptional humanitarians of two types—the dandified lord (Darlington, Illingworth, and Goring) and the poised and prosperous "fallen woman," two of whom (Mrs. Erlynne in *Lady Windermere's Fan* and Mrs. Chevely in *An Ideal Husband*) go in for wit and the other of whom (Mrs. Arbuthnot of *A Woman of No Importance*), though equally unrepentant, specializes in good works. Clever, epigrammatic conversation is what these characters do best; guilty secrets and the situational intricacies they weave are the strings for Wilde's verbal pearls.

In *Lady Windermere's Fan*, the initial secret is that Mrs. Erlynne, the runaway mother of whose continued existence Lady Windermere is utterly ignorant, has returned to London to regain a place in society and is blackmailing Lord Windermere, who seeks to protect his wife from knowledge of the blot on her pedigree. Misinterpreting her husband's patronage of a mysterious lady with a hint of a past, Lady Windermere is led to the brink of unconsciously repeating her mother's error by eloping with another man, thereby prompting Mrs. Erlynne to the one maternal gesture of her life: The older and wiser woman sacrifices her own reputation (temporarily, it turns out) to save that of her daughter.

In *A Woman of No Importance*, Gerald Arbuthnot, a youth reared in rural seclusion and apparent respectability by his mother, happens to encounter the man who is his father: worldly Lord Illingworth, who when young and untitled had seduced Gerald's mother and, on learning of her pregnancy, refused to marry her. This complex situation allows Wilde to expose several human inconsistencies. Previously uninterested in the child he had begotten and also unwilling to marry the beautiful young mother, Lord

Illingworth is now so full of paternal feeling that he offers to marry the middle-aged woman to retain the son. Gerald, who has just vowed to kill Lord Illingworth for attempting to kiss a prudish American girl, on hearing of Illingworth's past treachery to his mother wants her to let the offender "make an honest woman" of her. Mrs. Arbuthnot professes selfless devotion to her son but begs Gerald to forgo the brilliant prospects Illingworth can offer and remain with her in their provincial backwater.

In *An Ideal Husband*, the plot-initiating secret is a man's property rather than a woman's, and political intrigue rather than romantic. Sir Robert Chiltern, a high-principled politician with a rigidly idealistic young wife, encounters the adventuress Mrs. Chevely, who has evidence that Chiltern's career and fortune were founded on one unethical act—the selling of a political secret to a foreigner—and who attempts to use her knowledge to compel him to lend political support to a fraudulent scheme that will make her fortune. Acting against this resourceful woman is Chiltern's friend Lord Goring, an apparently effete but impressively capable man who can beat her at her own game. In brief, then, all three of these plays are formed of the highly theatrical matter that, in lesser hands, would form the stuff of melodrama.

Wilde's "pink lamp shade" comedies are difficult to stage because of the stylish luxury demanded of the actors, costumes, and sets, but the plays are not weaker for being so ornate: They accurately mirror a certain facet of late Victorian society. Similarly, the pervasive wit never becomes tiresome. The contrived reversals, artful coincidences, predictably surprising discoveries, and "strong curtains" may seem trite—but they work onstage. The defect that Wilde's first three comedies share is the problem of unreconciled opposites, implicit in *Salomé*. In *Lady Windermere's Fan*, *A Woman of No Importance*, and *An Ideal Husband*, part of Wilde is drawn to admire wit, style, vitality, and courage regardless of where they may be found, and part of him has a serious social or moral point to make. Even with this divided aim, Wilde wrote good comedies. When he solved the problem, he wrote a masterpiece: *The Importance of Being Earnest*.

What makes *The Importance of Being Earnest*, unlike the three Wilde comedies that precede it, a masterpiece of the theater rather than merely an eminently stageable play? Perhaps a good clue to the answer can be found in the play's subtitle, *A Trivial Comedy for Serious People*. This typically Wildean paradox has been variously interpreted. Whatever the author may have intended by it, one thing the phrase suggests to readers is that *The Importance of Being Earnest* is worth the attention of "serious people" because it, unlike Wilde's other three comedies, succeeds in being utterly trivial and thereby attains pure comic excellence. Eric Bentley has remarked of the play that "what begins as a prank ends as a criticism of life." Here at last Wilde offers witty wordplay and exuberant high spirits in an undiluted form. There are no melodramatic ambiguities or dark, complex emotions in *The Importance of Being Earnest*, where the chief events are flirtations that lead to engagements and prodigious consumption of tea, cucumber sandwiches, and muffins. Whereas *Lady Windermere's Fan*, *A Woman of No Importance*, and *An Ideal Husband* take place in the stylized but recognizably real world of contemporary London society, this play unfolds in a world apart, one which, despite its containing a Mayfair flat and a Hertfordshire manor, is as perfectly artificial yet completely valid as are Shakespeare's Forest of Arden in *As You Like It* and Athens in *A Midsummer Night's Dream*.

The Importance of Being Earnest contains some of the stock theatrical devices Wilde relied upon to galvanize his previous three comedies. There is mysterious parentage: Jack Worthing confesses to having been found in a handbag in Victoria Station. Characters run away from responsibility: Jack, in order to escape the country and get to town, has invented a wicked younger brother, Ernest, who lodges at the Albany; and Algernon Moncrieff, to escape from London to the country, has concocted an imaginary rural friend, the perennial invalid Bunbury. The comedy contains false identities: Both Jack and Algernon propose to and are accepted by their respective loves, the Honorable Gwendolyn Fairfax and Cecily Cardew, under the name "Ernest Worthing." There are misplaced possessions as significant as Lady Windermere's fan: Finding a cigarette case inscribed "From little Cecily, with her fondest love to her dear Uncle Jack," enables Algernon to discover his friend's double identity. The governess Miss Prism's unexpected, happy, eloquent reunion with the handbag she had mislaid twenty-eight years before brings the climactic revelation of the play: Through this recovery of the long-lost handbag, Jack, a comic Oedipus, discovers his true parentage. In all these cases, the dramatic machines of potential tragedy or melodrama are operated in the spirit of burlesque. There are no lapses or incongruities to drag down the lighthearted mood.

Similarly, the emotional developments, reversals, intrigues, and deceptions that were threatening in Wilde's other comedies are harmless in *The Importance of Being Earnest*, chiefly because the play is not about established relationships. It does not present married people with domestic differences; former lovers who should have married but failed to do so; present lovers already yoked to other people; parents, who through love, guilt, selfishness, or honor, influence the behavior of their children; or children who similarly manipulate their parents. The four principal characters Jack Worthing, Gwendolyn Fairfax, Algernon Moncrieff, and Cecily Cardew are all young, single, and, with the exception of Gwendolyn, parentless. The Reverend Dr. Chasuble and Miss Prism are, to use their own words, "ripe" but "celibate." Early in the play, Lane, Algernon's manservant, admits that, with regard to marriage, he has had "very little experience of it myself up to the present." Of all the characters, only the marvelous Lady Bracknell is mature, married, and encumbered with children. Even so, Lord Bracknell is completely under her control; that pitiful peer, who dines upstairs at her command, does and knows only what she prescribes. Her daughter Gwendolyn, on the other hand, is completely free from her domination; the poised young lady listens politely to her dogmatic mother and then acts precisely as she chooses. As a consequence, Lady Bracknell's personal essence and the behavior it determines are modified by neither spouse nor child.

With this array of singularly unfettered characters, *The Importance of Being Earnest* is not about domestic complications but about the act of committing oneself to domesticity. The social comedy of the play parallels the movement of a Jane Austen novel: Characters who exist as pure potential define and place themselves by choosing to marry and by selecting their particular mates. The choreography of this matrimonial ballet is exceptionally elegant, particularly in the commonly known three-act version. (The original four-act version, first staged by the New Vic in 1980, contains material that is not essential, though not uninteresting.) The dialogue is so uniformly delightful that it is impossible to single out a high point or two for quoting: For the first time, Wilde's comedy is a brilliant whole rather than a series of sparkling effects. Indeed, the play's final interchange between Lady Bracknell and her newfound nephew (soon-to-be son-in-law) Jack could be the dramatist talking to himself, for by taking comedy seriously enough to stay within its bounds, Wilde the dramatist finally achieved his goal of creating a play not merely well-made but perfect of its kind:

> LADY BRACKNELL: My nephew, you seem to be displaying signs of triviality.
>
> JACK: On the contrary, Aunt Augusta, I've now realized for the first time in my life the vital Importance of Being Earnest.

Other major works

NOVEL: *The Picture of Dorian Gray*, 1891.

SHORT FICTION: "The Canterville Ghost," 1887; *The Happy Prince and Other Tales*, 1888; *Lord Arthur Savile's Crime and Other Stories*, 1891; *A House of Pomegranates*, 1891.

POETRY: *Ravenna*, 1878; *Poems*, 1881; *Poems in Prose*, 1894; *The Sphinx*, 1894; *The Ballad of Reading Gaol*, 1898.

NONFICTION: *Intentions*, 1891; *De Profundis*, 1905; *Letters*, 1962 (Rupert Hart-Davies, editor).

MISCELLANEOUS: *Works*, 1908; *Complete Works of Oscar Wilde*, 1948 (Vyvyan Holland, editor); *Plays, Prose Writings, and Poems*, 1960.

Bibliography

Cohen, Philip K. *The Moral Vision of Oscar Wilde.* Rutherford, N.J.: Fair-leigh Dickinson University Press, 1978. Examines Wilde's writings as unified by his moral development through dialectical contraries of Old and New Testament codes. Notes Wilde's relationship with Walter Pater and stresses Wilde's attachment to a sister who died in childhood. The book shows signs of its dissertation origin. Contains illustrations, a select bibliography, and an index.

Ellmann, Richard. *Oscar Wilde.* London: Hamish Hamilton, 1987. A richly detailed, sympathetic account of Wilde's life and art, with balanced views of his accomplishments and significance for modern culture. Ellmann presents a forceful analysis of the events that caused Wilde's trial, imprisonment, and eventual early death. Contains many illustrations, notes, a select bibliography, two appendices of books by Wilde's parents, and an index.

Hyde, H. Montgomery. *Oscar Wilde: The Aftermath.* New York: Farrar, Straus, 1963. Interesting use of previously unavailable papers relating to Wilde's imprisonment. Hyde details the events that occurred during Wilde's time in prison and during the period after his release, and concludes with an account of the writing and publication of *The Ballad of Reading Gaol* and *De Profundis.* Includes footnotes, an index, and five appendices of excerpted materials.

McGhee, Richard D. "Elizabeth Barrett Browning and Oscar Wilde." In *Marriage, Duty, and Desire in Victorian Poetry and Drama.* Lawrence: Regents Press of Kansas, 1980. Comparing the art of Wilde and Browning, this study focuses on their contrasting emphases on duty and desire, with some similarity in their motives for attempting to reconcile the opposition between such values. Wilde's dramas are closely examined along with his lyric poems and critical essays. Notes and index.

Nassaar, Christopher S. *Into the Demon Universe: A Literary Exploration of Oscar Wilde.* New Haven, Conn.: Yale University Press, 1974. An insightful analysis of Wilde's major writings and a substantial account of the decadent movement. Wilde's thematic concerns with the demonic are traced to the Romantics and examined as the basis of a religious-aesthetic orientation. The dramas are closely examined, with a focus on *Salomé.* Includes an index and a bibliography.

Peter W. Graham
(Revised by *Richard D. McGhee*)

THORNTON WILDER

Born: Madison, Wisconsin; April 17, 1897
Died: Hamden, Connecticut; December 7, 1975

Principal drama

The Trumpet Shall Sound, pb. 1920, pr. 1927; *The Angel That Troubled the Waters and Other Plays*, pb. 1928 (includes 16 plays); *The Happy Journey to Trenton and Camden*, pr., pb. 1931 (one act); *The Long Christmas Dinner*, pr., pb. 1931 (one act: as libretto in German, 1961, translation and music by Paul Hindemith); *The Long Christmas Dinner and Other Plays in One Act*, pb. 1931 (includes *Queens of France*, *Pullman Car Hiawatha*, *Love and How to Cure It*, *Such Things Only Happen in Books*, *The Happy Journey to Trenton and Camden*); *Lucrece*, pr. 1932, pb. 1933 (adaptation of André Obey's *Le Viol de Lucrèce*); *A Doll's House*, pr. 1937 (adaptation of Henrik Ibsen's play); *The Merchant of Yonkers*, pr. 1938, pb. 1939 (adaptation of Johann Nestroy's *Einen Jux will er sich machen*); *Our Town*, pr., pb. 1938; *The Skin of Our Teeth*, pr., pb. 1942; *The Matchmaker*, pr. 1954, pb. 1956 (revision of *The Merchant of Yonkers*); *A Life in the Sun*, pr. 1955, pb. 1960 (in German), pb. 1977 (in English; commonly known as *The Alcestiad*; one act pb. 1952, pr. 1957 as *The Drunken Sisters*); *Plays for Bleecker Street*, pr. 1962 (3 one-acts: *Someone from Assisi*; *Infancy*, pb. 1961; and *Childhood*, pb. 1960).

Other literary forms

Thornton Wilder came to national prominence in 1927 with what has remained his best-known novel, *The Bridge of San Luis Rey*, which won for him the first of his three Pulitzer Prizes. The year before, his first published fiction, *The Cabala* (1926), had appeared, and in 1930 came his third novel, *The Woman of Andros*. These works were followed in 1934 by *Heaven's My Destination*—his first fictional work about the American experience—and, at lengthy intervals, by three additional novels: *The Ides of March*, the story of Caesar told from fictional diaries, letters, and records, and quite probably Wilder's most significant novel, appeared in 1948; *The Eighth Day*, winner of the National Book Award, was published in 1967; and his last novel, the semiautobiographical *Theophilus North*, was published in 1973. In 1942, Wilder cowrote the screenplay for Alfred Hitchcock's motion picture *Shadow of a Doubt* (1943). Over the years, Wilder wrote a number of essays, including several that develop his theory of drama; some that introduce works by other writers as varied as Sophocles, Gertrude Stein, James Joyce, and Emily Dickinson; and a few scholarly articles on the Spanish playwright Lope de Vega. These works have been collected posthumously in *American Characteristics and Other Essays* (1979).

Achievements

Thornton Wilder was a true man of letters, equally accomplished and highly regarded at various points in his career as both a novelist and a dramatist. None of his works of fiction, however, seems likely to endure as a classic in the way that two of his plays, *Our Town* and *The Skin of Our Teeth*, most assuredly will. Wilder admittedly has always been, as the foreword to *The Angel That Troubled the Waters* insists, a decidedly and deliberately religious playwright, not in any parochial sense of espousing a specific body of theological doctrine but in the larger sense of consistently posing moral and metaphysical questions. As he makes clear in that preface, however, if the religious artist today is to reach a sizable and responsive audience, that artist generally must couch his or her views "in that dilute fashion that is a believer's concession to a contemporary standard of good manners." By birth, Wilder was a Christian; by education and training, he was a humanist; by his own reading and intellectual inquiry later in life, he became an Existentialist. Several of the playlets in his first volume reveal the intersection of pagan and Christian myth, showing how the former is implicit in and fulfilled by the latter. Continually, Wilder emphasizes the "presentness" of the past and how the best that has been thought and said throughout the ages continues to be of value. Always he asserts the importance of reason even in ages of faith.

Wilder was one of the most learned and erudite of all American dramatists; throughout his life, he was a teacher as well as a writer, and his plays teach effortlessly, engagingly, and entertainingly. Much of American drama centers on the family, and Wilder's plays are no exception. His family, though, is the Family of Man, the human community throughout history. Because of the allegorical and parabolic nature of his plays, Wilder's works might appear at first to be lacking in subtlety and complexity, yet, through the simple means he employs, they touch on the most vital of ideas. The timeless rituals in which his families participate are the universal ones of birth and growth, love and marriage, sickness and death. If Wilder perhaps reflects Henri Bergson and Marcel Proust in his own philosophy of time as duration and memory as a simultaneous coexistence of all past experiences, he is a child of Ralph Waldo Emerson and Walt Whitman in his vague transcendentalism and almost religious belief in the value of democracy. Wilder insists that life has a purpose and a dignity, so it must be lived and cherished and nurtured. If this purpose and worth have become increasingly clouded, that simply makes artists all the more vital, for on them rests the task of revealing the divinity within human beings yet of showing them that they can become divine only by first being fully human.

Biography

Thornton Niven Wilder was born on April 17, 1897, in Madison, Wisconsin, into a family with a strong New England Protestant background—Congregationalist on his father Amos' side, Presbyterian on his mother Isabella's. An older brother, Amos, became a professor of theology and commentator on religious poetry, and among Wilder's three younger sisters was Isabel, with whom he would later make his home and share the closest emotional attachment of his life. When their father was appointed consul general to Hong Kong and later to Shanghai in the first decade of the new century, the family lived with him for brief periods in each city, though the young Wilder was educated mostly in California. After he was graduated from Berkeley High School in 1915, Wilder went to Oberlin College in Ohio, later transferring to Yale, from which he received his bachelor of arts degree in 1920. While in college, he wrote numerous "three-minute plays"—some of which would be included among the sixteen somewhat precious and pretentious closet dramas that reached print as *The Angel That Troubled the Waters and Other Plays*—as well as his first full-length effort, *The Trumpet Shall Sound*. Somewhat similar to Ben Jonson's *The Alchemist* (pr. 1610) in its incidents and thematic emphasis on justice, this early play was finally produced by the American Laboratory Theatre in New York in 1927.

While studying archaeology at the American Academy in Rome after college, Wilder began writing fiction. After returning to the United States, he taught French at the Lawrenceville School for Boys in New Jersey for much of the 1920's, staying there—with time out to attend Princeton for a masters of arts degree and for a stint writing at the MacDowell Colony in New Hampshire—until after the critical acclaim of his second novel, *The Bridge of San Luis Rey*, which was awarded the Pulitzer Prize for Fiction in 1928. In 1930, Wilder began lecturing for part of each academic year in comparative literature at the University of Chicago, where he made the acquaintance of Gertrude Stein, whose theories of time and language exercised a powerful influence on all of Wilder's subsequent writing for the theater. During the 1930's, Wilder published six additional one-act plays in his volume entitled *The Long Christmas Dinner and Other Plays in One Act*; in 1961, the title play became the libretto for an opera with music by Paul Hindemith. In addition, Wilder adapted both André Obey's *Le Viol de Lucrèce* (1931) and Henrik Ibsen's *A Doll's House* (1879) for Broadway before writing his most famous work, *Our Town*, which won for him the Pulitzer Prize for Drama in 1938. The same year saw the unsuccessful production, under the direction of Max Reinhardt, of *The Merchant of Yonkers*, later revised as *The Matchmaker* for performance at the Edinburgh Festival in Scotland in 1954 and in New York in 1955; in a still later transformation (1964), dressed up with a musical score by Jerry Herman, *The Matchmaker* became *Hello, Dolly!*, one of the greatest successes in the history of American musical comedy. While serving in the United States

Army Air Corps during World War II, Wilder won his second Pulitzer Prize for *The Skin of Our Teeth*, perhaps the most original and inventive of all American comedies.

At the beginning of the 1950's, Wilder was Charles Eliot Norton Professor of Poetry at Harvard, lecturing on the American characteristics in classic American literature. In 1955, his last full-length drama, *A Life in the Sun*, was performed at the Edinburgh Festival; in 1962, it, too, became the libretto for an acclaimed German opera, *Die Alkestiade*, with music by Louise Talma. Among the many honors that came to Wilder late in life were the Gold Medal for Fiction of the American Academy of Arts and Letters, the United States Presidential Medal of Freedom, and the National Medal for Literature. At the time of his death on December 7, 1975, he left incomplete two cycles of plays on which he had been working for more than a decade, "The Seven Deadly Sins" and "The Seven Ages of Man," whose titles suggest the allegorical and mythic nature of Wilder's best work for the theater. Perhaps the cumulative effect of the complete cycles would have been greater than the sampling of their parts that reached Off-Broadway production in 1962 under the collective title *Plays for Bleecker Street*. The three one-act plays, *Someone from Assisi*, *Infancy*, and *Childhood*, were Wilder's last original works produced for New York audiences.

Analysis

Thornton Wilder's contributions in style and technique to American drama are akin to the innovations that Alfred Jarry in France, Luigi Pirandello in Italy, and Bertolt Brecht in Germany made to world drama in the twentieth century. Basically, Wilder was an antirealistic playwright, reacting against the tenets and presuppositions underlying the type of drama that held sway during the nineteenth century and continues to be a potent force even today. During a play that, as part of its attempt to create the absolute illusion of reality, employs a box set so that the audience sees the action through an imaginary fourth wall, there is a complete separation between actors and audience, stage space and auditorium. The audience, even though it implicitly knows it is in a theater watching a play, pretends for the duration that it is seeing reality on the stage; in short, the audience makes believe that it is not making believe. On the other hand, in theater which makes no attempt at achieving such an absolute illusion of reality, the audience readily accepts that what it is seeing is make-believe or pretense. In his important essay "Some Thoughts on Playwriting" (1941), Wilder argues that the theater in its greatest ages—Periclean Athens and Elizabethan England, for example—has always depended heavily on conventions, what he calls "agreed-upon falsehoods" or "permitted lies." Such accepted conventions help to break down the artificial boundary between play and audience by inviting a fuller imaginative participation in the action; by increasing the audience's awareness of itself as audience; and by emphasizing the communal and ritualistic nature of the theatrical experience. In Wilder's view, the traditional box set, because it localizes the action to a particular place and restricts it to a definite time, renders the action less universal and hinders its ascent into the desirable realms of parable, allegory, and myth. In contrast, Wilder sought a theater wherein the large, recurrent outlines of the human story could be told through particular examples less important in themselves than the universal truths they stand for and embody.

Wilder's brand of minimalist theater—what the critic John Gassner has termed "theatricalism"—can be illustrated by looking at *The Happy Journey to Trenton and Camden*, which the dramatist himself regarded as the best of his one-act plays. The action is simple: The Kirby family (father, mother, son, and daughter) takes a brief automobile trip to visit a married daughter/sister, whose baby died shortly after birth. Since the literal journey is less important than the metaphoric one, it is appropriate that the bare brick walls of the backstage remain visible; that the automobile is merely suggested by four chairs and a platform, with Dad Kirby working an imaginary gearshift and steering wheel in pantomime; that the towns through which the family travels (including Lawrenceville, where Wilder once taught) are simply mentioned in the dialogue; and that a Stage Manager is available to serve as property man, to read the parts of all the minor characters, and to act the role of service station attendant. When the car must stop for an imaginary funeral procession to pass, it allows the family an opportunity to recall their son and brother Harold, who died in the war, and to remember that every human being must be ready for death. As is typical in Wilder, the central female figure carries the weight of the play's meaning and expresses the dramatist's simple faith. Ma Kirby is the Eternal Mother, preserver of the family, who is close to God and to the nature that shadows forth the divine. She understands the processive quality of existence: All things are born and they die; some, in fact, are born only to die. Further, she maintains her confidence in a providential order at work in the universe; although human beings cannot know the ways of God, they must continue in faith that all things in life are for the best. What tempers Wilder's optimism and often prevents it from becoming sentimental is that he always keeps before his audience the dark side of human nature—human beings' myopic vision that limits them from being all that they might become—and the dark side of human existence—the fact of death, especially of dying without ever having really lived.

When the Stage Manager steps out onto the stage at the beginning of *Our Town* and locates the mythical and microcosmic New England village of Grover's Corners, New Hampshire, firmly in time and space, he creates a place so palpably present to the American imagination that most people in the audience might expect to be able to find it on a map. This is, truly, anyone's and everyone's town, and the people who are born and grow up and live and marry and suffer and die there are clearly Everyman and Everywoman. Wilder's opening stage directions specify "No curtain. No scenery." The absence of a curtain conveys the timeless quality of elemental experiences; the action has no specific beginning, because these daily events have been occurring since time immemorial and will continue to go on, despite an ever-changing cast on the world's stage. The almost complete lack of scenery, with only "two arched trellises" permitted as a concession to the unimaginative and literal-minded in the audience, indicates that the action is unlocalized and not tied to only one place at one time, but could, and does, happen everywhere. The pantomimed actions—perhaps influenced by the style of the Chinese theater, with which Wilder was well acquainted—achieve the same effect; the audience has no difficulty recognizing them, precisely because they are common actions (such as getting meals) that everyone performs.

The play's action is as basic, and yet as universal, as the setting—neither more nor less than the archetypal journey of man and woman through life to death and beyond. In this respect, the title play from *The Long Christmas Dinner and Other Plays in One Act* serves as a precursor to *Our Town*. In that short work, Wilder presented ninety years in the life of the Bayard family. Characters enter through a portal on one side of the stage, which symbolizes birth; partake of a Christmas dinner over the years that symbolizes the feast of life; and then exit through a portal, on the opposite side of the stage, that symbolizes death. One generation replaces another, even uttering many of the same lines of dialogue. Act 1 of *Our Town*, called "Daily Life," focuses on the ordinary, day-to-day existence of two neighboring families: Editor Webb, his wife, older daughter, and younger son; and Doc Gibbs, his wife, older son, and younger daughter. In act 2, called "Love and Marriage," the playwright shows the courtship and wedding of George Gibbs and Emily Webb; the audience becomes an extension of the church congregation as the young couple enter and leave the ceremony via the theater aisles. Act 3, which is left untitled, is set in a cemetery with chairs for graves and an umbrella-protected group of mourners; it is the funeral of Emily, who died in childbirth and has been united in eternity with something like an Oversoul.

Although the action literally begins in May, 1901 (the hopeful springtime of a new century), *Our Town* is—unlike a play such as Eugene O'Neill's *Ah, Wilderness!* (pr. 1933)—more than simply a nostalgic recollection of a bygone era of American democratic egalitarianism. Nor is the picture of life from the dawn of the twentieth century to the outbreak of World War I as sentimentally one-sided and limited in its awareness of evil and the darker forces of existence as has sometimes been charged. Along with Simon Stimson, the town drunk and eventual suicide, Wilder portrays petty gossip and backbiting, even among the church choir ladies; lack of communication between husband and wife and parent and child; the pain of separation and loss through death; and (looking forward, since the action per se ends in 1913) war. The continuing importance of *Our Town*, however, should not be looked for on so basic a level as that of its story. Rather, it is a philosophical examination of time and the proper way of seeing, stressing the necessity for escaping from the narrow, myopic view of existence that human beings ordinarily take and embracing, with the poet's help, a God's-eye view of human history.

Wilder's attitude toward time as a continuum finds concretization in the way he conveys events that occurred prior to or will happen after the twelve-year scope of the action. Not only does the local expert, a college professor, Willard, provide a lengthy report about the geological formation of the region and the anthropological data of the area, but also the Stage Manager, in his casual shifting of verb tenses from present to future or future to past, points to a perspective that is both inside secular time and outside time, transcending it. Wilder's laconic Stage Manager, with his understated and homespun New England manner, performs several functions: He is narrator, bridging shifts in time and place, setting the scene for the audience; he is actor of minor roles, including drugstore owner and preacher at George and Emily's wedding; he is property man, constructing the soda fountain from a few boards; he is chorus, philosophizing for the audience; he is destroyer of the theatrical illusion, reminding the audience that they are in a theater watching a play. Distanced from the action that is filtered through his eyes, the audience begins to see with his sometimes ironic perspective. He possesses a Godlike omniscience, overseeing the progression of human history as God would. It is this kind of sight and insight that the audience, too, must develop. In a seemingly inconsequential exchange of dialogue (perhaps influenced by a similar passage in James Joyce's *A Portrait of the Artist as a Young Man*, 1916), Wilder hints at the idea on which the entire work pivots. George Gibbs's sister Rebecca tells about a letter that a minister sent to a sick friend; included as the final words of the address on the envelope was the location, "the Mind of God." Wilder, who himself acted the role of the Stage Manager in the Broadway production, tells his audience that if it could only plumb the mind of God, where everything—from least to most, from smallest to largest, past, present, and to come—exists simultaneously as part of a purposive, providential order, then they would live life wholly and even be able to cope with death.

The tension and tragedy of the human condition, however, arise because, paradoxically, it is possible to gain the perspective necessary for seeing life steadily and seeing it whole only after death. Emily dies giving birth, a poignant image not only of mutability but also of the way in which life and death are inextricably bound in nature's cycle. Only after she dies and is given the opportunity to relive the most "unimportant day" in her life does she see that even the most ordinary and banal of life's experiences is full of wonder and learn to treasure more what she has lost. Sadly, only the "saints and poets" seem to recognize this wonder and beauty while they are still alive. The end of a human life, union with some larger spirit, is in its beginning hinted at even in the most common events of daily living—if only that person, like the poet, could see.

While *Our Town* displays some affinities with medieval morality plays, *The Skin of Our Teeth* is influenced by the medieval mystery cycles in its structure: In capsule form (and stylistically akin somewhat to a comic strip), it recounts human history from the beginning of time to the present and on into the future. The Antrobuses, Wilder's Family of Man in this play, begin each of the three acts on the upswing, feeling positive about themselves and the human race; see their fortunes descend to a nadir, through either a natural disaster or human culpability; yet finally finish each act—and the play as a whole—having narrowly muddled through "by the skin of their teeth." In each instance, temptation is overcome, sinful action somehow compensated for. In act 1, with its echoes of the Garden of Eden story from Genesis, son Henry's killing of the neighbor boy (he earlier killed his brother, for which he received the mark of Cain) prompts Mr. Antrobus to despair, but daughter Gladys' ability to recite in school a poem by Henry Wadsworth Longfellow restores his faith. In act 2, with its underpinning of the Noah tale, the father's lack of faithfulness to Mrs. Antrobus sends shock waves through the family, as Gladys dons red stockings and Henry attacks a black person with a slingshot. Yet Mr. Antrobus, unlike the other conventioneers at Atlantic City who writhe in a snakelike dance, is among the remnant of faithful ones saved from the Deluge. Act 3 finds the family returning to normalcy after the war (any war), but the anarchic Henry threatens the stability of the family unit just as the forces of totalitarianism almost destroyed the world, until he is finally reconciled with his father, who puts his confidence in the best ideas from the past to sustain the human race. The overall structure, therefore, embodies Wilder's concept of cyclic time, with one result being that time can be handled anachronistically. The play, which began with a slide of the sun rising, ends with the equivalent lines from Genesis: "And the Lord said let there be light and there was light."

In its techniques, which extend the nonillusionistic style adopted in *Our Town*, *The Skin of Our Teeth* reflects the influence of Surrealism and even points forward to the multimedia effects of the 1960's and 1970's. The scenery, with its angles askew, the dozen lantern slides projected onto the set, the talking dinosaur and mammoth, the cardboard cutouts and flats, the lighting and noises—all contribute to a carnival atmosphere, anticipating the playful techniques of some Absurdist drama while also suggesting a dream happening without conscious control. Mr. Fitzpatrick, Wilder's director/stage manager here, not only stops the play so that he can rehearse volunteers taking over the parts of sick actors, but also is mildly satirized for his literal-mindedness and prosaicism; even Ivy, the costumer, understands the meaning of the play better than he does. Significantly, the substitute actors are needed to play the hours of the night who cross the stage; that they recite passages from Benedict de Spinoza, Plato, Aristotle, and the Bible (as similar characters also had in *Pullman Car Hiawatha*) demonstrates that the enduring ideas of the past are not out of reach of the common man. The illusion of reality is further destroyed when Lily Sabina Fairweather, a compound of temptress, mistress, camp follower, and maid, steps out of character and, as the actress Miss Somerset, speaks directly to the audience, requesting that they send up their chairs for firewood during the Ice Age of act 1 and, at the end of the play, sending them home to do their part in completing the history of the human race on earth.

Within the framework of his comic allegory of humankind's journey, Wilder's characters assume an archetypal dimension; each member of the Antrobus family, whom Wilder calls "our selves," seems to stand for an aspect of the archetypal man or woman's personality. Mr. Antrobus—the former gardener (Adam), self-made man, inventor of the wheel, the lever, gunpowder, the singing telegram, the brewing of beer and of grass soup—represents the power of the intellect, which can be a force for both creation and destruction. Appreciating the importance of the wisdom of past ages, he will not tolerate the burning of Shakespeare's works even to provide life-sustaining warmth. Mrs. Antrobus, inventor in her own right of the apron, the hem, the gore and the gusset, and frying in oil, is humankind's affective side; her watchword is the family and the promise of love between husband and wife that helps them endure and makes even suffering worthwhile. As one who insists that women are not the subservient creatures the media make them out to be, she stresses woman's role as transmitter of the Life Force. Lily Sabina (Lilith), with her philosophy of enjoying the present moment, embodies the hedonistic pleasure principle. The Antrobuses' daughter Gladys, who appears after the war with a baby, symbolically conveys hope for the future. Their son Henry is a representation of the strong, unreconciled evil that is always with man; though he is the enemy during the war and in general refuses to accept responsibility, he is still taken along on the ark at the end of act 2. In act 3, the actors playing Mr. Antrobus and Henry break out of their roles, moving from stereotypes to more rounded human beings as they reveal the tension between themselves as men rather than as characters. Something in the attitude of the actor playing Antrobus reminds the one portraying Henry of how authority figures have always blocked and hindered him, and so they clash personally. Through this tension, the actor playing Antrobus recognizes that there must indeed exist some lack within himself that triggered this negative response in the other, and so he promises to change. He ends confident that man, always on the edge of chaos and disaster, will ultimately endure and prevail, if only he accepts the chance to do the hard work that Providence demands of him.

Wilder, like George Bernard Shaw, has often been criticized for his romantic optimism, which seems out of keeping with the darker facts of human history—*The Skin of Our Teeth* opened, after all, only a year after Pearl Harbor and found its greatest success in post World War II Germany. Whether Wilder's optimistic belief in man's "spiral progression through trial and error" is found congenial or not, *The Skin of Our Teeth* remains a richly imaginative work and the seminal text of deliberately self-conscious art in the American theater.

Wilder's *The Matchmaker*—a revision of his *The Merchant of Yonkers*, an adaptation of Johann Nestroy's 1842 Viennese comedy *Einen Jux will er sich machen* (which, in turn, was based loosely on John Oxenford's 1835 English comedy *A Day Well Spent*)—belongs to that most venerable of dramatic traditions, the genre of romantic comedy. As such, it is characterized by a repressive authority figure who tries to thwart young love; mistaken identities and confusion between the sexes, including boys disguised as girls; and a ritualized dance to foreshadow the multiple marriages which resolve the plot. Along with these appear elements of good-natured, boisterous farce, including inopportune entrances and exits; hiding behind a screen, in closets, and under tables; and exploding cans of tomatoes shooting up through a trapdoor in the floor. What marks all of this traditional, even stereotypical material with Wilder's own signature are the themes and the manner in which he breaks down the illusion of stage reality.

A further alteration from the norm in romantic comedy is that in this play, the older couple, rather than the young ones, are the hero and heroine. Horace Vandergelder, the sly, miserly merchant from Yonkers (he seems a direct descendant of Ben Jonson's Volpone, the fox) forbids his sentimental young niece and ward Ermengarde to marry the penniless artist Ambrose Kemper. They ultimately circumvent his authority through the agency of two older women: Miss Flora Van Huysen, the spinster fairy godmother in the play, and Mrs. Dolly Gallager Levi, the inimitable matchmaker herself. Miss Van Huysen refuses to permit her own loneliness to be extended to others through the destruction of young love, and so she acts as the presiding deity over the three marriages: Ermengarde's to Ambrose; Cornelius Hackl's to Irene Molloy, the Irish widow and milliner; and

Barnaby Tucker's to Minnie, Mrs. Molloy's assistant. Dolly, who all along has her eyes on Horace for herself, is the only character among a cast of types permitted enough depth to probe into herself and her motives. In the manner in which she arranges the relationships of others and herself, there is something of the artist in Dolly Levi; her vocation is to make life interesting, to make people less selfish, to spread enjoyment, to see that the community renews and fructifies itself. She must, first of all, tutor Horace in adopting a proper attitude toward money; for her, money must "circulate like rain water" among the people and be "spread around like manure" if it is to encourage life and growth. She must also, however, tutor herself into giving up her widow's weeds, so to speak, and completely rejoining the human community. Ever since the death of her first husband, Ephraim, she has allowed herself to become like a dying leaf, and now must cure her underactive heart through marriage to Horace. For both Dolly and Horace, lonely old age is only narrowly averted. This emphasis on full participation in life and life's processes, of seeing that to everything there is a season and of not rushing before one's time toward death and decay, is peculiarly Wilder's. Also distinctively Wilder's is the emphasis on the need for "adventure" and "wonder," which are two of the key words spoken by nearly every one of the play's characters and are direct echoes of the attitudes espoused in *Our Town*.

The settings for the four acts of *The Matchmaker* are the most elaborately realistic box sets prescribed for any Wilder play. Precisely because they do form such a realistic background, replete with "obtrusive bric-a-brac," they make the several instances of direct address to the audience by the major characters all the more startling. The disjunction between the realistic sets and the very nonrealistic goings-on calls the audience's attention to the fact that it is watching a play and turns stage realism on its ear. *The Matchmaker* becomes, indeed, a playful and affectionate parody of the way that stage realism stifles life. To be doubly sure that the audience does not miss this point, Miss Van Huysen even repeats several times some variation of the line "Everything's imagination," which is another way of saying that all is make-believe and pretense—exactly what Wilder strives to provide for his theater audiences.

Wilder's *A Life in the Sun* is, both in form and content, linked closely to the Greek drama of the fifth century B.C. Its form, a play in three acts (each of which could almost stand alone as a self-contained episode) and a Satyr play, replicates that of the Greek trilogies, which were followed with a comic parody of the tragic action. Here, the Satyr play (entitled *The Drunken Sisters*, which tells how Apollo tricked the vain Fates into allowing Admetus to live) is added by Wilder to make the point that the tragic and comic experiences are incomplete in and of themselves; in life, the two kinds of perceptions must coexist. The content of Wilder's powerful retelling of the Alcestis story for modern man is religious and mythological in nature, with his act 2 corresponding closely to the material found in Euripides' original. Unlike T. S. Eliot's *The Cocktail Party* (pr. 1949), which uses the same myth allusively as a vague underpinning for a contemporary parable, or Eugene O'Neill's *Mourning Becomes Electra* (pr. 1931), which takes the outlines and psychology of the Orestes and Electra stories and redresses them at a different time and place, Wilder creatively adjusts the myth to reflect contemporary philosophical currents, especially Existentialism, as Jean-Paul Sartre had done in *The Flies* (pr. 1943).

Act 1 begins with a confrontation between Apollo, the force of light, and Death, the force of darkness, who introduce the issues that inform the entire play: the relationship between the divine and the human and the problem of discovering a meaning to life. Although Apollo admits that there exists much that human beings are incapable of understanding, he insists that what meaning does exist flows from him; Death, on the other hand—and later Tiresias, the wizened seer, will echo him—argues that it is the gods who cause human torment. By meddling in human affairs, the gods make people unhappy and distraught. On her wedding day, Alcestis decides not to marry the King of Thessaly unless she receives a clear sign from the gods; she will forsake man, finite and of this world, to love only God, infinite and other-worldly. Alcestis desires absolute certainty and the assurance that the gods have not abandoned humankind; without that, life is reduced to meaningless nonsense, and humankind is left in a condition similar to that of the Absurdists, with life made all the more unbearable because human beings have been given hope of some meaning only to see that hope dashed. The God Apollo, by becoming human in the form of one of Admetus' herdsmen, must save Alcestis by forcing her to recognize that God is within each and every person, that the divine can be found within the human, the infinite within the finite. When Admetus enters wearing a blue cloak like Apollo's, the sight is an epiphany for Alcestis, who pledges to marry him and live totally for him, ready even to die for him.

Act 2, which occurs twelve years later, finds Admetus at the point of death and Alcestis finally favored with the long-sought-for message from Delphi, which indicates that the gods do demand the difficult. The message challenges her to do what she was prepared to do at the close of act 1: die in place of Admetus. The Watchman, the old nurse Aglaia, and the Herdsman all offer to sacrifice themselves so that Admetus might live, but Alcestis insists that the role fall to her. It is not that Alcestis has no hesitation, for she dreads to cease to be, to leave the sunlight, and she still craves the right to understand the ways of God to man that would make man more than an animal. Finally, though, her love for Admetus dominates her love for life; she will die for him and, what is perhaps even harder, die from him, believing a divinity shapes her end. Yet, as Apollo intervenes in act 1, here Hercules, though in fear and trembling, descends into the Underworld to bring back from the dead the all-forgiving Alcestis, the "crown of women." The last image of the resurrected Alcestis led forth from Hell provides a further instance for the audience of the way in which classical and Christian myth and iconography fuse in Wilder: Apollo/Christ became man; Alcestis/Christ died and rose so that others might live.

If act 2 forms a meditation on death, act 3 is a metaphysical inquiry into the existence of human suffering, with Death taunting Apollo to explain why so many innocent in Thessaly have died in the pestilence: Do the gods make human beings suffer only so that people will remember rather than reject them? Admetus is now dead, and Alcestis is an old slave under King Agis. Epimenes, the only surviving son of the former queen, returns to what has become a wasteland, vowing butchery and revenge, only to have his hand stopped by his mother. Rejecting all of those who see God's influence only in the evil in the world and never in the good, Alcestis says that the gods' ways are not human ways; they do not love one minute and then turn against the loved one in the next. She counsels Agis, whose daughter Laodamia dies in the plague, that evil does have a purpose within the divine scheme and that suffering can make him open his eyes and learn wisdom. Her final visionary pronouncement recalls that of Emily in *Our Town*: Human beings should despair at the point of death only if they have not really lived, if they have failed to experience fully and treasure the here and now. The meaning of life is in the living of life. Alcestis herself becomes the sign that life does possess a meaning in and of itself, and, freed from the grave by the grace of Apollo, she experiences an apotheosis as her reward.

A Life in the Sun, as much a paean to woman and her role in the cosmic order as are *The Happy Journey to Trenton and Camden* and *The Skin of Our Teeth*, provides a dramatic summation of much of Wilder's philosophy: To become divine, human beings must first be fully human; the extraordinary is to be discovered in the ordinary; the power of myth is timeless, cutting across cultures and religions, synthesizing the past and the present, making the past ever new and vital. The Watchman's words in act 1 of *A Life in the Sun*, a play that is essentially an undiscovered country for all but ardent enthusiasts of Wilder, might be paraphrased as an epigraph for all Wilder's dramatic works: The essential facts of human life do not change, nor should humankind expect them to, from millennium to millennium, from year to year, from minute to minute. What must change is human beings' way of seeing.

Other major works

NOVELS: *The Cabala*, 1926; *The Bridge of San Luis Rey*, 1927; *The Woman of Andros*, 1930; *Heaven's My Destination*, 1934; *The Ides of March*, 1948;

The Eighth Day, 1967; *Theophilus North*, 1973.

NONFICTION: *The Intent of the Artist*, 1941; *American Characteristics and Other Essays*, 1979; *The Journals of Thornton Wilder, 1939-1961*, 1985.

SCREENPLAYS: *Our Town*, 1940 (with Frank Craven and Harry Chantlee); *Shadow of a Doubt*, 1943 (with Sally Benson and Alma Revelle).

TRANSLATION: *The Victors*, 1948 (of Jean-Paul Sartre's play *Morts sans sépulture*).

Bibliography

Burbank, Rex J. *Thornton Wilder.* 2d ed. Boston: Twayne, 1978. In this updated version of the 1962 edition, Burbank traces the history of critical controversy surrounding Wilder's work, offers insights into his methods of fictional and dramatic composition, and assesses his work's relative merits. Unlike many critics, Burbank does not adhere to the belief that a popular author cannot also be a good writer. Works such as *The Bridge of San Luis Rey*, *Our Town*, and *The Matchmaker*, he argues, all have the ingredients that appeal to young audiences in particular. Chronology, bibliography.

Goldstein, Malcolm. *The Art of Thornton Wilder.* Lincoln: University of Nebraska Press, 1965. In addition to providing a biographical sketch of the author, this brief but insightful analysis of Wilder's novels and plays offers a chronological discussion and general overview of Wilder's works. Particularly emphasized are thematic continuity and universality, language and characterization. Contains a bibliography.

Grebanier, Bernard. *Thornton Wilder.* Minneapolis: University of Minnesota Press, 1964. In this brief pamphlet intended for a general audience, the author presents an excellent overview of Wilder's major works. He focuses on Wilder's romanticism, his economy of expression, his preoccupation with the past, his concern with moral issues, and his profoundly American settings and locales. Good introduction to Wilder's work.

Haberman, Donald. *The Plays of Thornton Wilder: A Critical Study.* Middletown, Conn.: Wesleyan University Press, 1967. This excellent and scholarly study of Wilder's drama begins with some biographical information on the public and private sides of Wilder. It proceeds to discuss the religious dimension, the universal nature, the characterization and narrative technique, the language, and finally the mythic aspects of Wilder's work. Bibliography, appendix.

Papajewski, Helmut. *Thornton Wilder.* Translated by John Conway. New York: Frederick Ungar, 1968. This thoughtful study offers an assessment of Wilder's reception in Europe, particularly Germany. Considers both the novels and the plays. While addressing the qualities of independence and individuality in American literature, the author emphasizes the common traditions linking Wilder with Europe.

Wilder, Amos Niven. *Thornton Wilder and His Public.* Philadelphia: Fortress Press, 1980. An interesting account of the relationship between Wilder and his critical and reading public, written by Wilder's older brother, a theologian. His aim is to offer a sophisticated discrimination, both aesthetic and sociological, of his brother's work in the light of contemporary American reality, particularly its symbolism, dynamics, creative modes, and registers of meaning. Related subjects discussed are distinctive and recurrent patterns, styles, scenarios, genres, and themes (modes of language and fabulation), which reflect the basic orientation to this reality. Includes an appendix.

Thomas P. Adler
(Revised by *Genevieve Slomski*)

EMLYN WILLIAMS

Born: Mostyn, Wales; November 26, 1905
Died: London, England; September 25, 1987

Principal drama

Vigil, pr. 1925, pb. 1954 (one act); *Full Moon*, pr. 1927; *Glamour*, pr. 1928; *A Murder Has Been Arranged*, pr., pb. 1930; *Port Said*, pr. 1931 (revised as *Vessels Departing*, pr. 1933); *The Late Christopher Bean*, pr., pb. 1933 (adaptation of a work by Sidney Howard); *Spring 1600*, pr. 1934, pr. 1945 (revised), pb. 1946; *Night Must Fall*, pr., pb. 1935; *He Was Born Gay: A Romance*, pr., pb. 1937; *The Corn Is Green*, pr., pb. 1938; *The Light of Heart*, pr., pb. 1940; *The Morning Star*, pr. 1941, pb. 1942; *Pen Don*, pr. 1943; *The Druid's Rest*, pr., pb. 1944; *The Wind of Heaven*, pr., pb. 1945; *Thinking Aloud: A Dramatic Sketch*, pr. 1945, pb. 1946; *Trespass: A Ghost Story*, pr., pb. 1947; *Accolade*, pr. 1950, pb. 1951; *Someone Waiting*, pr. 1953, pb. 1954; *Beth*, pr. 1958, pb. 1959; *The Collected Plays*, pb. 1961; *Cuckoo*, pb. 1986.

Other literary forms

In addition to his stage and radio plays, Emlyn Wiliams wrote plays for television: in 1968, *A Blue Movie of My Own True Love*, about a love affair that results in murder; and in 1976, *The Power of Dawn*, about the final moments in the life of Leo Tolstoy.

Williams wrote the screenplays or provided dialogue for several motion pictures, including his *Friday the Thirteenth* (1933; with G. H. Moresby-White and Sidney Gilliat), *Evergreen* (1934; with Marjorie Gaffney), *The Man Who Knew Too Much* (1934; with A. R. Rawlinson and Edwin Greenwood), and *The Last Days of Dolwyn* (1949). His script for *The Citadel* (1938; with Frank Wead, Ian Dalrymple, Elizabeth Hill, and John Van Druten), based on the 1937 A. J. Cronin novel, was published in *Foremost Films of 1938.*

Williams also wrote two volumes of memoirs: *George: An Early Autobiography* (1961) and *Emlyn: An Early Autobiography, 1927-1935* (1973). The first tells the story of his childhood and youth in rural and urban Wales; the second chronicles his attempts to make a name for himself on the London stage as actor and playwright.

Williams' interest in the psychology of killers, a concern of several of his plays, led to his account of the 1963-1964 Moors murders in England, *Beyond Belief: A Chronicle of Murder and Its Detection* (1967).

In his youth, Williams wrote several novels, but it was not until he was seventy-five that he actually published a novel, *Headlong* (1980), a variation of the "if I were king" theme. Its hero, Jack Green, who is an actor struggling to achieve success on the London stage, turns out to be the only living heir to the English throne when the entire royal family is wiped out in a catastrophe.

Achievements

When one thinks of Wales in terms of theater, one thinks of Emlyn Williams, not only because he came from Wales but also because so many of his plays are filled with Wales. *The Corn Is Green*, his most popular play, is a hymn to the glory of life and to the distinctive virtues of the Welsh people. The play also won critical acclaim, receiving the New York Drama Critics Circle Award for Best Foreign Play of 1941.

Williams' studies of psychopathology are notable: His particularly chilling portrait of Dan in *Night Must Fall* was one of the first, and remains one of the most frightening, of several portraits of psychopathic killers who stalk their victims across countless reels and pages of twentieth century movies and books.

Williams has also been acclaimed for his acting ability, enjoying particular success for his impersonation of Charles Dickens reading his works and for his one-man show based on the works of Dylan Thomas.

For his distinguished career in the theater, Williams was named Commander of the Order of the British Empire in 1962.

Biography

George Emlyn Williams was born on November 26, 1905, in the village of Mostyn, Wales, the first surviving child of Richard and Mary Williams. Like most other children of his village, the young George spoke only Welsh until he was eight, and like most boys in that part of Wales, he could look forward to a life in the mines.

Williams was an imaginative child, however, and when he was ten he won a scholarship to the Holywell County School, where he came to the attention of Miss Grace Cooke, a London social worker and the model for Miss Moffat in *The Corn Is Green*. Recognizing his talents—especially his facility with languages—she helped him to secure a scholarship to Oxford, where he went in 1923. His choice of theater as a vocation was not surprising: As a child, he would create plays with characters cut out of illustrated catalogs; he would invent stories for them with himself as hero.

At Oxford, Williams—now using Emlyn as his first name—appeared in 1923 in his first play, a French farce; in 1924, he wrote his first play, a bittersweet version of Cinderella, never produced or published; in 1925, his first play was produced by the Oxford University Drama Society. *Vigil* is a one-act thriller about a cruel master who lures men to their deaths and who in turn is killed by his servant. As with so many of Williams' plays, there was a role in it for its author.

The year Williams received his M.A., 1927, was also the year the Drama

Society, under the direction of J. B. Fagan, produced Williams' first full-length play, *Full Moon*, a story of conflict between romantic and possessive love. Fagan, a playwright as well as a producer, thought enough of Williams as an actor to give him a role in his own play *And So to Bed*, in which Williams made his London debut in April, 1927, and his New York debut in November, 1927. During the New York run, Williams wrote *Glamour*, which in 1928 became his first play to be seen in London. Not until 1930 and *A Murder Has Been Arranged*, however, did he gain the attention of the critics. A murder mystery with supernatural overtones, it features a protagonist, Maurice Mullins, whose surface charm conceals his ruthlessness, anticipating Dan in *Night Must Fall* and Fenn in *Someone Waiting*. Reviews were good, but business was not.

The two plays that followed—*Port Said* (revised in 1933 as *Vessels Departing*) and *Spring 1600* (revised in 1945)—were neither critical nor popular successes. If Williams' career as playwright seemed at a standstill, however, his career as actor was flourishing, with roles in plays by Émile Zola, Sean O'Casey, Luigi Pirandello, Georg Kaiser, and Edgar Wallace.

The year 1935 was an important one for Williams. He married Molly O'Shann, and his first child, Alan Emlyn, was born. It was also the year in which *Night Must Fall* was produced. This psychological thriller ran for a year in London, provided Williams with one of his best roles, and established him as an important playwright. (Interestingly, 1935 is also the year in which the action of his novel *Headlong* occurs.)

He Was Born Gay, appearing two years later, did nothing to solidify Williams' reputation. Despite the presence in the cast of John Gielgud and Williams—his role of Lambert was another characterization in evil—the play barely lasted two weeks. Although its subtitle is *A Romance*, Williams could not decide whether the play was a romance, a comedy, or a tragedy.

The Corn Is Green, produced in 1938, is, with *Night Must Fall*, Williams' best work as a dramatist. An autobiographical comedy-drama about the efforts of an English schoolteacher to bring education to a small Welsh village, it was a success onstage in London with Sybil Thorndike and in New York with Ethel Barrymore, on-screen with Bette Davis, and on television with Katharine Hepburn.

The Light of Heart, Williams' next play, was written with an insider's knowledge of the theater. The character Maddoc Thomas, a Shakespearean actor in decline, is another of Williams' compelling portraits of an utterly self-absorbed, if charming, man, but the play is marred by sensationalism and lack of plausibility; it is difficult for the audience to believe that Thomas is as good an actor as Williams claims him to be.

Even less believable and more contrived is *The Morning Star*, a potboiler that served as the playwright's tribute to the courage of Londoners during the Blitz. Williams' heart was in the right place, but the incredible plot makes it difficult to take the play seriously. It was, however, a huge success in London. More significant contributions to the war effort were Williams' 1941 patriotic film, *This England*; his radio broadcasts, including readings from Charles Dickens; and his tours of various theaters of war to perform *Night Must Fall*, among other plays.

In *Pen Don*, Williams turned to medieval Wales for his setting and Welsh mythology for his subject matter. As far removed as *Pen Don* is from Williams' realistic plays, its theme—the conflict between innocence and experience—is a familiar one in his work.

Wales was also the setting for Williams' next two plays. *The Druid's Rest*, a comedy of misunderstanding, is steeped in local color. *The Wind of Heaven* is an ambitious play on the theme of the return of the Messiah in the guise of a boy during the time of the Crimean War. Ambrose Ellis, a Welsh apostate who tries to buy the boy for his circus, is another Williams protagonist caught between idealistic and materialistic motives. Save for him, however, the characters lack depth, and the conventions of the well-made play are at odds with the subject matter.

In comparison with the "kitchen sink" plays of the Angry Young Men that were setting the London theater on its heels with their scathing protests at the genteel Britain of yesteryear, Williams' postwar plays were tired and contrived: *Trespass*, a ghost story; *Accolade*, which fails to come to grips with its subject—the right of the artist to be free; *Someone Waiting*, a complicated mystery peopled with unpleasant characters; and *Beth*, his last play for the stage, which features a retarded heroine.

If these works added little to Williams' reputation as a playwright, he was, however, winning accolades as an actor, both in standard plays such as Henrik Ibsen's *The Wild Duck* (pb. 1884) and William Shakespeare's *The Merchant of Venice* (pr. c. 1596-1597) and in new works such as Terence Rattigan's *The Winslow Boy* (pr. 1946), which gave him one of his most acclaimed roles, as Sir Robert Morton. This seemingly heartless lawyer, who is revealed as a man with a caring heart, is much like those divided selves Williams created in his own plays.

Williams' career in films, which began in 1932, was also flourishing; among his works in this medium were *The Citadel*, for which he wrote dialogue; *Major Barbara* (1941), based on George Bernard Shaw's play; *The Last Days of Dolwyn*, an evocation of Welsh village life, which he wrote and directed; and *Ivanhoe* (1952), based on the novel by Sir Walter Scott.

Williams' greatest success in the theater came in 1951, not with a play but with a triumphant one-man show, his impersonation of Charles Dickens reading from his works. Williams assumed the characters' personas and re-created the storytelling genius of Dickens. He toured all over the world with this show, performing it more than two thousand times. In 1955, he turned to the work of a fellow Welshman, Dylan Thomas, for another one-man show, *Dylan Thomas Growing Up*, which also proved popular. A third program of solo readings, based on the work of H. H. Munro (Saki) and entitled *The Playboy of the Wicked World* (1978), was less successful.

Analysis

In genre, Emlyn Williams' plays range from fantasy to historical drama to psychological thriller to comedy; in time, from the days of King Arthur to Shakespeare's London to nineteenth century Wales to World War II London during the Blitz. Despite this variety and range, a majority of Williams' plays share common concerns: Wales, the theater, and the divided personality.

Seven of Williams' plays have Welsh settings; six others, though set elsewhere, feature Welsh characters, including Gwenny, Williams' first successful Welsh character, in his adaptation of Sidney Howard's *The Late Christopher Bean*. Dan, the psychopathic killer in *Night Must Fall* is Welsh. Mason, the heir to the throne of Louis XVI in *He Was Born Gay*, was smuggled out of France as a child and reared in Wales.

In Williams' plays, Welsh characters, such as Rhys Price Morris in *Glamour*, often affirm positive values. Ambrose Ellis, the expatriate Welshman in *The Wind of Heaven*, regains his religious faith at the same time as he regains his command of the Welsh language. *The Corn Is Green* and *The Druid's Rest* depict Welsh village life as hard but healthy, unrelenting but uncomplicated. These plays celebrate the lives and loving hearts of Welsh men and women. They are hearts filled with music, recalling the plays of Irish life of John Millington Synge and Sean O'Casey.

Theater is the subject matter of *Glamour*, *Spring 1600*, and *The Light of Heart*. The dramatic sketch *Thinking Aloud* records the thoughts and feelings of an actress who has murdered her husband. The stage of a theater is the setting for *A Murder Has Been Arranged*. Ambrose Ellis of *The Wind of Heaven* and Saviello of *Trespass* are showmen, one a circus owner, the other a medium.

If not actors by vocation, some Williams protagonists—Maurice Mullins in *A Murder Has Been Arranged* and Dan in *Night Must Fall*—constantly, even compulsively, act. Indeed, Dan cannot remember a time when he was not acting. These coldhearted killers mask their true nature under a veneer of charm.

Dan and Maurice are also studies in abnormal psychology, a preoccupation of Williams from *Vigil*, his first produced play, to *Beyond Belief*, his study of the Moors murders. Another example is Fenn in *Someone Waiting*. This ineffectual, insignificant tutor is actually a man of insane cunning, who nurtures and pursues revenge without remorse. Although no killer, Saviello in *Trespass* belongs with this group. This Italian medium is exposed as a sham, a draper from Cardiff; in a stunning reversal, however, he turns out to be, much against his will, a genuine and natural medium.

A variant on this theme of split personality is the dual life many of Williams' artists lead and the choices they must make. The genius of the painter in *The Late Christopher Bean* has gone unrecognized during his lifetime because of the very private life he has chosen to lead. Both Jill in *Glamour* and Ann Byrd in *Spring 1600* must decide between a life of rural innocence and a career in the theater. Maddoc Thomas in *The Light of Heart* is torn between the desire to hold on to his daughter and the equally strong pull to reestablish his career in the theater. Will Trenting, the prizewinning novelist about to be knighted in *Accolade*, has been leading a Jekyll-and-Hyde existence. Ambrose Ellis is a man at war with himself. Saint and sinner, he struggles between the attraction of worldly success as an impresario and his sense of divine mission.

The persistence in Williams' plays of characters with divided personalities or characters faced with the choice of two ways of life reflects, perhaps, Williams' own dual role as actor and playwright and his own dual existence as George, the hero of his first volume of autobiography recording his life in Wales, and as Emlyn, the hero of the second volume, covering the years during which he was making his way in the London theater.

Williams' interest in crime and in murder trials was heightened in 1934 by accounts in London newspapers of recent and past killers who had left their victims' corpses in trunks and of one killer, termed the "Butcher of Hanover," a seemingly nice young man who had set his mother on fire in order to get her insurance money. These stories of murder became the basis for *Night Must Fall*.

As Williams worked on his script, he decided that his victim could not possibly be his young man's mother. In real life, sons do kill their mothers, but such a situation onstage would, Williams believed, prove too horrible for an audience to accept. Even so, Dan, the young man, tells his prospective victim that she reminds him of his own mother—he even calls her Mother—and she treats him indulgently, like a son.

Night Must Fall is set in a cottage on the edge of a forest in Essex, occupied by Mrs. Bramson, an overbearing invalid constantly demanding attention. Although she has a maid, a cook, and a visiting nurse, much of the burden of her care falls on her niece, Olivia, a lonely, repressed young woman.

Into the household comes Dan, a bellboy from a nearby hotel. A former seaman, blackmailer, and pimp, he has now taken up murder—that of a woman guest from the hotel who has vanished and whose decapitated body turns up several days later. We are led to believe that Dan carries the severed head around with him in a hatbox.

With his childlike, innocent airs and his good humor, Dan is most beguiling and quickly wins Mrs. Bramson over. Olivia initially distrusts him, yet she feels drawn to him, even when, to her horror, she knows he has murdered. Dan, compelled to show off, takes pleasure in almost confessing his guilt to her. Although he is not subject to remorse, he does suffer sudden panics during which he confides in her. Playing upon her obvious attraction to him, he is able to keep her from giving him away.

Dan soon finds the opportunity he is seeking—to kill Mrs. Bramson and make off with her cashbox before the police become too suspicious of him. Reading to her one night from the Bible, he reminisces about mornings at sea when he was conscious of only the sun and himself. As the old lady reminds him, however, it is now night. Echoing Mrs. Bramson's remark, he loudly shuts the Bible and, singing a snatch of the same song heard before his first murder, picks up a cushion and smothers her.

In the play's final scene, Dan elatedly confesses to Olivia both the murder and his intention to burn the cottage with the body and Olivia in it. A beam from a police flashlight outside momentarily unnerves him, and Olivia, seeing him as an unprotected child, reaches out to him, but he soon regains his cocky self-assurance. As the police lead him off, he is looking forward to the attention women will give him at his trial, and he promises to give the spectators their money's worth. He passionately kisses Olivia, lights up a cigarette, and, with the same jauntiness that marked his first entrance, leaves.

Night Must Fall is no ordinary thriller. The audience knows from the prologue, set in the Court of Criminal Appeals, that the protagonist has been found guilty and condemned to death, a sentence with which the Lord Chief Justice finds no reason to interfere. Moreover, although the play provides a good deal of suspense, its emphasis is not on the twists and turns of plot but on the character of Dan.

Dan is a study in contrasts: raffish but ruthless, charming but callous, disarming but dangerous. Emotionally impregnable though he is, women find in him a vulnerability that fascinates them. He lives in the world of his imagination. There, nothing can touch him; there, everyone is under him. His masquerade feeds his vanity, and his vanity accounts for his constant desire to talk of himself.

There are enough chilling moments in the play to make palms sweat and pulses race. Williams places these moments most strategically at the end of each of the play's five scenes: Dan's singing "Mighty Lak a Rose" a few moments after we have learned the song was heard before the first victim disappeared; Olivia's look of horror as she stares into Dan's face at the news of the body's discovery; the murder of Mrs. Bramson as the lights dim and the music rises in crescendo; and Dan's final exit. No scene is more taut than the act 2 curtain. As the police inspector, suspicious of Dan, goes to open the hatbox, Dan sits drumming his fingers against the sofa and then wildly beats his fists against his head. Olivia claims the box as hers and walks off with it. The danger passed, Dan, left alone, crumples to the floor in a faint as the curtain quickly falls.

Night Must Fall is a tightly written play. Nowhere is this more evident than in Williams' handling of time. Although the action covers two weeks, each scene takes place just a little later in the day than the preceding one. The overall effect is that the play occurs in a single day, from morning to night. This telescoping of time adds to the play's growing suspense and tension. Also effective is the casual tone and banter of the opening scene and Williams' skillful use of humor. Both serve as a contrast to the dawning horror and lengthening shadows as night falls and envelops the cottage in darkness.

Night Must Fall ran in London for 435 performances with Dame May Whitty and the author in the leading roles. The play has been filmed twice, once in 1937 with Robert Montgomery and again in 1963 with Albert Finney.

The Corn Is Green tells the story of how a determined and dedicated schoolteacher in Wales discovers a literary talent among the local miners and exerts all of her power to make a success of him. A middle-aged English spinster, Miss Moffat, comes to a small Welsh village in the latter part of the nineteenth century to found a school for the children of Welsh miners. Though there is initial skepticism and resistance from some of the villagers and from the English Squire, who dominates the community through his ownership of the land, Miss Moffat perseveres, especially after she discovers a young boy, Morgan Evans, of great intellectual promise. She is resolved to release him into the world of enlightenment. She even plays up to the Squire to win his support.

Miss Moffat prepares Morgan well enough so that he can compete for an Oxford scholarship, but in the process she forgets that he is a human being. He rebels against her authority, turns to a local harlot, Bessie Watty, and gets her pregnant.

Months later, Morgan learns of Bessie's baby at the same time that he learns of winning the scholarship. Out of a sense of duty, he is ready to give up Oxford to marry Bessie, who does not love him and does not want the baby. Miss Moffat agrees to adopt the child, freeing Morgan to take the scholarship. When another promising youngster comes along, she will not be as clumsy as she was with Morgan. As the school bell rings clearly and confidently marking the beginning of another term, the curtain falls.

The Corn Is Green is a deeply felt play whose power derives in part from its autobiographical content. Because the material was too close to real life, Williams placed the action back in time. Morgan is the author's adolescent alter ego, although the playwright claimed that Morgan was not a self-portrait. Interestingly, Williams created the role of Morgan onstage. Certainly the relationship between teacher and pupil is autobiographical.

That relationship is the core of the play and accounts for the play's most dramatic and moving scenes: Miss Moffat's reading of Morgan's first essay, a lyric evocation of life in the mines; her impersonal treatment of him; his determination to climb over the stone wall behind which he has been a prisoner all his life and his acknowledgment that she has given him a leg up; his excited description to her of the Oxford examination; and their final confrontation and farewell, where they come together not as teacher and pupil, adult and youngster, but as two friends. Through her wisdom and understanding, Morgan now has the courage to become someone of whom Wales can be proud.

Miss Moffat is Williams' most surely drawn character and as close to a true heroine—or hero—as is any character in his plays. A woman of unbounded vitality, she will not be deterred from her goals—her pursuit of them makes her authoritative and tenacious—yet she is endowed with a genuine feeling for her fellowman.

Morgan, the play's second major character, is also well conceived; his growth from crude youngster to self-conscious rebel to serious scholar is most convincing. An impudent young man, he desperately wants to learn, but in his understandable distrust of the ways and means of learning, he resents the domineering hand of Miss Moffat.

The minor characters are winning, if stereotyped: the no-nonsense Cockney mother; her trollop daughter; a genteel English lady; the Squire who prides himself on not reading but who accepts the poet Alfred, Lord Tennyson because Tennyson attended Cambridge, the Squire's school. Williams mines the rich comic vein of such characters as Old Tom, who all of his life thought Shakespeare a place, and the volcanic John Gorowny Jones, harmless even while erupting.

The Corn Is Green is a ringing affirmation of education, an unusual theme for a contemporary play, but one that Williams invests with sincerity and excitement. At the same time, one might question whether an Oxford education is worth the sacrifice of personal responsibility and self-identity. The play takes up several social concerns as well: the plight of children sent to the mines, the status of women, and the relationship of the Welsh people and language to the English people and language.

If there is a weakness, it is in Williams' reliance on melodrama to bring matters to a climax—in this case, the illegitimate baby. In a play in which for two acts characterization shapes plot, it is disappointing to find, in the final scenes, plot molding characters. Still, Williams handles the mechanics of plot with a sure hand, and the play's theatrical quality never falters.

When Miss Cooke, the real-life prototype of Miss Moffat, received a copy of the script for her approval, she wrote to her former pupil that she did not believe audiences would want to see a play about education. Wrong as she was about the play's appeal, she was right when she told Williams that in his earlier plays she found the characters "a little out of focus." She added, though, that the people in *The Corn Is Green* were "straight from life. So it was, and so it is written."

Night Must Fall and *The Corn Is Green* are Williams' most satisfying plays, distinguished by strong characterization, a simple but effective narrative line, expert control of suspense and atmosphere, and an artful blend of pathos and humor. Because of these solid dramatic virtues, they continue to have a place on the international stage.

Other major works

NOVELS: *Headlong*, 1980; *Dr. Crippen's Diary: An Invention*, 1987.

NONFICTION: *George: An Early Autobiography*, 1961; *Beyond Belief: A Chronicle of Murder and Its Detection*, 1967; *Emlyn: An Early Autobiography, 1927-1935*, 1973.

SCREENPLAYS: *Friday the Thirteenth*, 1933 (with G.H. Moresby-White and Sidney Gilliat); *Evergreen*, 1934 (with Marjorie Gaffney); *The Man Who Knew Too Much*, 1934 (with A.R. Rawlinson and Edwin Greenwood); *The Divine Spark*, 1935 (with Richard Benson); *Broken Blossoms*, 1936; *The Citadel*, 1938 (with Frank Wead, Ian Dalrymple, Elizabeth Hill, and John Van Druten; based on A. J. Cronin's novel); *This England*, 1941 (with Bridget Boland and Rawlinson); *Major Barbara*, 1941 (based on George Bernard Shaw's play); *The Last Days of Dolwyn*, 1949; *Ivanhoe*, 1952 (based on Sir Walter Scott's novel).

TELEPLAYS: *A Month in the Country*, 1947; *Every Picture Tells a Story*, 1949; *In Town Tonight*, 1954; *A Blue Movie of My Own True Love*, 1968; *The Power of Dawn*, 1976.

RADIO PLAYS: *Pepper and Sand*, 1947; *Emlyn*, 1974 (adaptation of his book).

Bibliography

Burnham, David. "The Stage and Screen: *The Morning Star.*" Review of *The Morning Star. Commonweal* 36 (October 2, 1942): 565-566. While quite negative, Burnham's review offers insight into what the playwright's contemporaries expected from the theater. He considers Williams' mixture of techniques inappropriate for a play that depicts the horror of the London Blitz. The farcical scenes are not integrated to the main plot, yet they are superior to the scenes in which he exploits the techniques of photographic realism.

Dale-Jones, Don. *Emlyn Williams.* Cardiff: University of Wales Press, 1979. This monograph focuses on how Williams' Welsh background, including his studies in psychology and foreign literatures, determined his interest in the theater and influenced his plays. While it has a good bibliography, it lacks a table of contents and an index. Nevertheless, it is the most thorough study of Williams. Includes a photograph of the artist.

Hope-Wallace, Philip. "Emlyn Williams: Playwright, Actor, Producer." *Theatre Arts* 32 (January, 1948): 16-19. Acting experience contributed to the playwright's skill in writing dialogue and scenes of horror. Unfortunately, foreign audiences have failed to understand the essence of the plays because they do not understand the Welsh temperament. For example, the American film of *The Corn Is Green* lacks the charm of the play.

Krutch, Joseph Wood. "At Last." *The Nation* 151 (December 7, 1940): 585-587. The eminent drama critic offers a scholarly critique of *The Corn Is Green.* Williams infuses new life into conventional material, methods, and structures. While the types of characters may derive from textbook formulas, they become Welsh men and women. Autobiographical elements and intimacy with the landscape save the play from triteness.

Whitford-Roberts, Edward. *The Emlyn Williams Country.* Foreword by Emlyn Williams. Penarth, Wales: Penarth Times, 1963. This study attempts a further understanding of the Welsh content—characters, settings, atmosphere, and ethical principles—of Williams' plays. It includes a map of Flintshire and photographs of places that might have fueled the playwright's imagination and people who might have encouraged his career.

Richard B. Gidez
(Revised by *Irene Gnarra*)

TENNESSEE WILLIAMS
Thomas Lanier Williams

Born: Columbus, Mississippi; March 26, 1911
Died: New York, New York; February 25, 1983

Principal drama

Battle of Angels, pr. 1940, pb. 1945; *This Property Is Condemned*, pb. 1941, pr. 1946 (one act); *I Rise in Flame, Cried the Phoenix*, wr. 1941, pb. 1951, pr. 1959 (one act); *The Lady of Larkspur Lotion*, pb. 1942 (one act); *The Glass Menagerie*, pr. 1944, pb. 1945; *Twenty-seven Wagons Full of Cotton*, pb. 1945, pr. 1955 (one act); *You Touched Me*, pr. 1945, pb. 1947 (with Donald Windham); *Summer and Smoke*, pr. 1947, pb. 1948; *A Streetcar Named Desire*, pr., pb. 1947; *American Blues*, pb. 1948 (collection); *Five Short Plays*, pb. 1948; *The Long Stay Cut Short: Or, The Unsatisfactory Supper*, pb. 1948 (one act); *The Rose Tattoo*, pr., pb. 1951; *Camino Real*, pr., pb. 1953; *Cat on a Hot Tin Roof*, pr., pb. 1955; *Orpheus Descending*, pr. 1957, pb. 1958 (revision of *Battle of Angels*); *Suddenly Last Summer*, pr., pb. 1958; *The Enemy: Time*, pb. 1959; *Sweet Bird of Youth*, pr., pb. 1959 (based on *The Enemy: Time*); *Period of Adjustment*, pr. 1959, pb. 1960; *The Night of the Iguana*, pr., pb. 1961; *The Milk Train Doesn't Stop Here Anymore*, pr. 1963, pb. 1976 (revised); *The Eccentricities of a Nightingale*, pr., pb. 1964 (revision of *Summer and Smoke*); *Slapstick Tragedy: The Mutilated and The Gnädiges Fräulein*, pr. 1966, pb. 1970 (one acts); *The Two-Character Play*, pr. 1967, pb. 1969; *The Seven Descents of Myrtle*, pr., pb. 1968 (as *Kingdom of Earth*); *In the Bar of a Tokyo Hotel*, pr. 1969, pb. 1970; *Confessional*, pb. 1970; *Dragon Country*, pb. 1970 (collection); *The Theatre of Tennessee Williams*, pb. 1971-1981 (7 volumes); *Out Cry*, pr. 1971, pb. 1973 (revision of *The Two-Character Play*); *Small Craft Warnings*, pr., pb. 1972 (revision of *Confessional*); *Vieux Carré*, pr. 1977, pb. 1979; *A Lovely Sunday for Creve Coeur*, pr. 1979, pb. 1980; *Clothes for a Summer Hotel*, pr. 1980; *A House Not Meant to Stand*, pr. 1981.

Other literary forms

Besides his plays, Tennessee Williams produced short stories (many of which appear in collections), two volumes of poetry, a collection of essays, several screenplays, two novels, and a volume of memoirs.

Achievements

By common consensus, Williams ranks second—after Eugene O'Neill—among American dramatists. His major plays are performed all over the world, in spite of the fact that their usual locale, the American South, might seem too specialized for international appreciation. In this respect,

Williams may be compared to Anton Chekhov, who is in many ways his master and whose plays have also gained worldwide appreciation in spite of their intensely local ambience. Williams was unquestionably the most important American disciple of Chekhov—the most obvious resemblance lies in Williams' frequently superb use of symbol. His portrayal of frail characters in a cold and alien world is another immediate reminder of Chekhov. Williams' finest characterizations approach the archetypal; such figures as Blanche Dubois, Stanley Kowalski, Amanda Wingfield, and Big Daddy seem destined to join the great enduring characters of world theater. Like Chekhov's, Williams' characters are often repeated types—the gentleman caller, the helpless young woman, the witch-of-an-older-woman—but at their best, they are also highly individual and indeed unforgettable. Other characteristics which his plays share with Chekhov's are an apparent (though not actual) lack of structure, the use of settings and sound effects for atmospheric and thematic purposes, and poetic language. Yet what Williams drew from Chekhov he made distinctively his own. Williams was accused of pseudopoeticism, ineffective ambiguity, overly obvious use of symbolism, extremes of violence, and sentimentality, and at his worst, the blame is justified. At his best, however, he was one of the most dramatically effective and profoundly perceptive playwrights in the modern theater.

Biography

Tennessee Williams was born Thomas Lanier Williams in 1911 in Columbus, Mississippi, the son of Cornelius Coffin Williams and Edwina Dakin Williams. He lived his early years in the home of his grandparents, for whom he felt great affection. His grandfather was a minister, while Williams' father was a traveling salesman, apparently at home infrequently. In about 1919, his father accepted a nontraveling position at his firm's headquarters in St. Louis. The move from a more or less traditional Southern environment to a very different metropolitan world was extremely painful both for Williams and for his older sister, neither of whom ever really recovered from it.

The Glass Menagerie is clearly a play about the Williams family and its life in St. Louis, though Williams' *Memoirs* (1975) and other known facts make it clear that the play is by no means a precise transcription of actuality. On the other hand, *The Glass Menagerie* is by no means the only one of Williams' plays with biographical elements. His father, his mother, and his sister (who became mentally ill) are reflected in his characters in various plays. Williams' homosexuality, which he examines in some detail in his *Memoirs*, is also an important element in a number of his plays, including *A Streetcar Named Desire*, *Cat on a Hot Tin Roof*, and *Suddenly Last Summer*.

Williams attended the University of Missouri and Washington University and was graduated in 1938 from the University of Iowa. His adult life involved considerable wandering, with periods in such places as Key West, New Orleans, and New York. After various attempts at writing, some of which gained helpful recognition, Williams first won acclaim with *The Glass Menagerie*. Most of his plays from that point through *The Night of the Iguana* were successful, either on first production or later. He won Pulitzer Prizes for *A Streetcar Named Desire* and *Cat on a Hot Tin Roof*, and New York Drama Critics Circle Awards for those two and for *The Glass Menagerie* and *The Night of the Iguana*. The many plays that he wrote in the last twenty years of his life, however, achieved almost no success, either in the United States or abroad. Depending on one's point of view, either Williams' inspiration had run out, or he was writing a kind of play for which neither the public nor most critics are yet ready. Williams died in New York on February 25, 1983, having choked on a foreign object lodged in his throat.

Analysis

Tennessee Williams' *The Glass Menagerie* was regarded when first produced as highly unusual; one of the play's four characters serves as commentator as well as participant; the play itself represents the memories of the commentator years later, and hence, as he says, is not a depiction of actuality; its employment of symbolism is unusual; and in the very effective ending, a scrim descends in front of mother and daughter, so that by stage convention one can see but not hear them, with the result that both, but especially the mother, become much more moving and even archetypal. The play is also almost unique historically, in that it first opened in Chicago, came close to flopping before Chicago newspaper theater critics verbally whipped people into going, and then played successfully for months in Chicago before finally moving to equal success in New York.

One device which Williams provided for the play was quickly abandoned: a series of legends and images flashed on a screen indicating the central idea of scenes and parts of scenes. This device provides a triple insight into Williams: first, his skill at organizing scenes into meaningful wholes; second, his willingness to experiment, sometimes successfully, sometimes not; and third, his occasional tendency to spell out by external devices what a play itself makes clear.

The Glass Menagerie opens on a near-slum apartment, with Tom Wingfield setting the time (the Depression and Spanish-Civil-War 1930's); the play's method as memory, with its consequent use of music and symbol; and the names and relationships of the characters: Tom, his sister Laura, his mother Amanda, and an initially unnamed gentleman caller. A fifth character, Tom says, is his father, who, having deserted his family years before, appears only as a larger-than-life photograph over the mantel, which upon occasion—according to Williams' stage directions, but rarely in actual production—lights up.

Tom works in a shoe warehouse, writes poetry, and feels imprisoned by the knowledge that his hateful job is essential to the family's financial survival. Apparently, his one escape is to go to the movies. His relationship with his mother is a combination of love, admiration, frustration, and acrimony, with regular flare-ups and reconciliations. His relationship with his sister is one of love and sympathy. Laura is physically crippled as well as withdrawn from the outside world. She is psychologically unable (as one learns in scene 2) to attend business college, and lives in a world of her phonograph records and fragile glass animals. Amanda, a more complex character than the others, is the heart of the play: a constantly chattering woman who lives in part for her memories, perhaps exaggerated, of an idealized antebellum Southern girlhood and under the almost certain illusion that her son will amount to something and that her daughter will marry; yet she also lives very positively in the real world, aware of the family's poverty, keeping track of the bills, scratching for money by selling magazine subscriptions, taking advantage of her membership in the Daughters of the American Revolution. She is aware, too, that she must constantly remind her son of his responsibility to his family and that if her daughter is ever to marry, it must be through the machinations of mother and son. Yet, on the other hand, she is insufficiently aware of how her nagging and nostalgia drive her son to desperation and of how both son and daughter act upon occasion to protect her illusions and memories.

Scene 1 provides a general picture of this background; scene 2 is a confrontation between mother and daughter. Amanda has discovered that, rather than attending business college, Laura has simply left and returned home at the proper hours, spending her time walking in the park, visiting the zoo, or going to the movies. Amanda must accept the fact that a job for Laura is out of the question, and she therefore starts planning for the other alternative, marriage. The scene introduces a second symbol in a nickname that Laura says a boy gave her in high school: "Blue Roses." Roses are delicate and beautiful, like Laura and like her glass menagerie, but blue roses, like glass animals, have no real existence. Scene 3 shows Amanda trying unsuccessfully to sell magazine subscriptions on the telephone and ends in a shockingly violent quarrel between mother and son, concluding with Tom throwing his overcoat across the room in his rage and unintentionally destroying some of Laura's animals. One of Williams' most notable uses of lighting occurs in this scene. A pool of light envelops Laura as Tom and Amanda quarrel, so that one becomes aware without words that the devastating effect upon Laura is the scene's major point. Scene 4 shows Laura talking Tom into an apology and reconciliation, and Amanda taking advantage of Tom's remorse to persuade him to invite a friend from the warehouse home to dinner, in the hope that the "gentleman caller" will be attracted to Laura.

Scene 5 is long, building up suspense for Amanda and for the audience. Tom announces to his mother that he has invited a warehouse friend, Jim O'Connor, to dinner the next evening. Amanda, pleased but shocked at the suddenness of this new development, makes elaborate plans and has high expectations, but Tom tries to make her face the reality of Laura's physical and psychological limitations. Scene 6 shows the arrival of the guest and his attempt to accept Amanda's pathetic and almost comical Southern-belle behavior and elaborate "fussing," and Laura's almost pathological fright and consequent inability to come to the dinner table. Dialogue between Tom and Jim makes clear Jim's relative steadiness and definite if perhaps overly optimistic plans for a career. It also reveals Tom's near-failure at his job, his frustration over his family's situation, and his ripening determination to leave home: He has joined the merchant seamen's union instead of paying the light bill. The scene ends with the onset of a sharp summer storm. Laura, terrified, is on the sofa trying desperately not to cry; the others are at the dinner table and Tom is saying grace: a combination remarkable for its irony and pathos.

At the beginning of scene 7, the lights go out because of Tom's failure to pay the light bill, so the whole scene is played in candlelight. It is the climactic scene, and in it, Williams faced a problem faced by many modern playwrights: What kind of outcome does one choose, and by what means, in a situation where if things go one way they might seem incredible, and if they go the other, they might seem overly obvious? It is perhaps not a wholly soluble situation, but Williams did remarkably well in handling it. By Amanda's inevitable machinations after dinner, Jim and Laura are left alone. Jim—who has turned out to be the "Blue Roses" boy from high school, the boy with whom Laura was close to being in love—is a sympathetic and understanding person who, even in the short time they are alone together, manages to get more spontaneous and revealing conversation out of Laura than her family ever has, and even persuades her to dance. Clearly, here is a person who could bring to reality Amanda's seemingly impossible dreams, a man who could lead Laura into the real world (as he symbolically brought her glass unicorn into it by unintentionally breaking off its horn), a man who would make a good husband. For the play to end thus, however, would be out of accord with the facts of Williams' family life, with the tone of the whole play up to that point, and with modern audience's dislike of pat, happy endings in serious plays. Jim tells Laura that he is already engaged, a fact made more believable by Tom's unawareness of it. Laura's life is permanently in ruins. What might have happened will never happen. When Amanda learns the truth from Jim just before he leaves, the resulting quarrel with Tom confirms Tom in his plans to leave home permanently, abandoning his mother and sister to an apparently hopeless situation. Yet as he tells the audience—who are watching a soundless Amanda hovering over Laura to comfort her by candlelight—his flight has been unsuccessful. The memories haunt him; Laura haunts him. Speaking to her from a far-off world, he begs her to blow her candles out and thus obliterate the memory. She does, and the curtain falls.

Williams' next successful play, *A Streetcar Named Desire*, is generally regarded as his best. Initial reaction was mixed, but there would be little argument now that it is one of the most powerful plays in the modern theater. Like *The Glass Menagerie*, it concerns, primarily, a man and two women and a "gentleman caller." As in *The Glass Menagerie*, one of the women is very much aware of the contrast between the present and her Southern-aristocratic past; one woman (Stella) is practical if not always adequately aware, while the other (Blanche) lives partly in a dream world and teeters on the brink of psychosis; the gentleman caller could perhaps save the latter were circumstances somewhat different; and the play's single set is a slum apartment.

Yet these similarities only point up the sharp differences between the two plays. *A Streetcar Named Desire* is not a memory play; it is sharply naturalistic, with some use of expressionistic devices to point up Blanche's emotional difficulties. Blanche is not, as is Laura, a bond between the other two family members; she is, rather, an intolerable intruder who very nearly breaks up her sister's marriage. A more complex creation than anyone in *The Glass Menagerie*, she is fascinating, cultured, pathetic, vulgar, admirable, despicable: a woman who, unlike Amanda, cannot function adequately outside the safe, aristocratic world of the past, but who, like Amanda, can fight almost ferociously for what she wants, even when it is almost surely unattainable. Her opponent, Stella's husband, Stanley Kowalski, is also a much sharper figure than Tom Wingfield.

One of the major critical problems of *A Streetcar Named Desire* has been whose side one should be on in the battle between Blanche and Stanley. The answer may be one that some critics have been unable to accept: neither and both. Blanche's defense of culture, of the intellectual and aesthetic aspects of life, may be pathetic coming from one who has become a near-alcoholic prostitute, but it is nevertheless genuine, important, and valid. Life has dealt her devastating blows, to which she has had to respond alone; her sister has offered no help. Yet she herself is partly responsible for the horrible world in which she finds herself, and her attempts to find a haven from it are both pitiable and (because she is inadequately aware of the needs of others) repellent. Stanley, the sort of man who might, in later years, be called "macho," uncultured and uninterested in culture, capable (as Blanche also is in her own way) of violence, is nevertheless an intelligent man, a man who functions more capably than do any of his friends in the world in which he finds himself, a man who loves his wife and would be pathetically lost without her. Stanley would find any intrusion into his happy home intolerable, but he finds it doubly so when the intruder is a woman who stays on indefinitely, a woman with Blanche's affectations, her intolerance of any life-style other than that of her own childhood, her obvious dislike of her sister's marriage, and her corrupt sexual past which makes her attempts to attract one of Stanley's best friends more than Stanley can tolerate.

It is ironic that the play should end on a "happily-ever-after" note for Stanley and Stella (though surely Blanche can never be wholly forgotten), but this is life, not a model of life. Indeed, the life that both find, apparently, wholly satisfying and sufficient is itself a sort of irony. Stella has had to give up everything that Blanche believes in, everything from her own past, in order to accept it and welcome it.

The setting of *A Streetcar Named Desire* is the street and outdoor stairs of the building in which the Kowalskis live, and the interior of their two-room apartment. As scene 1 opens, neighbors are out front talking. Stanley and Mitch come in, prepared to go bowling. Stanley is carrying a package of meat. Stella comes out. Stanley throws the meat to her, and even the neighbors are amused at the symbolism. Stanley and Mitch proceed to the bowling alley, and Stella follows. Then Blanche comes around the corner, with her suitcase, dressed all in white—another ironic symbol—in a fashion appropriate to an upper-class garden party. In a stage direction, Williams compares her to a moth, and throughout the play, she fears the alluring but destructive light. She fears people seeing how she really looks. She fears facing the truth or having other people learn it. As she later says, she fibs because fibs are more pleasant; symbolically, she covers the overhead light bulb in the apartment with a paper lantern. Paper, indeed, is a recurring symbol throughout the play. For example, two of the melodies one hears from a distance are "Paper Doll" and "Paper Moon."

Blanche has never before seen Stella's apartment or met her sister's husband. To mark her progress through New Orleans to get to the apartment, Williams took advantage of actual New Orleans names (or former names); Blanche has to transfer from a streetcar called Desire to one called Cemeteries in order to arrive in the slum, called Elysian Fields. While the first of the streetcars gives the title to the play, Williams wisely makes use of the names only once after the opening scene. Blanche's progress in the play is from a wide range of desires (for culture, security, sex, and money) to a sort of living death, and while the slum may be an Elysian Fields for Stanley and Stella, it is a Tartarus for her. Williams also, like many earlier dramatists, gave some of his characters meaningful, and in this case, ironic names. Blanche DuBois is by no means a White Woods (though the name is a reminder of Anton Chekhov's *The Cherry Orchard*, 1904, and hence of the sort of life she has lost), and Stella is no Star. Such devices can be overdone: The name of their lost plantation, Belle Reve, may be an example.

A neighbor who owns the building lets Blanche into the apartment, and another neighbor goes for Stella. Blanche is alone. Like Laura on the night of the dinner, she is skittish, but her reaction is different: She spots a bottle of whiskey and takes a slug. Stella rushes in and, as is common in plays that begin with an arrival, the audience learns a great deal about both sisters as they talk—learns about their past, about Blanche's hostile attitude toward her environment, about the grim string of family illnesses and deaths, about the loss of the plantation. The sisters love each other but are obviously at odds in many respects. Blanche has been a schoolteacher, but one may doubt the reason she gives, a sort of sick leave, for being in New Orleans in early May while school at home is still in session. Stanley comes in with Mitch and another friend. Williams' description of him here, as the gaudy, dominant seed bearer, is famous. With Stella in the bathroom and his friends gone, Stanley encounters Blanche alone. He is surprised, but he tries to play the friendly host. Presently, he asks Blanche if she had not once been married. Blanche says that the boy died, promptly adding that she feels sick. The scene ends.

A prominent feature of this first scene, one that continues throughout the play, is the use of sound effects. There are sound effects in *The Glass Menagerie*, too, such as the glass menagerie thematic music and the music from the nearby dance hall, but in *A Streetcar Named Desire*, the sound effects are much more elaborate. As the curtain rises, one hears the voices of people passing and the sound of the "Blue Piano" in the nearby bar, and the piano becomes louder at appropriate points. Twice a cat screeches, frightening Blanche badly. As the subject of her husband and his death comes up, one hears—softly here but louder when Blanche reaches a crisis—the music of a polka, clearly a sound inside Blanche's head and hence an expressionistic device. At the end of scene 2, in which Blanche and Stanley have had a conversation which is both hostile and covertly sexual, a tamale vendor is heard calling "Red-hot!" Similar effects, notably of trains roaring past, occur throughout the play.

Scene 2 begins with a dialogue between Stanley and Stella. It is the next evening. Stella is taking Blanche out to dinner in order not to interfere with the poker night Stanley has planned. Stanley learns of the loss of the plantation and is angry, especially after he examines Blanche's trunk and finds it full of expensive clothes and furs. Stella has postponed telling Blanche that she is pregnant. Blanche enters and, seeing the situation, sends Stella on an errand so that she can have it out with Stanley. Stanley must accept the fact that the plantation has been lost because it was heavily mortgaged, and the mortgage payments could not be made. Blanche grows playful with him, and Stanley implies that she is being deliberately provocative. Stanley comes across Blanche's love letters from her dead husband, and Blanche becomes almost hysterical. Stanley tells Blanche of the coming baby. The men begin to arrive for poker. Stella returns and leads Blanche away.

Scene 3, entitled "The Poker Night," opens upon a garish and, Williams says, Van Gogh-like view of Stanley and his three friends playing poker. Stanley has had too much to drink and is becoming verbally violent. The women return from their evening out. Blanche encounters Mitch at the bathroom door—she wants to take another of her endless hot baths—and they are clearly attracted to each other. Stanley, hating the presence of women during a poker game, becomes physically violent, and (offstage) hits Stella. The other men, who are familiar with this behavior but feel great affection for Stanley, subdue him and leave. Blanche, horrified, has taken Stella to the upstairs apartment. Stanley realizes what has happened, sobs, and screams for Stella, who presently joins him on the outside stairs. They fall into a sexual embrace, and he carries her inside. Clearly, this series of events has occurred before; clearly, this is the usual outcome, and is one of the attractions which Stanley has for Stella. Blanche comes down the stairs, even more horrified, and Mitch returns and comforts her.

In scene 4, Blanche returns from upstairs the next morning and is shocked to learn that Stella accepts all that has happened and wants no change in her marital situation. With some justice, Blanche describes Stanley as an uncultured animal in a world where culture is essential—a speech which Stanley overhears. He comes in, and to Blanche's horror, Stella embraces him. It is in this scene that Blanche, uselessly and desperately, first thinks of an old boyfriend, now rich, as a source of rescue from her plight, a futile idea which she develops and tries harder and harder to believe in as her plight worsens. Scene 5 contains an example of Williams' occasionally excessive irony: Stanley asks Blanche her astrological sign, and it turns out that his is Capricorn and hers is Virgo. The major import of the scene is that Stanley confronts Blanche with stories he has heard about her life back home—and afterward Blanche admits to Stella that some of them are true. Blanche and Stella agree that marrying Mitch is the solution to Blanche's problem and Blanche is left alone. A young newsboy comes to collect money, and Blanche comes very close to trying, consciously and cynically, to seduce him. Clearly, sex, like alcohol, has been both a cause of and a response to her situation. Mitch arrives for a date, holding a bunch of roses, and the scene ends. Scene 6 opens with the return of the two from their date. Its major import is Blanche's telling Mitch about her dead husband, whom she encountered one evening in an embrace with an older man. Later that evening, while they were dancing to the polka she now keeps hearing, Blanche, unable to stop herself, told him he disgusted her. A few minutes later, he went outside and shot himself. Telling the story is a catharsis for Blanche and deeply enlists Mitch's sympathy. They are in each other's arms, and he suggests the possibility of marriage.

In scene 7, several months later, with Blanche still there and with the marriage idea apparently no further advanced, Stanley tells Stella of his now detailed and verified knowledge of Blanche's sordid sexual past, including her having seduced a seventeen-year-old student. As a result of this last action, Blanche lost her job, and Stanley, as he explains to Stella, has told Mitch the whole story. Stella is horrified, both at the facts themselves and at their revelation to Mitch. It is Blanche's birthday, there is a birthday cake, and Mitch has been invited. Scene 8 shows the women's mounting distress as Mitch fails to show up for the party; Stanley gives Blanche a "birthday present," a bus ticket back home for the following Tuesday; he makes it clear that Blanche's presence all this time has been almost too much to endure. Stella develops labor pains and leaves with Stanley for the hospital. Scene 9, later that evening, shows Mitch coming in with very changed intentions, tearing the paper lantern off and turning on the light to see Blanche plainly for the first time, telling her she is not clean enough to take home to his mother, and trying to get her to bed. She reacts violently, and he runs out.

In scene 10, the climactic scene, Stanley comes back. Blanche has been drinking and is desperately upset. With Stanley, she tries to retreat into fanciful illusions—Mitch has returned and apologized, her rich boyfriend has invited her on a Caribbean tour. Stanley exposes her lies, and her desperation grows, as indicated by lurid, darting shadows and other expressionistic devices. Their confrontation reaches a climax, and, after she tries to resist, he carries her off to bed. In scene 11, some weeks later, one learns that Blanche has told Stella that Stanley raped her, that Stella must believe that the rape is merely one of Blanche's psychotic illusions if her life with Stanley is to survive, and that Stella has made arrangements to place Blanche in a state institution. A doctor and nurse come to get her. Blanche is terrified. The nurse is cold and almost brutal, but the doctor gains Blanche's confidence by playing the role of a gentleman, and she leaves on his arm, clearly feeling that she has found what she has been seeking, a man to protect her. All this occurs while another poker game is in progress. The play ends with Stella in Stanley's arms, and with one of the other men announcing, "This game is seven-card stud."

The brutes have won, and Stella has permanently denied her heritage, yet one must remember that the "brutes" are not without redeeming qualities. Stanley has displayed intense loyalty to his friends, genuine love for his wife, and a variety of insecurities beneath his aggressive manner. The other men have displayed loyalty to Stanley, and Mitch has shown much sympathy and understanding. As Blanche has said early in the play, Stanley may be just what their bloodline needs, and that point is emphasized when, near the end of the final scene, the upstairs neighbor hands Stella her baby. Life must go on; perhaps the next generation will do better; but long before the play opens, life has destroyed a potentially fine and sensitive woman.

Of Williams' four plays analyzed here, *Cat on a Hot Tin Roof*, his next big success, is the only one which falls into a special Williams category: plays which at some stage or stages have been heavily revised. Williams has said that, because of advice from Elia Kazan, the director of the first Broadway production, he made changes in the third act. The changes include the appearance of one of the main characters, Big Daddy, who had been in the second act only, and adjustments changing the bare possibility of an affirmative ending to a probability. Revisions of considerably greater scope than this were made by Williams in other plays, including plays that were completely rewritten long after their original productions (*Summer and Smoke* into *The Eccentricities of a Nightingale*, and *Battle of Angels* into *Orpheus Descending*).

Cat on a Hot Tin Roof is famous for its somewhat expressionistic set, the bedroom of Brick and Margaret (Maggie) Pollitt. The two major pieces of furniture, both with symbolic value, are a large double bed and a combination radio-phonograph-television-liquor cabinet. The walls are to disappear into air at the top, and the set is to be roofed by the sky, as though to suggest that the action of the play is representative of universal human experience. The powerful expressionistic psychology of the play recalls the theater of August Strindberg, but *Cat on a Hot Tin Roof* is deeply embedded in revealed reality, with one major exception: One does not know the truth, one cannot know the truth, behind the crucial relationship between Brick and his dead friend Skipper; the degree (if any) of Brick's responsibility for Skipper's decline and death; or of Maggie's responsibility.

The bedroom, outside of which is a gallery running the length of the house, is in the plantation mansion of Brick's father, Big Daddy, on his twenty-eight-thousand-acre estate in the Mississippi delta. The first act is largely a monologue by Maggie, talking to a mostly inattentive and uninterested Brick, and interrupted only by brief appearances of Brick's mother, Big Mama, and his sister-in-law Mae and two of her five, soon to be six, children. Maggie, like Amanda and Blanche before her, is a loquacious and desperate woman who may be fighting for the impossible; unlike her predecessors, she lives entirely in the present and without major illusions, and hence fights more realistically. She wants Brick to return to her bed: She is a cat on a hot tin roof, sexually desperate but interested only in her husband. As the largely one-sided conversation continues, one learns the circumstances underlying Brick's loss of interest in her. Maggie tells Brick the news that his father is dying of cancer. Brick and Maggie have been living in the house for several months. Formerly an important athlete, a professional football player, and then a sports announcer, he has given up everything and lapsed into heavy drinking. He is on a crutch, having broken his ankle attempting, while drunk the previous night, to jump hurdles on the high school athletic field. Mae and her husband, Brick's older brother Gooper, a lawyer in Memphis, are visiting in hopes, as Maggie correctly guesses, of Big Daddy's signing a will in Gooper's favor, because, while Brick is Big Daddy's favorite, he will want the estate to go to a son who has offspring. Maggie is from a society background in Nashville, though her immediate family had been poor because of her father's alcoholism. Big Daddy himself is a Mississippi redneck who has worked his way to great wealth. Brick and Maggie met as students at the University of Mississippi. Formerly, according to Maggie, an excellent lover, Brick has made Maggie agree that they will stay together only if she leaves him alone. Unable to bear the frustration, Maggie is ready to break the agreement and fight to get Brick back.

The roots of Brick and Maggie's conflict are fitfully revealed when Maggie begins to speak of Skipper, their dead friend, any mention of whom greatly upsets Brick. In Maggie's version of the story, from college on, Brick's greatest loyalty was to Skipper. She says that Brick's standards of love and friendship were so pure as to have been frustrating to both Skipper and Maggie; that on an out-of-town football weekend when Brick had been injured and could not go, Maggie and Skipper, out of their common frustration, went to bed together; that Skipper could not perform, and that Maggie therefore, but in no condemnatory sense, assumed that he was unconsciously homosexual, though she believes that Brick is not. Maggie told Skipper that he was actually in love with her husband, and she now believes that it was this revelation which prompted Skipper to turn to liquor and drugs, leading to his death. Maggie now tells Brick that she has been examined by a gynecologist, that she is capable of bearing children, and that it is the right time of the month to conceive. Brick asks how it is going to happen when he finds her repellent. She says that that is a problem to be solved.

Act 2 is famous for consisting almost entirely of a remarkably effective and revealing dialogue between Brick and Big Daddy. The act opens, however, with the whole family there, as well as their minister, the Reverend Mr. Tooker. The minister is there ostensibly because of Big Daddy's birthday, and there is to be cake and champagne. From the family's point of view, he is also there because after the birthday party (which is as big a failure as Blanche's), they are going to tell Big Mama the truth about Big Daddy's cancer, and they want his help in the crisis. From his own point of view, he is there to hint at a contribution, either now or in Big Daddy's will or both, for ornamentation for his church. He is totally useless in the crisis and is therefore, in spite of Williams' deep affection for his own minister grandfather, typical of Williams' ministers.

The birthday party will take place in Brick and Maggie's bedroom because Brick is on a crutch: an ingenious pretext for limiting the play's action to a single setting. Big Daddy is one of Williams' most complex characters, and the contradictions in his nature are never fully examined, any more than they are with Blanche, because, as Williams says in a stage direction in act 2, any truly drawn characters will retain some mystery. Big Daddy is a loud, vulgar, apparently insensitive man who was originally a workman on the estate, then owned by a pair of homosexual men. He is now in a position of power and worth many millions. Desperately afraid to show any real feelings, he pretends to dislike his whole family, although in the case of Gooper and Mae and their children, the dislike is genuine and deep. One never learns his real attitude toward Maggie. Near the end of his talk with Brick, with great difficulty, Big Daddy expresses the love he has for him. His real attitude toward Big Mama remains uncertain. He has always teased her, made gross fun of her, and in his ostensibly frank conversation with Brick, he says that he has always disliked her, even in bed. He is clearly moved, however, when at the end of the family-scene part of the act, she, who is in her own way both as gross and as vulnerable as he, yells that she has always loved him. The conversation with Brick reveals his sensitivity in another direction: his distress over the intense poverty he has seen while traveling abroad and particularly an instance in Morocco when he saw a very small child being used as a procurer.

The motivation for the long father-and-son talk is that Big Daddy, hugely relieved at having been told, falsely, that he does not have cancer, wants to find out why Brick has given up working, given up Maggie (as everyone knows, because Gooper and Mae have listened in their bedroom next door), and turned to heavy drinking. Apparently, he has attempted frank talks with Brick in the past, with no success, even though each clearly loves and respects the other, and, because of Brick's lack of interest and determined reticence, it would appear that that is how the conversation is going now. Having just gone through a severe life crisis himself, however, Big Daddy is determined to help his son. He gets the beginning of an answer out of Brick by taking away his crutch so he cannot get at his liquor. Brick's answer is that he is disgusted with the world's "mendacity." Finding that answer insufficient, Big Daddy finally brings himself to make the climactic statement that the problem began when Skipper died; he adds that Gooper and Mae think the Brick-Skipper relationship was not "normal." Brick, at last unable to maintain his detachment, is furious. In a stage direction, Williams says that Skipper died to disavow the idea that there was any sexual feeling in the friendship, but whether Skipper did have such feelings is necessarily left uncertain. Brick himself, in his outrage, makes painfully clear that the very idea of homosexuality disgusts him. The relationship, he believes, was simply an unusually profound friendship, though he is finally forced to grant the likelihood that, from Skipper's point of view, though emphatically not his own, sexual love existed. (Whether Brick is himself bisexual is left uncertain, but it is clear that he could not face this idea if it were true.) He grants that liquor has been his refuge from a fact that Big Daddy (who has no prejudice against homosexuals) makes him face: that Brick's unwillingness to believe in the possibility of a homosexual reaction in Skipper, and to help Skipper recognize and accept it, is the major cause of Skipper's death. In a statement strongly reminiscent of some situations in the plays of O'Neill, Brick says that there are only two ways out: liquor and death. Liquor is his way, death was Skipper's. Then, in a state of strong emotional upheaval, Brick makes his father face the truth as his father has made him face it: He is dying of cancer. There is justice in Brick's remark that friends—and he and his father are friends—tell each other the truth, because the truth needs to be faced. As the act ends, Big Daddy is screaming at the liars who had kept the truth from him.

In the original version, as act 3 opens, the family and the Reverend Mr. Tooker enter. Big Daddy, one must assume, has gone to his bedroom to face his situation alone. The purpose of the gathering is to have the doctor, who presently comes in with Maggie, tell Big Mama the truth. Brick is in and out during the scene, but—in spite of appeals from Maggie and from Big Mama—he remains wholly aloof and is still drinking. If the shock of his conversation with Big Daddy is going to have an effect, it has not yet done so. After much hesitation, the doctor tells Big Mama the truth, to which she reacts with the expected horror. He tells her that Big Daddy's pain will soon become so severe as to require morphine injections, and he leaves a package. Big Mama wants comfort only from Brick, not from Gooper. The Reverend Mr. Tooker leaves promptly, and the doctor soon follows. Gooper tries to get Big Mama to agree to a plan he has drawn up to take over the estate as trustee. Big Mama will have it run by nobody but Brick, whom she calls her only son. She remarks what a comfort it would be to Big Daddy if Brick and Maggie had a child. Maggie announces that she is pregnant. Whether this lie is planned or spontaneous, one has no way of knowing, but Brick does not deny it. Gooper and Mae, whose behavior throughout the scene has been despicable, are shocked and incredulous. Big Mama has run out to tell Big Daddy the happy news. Gooper and Mae soon follow, but just before they go, a loud cry of agony fills the house: Big Daddy is feeling the pain the doctor has predicted. Maggie and Brick are left alone. Maggie thanks Brick for his silence. Brick feels the "click" that results from enough liquor and that gives him peace, and he goes out on the gallery, singing. Maggie has a sudden inspiration and takes all the liquor out of the room. When Brick comes in she tells him what she has done, says she is in control, and declares that she will not return the liquor until he has gone to bed with her. He grabs for his crutch, but she is quicker, and she throws the crutch off the gallery to the ground. Big Mama rushes in, almost hysterical, to get the package of morphine. Maggie reiterates that she is in charge and tells Brick she loves him. Brick, in the last speech of the play, says exactly what Big Daddy had said earlier when Big Mama said she loved him: "Wouldn't it be funny if that was true." Apparently, he has yielded. The curtain falls.

The ending is dramatically effective, but in a different way from Williams' earlier endings. *The Glass Menagerie*'s ending is final in one way, since it is all in the past, and *A Streetcar Named Desire*'s in another, since Blanche is escorted off, and Stanley and Stella are reconciled. In *Cat on a Hot Tin Roof*, one can only assume that Brick will "perform," that the result will be a pregnancy, and that the eventual effect of Maggie's use of force and of Big Daddy's shock tactics may be Brick's return to normality. Even in its original form, as here described, that is what the ending suggests, and Williams' instinct to leave an element of uncertainty seems correct.

The Night of the Iguana was Williams' next (and last) unmistakably successful play, after a series of plays of varying degrees of stage success but with more or less serious flaws. Unlike all of his earlier plays except *Camino Real*, *The Night of the Iguana* is set outside the United States and does not in any significant sense concern Southerners. It also differs from almost all the plays after *The Glass Menagerie* in being free of serious violence. Besides *A Streetcar Named Desire*, with the suicide of Blanche's husband, Williams had used castration, murder by blowtorch, death by cannibalism, and other extreme acts of violence, prompting the accusation, at times with some justice, of sensationalism.

The Night of the Iguana takes place on the veranda of a third-rate, isolated hotel in Mexico, in a rain forest high above the Pacific. Like several other Williams plays, it grew out of what was originally a short story. Unlike any of the others, except possibly the expressionistic *Camino Real*, its ending is affirmative, suggesting hope not only for the three major characters but for humanity in general. The central male character, a minister who has been locked out of his church because of fornication and what was regarded as an atheistic sermon, may be prepared in the end for a life of self-sacrifice—which may turn out to be richly fulfilling, since the woman to whom he may "sacrifice" himself is a woman who knows what genuine love means. The other woman, who is the central character, is Blanche's opposite: a New Englander instead of a quintessential Southerner, she is in no sense handicapped by the past; she retains a sense of humor; she sees things clearly; and she accepts her situation. She is tied to an elderly relative in a wheelchair but she is not bitter about it; the relative is neither a frustration nor an embarrassment. Finally, she uses whatever weapons she must to keep her grandfather and herself able, if sometimes only barely, to survive. Without being an obviously fierce fighter like Amanda, Blanche, or Maggie, she has come to terms with her circumstances and has prevailed. She is the first and only Williams character to do so, a new conception in his gallery of characters.

At the opening of act 1, Lawrence Shannon, the ex-minister, arrives at the hotel with a busload of female teachers and students on a Mexican tour for which he is the guide. He is in one of his periodic emotional breakdowns and has chosen to bring his tour party to this hotel in violation of the itinerary in order to get emotional support from his friends, the couple who run the hotel. It turns out, however, that the husband has recently drowned. The wife, now the sole owner, the brassy Maxine Faulk, clearly wants Shannon as a lover and may well be genuinely in love with him. Throughout the tour, and indeed on some previous tours, Shannon has ignored the announced tour route and facilities, leading the group where he chooses. He has also, and not for the first time, allowed himself to be seduced by a seventeen-year-old girl. The women are in a state of rebellion. Their leader, another of Williams' homosexuals, though an unimportant one, knows of the sexual liaison and later in the play reports the whole story to the tour company for which Shannon works, with the result that in act 3, he is replaced on the spot with another guide. He has the key to the tour bus, however, and refuses to relinquish it, so the passengers (most of whom never come up to the hotel) are helpless.

Shannon's situation is in some ways similar to, although milder than, Blanche's: He was pushed out of the church as Blanche was dismissed as a teacher; he is seriously distraught, and confused in his sexual orientation, he is attracted to young girls, as Blanche was to boys. Presently, there is another arrival at the hotel, Hannah Jelkes and her ninety-seven-year-old grandfather, whom she calls Nonno. She has pushed him up the hill and through the forest in his wheelchair. They are without funds, and she is desperate for a place for them to stay. Maxine, for all her rough exterior, cannot turn them away in their plight, but she is upset over their literal pennilessness. She is also upset over Hannah's desire to earn money, as she has done all over the world, by passing through hotel dining rooms so that, upon request, her grandfather may recite his poetry or she may make sketches of guests. The only other guests at the hotel, since it is the off-season, are a group of Nazis, whose presence in the play may seem puzzling, since they have nothing to do with the plot. They are in and out at various points, a raucous group, delighted with radio news of German successes in bombing Britain. Totally without feeling, they are probably in the play for contrast; their lack of feeling contrasts with Hannah's genuine sympathy for anything human except unkindness, with Nonno's sensitive artistry as a recognized minor poet, with Maxine's apparent ability to love, and with the growing evidence, as the play develops, of Shannon's potential for overcoming his self-centered and almost uncontrollable desperation.

The major focus in both act 2 and act 3 is on the dialogues between Hannah and Shannon, which, in revelation of character and effect on character, resemble the dialogue between Big Daddy and Brick. Indeed, act 2 and act 3 are so intertwined as to make it difficult to separate them. One learns about Hannah's past, about her having suffered from emotional problems similar to Shannon's, from which she recovered by sheer determination. In a sense, she has sacrificed her life to caring for her grandfather; she feels only pride and love for him, and concern over his age, his periods of senile haziness, and his inability to finish his first poem in twenty years. In a moment of symbolism, one sees that she is capable of lighting a candle in the wind. Seeking for God, she has so far found Him only in human faces. In sharp contrast, Shannon's view of the world is summed up in a memory of having seen starving persons searching through piles of excrement for bits of undigested food. Hannah's insight into Shannon's problem is deep, and she is adept in techniques, from sympathy to shock, to help bring him out of his somewhat self-indulgent despair. At one point in act 2, the Mexican boys who work for Maxine bring in an iguana and tie it to a post, planning to fatten it and eat it: a normal occurrence in their world. It escapes once and is recaptured. Maxine threatens to evict Hannah and Nonno but relents when Hannah makes her understand that she is not a rival for Shannon. Nonno provides embarrassing evidence of his intermittent senility. The act ends in the early evening with a heavy thunderstorm.

Early in act 3, later in the evening, Shannon's replacement arrives, and the bus key is taken from him by force. Shannon, growing more and more hysterical, tries to pull the gold cross from his neck and threatens to go down to the ocean and swim straight out to sea until he drowns. Maxine and her Mexican boys tie him in the hammock. Maxine tells Hannah that Shannon's behavior is essentially histrionic, and Hannah soon sees for herself that he is deriving a masochistic pleasure from the situation. She tells him, in a key speech, that he is enjoying an ersatz crucifixion, thus denying Shannon the role of Christ-figure which Williams had tried unsuccessfully to give his central male characters in certain earlier plays. Hannah as model and as psychiatrist begins to have an effect. He releases himself from the ropes, as she has told him all along he is able to do, and their conversation reveals enough about Hannah's past to make him admire her stamina, her hard-won stability, and her love of humanity, and to make him want, perhaps, to emulate her. He learns of the minimal, pathetic encounters she has had with male sexuality—in one instance, a man with a fetish for women's undergarments—and while they in no way disgusted her, since nothing does except cruelty, she is nevertheless a permanent virgin who is comfortable with her virginity. Shannon suggests that they should travel together, platonically. She rightly refuses, and puts in his mind the idea that Maxine needs him, as Nonno needs her, and that he needs to be needed in order to achieve stability. Hannah persuades Shannon to free the iguana, which is, as he has been, "at the end of its rope." Nonno wheels himself out of his room, shouting that he has finished his poem. He reads it, and they find it moving. Maxine persuades Shannon to stay with her permanently, though Williams seems undecided as to whether one should regard Shannon's acquiescence as a sacrifice. In any case, however, it is evidence that he may no longer be sexually askew, and that he may be capable of living a life that has some kind of meaning. The change is quicker than the change which may occur in Brick in *Cat on a Hot Tin Roof*, though both plays take place in a few hours, and though Williams says in a stage direction in *Cat on a Hot Tin Roof* that even if events have occurred which will result in changing a person, the change will not occur quickly. Perhaps one may say that the difference is justified in that Big Daddy, for all his love and honesty, is no Hannah—there are very few Hannahs in the world. Hannah's own trials are not over: After Maxine and Shannon go off together, as Hannah prepares to take Nonno back to his room, he quietly dies. Hannah is left alone. No one needs her any more. The curtain falls.

The play is notable for its atmosphere, its memorable characters, its compassion, its hard-won optimism. The ending of *The Glass Menagerie* is devastating. The ending of *A Streetcar Named Desire* may represent the best solution for Blanche and happiness for Stanley and Stella, but there is nevertheless a sense in which all three are victims. In *Cat on a Hot Tin Roof*, it is possible that the future will bring happiness to Brick and Maggie, but it is far from certain; the future means a horrible death from cancer for Big Daddy, a life deprived of much of its meaning for Big Mama, and wholly meaningless and despicable lives for Gooper and Mae. The contrast with *The Night of the Iguana* is enormous. With his poem, Nonno has at last, like his granddaughter, "prevailed," and one must assume that he is ready for death, a death which, in contrast to Big Daddy's, is swift and peaceful. Maxine is no longer alone and has someone to love. Shannon seems on the road to psychological recovery and a useful and satisfying life. Hannah, to be sure, is left alone, as Tom and Blanche are alone in their worlds, but the contrast between her and those others is sharp and unmistakable. She has faced previous crises, survived, prevailed. Happy endings in modern drama are rarely successful at a serious level. In *The Night of the Iguana*, Williams wrote that rare modern dramatic work: a memorable, affirmative play in which the affirmation applies to all the major characters and in which the affirmation is believable.

Other major works

NOVELS: *The Roman Spring of Mrs. Stone*, 1950; *Moise and the World of Reason*, 1975.

SHORT FICTION: *One Arm and Other Stories*, 1948; *Hard Candy: A Book of Stories*, 1954; *The Knightly Quest: A Novella and Four Short Stories*, 1967; *Eight Mortal Ladies Possessed: A Book of Stories*, 1974; *Collected Stories*, 1985.

POETRY: *In the Winter of Cities*, 1956; *Androgyne, Mon Amour*, 1977.

NONFICTION: *Memoirs*, 1975; *Where I Love: Selected Essays*, 1978.

SCREENPLAYS: *The Glass Menagerie*, 1950 (with Peter Berneis); *A Streetcar Named Desire*, 1951 (with Oscar Saul); *The Rose Tattoo*, 1955 (with Hal Kanter); *Baby Doll*, 1956; *The Fugitive Kind*, 1960 (with Meade Roberts, based on *Orpheus Descending*); *Suddenly Last Summer*, 1960 (with Gore Vidal); *Stopped Rocking and Other Screenplays*, 1984.

Bibliography

Bloom, Harold, ed. *Tennessee Williams.* New York: Chelsea House, 1987. Part of the Modern Critical Views series, this collection of critical essays carries an introduction by Bloom that places Williams in the dramatic canon of American drama and within the psychological company of Hart Crane and Arthur Rimbaud. Authors in this collection take traditional thematic and historical approaches, noting Williams' "grotesques," his morality, his irony, his work in the "middle years," and the mythical qualities in his situations and characters.

Rader, Dotson. *Tennessee: Cry of the Heart.* Garden City, N.Y.: Doubleday, 1985. The title and opening, explaining the author's first encounter with a recently "flipped out" Williams, give a flavor to this chatty biography. While it does not have the virtue of notes or a scholarly biography, it does have the appeal of a firsthand, fascinating account, filled with gossip and inside information, to be taken for what it is worth.

Spoto, Donald. *The Kindness of Strangers: The Life of Tennessee Williams.* Boston: Little, Brown, 1985. Spoto's literary biography begins with a description of Williams' parents, Cornelius and Edwina. Beginning with early separation, the Williams couple gave their children a stormy beginning in life. Spoto's lively chronicle details in ten chapters Williams' encounters with such diverse influences as the Group Theatre, Frieda and D. H. Lawrence, Senator Joseph R. McCarthy, Fidel Castro, Hollywood stars, and the homosexual and drug subcultures of Key West. Forty-two pages of notes, bibliography, and index make this study a valuable resource for further scholarship.

Williams, Dakin, and Shepherd Mead. *Tennessee Williams: An Intimate Biography.* New York: Arbor House, 1983. One of the more bizarre duos in biographical writing, Williams (Tennessee's brother) and Mead (Tennessee's childhood friend) produce a credible biography in a highly readable, well-indexed work. Their account of the playwright also helps to capture his almost schizophrenic nature. A solid index and extensive research assist the serious scholar and general reader.

Williams, Tennessee. *Tennessee Williams' Letters to Donald Windham, 1940-1965.* Edited by Donald Windham. New York: Holt, Rinehart and Winston, 1977. This extraordinary collection of letters contains extensive notes by Windham, as well as a nine-page index that reads like a literary, social, and cultural *Who's Who.* The value of this work is not only in its points of comparison with biographical works but also in its rare capturing of the ebb and flow of professional and personal relationships, as recorded in personal correspondence.

Jacob H. Adler
(Revised by *Rebecca Bell-Metereau*)

DAVID WILLIAMSON

Born: Melbourne, Australia; February 24, 1942

Principal drama

The Removalists, pr. 1971, pb. 1972; *Don's Party*, pr. 1971, pb. 1973; *Three Plays*, pb. 1974 (includes *The Coming of Stork*, pr. 1970; *Jugglers Three*, pr. 1972; *What If You Died Tomorrow*, pr. 1973); *The Department*, pr. 1974, pb. 1975; *A Handful of Friends*, pr., pb. 1976; *The Club*, pr. 1977, pb. 1978 (U.S. title, *Players*); *Travelling North*, pr. 1979, pb. 1980; *Celluloid Heroes*, pr. 1980; *The Perfectionist*, pr. 1982, pb. 1983; *Sons of Cain*, pr., pb. 1985; *Collected Plays*, pb. 1986 (includes *The Removalists*, *Don's Party*, and the titles in *Three Plays*); *Emerald City*, pr., pb. 1987; *Top Silk*, pr., pb. 1989; *Siren*, pr. 1990, pb. 1991; *Money and Friends*, pr., pb. 1992.

Other literary forms

David Williamson has written numerous screenplays for Australian and American films. Some he has adapted from his own work: *Stork* (1971), *The Removalists* (1974), *Don's Party* (1976), and *The Club* (1980). Others are original: *Petersen* (1974), *Eliza Frazer* (1976), *Partners* (1981), and *Pharlap* (1984). Two screenplays known internationally are *Gallipoli* (1981) and *The Year of Living Dangerously* (1982). He has also written the screenplay for *A Dangerous Life* (1988), the television miniseries *The Four-Minute Mile* (1988), and (with Kristin Williamson) two other Australian-produced television miniseries, *The Last Bastion* (1984) and *Princess Kate* (1988).

Achievements

Early in his career, Williamson gained recognition of the kind often considered most important to an Australian artist: the British George Devine Award in 1972 for his second play, *The Removalists*, while it was still onstage in Sydney. In 1973, the London *Evening Standard* conferred upon him the Most Promising Playwright Award for the London production of *The Removalists.*

At home, Williamson received in 1972 his first two "Awgies" (Australian Writers Guild Award) for *The Removalists*; in the next few years, he took additional Awgies for *Don's Party*, *The Club*, and *Travelling North*, as well as the Eric Award from Melbourne Critics for *Jugglers Three* in 1974. Williamson has won the Australian Film Institute Script Award three times, for *Petersen*, *Don's Party*, and *Gallipoli.* He has also been active in various Australian arts organizations, including the Australian Writers Guild, the Australia Council, and the Theatre Board of the Council. In 1988, he received an honorary doctorate from the University of Sydney.

Those early honors marking the achievements of so young a playwright must have been gratifying and encouraging to Williamson as he battled against the established Australian theater. He comments on that battle's victorious outcome in an article that appeared in *Meanjin* (1974), a journal that has long challenged Australia's traditional approach to art. Although entitled "*The Removalists:* A Conjunction of Limitations," the article includes, in addition to commentary on the play, some frank observations regarding the state of Australian theater when Williamson and his contemporaries decided that the country needed and deserved its own dramatic literature.

Theater in Australia, Williamson noted, has always flourished but only as an import business that considered its sole purpose the presentation of what was good from Europe and that would therefore educate and uplift "the barbarous beer-swilling populace" of Australia by showing them Europe's "more refined and sensitive values." Until the early 1970's, Williamson pointed out, plays by Australians about Australians held low priority, relegated as they were to coffeehouse theaters and small audiences. Such had been the fate of his first works.

By 1974, however, attitudes had changed so wholly that he could write: "As far as drama is concerned, the battle has been won." General audiences and the administrators of the large state-subsidized theaters had recognized at last the need to explore Australia on the stage and to support those dramatic explorations. Not many years earlier, when plays such as Williamson's *The Coming of Stork* were enjoying "short weekend seasons" in small theaters before meager audiences, so happy a denouement to such a long-standing conflict must have seemed unlikely. The work of Williamson and other playwrights who came into their own during the late 1960's and early 1970's now holds a secure place in Australian theatrical repertory. That their work has been made available in reader's editions also shows that the literary value of these dramas is appreciated and recognized.

Williamson's plays, especially, have gained acceptance abroad, even though each one stands firmly rooted in the Australian experience. Possibly, then, his greatest achievement lies in the talent to make universal that experience peculiar to Australians.

Biography

On the surface, David Keith Williamson's family background and early life hold little to suggest that he would someday help to revolutionize the Australian theater and in so doing emerge as one of Australia's major playwrights. Born in Melbourne in 1942, during the dark days of wartime Australia, this son of a bank official was reared and received his education for the most part in the small town of Victoria, northeast of Melbourne. He was graduated from Monash University in 1964 with an engineering degree, then took postgraduate work in psychology at the University of Melbourne. From 1966 until 1972, he lectured on thermodynamics and social psychology at Swinburne College of Technology. He married Carol Cranby in 1965, but seven years later he ended both his marriage and his teaching career. He then set out determined to fulfill his promise as a writer. In 1974, he remarried, this time to a journalist, Kristin Green; they moved to Birchgrove, an inner Harborside suburb of Sydney.

Although concentrating on engineering and psychology, Williamson showed interest in the theater during his university years, writing for campus production several satiric reviews and a short play. His first full-length work, *The Coming of Stork*, was produced in 1970 for "a short weekend season" by the Café La Mama Theatre in Melbourne. After this modest start, Williamson established himself the following year as a fresh and original voice in Australian theater when two more of his plays had successful seasons in Melbourne and Sydney. Both written in 1971, these two plays, *The Removalists* and *Don's Party*, moved in 1973 to London and New York, where they received attention rarely accorded Australian theatrical offerings, at least not since the 1950's, when Ray Lawler's steamy drama *Summer of the Seventeenth Doll* (pr. 1955) was produced; Lawler's account of Australian canecutters and barmaids in a Melbourne slum bore little resemblance, however, to the sophisticated and infinitely more universal plays Williamson sent abroad.

At home, Williamson continued to produce new work. That he was commissioned in 1973 to write a play to open the Drama Theatre of the new Sydney Opera House shows how far he had come in three years, from out-of-the-way coffeehouse and storefront theaters such as Café La Mama and The Pram Factory to the establishment's grand center of culture.

Not to be outdone, the officials of the South Australian Theatre Company in Adelaide commissioned a Williamson work to open the Playhouse at the new Adelaide Festival Centre in 1974; Williamson wrote *The Department* for that occasion. Two years later, the Playhouse introduced another of Williamson's plays, *A Handful of Friends.*

In 1978, Williamson's play *The Club* was produced even farther away from his Melbourne base, this time at the Kennedy Center in Washington, D.C., followed by a Broadway production (both productions were under the title *Players*). In 1980, *Travelling North* was produced in London. Although both plays had premiered earlier in Australia, their quick transport to England and the United States holds significance, for Australian artists are too often not taken seriously by many of their compatriots until they prove themselves abroad. Williamson had fulfilled that requirement, so those Australian critics still dubious about a writer whom some had called a "flash in the pan" were forced to accept their new playwright, one whose work had shaken the staid foundations of Australian theater much as Patrick White had a few years earlier altered forever the course of the Australian novel.

Even if Williamson had not established himself abroad as a playwright, he would have done so eventually as a screenwriter. In 1971, he adapted his first play, *The Coming of Stork*, into the film *Stork*, which was followed by several other adaptations and original screenplays. Not until 1981, though, did his screenwriting receive much attention outside Australia; the worldwide popularity of *Gallipoli* and *The Year of Living Dangerously* brought his work to millions, even though they may not have realized that the man who had written the scripts for those films was one of Australia's foremost playwrights. *Gallipoli* was based on various accounts of the Australian army landing on Gallipoli during World War I, an event that holds prominence in Australian history, while *The Year of Living Dangerously* was adapted from Australian novelist C. J. Koch's account of revolution in Indonesia. Intrigued by the events that led to the overthrow of the Marcos regime in the Philippines, Williamson wrote the screenplay for the Home Box Office (HBO) production about the revolution, *A Dangerous Life.* It showed in Australia, the United Kingdom, and the United States, and it was voted by American newspapers as one of the ten best television productions of 1988.

Williamson has said that writing for the film and television industries is not an especially "literary" activity, given the interference and whims of producers, directors, and financial backers. He has explained that he turned to these mediums because they provide opportunities, not possible on the stage, to address "epic" themes derived from historical and political events. He became involved in canceled projects considered too politically sensitive for general production, even though they were both based on true stories: one, the story of an American prisoner of war who was brainwashed by the Koreans, then accused by the McCarthy committee of collaborating with the Chinese; the other, an account of white South Africans who became victims of apartheid laws.

In the fall of 1984, Williamson's first major television effort, a miniseries entitled *The Last Bastion*, aired in Australia. The highly praised series, on which Williamson and his wife had worked for two years, chronicles the American presence in Australia during World War II. Other television projects include *Princess Kate*, a children's drama, and *The Four-Minute Mile*, which retells John Landy's triumph in breaking the record for running the mile.

Unlike many Australian artists in the past, Williamson has not fled his native land for the supposedly superior artistic environment he might find in Europe or the United States. Despite extensive travels and a growing international reputation, he continued to consider Australia his home. The screenplays may move into areas outside his native land, but the plays remain fixed in Australia. When a new production opens, which happens every two years or so, it always does well at the box office all across Australia, followed by productions abroad. Williamson once told an interviewer that he had ideas for at least ten new plays. He is not likely to quit writing drama that both entertains and challenges its audiences.

Analysis

The plays of David Williamson are distinguished by their naturalism, which they attain through disciplined structure, exact sense of place, honest and sympathetic treatment of characters, vivid language, and comedy. In each play, these elements combine to reveal believable characters caught up in familiar human conflicts. Yet the dramas consistently reach beyond the limitations of specific incidents, time, and place; in this reaching, however, they sidestep moralizing or didacticism, relying instead for their meaning on the mundane actions and often muddled responses of ordinary people.

In stage directions, Williamson stresses that the plays are "naturalistic" and should be produced accordingly. What he means by naturalistic, critics have debated, but notes from directors who have worked with Williamson reveal that naturalistic to the playwright means exactly what it says: The plays should be performed in a natural manner. The scripts, even when read, do possess a remarkable degree of naturalness, an outcome dependent in part on their disciplined structure.

Until *Travelling North* and *The Perfectionist*, Williamson followed the dictates of the well-made play, which makes his work more like George Bernard Shaw's, Henrik Ibsen's, or Anton Chekhov's than like that of many contemporary playwrights, who display a penchant for fragmentary scenes, unpredictable shifts of time and place, role doubling, and so on. Williamson has constructed these two plays with a series of short scenes set in varied places, but he has not permitted this departure from his usual method to shatter the sense of reality for which he strives. Whether the action takes a few minutes or an hour, he maintains the tension and conflict essential to his kind of drama. Believable characters come into conventional rooms, carry out everyday activities—eating, drinking, smoking, fighting, entering into conversations that may lead nowhere, that may be interrupted, or that may erupt in anger—and then leave the stage to continue their lives elsewhere. Rarely does a resolution take place.

Williamson has accepted the maxim that writers should write about what they know. Williamson knows urban Australia, especially the two major cities, Melbourne and Sydney; he knows Australians, too, particularly the middle-class, educated, city-dwelling ones; and he understands and sympathizes with their ambitions, frustrations, and quirks. He has put this thorough knowledge and understanding to good use in each of his plays.

Whether the action of a Williamson play takes place in a suburban living room or in a cluttered engineering laboratory at a technical college, the setting for that action is exact, made so by street names, references to climate, distance, city districts, commercial names, and so on. Many people outside Australia know only of the country's Outback—those vast stretches of land sparsely inhabited by sheep, kangaroos, weathered bushmen, and aborigines; few realize that seventy percent of Australians live in its five large cities. In part, this misconception stems from the tendency of Australian dramatists and fiction writers, until the 1970's or so, to set their works in the Outback, thereby giving the impression that Australia lacked an urban life. Williamson has helped to dispel that myth.

Australians have often been depicted by both their own writers and those abroad as bumptious colonials bragging and swaggering to hide their innate sense of insecurity. Williamson avoids such parody and stereotypical portrayals. Granted, his characters often swear and drink excessively, display crassness and greed, treat women as chattel, praise and indulge in violence, mouth racist slogans, and display all the other attitudes purported to be the mark of an Australian. Those characters caught up in the conflict of a Williamson play, however, never suffer unabated ridicule, for Williamson shows sympathy toward them in spite of the disagreeable habits and attitudes he takes such pains to point up. He makes it evident, first, that such qualities are not peculiar to Australians alone but indigenous to many Western nations. Second, he lends to the characters more than one dimension, so that they emerge as troubled and pained humans striving to grasp their predicament, a predicament shared by all men and women at some time or another.

The plays' language, like their structure, settings, and characters, never veers from the naturalistic tone Williamson demands of his art. The dialogue abounds in Australianisms, such as "poofter" for homosexual, "daks" for trousers, "uni" for university, and so on. An uninformed playgoer or reader might at first long for a glossary, but these words meld so perfectly into the dialogue that their meaning becomes evident in context. The words add color and help to capture the unique rhythm of Australian speech, which Williamson reproduces so splendidly.

Profanity, too, is excessive, almost at times to the point of annoyance, which may well be the purpose of all the "bloodies" and four-letter words. In *The Coming of Stork*, the play's namesake is notably foulmouthed, and after he suggests that one of his friends "piss off," that character analyzes the command: "There you are," he says. "Piss, a simple colloquial word meaning 'to urinate' and off, another simple word suggesting movement, but put them together and there's a rather telling forcefulness about the phrase." When in anger Stork shouts the words again, his friend replies: "Yes that's, er, very good Stork, but if you say it too often it does tend to lose its impact."

Australian critic Roslyn Arnold sees this profane and abusive language as more than superficial; in her 1975 article "Aggressive Vernacular: Williamson, Buzo and the Australian Tradition," she observes that the language "strikes down into the preoccupations and motivations of the characters, sheds light on social rituals, and raises questions about contemporary Australian life and the traditions informing it." At the conclusion of her discussion, however, Arnold finds it a "pity" that the new playwrights do not "extend that language to explore the possible depths" of relationships rather than their "width." Williamson seems to have done exactly that, for his later plays depend less on the "aggressive vernacular" and more on language that leads its speakers to probe the mysteries bound up in the human involvements with which they wrestle.

Although comedy may not seem appropriate for naturalistic theater, it remains a staple in Williamson's plays, to the extent that critics have accused him of relying on cheap gags, one-liners, and farcical situations. Disputing this charge, Williamson has said again and again that his work may be humorous but should neither be played for laughs nor taken as purely comic. The disparity between Williamson's subject matter and his comic treatment of it is best illustrated by the comments of a reviewer for the *International Herald Tribune.* He describes *The Removalists* as "a brutal play and also a hilarious one, an extraordinarily funny treatment of violence"; he then admits that "a comedy in which a man is beaten to a bloody and lifeless pulp" might seem "unlikely or contradictory," but the reviewer concludes that the play is neither. Williamson is certainly not the first writer to discover comedy as a weapon with which to bludgeon the unfunny people around him, but he has used the weapon with admirable originality, proving once more that a playwright can be serious while being funny.

Williamson's work has shown steady progress over the years. Those striking qualities that set apart even the defective first play, *The Coming of Stork*, he has continued to refine. To an extent, all Williamson's work for the stage has focused on a single theme: the perfection of relationships, a goal that forever eludes the characters. The plays are always open-ended, the suggestion left that the characters will continue their search and in so doing meet disappointments, make blunders, face defeat and humiliation, and, on occasion, succeed: In other words, they will continue to live out their lives. This view Williamson has explored in a variety of ways, so that the plays, although each an entity, may be placed in three groups: the plays about family and marriage, those about social relationships outside the family, and those about interactions in the larger world.

Jugglers Three, *What If You Died Tomorrow*, *Travelling North*, and *The Perfectionist* are all plays taking up the problems and the conflicts stemming from what Williamson perceives as the tyranny of family relationships and the fragility of marriage.

Set during the Vietnam War, *Jugglers Three* shows in part the adverse role that the war played in the lives of young Australians, but the work concerns itself more with marriage. A veteran returns to his home in Melbourne to discover that his wife has a lover, who is also married. This well-worn plot moves along at rapid pace and provides for a series of at once comic and sad scenes from which social commentary and an examination of marriage emerge. As the play closes, the lover departs, and the veteran and his wife engage in a ferocious game of table tennis, which turns into a sort of allegory of marriage. Whether they will reunite remains indefinite—and unimportant.

What If You Died Tomorrow dramatizes the havoc that fame can exert on both marriage and family relationships. Again set in Melbourne and focusing on a broken marriage and lovers, this play comes closest to farce of any of Williamson's work. A recently successful novelist, who has left his wife and children in order to live with a journalist, meets in the course of an evening an unlikely array of characters, including some literary types, his middle-class Australian parents just back from the requisite European tour, and a German afloat in Australia. By bedtime, not much has been settled, but much has been said about the artist and about the human engaged in the struggle to be human.

In *Travelling North*, the parent-child relationship comes into play when two older Australians engage in a twilight love affair, leaving their grown children, all unhappily married and generally alienated, to fend for themselves. Williamson reveals here a striking sensitivity toward the aging process with its accompanying physical deterioration, disappointment over failure, and crankiness. The title comes from the direction toward which the two aging lovers head: the Australian North, which is the equivalent of Florida.

The Perfectionist offers a microscopic examination of marriage and family and their consequent entanglements. Denmark is the setting for the first part of the play, which consists throughout of scenes that revive fragments of memory introduced by various characters. An Australian professor, serving as a visiting lecturer in a Danish university, and his wife engage in a quest to learn not only what marriage means but also what their independent lives mean. Once they have returned to Australia, the layers of protective illusions, jarred by their time abroad, begin to fall away, and they both face their denuded selves: the husband, whose striving for perfection has led him into pomposity, sycophancy, and isolation, and the wife, whose struggle against her helpmate role has led her into bitterness, an unsuccessful love affair, and dilettantism. They eventually separate, and at the play's closing, the possibility of their reunion is indefinite. Yet the action has reached a more forceful kind of completion, for the major characters have discarded many of their illusions and owned up to the need to reconstruct their lives. Whether that reconstruction will be accomplished remains as conjectural as their reunion.

Top Silk focuses on a family as well, this one consisting of a husband and wife who are well-established lawyers with a son who is a potential dropout. Not an altogether successful play, *Top Silk* follows both the conflicts within the home and the parallel ones outside, as the lawyers engage in politics, bribery, and other chicanery, while trying to figure out what to do about their marriage and son.

The Coming of Stork and *Don's Party* suggest that social relationships outside the family are equal in their complexity and delicacy to those within. *The Coming of Stork* carries all the excesses characteristic of plays of the 1960's and early 1970's; there is too much drinking, sex, and obscenity. Nevertheless, once the excesses are sifted out, what remains is a vivid series of vignettes depicting a group of educated, urban, young men and women seeking to establish themselves, not only in their professions but also in the larger task of being part of a social structure.

Don's Party bears a similarity to *The Coming of Stork*, but it handles the theme far more confidently and skillfully. Set during an Australian election night, with actual television coverage reproduced, the play at first appears to be about the election, but as the action unfolds, Australian politics recede and the ugly traits of Don's guests take the foreground—their fears, sexual repression, ambition, pettiness, selfishness, pretense, and lechery. The only definite resolution in the plot is the outcome of the election. Although unsatisfactory to most of Don's guests, the results produce little disappointment, so fully immersed are the revelers in their own problems. They leave the party unchanged—drunk, tired, frustrated by interrupted sexual liaisons—to resume their careers. Each may have approached some kind of epiphany but failed to recognize the moment.

Again depending on a party for its structure, *Money and Friends* depicts nine professionals sharing a weekend at the beach. One man is in dire financial trouble, but his friends find good reasons for not helping, even as they profess their devotion to him. Although the threat of financial ruin evaporates, the friends expose their weaknesses through the way they react to the request for assistance. A comedy of contemporary manners, the play ends as Williamson's plays always do: The personal engagements have not visibly altered the participants, and they revert to their muddled lives.

The theme of the individual interacting in the larger world provides the basis for *The Department*, *The Club*, *A Handful of Friends*, *Celluloid Heroes*, and *The Removalists.* The first two plays, one about a departmental meeting in a technical college, the other about behind-the-game politics in a Melbourne football club, spin out a web of forces that place all men and women on a common plane—that is, the forces of bureaucracy, compromise, and personal ambition. To escape may or may not be possible; the plays offer no solutions, only the dilemma. In *A Handful of Friends*, a film director, a journalist, an actress, a professor—all successful—meet and talk, and in so doing prove that outward attainment in the larger world does not assure inward peace in the private world. *Celluloid Heroes* focuses on the Australian film industry.

Among this group of plays, *The Removalists* stands out. The principal action of the play is simple enough: A man is slowly and methodically beaten to death. The plot is set in motion when two sisters ask for police protection from the husband of one of the sisters; they claim that he is violent. A corrupt police veteran and an idealistic newcomer offer to assist when the removalists (furniture movers) come to the couple's apartment. In an absurd, cruel, yet casual and hilarious way, the two sisters, the police officers, the husband, and a removalist complete the action, which, for no particular reason, seems inevitable. The police officers beat the husband while the mover takes out furniture, the sisters argue, and the older police officer intermittently attempts seduction. Once the others have left the apartment and the husband has died, the two officers engage in an orgy of violence, and the play ends.

Because of Australia's historical record of violence, it being a nation founded as a convict colony, critics there have tended to view the play as an expression of the country's lingering attraction to and acceptance of violent action. The play, however, has spoken in other historical contexts as well; it met with success in Poland when performed as a protest against oppressive rule before the fall of Communism.

Sons of Cain, constructed in forty or so scenes, blends comedy, moralism, and documentary realism to condemn corruption in high places and the media's inability—or refusal—to expose it. More direct in its condemnation of corruption than *The Removalists*, which relies heavily on metaphor, this play offers no solutions, only the hope that the righteous few will continue to battle the entrenched power. *Siren* also ostensibly focuses on public corruption as it follows a task force's attempt to compromise a bribe-taking mayor. The siren is the woman whom the force has hired to entrap the mayor in a motel. While waiting for their victim's arrival, the siren and her employers engage in exchanges, which lead to personal revelations unrelated to their original quest. As the play ends, the characters know more about themselves, but it is not clear whether that newfound knowledge will change them.

Sydney serves as the setting and inspiration for *Emerald City*, a place that will do its best to seduce the artist into greedy ways—in this case, a naïve scriptwriter. The sometimes comic play about personal corruption leads its protagonist through a series of moral dilemmas as he tries but fails to become rich and powerful. He concludes finally that he has succeeded in preserving at least a shred of moral integrity—and that is about all the artist or anyone can hope for in such a society.

Other major works

NONFICTION: "*The Removalists:* A Conjunction of Limitations," 1974 (in *Meanjin*).

SCREENPLAYS: *Stork*, 1971 (adaptation of *The Coming of Stork*); *Petersen*, 1974; *The Removalists*, 1974 (adaptation of his play); *Don's Party*, 1976 (adaptation of his play); *Eliza Frazer*, 1976; *The Club*, 1980 (adaptation of his play); *Gallipoli*, 1981; *Partners*, 1981; *The Year of Living Dangerously*, 1982; *Pharlap*, 1984; *A Dangerous Life*, 1988.

TELEPLAYS: *The Last Bastion*, 1984 (miniseries); *The Four-Minute Mile*, 1988 (miniseries); *Princess Kate*, 1988 (miniseries).

Bibliography

Carroll, Dennis. "David Williamson." In *Australian Contemporary Drama, 1909-1982.* New York: Peter Lang, 1985. Focuses on Williamson's depiction of the "ocker"—the stereotypical Australian male proud to be a colonial bumpkin, loud, rude, uncouth, uncultured, and generally obnoxious. A limited discussion. While many of the plays before the 1980's portray the "ocker," later ones have moved in other directions.

Kiernan, Brian. "David Williamson: Satiric Comedies." In *International Literature in English: Essays on the Major Writers*, edited by Robert Ross. New York: Garland, 1991. Contains a biographical sketch, an essay on the plays through 1989, a primary bibliography, and an annotated secondary bibliography. Kiernan argues that while the plays are highly "accessible" on any level, they exceed both satire and comedy to combine those forms into an original drama with a rare "human dimension."

____________. *David Williamson: A Writer's Career.* Port Melbourne, Australia: Heinemann, 1990. Called a "critical biography," this comprehensive study chronicles Williamson's personal life along with his development as a writer. Discusses each of the plays, providing background on productions as well as interpretation. Provides extensive information on Williamson's film and television career. Bibliographical materials. Most complete work on Williamson.

Williamson, David. *Williamson.* Edited by Peter Fitzpatrick. North Ryde, Australia: Methuen Australia, 1987. Describes Williamson as a "storyteller to the tribe" and "a shaper of cultural images." Uses this approach to analyze the plays to *The Perfectionist*, focusing on their handling of "ockerism," meaningful human relationships, and public institutions. The appendices provide a chronology of Williamson's career and a survey of the plays in performance. Select bibliography.

Zuber-Skerritt, Ortrun, ed. *David Williamson.* Amsterdam: Rodopi, 1988.

Offers excerpts from selected talks and articles by, and interviews with, Williamson. Provides an extensive bibliography of newspaper and magazine articles as well as international reviews.

Robert Ross

AUGUST WILSON

Born: Pittsburgh, Pennsylvania; April 27, 1945

Principal drama

Ma Rainey's Black Bottom, pr. 1984, pb. 1985; *Fences*, pr., pb. 1985; *Joe Turner's Come and Gone*, pr. 1986, pb. 1988; *The Piano Lesson*, pr. 1987, pb. 1990; *Two Trains Running*, pr. 1990, pb. 1992.

Other literary forms

Some of August Wilson's poetry was published in black literary journals, such as *Black World*, in 1969. He is known primarily for his plays.

Achievements

Critics have hailed Wilson as an authentic voice of African-American culture. His plays explore the black experience historically and in the context of deeper metaphysical roots in African culture. Between 1984 and 1992, his major plays have been successfully produced by regional theaters and on Broadway; in fact, he is the first African-American playwright to have had two plays running on Broadway simultaneously.

Wilson has received an impressive array of fellowships and awards: the Jerome Fellowship in 1980, the Bush Foundation Fellowship in 1982, membership in the New Dramatists starting in 1983, and the Rockefeller Fellowship in 1984. He has also been an associate of Playwrights Center, Minneapolis, and received the McKnight Fellowship in 1985, the Guggenheim Fellowship in 1986, five New York Drama Critics Circle Awards from 1985 to 1990, the Whiting Foundation Award in 1986, the Pulitzer Prize in drama in 1987 (for *Fences*) and 1990 (for *The Piano Lesson*), the Tony Award by the League of New York Theatres and Producers (for *Fences*), the American Theatre Critics Award in 1986, the Outer Circle Award in 1987, and the Drama Desk Award and John Gassner Award in 1987.

Wilson's goals are "to concretize the black cultural response to the world, to place that response in loud action, so as to create a dramatic literature as powerful and sustaining as black American music." While the form of his plays breaks no new ground, the substance and language produce powerful emotional responses. Rooted in the black experience, Wilson's plays touch universal chords.

Biography

August Wilson was born in Pittsburgh, Pennsylvania, on April 27, 1945, in the Hill District, a black neighborhood. He was one of six children born to Daisy Wilson from North Carolina, and a German baker, Frederick August Kittel, who eventually abandoned the family. Wilson left school at fifteen when a teacher refused to take his word that a twenty-page paper on Napoleon was his own work. He spent the next few weeks in the library, pretending to be at school. It was through reading, especially all the books he could find in the "Negro" subject section, that Wilson educated himself.

Later, he worked at odd jobs and spent time on street corners and at a cigar store called Pat's Place, listening to old men tell stories. Coming into adulthood during the Black Power movement of the 1960's, Wilson was influenced by it and participated in the Black Arts movement in Pittsburgh, writing and publishing poetry in black journals. With longtime friend Rob Penny, he founded the Black Horizons Theatre Company in Pittsburgh in 1968. He produced and directed plays, but his efforts at playwriting in those years failed, he later recalled, because he "didn't respect the way blacks talked" so he "always tried to alter it." He formed a connection with the Penumbra company in St. Paul and moved there in 1978. It was in this much smaller black community that he learned to regard the "voices I had been brought up with all my life" with greater respect.

Married in 1981 to Judy Oliver (he has a daughter, Sakina Ansari, from an earlier marriage), Wilson began to write scripts for the children's theater of a local science museum. This effort led him to submit his scripts to the National Playwrights Conference at the Eugene O'Neill Center in Waterford, Connecticut. His work caught the attention of conference director Lloyd Richards, who was also the dean of the Yale School of Drama and the artistic director of the Yale Repertory Company. Under Richards' direction, a staged reading of *Ma Rainey's Black Bottom* was performed in 1982 at the Eugene O'Neill Center, followed by a production at Yale and a Broadway success. The four succeeding plays by Wilson followed the same pattern, sometimes with intervening production at other regional theaters.

Divorced in 1990, Wilson moved to Seattle, Washington, where he continued to write another of his cycle of plays. He also participated as a dramaturge at the Eugene O'Neill Center when one of his own works was not being produced.

Analysis

Each of August Wilson's major plays dramatizes the African-American experience in a different decade of the twentieth century, and the action of each play is driven by the arrival or presence of a character who has what Wilson calls the "warrior spirit," the quality that makes a man dissatisfied and determined to change or disrupt the status quo. Each of the plays is affected by Wilson's feeling for the blues, music that he calls the "flag bearer of self-definition" for African Americans. Characters sing the blues, music is called for in scene transitions, and the rhythms of the dialogue reflect the blues. His plays are written to be performed on a single setting with action that is chronological. While he writes within the genre of psychological realism, each play displays a different degree of adherence to structure and plotting. His characters, mostly men, are African Americans uncertain of their own places in the world.

One of Wilson's greatest strengths is with language: The authenticity and rhythms of the dialogue and the colorful vitality of metaphor and storytelling connect him to the oral tradition of the African-American and African cultures. He discussed in an interview the indirect quality of black speech, with its circling of issues and answers that are not answers. Characters answer the question they think is intended, not necessarily the one that is expressed. This language, in fact, often becomes the unique poetry of his drama. The language is full of implied meanings and dependent on tonal quality for interpretation. Wilson also places increasing emphasis with each play on the superstitions and beliefs that affect his characters. These superstitions seem to come from a mixture of Christianity, ancient African religions, and street wisdom.

In *Ma Rainey's Black Bottom*, Wilson uses a historical figure, "Mother of the Blues" singer Ma Rainey, and invents a story around her. The setting is a simultaneous representation of a 1927 recording studio and a band-rehearsal room. Overlooking the studio from the control booth are Ma's white producer and white agent, their presence and location a graphic symbol of white society's control over black music.

The dialogue seems to meander through silly and inconsequential matters. The underlying seriousness of these matters becomes apparent as the characters reveal their ways of coping with the white world. Ma Rainey plays the prima donna (note the pun in the play's title) while she acknowledges to her band that, like all black artists, she is exploited. Her music is her "way of understanding life." Wilson centers her in the play, a dynamic and colorful presence, but the character central to the action is Levee.

Levee has that warrior spirit. The tragic irony is that when he lashes out and kills, he kills the only educated band member in the play. His urge for self-sufficiency (to have his own band and make his own music) becomes self-destructive. By application, Wilson suggests that the misplaced rage of his race can result in self-destruction. The grimly serious resolution to this play does not describe the tone of lightness and humor in much that precedes it. It is Levee's appetite that drives the play, sometimes comically, and it is his frustrated hunger that causes an unnecessary death.

Wilson's second major work, *Fences*, won a Pulitzer Prize in drama as well as Tony Awards for Wilson, the director, and two actors. It centers on the dynamic, volatile character Troy Maxson and takes place primarily in 1957. Troy is the warrior character whose spirit disrupts his own life as well as those of his sons and wife. Often inviting comparison with Arthur Miller's *Death of a Salesman* (pr. 1949), the play dramatizes the life of a baseball player prevented from realizing his big-league dreams by the color barrier, overcome too late for him. *Fences* is about a man's battle with life and his emotional, sometimes irrational way of facing unfairness, pain, love, hate. The fence that Troy built around his life, like that built around his home, could neither shut out the world's injustice nor protect his family or himself from his shortcomings. The final scene occurs after Troy's death in 1965, when others can express feelings about Troy that were not articulated before. This scene provides a quietly emotional contrast to the intensely alive Troy of the previous eight scenes. It is a necessary scene and yet points up the failure of father and son to express directly what they felt in their earlier confrontation.

Troy's brother, Gabriel, whose head injury from the war has made him believe himself to be God's angel Gabriel, provides a kind of mystical presence. Wilson uses his madness for a theatrically effective closing to the play. When Gabriel discovers that his horn will not blow to open the gates of heaven for Troy, he performs a weird "dance of atavistic signature and ritual" and howls a kind of song to open the gates. This marks the beginning of Wilson's increasing use of ritual, myth, and superstition in his plays.

In *Joe Turner's Come and Gone*, Wilson reaches farther back into the historical black experience. As in the old blues song of the same title, the brother of the governor of Tennessee, Joe Turner, found and enslaved groups of black men. Herald Loomis, the mysterious central character in this play, was so enslaved in 1901 and not released for seven years. The play dramatizes his search for his wife, which is actually a search for himself. His arrival at a Pittsburgh boardinghouse in 1911 disrupts and disturbs, creating the tension and significance of the drama.

Another boardinghouse resident, Bynum, establishes his identity as a "conjure man" or "rootworker" early in the play. Bynum's search for his "shiny man" becomes a thematic and structural tie for the play. At the end of the first act, during a joyous African call-and-response dance, Loomis has a sort of ecstatic fit, ending with his being unable to stand and walk. Some kind of dramatic resolution must relate Bynum's vision and Loomis' quest. It comes in the final scene when wife Martha returns and Loomis learns that his quest is still unrealized. Wilson describes Loomis' transformation in actions rather than words. His wife does not restore him; her religion does not restore him. In desperation, he turns a knife on himself, rubs his hands and face in his own blood, looks down at his hands, and says, "I'm standing. My legs stood up! I'm standing now!" It is at this point that he has found his "song of self-sufficiency." Wilson's rather poetic stage directions articulate a redemption that Loomis cannot verbalize, risking audience misinterpretation.

Bynum's final line of the play recognizes Loomis as a shiny man, the shiny man who can tell him the meaning of life. The suggestion of a Christ figure is unmistakable, and yet Loomis' soul is not cleansed through religious belief. He has denied the Christ of the white man, despite Martha's pleading. His epiphany is in finding himself. Joe Turner has come but he has also gone. Herald Loomis finds his identity in his own African roots, not in the slave identity that the white Joe Turner had given him.

With his fourth major play, Wilson crafts a more tightly structured plot. In fact, *The Piano Lesson* is stronger thematically and structurally than it is in character development. The characters serve to dramatize the conflict between the practical use of a family heritage to create a future, and a symbolic treasuring of that heritage to honor the past. The piano, which bears the blood of their slave ancestors, is the focus of the conflict between Boy Willie and his sister, Berniece. Its exotic carvings, made by their great grandfather, tell the story of their slave ancestors who were sold in exchange for the piano. Its presence in the northern home of Berniece and her Uncle Doaker represents the life of their father who died stealing it back from Sutter.

Berniece is embittered and troubled not only by the piano and her father's death but also by her mother's blood and tears which followed that death and by the loss of her own husband. In contrast, Boy Willie is upbeat and funny, an optimistic, ambitious, and boyish man who is sure he is right in wanting to sell the piano to buy Sutter's land. He has the warrior spirit. Throughout the play, the presence of Sutter's ghost is seen or felt. Sutter's ghost seems to represent the control that the white man still exerts over this family in 1937. Boy Willie chooses to ignore the ghost, to accuse his sister of imagining it, but ultimately it is Boy Willie who must wrestle with the ghost.

Wilson has said that this play had five endings because Berniece and Boy Willie are both right. The conflict is indeed unresolved as Boy Willie leaves, telling Berniece that she had better keep playing that piano or he and Sutter could both come back. The lesson of the piano is twofold: Berniece has learned that she should use her heritage, rather than let it fester in bitterness, and Boy Willie has learned that he cannot ignore the significance of this piano, which symbolizes the pain and suffering of all of his ancestors. There is little in the play that deviates from the central conflict. The skill of Wilson's writing is seen in the interplay of characters bantering and arguing, in the indirect quality of questions that are not answered, and in the storytelling. While characters may serve primarily as symbols and plot devices, they are nevertheless vivid and credible.

The disruptive character in Wilson's fifth play is Sterling, but the theme of *Two Trains Running*, set in 1969, is found in the character Memphis, the owner of the restaurant in which the action occurs. Memphis came north in 1936, driven away by white violence. He has always meant to return and reclaim his land. In the course of the play, he learns that he has to go back and "pick up the ball" so as not to arrive in the end zone empty handed. He must catch one of those two trains running south every day. He must not surrender.

The major characters in the play represent varying degrees of tenacity. Wilson skillfully builds a plot around two threads: Memphis' determination to get the city to pay his price for his property, and Sterling's determination to find a place for himself and gain the love of Risa. Hambone is a crazy character, driven mad almost ten years ago when the butcher Lutz across the street refused to pay him a ham for doing a good job of painting his fence. Hollaway, a commentator character, observes that Hambone may be the smartest of them all in his refusal to give up—each day going to Lutz and asking for his ham. The unfortunate fact is, though, that his life has been reduced to this one action; all he can say is "I want my ham. He gonna give me my ham." Risa, a woman determined not to be dependent on a sexual attachment, has scarred her own attractive legs to make herself less desirable. In spite of herself, she is attracted to the vitality and optimism of Sterling, and Sterling is most tenacious of all. His warrior spirit has landed him in prison and may do so again, but his zeal and good humor are compelling.

The constant reminders and presence of death give resonance to the lives and efforts of these people. When the play opens, the Prophet Samuel has already died and the offstage mayhem surrounding the viewing of his body is evident. Characters talk about several other deaths, and no sooner is Prophet Samuel buried than Hambone is discovered dead (again offstage). The reactions to his death comprise the ending of the play. Memphis and Sterling, trusting in the prophecies of the 322-year-old seer Aunt Ester, both triumph. Sterling runs across the street, steals a ham, and presents it to Mr. West, the undertaker, to put in Hambone's coffin. This final flourish of the play is an assertion of character identity and life. *Two Trains Running* may be Wilson's most accomplished work in blending character, plot, and theme.

Clearly, Wilson is an important playwright whose language, characters, storytelling, and themes enrich a limited body of work exploring the lives of African Americans. That he has written and seen produced several plays in one decade, reaching a wide audience, gives evidence that further development and output will occur.

Bibliography

Bigsby, C. W. E. *Modern American Drama, 1945-1990.* Cambridge, England: Cambridge University Press, 1992. The author interviewed Wilson for pertinent biographical data and includes some in-depth analysis of the first four plays.

Brustein, Robert. *Reimagining American Theatre.* New York: Hill & Wang, 1991. Brustein, critic and former artistic director of the Yale Repertory Theatre before Lloyd Richards, is one of the few negative voices criticizing Wilson's drama. He finds particular fault with the mechanisms and symbols of *The Piano Lesson* and hopes that Wilson will work to develop the poetic rather than historical aspects of his talent.

Harrison, Paul Carter. "August Wilson's Blues Poetics." In *August Wilson: Three Plays.* Pittsburgh: University of Pittsburgh Press, 1991. Harrison's essay, included as an afterword in this edition of Wilson's first three major plays, is a study that takes the view that Wilson's aesthetic is organically tied to his roots in the blues, which are in turn drawn from the ancient culture in Africa. He calls Wilson's work a "welcome model for future African-American dramaturgy." Wilson's preface to this volume provides insights into his thought and purpose.

Hill, Holly. "Black Theatre into the Mainstream." In *Contemporary American Theatre*, edited by Bruce King. New York: St. Martin's Press, 1991. Hill's analysis of the plays sets them in the context of their period.

Moyers, Bill. "August Wilson's America: A Conversation with Bill Moyers." *American Theatre* 6 (June, 1989): 12-17, 54-56. An excerpted and edited piece taken from *Bill Moyers: A World of Ideas* (1989), which is itself a transcription of television conversations broadcast on public television in October, 1989. Wilson expresses his ideas about race, his role as a dramatist, and the goals of his people. Contains photographs of Wilson and scenes from *Joe Turner* and *Ma Rainey's Black Bottom.*

Theater 9 (Summer/Fall, 1988). This special issue includes the script of *The Piano Lesson* with an earlier version of the ending, production photographs, and two informative essays. The articles "Wrestling Against History" and "The Songs of a Marked Man" explore Wilson's themes, especially the importance of myths and superstitions.

Wilson, August. "A Song in Search of Itself." Interview by Hilary De Vries. *American Theatre* 3 (January, 1987): 22-25. In this interview, Wilson reveals much about his motivations and intentions in the plays. Includes photographs of Wilson and scenes from *Ma Rainey's Black Bottom* and *Fences.*

Sally Osborne Norton

LANFORD WILSON

Born: Lebanon, Missouri; April 13, 1937

Principal drama

So Long at the Fair, pr. 1963 (one act); *Home Free!*, pr. 1964, pb. 1965 (one act); *The Madness of Lady Bright*, pr. 1964, pb. 1967 (one act); *No Trespassing*, pr. 1964 (one act); *Balm in Gilead*, pr., pb. 1965 (two acts); *Days Ahead: A Monologue*, pr. 1965, pb. 1967 (one scene); *Ludlow Fair*, pr., pb. 1965 (one act); *The Sand Castle*, pr. 1965, pb. 1970 (one act); *Sex Is Between Two People*, pr. 1965 (one scene); *This Is the Rill Speaking*, pr. 1965, pb. 1967 (one act); *The Rimers of Eldritch*, pr. 1966, pb. 1967 (two acts); *Wandering: A Turn*, pr. 1966, pb. 1967 (one scene); *Untitled Play*, pr. 1967 (one act; music by Al Carmines); *The Gingham Dog*, pr. 1968, pb. 1969; *The Great Nebula in Orion*, pr. 1970, pb. 1973 (one act); *Lemon Sky*, pr., pb. 1970; *Serenading Louie*, pr. 1970, pb. 1976 (two acts); *Sextet (Yes)*, pb. 1970, pr. 1971 (one scene); *Stoop: A Turn*, pb. 1970; *Ikke, Ikke, Nye, Nye, Nye*, pr. 1971, pb. 1973; *Summer and Smoke*, pr. 1971, pb. 1972 (libretto; adaptation of Tennessee Williams' play; music by Lee Hoiby); *The Family Continues*, pr. 1972, pb. 1973 (one act); *The Hot l Baltimore*, pr., pb. 1973; *Victory on Mrs. Dandywine's Island*, pb. 1973 (one act); *The Mound Builders*, pr. 1975, pb. 1976 (two acts); *Brontosaurus*, pr. 1977, pb. 1978 (one act); *Fifth of July*, pr., pb. 1978 (two acts); *Talley's Folly*, pr., pb. 1979 (one act); *A Tale Told*, pr. 1981 (pb. as *Talley and Son*, 1986; two acts); *Thymus Vulgaris*, pr., pb. 1982 (one act); *Angels Fall*, pr., pb. 1982 (two acts); *Three Sisters*, pr., pb. 1984 (translation of Anton Chekhov's play); *Balm in Gilead and Other Plays*, pb. 1985; *Say deKooning*, pr. 1985; *Sa-Hurt?*, pr. 1986; *A Betrothal*, pr., pb. 1986 (one act); *Burn This*, pr., pb. 1987; *A Poster of the Cosmos*, pr. 1988, pb. 1990 (one act); *Abstinence: A Turn*, pb. 1989 (one scene); *The Moonshot Tape and A Poster of the Cosmos*, pb. 1990; *Redwood Curtain*, pr. 1992.

Other literary forms

Besides stage plays, Lanford Wilson has written works in a number of other dramatic forms: several teleplays, *The Migrants* (1973, with Tennessee Williams), and *Sam Found Out* (1988), *Taxi!* (1978, not to be confused with the television series *Taxi*), and two unproduced screenplays, "One Arm," written in 1969 and based on a Tennessee Williams story, and "The Strike," based on the book *Last Exit to Brooklyn*, by Hubert Selby, Jr.

Achievements

During his first period of playwriting (1963-1972), Wilson struggled to learn his trade—mainly in the convivial atmosphere of Off-Off-Broadway, where it did not matter if sometimes audiences did not show up. His plays from this period, mostly one-acters, are clearly apprentice work. They contain echoes of Tennessee Williams, Arthur Miller, and the Theater of the Absurd; experiments include the use of overlapping and simultaneous speeches, free-floating time sequences, and characters who are figments of the main character's imagination. Perhaps the most effective of the plays from this decade are *Home Free!*, about a bizarre, incestuous relationship between brother and sister; *The Madness of Lady Bright*, about "a screaming preening queen" losing his beauty to middle age; and two impressionistic "montage" works which draw on Wilson's small-town Missouri background—*This Is the Rill Speaking* and *The Rimers of Eldritch*.

Except in *The Rimers of Eldritch*, a two-acter, Wilson during his apprentice decade had trouble sustaining longer plays; his longer works of this period tend to be uneven, diffuse, almost plotless. Their subject matter provides the main interest. *Balm in Gilead*, set in and around an all-night café on Upper Broadway, pictures the New York City subculture of pimps, prostitutes, pushers, and users (it also prefigures *The Hot l Baltimore*). *The Gingham Dog*, financially unsuccessful but favorably reviewed when it opened on Broadway, portrays the rancorous breakup of an interracial marriage. *Lemon Sky* is autobiographical—about a young man's efforts to reunite with his father, who fled years before and is rearing a second family in Southern California.

During his second and third periods (1973-1990) as a playwright, Wilson's work became more substantial in every sense: His plays of this period are generally longer, more conventional, more realistic, and more successful than those of the previous decade. Wilson's breakthrough was with *The Hot l Baltimore*, an Off-Broadway success (with 1,166 performances) produced in 1973. *The Hot l Baltimore* shows the playwright in control of his material, displays his sense of humor, and illustrates the format on which Wilson has relied (in lieu of plot) with repeated success—an updating of the old parlor or weekend drama which brings together a group of disparate characters in an interesting setting (usually threatened, usually around a holiday) and allows them to interact. Other plays falling into this format are *The Mound Builders*, *Fifth of July*, *Angels Fall*, *Talley and Son* (a revised version of the 1981 *A Tale Told*), and *Burn This*. Even the Pulitzer Prize-winning *Talley's Folly*, a romantic tour de force with only two characters, repeats the format on a smaller scale. Wilson reveals one source of this recurring device in his 1984 translation of Anton Chekhov's *Three Sisters*.

The public has been accurate in judging *The Hot l Baltimore*, *Talley's Folly*, and *Burn This* the best of Wilson's plays of the first two periods: They are the most tightly knit and evenly written, though some critics find them marred by sentimentality. *The Mound Builders*, his most ambitious work, is Wilson's favorite, but it shares, with *Fifth of July* and *Angels Fall*, a tendency toward rambling, uneven dialogue that is witty one moment and dull the next. *Angels Fall*, in particular, is burdened with intellectual baggage, something not found in Wilson's early work.

One simply does not look for highly structured, suspenseful plots from Wilson (the description "tightly knit," used above, is only relative), though his plays usually rise to a climax, even if it is sometimes forced or artificial. Rather, Wilson's work is significant for its characters and themes. His plays contain the greatest menagerie of characters in contemporary American drama—drag queens, freaks, prostitutes, academics, priests—for the most part likable, since Wilson has a special sympathy for the losers and lost of society (a category which, in his work, includes almost everybody). Wilson does not really need intellectual baggage, because his characters carry his themes much more powerfully: In the world of Wilson's plays, only "angels fall," since his characters are already down—but never out. This sense of humanity is Wilson's most sterling quality.

Biography

Lanford Eugene ("Lance") Wilson was born April 13, 1937, in Lebanon, Missouri, the son of Ralph Eugene and Violetta Tate Wilson. When he was five years old, his parents separated (and later divorced), his father leaving for California, his mother taking Lanford to Springfield, Missouri, where she worked in a garment factory and he attended school. When he was thirteen, his mother married again—a dairy inspector from Ozark, Missouri—and they moved to a farm. Wilson attended Ozark High School, where he painted, acted, and was on the track team.

Although his childhood was relatively happy, Wilson never quite recovered from his parents' marital breakup. At eighteen, after a term at Southwest Missouri State College, he headed for California for a reunion with his father, by then a San Diego aircraft-factory worker with a new wife and two younger sons. The reunion, painfully mirrored in Wilson's autobiographical play *Lemon Sky*, was unsuccessful: Wilson and his father were thoroughly incompatible. After a year in his father's household, during which he worked at his father's factory and attended San Diego State College, Wilson left for Chicago. He lived for six years in Chicago, where he worked as an artist in an advertising agency, studied playwriting at the University of Chicago, and wrote his first plays (none producible).

In 1962, Wilson moved to New York, worked as an office clerk—in a furniture store, at the Americana Hotel, and in the subscription office of the New York Shakespeare Festival—and surveyed the theatrical scene. He was disgusted by Broadway but stunned by an Off-Off-Broadway performance of Eugène Ionesco's *The Lesson* at Caffé Cino, a coffeehouse theater in Greenwich Village. Soon Wilson began waiting tables and writing plays for Caffé Cino: His first play produced was *So Long at the Fair*, in 1963, and he achieved his first success in 1964 with *The Madness of Lady Bright* (which was given 250 performances Off-Off-Broadway.) In 1966, Wilson had his first Off-Broadway success with *The Rimers of Eldritch*.

Wilson's rise had been swift, but then he began experiencing some setbacks. In 1967, he lost his home base at Caffé Cino when Joe Cino, the owner-manager, committed suicide; in 1968, *The Gingham Dog* failed on Broadway, followed in 1970 by *Lemon Sky*. After the failure of *The Gingham Dog*, Wilson became so despondent that he stopped writing for a time. He got back into playwriting by first doing mundane jobs for the Circle Repertory Company, which he had recently cofounded with actress Tanya Berezin, actor Rob Thirkield, and director Marshall W. Mason. In 1973, that company produced *The Hot l Baltimore*, and Wilson's career was back on track. All of his major plays during the following decade were initially produced by them and directed by Mason.

Wilson's plays have been produced throughout the United States and abroad; several have appeared on television, and *The Hot l Baltimore* was adapted as a television series. Wilson is the winner of numerous awards: a Vernon Rice Award (1967), Obies for *The Hot l Baltimore* and *The Mound Builders*, a Pulitzer Prize and a New York Drama Critics Circle Award (as best-of-best) for *Talley's Folly*, the Brandeis University Creative Arts Award, and fellowships from the Rockefeller and Guggenheim foundations.

Analysis

Lanford Wilson represents the most recent stage of an American cultural phenomenon that could be aptly termed "the heartland drama." Wilson's predecessor and fellow Missourian Mark Twain celebrated American innocence; Wilson mourns its loss. The loss occurred precisely on August 6, 1945, when Harry S Truman, the presidential Huck Finn, ordered that the atomic bomb be dropped on Hiroshima. America had been trying hard for a long time to lose its innocence, preferring instead to be sophisticated and worldly-wise. Now it seems like much more than innocence was lost, and many would like to turn back the clock. It appears that the famed innocence was the source of American wholeness, of Fourth of July optimism, of childlike wonder.

Lanford Wilson has centered his version of this American heartland drama on the family, where, according to Sigmund Freud, all the history of the world is played out. It is in the family, once the bastion of American innocence, that signs of the disintegration are most noticeable and its effects most far-reaching, and it is there that wholeness must be restored. Longing for the old innocence is expressed in Wilson's plays through titles which sound as if they are from nursery rhymes or children's games (some are). It is also expressed through the constant efforts to mend splintered families or to construct surrogate families. Yet the longing and the efforts are mostly in vain: The nursery-rhyme titles are mockeries, and the versions of home and family depicted are little better than cruel parodies.

Extreme examples can be found in *Home Free!*, where a brother and sister, huddled in their apartment in an attempt to shut out the world, play husband-wife and father-mother; in *The Madness of Lady Bright*, where the fading Lady Bright, lonely in his apartment, reminisces about former lovers (whose autographs are on the wall), talks with an imaginary "Boy" and "Girl," and waits in vain for a phone call; and in *The Hot l Baltimore*, where the condemned urban hotel of the title is the home of prostitutes and poor retirees. Unfortunately, in late-twentieth century America, these bizarre examples are only too real. For those seeking a substitute for the American family's lost wholeness, Wilson has some news: There is very little balm in Gilead, especially if one locates Gilead in such places as the New York City subculture of prostitutes and drug addicts.

Ultimately, in Wilson's work, the American heartland drama is not only played out in the family; the family itself—real or surrogate—mirrors and becomes a metaphor for the whole society. Such is the case in *Fifth of July*, where the extended Talley family and its holiday guests mirror the post-Vietnam state of the nation. The older generation is blessedly dead or slightly dotty; the middle generation, now over thirty, is burnt out, subsisting on drugs and memories of Berkeley idealism and sexual entanglements; and the younger generation has a precocious vocabulary and sophistication which leaves little doubt that the era of old-fashioned Fourth of July innocence is finished. Similarly, the surrogate family group (including real families) gathered for an archaeological dig in *The Mound Builders* mirrors the larger tensions in American society, particularly the tensions between preservation and development. In both plays, the sense of America's loss—of its values, its history—is acute.

In dramatizing America's loss, Wilson occasionally takes on the tones of an Old Testament prophet. Nowhere is this more the case than in *The Rimers of Eldritch*, the best example of Wilson's early experimental work. Reminiscent of Thornton Wilder's *Our Town* and Dylan Thomas' *Under Milk Wood*, though with a different emphasis, *The Rimers of Eldritch* treats a somewhat worn subject, now a television standard—the hypocrisy of a small town. Just one big down-home family, the town's citizens close ranks to heap their evil upon a poor scapegoat and thereby preserve their appearance of innocence, but the town's evil remains, its corruption confirmed. Appropriately, the printed play has the following epigraph from Jeremiah (the reference to balm in Gilead appears two verses later): "The harvest is past, the summer is ended, and we are not saved" (Jeremiah 8:20). *The Rimers of Eldritch* takes place during one spring, summer, and fall, but the play skips backward and forward in time, from one conversation to another, creating a montage effect rather than presenting a chronological sequence. Less confusing than it sounds, the montage dresses the worn subject in mystery and suspense, ironic juxtapositions, different versions of what happened (thereby mimicking small-town gossip), and a memory-like quality.

The town is named Eldritch and, true to the meaning of its name, Eldritch displays a weird collection of small-town characters, descendants of Sherwood Anderson's midwestern grotesques: farmers, a garage mechanic, a trucker; Cora Groves, owner of the Hilltop Café, who is carrying on with her young and transient lover; Patsy Johnson, prettiest girl at Centerville High, who gets pregnant by the transient lover and arranges a quick marriage to a hometown boy; Skelly Mannor, the town hermit, who goes about peeping into people's windows and who is suspected, according to an old rumor, of bestiality (boys follow him in the street shouting "Baaa!"); the town hero, a stock-car driver, now deceased, who was impotent and beat women; and a group of gossips who could substitute for the Eumenides. What characterizes the town, however, is not only its individual members but also its collective mentality. As Skelly says, the town's citizens see what they want to see and think what they want to think, all in the name of good Christian living.

The play's slight, makeshift plot dramatizes this observation. The plot revolves around an innocent fourteen-year-old crippled girl, who dreams of flying like Peter Pan and sowing autumn rime over the town. She compares the rime to sugar, but it turns out to be more like salt. Out of her sexual curiosity, she provokes her equally innocent boyfriend to try to rape her. Skelly happens on the scene and prevents the rape, but a nearby neighbor emerges with his gun and, naturally thinking that Skelly is the molester, kills him. The two "innocents" tell the Skelly-the-molester story to the judge and jury—a story the town is only too ready to believe. As the preacher (who doubles as judge) points out to the accompaniment of hymn-singing, the town is to blame for not shooting the fellow sooner.

Wilson's roots in the Bible Belt make him sound like the prophet Jeremiah in such plays as *Balm in Gilead* and *The Rimers of Eldritch*, but, in his *The Hot l Baltimore*, they also lead him to discover Mary Magdalene, whom he immediately forgave. An example of Wilson's mature work and his most popular play, *The Hot l Baltimore* is a warm and witty comedy—bittersweet, to be sure, but farcical at times. Apparently tired of turning his audiences into pillars of salt straining back toward the lost past, Wilson set out deliberately to entertain in *The Hot l Baltimore*—and happily succeeded with a realistic, conventional play that even observes the classical unities.

The play is set during one twenty-four-hour period ("a recent Memorial

Day") in the lobby of a seedy Baltimore hotel. Once an ornate showplace of the railroad era, the Hotel Baltimore is now scheduled for demolition. It is the home of the expected motley assortment of Wilson characters: hotel workers, retirees, transients, and—most notably—three warmhearted prostitutes. Like an extended family, from grandparents down to teenagers, they gather in the lobby to share each other's company and experiences. The prostitutes, in particular, share some ribald experiences concerning their clients. April observes, "If my clientele represents a cross section of American manhood, the country's in trouble," citing as one of the representative samples the fellow who scalds himself in the bathtub. Occasionally these scenes obtrude onstage, as at the hilarious end of act 1, when the outraged but otherwise unhurt Suzy, beaten and locked out of her room by a client, creates a commotion in the lobby by appearing wrapped in her towel and then nude.

Beneath the repartee and rough sexual humor, the audience is constantly reminded of the parallel between a troubled America and the rundown hotel. The hotel's residents will be losing their home, the workers, within a month, their jobs, and other people with troubles appear: Mrs. Bellotti, whose crazy, thieving, alcoholic son Horse has been kicked out of the hotel and whose diabetic husband has had his leg amputated; Paul Granger III, a refugee from a reform school who is searching for his lost grandfather; and Jackie and Jamie, a sister and brother who bought salty desert land in Utah and now lack money to get their car on the road. All represent typical cases of the American blues, just as the hotel setting represents the transience of American values and society in general.

Presiding over this scene, ministering to the troubled in spirit, is the trinity of prostitutes, Suzy, April Green, and the Girl. These angels of mercy provide not only sex but also therapy, laughter, and sympathy. Significantly, they, among all the characters, show the most concern about family ties—about Mr. Bellotti disowning Horse, about Paul Granger III giving up the search for his namesake grandfather, about Jackie's abandonment of Jamie; they also have the strongest feelings about the scheduled demolition of the hotel and the dispersal of its workers and residents. "We been like a family, haven't we?" says Suzy. "My family." She is so broken up that she moves in with a rotten pimp, because she needs "someone; . . . I need love!" The prostitutes have lost their illusions along with their innocence, but they retain their sense of values, their humanity. As the Girl says, "I just think it's really chicken not to believe in anything!" For Wilson, still mourning the loss of American innocence, the prostitutes were an important discovery: One takes one's balm, however little there is, wherever one can get it.

This philosophy of balm, discovered in *The Hot l Baltimore*, prevails in *Talley's Folly*, Wilson's Pulitzer Prize-winning work. *Talley's Folly* introduces two mature misfits who have about given up on love but finally find solace in each other's arms. As this simple plot suggests, *Talley's Folly*, like *The Hot l Baltimore*, observes the unities, only more so: Matt's wooing of Sally takes place entirely in an old boathouse (an ornate Victorian structure called Talley's Folly), and the time required coincides with the playing time (ninety-seven minutes, no intermission).

Family is a particularly important consideration in *Talley's Folly*, one of an ongoing series of Wilson plays about the Talley family of Lebanon, Missouri (the other plays are *Fifth of July* and *Talley and Son*). As in so many Wilson plays, however, here again the families depicted experience friction or breakup. Thirty-one-year-old Sally Talley is the family outcast, first because tuberculosis left her sterile and thus unfit to seal the Talley-Campbell family business partnership by marrying Harley Campbell, and second because her political views are anathema to the family, with its conservative small-town values (she sides with the union against the family's garment factory and is fired from teaching Sunday School). Forty-two-year-old Matt Friedman, a radical Jewish accountant, seems a likely mate for Sally, satisfying even her family's exacting requirements (though her brother Buddy runs Matt off with a shotgun). Matt does not even want children: Because the rest of his own family was wiped out in the Holocaust, he has resolved never to be responsible for bringing a child into this world.

Before the two can come together, they have to break down each other's solitary defenses. Matt has been melted down by Sally the summer before, with a few sessions in the boathouse, so now he takes the initiative. The play consists of their love sparring—Matt's persistence, Sally's attempts to chase him away, their anger, their jokes and repartee, their reminiscences, and finally their confessions—until Matt wins her hand. A fine vehicle for two good actors, *Talley's Folly* shows that, even in a bleak and hurtful world—no place to raise children—one can still find some balm in personal relationships.

The third play in the Talley family cycle, *Talley and Son*, a revision of the 1981 *A Tale Told*, is set in Lebanon, Missouri, on July 4, 1944, precisely the same evening as in *Talley's Folly.* A darker play than *Talley's Folly*, this play is about the financial and other machinations of three generations of Talleys, who, together with the Campbells, have run two of the most profitable businesses in Lebanon—the clothing factory and the bank. Because of the liberal use of plot devices, this story of meanness and greed has often been compared with Lillian Hellman's *The Little Foxes* (pr., pb. 1939).

Lest Wilson be accused of recommending retreat from the world, it should be added that in *Angels Fall*, he has used his family metaphor to extend the possibilities of reconciliation and hope. In *Angels Fall*, the surrogate family is a group of travelers taking shelter in a New Mexico mission church from a nearby nuclear accident. The play's title, perhaps implying that only angels stand tall enough to fall, suggests that Wilson has become reconciled to the loss of American innocence. Here the characters are all forgivably flawed and, in their mutual danger, in their mutual need, lean on one another and show a caring attitude. (Whether a nuclear accident is necessary to bring this about is unclear.) Even if the traditional American family is a dying institution, the play suggests, some of its values are still preserved in the bigger family of humankind—or perhaps in the family of God: What Wilson considers to be the fountainhead of these positive possibilities is implied in the setting (a church) and its presiding official, the genial Father Doherty.

Burn This, which premiered in January, 1987, is shocking, outrageous, and larger than life. It presents Wilson's views on art, human sexuality, and love. It is a poetic and cataclysmic work, in which art is seen as a sacrament, as an outward sign for inward, often chaotic but exhilarating truths. Many critics consider it to be Wilson's masterpiece. *Redwood Curtain*, a disturbing yet compassionate drama that depicts Vietnam veterans eking out primitive lives in the forests of Northern California, is perhaps equally powerful.

Whether Wilson has begun receiving his balm from the original source remains to be seen. Since he is still a practicing playwright, no one can say for sure where his thinking will lead, yet his religious development seems logical. Up to now, Wilson's work has been full of religious meaning, as he has moved steadily from a prophetic to a priestly stance, from the Old Testament vision of punishment toward the New Testament vision of love.

Other major works

TELEPLAYS: *The Migrants*, 1973 (with Tennessee Williams); *Taxi!*, 1978; *Sam Found Out: A Triple Play*, 1988.

Bibliography

Barnett, Gene A. *Lanford Wilson.* Boston: Twayne, 1987. The most valuable general study of Wilson. This book carries chapters on all the major plays through *Talley and Son.* It also includes a family genealogy and a family chronology for the entire Talley clan.

Bode, Walter. "Lanford Wilson." In *Contemporary Dramatists*, edited by D. L. Kirkpatrick. 4th ed. Chicago: St. James Press, 1988. Bode's brief article contains a complete primary bibliography through *Burn This.* The analysis that follows discusses Wilson's work as it relates to the conflict between the traditional values of the past and the "insidious pressures of modern life."

Dreher, Ann Crawford. "Lanford Wilson." In *Dictionary of Literary Biography*, edited by John MacNicholas. Vol. 7. Detroit: Gale Research, 1981. Dreher's essay traces literary influences and analyzes recurring themes in

Wilson's works: Wilson's interest in and respect for the past, his belief in the importance of a stable and loving family unit and the virtual impossibility of its continued existence, and his seemingly universal, Shakespearean love for humanity.

Herman, William. "Down and Out in Lebanon and New York: Lanford Wilson." In *Understanding Contemporary American Drama.* Columbia: University of South Carolina Press, 1987. Herman's chapter includes explications of Wilson's major plays. He praises Wilson for the "delicate poetic language at the heart of his style" and for his "epic encompassment of American experience and mythologies."

Robertson, C. Warren. "Lanford Wilson." In *American Playwrights Since 1945*, edited by Philip C. Kolin. New York: Greenwood Press, 1989. An accessible reference to primary and secondary sources through 1987. Robertson provides a complete primary bibliography of Wilson's works and brief discussions entitled "Assessment of Wilson's Reputation" and "Production History." The article also includes an informative survey of secondary sources and a complete secondary bibliography.

Harold Branam
(Updated by *James W. Robinson, Jr.*)

ROBERT WILSON

Born: Waco, Texas; October 4, 1941

Principal drama

Dance Event, pr. 1965; *Solo Performance*, pr. 1966; *Theater Activity*, pr. 1967; *Spaceman*, pr. 1967 (with Ralph Hilton); *ByrdwoMAN*, pr. 1968; *The King of Spain*, pr. 1969, pb. 1970; *The Life and Times of Sigmund Freud*, pr. 1969; *Deafman Glance*, pr. 1970; *Program Prologue Now, Overture for a Deafman*, pr. 1971; *Overture*, pr. 1972; *Ka Mountain, GUARDenia Terrace: a story about a family and some people changing*, pr. 1972; *king lyre and the lady in the wasteland*, pr. 1973; *The Life and Times of Joseph Stalin*, pr. 1973; *DIA LOG/A MAD MAN A MAD GIANT A MAD DOG A MAD URGE A MAD FACE*, pr. 1974; *The Life and Times of Dave Clark*, pr. 1974; *Prologue to a Letter for Queen Victoria*, pr. 1974; *A Letter for Queen Victoria*, pr. 1974, pb. 1977 (with Christopher Knowles); *To Street*, pr. 1975; *$ Value of Man*, pr. 1975; *DIA LOG*, pr. 1975 (with Knowles); *Einstein on the Beach*, pr., pb. 1976 (music by Philip Glass); *I Was Sitting On My Patio This Guy Appeared I Thought I Was Hallucinating*, pr. 1977, pb. 1978; *Prologue to the 4th Act of Deafman Glance*, pr. 1978; *DIALOG/NETWORK*, pr. 1978; *Death Destruction and Detroit*, pr. 1979; *DIALOG/Curious George*, pr. 1979; *Edison*, pr. 1979; *Medea*, pr. 1981; *The Golden Windows*, pr. 1982; *the CIVIL warS*, partial pr. 1983 and 1984 (includes *Knee Plays*); *Alcestis*, pr. 1985 (based on Euripides' play); *Knee Plays*, pr. 1986; *Cosmopolitan Greetings*, pr. 1988; *The Forest*, pr. 1988.

Other literary forms

Although Robert Wilson has produced some artwork, generated from his stage designs and exhibited in various galleries, no other substantial literary works are attributed to him.

Achievements

An experimental performing artist whose major work has been compared to Pablo Picasso's painting *Guernica* and Igor Stravinsky's ballet, *The Rite of Spring* (1913), and who has been characterized by Surrealist Louis Aragon as "a miracle," Wilson is considered by many to be the single most gifted and creative theater artist of the twentieth century. In scope, vision, imagination, and sheer size, Wilson's marathon "operas" (as he insists on calling them) are giant panoramas of all the possibilities of the stage, physical and temporal (one environmental event in Iran lasted a whole week). His reputation in Europe as the modern theater's most significant avant-garde director/

playwright is not so universally acknowledged in his native country, the United States, but, with the performance of major works on Broadway and at the Metropolitan Opera House, as well as the Brooklyn Academy of Music and the studios of Wilson's theater group, the Byrd Hoffman School of Byrds, his place in the history of American contemporary theater, especially the strong and widespread experimental movement of the 1960's and 1970's, is assured.

Wilson has won several distinguished European awards for his work, including the Grand Prize for *Einstein on the Beach* at the International Festival of Nations in Belgrade in 1977. In the United States, an Obie Special Award Citation for Direction was presented to Wilson in 1974; he has held numerous Guggenheim and Rockefeller Foundation fellowships.

Biography

Born in Waco, Texas, to white, middle-class, Protestant and Southern parents, Robert Wilson attended high school in his hometown. A gangly, shy, but likable young man he had a speech impediment that was "cured" by a dance teacher, Mrs. Byrd Hoffman, who simply made Wilson realize that he could "take his time" to express himself. Following his early impulse to be a visual artist, Wilson studied at the University of Texas and privately in Paris, graduating from Pratt Institute in Brooklyn in 1965. During these years his patience with and sympathy for learning disabilities led him to work with autistic and disturbed children in Texas, where he discovered not only a unique talent for helping them but also a personal metaphor for his own anguish at the virtually universal inability to communicate that is part of the existential condition.

After several striking visual projects such as "Poles" (an "installation" of more than six hundred telephone poles in rural Ohio) and the creation of giant puppets for Jean-Claude van Itallie's experimental play *America Hurrah* (1966), Wilson found that performance art offered the best medium for self-expression. Several small works in which Wilson was the primary performer were followed by increasingly ambitious projects, incorporating more and more "actors" (many of whom were untrained laypersons drawn to Wilson's charismatic personality) and more and more special effects, stage props, and scenery. By 1967, he had gathered a group of friends and theater experimenters into the Byrd Hoffman School of Byrds (named in honor of the woman who helped Wilson in high school) and began an impressive series of long performance works, first in the modest studios of downtown New York, then at the Brooklyn Academy of Music (BAM), and finally throughout Europe, where the combination of his genius and the more benign attitude of political and cultural institutions toward the support of experimental art allowed Wilson to create his best work.

Wilson began his experimental career with theater pieces, "demonstrations," workshops, and other alternative theater activities; often he tried "sound" pieces, whose function was to experience pure sound rather than the contextual tyranny of words. After his early "sound" works gained acceptance, Wilson tried an actual opera, *The Life and Times of Joseph Stalin*, with music by Alan Lloyd, Igor Demjen, and others. It previewed in Copenhagen as a production of the Byrd Hoffman School of Byrds but premiered at the Brooklyn Academy of Music in December of 1973. Truncated versions of the opera were subsequently performed, along with his next opera, *A Letter for Queen Victoria.* The following years continued Wilson's collaborations with his team of composers, choreographers, visual artists, and actors: *Einstein on the Beach*, one of the most successful of this series of works, with music by Philip Glass, premiered in France. The return of his work to the United States met with both unreserved acclaim and scathing criticism, culminating in the financial failure of the monumental multinational project *the CIVIL warS*, rehearsed and also performed, in part, in six separate countries and scheduled to be performed during the Olympics in Los Angeles in 1984. The only surviving portion of that work, the American connective sections known as *Knee Plays*, has toured the United States in truncated form.

Wilson continued to produce work for the stage and the opera fields, often revising earlier material and producing it in an entirely different way from the original concept. His imaginative direction of the plays of other playwrights has always included strongly experimental design elements, choreography, and alterations of the original text material to suit his unique style. Some later works are *Cosmopolitan Greetings*, based on the poems of Allen Ginsberg; *The Forest*, Wilson and David Byrne's version of the Gilgamesh legend; and a video piece, *La Femme à la Cafetière* (1989), dealing with the painting of that name by Paul Cézanne.

Analysis

Robert Wilson's "Theatre of Visions" can best be described as a series of stage tableaux and slowly moving, apparently nondramatic activities which, in the individual minds of the witnesses, connect to form a nonreductive, nonrhetorical, nonnarrative but subjectively unified theatrical experience. This experience may or may not bear a relationship to the piece's title, often referring to a famous person, as in *The King of Spain*, *The Life and Times of Sigmund Freud*, *A Letter for Queen Victoria*, and *Edison*. In the course of the performance (always extremely long by traditional standards), the witness is presented with an opportunity to form whatever subjective connections the images suggest, either intellectually or subconsciously, during which process new "bisociations" are created. Although appearing arbitrary and unrehearsed, the activities are carefully arranged for maximum visual effect. Wilson, however, does not prescribe that effect; it remains for the witness to make what he or she will of the series of "visions," adding to the mix the private experiences and perceptions each one brings to the theatrical event.

The Life and Times of Joseph Stalin, performed first in Denmark, then at BAM, provides access to Wilson's prevailing imagery, because it is in large part a retrospective of all of his work up to that time. In seven acts, each with its own prologue, the piece lasted twelve hours (7:00 P.M. to 7:00 A.M.) and survived four performances in December of 1973. The actors cross and move in seven planes parallel to the proscenium arch; objects hang from the flies against a sky backdrop; silent, immobile figures fill the stage (act 2 alone, originally part of *The King of Spain*, contains "a boy who stands on a stool for the entire act, a blind man and two other men who play chess, Freud, Anna, Stalin, a photographer who takes their picture, a piano player, and a walrus," as well as the King of Spain himself). Processions, choruses, minstrel-show performers, historically costumed, nude, and white-draped figures troop on and off; a cave, a pyramid, "two-dimensional trees and a three-dimensional house" are among the stage scenery; the menagerie includes four turtles with a pool on their backs, wooden fish that swim in it, a bull (beheaded during act 4), nine apes, and twenty dancing ostriches. Yet the huge size of the stage and the unimaginably long duration of the performance dwarf the props, performers, and action, and virtually every activity seems to take place in slow motion. The witness, partly lulled by the slow pace and absence of dramatic intensification, and partly prompted by its uniqueness to perceive everything with a new "vision," eventually succumbs to the rhythms of the performance, coming away from the experience freed from stale habits of passive receptivity and re-energized by the aesthetic euphoria of visual stimulation.

The dialogue passages in this monumental retrospective point to a transition in Wilson's work about this time. Earlier pieces (such as *Deafman Glance*) were essentially silent, with occasional songs, incomprehensible utterances, or sounds, but after the ambitious outdoor piece entitled *Ka Mountain, GUARDenia Terrace*, Wilson turned in another direction, marked by an increasingly concentrated examination of language as partial, failed, or desensitized communication. The spoken word, often in the form of seemingly meaningless phrases repeated and repeated, begins to draw the focus of the work. In stark contrast to the virtual silence of his early work, Wilson now exhaustively examined the nature of the word onstage.

A Letter for Queen Victoria is the best illustration of this new concern. The "text," edited by Bonnie Marranca with her introductory essay and a preface by Wilson, immediately identifies the nonnormative nature of Wilson's language experiments during this period. While the spoken word transliterates theoretically into the written word, no simple recitation of the "text" could reproduce the immediacy of the spoken performance, especially taking into account the participation of Christopher Knowles, a young man who shares authorship in the piece, clinically "autistic" but, according to Wilson, possessing perceptual powers different from but not inferior to normal perceptions. Knowles's and Wilson's "performance" of the phrases, neither linked nor "meaningful," reduces the text to "architectonic" sounds that express the actors' personal relationship in untranslatable ways.

From the backdrops of projected sound-words to the concrete layout of the poetry of the script page, Wilson's main arena of theatrical inquiry during this period becomes the word, the script, and its tenuous relationship to the spoken aspect of theatrical experience. For example, a "press conference" in Yugoslavia consisted of Wilson's repeating the word "dinosaur" for twelve hours while cutting an onion. A thwarted radio project called for actors to say "Hmm," "O.K.," and "There" for five hours. When a word is repeatedly uttered in this fashion, it loses its denotative meaning, resurfacing in the consciousness as pure sound, and, according to Wilson, helping to reestablish emotional responses which have been dulled by the everyday use of language. Wilson's close association with Knowles, Raymond Andrews, and other children with limited hearing and speech has inspired him to experiment with language as "weather," that is, as atmospheric pressures that alter accompanying movements and gestures, transforming them into highly subjective but effective personal communications.

The difficulties of "reading" a Wilson text should serve as a reminder: It is important to understand Robert Wilson's work as performance art rather than primarily as literary expression. While the "scripts" of Wilson's works are theoretically available, often in obscure and out-of-print formats, the complexity and visuality of the experiences are best captured in the form of "performance documentation." This genre, originating in such journals of experimental theater as *The Drama Review* and *Performing Arts Journal*, seeks to record nonscripted or partially scripted theatrical events by means of carefully detailed description of the nature, sequence, and duration of those events, told from the standpoint of a neutral, informed witness who avoids as much as is humanly possible any evaluative or subjective interpretations of those events. Necessarily, some interpretation is inevitable, but the reader can re-create, however imperfectly, some of the visual "semiotics" of the original performance. In Wilson's case, the German critic Stefan Brecht has reported all the significant performance pieces of the Byrd Hoffman Studio up to 1978 in his exhaustively comprehensive study, *The Theatre of Visions: Robert Wilson* (1978), a title which is descriptive of Wilson's whole aesthetic approach.

After a very successful European tour of *Einstein on the Beach* (a collaboration with experimental music composer Philip Glass) in 1976, culminating in sold-out performances at the Metropolitan Opera House in New York City, Wilson found himself with increasingly complex production difficulties, brought on by his limitless vision and his refusal to compromise it with the petty realities of financial exigency. Forced to try smaller works such as *I Was Sitting On My Patio This Guy Appeared I Thought I Was Hallucinating*, Wilson seemed to be gathering his energy for his masterpiece, *the CIVIL warS*, a work that was to combine the most striking scenes and activities from earlier work with new visions on a grand scale. Yet after years of preparation in six countries and countless fund-raising trips and meetings, Wilson was forced to abandon his epic cycle, expressly designed in scope and theme for the Olympic Arts Festival in 1984. Efforts to mount it in Austin, Texas, in 1986 fell to financial realities as well; American audiences could only glimpse the tattered fragments of the Wagnerian vision in a tour of the diminutive *Knee Plays*, whose original purpose was to link the larger segments together.

No discussion of modern opera or experimental theater can be complete without taking Wilson's work into account. He is a writer, designer, and director whose avant-garde, multifaceted works combine operatic size and musical complexity with the visual possibilities of the stage and the meditative concentration of philosophical speculation. Wilson's imaginative and demanding productions have forced opera to expand its self-definition to include works as far removed from nineteenth century notions as his collaborators—Meredith Monk, David Byrne, Allen Ginsberg, Christopher Knowles, Laurie Anderson, Richard Foreman, and many others—are different from their classical counterparts in dance, theater, and dramaturgy; he has claimed his place in theater and opera history. His theatrical vision has no limitations of size or duration, and he will be satisfied only when the world stages itself.

Bibliography

Bigsby, C. W. E. *Beyond Broadway.* Vol. 3 in *A Critical Introduction to Twentieth-Century American Drama.* Cambridge, England: Cambridge University Press, 1985. A full chapter on Wilson (in addition to numerous mentions throughout the book) covers his life, his early work with speech-impaired individuals, and his association with the Byrd Hoffman School of Byrds, and describes *Ka Mountain, GUARDenia Terrace*, *$ Value of Man*, and other stage pieces. Behind his work, Bigsby says, "there lies a romantic conviction about continuity, a touching faith about the possibility of communication and the essentially holistic nature of experience."

Byrne, David. "*The Forest*: A Preview of the Next Wilson-Byrne Collaboration." Interview by Laurence Shyer. *Theater* 19 (Summer/Fall 1988): 6-11. This interview with David Byrne discusses the nature of his collaboration with Wilson and contains many indirect Wilson quotations. Much on Wilson's forming a Berlin company in the fall of 1987 to make this Gilgamesh version (*The Forest*). Includes a seven-act breakdown of images in photographs and text.

Croyden, Margaret. *Lunatics, Lovers, and Poets: The Contemporary Experimental Theatre.* New York: McGraw-Hill, 1974. A description of the Byrd Hoffman School of Byrds, its "aesthetic of the Beautiful," and Wilson's experiences with brain-damaged children who "responded to dance and movement therapy." Much of the theatre of silence is wordless, Croyden notes, "and in some of his later workshop pieces, where words are uttered, the effect is that of silence nonetheless." Deals at length with *Deafman Glance.*

Deak, Frantisek. "Robert Wilson." In *The New Theatre: Performance Documentation*, edited by Michael Kirby. New York: New York University Press, 1974. A reprint of an article originally appearing in *The Drama Review* (June, 1974), unique in its fully illustrated (with photographs by Carl Paler) white-on-black pages. Gives a strong impression of the performance itself, in an act-by-act visual description accompanied by striking production shots.

Shyer, Laurence. *Robert Wilson and His Collaborators.* New York: Theatre Communications Group, 1989. The most complete and authoritative record of Wilson's busy artistic life and his relationships with his collaborators (arranged by artistic specialty). This indispensable volume is illustrated with photographs and drawings of most of Wilson's productions and is complemented by a strong chronology (with comments by contemporaries) and a select bibliography.

Zurbrugg, Nicholas. "Post-Modernism and the Multi-Media Sensibility: Heiner Muller's *Hamletmachine* and the Art of Robert Wilson." *Modern Drama* 31 (September, 1988): 439-453. Zurbrugg finds that "Wilson's aesthetic seems to hover somewhere between [Samuel] Beckett's and [John] Cage's antithetical explorations of form, ambiguity, chance and rule." Offers a strong discussion of Wilson's collaboration with the East German playwright and follows this article by Arthur Holmberg's "conversation" with Wilson and Heiner Muller.

Thomas J. Taylor

WILLIAM WYCHERLEY

Born: Clive(?), England; May 28, 1641(?)
Died: London, England; December 31, 1715

Principal drama

Love in a Wood: Or, St. James's Park, pr. 1671, pb. 1672; *The Gentleman Dancing-Master*, pr. 1672, pb. 1673 (adaptation of Pedro Calderón de la Barca's play *El maestro de danzar*); *The Country Wife*, pr., pb. 1675; *The Plain-Dealer*, pr. 1676, pb. 1677; *Complete Plays*, pb. 1967.

Other literary forms

Although William Wycherley's reputation among modern readers rests entirely upon his work as a playwright, he wrote poetry as well, most of it in his later years. Twenty-eight years after his last play, he published *Miscellany Poems: As Satyrs, Epistles, Love-Verses, Songs, Sonnets, Etc.* (1704), a collection of unremarkable pieces on a variety of subjects. The volume has lighter verses, songs of wine and women, but to the reader of the plays, there is matter of perhaps greater interest. Certain poems suggest that the dark vision of the later dramas continued to grow in Wycherley until he despaired of any hope for humanity.

Achievements

Wycherley's dramatic canon consists of only four plays, and his stature in English letters depends almost entirely on only one, *The Country Wife*. In his own day, *The Plain-Dealer* was his most popular comedy, but more recent criticism has called attention to certain problems with that play that have diminished its reputation. Interestingly, the play's flaws are a result of Wycherley's excessiveness in the very quality that makes his dramatic achievement unique. More than his contemporaries, Wycherley deals bluntly (some critics have said crudely) with the tendency of social conventions to corrupt natural human instincts. More specifically, he posits the need of men and women to come together in relationships of love and mutual respect, and he exposes the ills that result when that need is perverted by marriage for purely material reasons. As the real meaning for marriage, the strongest bond between two individuals, becomes infected and weakened by social concerns, so the more casual relationships between men and women suffer corruption as well. Finally, Wycherley's vision is a world of grotesques, moral cripples, through which a very few good people grope their way in search of honorable relationships.

Biography

It is not certain exactly where and when William Wycherley was born.

The year may have been 1640 or 1641 and the place Clive in Shropshire or Basing House in Hampshire. His father, Daniel Wycherley, was serving as teller to the Exchequer at the time of William's birth; later, he served as chief steward to the Marquis of Winchester and came under suspicion of embezzlement. In 1655, young Wycherley was sent for education to France, where he became a favorite of Madame de Montausier, who was instrumental in his conversion to Catholicism, although he returned to the Anglican Church in 1660. Wycherley stayed in France for four years, then returned to England and entered Queen's College at Oxford. He took no degree from Oxford and soon entered the Inner Temple. Law, however, was never a genuine interest for him. Court life held far greater appeal, and the ingratiating young man became a favorite of the Duchess of Cleveland, King Charles II's mistress. It was to her that he dedicated his first play, *Love in a Wood*, which opened in 1671 at the Theatre Royal in Drury Lane. He wrote only three more plays, and his entire career as a playwright spanned only a relatively few years.

In 1678, as a result of ill health, Wycherley was sent to Montpellier for a rest at the expense of Charles II. When Wycherley returned, the king offered him the position of tutor to his son, the young Duke of Richmond. The salary of fifteen hundred pounds a year, in addition to a pension when his services were no longer needed, was unusually generous. Unfortunately, Wycherley lost this fine opportunity and royal favor through a rash marriage. One day in 1679, he happened to meet a young woman in a London bookstore looking for a copy of *The Plain-Dealer*. Wycherley introduced himself to the young woman, who proved to be Countess Laetitia Isabella, daughter of the Earl of Radnor and widow of the Earl of Drogheda. Shortly after that meeting, they married in secret, but Charles and the Duchess of Cleveland soon found out and, furious, banished him from the court. Wycherley's new wife was ill-tempered and jealous, and her wealth was less than her debts.

Their marriage was short-lived and ended with Isabella's death in 1681. Wycherley fell ever deeper into debt and in 1685 was confined to Fleet Prison, but the new king, James II, who believed that Manly, the protagonist of *The Plain-Dealer*, was a representation of himself, arranged for Wycherley's release and partial payment of his debts. The grateful author became a Catholic once more.

Wycherley's later years were rather uneventful. In 1704, he published his *Miscellany Poems* and began a correspondence with Alexander Pope, who was then only sixteen. In 1715, he married young Elizabeth Jackson, the intent apparently being to deny any inheritance to a despised nephew. "Manly" Wycherley, as he was known after his most popular character, died only eleven days after his wedding. He was buried in St. Paul's, Covent Garden.

Analysis

When read in the sequence of their production on the stage, William Wycherley's four plays make an interesting study of a dramatist gaining mastery of his art. The early plays display a number of structural flaws and basic problems with dramatizing a story. Through what could only be deliberate experimentation, the several elements of drama are shaped, weighed, and positioned in a variety of ways until a near-perfect formula is achieved in *The Country Wife*.

The highest plot line of *Love in a Wood*, Wycherley's first play, concerns the adventures and trials of Valentine and Christina, idealized lovers who would seem more at home in a romance than a Restoration comedy of manners. Valentine, who had fled England for France after wounding a man in a duel, has secretly returned and is staying with his friend, Vincent. Ranger, another friend of Vincent, met Christina by chance while investigating the activities of his own mistress, Lydia. Through no fault of her own, Christina has now become the object of Ranger's desire, and this he has hastened to tell Vincent. Valentine concludes that Christina has been untrue, and five acts of the expected misunderstandings and confusions are needed to convince him that his jealousy is unfounded and to unite the pair in matrimony. A second level of the play concerns the adventures of Vincent and Ranger that do not directly involve Valentine. The fop, Dapperwit, also moves on this level, and together these three gallants generate the witty dialogue and bawdy action expected by a Restoration audience. The lowest level is occupied by an array of rogues and whores. Central are the efforts of the procuress, Mrs. Joyner, to match a mistress, a husband, and a particular suitor with the old usurer (Alderman Gripe), his sister, and his daughter, respectively.

Love in a Wood is much more complex than this simplified summary suggests. Minor characters and story lines clutter the action to such an extent that all but the most attentive viewers must, like the characters, find themselves lost in a wood. The play is obviously the work of a new playwright, one who is still learning the craft. Wycherley knew well all the things that might go into a drama. He knew Ben Jonson and the humors; he understood his age's fondness for wit and was himself at least witty enough to satisfy that appetite; he was aware that ideal, romantic love could always find an audience; he understood the importance of effective dialogue and could write it forcefully and naturally, if not elegantly. Unity, too, he was certain, was one of the several ingredients that a playwright should add to the pot.

Conscious attention to all of these elements can be seen in this first play, but also apparent is Wycherley's failure to understand that a cook need not empty his entire pantry to prepare one dish. *Love in a Wood* simply tries to do too much. There are too many characters, too many plots; unity, which should be the natural effect of careful plotting and characterization, is lost in the stew. The rather artificial attempts to build in a kind of unity are obvious. For example, the play begins on the level of the low plot, with Mrs. Joyner being berated by Gripe's sister, Lady Flippant, for not finding her a rich husband. More low characters are added before the action shifts to the level of the wits, as Ranger and Vincent prepare to seek new love in St. James's Park. Ranger encounters Christina, and the audience is introduced to the high plot. In only two acts, Wycherley, in sequence from low to high, introduces his principals and plots, but there the neat if obvious organization ends as the action shifts among characters and levels quickly and too often without clear purpose.

Another and again only partially successful unifying device is the use of certain key characters as links between the three major plot levels. Both Vincent and Ranger serve to tie the world of Valentine and Christina to that of the wits; Ranger is actually the catalyst for the action involving the ideal lovers. Dapperwit exists in a limbo between the wits and the low characters. He does keep company with Vincent and Ranger but is clearly more fop than wit, and unlike them, his existence affects but little the world of Valentine and Christina. Dapperwit is much more at home with Mrs. Joyner and Lady Flippant, and on this level he does help to move the action. Thus, the low is directly linked to the middle and the middle to the high. There is still, however, a quite obvious gap between the high and the low; no single character links the extremes.

Construction and theme cannot be separated, and Wycherley's failure to achieve effective unity of design is reflected in his ambiguous message. Happy marriage based on ideal love appears possible. Valentine and Christina exist in the real world of Restoration London, and their love survives nicely in that world, but there, too, live Gripe, Flippant, and Dapperwit, and their message must leave the audience quite confused as to what ideal love is really all about.

Wycherley's second play, *The Gentleman Dancing-Master*, adapted from Pedro Calderón de la Barca's *El maestro de danzar*, suggests that he was aware of the problems with *Love in a Wood*, but that he was unsure as to how to resolve them, for *The Gentleman Dancing-Master* is the pendulum at its opposite extreme. While *Love in a Wood* has three major plot levels and a host of minor intrigues and adventures, *The Gentleman Dancing-Master* has only one story to tell, and this it does with a cast of major characters only half the size of that of the first play. Hippolita, the fourteen-year-old daughter of Mr. Formal, is unhappily engaged to Mr. Paris, her cousin and an absurd Gallophile. Mr. Formal, almost as absurd in his devotion to Spanish manners and fashion, would do all in his power to preserve his daughter's virtue, and with the help of his widowed sister, Mrs. Caution, keeps her under careful watch. Hippolita, however, is smarter than the lot of them, and, with the unwitting help of Paris, she manages to conduct an affair with a young gallant, Mr. Gerrard, who at her suggestion poses as a dance instructor. The lovers plan an elopement, but Hippolita's doubts about Gerrard's motive—love or her money—and assorted other diversions postpone the nuptials until the end.

In his first play, Wycherley had aimed at too many targets. *The Gentleman Dancing-Master* aims at only one, a broad, comedic effect assisted by a large dose of farce. Wycherley himself was less than proud of this work as an indicator of his real literary skill, and critics have generally agreed that it has little to admire. First, there is the problem of the genre itself. Farce, while very popular with Restoration audiences, was held in low esteem by scholars. Truth to life was the principal criterion by which a play should be judged; so said most of the great English critics, including John Dryden, the leading dramatist, poet, and critic of the age. Believability is the least concern of a farce, for everything that contributes to a believable effect—fine characterization, realistic dialogue, tight plot development—must yield to the hilarity of the episode. Moreover, as farces go, *The Gentleman Dancing-Master* has been judged by many modern critics as especially uninventive.

To be sure, Wycherley's second play would never be studied as an example of Restoration comedy at its finest. Still, it is not without merit, and a brisk stage rendition reveals strengths that are lost in a closet reading. For example, the single plot line tends to hold together the broadly comic episodes, achieving a sense of unity that is most often lacking in farce. The play is about Hippolita's efforts to find a suitable husband, and a Hippolita well acted can keep that design always before the audience. Hippolita, certainly one of Wycherley's more interesting characters, is responsible for adding a rather larger dash of satire than is commonly found in farce, not so large a dash as to make the flavor noticeably bitter—after all, she does get her man—but still enough that the reader of Wycherley's later, darker comedies can look back to *The Gentleman Dancing-Master* and notice a hint of what was to come.

In this glimpse of Restoration society, a fourteen-year-old girl only recently returned home from boarding school is complete master of the revels. She rejects her father's choice of a husband, engineers her own courtship, and marries the man she wants, all under her father's roof and her aunt's close guard, and neither is aware of what has happened until the closing lines of the play. It is she who invents the dancing-master fiction and transforms a shallow young man, who is more interested in a dowry than a good marriage, into acceptable husband material. She displays the naïveté and frankness of a child and the insight and cleverness of a mature adult and can move between these extremes in a matter of a few lines. Yet all of this talent and effort is needed to obtain what ideally should be taken for granted: an assurance that the words of the wedding vow will be sincere, that her marriage will be based on mutual love, honesty, and respect. In Wycherley's world, however, such assurances are difficult to find. Even a child must be devious to accomplish what is right, when her own father and intended husband are themselves prime examples of misrepresentation.

Mr. Paris, who would be known as Monsieur de Paris, and Mr. Formal, who prefers to be called Don Diego, are as contemptible as they are absurd. Wycherley created the roles for James Nokes and Edward Angel, two of the most famous comic actors of the day. Indeed, Paris' part is the largest in the play, for it was doubtless Nokes as a French fool that the audience came to see. Both Formal and Paris have rejected what they are, Englishmen, to ape foreign manners: It is small wonder that they are so unaware of Hippolita's machinations. They have their own lies to live and would rather argue with each other as to whose lie is better than to see the reality of what is happening. That a fourteen-year-old girl with a sense of purpose can manipulate the adult world says little for that world. That the best husband available is a man so easily directed, a man who must be tested for sincerity before deemed acceptable, adds little reason for optimism, and finally that that fourteen-year-old is herself unsure of the true nature of her young man and is after all only adept at fooling fools must bring small reassurance. *The Gentleman Dancing-Master* is a comedy, a farce, but already the darker shadows have begun to fall.

With his third effort, Wycherley brilliantly overcame the problems of his first two plays. *The Country Wife* is generally acknowledged as one of the finest comedies of the Restoration, and it is still frequently acted, not so much as a historical curiosity but because it is good theater. The plot is somewhat more complex than that of *The Gentleman Dancing-Master*, but it is tightly unified by linking characters who have real business in the variety of situations; there is none of the baffling confusion of *Love in a Wood*. The main action is moved by Horner—who, as his name suggests, delights in making cuckolds of the London husbands. To that end, he has caused the false rumor of his own impotence to be spread about the town; as expected, husbands who would never let their wives near Horner have foolishly relaxed their guard. Lady Fidget, Mrs. Dainty Fidget, and Mrs. Squeamish are among his willing conquests.

The adventures of Margery Pinchwife, the title character, form a second but closely related plot. Jack Pinchwife married his country wife because he was hopeful that such a woman would be ignorant of the fashions of the city and the promiscuity of the gallants and ladies. This decision, however, was not motivated by a sense of higher morality; indeed, Pinchwife may well be the most immoral character in the play, for, as his name suggests, his every action is directed by his intense fear of being made a cuckold and by a jealousy that can move him to viciousness. Despite her husband, Margery has learned of the way of the world and is anxious to sample it. She realizes that there are better relationships than that which she enjoys with Pinchwife and so cultivates an affair with Horner. The third plot does not relate quite so directly to the main plot, but the characters and action provide some obvious contrasts that serve to clarify and further comment on the play's theme. Alithea, Pinchwife's sister, is engaged to Sparkish. She is an intelligent woman of genuine honor; he is the usual ridiculous fop that so delighted Restoration audiences. Fully aware that her fiancé is a fool, she is resolved to go through with their arranged marriage, though in fact she loves Harcourt, a friend of Horner, and he loves her. At the last, Sparkish's misunderstanding of Alithea's part in the typically confusing episodes and intrigues that follow results in a broken engagement and a clear way to her union with Harcourt.

While Alithea's role is a relatively minor and unimpressive one on the stage, she does make a significant contribution to an understanding of Wycherley's message. Alithea stubbornly insists on behaving honorably in a world where there is no honor. She is obliged by custom and contract to go through with the marriage arranged by Pinchwife and respects that obligation, though the union must result in a life of misery and wasted talent for her and in material gain for men who neither need nor deserve it. In Alithea, the audience sees real virtue turned against itself by corrupt marital customs that not only make cuckolds of fools, which may not be so bad, but also make honorable people victims of their own honor, which is intolerable. Still, at the end, it is only Alithea who appears to have a chance for real happiness. Mrs. Pinchwife's unhappy fate is to return to her husband, while the husbands return to their fool's paradise, as Horner convincingly reaffirms the lie about his impotency.

Before concluding that Wycherley's message is to proclaim the inevitable rewards that come to virtue, one should remember that he had little choice but to inject some measure of happiness at the ending (the play is a comedy), and that Alithea's deliverance from Sparkish has nothing to do with the power of virtue. She is freed from the contract by Sparkish's stupidity and the chance outcome of the intrigues of the other characters. In the world of *The Country Wife*, honor is as impotent as Horner pretends to be, and if anything is temporarily set right, it is only because of luck.

The corruptive power of marriage without love is seen from a different perspective in the title character, Margery Pinchwife. Alithea shows the system's effect on honor; Margery shows its effect on innocence. She enters the world of fashion a complete ingenue, and so Pinchwife would keep her, but all that is said to her and all that she sees writes on the blank slate of her character. Her jealous husband foolishly describes the pleasures of city life, pleasures to be avoided, and thus awakens her interest in them; he takes her to a play dressed as a man, so that she will not draw the attention of other men, which gives her the inspiration to assume a disguise when she visits Horner. Yet it would not be altogether accurate to say that Margery is corrupted, for at the end of the play, her naïve belief that she can exchange Pinchwife for Horner as her husband and live a happily married life ever after shows a character who has really learned nothing of how the system works. She does, indeed, do things that conventional morality would deem wicked, but she is merely aping what she has seen: These are the proper city responses, written on the slate by the characters around her, and against the background of her innocence, their conduct is brought into sharp relief. Hers is rightly the title role, for through her the audience clearly sees the nature of the other characters and the world they have created. There is no happy ending for Margery. Luck does not smile on her; she has not learned the true cunning of Horner that would allow her to make the best of the situation, and she is not one of the fools who can delude themselves with happy lies. She strikes a note at the end that is not quite comedy.

Mr. Harry Horner has been attacked by three hundred years of critics as one of the most immoral creations of the Restoration stage. In fact, there is no question of moral or immoral conduct in the high society in which he moves. The clearly moral alternative simply does not exist, and heroes are recognizable only by their superior wit and not at all by their deeds. Thus, though Horner does invent an obscene lie to help him bed other men's wives, his contempt for his victims manages to make him something more than simply another rake. He has honor of a sort, but certainly not Alithea's passive honor, not the honor of the martyr. Horner's honor allows him to use the weapons of the system against itself, and to him is the victory, for, with his lie still intact, he leaves the field strewn with cuckolds. That lie, however, is more than a tool for undoing fools; it is Wycherley's comment on the society. As the action moves the audience among various couples, it becomes increasingly clear that marriage has nothing to do with love or basic nature. It has become a thing arranged on paper and bought with money. Horner's impotence is a fiction. Ironically, the real sterility exists in the marriages of his victims.

Wycherley's final and longest play, *The Plain-Dealer*, confirms what was apparent in *The Country Wife*: The author had learned well the lessons of plot construction and structural unity. It poses other problems of characterization, however, that make it less a masterpiece than his third effort. The story is simple. There are only two plots, and all the principal characters occupy the same social level and have occasion to interact, thus creating a sense of unity. Captain Manly, the title character, is described by the author as honest, surly, and good-humored. He believes firmly in plain dealing, and the shortage of others who share that belief has led him to misanthropy. After losing his ship in the Dutch wars, Manly has returned to London to seek another vessel. He soon discovers that his mistress, Olivia, thought to be a plain dealer like him, has married another man and appropriated the money Manly had left in her care. Torn between contempt and affection, Manly sends his young aide, Fidelia, to arrange a meeting with Olivia. Instead, Olivia develops a passion for Fidelia, who in fact is a wealthy young heiress disguised as a boy to be near Manly, whom she loves. Manly next discovers that Olivia's secret husband is Vernish, the only man he really trusted. At Olivia's home, Manly fights Vernish, takes back the money, and discovers that Fidelia, who lost her wig in the commotion, is really a young woman. He immediately decides that Fidelia is a more proper object for his affection, and together the couple plan their future in the West Indies.

In the second plot, Lieutenant Freeman, a young friend of Manly, attempts to marry the cantankerous old Widow Blackacre for her fortune. The widow, whose only delight is in controlling her own business and suing people, wants no part of such an arrangement. When Freeman convinces the widow's stupid son to accept him as his guardian with full power over his inheritance, Widow Blackacre retaliates by claiming that her son is a bastard and not a legal heir. Freeman, however, discovers this to be a lie, and in order to avoid a charge of perjury, the widow is forced to grant him a handsome annuity.

Captain Manly is perhaps the most puzzling character in Restoration drama, and the difficulty of the audience in interpreting him obscures the theme of the play. Like that other famous voyager, Lemuel Gulliver, Manly suffers from misanthropy, and the distorted judgment to which it leads him makes it difficult to judge how representative a spokesman for the author he is intended to be. Certainly he has qualities to be admired. In relation to the collection of liars and frauds that surrounds him, his utter contempt is justified and his bluntness is refreshing. Still, he recognizes neither hypocrisy nor plain dealing when he sees them, and at times he is as willing to overlook or condone deliberate deception as he is at other times anxious to condemn it. Moreover, he is, like Horner, quite willing to practice a little deception of his own if it suits his purpose. Indeed, if Manly were not wrong and self-contradictory most of the time, there would be no play, for his mistakes move the plot. His greatest mistake is his choice of Olivia. She mouths the same philosophy of plain dealing as Manly but marries and steals in secret. Fidelia is the cause of another mistake; the plain dealer wanders through five acts unaware that his aide, the person with whom he plots revenge against Olivia, is a woman, and when her gender is discovered, he transfers his affection with embarrassing rapidity. Throughout those five acts, he has remained blind to the fact that Fidelia displays a faithfulness and devotion rare in a human being, and when he decides at last to love her, he is equally unconcerned that her disguise, while for a good purpose, was hardly consistent with plain dealing.

There is also the problem of Freeman. The lieutenant is really Manly's best friend, for Vernish turns out to be a villain. In fact, Freeman is the only character who deals plainly with Manly. He quite frankly tells his captain that truth is a handicap in the social world and honestly confesses his motives in the wooing of Widow Blackacre. Manly cannot tolerate the company of most dissemblers and hypocrites, but Freeman is an exception; apparently, honest hypocrites are acceptable.

Despite Manly's several mistakes and inconsistencies, he is still clearly the hero of the play, and Wycherley certainly intended the general audience response to be positive. After all, Manly does have the love of a good woman, who seems willing to suffer almost any humiliation for his sake, and he does have the sincere friendship of Freeman, something of a rogue, to be sure, but a likable rogue. The problems with Manly's philosophy of plain dealing are more apparent in a careful reading than they are in a lively performance, and his confusing behavior is in part a result of his being made to interact with Freeman and Fidelia, who have characterization problems of their own. Fidelia in almost any other play would present no difficulty. She is an idealized female who would be quite at home in a romance, but she seems strangely out of place in a world that requires a misanthrope for a hero. Moreover, her male disguise, which jars with Manly's love of plain dealing, is a conventional comedic device that would present no problem on another stage. Freeman, too, is a conventional figure, but confidant to Manly is not a proper job for a lovable rogue, and while Freeman would make an ideal friend for Horner, his role in *The Plain-Dealer* confuses the message.

Wycherley's final play, then, cannot be judged his best. It may well be, however, his darkest comment on society. Manly is certainly the closest thing to a direct spokesman that Wycherley ever created, and in *The Plain-Dealer* that spokesman was finally allowed to comment openly on the world of knaves and fools and hypocrites and whores that had been presented with increasing pessimism in the three earlier plays. The problems with Manly may well be the inevitable culmination of Wycherley's vision: Society corrupts honor and innocence and infects with confusion even the best efforts of the best people. There is no firm ground on which a plain dealer can stand.

Other major works

POETRY: *Miscellany Poems: As Satyrs, Epistles, Love-Verses, Songs, Sonnets, Etc.*, 1704.

Bibliography

Chadwick, W. R. *The Four Plays of William Wycherley: A Study in the De-*

velopment of a Dramatist. The Hague: Mouton, 1975. This study looks at each of the plays in chronological order to discover Wycherley's distinctive characteristics as a playwright, the reasons why he wrote, the type of comedy he enjoyed, his main concerns, and his development as a dramatist. Chadwick does not attempt to argue that posterity's overall assessment of the plays as stage pieces has been inaccurate. What is clear from the study is that Wycherley's attitude toward life and art was both comic and serious. Contains a biographical table, bibliography, and appendix.

Markley, Robert. *Two Edg'd Weapons: Style and Dialogue in the Comedies of Etherege, Wycherley, and Congreve.* New York: Oxford University Press, 1988. This excellent study is concerned with the comic style and language of Sir George Etherege, Wycherley, and William Congreve as a means of individual expression, as the rewriting or adaptation of systems of theatrical signification in predecessors, as the reflection of particular cultural codes of speech and behavior that would be accessible to their audience, and as a comment on the culture of which they and their audience were a part. Bibliography.

Rogers, Katharine M. *William Wycherley.* New York: Twayne, 1972. In this useful book for the general reader, the author argues that Wycherley's plays succeed both as brilliant comedies of wit and as significant social commentaries. After sketching the fashionable Restoration milieu in which Wycherley flourished, Rogers shows how the dramatist's early plays anticipated his two masterpieces. He examines in more detail the characters, humor, structure, and satire of Wycherley's major works, *The Country Wife* and *The Plain-Dealer.* Finally, he offers an account of the latter half of the dramatist's life, after he stopped writing plays, since this period has not been thoroughly presented elsewhere. Chronology, bibliography.

Vernon, P. F. *William Wycherley.* London: Longmans, Green, 1965. Vernon states that the playwright can be firmly placed in the mainstream of English satirists. His clear, incisive mind enabled him to seek out the false premises underlying various social habits. In this perceptive and sympathetic study, Wycherley's life and career as a dramatist are examined against the backdrop of his social milieu. Bibliography.

Zimbardo, Rose A. *Wycherley's Drama: A Link in the Development of English Satire.* New Haven, Conn.: Yale University Press, 1965. The author of this well-written book argues against using the label "Restoration comedy" to describe Wycherley's work. According to Zimbardo, from the beginning of his career Wycherley wrote in traditions that antedate and stretch beyond the forty-year period known as the Restoration to which the dramatist has been traditionally confined. Wycherley's mature plays, the critic states, span the gap between two great ages of English satire and point to the highest achievement in this genre, the satire of the Augustan Age.

William J. Heim
(Revised by *Genevieve Slomski*)

WILLIAM BUTLER YEATS

Born: Sandymount, near Dublin, Ireland; June 13, 1865
Died: Cap Martin, France; January 28, 1939

Principal drama

The Countess Cathleen, pb. 1892, pr. 1899; *The Land of Heart's Desire*, pr., pb. 1894; *Cathleen ni Houlihan*, pr., pb. 1902 (with Lady Augusta Gregory); *The Pot of Broth*, pr. 1902, pb. 1903 (with Lady Gregory); *The Hour-Glass*, pr. 1903, pr. 1912 (revised), pb. 1913; *The King's Threshold*, pr., pb. 1903 (with Lady Gregory); *On Baile's Strand*, pr. 1904, pb. 1905; *Deirdre*, pr. 1906, pb. 1907 (with Lady Gregory); *The Shadowy Waters*, pr. 1906, pb. 1907; *The Unicorn from the Stars*, pr. 1907, pb. 1908 (with Lady Gregory); *The Golden Helmet*, pr., pb. 1908; *The Green Helmet*, pr., pb. 1910; *At the Hawk's Well*, pr. 1916, pb. 1917; *The Player Queen*, pr. 1919, pb. 1922; *The Only Jealousy of Emer*, pb. 1919, pr. 1922; *The Dreaming of the Bones*, pb. 1919, pr. 1931; *Calvary*, pb. 1921; *Four Plays for Dancers*, pb. 1921 (includes *Calvary*, *At the Hawk's Well*, *The Dreaming of the Bones*, *The Only Jealousy of Emer*); *The Cat and the Moon*, pb. 1924, pr. 1931; *The Resurrection*, pb. 1927, pr. 1934; *The Words upon the Window-pane*, pr. 1930, pb. 1934; *The Collected Plays of W. B. Yeats*, pb. 1934, 1952; *The King of the Great Clock Tower*, pr., pb. 1934; *A Full Moon in March*, pr. 1934, pb. 1935; *The Herne's Egg*, pb. 1938; *Purgatory*, pr. 1938, pb. 1939; *The Death of Cuchulain*, pb. 1939, pr. 1949; *Variorum Edition of the Plays of W. B. Yeats*, pb. 1966 (Russell K. Alspach, editor).

Other literary forms

Throughout a literary career spanning a half century, William Butler Yeats distinguished himself principally by means of the production of some dozen volumes of lyric poems. His early work is most clearly indebted to the English Romantics, but his commitment to the cause of the Irish Literary Revival, of which he was the leader, and to the management of its showcase, the Abbey Theatre, gave him an increasingly public voice. The poetry of his last twenty years contains his most complex, modernist, and profound work and comprises the highest achievement in that genre during the twentieth century.

Yeats was also the author of a considerable body of essays, reviews, and introductions during a career of literary journalism, theatrical management, collecting and editing, and promoting the work of such collaborators as Lady Augusta Gregory and John Millington Synge: *Essays and Introductions* (1961), *Explorations* (1962), and *Uncollected Prose by W. B. Yeats* (2 volumes; 1970, 1976). Yeats's early excursions into short fiction are collected in *Mythologies* (1959). Autobiographical fragments are found in

Autobiographies (1926, 1955) and *Memoirs* (1972). *A Vision* (1925, 1937) sets forth a symbolic ordering of history and human character in a manner chiefly useful in explicating his poetry, while *The Senate Speeches of W. B. Yeats* (1960) gathers some of his public statements from the 1920's. The Yeats correspondence is partially collected in *The Letters of W. B. Yeats* (1954) and in *Ah, Sweet Dancer: W. B. Yeats, Margot Ruddock—A Correspondence* (1970).

Achievements

Yeats's reputation as one of the masters of modern literature rests mainly on his achievements in poetry, and his dramatic work has long been regarded less favorably as "poetry in the theater." This aspect of his oeuvre has, however, been reassessed in recent years, and he is currently regarded as one of the boldest and most original dramatists of the twentieth century. As one of the founders, first playwrights, and lifetime directors of the Abbey Theatre, Yeats was the central figure of the Irish Literary Revival. The example of efforts to develop a modern and national literature which drew on Celtic mythology, folklore, and the oral tradition of Ireland provided incentives for the latent talents of such dramatists as Lady Augusta Gregory, John Millington Synge, Padraic Colum, and Sean O'Casey.

Although Yeats experimented with several dramatic styles, including peasant realism, farce, and naturalism, his genius found its true métier in a highly sophisticated drama which combined poetry, dance, mask, and symbolic action to represent a world of ideals and pure passion. These plays, borrowed from the tradition of the Japanese Nō for their form and from Celtic heroic tales for their subjects, expressed Yeats's views of the primacy of imaginative or spiritual realities of which historical change and the differentiation of human character are emanations. Yeats was therefore at odds with modern realism and with its interest in individual character and social relations: An attitude of detachment and impersonality shaped his works into intensely ritualized expressions, having affinities both with religious drama and Absurdism.

Yeats lived through revolutions in politics and sensibility; most important, through a lifelong remaking of dramatic and lyric form and style, Yeats achieved a continuous renovation of his own spirit. Thus, he became one of those primarily responsible for the restoration to Ireland of its cultural heritage, at the same time forging an idiom which the modern world at large considers its own.

Biography

The eldest of the four children of John Butler Yeats, the painter, and his wife, Susan Pollexfen, William Butler Yeats was born in Sandymount, near Dublin. When he was nine years old, the family moved to London, where he attended the Godolphin School in Hammersmith, taking his holidays with his maternal grandparents in County Sligo in the rural west of Ireland. The Yeats family returned to Dublin in 1880, and the young Yeats thereafter completed his education at the high school and the Metropolitan Art School. During this time, from 1883 to 1886, he came under the influence of George Russell (Æ) and a circle of Dublin mystics, as well as John O'Leary, the aged Fenian leader.

These various influences turned the introverted boy from art to literature; from religious confusion (his mother was a Protestant, his father an agnostic) to Theosophy, the occult, and Rosicrucianism; and from the Oriental themes of his earliest literary efforts to Irish subjects. Yeats moved back to London in 1888. In 1890, he helped organize the Rhymers Club, where he made friends with many of the leading poets of the time, including Arthur Symons, William Morris, and Lionel Johnson, with whom he founded the Irish Literary Society in 1891.

In 1888, Yeats had met Maud Gonne, an actress and activist in behalf of Irish nationalism. A lifelong, unrequited obsession with her (she rejected marriage proposals in 1891 and again in 1916) accounts for the periodic intensification of his enthusiasm for nationalist politics, the subject of much of his poetry and two of his early plays, *The Countess Cathleen* and *Cathleen ni Houlihan*.

Yeats returned to Dublin in 1896, and in 1899, he collaborated with Edward Martyn and Lady Gregory in founding the Irish Literary Theatre, which in 1904 became the Abbey Theatre. The affairs of this theater—playwriting (peasant and Celtic themes), daily management, the promotion of playwrights with Irish subjects (Synge was the most notable)—were his preoccupations until about 1910.

After Ezra Pound introduced him to the Japanese Nō drama, Yeats wrote his *Four Plays for Dancers*: formal, symbolic, ritual plays based on Celtic, Irish, and Christian themes. He married Georgina Hyde-Lees in 1917 and, discovering her capacities as a medium, revived his interest in Spiritualism. With her assistance, he produced the systematized *A Vision*, which illuminates much of his mature drama and poetry. The Yeatses lived in Dublin and at Thoor Ballylee, a restored Norman tower in County Galway, and had two children. During the last twenty-five years of his life, Yeats produced his most mature work in poetry, prose, and drama. He was appointed a member of the Senate of the Irish Free State from 1922 to 1928, lectured widely in Europe and the United States, and received widespread recognition, including honorary doctorates and the Nobel Prize in Literature in 1923. In 1932, along with George Bernard Shaw and Æ, he founded the Irish Academy of Letters, and in 1936, he edited the controversial *Oxford Book of Modern Verse*. Failing health forced him to abandon Thoor Ballylee, and in the 1930's, he spent progressively more of each year in Italy and France. In 1939, shortly after completing his last play, *The Death of Cuchulain*, he died in the French Riviera and was temporarily buried there. His remains were returned to Drumcliff, County Sligo, his grandfather's parish, in 1948.

Analysis

William Butler Yeats's reputation justly rests upon his achievements in poetry, yet a considerable portion of that work is written for two or more voices: It is dramatic. Indeed, his first literary compositions were long dramatic poems, and throughout his life, he continued to publish his plays and poems side by side. Yeats believed that the language of poetry best represented imaginative reality, the life of the soul, or the introspective or subjective consciousness, as opposed to the spirit of science, the modern, extroverted age, the objective consciousness which draws its identity from external circumstances and which finds its appropriate expression in dramatic realism. Thus, throughout a career as a dramatist consisting of four distinct phases, Yeats's sympathies remained mystical, Symbolist, and removed from the mainstream of popular drama. Nevertheless, he is one of the genuinely original dramatists of the twentieth century, with influences on verse drama and the work of Samuel Beckett.

When Yeats joined talents and ambitions with Lady Gregory and Edward Martyn to form the Irish Literary Theatre in 1899, his first contributions to the venture were *The Countess Cathleen* and *Cathleen ni Houlihan*. The former is a rather static verse drama in which a heroic native aristocrat sells her soul to merchant-demons in order to save the starving peasants. The play aroused controversy over its doctrinal content in Catholic Ireland, and its author's doughty defense of independence in artistic and patriotic self-expression established a pattern that was often to repeat itself. His most dramatically successful early work, however, is *Cathleen ni Houlihan*, one of several peasant plays that Yeats wrote in collaboration with Lady Gregory.

The play depicts in realistic terms the diversion of a young man's intentions from his impending marriage to a phase of the 1798 rebellion in Ireland. An anonymous old woman becomes a young queen because of the heroic commitment of Michael Gillane. Here is *The Land of Heart's Desire* rewritten in nationalist terms: The thrifty realism of the peasants gradually yields to the incantatory power of the old woman's lament, and the political allegory is triumphantly announced in the famous curtain line. With Maud Gonne in the title role reciting the credo of nationalist Ireland, Yeats was accused of producing unworthy propaganda. He protested that it came to him in a dream, but like the subject matter of all of his early work, its origins are demonstrably in the native folklore which Yeats had been collecting and studying since his conversion to the cause of Ireland's cultural distinctiveness. The theme of this particular play is, indeed, traceable through popular ballad to the Gaelic *aisling* (vision) convention and to the theme of the lady and the king found in medieval Irish literature: Its power on an Irish stage is therefore attributable to more than its last line. Yeats was to wonder, with some justification, how much this play contributed to the Easter Rebellion of 1916.

Before the heroism of that week burst upon his and the nation's consciousness, Yeats was cultivating in himself and on the stage of the Abbey Theatre a renewed appreciation of the literature of ancient Ireland and its exaltation of heroic individualism, eloquence, aristocracy, and paganism. In the figure of Cuchulain, the hero of the Ulster Cycle, Yeats found the embodiment of these virtues, and he wrote a series of five plays dramatizing episodes from the hero's lone defense of Ulster, beginning with *On Baile's Strand*. Among Cuchulain's challengers is a young man in whom Cuchulain notes a resemblance to his abandoned wife, Aoife. Caught between his natural affinity for this image and his oath to King Conchubar to defend the province against intruders, Cuchulain is driven to combat. Too late, he discovers that the dead boy is his own son, and in his anguish he rushes, sword in hand, into the waves until he drowns.

This play marks a significant advance in technique on Yeats's early dramatic efforts in its tight control and complexity of theme. The theme of conflicting loyalties operates at several levels simultaneously, so that Cuchulain's roles as loyal soldier, independent hero, father, and son all conspire to bring on his tragic self-destruction. The framing device of the Fool and the Blind Man functions as an ironic low-life commentary on the serious central action, while at the same time casting up counterpart images of Conchubar and Cuchulain as creatures guided by similarly fitful lights.

Yeats went on to write four other Cuchulain plays, *The Golden Helmet*, *At the Hawk's Well*, *The Only Jealousy of Emer*, and *The Death of Cuchulain*, as well as several others drawn from Celtic sources made available by translators such as Lady Gregory. His dissatisfaction with modern realism, however, with its focus on the drama of individual character, distanced him from the kind of work that made the Abbey Theatre popular. When Ezra Pound introduced Yeats in 1913 to the Nō theater of Japan, Yeats recognized the tradition which would enable him to shape his own ideas into a successful poetic drama.

The Japanese Nō drama dates from the late Middle Ages, has strong Zen elements, and is highly stylized. It is a symbolic drama, developing the resources of mask, gesture, chanted dialogue, slow rhythmic dance, ornamental costume, chorus, and flute and drum to create an atmosphere of passionate reverie contained beneath an elegant repose. Yeats was attracted by the tone of gravity, detachment, mystery, grace, and nobility in these plays. His Spiritualist sympathies predisposed him to appreciate plays that featured figures in the process of "dreaming back" moments of extreme passion in their lives as they sought release from human desires and entrance into final peace. In his *Four Plays for Dancers*, especially *The Dreaming of the Bones* as well as in several later plays, these influences are evident. *The Dreaming of the Bones* is designed in two scenes joined by a choral interlude, according to the structure of a fantasy-style Nō such as *Nishikigi*. The Subordinate Player (here the Young Man) encounters the Main Players (here the Stranger and Young Girl) in a historical spot (the Abbey of Corcomroe) at a historical moment (1916). The Main Players tell the story of the place and ask for prayers and forgiveness of the Young Man, finally revealing themselves as the ghosts of Diarmuid MacMorrough and Dervorgilla (the twelfth century couple whose marriage was instrumental in the Norman invasion of Ireland). Because the Young Man is a modern Irish patriot for whom that liaison was the original sexual-political transgression, he refuses, and the couple is left to continue their purgatorial "dreaming back" of their tragic sin. The various themes of the play—dream, war, resurrection, cyclic change—coalesce in the emblems of the birds in the Musicians' final chorus. Subsequent experiments with the Nō form demonstrate Yeats's greater facility in adapting it to the expression of his own views of the afterlife and his mythologization of the Irish past—especially in *The Only Jealousy of Emer*, *The Words upon the Window-pane*, and *Purgatory*.

The Words upon the Window-pane is a daringly successful combination of Naturalism, Spiritualism, the "dreaming back" from the Nō, and Yeats's latter-day identification with eighteenth century Anglo-Ireland. In this dramatization of a Dublin séance, the tortured spirit of Jonathan Swift is invoked, though remaining unrecognized by any except the literary scholar John Corbet. Swift, the representative of intellectuality, classical ideals, and the natural aristocracy of Ireland, "dreams back" his rejection of the opportunity for fatherhood offered by Vanessa, thereby sharing Yeats's rejection of the "filthy modern tide" which would likely be their issue. In his management of middle-class character and dialogue, Yeats shows his capacities in the naturalistic style, but the dramatic coup here comes in the final scene, when these conventions are broken and the audience is left alone with an order of reality beyond the reach of skeptic or scholar.

In *Purgatory*, one of his last plays, Yeats achieved his most concentrated work for stage. The setting and action are symbolic, the language a brilliant fusion of colloquial and poetic idiom. The Old Man, the product of a marriage between a big house and a stable, lost his aristocratic mother at his birth and later murdered his drunken father. Now, accompanied by his son, the Old Man visits the scene of his parents' unfortunate wedding—unfortunate because it betrayed class and because it produced him, a parricide. In an attempt to break the chain of evil, the Old Man stabs his son, but to no avail: The spirits of his parents are trapped in a perpetual repetition of their crime, unless God intervenes. Here, Yeats has devised a complex dramatic symbol for the demise of aristocratic Anglo-Ireland, the approach of global conflict, and the relationship between the living conscience and the stages of spiritual purgation to be encountered after death. The play is thus a summary exposition of Yeats's social and philosophical views in the later years of his life, drawing on the disciplines of language and construction that he had refined over a lifetime of experimentation.

Other major works

SHORT FICTION: *John Sherman and Dhoya*, 1891, 1969; *The Celtic Twilight*, 1893; *The Secret Rose*, 1897; *The Tables of the Law and The Adoration of the Magi*, 1897; *Stories of Red Hanrahan*, 1904; *Mythologies*, 1959.

POETRY: *Mosada: A Dramatic Poem*, 1886; *Crossways*, 1889; *The Wanderings of Oisin and Other Poems*, 1889; *The Rose*, 1893; *The Wind Among the Reeds*, 1899; *In the Seven Woods*, 1903; *The Poetical Works of William B. Yeats*, 1906, 1907 (2 volumes); *The Green Helmet and Other Poems*, 1910; *Responsibilities*, 1914; *Responsibilities and Other Poems*, 1916; *The Wild Swans at Coole*, 1917, 1919; *Michael Robartes and the Dancer*, 1920; *The Tower*, 1928; *The Winding Stair and Other Poems*, 1933; *The Collected Poems of W. B. Yeats*, 1933, 1950; *A Full Moon in March*, 1935; *Last Poems and Plays*, 1940; *The Variorum Edition of the Poems of W. B. Yeats*, 1957 (Peter Allt and Russell K. Alspach, editors); *The Poems*, 1983; *The Poems: A New Edition*, 1984.

NONFICTION: *Ideas of Good and Evil*, 1903; *The Cutting of an Agate*, 1912; *Per Amica Silentia Lunae*, 1918; *Essays*, 1924; *A Vision*, 1925, 1937; *Autobiographies*, 1926, 1955; *A Packet for Ezra Pound*, 1929; *Essays, 1931-1936*, 1937; *The Autobiography of William Butler Yeats*, 1938; *On the Boiler*, 1939; *If I Were Four and Twenty*, 1940; *The Letters of W. B. Yeats*, 1954 (Allan Wade, editor); *The Senate Speeches of W. B. Yeats*, 1960 (Donald R. Pearce, editor); *Essays and Introductions*, 1961; *Explorations*, 1962; *Ah, Sweet Dancer: W. B. Yeats, Margot Ruddock—A Correspondence*, 1970 (Roger McHugh, editor); *Uncollected Prose by W. B. Yeats*, 1970 (volume 1, John P. Frayne, editor), 1976 (volume 2, Frayne and Colton Johnson, editors); *Memoirs*, 1972; *The Collected Letters of William Butler Yeats: Volume One, 1865-1895*, 1986.

MISCELLANEOUS: *The Collected Works in Verse and Prose of William Butler Yeats*, 1908.

Bibliography

Cowell, Raymond. *Critics on Yeats: Readings in Literary Criticism.* Coral Gables, Fla.: University of Miami Press, 1971. A short but useful summary of later scholarly views on Yeats's writing and also on his important role in the Celtic Renaissance.

Ellmann, Richard. *Yeats: The Man and the Masks.* New York: Macmillan, 1948. Rev. ed. New York: W. W. Norton, 1979. The classic study, written by the leading Yeats scholar less than a decade after Yeats's death, when many of his friends were alive, including Yeats's wife. Uses voluminous papers from Yeats's Dublin house.

Fletcher, Ian. *W. B. Yeats and His Contemporaries.* New York: St. Martin's Press, 1987. Places the Anglo-Irish Protestant Yeats firmly in his time and illuminates his work in the context of contemporary writers. The volume includes new essays and revised work on Yeats and the visual arts, and the resurgence in the 1890's of the political and religious movement central to Yeats's career as a poet, dramatist, critic, and nationalist leader.

Marcus, Philip L. *Yeats and the Beginning of the Irish Renaissance.* Ithaca, N.Y.: Cornell University Press, 1970. Draws on Yeats's abundant letters, reviews, articles, autobiographies, and papers to treat his literary career from 1855, when he first published poetry, to 1899, the formal debut of the Irish Literary Theatre.

Moore, John Rees. *Masks of Love and Death: Yeats as Dramatist.* Ithaca, N.Y.: Cornell University Press, 1971. Explains why a major poet felt compelled to become a playwright and why he was the most gifted poet to write for the theater since William Shakespeare.

Vendler, Helen Hennessy. *Yeats' Vision and the Later Plays.* Cambridge, Mass.: Harvard University Press, 1963. Explains Yeats's imagery and the nature of his poetic inspiration in his verse and dramas, demonstrating his position as the greatest poet of the modern era.

Cóilín D. Owens
(Revised by *Peter C. Holloran*)

PAUL ZINDEL

Born: Staten Island, New York; May 15, 1936

Principal drama

Dimensions of Peacocks, pr. 1959; *Euthanasia and the Endless Hearts*, pr. 1960; *A Dream of Swallows*, pr. 1964; *The Effect of Gamma Rays on Man-in-the-Moon Marigolds*, pr. 1965, pb. 1971; *And Miss Reardon Drinks a Little*, pr. 1967, pb. 1972; *The Secret Affairs of Mildred Wild*, pr. 1972, pb. 1973; *The Ladies Should Be in Bed*, pb. 1973; *Ladies at the Alamo*, pr. 1975, pb. 1977; *A Destiny with Half Moon Street*, pr. 1983; *Amulets Against the Dragon Forces*, pr. 1989.

Other literary forms

Paul Zindel once considered himself primarily a playwright, and in 1990 once said, "basically, I'm a dramatist"; he has, however, enjoyed great success as a writer of novels for teenagers, and it is in this capacity that he is best known. His first such work, *The Pigman* (1968), has sold in the millions, and sequels such as *The Pigman's Legacy* (1980) have followed. A 1989 book, *A Begonia for Miss Applebaum*, was critically well received, and the autobiographical *The Pigman and Me* was published in 1992. Zindel's teen characters confront the pangs and thrills of young adult reality as they reach for friendship, for romantic love, for mature perspectives on sexuality, and for success or at least survival in school or work. In 1984, Zindel published his first novel for adults, *When a Darkness Falls*.

Zindel has written screenplays for *Up the Sandbox* (1972), *Mame* (1974), *Runaway Train* (1983), and *Maria's Lovers* (1984), and a teleplay, *Let Me Hear You Whisper* (1966). He also writes for periodicals.

Achievements

Zindel's *The Effect of Gamma Rays on Man-in-the-Moon Marigolds* gained acceptance not only in the form of broadcasts on National Educational Television in New York but also through stage performance at the Alley Theatre in Houston, Texas. Zindel secured a Ford Foundation grant as a playwright-in-residence at the Alley in 1967. In 1970, the play opened in New York, Off-Broadway; then it moved to the New Theatre on Broadway. It closed on May 14, 1972, after 819 performances. *The Effect of Gamma Rays on Man-in-the-Moon Marigolds* received an Obie Award for the best Off-Broadway play in 1970. Also in 1970, Zindel won the New York Drama Critics Circle Award for Best American Play and the Vernon Rice Drama Desk Award as the most promising playwright of the season. In 1971, he received an honorary doctorate from his alma mater, Wagner

College, and a Pulitzer Prize for Drama.

The success of *The Effect of Gamma Rays on Man-in-the-Moon Marigolds* was followed in 1971 by a Broadway production of *And Miss Reardon Drinks A Little*, a play previously staged in Los Angeles in 1967. The Broadway production, starring Julie Harris, ran for 108 performances, and the play made the list of the ten best plays for the 1971 season. Zindel next brought a comedy to Broadway, *The Secret Affairs of Mildred Wild*, which lasted for only twenty-three performances.

Joining Actors' Studio in 1973, Zindel extensively revised earlier material to produce *Ladies at the Alamo*, which he himself directed at Actors' Studio for a two-week run in 1975. He directed the same play in a brief Broadway run in 1977, as well as a New York revival of *The Effect of Gamma Rays on Man-in-the-Moon Marigolds* in 1978. Finally, the Coconut Grove Playhouse in Coconut Grove, Florida, premiered Zindel's *A Destiny with Half Moon Street* in its 1982-1983 repertory.

Zindel's plays have moved from little and regional theaters to Broadway and back. Critics say that his later plays have not fulfilled the expectations raised by his initial success. Still, Zindel's plays continue to be performed in high school, college, touring company, and regional repertory productions.

Biography

Paul Zindel was born on May 15, 1936, in Staten Island, New York, to Paul and Betty (née Frank) Zindel. His father, a policeman, abandoned his wife and two small children, Paul and a sister. Betty Zindel, a practical nurse, launched into numerous ventures, ranging from real estate to dog breeding, and sometimes took in terminally ill patients for board and care. The family moved almost annually.

This transient life-style and his mother's unwillingness, if not inability, to form meaningful relationships acquainted young Zindel with various forms of loss. Pets allowed at one home might be forbidden by the next landlord. Dogs raised for sale would eventually be sold. Board-and-care patients would sometimes die. The frequent moves, too, kept the boy, more often than not, in the role of newcomer in a neighborhood. It grew simpler to enjoy the worlds of imagination and, when possible, the manageable environments of aquaria and terraria.

In school, Zindel occasionally acted in plays and skits, some of which he wrote himself. At fifteen, he contracted tuberculosis and spent about eighteen months in a sanatorium, the sole youth in an otherwise adult community. He learned some parlor games and studied piano during his stay; more important, he became an interested observer of adult behavior.

Returned to health and to high school, Zindel wrote a play for a contest sponsored by the American Cancer Society; it centered on a young pianist who recovers from a serious illness to play at Carnegie Hall. The play won for Zindel a Parker pen.

Zindel majored in chemistry at Wagner College in New York State. While completing his bachelor of science degree, he took a creative writing course with Edward Albee and wrote a play, *Dimensions of Peacocks*, during his senior year. Zindel was graduated in 1958, and after working briefly as a technical writer for a Manhattan chemical firm, he decided that he wanted to teach.

Completing a master of science degree at Wagner in 1959, Zindel began teaching chemistry and physics at Tottenville High School on Staten Island. His *Dimensions of Peacocks* received a minor staging; more significantly, he attended his first professional theater production, Lillian Hellman's *Toys in the Attic* (pr. 1960), and left with his appetite for theater whetted.

For the next several years, Zindel continued to teach and to write. A second play, *Euthanasia and the Endless Hearts*, had a brief coffeehouse production in 1960, and a third, *A Dream of Swallows*, managed a single performance Off-Broadway in 1964.

The Effect of Gamma Rays on Man-in-the-Moon Marigolds fared better. In 1965, it opened at the Alley Theatre in Houston, Texas. New York's National Educational Television ran four showings of its abridged teleplay format. Recognition grew, with the Ford Foundation underwriting Zindel as playwright-in-residence at the Alley in 1967. By 1969, Zindel felt sufficiently established in theater to resign from teaching. Playing in New York, *The Effect of Gamma Rays on Man-in-the-Moon Marigolds* accrued its various awards that prefaced the Pulitzer.

From the New York plaudits, Zindel went to writing screenplays in California. Paul Newman produced and directed a movie version of *The Effect of Gamma Rays on Man-in-the-Moon Marigolds* in 1972, and Zindel wrote screenplays for *Up the Sandbox* and *Mame*.

When *The Effects of Gamma Rays on Man-in-the-Moon Marigolds* was on the rise, a publisher suggested that Zindel should write fiction for the teen market. His first teen novel, *The Pigman*, was both a critical and a popular success, as were several subsequent teen novels. Some critics have complained that while the argot of the young constantly changes, the teen dialogue in Zindel's later novels is indistinguishable from that found in his novels of the late 1960's and early 1970's. In other ways, too, Zindel has been accused of merely repeating a successful formula.

In 1973, following the year in California, Zindel made two major decisions. He married Bonnie Hildebrand, a screenwriter with whom he later had two children, Elizabeth and David, and he joined the Actors' Studio in New York to learn the language of acting and directing as well as playwriting. At the same time, he resumed work on a manuscript which National Educational Television had turned down in 1970 as too explicit. In its earlier version, the play had centered on the exchanges and revelations of a group of women playing bridge and watching an exhibitionist in a building across the street. Zindel shifted the setting to a theater in Texas, and the conflict to a battle for control of the theater. To make the five characters more authentic, Zindel conducted in-depth interviews with five actresses from the Actors' Studio. The result was *Ladies at the Alamo.*

Beginning in the mid-1970's, Zindel became more active as a novelist than as a dramatist, but he continued to be involved in the theater, producing new work as well as adaptations. He occasionally traveled to regional productions of his plays as part of publicity campaigns (as he did for the 1990 Cleveland Playhouse revival of *The Effect of Gamma Rays on Man-in-the-Moon Marigolds*), and to be active as a moderator for the Actors Studio West, in the Los Angeles Playwrights' Unit. According to interviews, the process of filmmaking was destructive for him. His young adult novels are sometimes turned into plays; for example, *Confessions of a Teenage Baboon* (1977) began as a novel but became *Amulets Against the Dragon Forces*, produced at the Circle Repertory Theatre in 1989.

Analysis

Paul Zindel's plays closely follow his own life experience; certain features of his early years recur in his drama. His mother was bitter, transient, reclusive, and presumably uncertain of her place in life. Zindel's major plays commonly depict women struggling for identity and fulfillment, often damaged, if not destroyed, by betrayals or deaths of loved ones. Another recurring theme of Zindel's plays is the notion that modern secular society has abandoned traditional religion in favor of science, technology, and a humane concern for the present world, rather than interest in a world hereafter.

The Effect of Gamma Rays on Man-in-the-Moon Marigolds opens to observers the lives of Beatrice Hunsdorfer and her two teenage daughters, Ruth and Tillie. Beatrice, overtly modeled after Zindel's mother, is a cynical, verbally abusive paranoid schizophrenic. Her untidy home was once her father's vegetable store. Her husband left her long ago and later died of a heart attack. For income, Beatrice boards an aged woman who needs a walker to creep slowly from bed to table to bathroom and back to bed.

Ruth, the elder daughter, is the more physically attractive yet is emotionally unstable and subject to convulsions in times of stress. Tillie, the younger, is bright and eager to learn. Beatrice, more concerned about her girls' looks and marriageability than about their intellectual growth, badgers both daughters but is most severe with Tillie.

Act 1 opens with Tillie, in darkness, marveling that the atoms in her hand may trace back to a cosmic tongue of fire predating the birth of the sun and the solar system. As lights rise on the home scene, Beatrice fields a telephone call from Mr. Goodman, Tillie's science teacher. He is concerned about Tillie's absences. Beatrice responds with several defenses. She thanks Mr. Goodman for giving Tillie a pet rabbit and compliments him on his looks. Claiming that Tillie does not always want to go to school, Beatrice says that she does not want to put too much pressure on Tillie, lest she turn convulsive, as Ruth has done. The phone call ended, Beatrice derides Tillie and Mr. Goodman, then orders Tillie to stay home. The girl is anxious to see a cloud-chamber experiment in science class. Beatrice threatens to kill the rabbit if Tillie goes. In contrast, Beatrice encourages Ruth to go to school, lets her rummage through mother's purse for lipstick, and gives her a cigarette on request. Ruth scratches Beatrice's back and gives negative reports on Tillie's activities at school. She also reveals that she has seen the school file on the family. It records the parents' divorce, the absent father's death, and Ruth's nervous breakdown.

The scene fades to darkness, and again Tillie speaks. She describes the fountain of atoms visible in the cloud chamber, a phenomenon which could go on for eternity. Rising lights reveal Tillie preparing to plant irradiated seeds. Beatrice, scanning realty advertisements, mixes conjecture on the potential of various properties with questions about Tillie's science project. Nanny, the aged boarder, begins the slow trek to the table as Tillie tries to explain the concept of atomic half-life to Beatrice. Beatrice disparages Nanny, her daughters, and herself through derisive double meanings for the term "half-life."

Beatrice phones Mr. Goodman, expressing concern that Tillie's seeds were irradiated, turning aside his explanations. After several other demonstrations of instability and cruelty, Beatrice shows another aspect of her character. During a thunderstorm at night, Ruth suffers another seizure. Beatrice orders Tillie back to bed in typically harsh fashion but cradles Ruth with genuine compassion and tells how her father, Ruth's grandfather, used to sell fruit and vegetables from a horse-drawn wagon. Beatrice's mother had died quite early, and her father fell seriously ill while Beatrice was still rather young. Anxious for her future, he urged her to marry for security's sake. She still sees her father's face in her nightmares.

The following scene shows Beatrice again lashing out at Tillie and Nanny until Ruth dashes in. She reports excitedly that Tillie is a finalist in the science fair. The principal calls to ask Beatrice to attend the final judging and awards. Beatrice is rude and evasive. Her first thought is that people will ridicule her. Only after Tillie runs off in tears does Beatrice realize how her paranoiac response has hurt Tillie.

Act 2 opens with the Hunsdorfers about to leave for the final science fair presentations. Working as an attendance aide for Mr. Goodman, Ruth has overheard gossip about Beatrice, who used to be called "Betty the Loon." Ruth blackmails Tillie into giving her the rabbit by threatening to tell Beatrice the school gossip. Tillie concedes—she deeply wants her mother to share this one significant event in her life, even at the cost of her pet—but when Beatrice orders Ruth to stay home with Nanny, Ruth explodes with the epithet "Betty the Loon," and Beatrice crumbles emotionally. Ruth goes to school in Beatrice's place. In a scene change through a lighting shift, another science fair finalist, Janice Vickery, superficially explains the past, present, and future of her cat skeleton. Back at the Hunsdorfer home, Beatrice makes two phone calls. One is a bitter call to the high school. The other is to Nanny's daughter: Beatrice wants Nanny out of the house the next day. Finally, Beatrice heads upstairs with a bottle of chloroform.

In another shift by spotlight, Tillie cites the past, present, and future of her project. Lightly irradiated seeds produced normal plants. Moderately irradiated seeds produced various mutations. The heavily bombarded seeds either died or produced dwarfs. Knowing the range of effects, she believes some mutations will be good. She declares her faith in the strange, beautiful energy of the atom.

Beatrice is drunk when the girls get home. She has begun to refit the living room for a tea shop. Ruth brings the dead rabbit downstairs and goes into convulsions. The play closes with Tillie declaring her curiosity about the universe, her sense of place in the order of things, and her fascination with the atom.

The Effect of Gamma Rays on Man-in-the-Moon Marigolds presents a family, broken as Zindel's was, in financial straits, deriving income from a board-and-care patient, as Zindel's family had. Beatrice's unfinished real-estate and beauty classes mirror the varied attempts Zindel's mother made at supporting the family. The significance of Beatrice's preparation, in the last scene, for a tea shop is open to question. The move hints at growth in her character, yet she has killed the rabbit, the symbol of warmth and tenderness for the daughters. Tillie's success at least has stirred Beatrice to a new beginning.

Ruth has shifted from contempt for Tillie to pride in Tillie's achievement. That pride, however, seems rooted more in Ruth's concern for social status than in genuine understanding of either Tillie or the experiment. Tillie herself has not changed significantly in the play. At the outset, she speaks of her fascination with science. At the end, her success confirms her self-esteem and potential for growth in spite of the abuse from home.

Thus, the play relies on revelation of character more than on development of character in response to conflict. In a decade accustomed to "slice-of-life" literature and ambiguous if not bleak conclusions to many stories and plays, *The Effect of Gamma Rays on Man-in-the-Moon Marigolds* presents a positive faith in the future through science, and hope for one character in overcoming the emotional damage common in modern life.

And Miss Reardon Drinks a Little offers a different constellation of women but still mirrors several aspects of Zindel's personal experience. The three Reardon sisters, Ceil, Catherine, and Anna, embody many of the ills of teachers long settled in the education system, ills well-known to Zindel and anyone else with some teaching experience.

Of the three sisters, Ceil has been the assertive one. She has taken the courses necessary to carry her from classroom to administrative work with the board of education. She took the chance of marrying Edward Adams, although Catherine dated him first. Ceil, too, arranged for their dead mother's estate to be settled seven months prior to the night of the play's action, and now, Ceil is the one bringing papers for Anna's commitment for psychiatric care.

Act 1 begins with Mrs. Pentrano, the wife of the building superintendent, entering the Reardon sisters' apartment. She asks if the new lock has satisfied Anna and expresses concern for Anna's condition. A delivery boy brings groceries, including chopped meat, which Catherine arranges in a candy box. Untipped, the delivery boy exits with flippant sarcasm. Mrs. Pentrano has been pressing Catherine for a cosmetics and toiletries order despite Catherine's objections. Ceil arrives and dismisses Mrs. Pentrano with little more than a greeting.

Catherine berates Ceil for making scant contact since their mother's death. She also complains that her fellow faculty members believe that Catherine's position as assistant principal is a consequence of Ceil's being on the board of education. Ceil cuts through the criticism with questions about Anna; she also expresses her concern for Catherine, who, people say, has taken to drinking. During their exchanges, Catherine eats raw meat from the candy box. Since her breakdown, Anna has turned vegetarian and wants no meat or animal byproducts in the apartment. Slaughter of animals is too reminiscent of human death.

Catherine explains to Ceil the development of Anna's condition. During a trip to Europe after their mother's death, Anna suffered a cat bite. She grew convinced that she had rabies. She demanded shots for the disease and thereafter was on tranquilizers so that she could return to teaching in September. Suffering harassment by students, however, Anna eventually broke down, committing some unspecified form of sexual indiscretion with a male student.

Anna enters. Groggy with medication, she had forgotten that Ceil was due for dinner. Catherine goes about preparing fruits and vegetables for their meal. Anna worries about the presence of Mother's old pistol in the apartment. Ceil assures her that Mother kept only blanks in the gun. Anna searches desk and bookcase until she locates the pistol in an album. Anna rambles about her condition, criticizes Ceil for taking Edward away from Catherine, then fires the pistol. Catherine tries to humor Anna, retrieves the pistol, and puts it back in the album, saying that Ceil can take it away later.

The second act opens with the sisters, still at dinner, interrupted by Fleur Stein. Fleur, an acting guidance teacher at the school where Catherine and Anna work, brings an official faculty get-well gift. Her husband, Bob, is getting the package from the car. Fleur says she debated whether the gift should be religious. Anna responds with a long story of losing religion because she saw a puppy hit by a truck. When Bob presents the gift, Anna loses control. They have brought her leather gloves. She throws them across the room. Ceil explains Anna's aversion to animal products, and Catherine belatedly introduces Ceil to the Steins. Fleur is counselor for the boy involved in Anna's case, and she pressures Ceil for help in securing her guidance teacher's licensure. In return, she will persuade the boy's parents not to sue for damages. Fleur downplays judgment on the incident, attributing a loss of traditional religious attitudes to modern acceptance of science. Bob Stein, given certain provocations, bluntly attributes Anna's breakdown to lack of male companionship. He offers to get Anna a date for the evening and drapes Fleur's fox fur stole over Anna's shoulders. She screams and kicks the stole away, deploring the cruelty of the fur trade. Bob reacts in anger, insulting all three sisters in turn. Catherine suggests that Anna show Bob their mother's album.

As the third act opens, Anna fires the pistol at Bob's face. Bob grabs the gun, telling Anna that she has real problems. Anna, in response to an earlier comment by Fleur, asks Bob why he never uses his own bathroom at home. He retorts that he hates the soaps and rough paper that Fleur steals from the school. Fleur attempts to smooth over Bob's irate exit, assuring Ceil that she will do her best to help. With the Steins gone, Ceil wants to discuss business with Catherine alone, but Anna insists on staying. She reminisces about an eccentric principal they once knew. Ceil brings out the commitment papers and tells Catherine to get Anna packed for travel the next day.

Catherine rebels at the order. Anna asks Ceil how Edward makes love to her. Furious, Ceil shoves meat from the candy box in Anna's face. She screams and runs off to wash. Ceil keeps Catherine from following Anna. Catherine finally admits that she hates the dominance in both their late mother and Ceil. In return, Ceil rebukes Catherine for leaving her choices in life to others. Ceil throws the commitment papers down and leaves. Catherine now must take responsibility for either keeping Anna home or committing her for psychiatric care.

Examining the lives of professional educators, Zindel presents a family with the occupational stability and social standing he himself experienced in his first career. The Misses Reardon, like Tillie and Ruth Hunsdorfer, have suffered from an unhealthy family situation: an absent father and a domineering mother. Ceil, assertive in her own right, made choices that carried her out of Mother Reardon's sphere of control and eventually to the top echelon of her profession. Her progress is a logical extension of the strength of character Tillie Hunsdorfer maintains despite Beatrice's dominance. Catherine and Anna, in contrast, show the effects of remaining under Mother's control to the end. Catherine shrinks from asserting herself: She cannot briskly dismiss Mrs. Pentrano as Ceil can; rather than cope with awkward comments by the Steins, she runs the blender; instead of confronting Anna with her own preference of diet, she sneaks meat into the house and eats it raw. Both Catherine's craving for raw meat and Anna's indiscretion represent inordinate reactions to unfulfilled needs.

In addition to the parallels in family dynamics, there is another link between *And Miss Reardon Drinks a Little* and its predecessor. Tillie Hunsdorfer's youthful faith in science has evolved, in Fleur Stein, into the laconic conclusion that science has supplanted religious faith in modern life. Anna, in contrast, cannot rationalize pain and suffering; she traces the loss of her religion to the death of a pup. Ceil makes no claims regarding religion. She does live by the premise, however, that a person must accept responsibility for choices in life and must seize opportunities for change and growth. At the close of the play, she leaves Catherine with the choice of compensating for Anna's incapacity at home or committing her for psychiatric care. Catherine seems, at last, ready to accept the responsibility.

Zindel's strength as a dramatist lies in revelation of character through dialogue. In his plays, women of varying ages, varying degrees of assertiveness and self-esteem, and varying degrees of emotional damage contend for personhood, position, and power. Although many of these characters are powerfully realized, Zindel has not progressed significantly since the early success of *The Effect of Gamma Rays on Man-in-the-Moon Marigolds*, and critics and theatergoers are still waiting for him to fulfill the promise of that remarkable work.

Other major works

NOVEL: *When a Darkness Falls*, 1984.

SCREENPLAYS: *Up the Sandbox*, 1972; *Mame*, 1974; *Runaway Train*, 1983; *Maria's Lovers*, 1984.

TELEPLAYS: *Let Me Hear You Whisper*, 1966; *Alice in Wonderland*, 1985 (adapted from the story by Lewis Carroll); *A Connecticut Yankee in King Arthur's Court*, 1989 (adapted from the novel by Mark Twain).

CHILDREN'S LITERATURE: *The Pigman*, 1968; *My Darling, My Hamburger*, 1969; *I Never Loved Your Mind*, 1970; *I Love My Mother*, 1975; *Pardon Me, You're Stepping on My Eyeball!*, 1976; *Confessions of a Teenage Baboon*, 1977; *The Undertaker's Gone Bananas*, 1978; *A Star for the Latecomer*, 1980 (with Bonnie Zindel); *The Pigman's Legacy*, 1980; *The Girl Who

Wanted a Boy, 1981; *To Take a Dare*, 1982 (with Crescent Dragonwagon); *Harry and Hortense at Hormone High*, 1984; *The Amazing and Death-Defying Diary of Eugene Dingman*, 1987; *A Begonia for Miss Applebaum*, 1989; *The Pigman and Me*, 1992 (autobiography).

Bibliography

Barnes, Clive. "Troubled Times for a Teen." Review of *Amulets Against the Dragon Forces. Post* (New York), April 7, 1989. Barnes finds a "commonplace honesty" beneath the play's pretentiousness in this review of the Circle Repertory Company's production. Barnes finds "the same quality of compassion" as in *The Effects of Gamma Rays on Man-in-the-Moon Marigolds.* Barnes states that the play "[h]as the air of a work written to enable its author to get something off his chest."

DiGaetani, John L. *A Search for a Postmodern Theater: Interviews with Contemporary Playwrights.* New York: Greenwood Press, 1991. In one chapter, DiGaetani interviews Zindel about the influences of psychoanalysis on his work and the reasons for his gradual transition to young adult novels. Zindel's destructive relation with Hollywood is also discussed with considerable candor. Asked which playwrights Zindel admires, he replied, "I'm happy to say none."

Evett, Marianne. "'Moon-Marigolds' Author in Nostalgic Return Here." *Plain Dealer* (Cleveland), November 4, 1990. This preview of Cleveland Playhouse's revival of *The Effect of Gamma Rays on Man-in-the Moon Marigolds*, with Marlo Thomas in the role of Beatrice, includes a telephone interview with Zindel, who remembers the first productions and his "bubbly publicity agent (Bonnie Hildebrand). I ended up marrying her." He reports here that he "escaped East [from Hollywood] to keep my sanity intact."

Tate, Lori. "Script Is Flawed, but *Ladies at the Alamo* Fast and Funny." *State* (Columbia, S.C.), May 21, 1989. A seldom performed Zindel play from 1975 is reviewed here, a rare analysis of this work. Tate describes the theatrical setting of the play—"the theatre's board room"—and remarks that "what makes the characters so irresistible is the trash beneath the trappings."

Zindel, Paul. "Beyond Man-in-the-Moon Marigolds." Interview by Helen Dudar. *The New York Times*, April 2, 1989, p. B5. A long interview on the occasion of Zindel's later work, *Amulets Against the Dragon Forces*, twelve years after his last New York opening. He recaps his career, mostly in teen novels, and his sense of destructiveness in the maws of Hollywood. Good biographic profile, with a photograph.

Ralph S. Carlson
(Updated by *Thomas J. Taylor*)